The ETS Test Collection Catalog

The ETS Test Collection Catalog

Volume 5: Attitude Tests

Compiled by Test Collection,
Educational Testing Service

Table of Contents

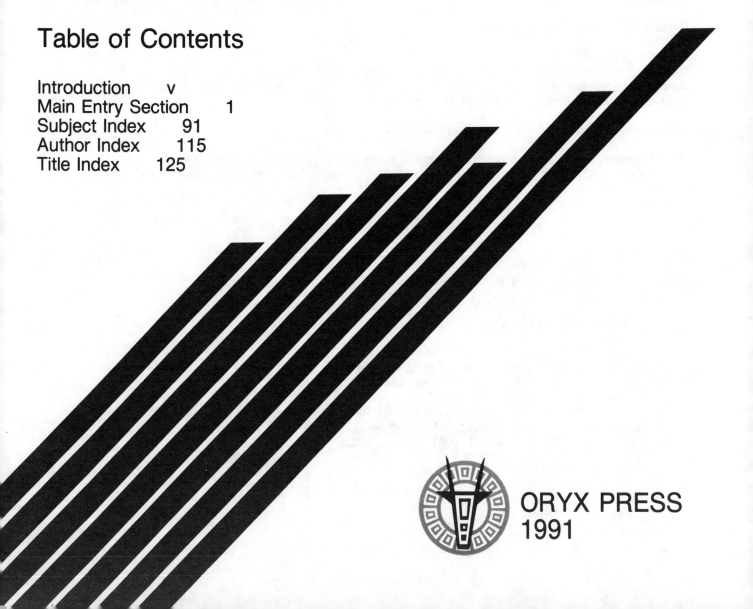

ORYX PRESS
1991

The rare Arabian Oryx is believed to have inspired the myth of the unicorn. This desert antelope became virtually extinct in the early 1960s. At that time several groups of international conservationists arranged to have 9 animals sent to the Phoenix Zoo to be the nucleus of a captive breeding herd. Today the Oryx population is nearly 800, and over 400 have been returned to reserves in the Middle East.

Copyright © 1991 by Educational Testing Service
Published by The Oryx Press
4041 North Central at Indian School
Phoenix, Arizona 85012-3397

Published simultaneously in Canada

Printed and Bound in the United States of America

∞ The paper used in this publication meets the minimum requirements of American National Standard for Information Science—Permanence of Paper for Printed Library Materials, ANSI Z39.48, 1984.

Library of Congress Cataloging-in-Publication Data
(Revised for vol. 5)

The ETS Test Collection catalog.

   Includes indexes.
   Contents: v. 1. Achievement tests and measurement devices — v. 2. Vocational tests and measurement devices —[etc.]—v. 5. Attitude tests.
   1. Educational tests and measurements—United States —Catalogs. 2. Achievement tests—United States— Catalogs. 3. Occupational aptitude tests—United States —Catalogs. 4. Educational Testing Service—Catalogs. I. Educational Testing Service. Test Collection.
LB3051.E79 1986   016.3712'6   86-678
ISBN 0-89774-248-6 (pbk. : v. 1)
ISBN 0-89774-617-1 (pbk. : v. 5)

INTRODUCTION

The Test Collection, Education Testing Service, is an extensive library of approximately 16,850 tests and other measurement devices. It was established to provide information on tests and assessment materials to those in research, advisory services, education, and related activities. As part of its function, the Test Collection acquires and disseminates information on hard-to-locate research instruments as well as on commercially available, standardized tests. Because the Test Collection deals only with tests and evaluation tools, it has been able to provide a reasonable amount of bibliographic control over what has historically been a scattering of information among many and diverse sources.

This volume, the fifth of *The ETS Collection Catalog* series, describes approximately 1,275 attitude measures. Other volumes in the series include *Volume 1: Achievement Tests and Measurement Devices; Volume 2: Vocational Tests and Measurement Devices; Volume 3: Tests for Special Populations;* and *Volume 4: Cognitive, Aptitude, and Intelligence Tests.* The tests described cover all age and grade levels.

Examples of the attitude measures in this volume include attitudes and/or opinions about nuclear arms, school curriculum, computers, male sexuality, stereotypes about females, marital satisfaction, honesty in the workplace, women in the military, life-style, secondary school mathematics, alcoholic beverages, organizational climate, life satisfaction of older adults, child rearing, death, reading, and homosexuality. Also included are instruments to assess managers' opinions of managerial style, teachers' attitudes toward principals' effectiveness, health care professionals' opinions toward organizational factors that influence patient care, and special education teachers' feelings about their abilities in the classroom. Vocational interest measures were excluded, although attitudes toward work and factors within the work situation are included.

For each entry in the main entry section of the directory, the following information is always present: test title, author, descriptors and/or identifiers (subject indexing terms), availability source, age or grade level, and an abstract. Other information, which is provided when available, includes publication or copyright date, subtests, number of test items, and the time required for an individual to complete the test. The test descriptions are arranged sequentially by the Test Collection's identification number in the main entry section.

There are three indexes that provide access to the Main Entry Section: Subject, Author, and Test Title. The Subject Index uses ERIC descriptors from the *Thesaurus of ERIC Descriptors, 11th Edition.* Each test title and its unique identification number is listed under the major descriptors assigned to it, so that there are several subject access points. Because all the instruments are attitude measures or opinionnaires, the descriptor "attitude measures" is not included in the Subject Index. In addition, some tests may be indexed under major identifiers, which are additional subject indexing terms not found in the *Thesaurus of ERIC Descriptors* but which help in describing the content of the test. In the Author Index, tests and their corresponding identification numbers are listed under the author's name. The Title Index is an alphabetical list of all tests included in the directory and their identification numbers.

Some of the tests referred to in the abstracts are listed in the Main Entry Section. Check the Title Index to locate these tests. For information about tests not included in this catalog, contact Test Collection at Educational Testing Service.

At the time the test catalog was compiled, all the tests included were still available from the test distributors indicated in the availability source. However, distribution of certain tests may be discontinued by test publishers or distributors and new tests developed and published.

The staff of the Test Collection will be happy to answer any questions about this catalog or other products and services. Inquiries may be addressed to Test Collection, Educational Testing Service, Princeton, NJ 08541.

Sample Entry

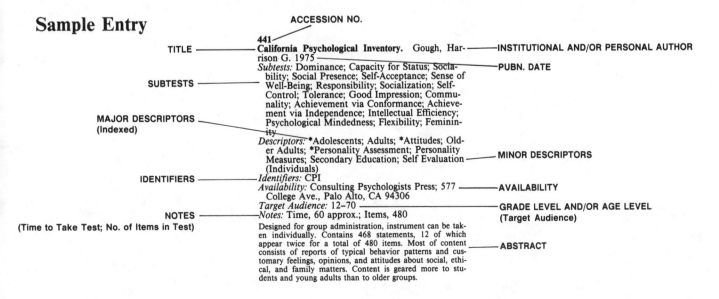

MAIN ENTRY SECTION

441
California Psychological Inventory. Gough, Harrison G. 1975
Subtests: Dominance; Capacity for Status; Sociability; Social Presence; Self-Acceptance; Sense of Well-Being; Responsibility; Socialization; Self-Control; Tolerance; Good Impression; Communality; Achievement via Conformance; Achievement via Independence; Intellectual Efficiency; Psychological Mindedness; Flexibility; Femininity
Descriptors: *Adolescents; Adults; *Attitudes; Older Adults; *Personality Assessment; Personality Measures; Secondary Education; Self Evaluation (Individuals)
Identifiers: CPI
Availability: Consulting Psychologists Press; 577 College Ave., Palo Alto, CA 94306
Target Audience: 12–70
Notes: Time, 60 approx.; Items, 480

Designed for group administration, instrument can be taken individually. Contains 468 statements, 12 of which appear twice for a total of 480 items. Most of content consists of reports of typical behavior patterns and customary feelings, opinions, and attitudes about social, ethical, and family matters. Content is geared more to students and young adults than to older groups.

706
School Interest Inventory. Cottle, William C. 1966
Descriptors: *Dropout Characteristics; Dropout Prevention; Females; Males; Predictive Measurement; *School Attitudes; Secondary Education; *Secondary School Students; *Student Attitudes
Availability: The Riverside Publishing Co.; 8420 Bryn Mawr Ave., Chicago, IL 60631
Grade Level: 7–12
Notes: Time, 20 approx.; Items, 150

Designed for use in the early detection, and possible prevention, of potential school dropouts. Scales established for males and females. Separate scoring masks available for each sex.

710
California Life Goals Evaluation Schedules. Hahn, Milton E. 1969
Descriptors: *Adolescents; *Adults; *Career Planning; Counseling Techniques; Higher Education; High Schools; *Individual Needs; *Majors (Students); *Motivation; *Older Adults; Rating Scales; Retirement
Identifiers: CLGES; Self Scoring Tests
Availability: Western Psychological Services; 12031 Wilshire Blvd., Los Angeles, CA 90025
Target Audience: 15–75
Notes: Time, 45 approx.; Items, 150

Assesses life goals in 10 areas including esteem, profit, fame, leadership, power, security, social service, interesting experiences, self-expression, and Independence. Useful for career and college planning, adjusting to aging or retirement, and career counseling. May be self- or examiner-scored and administered to individuals or groups.

714
Demos D Scale. Demos, George D. 1965
Subtests: Attitudes toward Teachers; Attitudes toward Education; Influences by Peers or Parents; School Behavior
Descriptors: Dropout Characteristics; *Potential Dropouts; Rating Scales; *School Attitudes; Secondary Education; *Secondary School Students; *Student Attitudes; Student Behavior
Identifiers: DDS; Self Administered Tests
Availability: Western Psychological Services; 12031 Wilshire Blvd., Los Angeles, CA 90025
Grade Level: 7–12
Notes: Items, 29

Designed to assess school attitudes of students in junior and senior high school. Scores may be converted to probabilities of dropping out of school.

789
Maferr Inventory of Feminine Values. Steinmann, Anne G.; Fox, David J. 1979
Descriptors: Adults; *Females; *Feminism; Finnish; French; German; Greek; Higher Education; Japanese; Life Satisfaction; Portuguese; Self Concept; *Sex Role; *Social Attitudes; Spanish; Undergraduate Students; *Values; Likert Scales; *Traditionalism
Identifiers: MIFV; Self Administered Tests
Availability: Maferr Foundation, Inc.; 1027 Reba Ridge, Great Falls, VA 20066
Grade Level: 13–16
Target Audience: Adults
Notes: Items, 34

Designed to distinguish between family, home, other-oriented women, those who find fulfillment through others in a traditional role and those women who seek fulfillment by actualizing their own potentialities. The inventory assesses a female's attitudes as traditional or liberal. Measures male and female perceptions of the female sex role. Five forms are available, 3 forms to be administered to women and 2 forms for men. Forms are available in several foreign languages.

790
Maferr Inventory of Masculine Values. Steinmann, Anne G.; Fox, David J. 1979
Descriptors: Adults; Finnish; French; German; Greek; Higher Education; Japanese; Life Satisfaction; *Males; Likert Scales; *Traditionalism; Portuguese; Self Concept; *Sex Role; *Social Attitudes; Spanish; Undergraduate Students; Values
Identifiers: MIMV; Self Administered Tests
Availability: Maferr Foundation, Inc.; 9 E. 81st St., New York, NY 10028
Grade Level: 13–16
Target Audience: Adults
Notes: Items, 34

Designed to distinguish between liberal men, those who fulfill themselves through the intermediary of others, and traditional men, those who are self-oriented and seek fulfillment by actualizing their own potentialities and abilities. Measures male and female perceptions of the male sex role. Five forms are available, 3 for administration to men and 2 for women. Forms are available in several foreign language translations.

877
How Supervise? File, Quentin W.; Remmers, H.H. 1971
Subtests: Supervisory Practices; Company Policies; Supervisor Opinions
Descriptors: Administrators; Adults; Beliefs; *Business Administration; *Human Relations; *Industrial Personnel; Middle Management; *Supervisors
Availability: Psychological Corp.; 555 Academic Ct., San Antonio, TX 78204-0952
Target Audience: 18–64
Notes: Time, 40 approx.

Designed to measure supervisor's knowledge of and insight into human relations in work situations. Forms A and B are equivalent and have 70 items each. Form M consists of 100 items and is useful at higher management levels.

1007
Pictorial Study of Values. Shooster, Charles N. 1957
Descriptors: Adult Literacy; *Adults; Culture Fair Tests; Higher Education; High Schools; *High School Students; *Illiteracy; *Non English Speaking; *Pictorial Stimuli; Political Attitudes; Religion; Social Values; *Undergraduate Students; *Values; *Visual Measures
Availability: Psychometric Affiliates; P.O. Box 807, Murfreesboro, TN 37133
Target Audience: 14–64
Notes: Time, 20 approx.; Items, 60

Designed to measure reactions to basic value areas of aesthetic, social, political, economic, religious, and theoretical. Nonlanguage test is composed of photographs. Suitable for illiterate and non-English-speaking persons as well as for literates.

1340
Study of Values: Third Edition. Allport, Gordon W.; And Others 1960
Descriptors: *Adults; *College Students; Higher Education; High Schools; *High School Students; Personality Measures; *Values
Availability: Riverside Publishing Co.; 8420 Bryn Mawr Ave., Chicago, IL 60631

Grade Level: 10–16
Target Audience: 15–64
Notes: Time, 20 approx.

Designed to measure relative prominence of 6 basic motives in personality. Classification is based on Edward Spranger's Types of Men. Instrument is based upon the assumption that individuals may be assessed through a study of their values or evaluative attitudes.

1650
Luther Hospital Sentence Completions. Thurston, John R.; And Others 1959
Subtests: Nursing; Self; Home-Family; Responsibility; Academic; Love-Marriage; Others
Descriptors: Counseling Techniques; Higher Education; *Nursing Education; Personality Assessment; Predictive Measurement; Projective Measures; Psychological Patterns; Self Concept; Student Attitudes; *Undergraduate Students
Identifiers: LHSC; Nursing Students; Sentence Completion Tests
Availability: Nursing Research Associates; 3752 Cummings St., Eau Claire, WI 54701
Grade Level: 13–16
Notes: Items, 90

Designed to evaluate attitudes and reactions of applicants and nursing students. Attitudinal areas related to performance in nursing school are evaluated. The Nursing Education Scale is a guideline developed for scoring this instrument. It may be used to quantify responses. Results of this instrument are frequently a good predictor of success in nursing school.

1651
Nursing Sentence Completions. Thurston, John R.; And Others 1974
Subtests: Nursing; Self; Home-Family; Responsibility; Academic; Love-Marriage; Others
Descriptors: Higher Education; *Nursing Education; Personality Assessment; Predictive Measurement; Projective Measures; Psychological Patterns; Self Concept; Student Attitudes; *Undergraduate Students
Identifiers: NSC; Nursing Students; Sentence Completion Tests
Availability: Nursing Research Associates; 3752 Cummings St., Eau Claire, WI 54701
Grade Level: 13–16
Notes: Items, 40

Designed to evaluate attitudes and reactions of applicants and nursing students. Instrument is a shorter form of Luther Hospital Sentence Completions (TC001650). Attitudinal areas related to performance in nursing school are evaluated. Results may be used as a predictor of successful achievement in nursing school. The Nursing Education Scale is a guideline developed for scoring this instrument. it may be used to quantify responses. Results of this instrument are frequently a good predictor of success in nursing school.

1652
Nurse Attitudes Inventory. Thurston, John R.; And Others 1966
Subtests: Nursing; Self; Home-Family; Responsibility; Academic; Love-Marriage; Others
Descriptors: Higher Education; *Nursing Education; Personality Assessment; Personality Measures; Psychological Patterns; *Undergraduate Students
Identifiers: NAI; *Nursing Students
Availability: Nursing Research Associates; 3752 Cummings St., Eau Claire, WI 54701
Grade Level: 13–16
Notes: Items, 70

Personality measure designed to elicit information concerning attitudes of nursing students. Designed to differentiate between potentially successful and unsuccessful students in nursing school. Use of the multiple-choice format replaced sentence completion technique used in other nursing attitude scales. The Nursing Education Scale is a guideline developed for scoring this instrument. It may be used to quantify responses.

1713
Organizational Survey. Nordli, Wilson Associates, Worcester, MA 1972
Descriptors: *Administrator Attitudes; *Administrators; Adults; *Employee Attitudes; *Employees; *Organizational Climate; Self Evaluation (Groups)
Identifiers: NW Organizational Survey

Availability: Psychological Services, International, Inc.; 311 Main St., Worcester, MA 10608
Target Audience: Adults
Notes: Items, 125

Designed to elicit individual perceptions and attitudes regarding a respondent's organization and its management.

1720
The Collett-Lester Fear of Death Scale. Lester, David; Collett, Lora-Jean 1974
Descriptors: Adults; *Death; *Fear; Neurosis
Identifiers: *Death Attitudes; *Fear of Death; TIM(A)
Availability: Tests in Microfiche; Test Collection, Educational Testing Service, Princeton, NJ 08541
Target Audience: Adults
Notes: Items, 36

Measures 4 dimensions of the general fear of death: death of oneself, death of others, dying of oneself, and dying of others. It can be administered to adults individually or in groups.

1721
Fear of Death Scale. Lester, David 1975
Descriptors: Adults; Beliefs; *Death; *Fear; Suicide
Identifiers: *Death Attitudes; *Fear of Death; TIM(A)
Availability: Tests in Microfiche; Test Collection, Educational Testing Service, Princeton, NJ 08541
Target Audience: Adults
Notes: Items, 21

A scale designed to measure the fear of death in an individual. In a study using this test, it was found that suicidal or suicide-prone students feared death less than less suicidal students. It is suggested that this type of information may aid in understanding the psychodynamics of suicidal persons.

1723
Thurston Sentence Completion Form. Thurston, John R. 1959
Descriptors: Adults; Child Rearing; Children; *Disabilities; Institutionalized Persons; *Parent Attitudes; *Parents; Projective Measures
Identifiers: TIM(C); TSCF
Availability: Tests in Microfiche; Test Collection, Educational Testing Service, Princeton, NJ 08541
Target Audience: Adults
Notes: Items, 45

Designed to elicit the attitudes and emotional reactions of the parents of handicapped children in 7 areas: personal reactions and concerns; attitudes regarding the child's satisfactions-discomfitures; reactions of brothers and sisters; reactions of community, friends, neighbors; attitudes toward the institution-hospital-treatment center and staff; attitudes relating to the hopes and expectations of the parent for the handicapped child; and attitudes of a general nature.

1749
S-C Teaching Inventory. Spier, Morris S. 1974
Descriptors: Adults; Forced Choice Technique; *Teacher Attitudes; *Teacher Behavior; *Teachers; Teacher Student Relationship; Teaching Methods; Teaching Styles
Identifiers: SCTI
Availability: University Associates, Inc.; 8517 Production Ave., P.O. Box 26240, San Diego, CA 92126
Target Audience: Adults
Notes: Time, 20 approx.

The S-C (Student-Content) Teaching Inventory was designed to assist respondents to focus on, organize, and understand their own experiences in the teacher-student interaction. Items are classified as centering on student orientation or content orientation. Instrument is available in the 1974 Annual Handbook for Group Facilitators.

1751
Problem-Analysis Questionnaire. Oshry, Barry; Harrison, Roger 1975
Subtests: Others; Organization; Self
Descriptors: Administrators; Adults; *Employees; *Human Relations; Interpersonal Relationship; *Locus of Control; *Work Attitudes; Work Environment
Availability: University Associates, Inc.; 8517 Production Ave., P.O. Box 26240, San Diego, CA 92126
Target Audience: Adults
Notes: Items, 48

Designed to identify problem situations in organizational environment and analyze the causes. Failure to resolve problems may result from deficiencies in areas of rational-technical analysis and openness. These failures may be found in others, in the organization, and in oneself. Human relations training may cause individuals to accept more responsibility for their problems, rather than blam-

ing external influences. This instrument is available as part of the Annual Handbook for Group Facilitators, 1975 edition.

1754
Lester Attitude toward Death Scale. Lester, David 1974
Descriptors: *Adults; Attitudes; *Death
Identifiers: TIM(J)
Availability: Tests in Microfiche; Test Collection, Educational Testing Service, Princeton, NJ 08541
Target Audience: Adults
Notes: Items, 21

Designed to assess an individual's attitude toward death. Examinee is presented with 21 statements and must indicate his or her agreement or disagreement with them.

1763
Correctional Institutions Environment Scale. Moos, Rudolf H. 1974
Subtests: Involvement; Support; Expressiveness; Autonomy; Practical Orientation; Personal Problem Orientation; Order and Organization; Clarity; Staff Control
Descriptors: *Adolescents; *Adults; *Correctional Institutions; *Institutional Environment; *Institutionalized Persons; Secondary Education; Secondary School Students; Social Environment
Identifiers: CIES; Social Climate Scales
Availability: Consulting Psychologists Press; 577 College Ave., Palo Alto, CA 94306
Grade Level: 7–12
Target Audience: 13–64
Notes: Time, 20 approx.; Items, 90

Designed to assess the effects of programs, staff training, and other factors on the social environment of juvenile and adult correctional facilities. The three dimensions assessed are relationship dimensions, treatment program dimensions, and system maintenance dimensions. This scale has been adapted to measure the ideal social environment (Form I) or the expectations one has of an environment (Form E). Short form (Form S) may be adapted from standard Form R. Alternate scales and their construction are described in the manual.

1764
University Residence Environment Scale. Moos, Rudolf H.; Gerst, Marvin S. 1974
Subtests: Involvement; Emotional Support; Independence; Traditional Social Orientation; Competition; Academic Achievement; Intellectuality; Order and Organization; Student Influence; Innovation
Descriptors: *Adults; *College Environment; *College Housing; Competition; Educational Environment; Higher Education; Residential Colleges; Social Environment; *Undergraduate Students; Dormitories
Identifiers: Social Climate Scales; URES
Availability: Consulting Psychologists Press; 577 College Ave., Palo Alto, CA 94306
Grade Level: 13–16
Target Audience: Adults
Notes: Time, 20 approx.; Items, 100

Designed to assess the social climates of university student living groups. Measures and describes student-student and staff-student relationships and organizational structure of the living group. Subscales are grouped into dimensions of relationship, personal growth or development, and system maintenance. This scale has been adapted to measure the ideal social environment (Form I), or the expectations one has of an environment (Form E). Short form (Form S) may be adapted from standard Form R. Alternate scales and their construction are described in the manual.

1765
Classroom Environment Scale. Moos, Rudolf H.; Trickett, Edison J. 1974
Subtests: Involvement; Affiliation; Teacher Support; Task Orientation; Competition; Order and Organization; Rule Clarity; Teacher Control; Innovation
Descriptors: *Classroom Environment; Competition; Peer Relationship; Secondary Education; *Secondary School Students; Secondary School Teachers; Social Environment; *Student Attitudes; Teacher Student Relationship
Identifiers: CES; Social Climate Scales
Availability: Consulting Psychologists Press; 577 College Ave., Palo Alto, CA 94306
Grade Level: 7–12
Notes: Time, 20 approx.; Items, 90

Designed to assess the social climate of secondary school classrooms. Interpersonal relationships between students and between students and teachers are measured as well as the type of organizational structure of a classroom. The nine subscales are grouped in dimensions of relationship, personal development, system maintenance, and system change. This scale has been adapted to measure the ideal social environment (Form I) or the expectations one has

of an environment (Form E). Short form (Form S) may be adapted from standard Form R. Alternate scales and their construction are described in the manual.

1766
Group Environment Scale. Moos, Rudolf H.; Humphrey, Barrie 1974
Subtests: Cohesion; Leader Support; Expressiveness; Independence; Task Orientation; Self-Discovery; Anger and Aggression; Order and Organization; Leader Control; Innovation
Descriptors: *Adults; Group Behavior; *Group Dynamics; Group Unity; Leaders; *Social Environment
Identifiers: GES; Social Climate Scales
Availability: Consulting Psychologists Press; 577 College Ave., Palo Alto, CA 94306
Target Audience: Adults
Notes: Time, 20 approx.; Items, 90

Designed to assess the social environment of psychotherapeutic, social, and task-oriented groups. Subscales are arranged in dimensions of relationship, personal growth, and system maintenance and system change. This scale has been adapted to measure the ideal social environment (Form I) or the expectations one has of an environment (Form E). Short form (Form S) may be adapted from standard Form R. Alternate scales and their construction are described in the manual.

1767
Work Environment Scale. Moos, Rudolf H.; Insel, Paul M. 1974
Subtests: Involvement; Peer Cohesion; Staff Support; Autonomy; Task Orientation; Work Pressure; Clarity; Control; Innovation; Physical Comfort
Descriptors: Adults; *Employee Attitudes; Employer Employee Relationship; Job Satisfaction; *Labor Relations; *Objective Tests; Productivity; *Social Environment; Supervisory Methods; *Work Environment
Identifiers: WES
Availability: Consulting Psychologists Press; 577 College Ave., Palo Alto, CA 94306
Target Audience: Adults
Notes: Items, 90

Assesses the social climate of work units, focusing on relationships among employees, between employees and supervisors, on the directions of personal growth available, and the unit's basic organizational structure and functioning. A tool for industrial psychologists evaluating correlates of productivity, worker satisfaction, supervisory methods. An alternate form, The 40-Item Short Form (Form S), of the WES was developed to permit rapid assessments of work group climate.

1782
Student Drug Survey. Hays, J. Ray 1971
Descriptors: Dropout Characteristics; *Drug Abuse; *Questionnaires; Secondary Education; *Secondary School Students; *Student Attitudes
Identifiers: TIM(B)
Availability: Tests in Microfiche; Test Collection, Educational Testing Service, Princeton, NJ 08541
Grade Level: 7–12
Notes: Items, 88

Designed to provide information on drug abuse among secondary school students and to identify similar characteristics among drug abusers. Also used to provide information on drug abuse and its correlation with prevalence of dropouts.

1808
Satisfaction of Values Inventory. Todd, Karen 1974
Subtests: At Home; At School; With Friends; In the Community; Affection; Respect; Skill; Enlightenment; Power; Wealth; Well-Being; Rectitude
Descriptors: *Adolescents; *Adults; *Children; Elementary School Students; Interpersonal Relationship; Need Gratification; Psychological Needs; Secondary School Students; *Student Attitudes
Identifiers: SAVI
Availability: Karen Rohne Todd; 403 N. Fullerton, Upper Montclair, NJ 07043
Target Audience: 11–64

Designed to measure value satisfaction in areas of affection, enlightenment, skill, wealth, power, rectitude, respect, and well-being. Assesses the contributions to value satisfaction made by significant others—home, school, peer group, and community. SAVI-I contains 32 items and is appropriate for children aged 11-13. SAVI-II is appropriate for adolescents and adults 14 and over. It contains 40 items.

2345
Survey of Personal Values. Gordon, Leonard V. 1967

Subtests: Practical Mindedness; Achievement; Variety; Decisiveness; Orderliness; Goal Orientation
Descriptors: *Adults; Career Counseling; Coping; Forced Choice Technique; Higher Education; High Schools; *High School Students; Job Applicants; *Undergraduate Students; *Values; *Work Attitudes
Identifiers: Self Administered Tests; SPV
Availability: London House; 1550 Northwest Hwy., Park Ridge, IL 60068
Grade Level: 9–16
Target Audience: Adults
Notes: Time, 15 approx.; Items, 30

Designed to measure critical values that help determine the manner in which an individual copes with problems of daily living. Useful in career counseling for high school and college students, as well as selection and placement of job applicants. Validation studies indicated instrument was predictive of job success in several areas.

2432
Family Adjustment Test. Elias, Gabriel 1952
Subtests: Attitudes toward Mother; Attitudes toward Father; Father-Mother Adjustment Quotient; Oedipal; Struggle for Independence; Parent-Child Friction-Harmony; Interparental Friction-Harmony; Family Inferiority-Superiority; Rejection of Child; Parental Qualities
Descriptors: Adjustment (to Environment); *Adolescents; *Adults; *Childhood Attitudes; *Children; *Emotional Adjustment; Family Attitudes; *Family Relationship; *Parent Child Relationship; Rejection (Psychology)
Identifiers: Elias Family Opinion Survey; FAT
Availability: Psychometric Affiliates; P.O. Box 807, Murfreesboro, TN 37133
Target Audience: 10–60
Notes: Time, 45 approx.; Items, 114

Designed to measure feelings of intrafamily homeyness-homelessness (H-ness) while appearing to be concerned only with the examinee's attitudes toward general community life. Homey feelings are defined as positive; they are full of warmth, love, and other unifying qualities. Homeless feelings are defined as negative, loveless, divisive, and full of friction.

2435
Human Relations Inventory. Bernberg, Raymond E. 1954
Descriptors: *Adults; *Conformity; *Delinquency; Higher Education; High Schools; *High School Students; Personality Measures; *Social Attitudes; *Social Behavior; *Undergraduate Students
Identifiers: HRI
Availability: Psychometric Affiliates; P.O. Box 807, Murfreesboro, TN 37133
Grade Level: 9–16
Target Audience: Adults
Notes: Items, 34

Designed to measure social conformity so that a prediction of antisocial behavior may be made. Discriminates between law violators and ordinary conformists.

2464
A Religious Attitudes Inventory. Crane, William E.; Coffer, J. Henry 1964
Descriptors: *Adults; Attitudes; *Beliefs; Clergy; Counseling Techniques; *Marriage Counseling; *Religion
Identifiers: CCRA; *Premarital Counseling
Availability: Family Life Publications, Inc.; P.O. Box 427, Saluda, NC 28773
Target Audience: Adults
Notes: Items, 107

Designed to provide an assessment of religious beliefs and to promote productive discussion toward resolution of conflicts in this area. Designed to enable counselees to verbalize feelings, doubts, basic attitudes, and fears concerning religious doctrine.

2492
A Study of Choices. Woodruff, Asahel D. 1948
Descriptors: Adolescents; Adults; *Personality Traits; *Political Attitudes; *Social Attitudes; *Values; *Work Attitudes
Identifiers: TIM(B)
Availability: Tests in Microfiche; Test Collection, Educational Testing Service, Princeton, NJ 08541
Target Audience: 16–65
Notes: Time, 120 approx.

Designed to measure a person's values. Included are such concepts as intellectual activity, home life, social life, personal improvement, friends, security, political power, comfort, excitement, wealth, society, and religion. The test is self-administering. It can be given to a group or to a single individual under supervision, or the subject can take the test away and bring it back completed. It is best to complete the test all in one sitting.

2516
Survey of Interpersonal Values. Gordon, Leonard V. 1960
Subtests: Support; Conformity; Recognition; Independence; Benevolence; Leadership
Descriptors: *Adults; Career Guidance; *College Students; Conformity; Counseling Techniques; Forced Choice Technique; Higher Education; High Schools; *High School Students; *Interpersonal Competence; *Values
Identifiers: Self Administered Tests; SIV
Availability: London House; 1550 Northwest Hwy., Park Ridge, IL 60068
Grade Level: 9–16
Target Audience: 14–64
Notes: Time, 15 approx.; Items, 30

Designed to measure certain values involving the individual's relationship with other people. Values assessed are important in the individual's personal, social, marital, and occupational adjustment. May be used for counseling or personnel selection. Manual was revised in 1976, but instrument items are unchanged.

2655
Sex-Attitude Sample Inventory. Schiller, Patricia 1966
Subtests: Dating; Marriage; Child Rearing; Sex Attitudes and Practices; Love-Meaning; Ego Strength
Descriptors: Adolescents; *Females; Secondary Education; *Secondary School Students; Self Concept; *Sexuality; *Student Attitudes
Identifiers: *Sexual Attitudes; Sexual Permissiveness
Availability: Patricia Schiller; 4224 38th St. N.W., Washington, DC 29016
Target Audience: 13–17
Notes: Items, 97

Designed to assess personal attitudes of secondary school girls, especially concerning dating, sex, and marriage.

2669
Attitudes toward Parental Control of Children. Stogdill, Ralph M.; Goddard, Henry H. 1936
Descriptors: Adults; *Child Rearing; Children; *Parent Attitudes; *Parents; Psychologists; Rating Scales
Identifiers: TIM(B)
Availability: Tests in Microfiche; Test Collection, Educational Testing Service, Princeton, NJ 08541
Target Audience: Adults
Notes: Items, 20

Questionnaire designed to assess ideas of parents and other individuals interested in children, concerning parental control of children and discipline. Experimental instrument.

2670
Attitudes toward Child Behavior. Stogdill, Ralph M.; Goddard, Henry H. 1936
Descriptors: Adults; *Child Rearing; Children; *Interpersonal Competence; *Parent Attitudes; Questionnaires; Rating Scales
Identifiers: TIM(B)
Availability: Tests in Microfiche; Test Collection, Educational Testing Service, Princeton, NJ 08541
Target Audience: Adults
Notes: Items, 40

Questionnaire elicits from parents some of their ideas about childrearing. Designed to reveal whether adults approve of an introvert or an extrovert social adjustment on the part of the child.

2706
The Orientation Inventory: Research Edition (1962). Bass, Bernard M. 1962
Subtests: Self-Orientation; Interactional-Orientation; Task-Orientation
Descriptors: *Adults; Counseling Techniques; *Goal Orientation; *Group Behavior; Higher Education; Individual Testing; Motivation; Student Attitudes; *Undergraduate Students; *Work Attitudes
Identifiers: *Organizational Behavior; ORI; Self Administered Tests
Availability: Consulting Psychologists Press; 577 College Ave., Palo Alto, CA 94306
Grade Level: 13–16
Target Audience: Adults
Notes: Time, 20 approx.; Items, 27

Designed to assess attitudes of individuals toward solution of problems or completion of tasks. Useful in personnel evaluation, as well as academic or vocational counseling. Scales are based on Bass's theory of interpersonal behavior in organizations. May be administered to groups or individuals.

2772
Scale for Measuring Attitudes toward Any Vocation. Miller, Harold E.; Remmers, H.H. 1960
Descriptors: Adolescents; *Adults; *Career Awareness; *College Students; *Occupations; *Secondary School Students; Social Attitudes; *Work Attitudes
Identifiers: Generalized Attitude Scales; Master Attitude Scales; PSAS; Purdue Master Attitude Scales; Purdue Research Foundation
Availability: University Book Store; 360 State St., West Lafayette, IN 47906
Target Audience: 12–64
Notes: Time, 10 approx.; Items, 85

Part of the Purdue Master Attitude Scales, formerly called Generalized Attitude Scales. Measures the subject's attitude toward any and all vocations. The subject is asked to agree or disagree with various statements about a specific vocation as named by the test administrator. Untimed. Comes in 2 Forms, Form A and B. Used with subjects from junior high level to adults.

2773
Scale for Measuring Attitude toward Any Defined Group. Grice, H.H.; Remmers, H.H. 1960
Descriptors: Adolescents; *Adults; *College Students; *Groups; *Secondary School Students; *Social Attitudes; *Social Bias
Identifiers: Generalized Attitude Scales; Master Attitude Scales; PSAS; Purdue Master Attitude Scales; Purdue Research Foundation
Availability: University Book Store; 360 State St., West Lafayette, IN 47906
Target Audience: 12–64
Notes: Time, 10 approx.; Items, 17

Part of the Purdue Attitude Scales, formerly called Generalized Attitude Scales. Measures the subject's attitude toward any and all groups. The subject is asked to agree or disagree with various statements about a specific group; the groups are selected by the test administrator. Untimed. Comes in 2 Forms, Form A and B. Used with subjects from junior high level to adults.

2774
Scale for Measuring Attitude toward Any Institution. Kelley, Ida B.; Remmers, H.H. 1960
Descriptors: Adolescents; *Adults; *College Students; *Institutions; *Organizations (Groups); *Secondary School Students
Identifiers: Generalized Attitude Scales; Master Attitude Scales; PSAS; Purdue Master Attitude Scales; Purdue Research Foundation
Availability: University Book Store; 360 State St., West Lafayette, IN 47906
Target Audience: 12–64
Notes: Time, 10 approx.; Items, 85

Part of the Purdue Attitude Scales, formerly called Generalized Attitude Scales. Measures the subject's attitude toward any and all institutions. The subject is asked to agree or disagree with various statements about 5 specific institutions; the institutions are chosen by the test administrator. Untimed. Comes in 2 Forms, Form A and B. Used with subjects from junior high level to adults.

2775
High School Attitude Scales. Gillespie, F.H.; Remmers, H.H. 1960
Descriptors: Adolescents; *Adults; *College Students; *High Schools; *Secondary School Students; *Social Attitudes; *Student Attitudes
Identifiers: Generalized Attitude Scales; Master Attitude Scales; PSAS; Purdue Master Attitude Scales; Purdue Research Foundation
Availability: University Book Store; 360 State St., West Lafayette, IN 47906
Target Audience: 12–64
Notes: Time, 10 approx.; Items, 85

Part of the Purdue Attitude Scales, formerly called Generalized Attitude Scales. Measures the subject's attitude toward high school, the environment, teachers, etc. The subject is asked to agree or disagree with various statements concerning high school life, etc. Untimed. Comes in 2 forms, Form A and B. Used with subjects from junior high level to adults.

2776
Scale for Measuring Attitudes toward Any Proposed Social Action. Thomas, Dorothy M.; Remmers, H.H. 1960
Descriptors: Adolescents; *Adults; Citizen Participation; *College Students; *Secondary School Students; *Social Action; *Social Attitudes
Identifiers: Generalized Attitude Scales; Master Attitude Scales; PSAS; Purdue Master Attitude Scales; Purdue Research Foundation
Availability: University Book Store; 360 State St., West Lafayette, IN 47906
Target Audience: 12–64
Notes: Time, 10 approx.; Items, 85

Part of the Purdue Attitude Scales, formerly called Generalized Attitude Scales. Measures the subject's attitude toward certain, specified social actions as chosen by the test administrator. The subject is asked to agree or disagree with various statements as they would apply to the proposed social actions. Comes in Form A and Form B. Untimed. Used with subjects from junior high level to adults.

2777
Scale for Measuring Attitudes toward Any Practice. Bues, H.W.; Remmers, H.H. 1960
Descriptors: *Activities; Adolescents; *Adults; *College Students; *Secondary School Students; *Social Attitudes
Identifiers: *Customs; Generalized Attitude Scales; Master Attitude Scales; PSAS; Purdue Master Attitude Scales; Purdue Research Foundation
Availability: University Book Store; 360 State St., West Lafayette, IN 47906
Target Audience: 12–64
Notes: Time, 10 approx.; Items, 85
Part of the Purdue Attitude Scales, formerly called Generalized Attitude Scales. Measures the subject's attitude toward certain, specified practices as chosen by the test administrator. The subject is asked to agree or disagree with various statements as they would apply to the practices. Comes in Form A and Form B. Untimed. Used with subjects from junior high level to adults.

2778
Scale for Measuring Attitude toward Any Home-Making Activity. Kellar, Beatrix; Remmers, H.H. 1960
Descriptors: Adolescents; *Adults; *College Students; *Homemakers; *Homemaking Skills; Home Management; *Secondary School Students; *Social Attitudes
Identifiers: Generalized Attitude Scales; Master Attitude Scales; PSAS; Purdue Master Attitude Scales; Purdue Research Foundation; Scale of Attitude toward Any Home Making Activity
Availability: University Book Store; 360 State St., West Lafayette, IN 47906
Target Audience: 12–64
Notes: Time, 10 approx.; Items, 85
Part of the Purdue Attitude Scales, formerly called Generalized Attitude Scales. Measures the subject's attitude toward certain, specific homemaker skills as chosen by the test administrator. The subject is asked to agree or disagree with various statements about homemaking. Comes in Form A and Form B. Untimed. Used with subjects from junior high level to adults.

2779
Scale for Measuring Individual and Group "Morale" Whisler, Laurence; Remmers, H.H. 1960
Descriptors: Adolescents; *Adults; *College Students; *Groups; Group Status; Labeling (of Persons); Morale; *Secondary School Students; *Social Attitudes; Social Bias; Social Class; Social Cognition; Social Structure
Identifiers: Generalized Attitude Scales; Master Attitude Scales; *Persons; PSAS; Purdue Master Attitude Scales; Purdue Research Foundation
Availability: University Book Store; 360 State St., West Lafayette, IN 47906
Target Audience: 12–64
Notes: Time, 10 approx.; Items, 17
Part of the Purdue Attitude Scales, formerly called Generalized Attitude Scales. Measures the subject's attitude toward persons or groups of persons (5 in number). The test administrator chooses the specific 5 persons or groups of persons. The subject is asked to agree or disagree with the statements as they apply to each person or group. Available as Form A and Form B. Untimed. Used with subjects from junior high level to adults.

2780
Scale to Measure Attitude toward Any School Subject. Silance, Ella B.; Remmers, H.H. 1960
Descriptors: Adolescents; *Adults; *College Students; *Courses; *Secondary School Students; *Student Attitudes
Identifiers: Generalized Attitude Scales; Master Attitude Scales; PSAS; Purdue Master Attitude Scales; Purdue Research Foundation
Availability: University Book Store; 360 State St., West Lafayette, IN 47906
Target Audience: 12–64
Notes: Time, 10 approx.; Items, 85
Part of the Purdue Attitude Scales, formerly called Generalized Attitude Scales. Measures the subject's attitude toward 5 school courses; the test administrator chooses the specific 5 courses. The subject is asked to agree or disagree with various statements as they apply to each of the 5 courses. Available as Form A and Form B. Used with subjects from junior high level to adults.

2935
Style of Mind Inventory: Trait, Value and Belief Patterns in Greek, Roman and Hebrew Perspectives. Fetler, Daniel 1961
Descriptors: Adults; *Beliefs; Cultural Traits; Ethics; Moral Values; *Personality Traits; Religious Cultural Groups; Self Evaluation (Individuals); *Values
Identifiers: TIM(A)
Availability: Tests in Microfiche; Test Collection, Educational Testing Service, Princeton, NJ 08541
Target Audience: Adults
Notes: Items, 33
Designed to identify an individual's style of mind by providing an indication of what percentage of his or her mind is Greek, Roman, and Hebrew in terms of traits, values, and beliefs. Appropriate for use with college students and adults.

2936
Mother-Child Relationship Evaluation. Roth, Robert M. 1961
Subtests: Acceptance; Overprotection; Overindulgence; Rejection; Confusion-Dominance
Descriptors: Adults; Child Rearing; Counseling Techniques; *Mother Attitudes; *Mothers; *Parent Child Relationship
Identifiers: MCRE
Availability: Western Psychological Services; 12031 Wilshire Blvd., Los Angeles, CA 90025
Target Audience: Adults
Notes: Time, 30 approx.; Items, 48
Designed to assess attitudes of a mother and how she relates to her child. Useful in determination of areas in the relationship which require improvement during counseling.

3014
Hannaford Industrial Safety Attitude Scale. Hannaford, Earle S. 1959
Descriptors: *Accident Prevention; *Administrator Attitudes; Adults; *Employee Attitudes; *Employees; *Industrial Personnel; Males; *Safety; *Supervisors; Work Attitudes; Work Environment
Identifiers: Industrial Safety Attitude Scale for Male Employ; Industrial Safety Attitude Scale for Male Supervisor; *Supervisor Attitudes
Availability: Center for Safety; Dept. of Occupational Health and Safety, School of Education, Health, Nursing, and Arts Prof., New York University, 715 Broadway, New York, NY 10003
Target Audience: Adults
Notes: Time, 15 approx.; Items, 20
Untimed instrument that evaluates both supervisors' and employees' attitudes toward safety. Designed to help the company locate accident risks and evaluate safety training programs as well as ascertain attitudes toward safety. Has also been used to stimulate discussion at safety meetings. Comes in 4 forms: Industrial Safety Attitude Scale for Male Supervisors Forms SA and SB; and Industrial Safety Attitude Scale for Male Employees Forms EA and EB. In each item, the subject is presented with a statement; he is asked whether he agrees or disagrees, or can't decide for each statement.

3110
A Marriage Analysis. Blazier, Daniel E.; Goosman, Edgar T. 1966
Subtests: Role Concept; Self-Image; Feelings toward Spouse; Emotional Openness; Knowledge of Spouse; Sexual Adjustment and Security; Common Traits; Meaning of Marriage
Descriptors: Adults; *Counseling Techniques; Emotional Adjustment; Marital Instability; Marriage; *Marriage Counseling; Role Perception; Self Concept; *Spouses
Identifiers: BGMA
Availability: Family Life Publications, Inc.; P.O. Box 427, Saluda, NC 28773
Target Audience: Adults
Notes: Time, 30 approx.; Items, 113
Designed to enable marriage counselor to identify problem areas in a marriage. Each spouse completes the instrument before seeing the counselor. A marriage profile may be drawn to indicate both spouses' beliefs on 8 factors deemed important to a successful marital relationship.

3130
Straus Rural Attitudes Profile. Straus, Murray A. 1956
Descriptors: Adults; Forced Choice Technique; *Rural Population; *Social Values
Identifiers: TIM(B)
Availability: Tests in Microfiche; Test Collection, Educational Testing Service, Princeton, NJ 08541
Target Audience: Adults
Notes: Time, 12; Items, 48

Inventory measures 4 variables which are hypothesized to be important value dimensions in contemporary American rural life: innovation proneness, rural life preference, primary group preference, and economic motivation. It is designed for self-administration by individuals with minimal reading skill. There are male and female forms of the test.

3144
Test of Basic Assumptions. Levit, Martin; Morrison, James H. 1959
Subtests: Organization of Effort and Problem Solving; Human Abilities and the Individual; General Philosophy of Life; Economics and Business
Descriptors: Adults; Counseling Techniques; Philosophy; *Values
Identifiers: TBA
Availability: James H. Morrison; 9804 Hadley Ave., Overland Park, KS 66212
Target Audience: Adults
Notes: Items, 20
Designed to assess attitudes toward 4 life areas. Useful in studying an individual's nonrational thinking process to enable a clinician to understand and predict behavior.

3149
C-R Opinionaire. Lentz, Theodore F. 1935
Descriptors: Adults; *Political Attitudes; *Conservatism
Identifiers: *Radicalism; Self Administered Tests
Availability: Theodore F. Lentz, Dir.; Peace Research Lab., 6251 San Bonita Ave., St. Louis, MO 63105
Target Audience: Adults
Notes: Time, 20 approx.; Items, 60
Designed to assess individual's attitudes as conservative or radical.

3154
Life Adjustment Inventory. Doll, Ronald C.; Wrightstone, J. Wayne 1951
Subtests: General Feeling of Adjustment to the Curriculum; Reading and Study Skills; Communication and Listening Skills; General Social Skills and Etiquette; Boy-Girl Relationships; Religion, Morals, and Ethics; Functional Citizenship; Vocational Orientation and Preparation; Education for Physical and Mental Health; Education for Family Living; Orientation to Science; Consumer Education; Development of Appreciation for and Creativity in the Arts; Education for Wise Use of Leisure Time
Descriptors: Curriculum Evaluation; High Schools; *High School Students; School Guidance; *Student Adjustment; *Student Attitudes
Availability: Psychometric Affiliates; P.O. Box 807, Murfreesboro, TN 37133
Grade Level: 9–12
Notes: Time, 25 approx.; Items, 180
Designed to measure students' general adjustment to their high school curriculum as well as their need for additional experiences in specific areas of daily life. May be used in curriculum evaluation and for diagnosis of curriculum maladjustments of individual students.

3164
Social Distance Scale. Bogardus, Emory S. 1954
Subtests: Ethnic Distance Scale (38); Occupational Distance (30); Religious Distance (30); Political and Economic Distance (20)
Descriptors: Adolescents; Adults; Attitude Change; Political Attitudes; Racial Attitudes; Secondary Education; *Social Attitudes; Vocational Interests
Identifiers: TIM(B)
Availability: Tests in Microfiche; Test Collection, Educational Testing Service, Princeton, NJ 08541
Target Audience: 13–65
Notes: Items, 118
Designed to measure personal attitudes, group attitudes, personal-group attitudes and changes in these areas.

3166
Fetler Self-Rating Test. Fetler, Daniel 1958
Descriptors: Adults; *Beliefs; Conflict; Ethics; *Personality Traits; *Religious Cultural Groups; Self Evaluation (Individuals); *Values
Identifiers: TIM(A)
Availability: Tests in Microfiche; Test Collection, Educational Testing Service, Princeton, NJ 08541
Target Audience: Adults
Notes: Items, 33
Designed to identify an individual's style of mind by providing an indication of what percentage of his mind is Greek, Roman, and Christian. It also indicates whether basic conflicts exist between values and beliefs. It may be

used to unearth various pathological patterns, to measure compatibility, and to study patterns of values in different occupations.

3330
Minnesota Satisfaction Questionnaire. Weiss, David; And Others 1977
Descriptors: Adults; *Employee Attitudes; *Employees; *Job Satisfaction; Rating Scales; Likert Scales
Identifiers: MSQ
Availability: Vocational Psychology Research; N620 Elliot Hall, University of Minnesota, 75 E. River Rd., Minneapolis, MN 55455
Target Audience: 18–65
Notes: Items, 100

Designed to measure employee's job satisfaction. Long form has 100 items, and short form has 20 items. Factors on the following scales are measured: ability utilization, achievement, activity, advancement, authority, company policies and practices, compensation, coworkers, creativity, independence, moral values, recognition, responsibility, security, social service, social status, supervision-human relations, supervision-technical, variety, and working conditions. Factor analysis of short form results in Intrinsic and Extrinsic Satisfaction as well as General Satisfaction score. Instrument is available for use only under the supervision of qualified psychologists, i.e., members of the American Psychological Association or persons with at least a Master's degree in psychology or its equivalent in training and experience. Graduate students may obtain materials for research use if their order is countersigned by their research adviser, who should be a qualified psychologist.

3351
College Interest Inventory. Henderson, Robert W. 1967
Descriptors: *College Bound Students; College Freshmen; *College Programs; Higher Education; High Schools; High School Students; *Interest Inventories; *Student Interests; Vocational Interests
Availability: Psychological Development Center; 7057 W. 130th St., Parma, OH 44130
Grade Level: 9–14
Notes: Items, 45

Measures student interest in college curricular areas. Designed to assist students in selection of college courses. Yields scores in areas of accounting, agriculture, biological science, business administration, civil engineering, education, electrical engineering, fine arts, foreign language, home economics, law, literature and journalism, mechanical engineering, physical science, and social science.

3503
Group Cohesiveness Scale. Goldman, Bernard 1957
Subtests: Individual Motives; Interpersonal Relations; Homogeneity of Attitude; Leadership
Descriptors: *Adults; Group Dynamics; Group Membership; *Group Unity; *Interpersonal Relationship; *Morale; Work Attitudes
Identifiers: Scale of Group Morale; Self Administered Tests
Availability: Psychometric Affiliates; P.O. Box 807, Murfreesboro, TN 37133
Target Audience: Adults
Notes: Time, 15 approx.; Items, 20

Designed to assess degree of cohesiveness within a group. Criteria for group morale include satisfaction of individual motives, homogeneity of attitudes, satisfaction of need for interpersonal relations, and respect for leadership.

3558
Forer Structured Sentence Completion Test. Forer, Bertram R. 1957
Descriptors: *Adolescents; *Adults; Aggression; Attitudes; Counseling Techniques; Females; Interpersonal Relationship; Males; Projective Measures; *Social Attitudes; *Values
Identifiers: FSSCT; Sentence Completion Tests
Availability: Western Psychological Services; 12031 Wilshire Blvd., Los Angeles, CA 90025
Target Audience: 13–64
Notes: Items, 100

Designed to assess attitude-value systems of counselees. Highly structured items force subjects to express attitudes in specific areas which have been determined in advance by the examiner. Technique illustrates individual differences, evasiveness, and defense mechanisms. Separate forms are available for men, women, adolescent boys, and adolescent girls.

3748
Leadership Opinion Questionnaire. Fleishman, Edwin A. 1960
Subtests: Consideration; Structure
Descriptors: *Administrator Attitudes; *Administrators; Adults; *Leadership; Leadership Styles; Personnel Selection; *Supervisors; Supervisory Training

Identifiers: LOQ; Self Administered Tests
Availability: London House; 1550 Northwest Hwy., Park Ridge, IL 60068
Target Audience: 18–64
Notes: Time, 15 approx.; Items, 40

Designed to measure leadership attitudes regarding basic dimensions of consideration and structure. Two scales are independent of one another. Consideration is the degree of rapport and 2-way communication with subordinates. Structure is the tendency to initiate ideas, plan, or direct a group toward organizational goals.

4021
JIM Scale. Frymier, Jack R. 1965
Descriptors: *Learning Motivation; *Overachievement; Questionnaires; Rating Scales; Secondary Education; *Secondary School Students; Student Evaluation; *Student Motivation; *Underachievement
Identifiers: Junior Index of Motivation; TIM(A)
Availability: Tests in Microfiche; Test Collection, Educational Testing Service, Princeton, NJ 08541
Grade Level: 7–12
Notes: Time, 30 approx.; Items, 80

Provides a measure of student motivation toward school.

4088
Omnibus Personality Inventory, Form F. Heist, Paul; Yonge, George 1968
Subtests: Thinking Introversion; Theoretical Orientation; Estheticism; Complexity; Autonomy; Religious Orientation; Social Extroversion; Impulse Expression; Personal Integration; Anxiety Level; Altruism; Practical Outlook; Masculinity-Femininity; Response Bias
Descriptors: Anxiety; Higher Education; *Personality Change; *Student Attitudes; *Student Behavior; *Undergraduate Students; Extraversion Introversion
Identifiers: Femininity; Masculinity; OPI
Availability: Psychological Corp.; 555 Academic Ct., San Antonio, TX 78204-0952
Grade Level: 13–16
Notes: Time, 60 approx.; Items, 385

Designed to assess attitudes, values and interests in areas of normal ego-functioning and intellectual activity. Developed for studies involving college students.

4184
Social Opinions Inventory. Finley, Cecile Bolton 1946
Subtests: World Better Without (125); World Better With (125); Of No Concern (125); Reject as Family Members (18); Reject as Friends (36); Reject from Groups (23); Keep Out of Country (19); Keep Country Out of International Federations (20)
Descriptors: Adolescents; Adults; Children; Ethnic Bias; *Maturity (Individuals); Questionnaires; Racial Bias; *Social Attitudes; Social Bias
Identifiers: TIM(A)
Availability: Tests in Microfiche; Test Collection, Educational Testing Service, Princeton, NJ 08541
Target Audience: 11–65
Notes: Time, 50; Items, 491

A measure of social maturity that elicits attitudes toward a variety of individuals and social institutions. Subject indicates which of a list of individuals the world would be better off without, better with, and those who do not concern the subject. Subject also selects those he or she would accept as family and group members.

4262
Dogmatism Scale. Rokeach, Milton
Descriptors: Adults; Beliefs; *Dogmatism; *Rating Scales
Identifiers: TIM(B)
Availability: Tests in Microfiche; Test Collection, Educational Testing Service, Princeton, NJ 08541
Target Audience: Adults
Notes: Items, 40

This instrument is designed to measure individual differences in openness or closedness of belief systems. Research instrument alternate form, D Scale, is available.

4287
Academic Interest Measures: Self-Scoring Form. Educational Testing Service, Princeton, NJ 1970
Descriptors: Adolescents; High Schools; *High School Students; *Interest Inventories; *Student Interests
Identifiers: AIM; TIM(C)
Availability: Tests in Microfiche; Test Collection, Educational Testing Service, Princeton, NJ 08541
Grade Level: 10–12
Notes: Items, 192

Designed to assess interest in 12 subject fields commonly included in secondary school curricula: biology, English, art, mathematics, social sciences, secretarial, physical sciences, foreign languages, music, industrial arts, home economics, and business. Twenty different forms are available.

4292
Face Scale. Kunin, Theodore 1955
Descriptors: *Adults; Measurement; *Measurement Techniques; Nonverbal Tests; Projective Measures
Identifiers: Facial Configuration
Availability: Personnel Psychology;v8 n1 p65-77, Spr 1955
Target Audience: Adults

Designed for use as a nonverbal response technique to assess attitudes and feelings. Two series of faces are illustrated—characterized and circular. Each set consists of 11 faces on a continuum from happy to sad. Faces may be used with any attitude measure where examiner does not want feelings filtered through the verbalization process.

4293
Group Toy Preference Test. Anastasiow, Nicholas J.
Descriptors: *Interest Inventories; *Males; *Pictorial Stimuli; Rating Scales; *Sex Role; *Toys; *Young Children
Identifiers: TIM(B)
Availability: Tests in Microfiche; Test Collection, Educational Testing Service, Princeton, NJ 08541
Target Audience: 5–6
Notes: Items, 45

Designed to provide an indication of a male child's adoption of a sex role as inferred from his toy preference patterns. The author's hypothesis is that 5-6 year old boys "who make consistent sex-typed toy preferences would show higher achievement test scores and be rated as more successful in school by their teachers".

4294
Hartman Value Profile. Hartman, Robert S.; Trigos, Mario Cardenas 1973
Descriptors: *Adolescents; *Adults; *Children; Psychological Testing; Self Concept; *Values
Identifiers: HVP
Availability: Research Concepts; Div. of Test Maker, Inc., 1368 E. Airport Rd., Muskegon, MI 49444
Target Audience: 5–64
Notes: Time, 30 approx.

An axiological measure of a person's capacity to value self and others. Designed to provide an understanding of the relationship between behavior and belief.

4307
Human Loyalty Expressionaire. Lentz, Theodore F. 1973
Descriptors: *Adults; *Global Approach; Political Attitudes; Social Attitudes; *Values
Identifiers: Loyalty
Availability: Peace Research Lab.; 6251 San Bonita Ave., St. Louis, MO 63105
Target Audience: Adults
Notes: Items, 104

Designed to measure attitudes concerning world-mindedness. Assesses humatriotism, loyalty to the whole of humanity. In *Humatriotism Human Interest in Peace and Survival*, instrument is appendices A, B, C of this book.

4325
How I Feel (Form Oz). Klopfer, Leopold E.; And Others 1970
Subtests: Attitude toward Science Class and Science; Anxiety about Science Class
Descriptors: Anxiety; *Elementary School Science; *Elementary School Students; *Grade 2; *Grade 3; Primary Education; *Student Attitudes
Identifiers: HIF; Oral Testing; TIM(E)
Availability: Tests in Microfiche; Test Collection, Educational Testing Service, Princeton, NJ 08541
Grade Level: 2–3
Notes: Time, 30 approx.; Items, 30

Designed to elicit students' attitudes toward their science classes, their study of science, and certain science learning activities. The questionnaire includes 2 scales: attitude toward science class and science, and anxiety about science class. It was originally developed for use with an individualized science program in grades 2 and 3.

4340
T.A.P. Social Attitude Battery. Levinson, Daniel J. 1960
Subtests: Authoritarianism; Ethnocentrism; Religious Conventionalism; Politico-Economic Conservatism; Traditional Family Ideology

Descriptors: Adults; Authoritarianism; Economics; Egocentrism; Family Attitudes; Political Attitudes; Racial Attitudes; Religion; *Social Attitudes
Identifiers: E Scale; PEC Scale; TIM(B); Traditional Family Ideology Scale
Availability: Tests in Microfiche; Test Collection, Educational Testing Service, Princeton, NJ 08541
Target Audience: Adults
Notes: Items, 69

A shortened version combining the author's F Scale, E Scale (TC009355), PEC Scale, Traditional Family Ideology Scale (TC009740), and RC Scale. Measures various social, political, economic, religious, and racial attitudes. Sixty-four of the items are statements to which the respondent indicates the degree of his or her agreement or disagreement. The remaining 5 items are open-ended questions. The Scoring Key for Revised Form FERPT is dated June 1959. Larry Kerpelman's PEC-F test (TC005126) is a revised version of the economic and political items in this test.

4748
Teacher's Subjective Evaluation of the Roslyn High School System of Selective Academic Placement. Rosengarten, William 1969
Descriptors: Adults; *Homogeneous Grouping; Program Evaluation; Rating Scales; Secondary School Teachers; *Student Placement; *Teacher Attitudes
Availability: ASIS/NAPS; c/o Microfiche Publications, P.O. Box 3513, Grand Central Station, New York, NY 10163-3513 (Doc. No. 00705)
Target Audience: Adults
Notes: Items, 6

Assesses Teachers' opinions of and reaction to, homogeneous grouping of students.

4795
Religious Belief Questionnaire. Apfeldorf, Max; Smith, Walter J. 1969
Descriptors: Adolescents; Adults; *Attitudes; Behavior; *Beliefs; Patients; Rating Scales; *Religion; *Veterans
Identifiers: TIM(E)
Availability: Tests in Microfiche; Test Collection, Educational Testing Service, Princeton, NJ 08541
Target Audience: 13-65
Notes: Items, 64

Designed to assess an individual's religious beliefs, attitudes, feelings, and practices. The questionnaire is multidenominational and covers God, prayer, Bible, good and evil and their consequences, organized religion, religious practices, and duties of daily living. One of 3 instruments developed for use in a study of how and to what extent religious beliefs influence behavior. Data were collected from 53 veterans in a Veterans Administration Hospital and 122 male and female high school students. Two parallel forms are available.

4811
Attitudes Inventory for Youth. French, J.L.; Cardon, B.W. 1969
Subtests: Planning (6); Attitudes toward School and Teachers (45); Personal Traits (36); Goals (17)
Descriptors: *Dropouts; High Schools; *High School Students; Objectives; Personality Traits; Planning; Rating Scales; School Attitudes; Self Concept; *Student Attitudes; Teachers
Identifiers: TIM(A)
Availability: Tests in Microfiche; Test Collection, Educational Testing Service, Princeton, NJ 08541
Grade Level: 9-12
Notes: Items, 104

Designed for use in a study of bright dropouts. A 325-item long form was also used. Students responded to statements on a 5-point agree/disagree scale and checked off traits they feel they possess.

4931
Organizational Frustration Scale. Spector, Paul E. 1975
Descriptors: Adults; *Job Satisfaction; Rating Scales; Supervisors; *Work Attitudes; Work Environment
Identifiers: *Frustration; TIM(A)
Availability: Tests in Microfiche; Test Collection, Educational Testing Service, Princeton, NJ 08541
Target Audience: Adults
Notes: Items, 29

Designed to investigate the reactions of employees to frustration in the actual work setting. Frustration is defined as the interference with an ongoing overt or covert response sequence. Items concern aspects of the job, supervisor, or job environment.

4932
Activity Scale. Kerpelman, Larry C.; Weiner, Michael J. 1969
Subtests: Actual Activities (12); Desired Activities (12)
Descriptors: *Activism; Citizen Participation; Communication (Thought Transfer); Higher Education; Information Seeking; *Political Attitudes; Questionnaires; *Undergraduate Students
Identifiers: TIM(A)
Availability: Tests in Microfiche; Test Collection, Educational Testing Service, Princeton, NJ 08541
Grade Level: 13-16
Notes: Time, 12; Items, 24

Survey measure of sociopolitical activism. Covers length of time respondent actually participated in activities and elicits information on the amount of time the respondent would have preferred to spend on such activities. Deals with 3 areas of potential involvement: action participation, communication activities, and information gathering.

4933
Academic Interest Inventory, Revised Edition. Bild, Bernice; Dutton, Eugene 1951
Descriptors: *College Curriculum; *College Freshmen; *Course Content; Higher Education; *Interest Inventories; Undergraduate Students
Identifiers: *Academic Interests; TIM(E)
Availability: Tests in Microfiche; Test Collection, Educational Testing Service, Princeton, NJ 08541
Grade Level: 13-16
Notes: Time, 20 approx.; Items, 132

Designed to measure a college student's interest in 12 areas of academic work: commerce and business administration; engineering and architecture; mathematics; chemistry and physics; geology and geography; biological science, sociology and psychology; education; history, government, and political science; English, journalism and speech; foreign language; and fine arts. The test may be used to help students select a major field of specialization, and it also may aid in the selection of specific courses.

4934
Learning Environment Inventory. Walberg, Herbert J.; Anderson, Gary J. 1967
Subtests: Cohesiveness; Diversity; Formality; Speed; Environment; Friction; Goal Direction; Favoritism; Cliqueness; Satisfaction; Disorganization; Difficulty; Apathy; Democratic; Competitiveness
Descriptors: Adolescents; *Classroom Environment; Group Dynamics; Interpersonal Relationship; Rating Scales; School Attitudes; Secondary Education; *Secondary School Students; *Student Attitudes; *Teacher Student Relationship
Identifiers: LEI; TIM(C)
Availability: Tests in Microfiche; Test Collection, Educational Testing Service, Princeton, NJ 08541
Target Audience: 12-18
Notes: Time, 40 approx.; Items, 105

Designed to assess an individual student's perceptions of his or her class, or to gauge the learning environment of the class as a group. Subscores include cohesiveness, diversity, formality, speed, environment, friction, goal direction, favoritism, cliqueness, satisfaction, disorganization, difficulty, apathy, democratic, and competitiveness. Research instrument.

4936
Purpose in Life Test. Crumbaugh, James C.; Maholick, Leonard T. 1969
Descriptors: *Adults; Alcoholism; Counseling Techniques; *Disabilities; High Schools; *High School Students; *Life Satisfaction; Neurosis; Older Adults; Quality of Life; Rating Scales
Identifiers: PIL; Sentence Completion Test
Availability: Psychometric Affiliates; P.O. Box 807, Murfreesboro, TN 37133
Grade Level: 9-12
Target Audience: Adults
Notes: Items, 33

Designed to measure the degree to which meaning in life has been found. Constructed from the orientation of logotherapy, a system of existential therapy originated by Viktor E. Frankl of the University of Vienna Medical School. Instrument is designed to detect an existential vacuum. Especially pertinent to alcoholic, retired, and handicapped populations. The Seeking of Noetic Goals Test (TC005869) was developed to complement this instrument.

4946
Fear of Death and Fear of Dying Scale. Lester, David
Descriptors: Adults; *Death; *Fear; Rating Scales

Availability: ASIS/NAPS; c/o Microfiche Publications, P.O. Box 3513, Grand Central Station, New York, NY 10163-3513 (Doc. No. 00418)
Target Audience: 18-64
Notes: Items, 36

Designed to measure fear of death of self, others, fear of the act of dying of self, others. Uses 6-point agree-disagree scale.

4949
Fascination Inventory C-M. Dutton, Eugene; Shaw, Franklin J. 1962
Subtests: Thinking; Managing; Helping; Doing
Descriptors: Adults; Career Planning; *College Students; Higher Education; *Interest Inventories; Talent
Identifiers: TIM(E)
Availability: Tests in Microfiche; Test Collection, Educational Testing Service, Princeton, NJ 08541
Grade Level: 13-16
Notes: Items, 108

Designed to predict the kinds of general activities or preferred behavior responses from which an individual is likely to receive the strongest satisfactions, by which he or she is most likely to be thoroughly challenged, and to which he or she is most likely to dedicate the greatest efforts. Four scores, or flair areas, are provided: thinking, managing, helping, and doing. The thinking variable measures preference for planning, for symbolic manipulations, reasoning, anticipating, and philosophizing. The managing variable indicates preference for organizing and directing, and for motivating and controlling human and natural events. The helping variable measures preference for coaching, assisting, and sympathizing and for working in mutual teamwork activities. The doing variable indicates a preference for action and for accomplishing programs, projects, and plans. Designed for use with college students, the inventory is based on Frank Shaw's work concerned with conservation, development, and stimulation of human talent.

4950
Work Values Inventory. Super, Donald E. 1970
Descriptors: *Adults; Higher Education; *Job Satisfaction; Secondary Education; *Secondary School Students; *Undergraduate Students; *Values
Identifiers: Self Description Questionnaire; WVI
Availability: Riverside Publishing Co.; 8420 Bryn Mawr Ave., Chicago, IL 60631
Target Audience: 12-64
Notes: Time, 15 approx.; Items, 45

Developed to assess goals that motivate individuals to work. Measures intrinsic and extrinsic values related to an occupation. May be used with students planning for college or careers.

4999
The Environmental Assessment Technique. Astin, Alexander W.; Holland, John L.
Descriptors: *College Environment; *College Seniors; Higher Education; *Student Attitudes; Undergraduate Students
Identifiers: EAT
Availability: Journal of Educational Psychology;v54 n4 p217-26, 1963
Grade Level: 13-16
Notes: Items, 39

Designed to assess college environment based on 8 attributes of the student body, size of student body, intelligence level, and personal orientations of students as indicated by percentage of students in each of 6 classes of major fields (Realistic, Intellectual, Social, Conventional, Enterprising, and Artistic).

5090
A Scale for the Measurement of Attitudes toward Healthful Living. Meise, William C.
Subtests: Social and Biological Background; Nutrition and Diet; Excretion and Cleanliness; Exercise and Body Mechanics; Fatigue and Rest; Mental Health and Integration; Reproduction and Heredity; Prevention and Control Disease; Health of the Special Organs; Environmental Health; Medical Care and Advice
Descriptors: Health; Higher Education; Life Style; *Physical Health; *Student Attitudes; *Undergraduate Students
Availability: William C. Meise; Slippery Rock State College, Slippery Rock, PA 16057
Grade Level: 13-16
Notes: Time, 35 approx.; Items, 100

Designed to assess attitudes of college students toward healthful living.

5141
Institutional Goals Inventory. Educational Testing Service, Princeton, NJ 1972

Descriptors: *Administrator Attitudes; Career Development; College Faculty; College Students; Cultural Context; Educational Development; *Educational Objectives; Educational Planning; French; *Higher Education; *Organizational Objectives; Rating Scales; Research; Social Values; Spanish; Student Attitudes
Identifiers: *Faculty Attitudes
Availability: Educational Testing Service; School and Higher Education Programs, Princeton, NJ 08541
Grade Level: 13–17
Notes: Time, 45; Items, 118

Designed to assist colleges and universities in defining educational goals, establishing priorities among goals and assisting with present and future planning. Respondents indicate views of these goals on a 5-point scale of importance. Areas covered include academic and personal development, intellectual orientation, humanism/altruism, cultural and aesthetic awareness, vocational preparation, advanced training research, public service, social egalitarianism, criticism, and activism.

5192
Elementary Science "Beliefs" Inventory. Good, Ronald G. 1971
Descriptors: Adults; *Elementary School Science; *Elementary School Teachers; Higher Education; *Student Attitudes; *Teacher Education Curriculum; *Undergraduate Students
Availability: Journal of Research in Science Teaching;v8 n3 p255-62, 1971
Grade Level: 13–16

Designed to assess opinions of elementary school teachers and undergraduates in elementary school education. Beliefs about science and science education are specifically assessed. Developed to assess attitudes related to the objectives of a student-structured approach to science-education course. Instrument is also available from the author: Ronald Good; Dept. of Science Education, Florida State University, Tallahassee, FL 32306.

5224
University Alienation Scale. Burbach, Harold J. 1972
Descriptors: *Black Students; College Environment; Higher Education; Social Attitudes; *Student Alienation; *Undergraduate Students; Likert Scales
Identifiers: UAS
Availability: Harold J. Burbach; Foundations of Education, School of Education, University of Virginia, Charlottesville, VA 22093
Grade Level: 13–16
Notes: Items, 24

Designed to assess feelings of alienation among black students at various institutions of higher education. Alienation in this context was defined as the concept of powerlessness, meaninglessness, and social estrangement.

5278
Opinionnaire on Attitudes toward Education. Lindgren, Henry Clay; Kelley, Ida B. 1958
Descriptors: Adults; Authoritarianism; Classroom Techniques; Culture Fair Tests; *Discipline Policy; *Elementary School Teachers; *Secondary School Teachers; Student Behavior; *Student Centered Curriculum; Student Teachers; *Teacher Attitudes; Teacher Student Relationship; *Teaching Styles
Identifiers: ATE Opinionnaire; TIM(B)
Availability: Tests in Microfiche; Test Collection, Educational Testing Service, Princeton, NJ 08541
Target Audience: Adults
Notes: Time, 30 approx.; Items, 50

Designed to measure the degree of acceptance of child-centered educational policies, this self-administered questionnaire covers 3 areas of educational policy: the desirability of understanding the behavior of students, particularly in terms of its psychological causation; the desirability of the teacher's using authoritarian methods as means of controlling the behavior of students; and subject-matter centeredness vs. learner-or child-centeredness. A long (50-item) and a short (30-item) form of the opinionnaire are included. The short form has only 2 response choices, agree or disagree.

5331
Color Meaning Test II. Williams, John E.
Descriptors: *Preschool Children; Preschool Education; *Racial Attitudes; Racial Bias
Identifiers: CMTII; TIM(A)
Availability: Tests in Microfiche; Test Collection, Educational Testing Service, Princeton, NJ 08541
Target Audience: 2–5
Notes: Items, 24

Assesses the evaluative responses of preliterate children to the colors black and white and provides an index of black-white bias. The child is given 24 opportunities to choose a black or a white animal in response to stories containing

one of 12 positive evaluative adjectives or one of 12 negative evaluative adjectives. Pictures required to administer the test must be rented or purchased from the author.

5499
Anxiety Self-Report. Parsons, Jane S. 1973
Descriptors: Adults; *Anxiety; Rating Scales; Self Evaluation (Individuals); *Teacher Attitudes; Teacher Evaluation; *Teachers
Identifiers: Anxiety Self Report; ASR
Availability: ERIC Document Reproduction Service; 3900 Wheeler Ave., Alexandria, VA 22304 (ED079330, 61 pages)
Target Audience: Adults
Notes: Items, 4

An abbreviated scale designed to obtain a measure of anxiety about teaching as well as general feelings of anxiety.

5568
The Family Relations Inventory. Brunkan, R.; Crites, John O.
Descriptors: *Childhood Attitudes; Child Rearing; Fathers; Higher Education; Mothers; *Parent Child Relationship; *Undergraduate Students
Availability: John O. Crites; Dept. of Psychology, University of Maryland, College Park, MD 20742
Grade Level: 13–16
Notes: Items, 202

Designed to assess individual's attitudes and perceptions about relationship with either one or both parents.

5596
Satisfaction Scale. Tuckman, Bruce W. 1968
Descriptors: *Course Evaluation; High Schools; *High School Students; Rating Scales; *Student Attitudes; Student Evaluation of Teacher Performance; Satisfaction
Availability: ERIC Document Reproduction Service; 3900 Wheeler Ave., Alexandria, VA 22304 (ED028990, 119 pages)
Grade Level: 9–12
Notes: Items, 9

Designed to measure student's subjective assessment of a course and instructor.

5618
Ambiguity Tolerance Scale: 20 Item Version. MacDonald, A.P. 1970
Descriptors: *Adults; *Ambiguity; Dogmatism; Personality Assessment; Personality Measures; *Undergraduate Students
Identifiers: AT(20); Rydell Rosen Ambiguity Tolerance Scale
Availability: Psychological Reports;v26 p791-98, 1970
Grade Level: 13–16
Target Audience: Adults
Notes: Items, 20

Instrument is a revision of the Rydell-Rosen Ambiguity Tolerance Scale, which consists of the first 16 items in this revised 20-item version. Intolerance of ambiguity is the tendency to perceive ambiguous materials or situations as threatening. Results of this study proved a high correlation between ambiguity tolerance and superior performance of ambiguous tasks. Intolerance was associated with rigidity, dogmatism and frequent church attendance.

5627
Maryland Parent Attitude Survey. Pumroy, Donald K.
Descriptors: Adults; *Child Rearing; Forced Choice Technique; *Parent Attitudes; Parents
Identifiers: MPAS; TIM(B)
Availability: Tests in Microfiche; Test Collection, Educational Testing Service, Princeton, NJ 08541
Target Audience: Adults
Notes: Items, 95

Designed to elicit parents' attitudes toward childrearing. The test is scored for 4 different types of parents: disciplinarian, indulgent, protective, and rejecting. An experimental research instrument.

5656
Curriculum Accommodation Questionnaire. Jones, John A. 1974
Subtests: Educational Conservatism; Educational Progressivism; Moral Flexibility; Permissiveness; Puritanism; Rugged Individualism; Bigotry; Curriculum Defined by Society; Teacher Distrust of Authority; Equality of Educational Opportunity; Rigidity toward Change; Academic Elitism; Law and Order
Descriptors: Adults; *Educational Innovation; Rating Scales; *Teacher Attitudes; *Teachers; *Values
Identifiers: CAQ

Availability: ERIC Document Reproduction Service; 3900 Wheeler Ave., Alexandria, VA 22304 (ED091436, 36 pages)
Target Audience: 18–64
Notes: Items, 56

Designed to measure differences in values and attitudes between teachers possessing differing degrees of innovativeness. Factor variables generally were better at revealing attitudes and values negatively associated with teacher innovativeness.

5745
Inventory of Roles and Values of Students, Faculty, and Administration in College and University Decision-Making. Troyer, Maurice E. 1967
Subtests: Part I Role of Decision Maker for Areas and Issues Calling for Policy and Decision Making; Part II Value Orientations Supportive of Perceived Roles
Descriptors: College Administration; College Faculty; College Students; *Decision Making; *Democratic Values; Higher Education; *Policy Formation; *Teacher Student Relationship; *Teacher Administrator Relationship; *Values
Identifiers: TIM(E)
Availability: Tests in Microfiche; Test Collection, Educational Testing Service, Princeton, NJ 08541
Grade Level: Higher Education
Notes: Items, 72

Part I of the inventory is designed to measure attitudes toward the roles of college students, faculty, and administration in decision making about the university's program, the library, the faculty and administration, control and regulation of dormitories and campus conduct, financial matters, campus development and use of facilities, student organizations and activities, and public relations. Part II is designed to quantify and rank the values used as a basis for the roles expressed in Part I.

5773
Parental Attitude Research Instrument, Form IV. Schaefer, Earl S.; Bell, Richard Q. 1958
Subtests: Encouraging Verbalization; Fostering Dependency; Seclusion of the Mother; Breaking the Will; Martyrdom; Fear of Harming the Baby; Marital Conflict; Strictness; Irritability; Excluding Outside Influences; Deification; Suppression of Aggression; Rejection of the Homemaking Role; Equalitarianism; Approval of Activity; Avoidance of Communication; Inconsiderateness of the Husband; Suppression of Sexuality; Ascendance of the Mother; Intrusiveness; Comradeship and Sharing; Acceleration of Development; Dependency of the Mother
Descriptors: Adults; *Child Rearing; Family Life; *Parent Attitudes; Parent Child Relationship; Parent Influence; *Parents; *Personality Development
Identifiers: Inventory of Attitudes on Family Life and Children; PARI
Availability: Child Development;v29 n3 p339-61, Sep 1958
Target Audience: 18–64
Notes: Time, 20 approx.; Items, 115

Designed to assess parental attitudes toward child rearing and family life. Useful in research to determine parental influence on child's personality development.

5774
A Semantic Differential for Measurement of Global and Specific Self-Concepts. Corbett, Lois Stilwell
Descriptors: Elementary Education; *Elementary School Students; *Self Concept; Self Concept Measures; Semantic Differential; Student Attitudes
Availability: Dr. Lois Stillwell Corbett; Office of Child Study and Guidance, Akron Public Schools, 70 N. Broadway, Akron, OH 44308
Grade Level: 2–6

Designed to assess student attitudes toward self and others. Primary form consists of 9 items with a 3-point scale. The intermediate form consists of 9 items with a 5-point scale. Areas to be rated are determined by the examiner.

5803
Preschool Self-Concept Picture Test. Woolner, Rosestelle B. 1966
Descriptors: Nonverbal Tests; *Personality Traits; *Preschool Children; Preschool Education; Preschool Teachers; Pretests Posttests; *Self Concept; *Self Concept Measures; *Student Attitudes
Identifiers: PSCPT
Availability: Rosestelle B. Woolner; 3551 Aurora Cir., Memphis, TN 38111
Target Audience: 2–5
Notes: Items, 10

Designed to assist preschool teachers in assessing students' self-concept. Author recommends administration of the test at the beginning and the end of the school year.

5829
Political and Cultural Elicitation Routine. Candee, Dan 1974
Descriptors: *Activism; Adolescents; Adults; Autobiographies; Higher Education; *Political Affiliation; *Political Attitudes; Projective Measures; *Undergraduate Students
Identifiers: PACER; TIM(B)
Availability: Tests in Microfiche; Test Collection, Educational Testing Service, Princeton, NJ 08541
Grade Level: 13-16
Notes: Items, 109
PACER is a semistructured questionnaire designed to measure political ideology. Responses are coded according to 8 types of political thinking: affect, projection, traits, pragmatic, cognitive stimulation, personal growth, higher values, and analysis.

5858
Group Atmosphere Scale. Fiedler, Fred E.
Subtests: Group Atmosphere; Least Preferred Coworker
Descriptors: Adults; *Employee Attitudes; Leadership Qualities; *Organizational Climate; Organizational Effectiveness; *Personnel; Semantic Differential; *Sociometric Techniques
Availability: Dr. Fred E. Fiedler; Dept. of Psychology, Guthrie Hall, University of Washington, Seattle, WA 98195
Target Audience: Adults
Notes: Items, 28
Semantic differential scores assess group atmosphere and least preferred coworker. Designed to assess relationship of leader behavior and group atmosphere and employee interaction.

5869
Seeking of Noetic Goals Test. Crumbaugh, James C. 1977
Descriptors: *Adults; High Schools; *High School Students; *Life Satisfaction; *Motivation; Quality of Life; Rating Scales
Identifiers: SONG
Availability: Psychometric Affiliates; P.O. Box 807, Murfreesboro, TN 37133
Target Audience: Adults
Notes: Time, 10 approx.; Items, 20
Designed to measure individual's strength of motivation to find life meaning. Derived from logotherapy, a system of existential therapy developed by Viktor E. Frankl of the University of Vienna Medical School. Developed to complement the Purpose in Life Test (TC004936). A high score on SONG indicates individual lacks life purpose and has a motivation to find it. It would indicate a potential candidate for logotherapy.

5940
Parent Attitude Inquiry; Research Edition III. Baumrind, Diana 1967
Descriptors: Adults; *Child Rearing; Discipline; Maturity (Individuals); *Parent Attitudes; Parent Child Relationship; *Preschool Children; Questionnaires; Values
Availability: Family Socialization Project; Institute of Human Development, Tolman Hall 1203, University of California, Berkeley, CA 94720
Target Audience: 18-64
Notes: Items, 117
Questionnaire measuring parents' attitudes toward child rearing for parents of preschool age children. Items cover early maturity demands, values, conformity, anger over lack of control, firm enforcement, promotes nonconformity, discourages infantile behavior, authoritative, impatient, consistent, articulated, child-rearing philosophy.

6021
Sexual Attitude Survey. Kilpatrick, Dean G.; And Others
Descriptors: *College Students; Higher Education; Questionnaires; *Sexuality; Undergraduate Students
Identifiers: SAS; TIM(A)
Availability: Tests in Microfiche; Test Collection, Educational Testing Service, Princeton, NJ 08541
Grade Level: 13-16
Notes: Items, 29
Questionnaire measures reported sexual liberality of attitudes and behavior of individuals in a college population.

6061
A Love Attitudes Inventory. Knox, David 1971

Descriptors: *Adults; *Attitudes; *Counseling Techniques; *Family Life Education; Higher Education; High Schools; *High School Students; Marriage Counseling; Rating Scales; *Undergraduate Students; *Love
Identifiers: LAI; Premarital Counseling
Availability: Family Life Publications, Inc.; P.O. Box 427, Saluda, NC 28773
Grade Level: 9-16
Target Audience: 15-64
Notes: Items, 30
Designed to indicate student's attitudes toward love. Assesses attitude as romantic or realistic. May be used in adolescent and adult family living and marriage classes, marital and premarital counseling, and for counseling individuals who experience difficulty in forming lasting relationships.

6068
Program Aide Attitude Test. University of Arizona, Univ., Tucson, Arizona Center for Educational Research and Development 1970
Descriptors: Adults; *Attitude Change; Disadvantaged; *Educational Attitudes; Primary Education; *Teacher Aides
Identifiers: PAAT; Tucson Early Educational Model
Availability: The Journal of Experimental Education;v38 n4 p88-92, Sum 1970
Target Audience: Adults
Notes: Items, 35
Designed to assess changes in educational attitudes of teacher aides. Instrument is to be administered twice during the school year—fall and spring. Aides received no formal training and were trained by the classroom teacher. This instrument is a modified form of the Survey of Educational Attitudes developed for the Tucson Early Education Model.

6098
Intellectual Achievement Responsibility Questionnaire. Crandall, Virginia C.; And Others
Subtests: Success; Failure
Descriptors: *Academic Achievement; Adolescents; Attribution Theory; Children; *Educational Attitudes; *Elementary School Students; Elementary Secondary Education; *Forced Choice Technique; *Locus of Control; Questionnaires; *Secondary School Students
Identifiers: IAR; TIM(A)
Availability: Tests in Microfiche; Test Collection, Educational Testing Service, Princeton, NJ 08541
Grade Level: 3-12
Notes: Items, 34
Forced-choice measure provides assessments of children's beliefs that they, rather than others, are responsible for their intellectual and academic successes and failures. Subscale scores assess internal-external control separately in success and failure situations.

6099
Children's Social Desirability Questionnaire. Crandall, Virginia C.
Descriptors: Adolescents; Children; *Conformity; *Elementary School Students; Elementary Secondary Education; Individual Testing; Questionnaires; *Secondary School Students; *Social Attitudes
Identifiers: CSD; TIM(A)
Availability: Tests in Microfiche; Test Collection, Educational Testing Service, Princeton, NJ 08541
Grade Level: 3-12
Notes: Items, 48
Questionnaire measures the tendency to give socially approved responses by asking the respondent questions to determine whether he or she behaves according to approved middle-class mores, whether he or she ever behaves in a deviating fashion, or whether he or she sometimes thinks or acts in an acceptable manner. A true-false form of the scale is recommended for group administration to children in grades 6-12; a direct-question form (yes-no answer) is recommended for individual administration to children in grades 3-5.

6105
Job Satisfaction Blank No. 5. Hoppock, Robert 1970
Descriptors: Adults; Career Change; *Job Satisfaction; Questionnaires; Work Attitudes
Identifiers: TIM(A)
Availability: Tests in Microfiche; Test Collection, Educational Testing Service, Princeton, NJ 08541
Target Audience: Adults
Notes: Items, 28
Designed to assess the respondents' feelings about their job, how much of the time they are satisfied, their feelings about changing jobs, and job-related attitudes as compared

to those of other people. Percentiles are provided based on data obtained from 301 employed adults in New Hope, PA, which was, in 1933, a manufacturing village.

6109
Reading Teacher Survey. Askov, Eunice Nicholson 1971
Descriptors: Adults; *Individualized Reading; *Reading Teachers; Semantic Differential; *Teacher Attitudes
Identifiers: WDRSD; Wisconsin Design for Reading Skill Development
Availability: ERIC Document Reproduction Service; 3900 Wheeler Ave., Alexandria, VA 22304 (ED048349, 19 pages)
Target Audience: Adults
Notes: Items, 11
Designed to assess attitudes of reading teachers toward individualizing reading instruction. Used to determine teachers' attitudes toward adoption of the Wisconsin Design for Reading Skill Development. For detailed study, see ERIC Document ED040080.

6119
Prueba de la Terminacion de la Frase de Fehrenbach. Fehrenbach, Alice 1974
Subtests: Self-Attitudes; Attitudes toward Others; Attitudes toward Authority; Attitudes toward School; Self-Adequacy; Past and Future
Descriptors: *Emotional Adjustment; Individual Testing; *Leadership; Projective Measures; School Attitudes; Secondary Education; Self Concept; *Social Adjustment; Spanish Speaking
Identifiers: Authority; Frustration; Future; Past; *Sentence Completion Form; TIM(G)
Availability: Tests in Microfiche; Test Collection, Educational Testing Service, Princeton, NJ 08541
Grade Level: 7-12
Notes: Time, 60; Items, 100
Discriminates between students with potential leadership qualities in terms of outstanding or average adjustment or those who have adjustment difficulties. Can be used to gather information prior to counseling or to provide teachers with insight into the hopes and fears of children. Manual and inventory are in Spanish. Can be administered individually or to groups. Group administration in which the students themselves write in the information often exposes more difficulties in communication that the student may have.

6160
The School Counselor Attitude Inventory. Baker, Stanley B. 1971
Descriptors: Adults; Change Agents; *Counselor Attitudes; Multiple Choice Tests; *School Counselors
Identifiers: SCAI; TIM(B)
Availability: Tests in Microfiche; Test Collection, Educational Testing Service, Princeton, NJ 08541
Target Audience: Adults
Notes: Items, 20
This 20-item instrument is designed to measure counselors' preferred behaviors on the continuum from status quo through counselor model to change agent. The respondent is presented with a client problem and is asked to choose, from 6 responses, the one which best suits his or her style as a counselor. Each of the 6 responses represents one of the following categories: strong status quo advocate, status quo advocate with secondary interest in the client, status quo-oriented counselor, change-oriented counselor, semi-active change agent, and strong change agent.

6168
Learning Climate Questionnaire. Bowen, Donald D.; Kilmann, Ralph H. 1973
Subtests: Grading Process; Physical Environment; Task Relationships with Faculty; Social Relationships with Faculty; Course Material Presentation
Descriptors: *Business Administration Education; *College Environment; *Graduate Students; Graduate Study; Higher Education; *Masters Programs; Organizational Climate; Rating Scales; *Student Attitudes
Identifiers: LCQ
Availability: Dr. Ralph H. Kilmann; Graduate School of Business, University of Pittsburgh, Pittsburgh, PA 15260
Grade Level: 17-20
Target Audience: Adults
Notes: Items, 51
Designed to assess the learning climate of professional schools. Originally developed for use with students in a Masters of Business Administration program. May be used to investigate organizational dynamics of professional schools in other areas of study.

6172
Writing Apprehension Measure. Miller, Michael D.; Daly, John A. 1975
Descriptors: Adults; *Anxiety; *Emotional Response; Rating Scales; Undergraduate Students; Verbal Communication; *Writing (Composition); Likert Scales
Identifiers: TIM(B); WAT
Availability: Tests in Microfiche; Test Collection, Educational Testing Service, Princeton, NJ 08541
Target Audience: Adults
Notes: Items, 26
Self-report questionnaire is designed to measure general anxiety about encoding written communication. The respondent indicates the degree of his or her agreement or disagreement with each of 26 items which deal with tendencies to avoid writing, attitudes toward written communication, and feelings experienced during writing.

6182
The Nature and Function of Social Work Questionnaire. Taber, Merlin; Vattano, Anthony J. 1970
Descriptors: Adults; Attitudes; *Job Satisfaction; Rating Scales; *Social Workers; *Work Attitudes
Identifiers: TIM(B)
Availability: Tests in Microfiche; Test Collection, Educational Testing Service, Princeton, NJ 08541
Target Audience: Adults
Notes: Items, 71
Designed to assess the attitudes of social workers and others who are well oriented to social work toward the profession. It encompasses 5 professional orientations: psychodynamic-mindedness, social action, social-environment-mindedness, title-protection and training, and private practice. The instrument is recommended for group rather than individual analysis.

6190
Fehrenbach Children's Questionnaire. Fehrenbach, Alice 1957
Descriptors: *Children; Elementary School Students; Parent Child Relationship; Peer Relationship; Questionnaires; School Attitudes; School Counselors; School Psychologists; *Self Evaluation (Individuals); *Spanish; Spanish Speaking; Teacher Student Relationship
Identifiers: TIM(I)
Availability: Tests in Microfiche; Test Collection, Educational Testing Service, Princeton, NJ 08541
Target Audience: 6-12
Notes: Items, 60
A questionnaire which may be administered individually or to groups. Responses to questions will reflect children's attitudes toward themselves, peers, parents, teachers, school, degree of frustration. Questionnaire is also available in Spanish. Is not intended as a diagnostic instrument, but to serve as a point of departure for counseling or therapy.

6192
Piers-Harris Children's Self-Concept Scale. Piers, Ellen V.; Harris, Dale B. 1969
Subtests: Behavior; Intellectual and School Status; Physical Appearance and Attributes; Anxiety; Popularity; Happiness and Satisfaction
Descriptors: Anxiety; *Elementary School Students; Elementary Secondary Education; Individual Testing; School Attitudes; *Secondary School Students; *Self Concept; *Self Concept Measures; Student Attitudes
Identifiers: The Way I Feel about Myself
Availability: Western Psychological Services; 12031 Wilshire Blvd., Los Angeles, CA 90025
Grade Level: 3-12
Notes: Time, 20 approx.; Items, 80
Designed to assess self-attitudes of children in grades 3-12. Requires a third grade reading level. May be administered individually to children below that level. Measures self-concept in areas of behavior, intellectual and school status, physical appearance, anxiety, popularity, and happiness-satisfaction.

6225
Attitudes toward Riding the School Bus. Barker, Donald G. 1966
Descriptors: High Schools; *High School Students; Rating Scales; *School Buses; *Student Attitudes
Availability: Psychology in the Schools;v3 n3 p278-81, Jul 1966
Grade Level: 9-12
Notes: Items, 24
Designed to measure attitudes of high school students concerning riding the school bus.

6226
Attitudes toward a Guidance Program. Barker, Donald G. 1966

Descriptors: *Adults; Higher Education; *Parent Attitudes; *School Guidance; *Student Attitudes; *Teacher Attitudes; *Undergraduate Students
Identifiers: Self Administered Tests
Availability: Personnel and Guidance Journal;v44 n5 p1077-83, Jun 1966
Grade Level: 13-16
Target Audience: Adults
Notes: Time, 5 approx.; Items, 20
Designed to assess attitudes toward school guidance programs. May be completed by students, parents, or teachers.

6271
Faculty Morale—Institutional Climate Scale. Bowers, Orville E. 1968
Subtests: Working Conditions and Services (10); Personnel Policies and Practices (10); Faculty-Administrator Relationships (10); Student Relationships (10); Colleague Relationships (10)
Descriptors: Adults; *College Faculty; *Faculty College Relationship; Interprofessional Relationship; *Morale; Personnel Policy; Teacher Student Relationship; Teacher Administrator Relationship; *Teacher Attitudes; Work Environment
Identifiers: TIM(A)
Availability: Tests in Microfiche; Test Collection, Educational Testing Service, Princeton, NJ 08541
Target Audience: Adults
Notes: Time, 35; Items, 50
Designed to identify the elements that describe institutional climate and faculty morale prevailing on a college campus. The items are grouped in the following areas: working conditions and services, personnel policies and practices, faculty-administrator relationships, colleague relationships, and student relationships.

6341
Aggression Scale. Larsen, Knud S. 1971
Descriptors: *Adults; *Aggression; Attitudes
Availability: Journal of Personality Assessment;v35 n3 p275-81, 1971
Target Audience: Adults
Subject is asked to agree or disagree with a series of attitudinal statements. The responses given yield a measure of aggression. Form A consists of 20 items. Form B has 17 items.

6358
Pupil Situational Inventory: A Measure of Experimental Attitude. Cheong, George S.C. 1964
Descriptors: *Elementary School Students; Intermediate Grades; Rating Scales; School Attitudes; *Student Attitudes
Identifiers: Dewey (John); PSI
Availability: The Journal of Experimental Education;v38 n2 p24-30, Win 1969
Grade Level: 4-6
Notes: Items, 25
Designed to measure experimental attitude of students in grades 4 to 6, specifically in terms of John Dewey's philosophy of experimentalism.

6403
Preschool Racial Attitude Measure II. Williams, John E. 1975
Subtests: Racial Attitude (36); Sex Role (12)
Descriptors: *Preschool Children; *Racial Attitudes; Racial Identification; *Sex Role; Young Children
Identifiers: PRAM II; TIM(A)
Availability: Tests in Microfiche; Test Collection, Educational Testing Service, Princeton, NJ 08541
Target Audience: 3-7
Notes: Items, 36
Designed to assess racial attitudes in preschool children. It yields racial attitude and sex-role scores. Stimulus materials consist of 36 color photographs, 24 racial attitude pictures, and 12 sex-role pictures. PRAM II may also be used to obtain a measure of racial identification. The pictures required to administer the test must be rented or purchased from the author.

6410
Tandy's Semantic Attitude Scale for Attitudes toward Smoking. Tandy, Ruth Elizabeth
Descriptors: Adolescents; Adults; *Semantic Differential; *Smoking; Likert Scales
Identifiers: Hawthorne Effect; TIM(E)
Availability: Tests in Microfiche; Test Collection, Educational Testing Service, Princeton, NJ 08541
Target Audience: 12-65
Notes: Items, 12
Evaluates 12 concepts through the use of 10 sets of bi-polar adjectives rated on a 9-point scale. It was designed for use in a study of seventh graders' attitudes toward

smoking and is purported to be applicable to subjects in higher grades and adults. Six concepts are concerned with cigarette smoking. Another 6 are inserted to disguise the smoking concepts and prevent the Hawthorne effect.

6423
Interest Assessment Scales: Form III. Ronning, Royce R.; And Others 1963
Descriptors: Adolescents; Adults; Higher Education; High Schools; High School Students; *Interest Inventories; Interests; Rating Scales; Undergraduate Students
Identifiers: IAS; TIM(B)
Availability: Tests in Microfiche; Test Collection, Educational Testing Service, Princeton, NJ 08541
Target Audience: 14-65
Notes: Items, 81
Interest assessment device consists of 8 factors: adventure, order, influencing others, nurturance, concrete means, written expression, abstract ideas, and aesthetic. Research instrument.

6447
Creativity Attitude Survey. Schaefer, Charles E. 1971
Subtests: Confidence in Own Ideas; Appreciation of Fantasy; Theoretical and Aesthetic Orientation; Openness to Impulse Expression; Desire for Novelty
Descriptors: *Creativity; Creativity Tests; *Elementary School Students; Intermediate Grades; *Student Attitudes
Identifiers: CAS
Availability: Psychologists and Educators; P.O. Box 513, St. Louis, MO 63017
Grade Level: 4-6
Notes: Time, 10 approx.; Items, 32
Designed to measure levels of creativity and attitudes toward creative expression.

6457
Self-Esteem Inventory: School Form. Coopersmith, Stanley 1981
Subtests: General Self; Social Self-Peers; Home-Parents; School Academic, Lie Scale
Descriptors: *Adolescents; *Children; Elementary School Students; Parent Child Relationship; Peer Relationship; *School Attitudes; Secondary School Students; *Self Concept Measures; *Self Esteem; Social Attitudes; *Student Attitudes; Test Wiseness
Identifiers: SEI
Availability: Consulting Psychologists Press; 577 College Ave., Palo Alto, CA 94306
Target Audience: 8-15
Notes: Time, 10 approx.; Items, 58
Designed to measure evaluative attitudes toward the self in social, academic, family, and personal areas of experience. This form was previously known as Form A or Long Form. May be administered to groups or individuals.

6471
World Regions Perception Survey. Carnegie-Mellon University., Pittsburgh, PA, Project Africa 1967
Descriptors: Association Measures; Cultural Awareness; Geographic Concepts; Geographic Regions; Secondary Education; *Secondary School Students; Social Studies; *Student Attitudes; *World Geography
Identifiers: Africa; Project Africa
Availability: ERIC Document Reproduction Service; 3900 Wheeler Ave., Alexandria, VA 22304 (ED030010, 16 pages)
Grade Level: 7-12
Notes: Time, 30 approx.; Items, 90
Designed to assess student's perceptions of Africa south of the Sahara. Respondents must identify stimulus terms with any of 7 regions of the world.

6502
Snyder Jewish Drinking Practices Interview Schedule. Snyder, Charles B. 1958
Descriptors: Adults; *Alcoholic Beverages; Cultural Influences; *Drinking; Interviews; *Jews; Social Attitudes
Availability: Snyder, Charles B.; Alcohol and the Jews: A Cultural Study of Drinking and Sobriety.Carbondale, IL: Southern Illinois University Press, 1978, C1958
Target Audience: Adults
Notes: Items, 72
Designed to assess drinking practices and attitudes toward alcoholism of Jewish adults.

6598
University of Maryland Marijuana Use Questionnaire. McKenzie, James D. 1983

Descriptors: Alcoholic Beverages; *Drug Abuse;
Higher Education; *Marijuana; Questionnaires;
*Student Attitudes; Student Behavior;
*Undergraduate Students
Availability: Division of Testing, Research and
Data Processing; The Counseling Center, Shoe-
maker Bldg., University of Maryland, College
Park, MD 20742
Grade Level: 13–16

A series of anonymous questionnaires used to assess drug
and alcohol use among undergraduate students. Attitudes
toward drug use are also assessed.

6691
Marriage Scale. White, J. Gustav 1970
Descriptors: Adults; *Beliefs; *Counseling Tech-
niques; Interpersonal Relationship; *Marriage
Counseling; Mate Selection; Rating Scales;
*Spouses
Identifiers: *Engaged Couples; *Premarital Coun-
seling; Self Administered Tests
Availability: Psychologists and Educators; P.O.
Box 513, St. Louis, MO 63017
Target Audience: 18–64
Notes: Time, 15 approx.; Items, 21

Designed primarily for use in premarital counseling. Used
to expose couples' attitudes toward major factors in a
happy marriage. The areas of agreement and disagreement
are thus opened for discussion. May be used for married
couples as well as for engaged couples. Factors assessed
include mutual understanding, outlook on life, religion,
love, intercommunication, objectionable habits, pleasures,
relatives, children, sex, occupation, finances, and major
plans. Not suitable for persons with below average reading
level.

6698
School Morale Scale. Wrightsman, Lawrence S.;
And Others 1968
Subtests: School Plant; Instruction; Administra-
tion, Regulations and Staff; Community; Other
Students; Teacher Student Relationships; Gen-
eral School Feelings
Descriptors: *Elementary School Students; Inter-
mediate Grades; *Interpersonal Relationship;
Morale; *School Attitudes; Secondary Educa-
tion; *Secondary School Students; *Student At-
titudes
Identifiers: SM Scale
Availability: Lawrence S. Wrightsman; Dept. of
Psychology, University of Kansas, Lawrence, KS
66045
Grade Level: 5–12
Notes: Items, 84

Designed to assess students attitudes about several aspects
of school. Assesses overall school morale.

6699
Philosophies of Human Nature Scale. Wrights-
man, Lawrence S. 1964
Subtests: Trustworthiness; Strength of Will and
Rationality; Altruism; Independence from
Group Pressures; Complexity; Variability
Descriptors: Adults; *Beliefs; *Human Relations;
Rating Scales; Likert Scales
Identifiers: *Human Nature; PHN; TIM(I)
Availability: Tests in Microfiche; Test Collection,
Educational Testing Service, Princeton, NJ
08541
Target Audience: 18–64
Notes: Items, 84

Attempts to measure a person's beliefs about human nature, specifically one's beliefs about the interpersonal aspects of human nature. The author delineates 6 basic
dimensions: trustworthiness or the extent to which people
are seen as honest, moral, and reliable; altruism, the extent of sympathy, unselfishness, and concern for others;
independence, the extent to which a person holds to his or
her convictions despite pressures to conform; strength of
will and rationality, the extent to which people understand
the motives behind their behavior and exert control over
the outcomes of their behavior; complexity, the extent to
which people are difficult or easy to understand; and
variability, which relates to an individual's changeability.

6746
Attitudes toward Self and School. Cincinnati Pub-
lic Schools, Ohio Dept. of Program Research and
Design 1966
Descriptors: *Childhood Attitudes; Primary Edu-
cation; *Self Concept; Self Concept Measures;
Young Children
Identifiers: TIM(A)
Availability: Tests in Microfiche; Test Collection,
Educational Testing Service, Princeton, NJ
08541
Grade Level: 1–3
Notes: Items, 18

Device is orally administered to groups of primary school
children to measure self-concept and school motivation.

6755
Background and Experience Questionnaire. Edu-
cational Testing Service, Princeton, NJ 1963
Descriptors: Adolescents; *Biographical Inven-
tories; Extracurricular Activities; High Schools;
*High School Seniors; *Predictive Measurement;
Questionnaires; *Student Interests
Identifiers: BEQ; TIM(B)
Availability: Tests in Microfiche; Test Collection,
Educational Testing Service, Princeton, NJ
08541
Grade Level: 12
Notes: Items, 168

Designed to measure the behavior and interests of adolescents as they reflect an orientation toward the adult or
adolescent culture. The values, beliefs, and norms characterizing each orientation are emphasized.

6756
**Background and Experience Questionnaire: Grade
7.** Educational Testing Service, Princeton, NJ
1963
Descriptors: Adolescents; *Biographical Inven-
tories; *Extracurricular Activities; Junior High
Schools; *Junior High School Students;
*Predictive Measurement; Questionnaires;
*Student Interests
Identifiers: BEQ; TIM(B)
Availability: Tests in Microfiche; Test Collection,
Educational Testing Service, Princeton, NJ
08541
Grade Level: 7
Notes: Items, 169

Designed to measure the behavior and interests of adolescents as they reflect an orientation toward either the adult
or adolescent culture. Emphasis is placed on the values,
beliefs, and norms characterizing each orientation.

6757
**Background and Experience Questionnaire: Grade
9.** Educational Testing Service, Princeton, NJ
1963
Descriptors: Adolescents; *Biographical Inven-
tories; *Extracurricular Activities; *High School
Freshmen; High Schools; Predictive Measure-
ment; Questionnaires; *Student Interests
Identifiers: BEQ; TIM(B)
Availability: Tests in Microfiche; Test Collection,
Educational Testing Service, Princeton, NJ
08541
Grade Level: 9
Notes: Items, 169

Designed to measure the behavior and interests of adolescents as they reflect an orientation toward either the adult
or adolescent culture. The values, beliefs, and norms characterizing each orientation are emphasized.

6758
**Background and Experience Questionnaire: Grade
11.** Educational Testing Service, Princeton, NJ
1963
Descriptors: Adolescents; *Biographical Inven-
tories; Extracurricular Activities; High Schools;
*High School Students; *Predictive Measure-
ment; Questionnaires; *Student Interests
Identifiers: BEQ; TIM(B)
Availability: Tests in Microfiche; Test Collection,
Educational Testing Service, Princeton, NJ
08541
Grade Level: 11
Notes: Items, 169

Designed to measure the behavior and interests of adolescents as they reflect an orientation toward either the adult
or adolescent culture. The values, beliefs, and norms characterizing each orientation are emphasized.

6759
**Background and Experience Questionnaire: Revised
Edition Grades 7-9.** Educational Testing Service,
Princeton, NJ 1965
Descriptors: Adolescents; *Biographical Inven-
tories; *Extracurricular Activities; Junior High
Schools; *Junior High School Students;
*Predictive Measurement; Questionnaires;
*Student Interests
Identifiers: BEQ; TIM(B)
Availability: Tests in Microfiche; Test Collection,
Educational Testing Service, Princeton, NJ
08541
Grade Level: 7–9
Notes: Time, 45 approx.; Items, 124

Provides a measure of interests and how much time is
spent in activities such as watching television, reading,
studying, and working. Also covered are educational-voca-
tional plans, home background, and school achievement.

6760
**Background and Experience Questionnaire: Revised
Edition: Grades 10-12.** Educational Testing Ser-
vice, Princeton, NJ 1965

Descriptors: Adolescents; *Biographical Inven-
tories; *Extracurricular Activities; High Schools;
*High School Students; *Predictive Measure-
ment; Questionnaires; *Student Interests
Identifiers: BEQ; TIM(B)
Availability: Tests in Microfiche; Test Collection,
Educational Testing Service, Princeton, NJ
08541
Grade Level: 10–12
Notes: Time, 45 approx.; Items, 131

Provides a measure of interest and how much time is
spent in various activities such as reading, working, and
watching television. Also covered are educational-voca-
tional plans, home background, and school achievement.

6772
San Diego County Inventory of Reading Attitudes.
San Diego County Dept. of Education, California
1961
Descriptors: Elementary Education; *Elementary
School Students; *Reading Attitudes; Student
Attitudes
Availability: ERIC Document Reproduction Ser-
vice; 3900 Wheeler Ave., Alexandria, VA 22304
(ED196938, 145 pages)
Grade Level: 1–6
Notes: Items, 25

Designed to assess attitudes of elementary school students
toward reading. Further information concerning this instrument may be obtained from Glen N. Pierson, San
Diego County Department of Education, 6401 Linda Vista
Road, San Diego, CA 92111. Instrument is included in
Measuring Attitudes toward Reading, ERIC/TM Report
73, available through ERIC.

6777
Dental Auxiliary Image Test. Chambers, David
W. 1971
Descriptors: Adults; *Attitudes; *Dental Assistants;
*Dental Hygienists; *Patients; *Projective Mea-
sures
Identifiers: DAIT; TIM(B)
Availability: Tests in Microfiche; Test Collection,
Educational Testing Service, Princeton, NJ
08541
Target Audience: Adults
Notes: Time, 5; Items, 15

Projective instrument designed to elicit perceptions of
dental assistants and dental hygienists. Responses are
scored according to 10 coding categories: tasks, human
relations, significant contributions, competence and confidence, integrity, qualifications, health, job opportunity,
work constraints, and negative image. Instrument may be
administered to individuals or small groups. Suitable for
dental patients, dental students and dental assisting students, as well as for practicing dental professionals.

6790
Paulson Survey on Drugs. Paulson, Patricia Cal-
lahan 1971
Descriptors: Community Colleges; Drug Abuse;
*Drug Use; *Student Attitudes; Two Year Col-
leges; *Two Year College Students
Availability: University Microfilms International;
Dissertation Copies, P.O. Box 1764, Ann Arbor,
MI 48106 (Order No. 71-6933)
Grade Level: 13–14
Notes: Items, 23

Developed as a research instrument to investigate attitudes and practices toward drugs by both users and nonusers in a community college. Statements in the questionnaire cover demographic data, attitudes toward drugs and
drug use, reasons for using drugs, facts about users, self-
image, success-failure motivation, and self-esteem. Many
of the questions have multiple parts.

6911
Purdue Teacher Opinionaire. Bentley, Ralph R.;
Rempel, Averno M. 1967
Subtests: Teacher Rapport with Principal; Satis-
faction with Teaching; Rapport among Teach-
ers; Teacher Salary; Teacher Load; Curriculum
Issues; Teacher Status; Community Support of
Education; School Facilities and Services; Com-
munity Pressures
Descriptors: Adults; *Opinions; Teacher Admin-
istrator Relationship; *Teacher Attitudes;
*Teacher Morale; Teachers; Teacher Supervi-
sion; Teaching Conditions
Identifiers: PTMI; PTO; Purdue Teacher Morale
Inventory; Purdue Teacher Opinionaire Supple-
ment
Availability: University Book Store; 360 State St.,
West Lafayette, IN 47906
Target Audience: Adults
Notes: Time, 30 approx.; Items, 100

Untimed instrument that gives teachers the opportunity to
express their opinions about their school (working) environment and measures their morale. Used as an aid for
school boards, superintendents, administrators, and teachers in the improvement of the educational program. In a

Likert-type scale, the teacher agrees or disagrees with the statement in each item. Available as (1) Form A (copyright 1976); (2) Form B (copyright 1964); and (3) a Supplement in which the teachers express their opinions concerning the school board, the superintendent of schools, and their department head (30 additional items, copyright 1972). Previously issued under the title Purdue Teacher Morale Inventory.

6929
Opinions toward Adolescents. Martin, William T. 1972
Subtests: Conservative-Liberal; Permissive-Punitive; Morally Accepting-Morally Restrictive; Democratic-Authoritarian; Trust-Mistrust; Acceptance-Prejudice; Understanding-Misunderstanding; Sincerity-Skepticism
Descriptors: *Adolescents; *Adults; Attitudes; Higher Education; Rating Scales; Screening Tests; *Social Attitudes; Undergraduate Students
Identifiers: *Adult Attitudes; OTA; Self Administered Tests
Availability: Psychologists and Educators; P.O. Box 513, St. Louis, MO 63017
Grade Level: 13–16
Target Audience: Adults
Notes: Items, 89

Designed to assess adults' opinions of adolescents. May be used as screening device for persons seeking positions to work with adolescents. Useful in staff education programs and research. Items are written on readability level of grades 5-7.

6936
Psychological Audit for Interpersonal Relations. Stephenson, Richard R. 1966
Subtests: Social Status; Intellectual Rigidity; Family Cohesiveness; Social Extraversion; Political Conservatism; Self-Rejection; Aggressive Hostility; Physical Affection; Monetary Concern; Change and Variety; Dominant Leadership; Nurturant Helpfulness; Order and Routine; Esthetic Pleasures; Submissive Passivity; Psychological Support; Emotional Control; Dependent Suggestibility; Self-Acceptance
Descriptors: *Adults; Counseling Techniques; Industrial Personnel; *Interpersonal Relationship; *Marriage Counseling; Mate Selection; *Personality Assessment; Personality Measures; Personnel Selection
Identifiers: *Premarital Counseling; The PAIR Test
Availability: Richard R. Stephenson; 3745 4th Ave., San Diego, CA 92103
Target Audience: 18–64
Notes: Time, 60 approx.; Items, 500

Designed to assess interest, personality, and attitude dimensions. Useful in situations where it is important to select or match people on the basis of increased probability of psychological compatibility. Primarily used in premarital and postmarital compatibility assessment and counseling.

6983
Sentence Completion Test. Irvin, Floyd S. 1972
Subtests: Self-Concept; Parental Attitude; Peer Attitude; Need for Achievement; Learning Attitude; Body Image
Descriptors: Achievement Need; Adolescents; Affective Measures; Body Image; Higher Education; High Schools; *High School Students; Individual Testing; Self Concept; *Undergraduate Students
Identifiers: SCT
Availability: Psychologists and Educators; P.O. Box 513, St. Louis, MO 63017
Grade Level: 9–16
Notes: Time, 15 approx.; Items, 35

Designed to assess attitudes and opinions concerning self-concept, parental attitude, peer attitude, and need for achievement. Individual administration should be used when instrument is used in a clinical setting.

6991
M-Scale. Morrison, James H. 1969
Descriptors: *Adults; *Racial Attitudes; Racial Relations
Identifiers: United States
Availability: James H. Morrison; 9804 Hadley Ave., Overland Park, KS 66212
Target Audience: Adults
Notes: Time, 20 approx.; Items, 28

Designed to measure attitudes toward black-white relations in the United States. May be used to initiate discussion of black-white issues in sensitivity training.

6999
Pair Attraction Inventory. Shostrom, Everett L. 1970

Subtests: Mother-Son; Daddy-Doll; Bitch-Nice Guy; Master-Servant; Hawks; Doves; Rhythmic Score
Descriptors: Adults; Affective Measures; *Females; Interpersonal Attraction; *Interpersonal Relationship; *Males; Marriage Counseling; *Mate Selection; Spouses
Identifiers: PAI; Premarital Counseling; Self Administered Tests
Availability: Educational and Industrial Testing Service; P.O. Box 7234, San Diego, CA 92107
Target Audience: Adults
Notes: Time, 30 approx.; Items, 224

Designed to measure aspects contributing to mate or friend selection. Measures complementarity and symmetry in pair relationships. Useful in premarital and marital counseling. Assesses feelings and attitudes about the male-female relationship with another person. Separate forms for men and women.

7004
Sensation Seeking Scale Form IV. Zuckerman, Marvin 1975
Descriptors: Adults; *Attitudes; Forced Choice Technique; Higher Education; High Schools; *High School Students; Personality Traits; *Sensory Experience; *Undergraduate Students
Identifiers: SSS; TIM(B)
Availability: Tests in Microfiche; Test Collection, Educational Testing Service, Princeton, NJ 08541
Target Audience: 14–65
Notes: Items, 72

Designed to measure the propensity to seek varied and changing sensations for the purpose of maintaining an optimal level of arousal. Subscores are thrill and adventure seeking, experience seeking, disinhibition, boredom susceptibility, and general.

7005
Occupational Prestige Scale. Thompson, Donald L.; Tseng, M.S. 1972
Descriptors: Adults; Career Counseling; *Grade 11; *Grade 12; Higher Education; High Schools; *High School Students; *Occupations; Predictor Variables; *Student Attitudes; *Undergraduate Students; *Prestige
Identifiers: North Hatt Scale
Availability: Dr. Donald L. Thompson; University of Connecticut, Storrs, CT 06268
Grade Level: 11–16
Target Audience: 18–45
Notes: Time, 10 approx.; Items, 20

A shortened version of the North-Hatt Scale (National Opinion Research Center, 1947) which assesses an individual's perception of the prestige hierarchy of occupations. Examinee is given an alphabetical list of 20 occupations which he must rank in order of prestige associated with it. It was found that subjects in whom need for achievement exceeded fear of failure showed more accurate perceptions of occupational prestige hierarchy as compared to a cross-sectional standardization sample. Respondents who had more accurate perceptions were more likely to seek vocational counseling. Thus the instrument has predictive validity.

7024
Curriculum Attitude Inventory. Langenbach, Michael 1970
Descriptors: Adults; *Curriculum Development; Rating Scales; *Teacher Attitudes; *Teachers
Identifiers: CAI
Availability: Michael Langenbach; College of Education, University of Oklahoma, 820 Van Vleet Oval, Norman, OK 73069
Target Audience: Adults
Notes: Items, 50

Designed to measure teachers' attitudes toward curriculum use and planning.

7044
Allen Scale of Beliefs. Allen, B.J. 1972
Descriptors: Beliefs; High Schools; *High School Students; *Political Attitudes; *Social Attitudes
Identifiers: ASOB; TIM(A)
Availability: Tests in Microfiche; Test Collection, Educational Testing Service, Princeton, NJ 08541
Grade Level: 9–12
Notes: Items, 46

Assesses the extent to which students are committed to American sociopolitical values.

7054
Questionnaire Psychologique. Gough, Harrison G. 1975

Subtests: Dominance; Capacity for Status; Sociability; Social Presence; Self-Acceptance; Sense of Well-Being; Responsibility; Socialization; Self-Control; Tolerance; Good Impression; Communality; Achievement via Conformance; Achievement via Independence; Intellectual Efficiency; Psychological-Mindedness; Flexibility; Femininity
Descriptors: *Adolescents; Adults; *Attitudes; *French; Older Adults; *Personality Assessment; Personality Measures; Secondary Education; Self Evaluation (Individuals)
Identifiers: *CPI
Availability: Consulting Psychologists Press; 577 College Ave., Palo Alto, CA 94306
Target Audience: 12–70
Notes: Time, 60 approx.; Items, 480

Designed for group administration, instrument can be taken individually. Contains 468 statements, 12 of which appear twice for a total of 480 items. Most of content consists of reports of typical behavior patterns and customary feelings, opinions, and attitudes about social, ethical, and family matters. Content is geared more to students and young adults than to older groups.

7055
Questionario Psicologico. Gough, Harrison G. 1975
Subtests: Dominance; Capacity for Status; Sociability; Social Presence; Self-Acceptance; Sense of Well-Being; Responsibility; Socialization; Self-Control; Tolerance; Good Impression; Communality; Achievement via Conformance; Achievement via Independence; Intellectual Efficiency; Psychological-Mindedness; Flexibility; Femininity
Descriptors: *Adolescents; Adults; *Attitudes; *Italian; Older Adults; *Personality Assessment; Personality Measures; Secondary Education; Self Evaluation (Individuals)
Identifiers: *CPI
Availability: Consulting Psychologists Press; 577 College Ave., Palo Alto, CA 94306
Target Audience: 12–70
Notes: Time, 60 approx.; Items, 480

Designed for group administration, instrument can be taken individually. Contains 468 statements, 12 of which appear twice for a total of 480 items. Most of content consists of reports of typical behavior patterns and customary feelings, opinions, and attitudes about social, ethical, and family matters. Content is geared more to students and young adults than to older groups.

7056
Psychologischer Test. Gough, Harrison G. 1975
Subtests: Dominance; Capacity for Status; Sociability; Social Presence; Self-Acceptance; Sense of Well-Being; Responsibility; Socialization; Self-Control; Tolerance; Good Impression; Communality; Achievement via Conformance; Achievement via Independence; Intellectual Efficiency; Psychological-Mindedness; Flexibility; Femininity
Descriptors: *Adolescents; Adults; *Attitudes; *German; Older Adults; *Personality Assessment; Personality Measures; Secondary Education; Self Evaluation (Individuals)
Identifiers: *CPI
Availability: Consulting Psychologists Press; 577 College Ave., Palo Alto, CA 94306
Target Audience: 12–70
Notes: Time, 60 approx.; Items, 480

Designed for group administration, instrument can be taken individually. Contains 468 statements, 12 of which appear twice for a total of 480 items. Most of content consists of reports of typical behavior patterns and customary feelings, opinions, and attitudes about social, ethical, and family matters. Content is geared more to students and young adults than to older groups.

7057
Inventario Psicologico. Gough, Harrison G. 1975
Subtests: Dominance; Capacity for Status; Sociability; Social Presence; Self-Acceptance; Sense of Well-Being; Responsibility; Socialization; Self-Control; Tolerance; Good Impression; Communality; Achievement via Conformance; Achievement via Independence; Intellectual Efficiency; Psychological-Mindedness; Flexibility; Femininity
Descriptors: *Adolescents; Adults; *Attitudes; Older Adults; *Personality Assessment; Personality Measures; Secondary Education; Self Evaluation (Individuals); *Spanish
Identifiers: *CPI
Availability: Consulting Psychologists Press; 577 College Ave., Palo Alto, CA 94306
Target Audience: 12–70
Notes: Time, 60 approx.; Items, 480

Designed for group administration, instrument can be taken individually. Contains 468 statements, 12 of which appear twice for a total of 480 items. Most of content consists of reports of typical behavior patterns and customary feelings, opinions, and attitudes about social, ethical, and family matters. Content is geared more to students and young adults than to older groups.

7062
Personnel Reaction Blank. Gough, Harrison G. 1970
Descriptors: Adults; Interest Inventories; *Job Applicants; *Reliability; Semiskilled Workers; *Work Attitudes
Identifiers: PRB
Availability: Consulting Psychologists Press; 577 College Ave., Palo Alto, CA 94306
Target Audience: 15–64
Notes: Time, 15 approx.; Items, 70
Designed to assess dependability-conscientiousness personality factor to predict job performance in routine, non-managerial situations.

7068
Henderson Environmental Learning Process Scale (HELPS). Henderson, Ronald W.; And Others 1972
Descriptors: Academic Achievement; Adults; Cultural Influences; *Family Environment; *Parent Attitudes; Rating Scales; *School Attitudes; Spanish; *Spanish Speaking; Young Children
Identifiers: HELPS; TIM(A)
Availability: Tests in Microfiche; Test Collection, Educational Testing Service, Princeton, NJ 08541
Target Audience: Adults
Notes: Time, 30 approx.; Items, 55
HELPS is designed to measure characteristics of the home environment related to the intellectual and scholastic performance of young children. The interview schedule elicits information on the aspiration level of the home, the range of environmental stimulation available to the child, the parental guidance or direct teaching provided, the range of adult models available, and the nature of reinforcement practices used to influence the child's behavior. Both English and Spanish forms of the scale are available, and the interview is conducted in the language of choice of the respondents.

7120
Job Descriptive Index. Smith, Patricia C. 1975
Subtests: Work on Present Job; Present Pay; Opportunities for Promotion; Supervision on Present Job; People on Your Present Job
Descriptors: Adults; *Employee Attitudes; Employees; *Job Satisfaction; *Work Attitudes
Identifiers: JDI
Availability: Patricia C. Smith; Dept. of Psychology, Bowling Green State University, Bowling Green, OH 43403
Target Audience: Adults
Designed to elicit employees' attitudes concerning their job and work climate.

7128
Death Anxiety Scale. Templer, Donald I. 1970
Descriptors: Adults; *Anxiety; *Death
Identifiers: DAS
Availability: Donald I. Templer; California School of Professional Psychology, 1350 M St., Fresno, CA 93721
Target Audience: Adults
Notes: Items, 15
Designed to assess attitudes concerning death.

7131
Verbal Check List. Lerner, Richard M.
Subtests: Physique and Physical; Social; Personal
Descriptors: Body Image; Elementary School Students; Elementary Secondary Education; Higher Education; *Individual Testing; *Physical Characteristics; *Pictorial Stimuli; Secondary School Students; Undergraduate Students; Visual Measures
Identifiers: TIM(C); VCL
Availability: Tests in Microfiche; Test Collection, Educational Testing Service, Princeton, NJ 08541
Target Audience: 5–20
Notes: Items, 56
A list of adjectives or descriptive phrases designed to elicit information concerning certain dimensions of body-build stereotyping. The items are arranged into 3 categories of attributes: physical, social, and personal. Stimulus pictures consisting of figure drawings of male endomorphs, mesomorphs, and ectomorphs are used in administering the test. Individual administration.

7132
Study Attitudes and Methods Survey. Michael, William B.; And Others 1972

Descriptors: *Counseling Techniques; Higher Education; Rating Scales; Secondary Education; *Secondary School Students; *Student Attitudes; Student Motivation; *Study Habits; *Undergraduate Students
Identifiers: SAMS
Availability: Educational and Industrial Testing Service; P.O. Box 7234, San Diego, CA 92107
Grade Level: 7–16
Notes: Time, 30 approx.; Items, 150
Designed to assess noncognitive factors associated with success in school. Assesses dimensions of attitude, motivation and study habits important to academic success. May be used to identify students who may be helped by individual counseling. Factor dimensions measured are academic interest—love of learning, academic drive—conformity, study methods, study anxiety, manipulation, and alienation toward authority.

7153
FIRO Scales: VAL-ED. Schutz, Will 1977
Subtests: Importance; Mind; Teacher-Student: Control; Teacher-Student: Affection; Administrator-Teacher: Inclusion; Administrator-Teacher: Control; Administrator-Teacher: Affection; Teacher-Community: Inclusion; Teacher-Community: Control; Teacher-Community: Affection; Administrator-Community: Control; Administrator-Community: Affection
Descriptors: Administrators; Adults; *Interpersonal Relationship; Personality Measures; Rating Scales; School Attitudes; *School Community Relationship; Social Attitudes; *Teacher Student Relationship; *Teacher Administrator Relationship; Teachers; *Value Judgment
Identifiers: Educational Values; Fundamental Interpersonal Relations Orientation
Availability: Consulting Psychologists Press; 577 College Ave., Palo Alto, CA 94306
Target Audience: 18–64
Notes: Time, 15 approx.; Items, 126
Designed to assess values regarding several aspects of education. FIRO theory is applied to the interpersonal aspects of education.

7168
Personal Beliefs Inventory: Forms A and B. Brown, Bob Burton
Subtests: Personal Beliefs Inventory (40); Teacher Practices Inventory (40); Personal Opinion Questionnaire (66)
Descriptors: Adults; *Beliefs; *Opinions; *Rating Scales; *Social Values; *Teacher Attitudes; Teacher Behavior; *Teachers; *Teaching Methods
Identifiers: TIM(B)
Availability: Tests in Microfiche; Test Collection, Educational Testing Service, Princeton, NJ 08541
Target Audience: Adults
Notes: Items, 146
As part of the Experimentalism Scale, this inventory was designed to measure agreement-disagreement with Dewey's philosophy of experimentalism. Items concern belief in the continuity or the dualism of the following: mind and body, permanence and change, science and morals, emotions and intellect, freedom and authority, and knowing and doing. Untimed.

7187
Achievement Scales: Female. Mehrabian, Albert 1968
Descriptors: *Achievement Need; Adults; *Females; Motivation; Rating Scales; Self Evaluation (Individuals)
Identifiers: Achievement Scale for Females
Availability: Albert Mehrabian; 17141 Rayen St., Northridge, CA 91325
Target Audience: Adults
Notes: Items, 26
Designed to elicit personal attitudes of women to discriminate between high and low achievers.

7188
Achievement Scales: Male. Mehrabian, Albert 1968
Descriptors: *Achievement Need; Adults; *Males; Motivation; Rating Scales; *Self Evaluation (Individuals)
Identifiers: Achievement Scale for Males
Availability: Albert Mehrabian; 17141 Rayen St., Northridge, CA 91325
Target Audience: Adults
Notes: Items, 26
Designed to elicit personal attitudes of men in an attempt to discriminate between high and low achievers.

7199
Attitudes toward Women Scale: Short Form. Spence, Janet T.; And Others

Descriptors: Adults; *Females; Rating Scales; *Sex Role; Likert Scales
Identifiers: AWS; TIM(A)
Availability: Tests in Microfiche; Test Collection, Educational Testing Service, Princeton, NJ 08541
Target Audience: Adults
Notes: Items, 25
A shortened version of the original scale which was devised to measure attitudes toward the rights and roles of women in modern society. The items cover the vocational, educational, and intellectual roles of women, as well as their freedom and independence, dating and courtship patterns, etiquette, sexual behavior, and marital relationships and obligations.

7211
Conformity Scale. MacDonald, A.P.
Descriptors: Adults; *Conformity
Identifiers: Opinion Survey C20; TIM(C)
Availability: Tests in Microfiche; Test Collection, Educational Testing Service, Princeton, NJ 08541
Target Audience: Adults
Notes: Items, 20
Conformity scale controlled for acquiescence response set. The scale is based upon items developed by Barron and Crutchfield. Equal number of true and false answers are used to produce a balanced scale.

7224
How I Feel about Television in School. Ayers, Jerry B.
Descriptors: *Educational Television; Elementary School Students; Primary Education; Rating Scales; *Student Attitudes; Television; Television Teachers; *Young Children
Identifiers: Oral Tests; TIM(A)
Availability: Tests in Microfiche; Test Collection, Educational Testing Service, Princeton, NJ 08541
Grade Level: 1–3
Designed to measure attitudes toward the use of instructional television in the classroom. Two forms are available. The written form has 22 items consisting of a rating scale and sentence completions. The second form is administered orally. The student responds to the 20 items by marking one of 4 faces to indicate his or her feelings about the question. The faces range from smiling to frowning.

7241
Student Instructional Report. Educational Testing Service, Princeton, NJ 1973
Descriptors: *College Students; *Course Evaluation; *Higher Education; Questionnaires; Spanish; *Spanish Speaking; Student Attitudes; *Student Evaluation of Teacher Performance; Teacher Student Relationship; *Two Year Colleges; *Vocational Schools
Availability: School and Higher Education Programs; Educational Testing Service, Princeton, NJ 08541
Grade Level: 13–16
Notes: Items, 49
Questionnaire designed to measure student perceptions of the organization and structure of courses, teaching techniques and student-teacher rapport for 2- and 4-year colleges, universities, and technical institutions. Thirty academic fields are represented. Also available in Spanish.

7242
Themes Concerning Blacks. Williams, Robert L. 1972
Descriptors: *Adolescents; *Adults; *Black Attitudes; *Blacks; Pictorial Stimuli; *Projective Measures
Identifiers: TCB
Availability: Williams and Associates; Black Community Psychology, 6373 Del Mar Blvd., St. Louis, MO 63130
Target Audience: 13–64
Notes: Items, 15
Designed to elicit from black subjects themes of achievement, pride, awareness, as well as negative themes of hate, aggression, and depression. Subject is shown a picture and asked to construct a story about what took place prior to the picture, what is occurring in the picture, and what will be the outcome.

7243
Williams Awareness Sentence Completion. Williams, Robert L. 1972
Descriptors: Adolescents; Adults; *Black Attitudes; *Blacks; Projective Measures; Racial Bias; Whites
Identifiers: Sentence Completion Tests; WASC
Availability: Williams and Associates; Black Community Psychology, 6373 Del Mar Blvd., St. Louis, MO 63130
Target Audience: 13–64
Notes: Items, 40

Designed to elicit feelings of conflict of black people regarding their race and prejudicial and/or positive white attitudes toward black people.

7261
Organizational Value Dimensions Questionnaire: Business Firm. Shartle, Carroll L.; Stogdill, Ralph M.
Subtests: Magnitude, Structure, and Growth; Consideration of Employee Welfare, Parentalism; Strategy, Shrewdness, Ruthlessness; Social and Ethical Responsibility; Quality of Product or Service; Stability, Lack of Change; Control over Employee Identification; External Political Participation; Member Equality
Descriptors: *Adults; *Business; Moral Values; Rating Scales; *Values; Work Attitudes
Identifiers: OVDQ; Value Scale (The Business Firm)
Availability: Administrative Science Research; Ohio State University, 1775 College Rd., Columbus, OH 43210
Target Audience: Adults
Notes: Items, 100
Designed to measure attitudinal values relating to business and industrial firms in general.

7265
Attitudes toward Vocational Education Scale. Engler, John P. 1975
Descriptors: *Administrator Attitudes; Administrators; Adults; *High Schools; Rating Scales; *Vocational Education; Likert Scales
Identifiers: ATVE Scale; TIM(A)
Availability: Tests in Microfiche; Test Collection, Educational Testing Service, Princeton, NJ 08541
Target Audience: Adults
Notes: Items, 67
Developed to measure the attitudes of high school administrators toward vocational education.

7266
The Semantic Study. Engler, John P.
Descriptors: *Administrator Attitudes; Adults; Institutions; *Occupations; *School Administration; *Secondary Education; *Semantic Differential
Identifiers: TIM(E)
Availability: Tests in Microfiche; Test Collection, Educational Testing Service, Princeton, NJ 08541
Target Audience: Adults
Notes: Items, 36
Designed to assess attitudes of secondary school administrators toward basic concepts of vocational and technical education. Thirty-six related concepts in 3 categories, vocational, academic, and unclassified, are evaluated through the use of 9 pairs of bipolar adjectives.

7281
The Knowledge about Psychology Test. Costin, Frank 1975
Descriptors: *College Students; Higher Education; *Knowledge Level; Multiple Choice Tests; *Psychologists; Psychology; *Student Attitudes
Identifiers: KAP; TIM(A)
Availability: Tests in Microfiche; Test Collection, Educational Testing Service, Princeton, NJ 08541
Grade Level: 13–16
Notes: Time, 30 approx.; Items, 60
Test of general knowledge about psychology and psychologists is based on the Facts about Science Test (TC001333). It is intended for research purposes only. The test consists of 2 scales of 30 items each. Scale S measures students' understanding of scientific and professional characteristics of psychology. Scale P measures students' perception of personal characteristics of psychologists.

7318
Student Evaluation of Teaching. Center for Educational Research, Seattle, WA 1973
Descriptors: *College Faculty; *College Students; Course Evaluation; Feedback; Higher Education; School Attitudes; Student Attitudes; *Student Evaluation of Teacher Performance
Identifiers: SET
Availability: Center for Educational Research; P.O. Box 85110, University Station, Seattle, WA 98105
Grade Level: 13–20
Notes: Time, 20 approx.; Items, 46
Designed to measure student's attitudes and opinions about quality of teaching and course content. Developed to assist college faculty with information to improve teaching methods. Respondent completes instrument anonymously to encourage honest evaluation.

7319
Maternal Attitude Scale. Cohler, Bertran J. 1970

Subtests: Control of Child's Aggressive Impulses; Reciprocal Relationship with Child; Appropriate versus Inappropriate Closeness; Acceptance versus Denial of Emotional Complexity; Comfort versus Discomfort in Understanding and Meeting the Child's Needs; Encouragement of Positive Interaction with the Child versus Maternal Hostility towards Childrearing
Descriptors: *Adjustment (to Environment); Adults; *Affective Measures; Emotional Disturbances; *Mother Attitudes; *Parent Child Relationship; Parent Role; *Rating Scales
Identifiers: MAS; TIM(B)
Availability: Tests in Microfiche; Test Collection, Educational Testing Service, Princeton, NJ 08541
Target Audience: Adults
Notes: Items, 233
Designed to elicit attitudes versus behavior of mothers of infants and young children toward child-rearing. It contains forced choice items based upon a devised 10 Mother-Child Interaction Issues which have 3 subscales: Female Sexuality, Childbirth, and a Lie Scale.

7320
Teaching Attitudes Questionnaire. Wright, Benjamin D.; Tuska, Shirley A. 1962
Descriptors: Adults; *Career Choice; Motivation; Parent Child Relationship; *Parent Influence; Self Concept; Teacher Student Relationship; *Teacher Attitudes; Teacher Evaluation; *Teachers
Identifiers: TATSO Questionnaire
Availability: Benjamin D. Wright; Dept. of Education, University of Chicago, 5835 Kimbark Ave., Chicago, IL 60637
Target Audience: Adults
Designed to assess attitudes of teachers and students preparing to enter the teaching profession. Attempts to determine factors that influence individual to become a teacher. Measures attitudes toward parents and teachers.

7325
Student Attitude Scale. Seagren, Alan T. 1967
Descriptors: High Schools; *High School Students; *Interpersonal Competence; *Peer Relationship; *Student Evaluation of Teacher Performance; *Student School Relationship; *Teacher Student Relationship
Identifiers: Student Teacher Impact Study; TIM(A)
Availability: Tests in Microfiche; Test Collection, Educational Testing Service, Princeton, NJ 08541
Grade Level: 10–12
Notes: Items, 65
Designed to elicit students' attitudes in 5 categories: school, teachers, interpersonal relationships with teachers, peers, and self.

7335
Projective Prejudice Test. Katz, Phyllis A.; Zalk, Susan R. 1973
Descriptors: Elementary Education; *Elementary School Students; *Racial Attitudes; Slides; *Social Bias; Student Attitudes
Identifiers: Katz Zalk Opinion Questionnaire
Availability: Dr. Phyllis A. Katz; Dept. of Educational Psychology, City University Graduate Center, 33 W. 42nd St., New York, NY 10036
Grade Level: 2–6
Notes: Items, 24
Designed to measure racial attitudes of children. Subjects are shown a series of 24 slides depicting children in ambiguous interracial situations. They must indicate their response in a picture booklet.

7343
Alienation Scale. Dean, Dwight G.
Subtests: Powerlessness; Normlessness; Isolation
Descriptors: Adults; *Alienation; *Apathy; Rating Scales; *Role Conflict; *Social Isolation
Identifiers: Dean Alienation Scale; Dean Scale; TIM(B)
Availability: Tests in Microfiche; Test Collection, Educational Testing Service, Princeton, NJ 08541
Target Audience: Adults
Notes: Items, 24
Designed to measure the 3 major components of alienation: powerlessness, normlessness, and isolation.

7356
Attitudes toward Homosexuality Scale. Dunbar, John; And Others 1972
Descriptors: *Adults; Higher Education; *Homosexuality; Student Attitudes; *Undergraduate Students
Identifiers: *Sexual Attitudes

Availability: ASIS/NAPS, c/o Microfiche Publications; P.O. Box 3513, Grand Central Station, New York, NY 10163-3513 (Doc. No. 02005).
Grade Level: 13–16
Target Audience: Adults
Notes: Items, 14
Designed to assess attitudes toward homosexuality.

7357
Sexual Liberalism-Conservatism Scale. Dunbar, John; And Others 1973
Descriptors: Adults; *Sexuality; Conservatism; Liberalism
Availability: ASIS/NAPS, c/o Microfiche Publications; P.O. Box 3513, Grand Central Station, New York, NY 10163-3513 (Doc. No. 02005).
Target Audience: 18–64
Notes: Items, 17
Designed to measure attitudes toward a variety of heterosexual sex practices and toward general issues concerned with sexual freedom.

7358
Sex Concern-Guilt Scale. Dunbar, John; And Others
Descriptors: *Adults; Homosexuality; *Self Esteem; *Sexuality
Identifiers: CG; *Guilt; *Sexual Attitudes; Sexual Behavior
Availability: ASIS/NAPS, c/o Microfiche Publications; P.O. Box 3513, Grand Central Station, New York, NY 10163-3513 (Doc. No. 02005)
Target Audience: Adults
Notes: Items, 11
Designed to measure personal sex guilt of respondents and how these feelings affected attitudes toward homosexuality.

7375
Psychotherapy Questionnaire: Patient's Form. Strupp, Hans H. 1964
Descriptors: *Adults; *Physician Patient Relationship; *Psychotherapy
Identifiers: *Patient Attitudes
Availability: Dr. Hans H. Strupp; Dept. of Psychology, 134 Wesley Hall, Vanderbilt University, Nashville, TN 37203
Target Audience: Adults
Notes: Items, 89
Designed to assess attitudes of former patients concerning their therapeutic experience and relationship with psychotherapist.

7376
Psychotherapy Questionnaire: Therapist's Form. Strupp, Hans H.
Descriptors: Adults; Physician Patient Relationship; *Psychotherapy; Rating Scales; *Therapists
Availability: Dr. Hans H. Strupp; Dept. of Psychology, 134 Wesley Hall, Vanderbilt University, Nashville, TN 37203
Target Audience: Adults
Notes: Items, 23
Designed to assess psychotherapist's attitudes and opinions concerning former patients. Therapist is asked to rate each patient in comparison with other patients he or she has treated.

7386
Education Apperception Test. Thompson, Jack M.; Sones, Robert A. 1973
Descriptors: Adolescents; Elementary Education; *Elementary School Students; Individual Testing; Peer Relationship; Pictorial Stimuli; *Preschool Children; Preschool Education; Projective Measures; *School Attitudes; Student School Relationship
Identifiers: EAT
Availability: Western Psychological Services; 12031 Wilshire Blvd., Los Angeles, CA 90025
Grade Level: K–6
Target Audience: 4–6
Notes: Items, 18
Designed to assess child's perception of school and the educative process. EAT consists of 18 pictures depicting middle elementary school students in school and school-related activities. Instrument is designed to evoke responses in 4 major areas: reaction toward authority, reaction toward learning, peer relationships, and home attitude toward school. Also useful with adolescents.

7391
Motoric Ideational Sensory Test. Stein, Kenneth B.; Lenrow, Peter 1970
Subtests: Sensory Dimension; Ideational Dimension; Motoric Dimension
Descriptors: *Cognitive Style; Cognitive Tests; *College Students; Higher Education; Interest Inventories; Rating Scales; Student Interests
Identifiers: MIST

*Availability: Journal of Personality and Social Psychology;*v16 n4 p656-64, 1970
Grade Level: 13–20
Notes: Items, 45

Designed to measure the motoric, ideational, and sensory perceptual expressive dimensions. These dimensions are defined by self-endorsed statements pertaining to activity preferences. Individual's expressive style may be determined from test results.

7400
Multifactor Racial Attitude Inventory: Form C-8.
Woodmansee, John J.; Cook, Stuart W. 1970
Subtests: Negro Militance; Negro Superiority; Integration-Segregation Policy; Acceptance in Close Personal Relationships; Negro Inferiority; Ease in Interracial Contacts; Derogatory Beliefs; Local Autonomy; Private Rights; Acceptance in Status Superior Relationships; Gradualism; Interracial Marriage; Approaches to Negro Progress
Descriptors: Activism; Adults; *Black Stereotypes; *Racial Attitudes; Racial Integration; *Racial Relations; Racial Segregation
Identifiers: MRAI; TIM(C)
Availability: Tests in Microfiche; Test Collection, Educational Testing Service, Princeton, NJ 08541
Target Audience: Adults
Notes: Time, 30 approx.; Items, 130

Designed to measure different aspects of attitude toward blacks. The subscales include integration-segregation policy, acceptance in close personal relationships, Negro inferiority, ease in interracial contacts, derogatory beliefs, local autonomy, private rights, acceptance in status-superior relationships, gradualism, interracial marriage, approaches to Negro progress, Negro militance, and Negro superiority.

7401
Judging Arguments: Form C-2. Cook, Stuart
Descriptors: *Adults; *College Students; Higher Education; *Persuasive Discourse; *Racial Attitudes; Racial Bias; Racial Integration; Racial Relations; Racial Segregation; Rating Scales; Student Attitudes
Availability: Stuart W. Cook; Institute of Behavioral Science, University of Colorado, Boulder, CO 80302
Grade Level: 13–16
Target Audience: Adults
Notes: Items, 40

Designed to assess individual's ratings of plausibility of arguments for and against segregation. Studies have indicated a high correlation between ratings of plausibility of statements about segregation and rater's racial attitudes as indicated by a self-report inventory.

7402
Information Test: Form C-4. Institute of Behavioral Science, Boulder, CO
Descriptors: Adults; *American Indians; *Blacks; Hispanic Americans; Minority Groups; *Puerto Ricans; *Racial Attitudes; *Racial Bias; Social Attitudes
Availability: Stuart W. Cook; Institute of Behavioral Science, University of Colorado, Boulder, CO 80302
Target Audience: Adults
Notes: Items, 74

Designed to assess ways in which apparently factual information can be used to reflect the influence of one's own attitudinal position. Measures attitudes toward 3 minority groups—American Indians, American blacks, and Americans of Puerto Rican descent.

7403
Fact and Opinion: Form C-2 (B). Institute of Behavioral Science, Boulder, CO
Descriptors: *Adults; Blacks; *Black Stereotypes; Opinions; *Racial Attitudes; Racial Relations; Rating Scales
Availability: Stuart W. Cook; Institute of Behavioral Science, University of Colorado, Boulder, CO 80302
Target Audience: Adults
Notes: Items, 30

Designed to assess respondent's ability to distinguish between fact and opinion. Results provide an indication of the examinee's attitudes covering race relations.

7404
Multifactor Racial Attitude Inventory: Short Form.
Ard, Nicholas; Cook, Stuart 1970
Descriptors: Adults; *Black Stereotypes; *Racial Attitudes; Racial Relations; Social Attitudes
Identifiers: Measurement of Verbal Racial Attitudes; MRAI; TIM(C)
Availability: Tests in Microfiche; Test Collection, Educational Testing Service, Princeton, NJ 08541

Target Audience: Adults
Notes: Time, 5; Items, 12

This short form adaptation employs single items to assess each of the factors comprising the long form (TC007400). May also be suitable for use with high school and college students.

7405
Personnel Evaluation: Form C-4. Institute of Behavioral Science, Boulder, CO
Descriptors: *Adults; Peer Evaluation; Personality Assessment; *Racial Attitudes; Semantic Differential; *Social Attitudes
Availability: Stuart W. Cook; Institute of Behavioral Science, University of Colorado, Boulder, CO 80302
Target Audience: Adults
Notes: Items, 38

Designed to assess racial and social attitudes. Subject is shown a photograph and given a brief personality description of 38 people. Examinee is asked to rate individual's personality on a semantic differential scale. Examinee is also asked to rate degree to which he or she would prefer to interact with the person described.

7435
CPH Patient Attitude Scale. Kahn, Marvin W.; Jones, Nelson F. 1974
Descriptors: Adults; Group Testing; Individual Testing; *Mental Disorders; *Patients; *Psychiatric Hospitals; Rating Scales
Identifiers: Patient Attitudes; TIM(A)
Availability: Tests in Microfiche; Test Collection, Educational Testing Service, Princeton, NJ 08541
Target Audience: Adults
Notes: Items, 45

Designed to measure the attitudes of mental patients toward mental hospital activities and personnel. Also measures their attitudes about the nature, cause, and treatment of mental illness. Scale can be administered individually or in groups.

7439
The Gottesfeld Community Mental Health Critical Issues Test. Gottesfeld, Harry 1974
Subtests: Community Context; Radicalism; Traditional Psychotherapy; Prevention; Extending the Definition of Mental Health; Role Diffusion
Descriptors: Adults; Community Health Services; Mental Disorders; *Mental Health Programs; *Social Attitudes; *Mental Health Workers
Availability: Human Sciences Press; 72 5th Ave., New York, NY 10011
Target Audience: Adults
Notes: Items, 72

Designed to assess attitudes concerning major issues in the community mental health field.

7447
Irrational Belief Test. Sweney, Arthur B.; Jones, R. Garner 1969
Descriptors: Adults; *Beliefs; Social Values
Identifiers: Irrational Belief Scale (Ellis)
Availability: Test Systems, Inc.; P.O. Box 18432, Wichita, KS 67218
Target Audience: 18–64
Notes: Items, 100

Designed to measure the extent to that an individual has incorporated certain socially communicated values or beliefs that are essentially irrational and inconsistent. Based on Ellis' irrational belief system. Uses 5-point agree/disagree scale.

7460
Milwaukee Academic Interest Inventory. Baggaley, Andrew R. 1973
Descriptors: *College Bound Students; Counseling Techniques; Higher Education; High Schools; *Interest Inventories; *Majors (Students); *Student Educational Objectives; *Undergraduate Students; *Vocational Interests
Availability: Western Psychological Services; 12031 Wilshire Blvd., Los Angeles, CA 90025
Grade Level: 12–14
Notes: Time, 20 approx.; Items, 150

Designed to aid students in selection of college major course of study. Questions are structured to compare student's academic interests with those of typical students in specified fields. May be used for individual or group testing. Yields interest scores for Physical Science; Healing Occupations; Behavioral Science; Economics; Humanities-Social Studies; and Elementary Education.

7469
Lyons Relationship Scales. Goucher, Elizabeth L.; Efron, Herman Y.
Subtests: The Relationship from the Viewpoint of the Patient; The Relationship from the Viewpoint of the Relative

Descriptors: Adults; Family Attitudes; *Family Relationship; Interaction; *Interviews; *Patients; *Psychiatric Hospitals; Rating Scales
Identifiers: Patient Attitudes; *Psychiatric Patients; TIM(C)
Availability: Tests in Microfiche; Test Collection, Educational Testing Service, Princeton, NJ 08541
Target Audience: Adults
Notes: Time, 45 approx.; Items, 29

Designed to assess changes in the psychiatric patient-family relationship. The instrument consists of 2 parts: Schedule I, the relationship from the viewpoint of the patient; and Schedule II, the relationship from the viewpoint of the relative. The scales are intended for use after an interview with both the patient and the relative.

7470
Survey of Opinions. Efron, Herman Y. 1967
Subtests: Segregation via Institutionalization; Cultural Deprivation; Nonparadoxical Etiology; Personal Exclusion; Authoritarianism; Hopelessness
Descriptors: *Adults; *Mental Retardation; Special Education; *Special Education Teachers; *Teacher Attitudes
Availability: Herman Efron; 909 Brentwood Ln., Silver Spring, MD 20902
Target Audience: Adults
Notes: Items, 70

Designed to assess attitudes toward mental retardation and educable retarded subjects. Developed primarily for use with individuals in special and general education.

7472
Attitude toward Hospitalization Scale. Garlington, Warren K.; Stotland, Ezra
Subtests: Openness of Communication between Patients; Communication between Patients and Staff; Purpose of Hospital Activities (for Patient of Hospital); Hospital as Refuge or for Active Treatment; Value Judgments toward Mental Illness; Individuality vs. Conformity
Descriptors: Adults; Attitudes; *Hospital Personnel; Mental Disorders; *Patients; *Psychiatric Hospitals; Rating Scales
Identifiers: ATHS; TIM(B)
Availability: Tests in Microfiche; Test Collection, Educational Testing Service, Princeton, NJ 08541
Target Audience: Adults
Notes: Items, 60

Developed to measure attitudes concerning the purpose and methods of mental hospitals and the nature of mental illness as perceived by patients, staff, and the general public. Six subscales comprise the instrument.

7485
Teacher's Evaluation Form. Dorr, Darwin; Cowen, Emory L. 1971
Subtests: Communication; Service; Comparison with Other Mental Health Services
Descriptors: Adults; *Elementary School Teachers; *Mental Health Programs; *Program Evaluation; Rating Scales; *Teacher Attitudes
Identifiers: *Primary Mental Health Project
Availability: Darwin Dorr; Washington University, Dept. of Psychology, St. Louis, MO 63130
Target Audience: Adults
Notes: Items, 9

Designed to determine teacher attitudes toward the Primary Mental Health Project (PMHP).

7504
Parent-Child Interaction Rating Scales. Heilbrun, Alfred B.
Descriptors: Higher Education; *Parent Child Relationship; Rating Scales; *Student Attitudes; *Undergraduate Students
Identifiers: TIM(B)
Availability: Tests in Microfiche; Test Collection, Educational Testing Service, Princeton, NJ 08541
Grade Level: 13–16
Notes: Items, 8

Measure of parental nurturance of the child is designed to elicit students' perceptions of the way their parents related to them during their formative years. The subject rates each parent on 8 modes of nurturant behavior: degree of affection felt for the subject, degree of affection physically expressed toward the subject, approval of the subject and his or her behavior, sharing of personal feelings and experiences, concrete giving (gifts, money, etc.), encouragement of the subject in meeting responsibilities and pursuing personal interests, trust placed in the subject, and sense of security felt by the subject in relations with his or her parents.

7505
Child Rearing Practices Report. Block, Jeanne 1965

Descriptors: Adolescents; Adults; Cantonese; *Child Rearing; *Cross Cultural Studies; Dutch; Finnish; Norwegian; *Parent Attitudes; Parent Child Relationship; Parents; *Q Methodology; Swedish
Identifiers: *Croation (Language); CRPR; *Danish (Language); TIM(B)
Availability: Tests in Microfiche; Test Collection, Educational Testing Service, Princeton, NJ 08541
Target Audience: 16–50
Notes: Items, 91
Designed to identify child-rearing attitudes and values. The report may be completed by the parent to describe his or her own child-rearing behavior or by the child to describe the child-rearing orientations of his or her parents. The instrument employs the Q-sort technique. Two forms are available, one for child and one for parent.

7514
Children's Audience Sensitivity Inventory. Paivio, Allan 1961
Subtests: Exhibitionism; Self-Consciousness; Audience Anxiety
Descriptors: Anxiety; *Audiences; Elementary Education; *Elementary School Students; *Self Concept; Self Concept Measures; *Student Attitudes; Extraversion Introversion
Identifiers: CASI
Availability: Child Development, v32 p721-30, 1961
Grade Level: 3–6
Notes: Items, 35
Designed to measure feelings of anxiety, exhibitionism, and avoidance of public exposure by children in the presence of an audience.

7521
Rucker-Gable Educational Programming Scale. Rucker, Chauncy N.; Gable, Robert K. 1974
Descriptors: Adults; *Emotional Disturbances; *Knowledge Level; *Learning Disabilities; *Mental Retardation; *Student Placement; *Teacher Attitudes; *Teachers
Availability: Rucker Gable Associates; P.O. Box 97, Storrs, CT 06268
Target Audience: Adults
Notes: Items, 30
Designed to measure teachers' knowledge of appropriate program placements for handicapped children. Thirty brief descriptions of children's classroom behavior are given. Responding teachers assign each child to one of 7 placements ranging from "regular classroom" to "not for public education." Six attitude scores are calculated by summing weighted responses to these items. They represent attitudes toward children with mental retardation, emotional disturbance, and learning disabilities and the degree of disability, mild, moderate, and severe.

7525
Questionnaire on the Occupational Status of Women. Bingham, William C.; House, Elaine
Descriptors: Adults; Career Counseling; *Counselor Attitudes; Counselor Educators; *Equal Opportunities (Jobs); *Negative Attitudes; School Counselors; *Sex Role; *Sex Stereotypes
Identifiers: TIM(A)
Availability: Tests in Microfiche; Test Collection, Educational Testing Service, Princeton, NJ 08541
Target Audience: Adults
Notes: Items, 50
Designed to assess knowledge of and attitudes toward the occupational status of women. The questionnaire was intended to investigate the extent to which misinformation and negative attitudes toward women and work prevail among counselors and counselor educators.

7526
A Study of Young People. Blacker, Edward; And Others
Descriptors: Adolescents; *Alcoholism; *Delinquency; *Drinking; *Males; Social Attitudes
Identifiers: TIM (A)
Availability: Tests in Microfiche; Test Collection, Educational Testing Service, Princeton, NJ 08541
Target Audience: Adolescents
Notes: Items, 174
Designed to collect information regarding the drinking attitudes and practices of male adolescents, particularly among delinquent male adolescents, among whom alcoholism is a problem.

7527
Marijuana Attitude Scale. Baer, Daniel J. 1973

Descriptors: Drug Abuse; *Drug Legislation; Higher Education; High Schools; *High School Students; *Marijuana; *Political Attitudes; *Social Attitudes; *Undergraduate Students
Availability: Daniel J. Baer; Psychology Dept., McGuinn Hall, Boston College, Chestnut Hill, MA 02167
Grade Level: 9–16
Notes: Items, 44
Designed to assess attitudes toward use and legalization of marijuana. Political views and drug experience were found to influence responses. Scale may be divided into 2 22-item forms.

7553
Management Appraisal Survey. Hall, Jay; And Others 1973
Subtests: Philosophy; Planning; Implementation; Evaluation
Descriptors: *Administrative Principles; *Administrator Evaluation; Adults; *Employee Attitudes; Interpersonal Competence; *Leadership Styles; Measures (Individuals); Motivation; *Profiles; *Surveys
Identifiers: Leadership Effectiveness; MAS
Availability: Teleometrics International; 1755 Woodstead Ct., The Woodlands, TX 77380
Target Audience: Adults
Notes: Items, 12
This survey is an assessment of managerial practices and attitudes as viewed through the eyes of employees. Subordinate ratings may be compared by the manager with self-ratings from the Styles of Management Inventory (TC007562) on overall management style and 4 management components of philosophy, planning, implementation, and evaluation.

7562
Styles of Management Inventory. Hall, Jay; And Others 1973
Subtests: Philosophy; Planning; Implementation; Evaluation
Descriptors: *Administrative Principles; *Administrator Attitudes; Adults; Interpersonal Competence; *Leadership Styles; Motivation; *Profiles; *Self Evaluation (Individuals)
Identifiers: Leadership Effectiveness; SMI
Availability: Teleometrics International; 1755 Woodstead Ct., The Woodlands, TX 77380
Target Audience: 18–64
The Styles of Management Inventory provides managers with a means of relating their behavior to their on-the-job practices and of discovering areas in need of change. Normative data and conversion tables afford personal comparison with both the average manager and a theoretical field.

7584
Social Interest Index. Greever, Kathryn B.; And Others 1973
Subtests: Work; Friendship; Love; Self-Significance
Descriptors: *Adults; Higher Education; Self Concept Measures; *Self Evaluation (Individuals); *Social Attitudes; *Undergraduate Students
Identifiers: Adler (Alfred); *Social Interest
Availability: Dr. Kathryn B. Greever; Research and Training Center, 509 Allen Hall, West Virginia University, Morgantown, WV 26506
Grade Level: 13–16
Target Audience: Adults
Notes: Items, 32
Designed to measure level of social interest an individual has attained. Alfred Adler's concept of social interest was defined as useful contributions to society through democratic cooperation. The degree to which social interest is developed governs the way an individual moves toward self-significance.

7592
Value Socialization Scales. Gorsuch, Richard L. 1970
Subtests: Value Socialization Scale; Semantic Differential Value Scale
Descriptors: *Elementary School Students; Intermediate Grades; Rating Scales; Social Attitudes; *Social Development; Subcultures; *Values
Identifiers: TIM(B)
Availability: Tests in Microfiche; Test Collection, Educational Testing Service, Princeton, NJ 08541
Grade Level: 4–6
Notes: Items, 58
Designed to reflect the degree to which a child has learned those values necessary to fit into any society or to choose among the subcultures available to him or her. The device consists of 2 scales. With the first, the child is asked to rate a series of behaviors reflecting basic social values. In the second, he or she is asked to indicate how much he or she admires a child who performs various acts. The scales are intended for research use.

7597
Authority Figure Perception Test. Ferguson, Ben; Kennelly, Kevin 1974
Subtests: Encouraging vs. Discouraging Constructive Environmental Manipulations; Supporting vs. Rejecting When Difficulty Encountered; Positive vs. Negative Reinforcers; Predictable vs. Unpredictable Standards; Acting upon Issue Oriented Reason vs. Arbitrary Rule
Descriptors: High Schools; *High School Students; *Locus of Control; *Student Attitudes
Identifiers: *Authority Figures
Availability: ASIS/NAPS; c/o Microfiche Publications, P.O. Box 3513, Grand Central Station, New York, NY 10163-3513 (Doc. No. 02379)
Grade Level: 9–12
Target Audience: 14–18
Notes: Items, 54
Designed to measure adolescents' perceptions of authority figures.

7603
Helping Relationship Inventory. Jones, John E. 1973
Subtests: Understanding; Probing; Interpretive; Supportive; Evaluative
Descriptors: *Adults; *Helping Relationship; Interpersonal Communication
Identifiers: HRI
Availability: University Associates, Inc.; 8517 Production Ave., P.O. Box 26240, San Diego, CA 92126
Target Audience: Adults
Notes: Items, 25
Designed to assess individual's attitudes and feelings concerning the relationship between 2 persons when one is attempting to help the other. Instrument is available in the 1973 Annual Handbook for Group Facilitators.

7606
Lead Questionnaire. Dore, Russell 1973
Descriptors: *Adults; *Leadership Styles; Questionnaires; *Supervisors; Supervisory Methods; *Work Attitudes
Availability: University Associates, Inc.; 8517 Production Ave., P.O. Box 26240, San Diego, CA 92126
Target Audience: 18–64
Notes: Items, 60
Designed to measure individual's attitudes toward different methods of leadership. Instrument is available in the 1973 Annual Handbook for Group Facilitators.

7608
Environmental Response Inventory. McKechnie, George E. 1974
Subtests: Pastoralism; Urbanism; Environmental Adaptation; Stimulus Seeking; Environmental Trust; Antiquarianism; Need Privacy; Mechanical Orientation; Communality
Descriptors: Adjustment (to Environment); *Adolescents; *Adults; Attitudes; Environmental Influences; *Environmental Research; *Older Adults; Personality Measures; *Physical Environment; Rating Scales
Identifiers: ERI
Availability: Consulting Psychologists Press; 577 College Ave., Palo Alto, CA 94306
Target Audience: 15–75
Notes: Time, 30 approx.; Items, 184
Designed to assess people's attitudes toward their physical environment. Explores personality differences in relation to environmental psychology.

7609
Ward Atmosphere Scale. Moos, Rudolf H. 1974
Subtests: Involvement; Support; Spontaneity; Autonomy; Practical Orientation; Personal Problem Orientation; Anger and Aggression; Order and Organization; Program Clarity; Staff Control
Descriptors: Adults; Hospital Personnel; *Hospitals; *Patients; Psychiatric Hospitals; *Psychiatric Services; *Social Environment
Identifiers: *Psychiatric Patients; Social Climate Scales; WAS
Availability: Consulting Psychologists Press; 577 College Ave., Palo Alto, CA 94306
Target Audience: Adults
Notes: Time, 20 approx.; Items, 100
Designed to assess the social environment of hospital-based psychiatric treatment programs. The subscales are arranged in dimensions of relationship, treatment program, and system maintenance. May be completed by patients or staff members. This scale has been adapted to measure the ideal social environment (Form I), or the expectations one has of an environment (Form E). Short form (Form S) may be adapted from standard Form R. Alternate scales and their construction are described in the manual.

7610

Community Oriented Programs Environment Scale.
Moos, Rudolf H. 1974
Subtests: Involvement; Support; Spontaneity;
Autonomy; Practical Orientation; Personal
Problem Orientation; Anger and Aggression; Or-
der and Organization; Program Clarity; Staff
Control
Descriptors: *Adults; *Community Health Ser-
vices; Group Homes; *Psychiatric Services; Re-
habilitation Centers; Sheltered Workshops;
*Social Environment
Identifiers: COPES; Patient Attitudes; *Psychiatric
Patients; Social Climate Scales
Availability: Consulting Psychologists Press; 577
College Ave., Palo Alto, CA 94306
Target Audience: Adults
Notes: Time, 20 approx.; Items, 100

Designed to assess the social environment of community-
based psychiatric treatment programs, such as halfway
houses and sheltered workshops. This scale has been
adapted to measure the ideal social environment (Form I),
or the expectations one has of an environment (Form E).
Short form (Form S) may be adapted from standard Form
R. Alternate scales and their construction are described in
the manual.

7613

Teacher Image Questionnaire. Educator Feedback
Center, Kalamazoo, MI
Descriptors: Feedback; Secondary Education; Sec-
ondary School Students; *Secondary School
Teachers; Student Attitudes; *Student Evalua-
tion of Teacher Performance; *Teacher Effec-
tiveness; Teacher Evaluation
Availability: Evaluation Center; Western Michigan
University, Kalamazoo, MI 49008
Grade Level: 7–12
Notes: Time, 15 approx.; Items, 16

Designed to elicit information from students concerning
their perceptions of a teacher's effectiveness. Information
is used to provide feedback to teachers and to construct a
teacher image profile.

7615

Imber Children's Trust Scale. Imber, Steve C.
1971
Subtests: Father Trust; Mother Trust; Peer Trust;
Teacher Trust
Descriptors: Academic Achievement; *Elementary
School Students; Intermediate Grades; *Parent
Child Relationship; *Peer Relationship;
*Student Attitudes; *Teacher Student Relation-
ship
Identifiers: ICTS; Oral Testing; *Trust
Availability: Steve C. Imber; Assistant Professor,
Special Education, Rhode Island College, 600
Mt. Pleasant Ave., Providence, RI 02908
Grade Level: 4–5
Notes: Items, 40

Designed to measure a child's trust of his or her father,
mother, peers, and teachers. May be used to examine
relationship between trust and academic performance.

7628

**Scales to Measure Attitudes toward Industrial Psy-
chology and Psychological Testing.** Rhoads, Rod-
ney F.; Landy, Frank J.
Subtests: The Use of Psychologists in Business
and Industry; The Use of Personnel Tests in
Business and Industry
Descriptors: Adults; *Employee Attitudes;
*Industry; *Personnel Evaluation;
*Psychological Testing
Identifiers: TIM(A)
Availability: Tests in Microfiche; Test Collection,
Educational Testing Service, Princeton, NJ
08541
Target Audience: Adults
Notes: Items, 96

Designed to assess the magnitude and direction of attitudes toward industrial psychology and psychological
testing among a broad range of industrial groups.

7630

The Long Term Family Interview Schedule. Blum,
Richard H.
Subtests: Section 1, Family Description; Section 2,
Mother Interview; Father Interview; Section 3,
Child Description; Section 4, Family Organiza-
tion; Section 5, Whole Family Observation; Sec-
tion 6, Family Study; Student Interview; Dealer
Section; Interview for Children under 13; Drug
and Medicine Survey
Descriptors: Adolescents; Adults; Children; *Drug
Abuse; *Family Attitudes; *Family Counseling;
*Family Environment; *Family Relationship;
Lysergic Acid Diethylamide; Marijuana; *Parent
Attitudes; Questionnaires; Sedatives; Stimulants
Identifiers: TIM(A)

Availability: Tests in Microfiche; Test Collection,
Educational Testing Service, Princeton, NJ
08541
Target Audience: 5–64
Notes: Items, 277

Designed to investigate and identify those familial variables related to the development of drug problems and
illicit drug use in children. Ten-part questionnaire.

7631

Standard Student Interview Form. Blum, Richard
H. 1969
Descriptors: *Biographical Inventories; *College
Students; *Drug Abuse; *Family Characteristics;
Higher Education; Parent Attitudes; Political
Attitudes; Questionnaires; Social Attitudes;
*Student Attitudes
Identifiers: National Institute of Mental Health;
TIM(E)
Availability: Tests in Microfiche; Test Collection,
Educational Testing Service, Princeton, NJ
08541
Grade Level: 13–20
Notes: Items, 78

Extensive questionnaire developed for use in the National
Institute of Mental Health Cooperative Collegiate Study.
It is designed to record specific information on respondent's background, drug preferences and experience, political and social attitudes of self and parents, and parental
practices and attitudes toward drug and medicine use.

7633

**Attitude toward the Use of Lie Detectors in Busi-
ness and Government Questionnaire.** Sistrunk,
Frank; Spector, Paul E. 1974
Descriptors: Adults; *Business; *Government
(Administrative Body); Personnel Selection;
*Polygraphs; Likert Scales
Identifiers: TIM(A)
Availability: Tests in Microfiche; Test Collection,
Educational Testing Service, Princeton, NJ
08541
Target Audience: Adults
Notes: Items, 25

Likert-type questionnaire is concerned with the general
public's attitude toward the use of lie detectors, in various
situations, such as personnel selection, general use in business to screen employees for thefts, and also more common usage in legal procedures.

7662

General Beliefs. Coan, Richard W.; And Others
Descriptors: Adults; *Moral Values; *Personality
Assessment; *Social Values
Identifiers: TIM(A)
Availability: Tests in Microfiche; Test Collection,
Educational Testing Service, Princeton, NJ
08541
Target Audience: Adults
Notes: Items, 73

Deals with general beliefs and attitudes of adults. The
inventory yields scores for the following 6 factors: conventional theistic religion vs. nontheistic viewpoint, future
productive vs. present spontaneous orientation, detachment vs. involvement, relativism vs. absolutism, scientism
vs. determinism, and optimism vs. pessimism.

7663

Personal Opinion Survey. Coan, Richard W.;
Fairchild, Marcia T.
Descriptors: Adults; Higher Education; *Individual
Power; Interpersonal Competence; *Locus of
Control; *Personality Assessment; *Self Deter-
mination
Identifiers: TIM(A)
Availability: Tests in Microfiche; Test Collection,
Educational Testing Service, Princeton, NJ
08541
Grade Level: Higher Education
Target Audience: Adults
Notes: Time, 30 approx.; Items, 120

Assesses several aspects of the experience of control. Provides scores for 7 factors: achievement through conscien-
tious effort, personal confidence in ability to achieve mastery, capacity of mankind to control its destiny vs. supernatural power of fate, successful planning and organization, self-control over internal processes, control over
large-scale social and political events, and control in immediate social interaction.

7684

Measure of Values: Form III. Pierce, Robert A.;
Schwartz, Allan J. 1972
Descriptors: Higher Education; *Undergraduate
Students; *Values; Likert Scales
Identifiers: TIM(A)
Availability: Tests in Microfiche; Test Collection,
Educational Testing Service, Princeton, NJ
08541
Grade Level: 13–16
Notes: Items, 134

Inventory of personal values developed using college students as respondents. There are separate forms yielding 11
scales for men and 12 for women. The scales for women
are independence, wealth, achievement, righteousness, athletic competence, love and marriage, altruistic service,
politics, family good times, thoughtful solitude, and religious involvement. The scales for men are warmth and
fun, status and power, wealth and achievement, aesthetic
and intellectual wonder, politics, independence, athletic
competence, altruistic service, religion, thoughtful solitude,
and affection for parents.

7685

Inventory of Temporal Experiences. Form J.
Yonge, George D. 1973
Descriptors: Higher Education; Rating Scales; Stu-
dent Attitudes; *Time Perspective;
*Undergraduate Students
Identifiers: ITE; TIM(B)
Availability: Tests in Microfiche; Test Collection,
Educational Testing Service, Princeton, NJ
08541
Grade Level: 13–16
Notes: Items, 101

An inventory of temporal experiences and perceptions that
yields 4 scores: human time, animal time, vital time, and
physical time.

7692

Sexual Attitude Change Scale. Annon, Jack S.;
Robinson, C.H. 1971
Descriptors: Adults; Rating Scales; *Sexuality
Identifiers: SACS; Sexual Behavior; TIM(A)
Availability: Tests in Microfiche; Test Collection,
Educational Testing Service, Princeton, NJ
08541
Target Audience: Adults
Notes: Time, 7 approx.; Items, 78

Designed as part of a study on sexual anxiety, sexual
attitudes, and attitude change. Elicits attitudes toward sexually related activities and feelings about one's own and
one's partner's body. Male and female forms are available.

7700

Role Perception Battery. Sterling, James W.
Subtests: Role Conflict; Perceptions of Reference
Groups; Aggregate Role; Role Attributes; Per-
ception of Danger Attitudinal Orientations to
Role
Descriptors: Adults; *Police; Rating Scales; *Role
Perception
Identifiers: TIM(E)
Availability: Tests in Microfiche; Test Collection,
Educational Testing Service, Princeton, NJ
08541
Target Audience: Adults

Designed to assess 6 factors of the police officer's role.
The Role Conflict Schedules ask the officer to describe the
way that various community groups might view the officer's role and to rate the extent to which s/he is bothered
by conflicting views. Semantic Differential Scales are used
to measure the officer's perception of reference groups as
role reciprocals and evaluators. The Position Inventory is
designed to measure the subjects' concept of the aggregate
role of the police. The Wetteroth Trait Image Survey is
used to discover the attributes thought to be essential to
the enactment of the police role. The Danger Scales are
designed to determine the degree of danger perceived by
police in typical work assignments. The Police Opinion
Poll includes a variety of attitudinal orientations related to
the police role.

7701

**Parental Attitude Research Instrument: Short
Form.** Cross, Herbert J.; Kawash, George F. 1968
Descriptors: Adults; *Authoritarianism; *Child
Rearing; Family Life; Higher Education;
*Parent Attitudes; Parent Child Relationship;
Parent Influence; *Parents; *Undergraduate Stu-
dents
Identifiers: Inventory on Family Life and Atti-
tudes; PARI
Availability: Psychological Reports; v23 p91-98,
1968
Grade Level: 13–16
Target Audience: Adults
Notes: Items, 45

A revised and shortened form of the Parental Attitude
Research Instrument Form IV (TC005773) designed to
assess authoritarianism and warmth. Useful in assessing
authoritarian attitudes toward childrearing.

7707

Grasha-Riechmann Student Learning Styles.
Riechmann, Sheryl Wetter; Grasha, Anthony F.
Descriptors: Classroom Techniques; *Cognitive
Style; Higher Education; Rating Scales; Student
Attitudes; Student Evaluation of Teacher Per-
formance; *Undergraduate Students
Identifiers: GRSLSS; TIM(B)

Availability: Tests in Microfiche; Test Collection, Educational Testing Service, Princeton, NJ 08541
Grade Level: 13–16
Notes: Items, 90

Developed to assess 6 student-learning styles: independent, dependent, avoidant, participant, collaborative, and competitive. Each response style is defined around 3 classroom dimensions: student attitudes toward learning, view of teachers and/or peers, and reactions to classroom procedures. Both specific and general class versions of the 90-item questionnaire are available.

7711
Family Agreement Measure. Bodin, Arthur M. 1966
Subtests: Strengths; Problems; Authority; Communication; Defensiveness; Discipline
Descriptors: Adults; Child Rearing; Family Environment; Family Relationship; *Interaction; *Parent Attitudes; *Parents; Rating Scales
Identifiers: BFAM; Bodin Family Agreement Measure
Availability: Dr. Arthur M. Bodin; Mental Research Institute, 555 Middlefield Rd., Palo Alto, CA 94301
Target Audience: Adults
Notes: Items, 12

Designed to assess agreement between parents concerning child-rearing attitudes and family interaction.

7716
Schwirian Science Support Scale. Schwirian, Patricia M. 1967
Subtests: Rationality; Utilitarianism:; Universalism; Individualism; Progress and Meliorism
Descriptors: Adolescents; *Adults; Attitudes; Rating Scales; Science Education; *Sciences; *Scientists; Self Concept Measures; Student Attitudes; *Undergraduate Students; Values; Likert Scales
Identifiers: Science Support Scale; TRI S Scale
Availability: Science Education;v52 n2 p172-79, Mar 1968
Target Audience: 18–64
Notes: Time, 30 approx.; Items, 40

To determine the attitudes of undergraduate students and adults toward science and scientists. To be used as an initial step toward the development of healthy, positive attitudes in science education. Based upon the values given in Bernard Barber's book, *Science and the Social Order.*

7723
What I Like to Do: Second Edition. Meyers, Charles E.; And Others 1975
Subtests: Play; Academic; The Arts; Occupations; Reading
Descriptors: Elementary Education; *Elementary School Students; *Interest Inventories; Intermediate Grades; Reading Interests; *Student Interests; Vocational Interests
Identifiers: Self Administered Tests
Availability: Science Research Associates; 155 N. Wacker Dr., Chicago, IL 60606
Grade Level: 4–6
Notes: Time, 45 approx.; Items, 150

Designed to reveal interest patterns of youngsters' preferences in areas of play, academics, arts, occupations, and reading. Yields individual and class interest profiles.

7734
Sex Knowledge and Attitude Test, Second Edition. Lief, Harold I. 1972
Descriptors: Adults; Foreign Countries; Knowledge Level; Sex Education; *Sexuality; Social Attitudes
Identifiers: England; *Sexual Attitudes; SKAT; Sweden
Availability: Marriage Council of Philadelphia, Inc., Center for the Study of Sex Education in Medicine, 4025 Chestnut St. (2nd Fl.), Philadelphia, PA 19104
Target Audience: Adults
Notes: Time, 30 approx.; Items, 149

Test represents an institutional research tool and/or classroom teaching aid, and an efficient system for tabulating, scoring, and reporting data on sexual knowledge and attitudes from a variety of institutions and groups.

7736
Defining Issues Test. Rest, James R. 1972
Descriptors: Adolescents; Adults; Higher Education; High Schools; *High School Students; Moral Development; *Moral Values; Social Attitudes; Social Values; Student Attitudes; *Undergraduate Students; *Value Judgment
Identifiers: DIT
Availability: James R. Rest; University of Minnesota, 330 Burton Hall, Minneapolis, MN 55455
Grade Level: 9–16

Notes: Time, 50 approx.; Items, 6
Designed to assess development of moral judgment. Respondent indicates priorities in dealing with 6 moral dilemmas by ranking a series of solutions.

7737
Courtship Questionnaire. Wilson, Warner R. 1965
Descriptors: *Adjustment (to Environment); Higher Education; *Sexuality; Social Attitudes; *Undergraduate Students
Identifiers: *Courtship; *Sexual Attitudes; Sexual Permissiveness
Availability: Psychological Reports;v17 p371-78, 1965
Grade Level: 13–16
Notes: Items, 6

Designed to assess students' attitudes toward sexual intimacy. Students were given the questionnaire and each of 4 groups was given different instructions. Instructions were given to answer questions in terms of peer approval, parent approval, individual approval, and how subject would behave in a given situation. Attitudes to sexual intimacy were studied in relation to avowed happiness and religiosity.

7739
Social Customs Questionnaire. Wilson, Warner R. 1970
Descriptors: *Adults; Racial Attitudes; *Racial Bias; Racial Integration; *Social Attitudes
Availability: Warner R. Wilson; Dept. of Psychology, Wright State University, Col. Glenn Hwy., Dayton, OH 45431
Target Audience: Adults
Notes: Items, 28

Designed to assess attitudes of racial and social groups toward integration and equal rights.

7773
Characteristics Scale. Elmore, Patricia B.; Beggs, Donald L.
Descriptors: Elementary Education; *Elementary School Students; Elementary School Teachers; Student Behavior; Student Characteristics; *Teacher Attitudes
Availability: Dr. Patricia B. Elmore; Guidance and Educational Psychology, Southern Illinois University, Carbondale, IL 62901
Grade Level: K–6
Notes: Items, 16

Designed to assess teachers' opinions concerning characteristics of importance for the satisfactory or acceptable behavior of a student in the classroom.

7774
Parental Acceptance Scale. Porter, Blaine R.
Descriptors: Adults; Affection; Child Rearing; Parent Attitudes; *Parent Child Relationship; *Parents; Rating Scales; Self Evaluation (Individuals)
Identifiers: Acceptance
Availability: Dr. Blaine R. Porter; University Professor, 2240 Smith Family Living Center, Brigham Young University, Provo, UT 84602
Target Audience: Adults
Notes: Time, 30 approx.; Items, 40

Designed to assess parent's acceptance of his/her child. Parents rate themselves based upon feelings they have and actions they take in relationship to their child.

7776
The Perceived Equity Scale. Spector, Paul E.; And Others 1975
Descriptors: Adults; *Compensation (Remuneration); *Employee Attitudes; Employees; *Job Satisfaction; Rating Scales; Work Attitudes; *Likert Scales
Identifiers: PES; TIM(C)
Availability: Tests in Microfiche; Test Collection, Educational Testing Service, Princeton, NJ 08541
Target Audience: Adults
Notes: Items, 19

Designed to measure whether or not an individual feels equitably compensated in his or her job. The items pertain to rewards or inducements that an employer or organization can give an employee. The respondents are required to compare the rewards they receive with the effort they must make.

7781
Negative Attitudes toward Masturbation Inventory. Abramson, Paul R.; Mosher, Donald L. 1975
Descriptors: *Adults; Higher Education; *Negative Attitudes; Rating Scales; *Sexuality; Undergraduate Students
Identifiers: Guilt; *Masturbation; Self Administered Tests
Availability: Paul R. Abramson; Dept. of Psychology, University of California, 405 Hilgard Ave., Los Angeles, CA 90024

Grade Level: 13–16
Target Audience: Adults
Notes: Items, 30

Designed to assess negative attitudes toward masturbation and the relationship between these attitudes and sex guilt or frequency of masturbation.

7792
Intellectualism-Pragmatism Scale. Yuker, Harold E.; Block, J.R. 1965
Descriptors: *Graduate Students; Higher Education; *Student Attitudes; *Undergraduate Students
Identifiers: Intellectual Pragmatism Scale (Yuker and Block); IP Scale; Pragmatism
Availability: Dr. Harold E. Yuker; Psychology Dept.; Hofstra University, Hempstead, NY 11550
Grade Level: 13–20
Notes: Items, 30

Designed to assess intellectual versus pragmatic attitudes of college students.

7795
Personal Attributes Questionnaire. Spence, Janet T.; And Others 1973
Subtests: Male-Valued; Female-Valued; Sex Specific
Descriptors: Adults; *College Students; Rating Scales; Self Evaluation (Individuals); *Sex Stereotypes; Social Attitudes
Identifiers: PAQ; TIM(C)
Availability: Tests in Microfiche; Test Collection, Educational Testing Service, Princeton, NJ 08541
Target Audience: Adults
Notes: Items, 110

Provides a measure of sex-role stereotypes; that is, beliefs that men and women differ in many of their characteristics. Respondents rate themselves and then a typical male and female on a series of items. The ratings are divided into male-valued, female-valued, and sex-specific items. The questionnaire is a revision of the Sex Role Stereotyping Questionnaire.

7800
Death Concern Scale. Dickstein, Louis S. 1972
Descriptors: *Anxiety; *Death; Higher Education; *Undergraduate Students
Availability: Psychological Reports;v30 p563-71, Apr 1972
Grade Level: 13–16
Notes: Items, 30

Designed to measure individual differences in the degree to which an individual consciously confronts death and is disturbed by its implications. Instrument is also available from the author: Louis S. Dickstein; 71 Clinton Place, Newton Centre, MA 02159.

7814
Student Attitude Measure. Colwell, David; And Others 1975
Subtests: General School Attitude; Interpersonal Self-Concept; Intrapersonalized Self-Concept
Descriptors: Elementary Education; *Elementary School Students; Peer Relationship; Primary Education; *School Attitudes; Self Concept; *Student Adjustment; *Student Attitudes; Videotape Recordings
Availability: ERIC Document Reproduction Service; 3900 Wheeler Ave., Alexandria, VA 22304 (ED110475, 42 pages)
Grade Level: 1–4
Notes: Time, 45 approx.; Items, 24

Designed to assess education-related attitudes of young children in grades 1 through 4. Test administration may be oral or presented on videotape.

7815
Minneapolis Student Opinion Questionnaire. Johnson, Lary; Taunce, R.W. 1972
Subtests: Liking of School; Interest in Learning; Unfair Punishment; Self-Concept; Friendly Atmosphere; Involvement in Decision Making; Class Discussions; Positive Reinforcement; Curriculum Relevance; Fear of Asking Questions; Perceptions of Progress in Learning; Racial Items; Factor Y; Factor X
Descriptors: Feedback; Racial Attitudes; *School Attitudes; Secondary Education; *Secondary School Students; Secondary School Teachers; Self Concept; *Student Adjustment; *Student Attitudes
Identifiers: SOQ
Availability: ERIC Document Reproduction Service; 3900 Wheeler Ave., Alexandria, VA 22304 (ED084303, 49 pages)
Grade Level: 7–12
Notes: Items, 93

Designed to assess student attitudes toward school, teachers, peers, curriculum, and other education-related areas.

7825
Authoritarian Family Ideology Scale. Ernhart, Claire B.; Loevinger, Jane 1969
Descriptors: Adults; *Authoritarianism; *Child Rearing; Mothers; *Parent Attitudes; Parents
Identifiers: AFI
Availability: Dr. Claire B. Ernhart; Dept. of Psychiatry, Cleveland Metropolitan General Hospital, Cleveland, OH 44109
Target Audience: Adults
Notes: Items, 42

Designed to assess child-rearing attitudes of parents, especially mothers. Measures preference for authoritarian family structure.

7839
Bilingual Center Parent Questionnaire. Chicago Area Bilingual Centers, Illinois 1974
Subtests: Background and Language; About the Bilingual Center; Parents Feelings
Descriptors: Adults; Arabic; *Bilingualism; *Bilingual Students; Chinese; Greek; Italian; Japanese; Korean; *Parent Attitudes; Parents; *Program Evaluation; Spanish; Spanish Speaking; Tagalog
Identifiers: TIM(E)
Availability: Tests in Microfiche; Test Collection, Educational Testing Service, Princeton, NJ 08541
Target Audience: Adults
Notes: Items, 38

Designed to assess the attitudes of parents, whose children attend the Chicago Area Bilingual Centers, toward the centers themselves. Questions are included that gather information on dominant language, language used in various situations, and communication ease in English. Forms are available in English, Greek, Chinese, Arabic, Italian, Korean, Japanese, and Tagalog.

7859
Ivie Attitudinal Test. Ivie, Richard P. 1975
Subtests: Self-Concept; Attitude toward School; Peer Relations
Descriptors: *Elementary School Students; Elementary Secondary Education; *Peer Relationship; Personality Measures; Personality Traits; Psychological Testing; *Rating Scales; *Secondary School Students; Self Concept; *Self Concept Measures; *Spanish; Spanish Speaking; Student Adjustment; *Student Attitudes; Student Characteristics
Identifiers: IAT; Ivie Prueba De Comportamiento
Availability: Bilingual Leadership through Speech and Drama; Pomona Unified School District, 800 S. Garey Ave., P.O. Box 2900, Pomona, CA 91769
Grade Level: 6–12
Notes: Time, 15 approx.; Items, 59

Questionnaire and rating scale designed to measure student activities and feelings toward school, home, parents, and community. Available in both Spanish and English.

7869
Family Background. Cohen, Donald; Dibble, Eleanor 1972
Descriptors: Adolescents; Children; *Parent Attitudes; *Parent Child Relationship; Parents; Questionnaires; *Twins
Identifiers: Zygosity
Availability: Dr. Donald Cohen; Yale Child Study Center, 333 Cedar St., New Haven, CT 06510
Target Audience: 0–18
Notes: Items, 21

Designed to assess parental perceptions of twins and how parents treat them.

7878
Student Questionnaire. Knox, Alan B.; And Others 1973
Descriptors: *Adult Basic Education; Adults; *Program Evaluation; Questionnaires; *Student Attitudes
Availability: ERIC Document Reproduction Service; 3900 Wheeler Ave., Alexandria, VA 22304 (ED091537, 160 pages)
Target Audience: 18–64
Notes: Items, 7

Questionnaire designed for use in evaluating adult basic education programs. Covers reasons for attendance and feelings about classes themselves. Completed by students.

7892
Chabassol Adolescent Structure Inventory. Chabassol, David J. 1970
Subtests: Wants Structure; Has Structure
Descriptors: *Adolescent Development; *Adolescents; Parent Child Relationship; *Parent Influence; Personal Autonomy; Secondary Education; *Secondary School Students; Student Attitudes; Teacher Student Relationship
Identifiers: CASI

Availability: David J. Chabassol; Dept. of Education, University of Victoria, Box 1700, Victoria, BC, V8W2Y2, Canada
Target Audience: 13–17
Notes: Items, 47

Designed to measure the extent to which adolescents want structure and perceive themselves as having such structure. In the context of this instrument, structure is defined as guidance, advice, information, clarity, or direction offered to the adolescent by an adult authority figure.

7900
School Motivation Analysis Test: Revised Edition. Sweney, Arthur B.; And Others 1976
Subtests: Assertiveness; Mating; Fear; Narcissism; Pugnacity; Protectiveness; Self-Sentiment; Superego; School; Home
Descriptors: *Adolescents; Attitudes; *Counseling Techniques; *Motivation; *Psychological Needs; Secondary Schools; *Secondary School Students; Values
Identifiers: Drives (Personality); SMAT
Availability: Institute for Personality and Ability Testing; P.O. Box 188, Champaign, IL 61820
Target Audience: 12–17
Notes: Time, 60 approx.; Items, 183

Developed to measure motivation, drive strengths, and interests in adolescents aged 12 to 17. Six scales measure basic drives including assertiveness, mating (sex), fear, narcissism, pugnacity-sadism, and protectiveness (pity). Four scales measure sentiments including self-sentiment, superego, school, and home. Material is written at a reading grade level of 4.6. Adult version of scale is Motivation Analysis Test (TC000609).

7911
Marriage Skills Analysis. Henderson, Robert W.; Wiggins, Jack G. 1970
Subtests: Physical; Sex; Loving; Togetherness; Talking; Listening; Adapting and Conforming; Money Management; Learning; Family Goal Setting; Reconciliation; Creating; Helping; Sense of Humor; Aggression
Descriptors: Adults; Affective Measures; *Counseling Techniques; Interest Inventories; *Interpersonal Relationship; *Marriage Counseling; *Spouses
Identifiers: *Premarital Counseling; Self Administered Tests
Availability: Psychological Development Center; 7057 W. 130th, Parma, OH 44130
Target Audience: Adults
Notes: Items, 40

Designed to enable individual to express interests and activities in several aspects of married life. Consists of 15 scales, each of which contains 4 areas: feeling, thinking, acting, and people. May be used for married couples and for couples contemplating marriage.

7930
Parent Questionnaire. Bailey, John E.; Ellis, David B. 1974
Descriptors: Adults; *Behavioral Objectives; Child Development; Child Rearing; Early Childhood Education; *Educational Needs; *Parent Aspiration; *Parent Attitudes; Parent Child Relationship; *Parents; Preschool Children; Young Children
Availability: ERIC Document Reproduction Service; 3900 Wheeler Ave., Alexandria, VA 22304 (ED109219, 57 pages)
Target Audience: Adults

Designed to survey the educational attitudes of preschool children's parents. Developed to elicit information for an educational needs analysis model. Measures factors that parents perceive as affecting their ability to raise their child and competencies parents desire their children to have attained by age 6.

7932
Racial Attitudes and Cultural Expressions Test. Samph, Thomas; Sayles, Felton 1972
Descriptors: *Black Youth; *Elementary School Students; Primary Education; *Racial Attitudes; Sociometric Techniques; *White Students
Identifiers: RACE
Availability: ERIC Document Reproduction Service; 3900 Wheeler Ave., Alexandria, VA 22304 (ED101013, 87 pages)
Grade Level: 1–3
Notes: Items, 12

Designed to measure racial attitudes of primary grade students.

7934
Goal-Priority Instrument. House, Ernest R. 1973
Descriptors: Administrators; *Adults; Citizen Participation; Community Attitudes; *Educational Objectives; Parents; *Program Evaluation; Rating Scales; *State Departments of Education; Teacher Attitudes; Teachers

Availability: ERIC Document Reproduction Service; 3900 Wheeler Ave., Alexandria, VA 22304 (ED078085, 35 pages)
Target Audience: Adults

Designed to assess educational priorities. Respondents were asked to rate 9 specific goals in terms of importance, likelihood of accomplishment, and amount of money to be spent to implement them. Developed for the Illinois Office of the Superintendent of Public Instruction. May be applicable in other states.

7944
Scales to Measure Attitudes toward Marijuana and Marijuana Users. Colaiuta, Victoria; Breed, George 1974
Subtests: Psychological, Physiological and Sociological Effects of Marijuana on Users; Marijuana as a Psychosocial Panacea; Liberal/Conservative Ambivalence toward the Usage of Marijuana
Descriptors: Adults; *College Students; *Drug Use; *Marijuana; *Predictive Measurement; *Student Attitudes
Identifiers: TIM(C)
Availability: Tests in Microfiche; Test Collection, Educational Testing Service, Princeton, NJ 08541
Grade Level: 13–20
Target Audience: Adults
Notes: Items, 22

Instrument used to predict classifications of student marijuana users and nonusers.

7955
Personal Inventory. Hill, Harris E.; Monroe, Jack J. 1975
Descriptors: Adults; *Attitudes; Biographical Inventories; *Drug Abuse; *Drug Addiction; *Males; Personality Traits; Predictive Measurement; Psychotherapy; *Self Concept
Identifiers: *Drug Addicts; PI; TIM(D)
Availability: Tests in Microfiche; Test Collection, Educational Testing Service, Princeton, NJ 08541
Target Audience: Adults
Notes: Items, 220

Designed to measure personality and drug-related experiences of opiate addicts, with the intent of predicting their suitability for psychotherapy. The items cover personality characteristics, drug preference, effect of drugs on personal experiences, and history of use.

7956
Inventory of Habits and Attitudes. Monroe, Jack J.; Hill, Harris E. 1970
Descriptors: Adults; *Alcoholism; *Attitudes; Biographical Inventories; *Males; Personality Traits
Identifiers: *Alcoholism Questionnaire; IHA; TIM(D)
Availability: Tests in Microfiche; Test Collection, Educational Testing Service, Princeton, NJ 08541
Target Audience: Adults
Notes: Items, 200

Developed for the evaluation and description of presumably stable characteristics of alcoholics. Covers experiences, sentiments, and attitudes concerning alcohol and alcoholics as well as a variety of demographic variables, personality, adjustment, familial relationships, and attitudes about treatment.

7960
A Study of Generations: Phase A-Family Relations, Phase B. Bengtson, Vern L.; And Others 1972
Descriptors: Adolescents; Adults; *Attitudes; *Biographical Inventories; *Family Attitudes; Opinions; *Parent Child Relationship; *Self Concept; Values; Life Events
Identifiers: TIM(C)
Availability: Tests in Microfiche; Test Collection, Educational Testing Service, Princeton, NJ 08541
Target Audience: 13–65
Notes: Items, 448

Collection of instruments developed to elicit the attitudes and feelings of parents, grandparents, and young adults concerning similarities and differences that exist between age groups in contemporary American society. The instruments include your opinions, family relations in 3 generations, activities, relations, you and your parents, you and your grandparents, other aspects of family life, relations with in-laws, more opinions, values, behaviors, feelings, opinions about families, goals, religion, your parents' opinions, your own views, and background information. Phase B is an autobiographical inventory. Subscales include schedule of life events, area of change, who are you?, questions on generations, attitudes, opinions, and behaviors.

7964

Survey of School Attitudes: Primary. Hogan, Thomas P. 1975
Subtests: Reading/Language; Mathematics; Science; Social Studies
Descriptors: Affective Measures; *Elementary School Curriculum; Elementary School Science; *Elementary School Students; Language Arts; Mathematics; Primary Education; *School Attitudes; Social Studies; *Student Attitudes
Identifiers: Oral Testing; SSA
Availability: Psychological Corp.; 555 Academic Ct., San Antonio, TX 78204-0952
Grade Level: 1–3
Notes: Time, 40 approx.; Items, 72
Designed to measure student reactions to 4 major areas of school curriculum. These include language arts and reading, mathematics, science, and social studies. Teacher reads item stems to students so that no reading is required of students. Instrument should be administered in 2 sittings. Forms A and B are available.

7965

Survey of School Attitudes: Intermediate. Hogan, Thomas P. 1975
Descriptors: Affective Measures; *Elementary School Curriculum; *Elementary School Students; Intermediate Grades; Junior High Schools; *Junior High School Students; Language Arts; Mathematics; *School Attitudes; Sciences; Social Studies; *Student Attitudes
Identifiers: SSA
Availability: Psychological Corp.; 555 Academic Ct., San Antonio, TX 78204-0952
Grade Level: 4–8
Notes: Time, 30 approx.; Items, 72
Designed to measure student reactions to 4 major areas of school curriculum. These include language arts and reading, mathematics, science, and social studies. Vocabulary of items is at, or below, a fourth grade reading level. Forms A and B are available.

8000

Chasen Diagnostic Sex-Role Bias Scale. Chasen, Barbara; Weinberg, Sharon 1974
Descriptors: Adults; Case Studies; Rating Scales; *School Psychologists; *Sex Bias; Sex Role
Identifiers: TIM(C)
Availability: Tests in Microfiche; Test Collection, Educational Testing Service, Princeton, NJ 08541
Target Audience: Adults
Notes: Items, 40
Designed to measure sex-role bias toward children. The scale consists of case histories focusing on the somewhat unhealthy aspects of 2 main factors of behavior: activity (composed of independence and aggression) and passivity (composed of dependence and nonaggression).

8038

Parental Attitude Research Instrument (Glasser-Radin Revision). Glasser, Paul; Radin, Norma 1965
Descriptors: Adults; *Child Rearing; Disadvantaged; Low Income; *Mothers; *Parent Attitudes; *Parent Education; Preschool Children; Rating Scales; Likert Scales
Identifiers: PARI; TIM(E)
Availability: Tests in Microfiche; Test Collection, Educational Testing Service, Princeton, NJ 08541
Target Audience: Adults
Notes: Items, 36
Revision of the original instrument for measuring child-rearing attitudes by Schaefer and Bell was developed for use in a study of disadvantaged parents. Statements are evaluated on a 4-point, Likert-type forced-choice scale from strongly agree to strongly disagree.

8096

Purdue Social Attitude Scales for Preschool Children. Cicirelli, Victor G.
Subtests: Attitude toward Peers; Attitude toward School; Attitude toward Home; Attitude toward Community
Descriptors: Affective Behavior; Affective Measures; *Individual Testing; Pictorial Stimuli; *Preschool Children; Preschool Education; *Social Attitudes; Student Attitudes
Identifiers: Oral Testing; PSAS; TIM(C)
Availability: Tests in Microfiche; Test Collection, Educational Testing Service, Princeton, NJ 08541
Target Audience: 2–5
Notes: Time, 20 approx.; Items, 40
Designed to assess children's feelings and evaluations about persons, objects and situations that represent peers, school, community, and home. Items are a series of cartoon picture stories. Scales should be individually administered and are intended for use in research studies only and not for individual diagnosis of children.

8097

Purdue Social Attitude Scales for Primary Grade Children. Cicirelli, Victor G.
Descriptors: Affective Behavior; Affective Measures; Individual Testing; Pictorial Stimuli; Primary Education; *Social Attitudes; Student Attitudes; *Young Children
Identifiers: Oral Testing; TIM(E)
Availability: Tests in Microfiche; Test Collection, Educational Testing Service, Princeton, NJ 08541
Grade Level: 1–3
Notes: Time, 30 approx.; Items, 40
Designed to assess children's attitudes toward peers, school, community, and home. The scales are intended for research use and not for the individual diagnosis of children. Small group or individual administration.

8100

Purdue Interview Schedule for Parents of Primary Grade Children. Cicirelli, Victor G.
Subtests: Achievement Aspirations; Learning Environment; Concern for Child's Education; Maturity Demands; Television Habits; Parent Activities; Attitudes toward Education; Attitude toward Child; Permissiveness; Restrictiveness; Authorization Attitude; Demographic SES Variables
Descriptors: *Academic Achievement; Adults; Child Rearing; *Family Environment; *Parent Aspiration; *Parent Attitudes; *Parent Influence; Parent Role; Parents; Parent Student Relationship; Primary Education; *Students; Likert Scales
Identifiers: TIM(C)
Availability: Tests in Microfiche; Test Collection, Educational Testing Service, Princeton, NJ 08541
Target Audience: Adults
Notes: Items, 116
Designed to elicit information concerning parent characteristics related to their children's social-emotional and intellectual characteristics. Experimental edition.

8102

Attitudes in Vocational Choice. Blum, Stuart Hollander 1961
Descriptors: Career Choice; *College Students; Higher Education; *Males; Student Attitudes; Student Motivation; *Work Attitudes
Identifiers: Security Inventory
Availability: Stuart H. Blum; Dept. of Education, Brooklyn College, Bedord Ave. and Ave. H, Brooklyn, NY 11210
Grade Level: 13–20
Notes: Time, 25 approx.; Items, 40
Designed to measure the degree of emphasis placed upon security as a factor in vocational choice.

8169

Client Attitude Questionnaire. Morrison, James K. 1973
Descriptors: Adults; Biological Influences; Institutionalized Persons; Institutional Personnel; *Mental Disorders; *Psychiatrists; Questionnaires; Social Influences
Identifiers: CAQ; TIM(D)
Availability: Tests in Microfiche; Test Collection, Educational Testing Service, Princeton, NJ 08541
Target Audience: Adults
Notes: Items, 20
Twenty-item rating scale designed to elicit respondents' attitudes toward mental illness and the degree of their endorsement of the psychosocial approach to psychiatric ideology and practice. Two versions of the questionnaire are available, the CAQ-A and CAQ-B, with the CAQ-B being more efficient for tapping the psychosocial attitudes of the subject being tested.

8189

Quality of School Life Scale. Epstein, Joyce L.; McPartland, James M. 1976
Subtests: Satisfaction; Commitment to Classwork; Reactions to Teachers
Descriptors: Educational Experience; *Elementary School Students; Intermediate Grades; *School Attitudes; Secondary Education; *Secondary School Students; Student Attitudes; Teacher Student Relationship
Identifiers: QSL
Availability: Riverside Publishing Co.; 8420 Bryn Mawr Ave., Chicago, IL 60631
Grade Level: 4–12
Notes: Time, 20 approx.; Items, 27
Designed to elicit a student's attitudes toward school, teachers, and course content. Respondent evaluates his/her school experience.

8267

Arlin-Hills Attitude Surveys: Primary. Arlin, Marshall 1976
Subtests: Teachers; Learning Processes; Mathematics; Language Arts
Descriptors: *Elementary School Students; Primary Education; *School Attitudes; *Student Attitudes
Availability: Psychologists and Educators; P.O. Box 513, St. Louis, MO 63017
Grade Level: K–3
Notes: Items, 15
Four cartoon instruments of 15 items each are designed to be administered and interpreted on a group basis. An efficient and inexpensive manner of using instruments is to distribute the 4 instruments at random to students within a classroom. Students may also complete anywhere from 2 to 4 instruments if the total number in class is small. Student anonymity must be protected to produce honest reporting of attitudes.

8268

Arlin-Hills Attitude Surveys: Elementary. Arlin, Marshall 1976
Subtests: Teachers; Learning Processes; Mathematics; Language Arts
Descriptors: *Elementary School Students; Intermediate Grades; *School Attitudes; *Student Attitudes
Availability: Psychologists and Educators; P.O. Box 513, St. Louis, MO 63017
Grade Level: 4–6
Notes: Items, 15
Four cartoon instruments of 15 items each are designed to be administered and interpreted on a group basis. An efficient and inexpensive manner of using instruments is to distribute the 4 instruments at random to students within a classroom. Students may also complete anywhere from 2 to 4 instruments if the total number in class is small. Student anonymity must be protected to produce honest reporting of attitudes.

8269

Arlin-Hills Attitude Surveys: Secondary. Arlin, Marshall 1976
Subtests: Teachers; Learning Processes; Mathematics; Language Arts
Descriptors: *School Attitudes; Secondary Education; *Secondary School Students; *Student Attitudes
Availability: Psychologists and Educators; P.O. Box 513, St. Louis, MO 63017
Grade Level: 7–12
Notes: Items, 15
Four cartoon instruments of 15 items each are designed to be administered and interpreted on a group basis. An efficient and inexpensive manner of using instruments is to distribute the 4 instruments at random to students within a classroom. Students may also complete anywhere from 2 to 4 instruments if the total number in class is small. Student anonymity must be protected to produce honest reporting of attitudes.

8271

Evaluative Disposition toward the Environment. Milchus, Norman J. 1976
Subtests: Aesthetic versus Indifferent to Beauty; Experiential versus Avoidance of First-Hand Experience; Knowledge Seeking versus Disinterest in Information; Prudent versus Immediate/ Exploitive; Active versus Passive to Duty; Responsible versus Unclear of Duty; Practical versus Sentimental
Descriptors: *Conservation (Environment); *Environmental Education; Higher Education; High Schools; *High School Students; *Program Evaluation; *Undergraduate Students; *Values
Identifiers: EDEN
Availability: Person-O-Metrics; 20504 Williamsburg Rd., Dearborn Heights, MI 48127
Grade Level: 9–16
Notes: Time, 45; Items, 70
Designed to elicit information on a person's values, opinions, and interests related to the environment and energy. Measures 7 environmental factors: aesthetic vs. indifference to beauty; experiential vs. avoidance of first-hand experience; knowledge seeking vs disinterest in information; prudent vs. immediate/exploitive; active vs. passive to duty; responsible vs. unclear of duty; and practical vs. sentimental.

8274

Self-Esteem Inventory: Adult Form. Coopersmith, Stanley 1981
Descriptors: *Adolescents; *Adults; Family Relationship; Peer Relationship; *Self Concept Measures; *Self Esteem; *Social Attitudes
Identifiers: SEI
Availability: Consulting Psychologists Press; 577 College Ave., Palo Alto, CA 94306
Target Audience: 16–64
Notes: Time, 10 approx.; Items, 25

Designed for use with persons aged 16 years and above. Adapted from the SEI School Short Form (TC005452). Assesses attitudes toward self in social and personal contexts.

8288
Attitudes toward Homosexuality Scale. McDonald, A.P., Jr.; Huggins, Jim 1976
Descriptors: Adults; *Homosexuality; *Lesbianism; Likert Scales
Availability: Center for the Study of Human Sexuality; 1405 Medical Pwy., Ste. 205, Austin, TX 78756
Target Audience: Adults
Notes: Items, 28

A measure of attitudes in 3 forms: male, female, and general using a 9-point Likert-Type scale. A discussion of the reliability, validity, and norms can be found in: *The Homosexual Counseling Journal*; v1 n4 p169-80, 1974.

8290
Employment Readiness Scale. Alfano, Anthony M. 1973
Descriptors: Adults; Unemployment; *Work Attitudes
Identifiers: TIM(J)
Availability: Tests in Microfiche; Test Collection, Educational Testing Service, Princeton, NJ 08541
Target Audience: Adults
Notes: Items, 43

The scale was developed to measure attitudes toward work and to help determine the relation between length of unemployment time and work attitudes.

8294
Fear of Success Scale. Zuckerman, Miron; Allison, Stephen 1976
Descriptors: *Achievement Need; Adults; Attitudes; *Fear of Success; Motivation; Rating Scales
Identifiers: FOSS; TIM(D)
Availability: Tests in Microfiche; Test Collection, Educational Testing Service, Princeton, NJ 08541
Target Audience: Adults
Notes: Items, 27

Developed to assess individual differences in the motive to avoid success. Items describe the benefits of success, the cost of success, and the respondent's attitudes toward success when compared to other alternatives.

8302
Index of Marital Satisfaction. Hudson, Walter W. 1974
Descriptors: Adults; *Marital Instability; *Marriage; *Marriage Counseling; Rating Scales; *Spouses; *Marital Satisfaction
Identifiers: IMS; TIM(D)
Availability: Tests in Microfiche; Test Collection, Educational Testing Service, Princeton, NJ 08541
Target Audience: Adults
Notes: Time, 5 approx.; Items, 25

Designed to measure the degree of satisfaction people have with their present marriage. Items elicit feelings about a number of components, behaviors, attitudes, and events that occur within and characterize the degree of discord or dissatisfaction in a marital relationship. One of 4 scales intended to be administered at regular intervals to enable therapists to monitor and evaluate their clients' response to treatment.

8303
Index of Sexual Satisfaction. Hudson, Walter W. 1974
Descriptors: Adults; Attitudes; *Interpersonal Relationship; *Rating Scales; *Sexuality
Identifiers: ISS; *Sexual Adjustment; Sexual Attitudes; TIM(D)
Availability: Tests in Microfiche; Test Collection, Educational Testing Service, Princeton, NJ 08541
Target Audience: Adults
Notes: Time, 5 approx.; Items, 25

Designed to measure the degree of satisfaction couples achieve in the sexual component of their relationship. Scale is intended to be administered at regular intervals to enable therapists to monitor and evaluate their clients' response to treatment.

8304
Child's Attitude toward Mother. Hudson, Walter W. 1976
Descriptors: Adolescents; Adults; Family Counseling; *Family Problems; *Mothers; *Parent Child Relationship; Rating Scales
Identifiers: CAM; TIM(D)
Availability: Tests in Microfiche; Test Collection, Educational Testing Service, Princeton, NJ 08541
Target Audience: 12-65

Notes: Items, 25

Designed to measure the degree of contentment a child (ages 12 and older) has with his or her mother. The scale is intended to indicate the magnitude of a relationship problem between mother and child. One of a series of 3 tests to be administered by therapist at regular intervals to measure progress of treatment.

8305
Child's Attitude toward Father. Hudson, Walter W. 1976
Descriptors: Adolescents; Adults; Family Counseling; *Family Problems; *Fathers; *Parent Child Relationship; Rating Scales
Identifiers: CAF; TIM(D)
Availability: Tests in Microfiche; Test Collection, Educational Testing Service, Princeton, NJ 08541
Target Audience: 12-65
Notes: Items, 25

Designed to measure the degree of contentment a child (ages 12 and older) has with his or her father. The scale is intended to indicate the extent of a relationship problem between father and child. One of a series of 3 tests to be administered by a therapist at regular intervals to measure progress of treatment.

8306
Index of Parental Attitudes. Hudson, Walter W. 1976
Descriptors: Adults; *Family Counseling; Family Problems; *Parent Attitudes; *Parent Child Relationship; *Parents; Rating Scales
Identifiers: IPA; TIM(D)
Availability: Tests in Microfiche; Test Collection, Educational Testing Service, Princeton, NJ 08541
Target Audience: Adults
Notes: Items, 25

Designed to measure the magnitude of a parent's relationship problem with a specific child. One of a series of 3 tests to be administered by a therapist at regular intervals to measure progress of treatment.

8309
Pennsylvania Assessment of Creative Tendency. Rookey, Thomas J. 1973
Descriptors: *Creativity; *Curiosity; *Divergent Thinking; *Elementary School Students; Evaluative Thinking; Intermediate Grades; Rating Scales
Identifiers: PACT; TIM(D)
Availability: Tests in Microfiche; Test Collection, Educational Testing Service, Princeton, NJ 08541
Grade Level: 4-6
Notes: Items, 45

An attitude inventory developed to measure students' creative tendencies. Creativity is defined as the conception by an individual of an event or relationship which, in the experience of that individual, did not exist previously. The items were constructed in terms of 9 traits derived from a profile of the creative child: self-direction, evaluative ability, flexible thinking, original thinking, elaborative thinking, willingness to take risks, ease with complexity, curiosity, and fluent thinking ability. Five alternate forms of this test are included: Form 39, Form 19A, Form 19B, Form 13A, Form 13B.

8310
Sex Stereotype Measure II. Williams, John E.; Best, Deborah L. 1976
Descriptors: Elementary Education; *Elementary School Students; Individual Testing; *Pictorial Stimuli; *Sex Stereotypes; *Student Attitudes
Identifiers: Oral Testing; SSM II; TIM(D)
Availability: Tests in Microfiche; Test Collection, Educational Testing Service, Princeton, NJ 08541
Grade Level: K-6
Target Audience: 5-12
Notes: Time, 20 approx.; Items, 32

Developed to assess children's knowledge of adult-defined, conventional, sex-trait stereotypes. It employs human figure silhouettes and brief stories designed to represent traits that adults define as descriptive of the male and female stereotypes. SSM II may be individually administered to younger children and group administered to older ones.

8311
Sex Attitude Measure. Williams, John E.; Best, Deborah L. 1976
Descriptors: Elementary Education; *Elementary School Students; *Individual Testing; Pictorial Stimuli; Sex Bias; *Sex Role; *Sex Stereotypes; *Student Attitudes
Identifiers: SAM; TIM(D)
Availability: Tests in Microfiche; Test Collection, Educational Testing Service, Princeton, NJ 08541
Grade Level: K-6

Target Audience: 5-12
Notes: Time, 15 approx.; Items, 24

Designed to assess children's attitudes or evaluative bias toward male and female persons, independent of their stereotype knowledge. The procedure employs brief stories and human figure silhouettes. It can be individually or group administered. High total scores indicate pro-female/anti-male bias, low scores indicate pro-male/anti-female bias, and midrange scores indicate no consistent bias in the evaluation of male and female persons.

8326
Degree of Incapacitation Scale. Herson, Phyllis F.
Descriptors: Adults; *Disabilities; *Elementary School Teachers; *Secondary School Teachers; Situational Tests; Students; *Teacher Attitudes
Identifiers: TIM(D)
Availability: Tests in Microfiche; Test Collection, Educational Testing Service, Princeton, NJ 08541
Target Audience: Adults
Notes: Items, 20

Designed to elicit information from elementary and secondary teachers on the views about possible policy and procedures with regard to a hypothetical pupil who may be psychologically incapacitated or abnormal. The teachers are asked to indicate their agreement with a variety of statements regarding such things as the extent to which the behavior is abnormal, the prognosis, the type of treatment needed, and the kind of effect the pupil has on his or her peers.

8333
Social Interest Scale. Crandall, James E. 1975
Descriptors: Adults; Empathy; *Forced Choice Technique; *Personality Traits; *Prosocial Behavior; Quality of Life; *Social Attitudes; Values
Identifiers: Personal Trait Value Scale; SIS; TIM(D)
Availability: Tests in Microfiche; Test Collection, Educational Testing Service, Princeton, NJ 08541
Target Audience: Adults
Notes: Items, 24

Designed to assess a person's interest in the welfare of others, this self-report instrument requires the individual to choose which of 2 values he considers to be more important. Each of the pairs of values includes one closely related to social interest and one less relevant.

8340
Situational Attitude Scale—Simplified. Rovner, Robert; Sedlacek, William E. 1974
Descriptors: Adults; Blacks; *Racial Attitudes; Semantic Differential; Social Attitudes; *Whites
Identifiers: SASS
Availability: William E. Sedlacek; Counseling Center, University of Maryland, College Park, MD 20742
Target Audience: Adults
Notes: Items, 10

Designed to assess attitudes of noncollege-trained white population toward blacks. Consists of 10 bipolar semantic differential scales.

8354
Faces Attitude Inventory: Form M. Rim, Eui-Do 1977
Subtests: Attitude toward School; Attitude toward Mathematics
Descriptors: *Elementary School Students; *Mathematics; Mathematics Anxiety; Pictorial Stimuli; Primary Education; *School Attitudes; *Student Attitudes; *Visual Measures
Identifiers: FAI; Oral Testing; TIM(D)
Availability: Tests in Microfiche; Test Collection, Educational Testing Service, Princeton, NJ 08541
Grade Level: K-3
Notes: Time, 25 approx.; Items, 20

Designed to measure children's attitudes toward school, and toward mathematics. Each item consists of a question about a specific problem situation and a corresponding picture depicting the situation. The children indicate their responses by marking 1 of 3 faces (happy, plain, unhappy) printed beneath each picture.

8355
How I Describe My Feelings. Rim, Eui-Do 1977
Subtests: School Attitudes; Mathematics Attitudes; Self-Evaluation; Others Opinion of Self
Descriptors: *Elementary School Students; Elementary Secondary Education; *Mathematics; Peer Evaluation; Rating Scales; *School Attitudes; *Secondary School Students; *Self Concept; *Student Attitudes
Identifiers: TIM(D)
Availability: Tests in Microfiche; Test Collection, Educational Testing Service, Princeton, NJ 08541
Grade Level: 3-12

Notes: Items, 44

Employs the semantic differential technique to measure students' self-concept and attitudes toward school and mathematics.

8356
How I Feel about Science: Form S. Rim, Eui-Do 1971
Descriptors: *Elementary School Students; *Preschool Children; Preschool Education; Primary Education; *School Attitudes; *Sciences; *Student Attitudes; *Young Children
Identifiers: HIF; Oral Testing; TIM(D)
Availability: Tests in Microfiche; Test Collection, Educational Testing Service, Princeton, NJ 08541
Target Audience: 3-8
Notes: Time, 50 approx.; Items, 36
Measures 6 aspects of children's attitudes toward science: attitude toward science class, liking for science in comparison with other school subjects, anxiety about science class, self-direction in science, attitude toward science and science professions, and general attitude toward school.

8363
Stuttering Attitudes Checklist. Cooper, Eugene B. 1976
Descriptors: *Adolescents; Attitudes; *Children; *Self Concept; Self Concept Measures; *Self Evaluation (Individuals); Speech Evaluation; Speech Therapy; *Stuttering
Identifiers: Personalized Fluency Control Therapy; PFC Therapy
Availability: DLM Teaching Resources; 1 DLM Park, P.O. Box 4000, Allen, TX 75002
Target Audience: 9-16
Notes: Time, 15 approx.; Items, 25
Part of the Personalized Fluency Control Therapy, a program of behavioral and attitudinal therapy, designed to modify stuttering in adults and children. This instrument is for older children and adolescents who are required to mark their agreement, or their disagreement (only 2 answers possible) with the given statements.

8365
Parent Attitudes toward Stuttering Checklist. Cooper, Eugene B. 1976
Descriptors: *Adolescents; *Children; *Parent Attitudes; Speech Evaluation; *Speech Habits; Speech Therapy; *Stuttering
Identifiers: Personalized Fluency Control Therapy; PFC Therapy
Availability: DLM Teaching Resources; 1 DLM Park, P.O. Box 4000, Allen, TX 75002
Target Audience: 2-16
Notes: Time, 15 approx.; Items, 25
Part of the Personalized Fluency Control Therapy, a program of behavioral and attitudinal therapy, designed to modify stuttering in adults and in children. This instrument is designed to elicit information from parents on their attitudes toward their child's stuttering. For each item, the parent is to mark either his or her agreement or disagreement (only 2 answers possible) with the given statement.

8403
Parent Evaluation Scales. Cooper, Joseph B. 1966
Subtests: The Mother Scale; The Father Scale
Descriptors: *Childhood Attitudes; *Fathers; Higher Education; High Schools; *High School Students; *Mothers; Parent Child Relationship; Parents; Pretests Posttests; Rating Scales; *Undergraduate Students
Availability: The Journal of Genetic Psychology;v108 p49-53, 1966
Grade Level: 9-16
Notes: Items, 52
Designed to assess student's attitudes toward his/her parents. Separate 26-item scales for mother and father.

8417
Morrison's Passive Aggression Scale for Pupils. Morrison, Evelyn 1977
Descriptors: *Aggression; Behavior Rating Scales; *Elementary School Students; Intermediate Grades; Secondary Education; *Secondary School Students; *Student Evaluation; *Teacher Attitudes; Likert Scales
Identifiers: TIM(D)
Availability: Tests in Microfiche; Test Collection, Educational Testing Service, Princeton, NJ 08541
Grade Level: 5-12
Notes: Items, 15
Designed to measure passive aggression on the part of the pupil as perceived by the teacher. The items reflect such attitudes as quiet rebellion, negativism, obstinacy, and lack of responsibility.

8418
Achievement-Related Affect Scale. Solomon, Daniel; Yaeger, Judy
Descriptors: *Achievement Need; *Elementary School Students; Elementary Secondary Education; *Secondary School Students; *Student Motivation; Success
Availability: Daniel Solomon; Child Development Project, 111 Deerwood Pl., Ste. 165, San Ramon, CA 94583
Target Audience: 8-17
Notes: Items, 20
Designed to assess student's achievement motivation in situations involving academic achievement, peer competition in sports, and other individual achievement efforts.

8457
Children's Achievement Motivation Scale. Weiner, Bernard
Descriptors: *Achievement Need; Adolescents; Children; Forced Choice Technique; *Self Evaluation (Individuals)
Identifiers: TIM(D)
Availability: Tests in Microfiche; Test Collection, Educational Testing Service, Princeton, NJ 08541
Target Audience: 6-14
Notes: Items, 20
Developed to assess the achievement motivation of children. The items tap the kind of affect (hope or fear), the direction of behavior (approach or avoidance), and the preference for risk (intermediate vs. easy or difficult) expressed in achievement situations.

8479
Staff Child Rearing Philosophy. Thomas, George 1972
Subtests: Harshness; Strictness; Rewards/Punishment; Tolerance; Sharing Decision-Making; and Protectiveness
Descriptors: Adults; Attitudes; *Child Caregivers; *Child Rearing; Institutional Schools; Philosophy; Professional Personnel
Identifiers: Effectiveness of Child Caring Institutions
Availability: Regional Institute of Social Welfare Research, Inc.; 455 N. Milledge Ave., P.O. Box 152, Athens, GA 30603
Target Audience: Adults
Notes: Items, 30
One of a series of instruments developed for use in a research study on community-oriented care in children's institutions. Adapted from the Parental Attitude Research Instrument Form IV (TC005773) to assess child-rearing philosophy of professional staff in children's institutions.

8480
Community Orientedness Scale. Thomas, George 1972
Descriptors: Adults; Attitudes; *Child Caregivers; *Community Coordination; Institutional Schools; Professional Personnel
Identifiers: Effectiveness of Child Caring Institutions
Availability: Regional Institute of Social Welfare Research, Inc.; 455 N. Milledge Ave., P.O. Box 152, Athens, GA 30603
Target Audience: Adults
Notes: Items, 12
One of a series of instruments developed for use in a research study on community-oriented care in children's institutions. Designed to assess attitudes of institutional child care staff toward community involvement in institutional activities.

8484
PPP School Sentence Form. Fineman, Carol; Levine, Eleanor 1973
Subtests: Areas of Positive Motivation; Areas of Negative Motivation; Feelings about School Topics; Feelings about Peer Topics; General Self-Concept
Descriptors: *Attitude Change; Elementary Education; *Elementary School Students; *Learning Disabilities; Peer Relationship; Projective Measures; *Self Concept; Student Attitudes; *Student Motivation
Identifiers: Oral Testing; Prescriptive Profile Procedure; Tim(D)
Availability: Tests in Microfiche; Test Collection, Educational Testing Service, Princeton, NJ 08541
Target Audience: 5-12
Notes: Items, 20
Elicits information concerning children's feelings about school-related topics. It can provide the following information: areas of positive motivation, areas of negative motivation, feelings about school topics, feelings about peer topics, and general self-concept. The form was developed in connection with the Prescriptive Profile Procedure for Children with Learning Disabilities and may be used at

intervals to assess change in attitude and self-concept. There is a 20-item form and a 22-item supplementary completion form which may be used at the teacher's discretion.

8489
Parent Discipline Inventory. Dlugokinski, Eric L. 1973
Descriptors: Adolescents; Children; *Discipline Policy; Elementary Secondary Education; *Empathy; *Induction; *Mothers; Parent Child Relationship; *Peer Relationship; Rating Scales; Situational Tests
Identifiers: TIM(D)
Availability: Tests in Microfiche; Test Collection, Educational Testing Service, Princeton, NJ 08541
Target Audience: 8-15
Notes: Items, 6
Designed to assess children's perceptions of maternal disciplinary style in terms of inductive responses to peer-conflict situations. Induction refers to attempts at communicating to the child the consequences of his or her actions for others and involves using reasoning to develop empathy or perception of the needs of others.

8496
Martin-Larsen Approval Motivation Scale. Martin, Harry J.; Larsen, Knud 1976
Descriptors: *Adjustment (to Environment); Adults; *Conformity; Interviews; *Locus of Control; *Personality Traits; Social Attitudes; *Undergraduate Students; Likert Scales
Identifiers: *Frustration; MLAM; TIM(D)
Availability: Tests in Microfiche; Test Collection, Educational Testing Service, Princeton, NJ 08541
Target Audience: Adults
Notes: Items, 20
Developed to measure attitudes toward approval seeking and to examine the relationship between approval seeking, social cost, and aggression. The scale encompasses 5 factors: conformity, social cost, Machiavellianism, internal vs. external control, and need for social acceptance.

8500
Children's Dependency Scale. Golightly, Carole; And Others 1970
Descriptors: *Achievement Need; *Elementary School Students; Intermediate Grades; Motivation; *Parent Child Relationship; *Socialization; *Student Attitudes; *Dependency (Personality)
Identifiers: CDS; Grade School Attitude Questionnaire; TIM(D)
Availability: Tests in Microfiche; Test Collection, Educational Testing Service, Princeton, NJ 08541
Grade Level: 4-6
Notes: Items, 65
Developed to provide an objective measure of both instrumental and emotional dependency in children ages 8 to 12. The items are representative of home, school, and play situations.

8510
The Personal Attribute Inventory. Parish, Thomas S.; And Others 1976
Descriptors: *Affective Measures; College Students; Higher Education; Self Concept Measures; Self Evaluation (Individuals)
Identifiers: Oklahoma State University; PAI
Availability: Thomas S. Parish; Dept. of Administration and Foundations, College of Education, Holton Hall, Kansas State University, Manhattan, KS 66506
Grade Level: 13-16
Notes: Items, 100
The Personal Attribute Inventory (PAI) is an interpersonal assessment instrument which consists of 50 positive and 50 negative adjectives from Gough's Adjective Check List. The subject is to select 30 which are most descriptive of the target group or person in question. This instrument was specifically designed to tap affective reactions and may be used in either assessing attitudes toward others or as a self-concept scale. The PAI was used by college students at Oklahoma State University but could be used by younger and older groups.

8519
Supervisory Attitudes: The X-Y Scale. Ford, Robert N. 1972
Descriptors: Administrator Attitudes; Adults; Behavior Rating Scales; Leadership Styles; *Self Evaluation (Individuals); Supervision; *Supervisors
Identifiers: Theory X; Theory Y
Availability: Pfeiffer, J.W., and Jones, J.E.; The 1972 Annual Handbook for Group Facilitators.La Jolla, CA: University Associates, 1972
Target Audience: Adults

Designed to determine supervisory behavior in relation to subordinates. Assesses supervisor's attitudes toward subordinates in terms of McGregor's Theory X and Theory Y.

8553
Pupil Behavior Checklist. Rhodes, Fen 1971
Descriptors: *Behavior Rating Scales; Elementary Education; *Elementary School Students; Elementary School Teachers; Observation; *School Attitudes; Student Attitudes; *Student Behavior
Availability: Dr. Fen Rhodes; Instructional Support, School of Social and Behavioral Sciences, California State University at Long Beach, Long Beach, CA 90840
Grade Level: K–6
Notes: Items, 45

Designed to assess student attitudes toward school and learning. Classroom teacher observes and records behaviors judged to be reflective of attitudes.

8559
Children's Self-Social Constructs Test: Preschool Form. Henderson, Edmund H.; And Others 1967
Subtests: Preference; Esteem; Realism Size; Identification with Mother, Father, Friends or Teacher; Social Interest-Dependency; Minority Identification
Descriptors: Body Image; *Elementary School Students; Friendship; Identification (Psychology); Individual Testing; *Interpersonal Relationship; Minority Groups; Nonverbal Tests; Parents; *Self Concept Measures; Teachers; *Young Children; Dependency (Personality)
Identifiers: TIM(G)
Availability: Tests in Microfiche; Test Collection, Educational Testing Service, Princeton, NJ 08541
Target Audience: 3–8
Notes: Time, 10; Items, 26

Individually administered, nonverbal measure of self-perception in relation to significant others: mother, father, friends, teachers. The tested child arranges figures representing himself and others via paper and pencil. From the arrangements the testees' feelings can be inferred.

8565
Sex Attribution Questionnaire. Greenberg, Roger P.; Zeldow, Peter B. 1975
Descriptors: Adults; *Females; *Males; *Sex Bias; Sex Role; *Sex Stereotypes; Social Attitudes
Identifiers: Sexual Attitudes
Availability: Roger P. Greenberg; State University of New York, Upstate Medical Center, Syracuse, NY
Target Audience: Adults
Notes: Items, 24

Developed to assess attitudes concerning behavior of members of a specific sex. Sex attribution is defined as any explanation of behavior that specifies sex of the performer as a causal agent. Equivalent forms available for male and female respondents.

8612
Fennema-Sherman Mathematics Attitudes Scales. Fennema, Elizabeth; Sherman, Julia A. 1976
Subtests: Attitude toward Success in Mathematics Scale; Mathematics as a Male Domain Scale; Father Scale; Mother Scale; Teacher Scale; Confidence in Learning Mathematics Scale; Mathematics Anxiety Scale; Effectance Motivation in Mathematics Scale; Usefulness of Mathematics
Descriptors: High Schools; *High School Students; *Mathematics; Mathematics Anxiety; Motivation; Self Esteem; *Sex Stereotypes; *Student Attitudes; Success; Likert Scales
Identifiers: TIM(D)
Availability: Tests in Microfiche; Test Collection, Educational Testing Service, Princeton, NJ 08541
Grade Level: 9–12
Notes: Items, 108

Measures some important, domain specific, attitudes which the authors feel are related to the learning of mathematics by all high school students and/or the cognitive performance of females. The Father, Mother, and Teacher Scales measure the perceptions by students of the attitudes of father, mother or teacher toward the student as a learner of mathematics.

8623
Scale of Reading Attitude Based on Behavior. Rowell, C. Glennon 1972
Subtests: Reading in the Content Areas; Reading for Pleasure; Reading in Reading Classes
Descriptors: *Behavior Rating Scales; *Elementary School Students; Intermediate Grades; *Reading Attitudes; Student Attitudes; Student Behavior
Availability: The Reading Teacher;v25 n5 p442–47, Feb 1972
Grade Level: 4–6
Notes: Items, 16

Designed to assess student's attitude toward reading by observing and recording his/her behavior in reading situations. Observer should evaluate child over a prolonged period of time.

8624
Incomplete Sentence Projective Test. Boning, Thomas; Boning, Richard 1957
Descriptors: Elementary Education; *Elementary School Students; *Projective Measures; *Reading Attitudes; Self Concept; Student Adjustment; Student Attitudes
Identifiers: Sentence Completion Tests
Availability: The Reading Teacher;v10 p196-200, Apr 1957
Grade Level: 1–8
Notes: Items, 42

Designed to assess student attitudes toward reading. Adapted from Ruth Strang's Incomplete Sentence Test.

8633
Anttonen Arithmetic Scale. Anttonen, Ralph G. 1970
Descriptors: *Arithmetic; Children; *Elementary School Students; *Student Attitudes
Identifiers: Revised Hoyt Minnesota Pupil Opinion Scale; TIM(D)
Availability: Tests in Microfiche; Test Collection, Educational Testing Service, Princeton, NJ 08541
Target Audience: 8–12
Notes: Items, 28

Designed to determine how positively or negatively children feel toward arithmetic. The children answer either yes or no.

8642
Behavior Rating Scales for School Beginners. Long, Barbara H.; Henderson, Edmund H. 1971
Descriptors: Behavior Rating Scales; *Elementary School Students; *Grade 1; Primary Education; *Racial Attitudes; Student Behavior; *Teacher Attitudes
Availability: Sociology of Education;v44 p358-68, Sum 1971
Grade Level: 1
Notes: Items, 24

Designed for teachers to rate classroom behavior of first grade students. Teacher's attitudes and racial opinions affected their rating of children.

8665
A Scale to Measure Populist Attitudes. Farrell, James J.; Laughlin, Patrick R. 1976
Descriptors: *Adults; *Older Adults; *Political Attitudes
Identifiers: *Populism
Availability: The Journal of Psychology;v94 p33-38, 1976
Target Audience: 18–69
Notes: Items, 20

Designed to assess populist attitudes of adult population.

8667
Sexism in Occupations. Rich, Roy; And Others 1977
Descriptors: Adolescents; Adults; Children; *Feminism; *Occupations; *Sex Bias; *Sex Role
Identifiers: Beliefs about Equal Rights for Men and Women; TIM(D)
Availability: Tests in Microfiche; Test Collection, Educational Testing Service, Princeton, NJ 08541
Target Audience: 8–64
Notes: Items, 78

Measures attitudes and biases regarding various occupations and the male-female roles associated with them. The respondent places each of 50 cards listing occupations along a 9-point male-female continuum. The respondent also completes a separate, 28-item sexism test, entitled Beliefs about Equal Rights for Men and Women. Tester is required to make his or her own set of cards and the sorting board.

8672
Sex Role Ideology And Family Orientation Scale. Angrist, Shirley S.; And Others 1976
Descriptors: Family Life; High Schools; *High School Students; *Parent Child Relationship; *Parent Role; Rating Scales; *Sex Role; Sex Stereotypes; *Student Attitudes; Likert Scales
Identifiers: TIM(D)
Availability: Tests in Microfiche; Test Collection, Educational Testing Service, Princeton, NJ 08541
Grade Level: 9–12
Notes: Items, 37

Developed to assess students' attitudes toward sex roles and the family as an institution, the scale can be used to evaluate the effectiveness of programs designed to reduce traditional stereotypic attitudes.

8695
Feminism Scales. Dempewolff, Judy 1972
Descriptors: Adults; *Feminism; *Sex Bias; Sex Role; *Sex Stereotypes; Likert Scales
Identifiers: TIM(D)
Availability: Tests in Microfiche; Test Collection, Educational Testing Service, Princeton, NJ 08541
Target Audience: Adults
Notes: Items, 28

Four-point Likert-type scale developed to measure attitude toward feminism. Includes 2 forms (A and B), which consist of 28 questions each. Form A endorses feminism, and Form B supports traditional roles.

8697
Attitudes toward Old Persons Scale. Block, J.R. 1966
Descriptors: *Adults; *Older Adults; *Social Attitudes
Identifiers: ATOP
Availability: Dr. J.R. Block; Exec. Dir. for Research and Resource Development, Hofstra University, Hempstead, NY 11550
Target Audience: Adults
Notes: Items, 18

Designed to assess negative and positive attitudes of younger adults to old persons.

8698
Revised Math Attitude Scale. Aiken, Lewis R. 1963
Descriptors: *Females; Higher Education; *Mathematics Anxiety; Predictive Measurement; Student Attitudes; *Undergraduate Students
Availability: The Journal of Educational Research;v56 n9 p476-80, May-Jun 1963
Grade Level: 13–16
Notes: Items, 20

Designed to assess attitudes toward mathematics, particularly those of women. Research has shown this instrument to be a reliable and valid predictor for college women of success in mathematics when used in conjunction with a test of mathematical ability.

8709
Questionnaire on Parent and Educator Knowledge of the Attitudes toward Sexism and the Law. Powell, C.; Mullally, B.
Descriptors: Adults; *Knowledge Level; *Laws; *Parent Attitudes; Parent Participation; *Sex Bias; *Teacher Attitudes; Teacher Participation
Identifiers: Project ASPIRE
Availability: Clyde Powell; Dept. of Education; Eastern New Mexico University, Portales, NM 88130
Target Audience: Adults
Notes: Items, 61

Instrument developed to investigate parent and educator knowledge of, and attitudes toward, sexism and the law as it now stands. First section of the test pertains to knowledge, and the second section pertains to attitudes.

8733
Semantic Differential Scale. Greenberg, Judith W.
Subtests: Teacher; ME; Reading; Mother; School Work; Father
Descriptors: Academic Achievement; *Adolescents; *Elementary School Students; Elementary Secondary Education; Parent Child Relationship; *School Attitudes; Self Concept; *Semantic Differential; *Student Attitudes
Identifiers: TIM(D)
Availability: Tests in Microfiche; Test Collection, Educational Testing Service, Princeton, NJ 08541
Target Audience: 8–16
Notes: Items, 72

Designed to measure meanings children attach to and their attitude toward certain significant concepts and persons that may be related to their school achievement. Three scale dimensions are evaluative, activity, and potency.

8738
Evaluation Survey. Fine, Jo Renee 1977
Subtests: Opinions; The School; Language and Materials; Facts
Descriptors: Adults; *Course Evaluation; *Inservice Education; Rating Scales; *Sex Bias; *Sex Stereotypes; Student Behavior; *Teacher Attitudes; Teachers; Likert Scales
Identifiers: TIM(D)
Availability: Tests in Microfiche; Test Collection, Educational Testing Service, Princeton, NJ 08541
Target Audience: Adults
Notes: Items, 74

Developed to evaluate an inservice teacher training program in nonsexist education, the survey elicits information on teachers' attitudes, behaviors, and knowledge concerning sexism.

8789
Attitudes toward Sex Roles Scale. Hawley, Peggy 1977
Descriptors: *Adults; Androgyny; *Females; High Schools; *High School Students; *Males; *Sex Role; Sex Stereotypes; *Social Attitudes; *Spanish
Identifiers: Sexual Attitudes
Availability: Peggy Hawley; Dept. of Counselor Education, San Diego State University, 5300 Campanile Dr., San Diego, CA 92182-0430
Grade Level: 9-12
Target Audience: 15-64
Notes: Time, 30 approx.; Items, 35
Designed to assess attitudes toward sex role behavior ranging from dichotomous to androgynous. A Spanish-language version is available.

8790
Assessment of Student Attitudes toward Learning Environments. Research for Better Schools, Inc., Philadelphia, PA 1976
Subtests: Attitude toward Education in General; School Curriculum; School Resources; School Counseling
Descriptors: Adjustment (to Environment); Career Education; Career Guidance; High Schools; *High School Students; *Learning Experience; *Rating Scales; School Community Programs; *Student Adjustment; *Student Attitudes; Student Characteristics; *Student Experience; Work Experience Programs; Likert Scales
Identifiers: ASA; Blair (Mark W); Career Education Evaluation Program; RBS Career Education Evaluation Package
Availability: Research for Better Schools; 444 N. 3rd St., Philadelphia, PA 19123
Grade Level: 9-12
Notes: Time, 15 approx.; Items, 26
Untimed instrument that measures students' attitudes toward traditional and nontraditional learning environments. Items from this instrument used in the authors' Student attitude Survey 1976 Form (TC008793). Renders 4 subscales: Attitude toward education in general, school curriculum, school resources, and school counseling. For each item the subject is asked to indicate his or her agreement or disagreement with the statement (from strongly disagree to strongly agree). Part of the RBS Career Education Evaluation Package.

8791
Community Participant Opinion Survey. Research for Better Schools, Inc., Philadelphia, PA 1976
Descriptors: *Adults; *Business; Career Education; Career Exploration; Community Involvement; *Curriculum Evaluation; *Opinions; School Business Relationship; *School Community Programs; Secondary School Curriculum; *Work Experience Programs; Likert Scales
Identifiers: Blair (Mark W); Career Education Evaluation Program; CPOS; RBS Career Education Evaluation Package
Availability: Research for Better Schools; 444 N. 3rd St., Philadelphia, PA 19123
Grade Level: 9-12
Target Audience: Adults
Notes: Time, 15 approx.; Items, 15
An untimed, Likert-type scale, used to obtain the attitudes and opinions of community participants concerning any educational programs similar to the RBS Career Education program. The last 2 items are open-ended questions, requiring a written response from the subject. The authors feel that this instrument may be administered in person, by mail, or by telephone. Usually group administered.

8792
Parent Opinion Survey. Research for Better Schools, Inc., Philadelphia, PA 1976
Descriptors: Adults; Career Education; *Curriculum Evaluation; *High School Students; Opinions; *Parent Attitudes; *Parents; Parent School Relationship; *Rating Scales; School Community Programs; Secondary School Curriculum; Student Centered Curriculum; *Work Experience Programs; Likert Scales
Identifiers: Blair (Mark W); Career Education Evaluation Program; POS; RBS Career Education Evaluation Package
Availability: Research for Better Schools; 444 N. 3rd St., Philadelphia, PA 19123
Grade Level: 9-12
Target Audience: Adults
Notes: Time, 15 approx.; Items, 15

Untimed survey that measures the attitudes and opinions of those parents whose children are enrolled in high school career education programs similar to RBS Career Education Evaluation Package or Program. Covers various program elements, opinions on program benefits, and comparisons of the program to standard curricular offerings. The first 13 items require a Likert Scale type of answer; the last 2 items are open-ended questions, which require a written answer on the part of the parent. Part of the authors' RBS Career Education Evaluation Package. The authors suggest that this instrument may be administered via phone interview or in person during various parent meetings or other gatherings. Usually group administered.

8793
Student Attitude Survey, 1976 Form. Research for Better Schools, Inc., Philadelphia, PA 1976
Descriptors: *Career Education; Career Exploration; High Schools; *High School Students; *Rating Scales; School Community Programs; Self Concept; *Self Concept Measures; Self Evaluation (Individuals); *Student Attitudes; Student Characteristics; Student Experience; Student Interests; *Work Experience Programs; Likert Scales
Identifiers: Blair (Mark W); Career Education Evaluation Program; Kershner (Keith M); RBS Career Education Evaluation Package; RBS Student Attitude Survey; SAS
Availability: ERIC Document Reproduction Service; 3900 Wheeler Ave., Alexandria, VA 22304 (ED133358, 46 pages).
Grade Level: 9-12
Notes: Time, 30 approx.; Items, 80
Untimed instrument designed to assess student attitudes toward school, work, self, and others. Based upon developers' hypothesis that student attitudes in these areas are relevant to the intended effects of an experience-based career education program. Includes both preexisting and new items. The school-related items were taken from the authors' Assessment of Student Attitudes toward Learning Environments (TC008790); the scales for attitudes toward themselves and others were adapted from the Berger Acceptance of Self and Other Scales. New scales were developed for the remaining test items. Gives 4 subscales: attitudes toward learning environments (education in general, curriculum, resources, counseling), attitudes related to careers (knowledge, planning, etc.), acceptance of self, and acceptance of others. For each item the subject is asked to indicate his or her agreement or disagreement with the statement (from strongly disagree to strongly agree).

8794
Student Opinion Survey. Research for Better Schools, Inc., Philadelphia, PA 1976
Descriptors: Career Education; Career Exploration; *Curriculum Evaluation; High Schools; *High School Students; *Opinions; Rating Scales; Secondary School Curriculum; *Student Attitudes; Student Centered Curriculum; *Student Experience; *Work Experience Programs; Likert Scales
Identifiers: Blair (Mark W); Career Education Evaluation Program; RBS Career Education Evaluation Package; SOS
Availability: Research for Better Schools; 444 N. 3rd St., Philadelphia, PA 19123
Grade Level: 9-12
Notes: Time, 15 approx.; Items, 23
Untimed survey used to obtain student opinions concerning any career education program which is similar to RBS Career Education Program. Includes various program elements, program benefits, and a comparison of the program to standard curricular programs and courses. Part of the authors' RBS Career Education Evaluation Package. Most items use a Likert-type scale; a few are open-ended, and require a written response from the subject.

8832
The AVJ Scale of Attitude toward Mathematics. Adams, Sam; And Others 1977
Descriptors: *Education Majors; Higher Education; *Mathematics; *Student Attitudes; Teacher Education; Undergraduate Students
Availability: ADI Auxiliary Publications Project; Photoduplication Service, Library of Congress, Washington, DC 20540 (Doc. No. 9581)
Grade Level: 13-16
Notes: Items, 25
Designed to assess attitudes toward mathematics of undergraduate students of education. For a description of the scale see *Journal of Educational Measurement*; v4 n4, Win 1967.

8834
Inquiry Skill Measures. Nelson, N.A.; Abraham, E.C. 1973
Descriptors: *Elementary School Science; Elementary School Students; Fundamental Concepts; *Grade 6; Individual Testing; Intermediate Grades; *Science Tests; Scientific Attitudes; Scientific Literacy; Verbal Tests
Identifiers: Interactive Communication; ISM

*Availability: Journal of Research in Science Teaching;*v10 n4 p291-97, 1973
Grade Level: 6
Instrument designed to measure 4 science processes (knowledge, cognitive skills, attitudes, and psychomotor skills) which purportedly are developed in children as a result of experiencing the newer science curricula.

8836
Seaman's Attitude Inventory. Seaman, Janet A.
Subtests: Social Aspects; Psychological Aspects; Administrative Aspects; Physical Aspects
Descriptors: *Disabilities; *Elementary School Students; Grade 6; Intermediate Grades; *Physical Education; School Attitudes; Secondary Education; *Secondary School Students; *Student Attitudes
Availability: Educational Studies Center for Adapted Physical Education; Dept. of Physical Education, California State University, 5151 State University Dr., Los Angeles, CA 90032
Grade Level: 6-12
Notes: Items, 40
Designed to assess attitudes of handicapped students toward physical education instruction. Useful with students possessing a minimum reading level of sixth grade.

8840
Croake-Hinkle Children's Fears Assessment Instrument. Croake, James W.; Catlin, Nancy 1970
Subtests: Animals; Supernatural; Personal Relations; Political; Safety; Natural Phenomena; School-Related Fears; Drugs; Ecological; Home; Future
Descriptors: Anxiety; Check Lists; Elementary Education; *Elementary School Students; *Fear; *Student Attitudes
Availability: Dr. James W. Croake; Dept. of Psychiatry and Behavioral Sciences, University of Washington, Seattle, WA 98195
Grade Level: 3-9
Target Audience: 8-14
Notes: Items, 71
Designed to elicit children's fears in several areas, including school-related situations.

8841
Attitudes toward Child Rearing Scale. Croake, James W.; Hinkle, Dennis E.
Descriptors: Adults; *Child Rearing; *Parent Attitudes; *Parents; Power Structure
Identifiers: ATCRS
Availability: Dr. James W. Croake; Dept. of Psychiatry and Behavioral Sciences, University of Washington, Seattle, WA 98115
Target Audience: Adults
Notes: Items, 40
Designed to assess authoritarian or democratic attitudes of parents toward child rearing.

8845
Adolescent Value-Orientation Profile. Ulin, Richard O.
Subtests: Peer Group; Family Allegiance; Athletics; Dating; Financial Security; Urge for Upward Mobility; Respect for Academic Achievement
Descriptors: *Adolescents; *Opinions; Self Evaluation (Individuals); *Values
Identifiers: TIM(E); Values Questionnaire
Availability: Tests in Microfiche; Test Collection, Educational Testing Service, Princeton, NJ 08541
Target Audience: Adolescents
Notes: Items, 42
Measures adolescent's degree of adherence to each of 7 values. Each item presents a situation with a choice of 2 possible actions.

8878
Survey Instrument: Geometry Test and Teaching Geometry Test. Backman, Carl Adolph 1969
Subtests: Information Sheet; Attitude Survey; The Teaching of Geometry in the Elementary School; Geometry
Descriptors: Adults; *Elementary School Teachers; Geometric Concepts; *Geometry; Multiple Choice Tests; Surveys; *Teacher Attitudes; *Teacher Characteristics; Teacher Education; *Teacher Qualifications; Likert Scales
Identifiers: TIM(E)
Availability: Tests in Microfiche; Test Collection, Educational Testing Service, Princeton, NJ 08541
Target Audience: Adults
Notes: Items, 127
Used to collect information on elementary school teachers' presage characteristics relevant to teacher preparation. The 4 parts give the following types of information: (1) background, training/experience; (2) attitudes toward geometry

and teaching geometry; (3) teacher's familiarity with both the techniques and problems related to teaching of geometry; and (4) teacher's familiarity with geometric concepts. Teachers are allowed to keep the test for 2 weeks.

8879

Children's Sex-Stereotypes of Adult Occupations. Schau, Candace Garrett; Kahn, Lynne 1978
Descriptors: Elementary Education; *Elementary School Students; *Occupations; *Rating Scales; *Sex Role; *Sex Stereotypes; *Student Attitudes
Identifiers: TIM(E)
Availability: Tests in Microfiche; Test Collection, Educational Testing Service, Princeton, NJ 08541
Grade Level: 1–5
Notes: Time, 45 approx.; Items, 21

Designed for elementary school children to assess the sex stereotypes of 21 adult occupations. (Preceding the actual test is a language lesson which tests the children's knowledge of the words is, should, and can.) The tester reads the definition of each occupation twice, one time the child is asked to rate according to ability (who can be?) and the other time, to rate according to prescription (who should be?). The rating is done according to a 5-point pictorial scale (more women than men, more men than women, or equal number of each sex). Suggested that additional adults assist if group is larger than 15 or with younger children.

8883

Paired Hands Test. Zucker, Karl B.; Barnett, David W. 1977
Descriptors: *Adolescents; *Adults; *Children; *Interaction; Intermediate Grades; Interpersonal Relationship; Pictorial Stimuli; Projective Measures; Secondary Education; *Social Attitudes
Identifiers: Others (Concept); PHT
Availability: McCarron-Dial Systems; P.O. Box 45628, Dallas, TX 75245
Grade Level: 4–12
Target Audience: 9–64
Notes: Time, 15 approx.; Items, 20

Designed to measure the "others-concept," which is defined as one's general expectancies or perceptions about other people along a positive-negative continuum. Three forms are available: Elementary for grades 4-6; Secondary for grades 7-12; and Adult. All forms use same photographs but multiple-choice options vary for each form.

8886

Group Instrument to Measure Young Children's Attitudes toward School. Beere, Carole A. 1970
Descriptors: Primary Education; *School Attitudes; Student Adjustment; *Student Attitudes; *Visual Measures; *Young Children; Likert Scales
Identifiers: Oral Testing; TIM(E)
Availability: Tests in Microfiche; Test Collection, Educational Testing Service, Princeton, NJ 08541
Grade Level: K–3
Notes: Time, 45 approx.; Items, 40

Nonverbal Likert-type scale is designed to measure the attitudes toward school of preliterate early elementary school children. Items are presented orally and in picture form. Response choices are also presented pictorially in the form of 5 line-drawn, neuter and nonracial round faces with expressions ranging from a pronounced smile to a pronounced frown.

8902

Stages of Concern Questionnaire. Hall, Gene E.; And Others 1974
Descriptors: Adults; Attitude Change; *College Faculty; Educational Change; *Educational Innovation; *Elementary School Teachers; *Instructional Innovation; Mainstreaming; Special Education; *Teacher Attitudes
Identifiers: Concerns Based Adoption Model; SoCQ
Availability: ERIC Document Reproduction Service; 3900 Wheeler Ave., Alexandria, VA 22304 (ED147342, 36 pages)
Target Audience: Adults
Notes: Items, 35

Developed to assess teacher's concerns about innovations in curriculum and methods. Assesses faculty and administration concerns about changes in schools and universities. Supplementary materials are available from the Research and Development Center for Teacher Education, Educational Annex, University of Texas, Austin, TX 78703.

8920

Attitudes toward Handicapped Individuals Scale. Lazar, Al 1971
Descriptors: Adults; *Disabilities; Individual Testing; Negative Attitudes; *Rejection (Psychology); *Social Attitudes; Likert Scales
Identifiers: ATHI; Oral Testing; TIM(E)

Availability: Tests in Microfiche; Test Collection, Educational Testing Service, Princeton, NJ 08541
Target Audience: Adults
Notes: Time, 12 approx.; Items, 20

Adaptation of the Attitudes toward Disabled Persons (ATDP) by Yuker, Block and Young consists of 20 items rated on a 6-point Likert-type scale from agree very much to disagree very much. Its purpose is to measure attitudes of acceptance or rejection.

8925

Test Anxiety Questionnaire. Mandler, George; Sarason, Seymour 1952
Descriptors: Higher Education; Stress Variables; *Student Attitudes; *Test Anxiety; *Undergraduate Students
Availability: Seymour Sarason; Center for the Study of Education, 70 Sachem St., New Haven, CT 06520
Grade Level: 13–16
Notes: Items, 39

Designed to assess student attitudes toward group intelligence or aptitude testing, course examinations, and individual intelligence testing. Developed as a measure of test anxiety.

8928

Parent Behavior Form. Worrell, Leonard; Worrell, Judith
Subtests: Acceptance; Active Involvement; Equalitarianism; Cognitive Independence; Curiosity; Cognitive Competence; Lax Control; Conformity; Achievement; Strict Control; Punitive Control; Hostile Control; Rejection
Descriptors: *Adolescents; Adults; Behavior Rating Scales; *Childhood Attitudes; Child Rearing; Fathers; Mothers; *Parent Child Relationship; *Rejection (Psychology)
Identifiers: *Acceptance; PBF; TIM(N)
Availability: Tests in Microfiche; Test Collection, Educational Testing Service, Princeton, NJ 08541
Target Audience: 13–64
Notes: Items, 270

Designed to access child's attitudes toward parent's child-rearing practices. Results of instrument indicate acceptance or rejection of parent's behavior. Separate forms for mothers and fathers. Measures the presence of various positive and negative parenting behaviors.

8944

UCLA Drug Abuse Questionnaire. Churchman, David; Erlich, Oded 1975
Subtests: Knowledge of Drug Abuse; Attitudes toward Drug Abuse
Descriptors: Achievement Tests; *Drug Abuse; Drug Addiction; Higher Education; Knowledge Level; *Student Attitudes; *Undergraduate Students; Likert Scales
Identifiers: Drug Abuse Scales
Availability: ERIC Document Reproduction Service; 3900 Wheeler Ave., Alexandria, VA 22304 (EC117123, 27 pages)
Grade Level: 13–16
Notes: Items, 79

Designed to measure knowledge of drug abuse and attitudes toward drug abuse and drug addicts.

8947

Motivational Needs Inventory. Smith, Janice P. 1971
Descriptors: *Achievement Need; *Affiliation Need; Motivation; School Attitudes; Secondary Education; *Secondary School Students; Secondary School Teachers; *Student Evaluation; *Student Motivation; *Teacher Attitudes
Identifiers: MNI
Availability: ERIC Document Reproduction Service; 3900 Wheeler Ave., Alexandria, VA 22304 (ED128467, 30 pages)
Grade Level: 7–12
Notes: Items, 35

Designed to elicit teacher's opinion of a student in the school environment. Assesses student motivation as achievement or affiliation oriented.

8949

Evaluation Characteristics Survey. Kelly, Edward F.; Bunda, Mary Anne 1971
Subtests: Decision; Relationships; Judgments; Standards; Description; Cost; Personnel; Design; Rationale; Instrumentation; Analysis; Conclusions; Language; Information; Services; Coordination; Planning; Objectives
Descriptors: *Administrators; Adults; Community Attitudes; Educational Assessment; Evaluation Criteria; Evaluation Methods; Evaluators; Needs Assessment; Surveys

Availability: ERIC Document Reproduction Service; 3900 Wheeler Ave., Alexandria, VA 22304 (ED049317, 26 pages)
Target Audience: Adults
Notes: Items, 85

Designed to assess priorities held by various groups concerning school evaluation planning. The groups were professional evaluators, ESEA Title III staff, graduate students, local school staff, and administrators.

8962

Attitudes toward Old People Scale. Tuckman, Jacob; Lorge, Irving 1952
Subtests: (Old People) Physical; Mental Deterioration; Family; Activities and Interests; Conservatism; Best Time of Life; Financial; Attitude toward Future Personality Traits; Insecurity; (Older Worker) Physical; Mental; Interpersonal; Resistance of New; Employer Attitudes
Descriptors: Adults; *Employer Attitudes; Interpersonal Relationship; Mental Health; *Older Adults; Physical Characteristics; Retirement; *Social Attitudes
Availability: Journal of Educational Psychology;v43 p400-07, 1952
Target Audience: Adults
Notes: Items, 40

Designed to assess attitudes toward old people and older workers. Questionnaire is divided into 2 broad categories—Old People and Older Workers.

8965

Assessment of Law-Related Competencies. Schell, Robert L. 1976
Subtests: Groups Establish Certain Acceptable Behavior; Groups Differentiate between Acceptable and Unacceptable Behavior; Groups React in Varied Ways to Acceptable and Unacceptable Behavior
Descriptors: *Achievement Tests; Citizenship Responsibility; *Elementary School Students; Elementary Secondary Education; Justice; Knowledge Level; Law Enforcement; Laws; *Legal Education (Professions); Political Attitudes; *Political Science; *Secondary School Students; Student Attitudes
Identifiers: Pennsylvania Department of Education
Availability: ERIC Document Reproduction Service; 3900 Wheeler Ave., Alexandria, VA 22304 (ED142561, 81 pages.)
Grade Level: K–12
Notes: Time, 60 approx.

Designed to measure cognitive knowledge of law-related concepts in political science and government. Student's political attitudes in relation to legal system are also assessed. Three forms are available. Primary level is for use in grades K-4. It consists of 75 items to be completed in 60 minutes. The intermediate level is for use in grades 5-8. It consists of 66 items to be completed in 45 minutes. The secondary level is for use in grades 9-12. It consists of 100 items to be completed in 45 minutes.

8974

Sibling Behavior Inventory. Aaronson, May; Schaefer, Earl S. 1971
Subtests: Positive Relationship; Conscience-Ridden; Troublemaking; Active Helpfulness; Possessiveness; Argumentativeness; Teaching; Dominance; Withdrawal of Relationship; Respecting Autonomy; Rivalry; Physical Cruelty; Confiding; Submissiveness; Mental Cruelty; Negative Relationship; Companionship; Leadership; Hostile Detachment; Destructiveness; Detachment; Dependency; Acceptance
Descriptors: Behavior Rating Scales; Childhood Attitudes; *Children; Elementary Education; *Elementary School Students; Family Relationship; *Siblings
Identifiers: SBI
Availability: May Aaronson; National Institutes of Mental Health, Dept. of Health, Education and Welfare, Rm. 11C06, Parklawn Bldg, 5600 Fishers Ln., Rockville, MD 20352
Grade Level: K–6
Notes: Items, 115

Designed to assess child's perception of sibling's relationship toward him or her on a series of 23 scales. Useful in studies concerning psychology of relationships.

9013

Student Perceptions of Learning and Teaching. McKeachie, W.J.
Subtests: Impact on Students; Instructor Effectiveness; Rapport; Group Interaction; Difficulty; Structure; Feedback; Student Responsibility; Overall Evaluation

Descriptors: College Instruction; *College Students; Higher Education; *Rating Scales; *Student Attitudes; *Student Evaluation of Teacher Performance; Teacher Evaluation; *Teaching Styles
Identifiers: TIM(E)
Availability: Tests in Microfiche; Test Collection, Educational Testing Service, Princeton, NJ 08541
Grade Level: 13–16

Designed to determine students' perceptions of their own learning and an instructor's effectiveness. Statements related to course impact on the student, teacher effectiveness, teacher rapport, group interaction, course difficulty and structure, and feedback are rated on a 6-point scale from almost never to almost always. Separate 5-point scales measure students' feelings of responsibility toward learning and general evaluation of course and instructor. Two forms are available. Students may comment on each question.

9017
Motivation Feedback Opinionnaire. University Associates, San Diego, CA 1973
Subtests: Self-Actualization; Esteem; Belonging; Safety; Basic
Descriptors: *Adults; *Employee Attitudes; *Employees; Job Satisfaction; Motivation; Needs Assessment; Peer Acceptance; Psychological Needs; Self Actualization; Self Esteem
Availability: University Associates, Inc.; 8517 Production Ave., P.O. Box 26240, San Diego, CA 92126
Target Audience: Adults
Notes: Items, 20

Designed to assess employees' attitudes about their jobs and working conditions. A separate scoring sheet identifies 5 areas of needs motivation.

9018
Political World Interview (Short Version). Crain, William C. 1974
Descriptors: *Adolescents; *Political Attitudes; Secondary Education; *Secondary School Students; Social Attitudes; Social Values; Student Attitudes
Identifiers: Reasoning Ability
Availability: ERIC Document Reproduction Service; 3900 Wheeler Ave., Alexandria, VA 22304 (ED109145, microfiche only)
Target Audience: 13–17
Notes: Items, 19

Designed to assess reasoning ability and social and political attitudes. Subject is asked to imagine a group of people going to an island where they must establish a government and a set of laws. Items deal with issues faced by a democratic government. Instrument is also available from author. William C. Crain; Department of Psychology, City College of the City University of New York, New York, NY 10031.

9037
What Is Your Attitude toward Science? A Scientific Attitude Inventory. 1970
Descriptors: High Schools; *High School Students; Science Education; *Scientific Attitudes; Secondary School Science; *Student Attitudes
Availability: Journal of Research in Science Teaching;v7 p85-94, 1970
Grade Level: 9–12

Designed to assess scientific attitudes of high school students. The attitudes assessed are both intellectual and emotional.

9052
The Environmental Preference Scales. McCall, John N.
Subtests: Comfortable; Exciting; Natural; Social; Urban
Descriptors: Adolescents; Adults; *Design Preferences; *Environment; Forced Choice Technique; Physical Environment; Rural Environment; Social Environment; Urban Environment
Identifiers: TIM(E)
Availability: Tests in Microfiche; Test Collection, Educational Testing Service, Princeton, NJ 08541
Target Audience: 15–65
Notes: Items, 75

Designed to determine a subject's preferences in living, working, or recreation areas. The 5 preference types are comfortable, exciting, natural, social, or urban.

9073
Survey of Student Interests in and Opinions of Mathematics. Michaels, Linda A. 1976
Subtests: Enjoyment of Word Problems; Enjoyment of Pictorial Problems; Appreciation of the Utility of Mathematics; Security with Mathematics

Descriptors: *Grade 7; Junior High Schools; *Junior High School Students; Rating Scales; *Secondary School Mathematics; *Student Attitudes
Identifiers: TIM(E)
Availability: Tests in Microfiche; Test Collection, Educational Testing Service, Princeton, NJ 08541
Grade Level: 7
Notes: Items, 38

Designed for use with junior high school students. It is intended to measure the following 4 facets of the student's attitude toward mathematics: enjoyment of word problems, enjoyment of pictorial problems, appreciation of the utility of mathematics, and security with mathematics.

9074
Semantic Differential Instrument for Measuring Attitude toward Mathematics. McCallon, Earl L.; Brown, John D. 1971
Descriptors: *Graduate Students; Graduate Study; Higher Education; *Mathematics; School Attitudes; Semantic Differential; *Student Attitudes
Availability: Journal of Experimental Education;v39 n4 p69-72, 1971
Grade Level: 17–20
Notes: Items, 15

Designed to assess attitudes toward mathematics of graduate students who are not mathematics majors.

9088
Adolescent Rating Scales. Baumrind, Diana 1972
Descriptors: *Adolescents; Behavior Rating Scales; High Schools; *High School Students; Interviews; Parent Child Relationship; *Student Attitudes; *Student Behavior
Identifiers: Parental Authority Research Project
Availability: Dr. Diana Baumrind; Institute of Human Development, University of California, Tolman Hall 1203, Berkeley, CA 94720
Grade Level: 9–12
Target Audience: 13–18
Notes: Items, 18

Designed to assess adolescent's attitudes and behaviors based upon rater's interpretation of responses to several interview questions.

9089
Parent Rating Scales. Baumrind, Diana 1972
Subtests: Firm vs. Lax Enforcement; Directive and Demanding vs. Nondirective and Undemanding; Assertive and Self-Confident vs. Passive and Lacking in Self-Confidence; Encourages vs. Does Not Encourage Individuality and Self-Awareness; Values and Encourages vs. Does Not Value or Encourage Rationality in Self and Child; Values vs. Does Not Value Autonomy of Thought and Action; Loving, Supportive vs. Rejecting, Neglecting
Descriptors: Adolescents; Adults; Behavior Rating Scales; *Child Rearing; *Parent Attitudes; *Parent Child Relationship; *Parents; Power Structure
Identifiers: Parental Authority Research Project
Availability: Dr. Diana Baumrind; Institute of Human Development, University of California, Tolman Hall 1203, Berkely, CA 94720
Target Audience: Adults
Notes: Items, 102

Developed as part of the Parental Authority Research Project to assess relationship between parents and their adolescent children.

9090
Semantic Differential Scale. Harvill, Leo M. 1971
Descriptors: Arithmetic; Art; *Elementary School Students; Grade 2; Grade 3; Primary Education; Reading Attitudes; *School Attitudes; Semantic Differential; *Student Attitudes
Availability: ERIC Document Reproduction Service; 3900 Wheeler Ave., Alexandria, VA 22304 (ED056059, 38 pages)
Grade Level: 2–3
Notes: Items, 35

Designed to assess children's attitudes toward arithmetic, reading, and art.

9091
Millimeter Scale. Harvill, Leo M. 1971
Descriptors: Arithmetic; Art; *Elementary School Students; Grade 2; Grade 3; Primary Education; Rating Scales; Reading Attitudes; *School Attitudes; *Student Attitudes
Availability: ERIC Document Reproduction Service; 3900 Wheeler Ave., Alexandria, VA 22304 (ED056059, 38 pages)
Grade Level: 2–3
Notes: Items, 9

Designed to assess students' attitudes about arithmetic, reading, and art. Student must indicate degree of his or her attitude by noting his or her preference on a 100 millimeter vertical line.

9092
Box Scale. Harvill, Leo M. 1971
Descriptors: Arithmetic; Art; *Elementary School Students; Grade 2; Primary Education; Rating Scales; Reading Attitudes; *School Attitudes; Student Attitudes
Availability: ERIC Document Reproduction Service; 3900 Wheeler Ave., Alexandria, VA 22304 (ED056059, 38 pages)
Grade Level: 2
Notes: Items, 13

Designed to assess students' attitudes toward school tasks, especially arithmetic. Subject is asked to mark 1 of 5 succeedingly smaller size boxes to indicate attitude toward a specific task.

9093
Forced Choice Scale. Harvill, Leo M. 1971
Descriptors: Arithmetic; Art; *Elementary School Students; Forced Choice Technique; Grade 2; Grade 3; Primary Education; Reading Attitudes; *School Attitudes; *Student Attitudes
Identifiers: Ipsative Measurement
Availability: ERIC Document Reproduction Service; 3900 Wheeler Ave., Alexandria, VA 22304 (ED056059, 38 pages)
Grade Level: 2–3
Notes: Items, 18

An ipsative scale composed of triads of statements concerning school tasks. Assesses students' attitudes toward reading, arithmetic, and art.

9094
Picture Scale. Harvill, Leo M. 1971
Descriptors: Arithmetic; Art; *Elementary School Students; Grade 2; Grade 3; Pictorial Stimuli; Primary Education; Reading Attitudes; *School Attitudes; *Student Attitudes
Identifiers: Ipsative Measurement
Availability: ERIC Document Reproduction Service; 3900 Wheeler Ave., Alexandria, VA 22304 (ED056059, 38 pages)
Grade Level: 2–3
Notes: Items, 21

Designed to measure students' attitudes toward arithmetic, reading, and art. Student is asked to indicate which pictured activity most closely reflects his or her attitude.

9128
Faculty Attitudes towards the Goals and Objectives of College Unions in American Higher Education. Adair, Carolyn M.
Descriptors: *College Faculty; Higher Education; *Organizational Objectives; *Student Unions; *Teacher Attitudes
Identifiers: TIM(E)
Availability: Tests in Microfiche; Test Collection, Educational Testing Service, Princeton, NJ 08541
Grade Level: 13–16
Notes: Items, 33

Developed to measure college faculty attitudes toward specifically stated goals of student unions.

9136
World Hypotheses Scale. Bethel, Maxine Harris; And Others
Subtests: Formist; Mechanist; Contextualist; Organicist
Descriptors: *Cognitive Structures; Higher Education; Philosophy; Social Attitudes; *Student Attitudes; *Undergraduate Students
Identifiers: WHS
Availability: ASIS/NAPS, c/o Microfiche Publications; P.O. Box 3513, Grand Central Station, New York, NY 10163-3513 (Doc. No. 02809)
Grade Level: 13–16
Notes: Items, 12

Designed to assess an individual's preferences for the 4 world hypotheses developed by Stephen Pepper. These hypotheses are used to explain and understand life events. The subject is given 12 behavioral events. He or she must rank 4 explanations for each event according to his or her preference. Each explanation represents one of the world hypotheses—formism, mechanism, organicism, and contextualism.

9162
Attitudes toward Feminist Issue Scale. Brodsky, Annette 1975
Subtests: Human Reproduction; Child Care; Politics and Legislation; Employment; Overcoming Self-Denigration; Marriage and Family; Consciousness-Raising in Media; Religion; Education

Descriptors: *College Students; *Females;
*Feminism; Higher Education; *Political Attitudes; *Political Issues; Rating Scales; Social Attitudes
Identifiers: TIM(E)
Availability: Tests in Microfiche; Test Collection, Educational Testing Service, Princeton, NJ 08541
Grade Level: 13–16
Notes: Items, 120

The resolutions from the 1970 convention of the National Organization for Women were paraphrased to form items to measure attitudes toward feminist issues. The topics covered are human reproduction, child care, politics and legislation, overcoming self-denigration, marriage and family, consciousness-raising in media, religion, education. All the items were written to reflect the positive feminist direction.

9163
Vocational Director Opinionnaire Form. Cheek, Jimmy G.; Christiansen, James E. 1975
Subtests: Role Statements; Issues; Background Information
Descriptors: *Administrator Attitudes; Adults; *Career Counseling; *Counselor Role; Opinions; Program Evaluation; *Role Perception; *Secondary Education; *Vocational Directors; Likert Scales
Identifiers: Texas; TIM(E)
Availability: Tests in Microfiche; Test Collection, Educational Testing Service, Princeton, NJ 08541
Target Audience: Adults
Notes: Items, 88

Assesses the perceived role of the vocational counselor by vocational directors in Texas. To be used with and given to the vocational counselors (TC009164), the secondary school principals (TC009165), and the secondary school counselors (TC009166). Has 2 sections: (1) closed-form opinionnaire regarding the role of and current issues concerning vocational counselors in Texas; (2) background information.

9164
Vocational Counselor Opinionnaire Form. Cheek, Jimmy G.; Christiansen, James E. 1975
Subtests: Role Statements; Issues; Background
Descriptors: Adults; *Career Counseling; *Counselor Attitudes; *Counselor Role; Opinions; Program Evaluation; *Role Perception; *School Counselors; *Secondary Education; Likert Scales
Identifiers: Texas; TIM(E)
Availability: Tests in Microfiche; Test Collection, Educational Testing Service, Princeton, NJ 08541
Target Audience: Adults
Notes: Items, 88

Self-assessment of the perceived role of the vocational counselor in Texas. To be used with and given to the vocational directors (TC009163), the secondary school principals (TC009165), and the secondary school counselors (TC009166). Has 2 sections: (1) closed-form opinionnaire regarding the role of and current issues concerning vocational counselors in Texas; and (2) background information.

9165
Secondary School Principal Opinionnaire. Cheek, Jimmy G.; Christiansen, James E. 1975
Subtests: Role Statements; Issues; Background Information
Descriptors: *Administrator Attitudes; Adults; *Career Counseling; *Counselor Role; Opinions; *Principals; Program Evaluation; *Role Perception; *Secondary Education; Likert Scales
Identifiers: Texas; TIM(E)
Availability: Tests in Microfiche; Test Collection, Educational Testing Service, Princeton, NJ 08541
Target Audience: Adults
Notes: Items, 88

Assessment by secondary school principals in Texas of the perceived role of the vocational counselor in Texas. To be used with and given to the vocational directors (TC009163), the vocational counselors (TC009164), and the secondary school counselors (TC009166). Has 2 sections: (1) closed-form opinionnaire regarding the role of and current issues concerning vocational counselors in Texas; and (2) background information.

9166
Secondary School Counselor Opinionnaire Form. Cheek, Jimmy G.; Christiansen, James E. 1975
Subtests: Role Statements; Issues; Background Information
Descriptors: Adults; *Career Counseling; *Counselor Attitudes; *Counselor Role; Opinions; Program Evaluation; *Role Perception; *School Counseling; *Secondary Education; Likert Scales

Identifiers: Texas; TIM(E)
Availability: Tests in Microfiche; Test Collection, Educational Testing Service, Princeton, NJ 08541
Target Audience: Adults
Notes: Items, 88

Assesses the perceived role of the vocational counselor in Texas by secondary school counselors. To be used with and given to the vocational directors (TC009163), the vocational counselors (TC009164), and the secondary school principals (TC009165). Has 2 sections: (1) closed-form opinionnaire regarding the role of and current issues concerning vocational counselors in Texas; and (2) background information.

9167
San Francisco 1962 Drinking Practices Questionnaire. Knupfer, Genevieve 1962
Descriptors: Adults; *Alcoholic Beverages; *Behavior Patterns; *Drinking; Individual Characteristics; Questionnaires; Social Attitudes; Social Background
Identifiers: Alcoholics; Knupfer Drinking Practices Study
Availability: CARRF; Center of Alcohol Studies, Rutgers University, Allison Rd., Piscataway, NJ 08854
Target Audience: Adults
Notes: Items, 99

Designed to assess attitudes of adults concerning alcohol consumption. Also elicits information on individual's drinking practices and social background. Instrument is available as entry 2.1/9A.

9172
Washington Alcohol Poll Questionnaire. Maxwell, M. 1951
Descriptors: *Adults; *Alcoholic Beverages; Alcoholism; *Behavior Patterns; *Drinking; Interviews; Questionnaires
Identifiers: Alcoholics
Availability: CARRF; Center of Alcohol Studies, Rutgers University, Allison Rd., Piscataway, NJ 08854
Target Audience: Adults
Notes: Items, 77

Designed to assess attitudes toward drinking as well as drinking practices. Developed for use in a quantity-frequency survey of drinking behavior. Instrument is available as entry 2.1/3.

9173
ARF Alcoholism Questionnaire. Marcus, A.M. 1963
Subtests: Emotional Difficulties as Causes of Alcoholism; Loss of Control; Prognosis for Recovery; Alcoholic as a Steady Drinker; Alcoholism and Character Defect; Social Status of the Alcoholic; Alcoholism as an Illness; Harmless Voluntary Indulgence; Addiction Liability
Descriptors: *Adults; *Alcoholism; *College Students; Drinking; Higher Education; *Student Attitudes
Identifiers: Alcoholics; Marcus Attitudes toward Alcohol Scale
Availability: CARRF; Center of Alcohol Studies, Rutgers University, Allison Rd., Piscataway, NJ 08854
Grade Level: 13–16
Target Audience: Adults
Notes: Time, 30 approx.; Items, 40

Designed to assess attitudes toward alcoholism and alcoholics. Instrument is available as entry 1.3.

9174
Questionnaire on Alcoholism. Connor, R.G. 1960
Descriptors: Adults; *Alcoholism; *Behavior Patterns; Biographical Inventories; *Drinking; Drug Use; Family Influence; Parent Attitudes; Questionnaires; Religious Factors
Identifiers: Alcoholics
Availability: CARRF; Center of Alcohol Studies, Rutgers University, Allison Rd., Piscataway, NJ 08854
Target Audience: Adults
Notes: Items, 139

A questionnaire designed for completion by alcoholics. Assesses areas of parental attitudes toward alcohol, history of drinking behaviors, religious background, and attitudes of family and friends concerning respondent's drinking habits. Instrument is entry 2.7/214.

9175
Attitudes of Parents Questionnaire. Jackson, J.K.; Connor, R.G. 1953
Descriptors: Adults; *Alcoholism; *Behavior Patterns; *Drinking; Family Influence; *Parent Attitudes; Questionnaires; *Social Attitudes
Availability: CARRF; Center of Alcohol Studies, Rutgers University, Allison Rd., Piscataway, NJ 08854

Target Audience: Adults
Notes: Items, 20

Designed to assess attitudes toward alcoholism. Developed to specifically assess attitudes of temperance people. Instrument is entry 1.1.

9177
North Carolina Study of Youth Questionnaire. Alexander, C.N.; Campbell, E.Q. 1961
Descriptors: *Alcoholic Beverages; Behavior Patterns; *College Freshmen; *Drinking; Higher Education; Questionnaires; Student Attitudes; Student Behavior
Identifiers: North Carolina
Availability: CARRF; Center of Alcohol Studies, Rutgers University, Allison Rd., Piscataway, NJ 08854
Grade Level: 13
Notes: Items, 79

Designed to assess attitudes and influences concerning collegiate drinking patterns. Assesses drinking practices of college freshmen. Instrument is available as entry 2.3/304A. Developed for use in the study of Influences and Collegiate Drinking Patterns at 21 North Carolina Colleges.

9178
North Carolina Study of Seniors Questionnaire. Alexander, C.N.; Campbell, E.Q. 1965
Descriptors: *Alcoholic Beverages; Behavior Patterns; *College Seniors; *Drinking; Followup Studies; Higher Education; Questionnaires; Student Attitudes; Student Behavior
Identifiers: North Carolina
Availability: CARRF; Center of Alcohol Studies, Rutgers University, Allison Rd., Piscataway, NJ 08854
Grade Level: 16
Notes: Items, 69

Designed to assess attitudes and drinking patterns of college seniors. Developed for use with students who had completed the North Carolina Study of Youth Questionnaire (TC009177) as college freshmen. Instrument is available as entry 2.3/304B. Developed for use in the study of Influences and Collegiate Drinking Patterns at 21 North Carolina Colleges.

9192
Values Inventory for Children. Gilford, Joan S.; And Others 1971
Subtests: Asocial; Social Conformity; Me First; Academic/Health; Masculinity; Adult Closeness; Aesthetics; Sociability
Descriptors: *Childhood Attitudes; Cultural Differences; *Elementary School Students; Ethnic Groups; Forced Choice Technique; Individual Needs; Nonverbal Tests; *Picture Books; Primary Education; *Self Concept Measures; Spanish; Spanish Speaking; *Student Attitudes; *Values; Visual Measures
Identifiers: Faking (Testing)
Availability: ERIC Document Reproduction Service; 3900 Wheeler Ave., Alexandria, VA 22304 (ED050178, 278 pages)
Grade Level: 1–3
Notes: Time, 30 approx.; Items, 30

A nonverbal, self-administering inventory of values, which is used to measure 7 dimensions of value based upon 7 categories of needs: physiological, safety, love, esteem, aesthetic, self-actualization, and aggression. In this instrument, values are interpreted to be reflected by attitudes as determined by the affective responses to the activities and situation presented in the picture books. Moral attitudes (or values) have also been included even though they are not synonymous with the term values as defined herein. There are 2 alternate forms: (1) Form X (the child responds to a single picture by choosing the extent of his or her like or dislike on a graded, 4-point scale; the child circles the face that describes his or her feelings); and (2) Form Y (the child selects which of the 2 pictures in each item he or she likes better). Instructions for administering the instrument are available in both Spanish and English.

9198
Environment Rating Scale. Pedersen, Darhl M. 1977
Descriptors: Environmental Research; Higher Education; High Schools; *High School Students; *Physical Environment; Rating Scales; *Student Attitudes; *Undergraduate Students
Availability: Darhl M. Pedersen; Dept. of Psychology, Brigham Young University, Provo, UT 84602
Grade Level: 9–16

Semantic differential scale designed to assess students' attitudes concerning physical environment in large city, small town, forest, desert, and beach.

9200
When I Was Born. Clifford, Edward 1974
Subtests: Parental Emotion; Parental Apprehension; Parental Pride; Parental Nurturance

Descriptors: *Adolescents; *Childhood Attitudes; Fathers; Mothers; Parent Attitudes; Parent Child Relationship; *Young Adults
Availability: Dr. Edward Clifford; Dept. of Psychology, Box 3894, Duke University Medical Center, Durham, NC 27710
Target Audience: 11–20
Notes: Items, 32

Designed to measure adolescents' perceptions of parental reactions at the time of their births. Current feelings are assumed to be projected as perceptions of what occurred at birth. Perceptions of adolescents with congenital and acquired anomalies differed significantly from the normal sample.

9211
Our World of Today, Our World of Tomorrow. Voelker, Alan M.
Descriptors: *Elementary School Students; *Futures (of Society); Intermediate Grades; Secondary Education; *Secondary School Students; Semantic Differential; Student Attitudes; World Affairs; *World Problems
Availability: Alan M. Voelker; Curriculum and Instruction, Northern Illinois University, DeKalb, IL 60115
Grade Level: 5–12
Notes: Items, 20

Designed to assess student opinions concerning the world of today and the world of the future.

9212
Some Ideas I Have. Voelker, Alan M.
Descriptors: Ecological Factors; *Elementary School Students; *Environmental Education; Intermediate Grades; Junior High Schools; *Junior High School Students; *Pollution; School Attitudes; *Student Attitudes
Availability: Alan M. Voelker; Curriculum and Instruction, Northern Illinois University, DeKalb, IL 60115
Grade Level: 5–8
Notes: Items, 37

Designed to assess students' opinions concerning school and environmental factors, such as pollution and environmental protection.

9213
Stories about Real Life Problems. Voelker, Alan M.
Descriptors: Ecological Factors; *Elementary School Students; *Environmental Education; Intermediate Grades; Junior High Schools; *Junior High School Students; *Problem Solving; *Social Attitudes; Social Problems; Student Attitudes
Availability: Alan M. Voelker; Curriculum and Instruction, Northern Illinois University, DeKalb, IL 60115
Grade Level: 5–8
Notes: Items, 52

Designed to assess students' social attitudes and problem-solving ability. Descriptions of community problems are presented with possible solutions. Subject is asked to evaluate solutions and suggest others.

9232
Scale of Economic Liberalism. O'Kane, James M. 1970
Descriptors: Economic Factors; High Schools; *High School Seniors; Males; *Political Attitudes; Rating Scales; Social Mobility; Student Attitudes; *Working Class; *Liberalism
Availability: James M. O'Kane; Dept. of Sociology, Drew University, Madison, NY 07940
Grade Level: 12
Notes: Items, 20

Designed to assess political attitudes of upwardly mobile Catholic, male, working class adolescents. Attitudes are measured in terms of economic liberalism.

9233
Questionnaire on Attributes of Psychological Journal Articles. Gottfredson, Stephen D.; Garvey, William D. 1976
Descriptors: Adults; Psychological Studies; Psychology; *Quality Control; *Scholarly Journals; Social Science Research; *Editors
Identifiers: Journal Articles
Availability: American Psychologist;v33 n10 p920-34, Oct 1978
Target Audience: Adults
Notes: Items, 83

Designed to assess attitudes and opinions of editors of selected psychological journals concerning criteria upon which assessments of articles may be made.

9269
Wharton Attitude Survey. Wharton, Kenneth 1978

Descriptors: *Behavior Problems; Classroom Environment; Classroom Techniques; Discipline Problems; *Peer Evaluation; Secondary Education; *Secondary School Students; *Student Attitudes
Identifiers: Disruptive Behavior
Availability: Amidon Publications; 1966 Benson Ave., St. Paul, MN 55116-9990
Grade Level: 7–12
Notes: Time, 15 approx.; Items, 11

Designed to assess students' attitudes concerning classroom environment and disruptive students. Students are asked to identify students who disrupt classroom activities. Survey should be administered by someone other than the regular teacher. Instrument should be completed anonymously.

9272
National Smoking Test. Loewenwarter, Paul 1968
Descriptors: *Adults; Behavior Patterns; Knowledge Level; Rating Scales; *Smoking; *Social Attitudes; Tobacco
Availability: Congressional Record;v114 p1132-37, Jan 26 1968
Target Audience: Adults

Designed to assess attitudes toward smoking, knowledge of effects of smoking, and assessment of own smoking habits. Developed to present reputable, factual material about smoking to a national television audience.

9274
Chicago Smoking Behavior Intensive Questionnaire. Straits, Bruce C. 1962
Descriptors: Adults; Behavior Patterns; Drug Use; Interviews; *Smoking; Social Attitudes; Social Environment; Tobacco
Availability: Bruce C. Straits; Dept. of Sociology, University of California, Santa Barbara, CA 93106
Target Audience: Adults

Designed to assess attitudes, practices and interpersonal environment of smokers through individual interviews. Used to study reasons for success and failure of smokers to quit the habit.

9280
Heubach Smoking Habits and Attitudes Questionnaire. Heubach, Philip G. 1964
Descriptors: Adolescents; *Behavior Patterns; High Schools; *High School Seniors; High School Students; *Smoking; Social Attitudes; *Student Attitudes; Tobacco
Availability: ERIC Document Reproduction Service; 3900 Wheeler Ave., Alexandria, VA 22304 (ED053218, 152 pages)
Grade Level: 9–12
Notes: Items, 74

A questionnaire designed to assess smoking practices and attitudes toward smoking. Designed for high school students, particularly seniors.

9283
Passey-Pennington Attitudes toward Alcohol and Its Uses Scales. Passey, George E.; Pennington, Dempsey F. 1959
Subtests: Treatment of Alcoholism; Alcohol Education; Legal and Social Control of Alcohol; Moderate (Social) Drinking; Alcoholism and the Alcoholic
Descriptors: Adults; Alcohol Education; *Alcoholism; Higher Education; High Schools; *High School Students; Social Attitudes; *Student Attitudes; *Undergraduate Students
Identifiers: Self Administered Tests
Availability: CARRF; Center of Alcohol Studies, Rutgers University, Allison Rd., Piscataway, NJ 08854
Grade Level: 9–16
Notes: Items, 60

Designed to assess attitudes toward alcohol and its use. Subject is requested to agree or disagree with statements concerning alcohol education, treatment of alcoholism, legal and social control, social drinking, and alcoholism. Forms A and B are available. Order number for this instrument is 1.8A.

9284
Holloway Student Drinking and Alcohol Knowledge Questionnaire. Holloway, R. 1963
Descriptors: *Alcoholic Beverages; Alcoholism; Behavior Patterns; *Drinking; High Schools; *High School Students; Knowledge Level; Parent Attitudes; Social Attitudes; Student Attitudes; Student Behavior
Availability: CARRF; Center of Alcohol Studies, Rutgers University, Allison Rd., Piscataway, NJ 08854
Grade Level: 9–12
Notes: Items, 50

Designed to assess behavior, attitudes and knowledge of high school students with respect to alcoholic beverages. Items elicit information about parent attitudes and family background. Available as entry 2.3/203.

9290
American Drinking Practices Questionnaire. Cahalan, Don; And Others 1964
Descriptors: Adults; *Alcoholic Beverages; Attitudes; *Behavior Patterns; *Drinking; Family Characteristics; Interviews; Questionnaires; Social Influences
Identifiers: National Survey of Attitudes and Interests
Availability: CARRF; Center of Alcohol Studies, Rutgers University, Allison Rd., Piscataway, NJ 08854
Target Audience: Adults
Notes: Items, 89

Designed to assess attitudes and drinking practices of representative adult population. Many items are concerned with alcohol consumption. Instrument is available as entry 2.1/13.

9293
Allardt Drinking Norms and Drinking Habits Questionnaire. Allardt, Erik; And Others 1956
Descriptors: Adults; *Alcoholic Beverages; Alcoholism; *Behavior Patterns; *Drinking; *Finnish; Foreign Countries; Interviews; Social Attitudes
Identifiers: Finland (Helsinki)
Availability: CARRF; Center of Alcohol Studies, Rutgers University, Allison Rd., Piscataway, NJ 08854
Target Audience: Adults
Notes: Items, 64

An individual interview developed to assess drinking habits, attitudes, and norms in Helsinki, Finland. Finnish and English forms are available. Instrument is available as entry 2.1/34.

9299
Kansas Attitudes toward Alcoholic Beverages Questionnaire. McCluggage, Marston M.; And Others 1956
Descriptors: *Alcoholic Beverages; Behavior Patterns; *Drinking; High Schools; *High School Students; Social Attitudes; *Student Attitudes
Identifiers: Kansas
Availability: CARRF; Center of Alcohol Studies, Rutgers University, Allison Rd., Piscataway, NJ 08854
Grade Level: 9–12
Notes: Items, 43

Designed to assess drinking attitudes and practices among high school students. Survey was developed for high school populations in Eastern Kansas. Available as entry 2.3/201C.

9308
Berkeley Drinking Practices Questionnaire. Knupfer, Genevieve 1960
Descriptors: Adults; *Alcoholic Beverages; *Behavior Patterns; Biographical Inventories; *Drinking; Interviews; Questionnaires; *Social Attitudes; Socioeconomic Background
Identifiers: California (Berkeley)
Availability: CARRF; Center of Alcohol Studies, Rutgers University, Allison Rd., Piscataway, NJ 08854
Target Audience: Adults
Notes: Items, 59

A structured interview designed to assess drinking habits, practices and attitudes. Used in a comparison study of drinkers and abstainers in a large California city. Instrument is available as entry 2.1/6.

9314
College Drinking Questionnaire. Straus, Robert; Bacon, S.D. 1953
Descriptors: *Alcoholic Beverages; Behavior Patterns; *Drinking; Higher Education; Questionnaires; Socioeconomic Background; Student Attitudes; *Undergraduate Students
Availability: CARRF; Center of Alcohol Studies, Rutgers University, Allison Rd., Piscataway, NJ 08854
Grade Level: 13–16
Notes: Items, 70

Designed to assess college students' drinking practices, socioeconomic background and attitudes toward alcohol. Instrument is available in 3 alternate forms as entry 2.3/301.

9315
Williams Questionnaire on Attitudes toward Temperate and Irresponsible Use of Alcoholic Beverages. Williams, Allan F. 1965

Descriptors: Adolescents; Alcohol Education;
  *Alcoholic Beverages; *Drinking; High Schools;
  *High School Students; Social Attitudes;
  *Student Attitudes
Identifiers: Attitudes about Drinking
Availability: CARRF; Center of Alcohol Studies,
  Rutgers University, Allison Rd., Piscataway, NJ
  08854
Grade Level: 9–12
Notes: Items, 57

Designed to assess attitudes of adolescents concerning use
of alcoholic beverages. Instrument is available as entry
2.3/204.

9316
Richardson Alcohol Attitude Scales. Richardson,
Jack J. 1964
Descriptors: Adults; *Alcoholic Beverages;
  *Drinking; Higher Education; Parent Attitudes;
  Student Attitudes; *Undergraduate Students
Availability: Jack J. Richardson; Dept. of Health
  Education, Southern Illinois University, Carbon-
  dale, IL 62901
Grade Level: 13–16
Target Audience: Adults

Designed to measure attitudes of college students and
their parents toward consumption of alcohol. Student
completes one form to express own attitude. Separate
forms are completed as student believes mother and father
would complete them. Each parent completes two forms—
one to express own attitudes, the other completed as he/
she believes their child would respond.

9346
Responsibility Denial Scale. Schwartz, Shalom H.
1968
Descriptors: Adults; Rating Scales; *Responsibility;
  Social Attitudes; Social Responsibility
Identifiers: AR Scale
Availability: Shalom H. Schwartz; Dept. of Psy-
  chology, Hebrew University, Jerusalem, Israel
  91905
Target Audience: Adults
Notes: Items, 28

Designed to assess subject's attitudes toward assuming
responsibility for his/her actions.

9353
Biographical and Personality Inventory. Force,
Ronald C. 1972
Descriptors: Adolescents; *Attitudes; *Biographical
  Inventories; *Delinquency; *Delinquent Reha-
  bilitation; *Drug Abuse; *Personality Assess-
  ment; *Recidivism; Young Adults
Availability: Test Systems, Inc.; P.O. Box 18432,
  Wichita, KS 67218
Target Audience: 13–19
Notes: Time, 60; Items, 200

Individual or group-administered objective test designed
to predict the recovery potential of delinquent youth. Low
scores indicate need only for housing and care by own or
foster family. Highest scores indicate need for controlled
environment. Separate forms for boys and girls are available. Items are multiple choice and true/false. Requires
fifth grade reading ability. Scoring procedure available
indicating drug or alcohol problems. May be administered
prior to sentencing or treatment and only by a certified
psychologist.

9355
E Scale. Adorno, T.W.; And Others 1950
Subtests: Negroes; Minorities; Patriotism
Descriptors: *Adults; Bias; *Ethnocentrism; Higher
  Education; Racial Attitudes; *Undergraduate
  Students; Likert Scales
Availability: Adorno, T.W., and Others; *The Au-
  thoritarian Personality.*New York: Harper &
  Row Publishers, 1950.
Grade Level: 13–16
Target Audience: Adults
Notes: Items, 34

Designed to measure ethnocentrism that means provincial-
ism or cultural narrowness. It is a concept that implies a
consistent frame of mind concerning "outgroups," those
groups with whom the respondent does not identify. Form
78 is a 14-item version of the E Scale. All items are
negatively stated.

9365
**Differential Attitudes of Black and White Patients
toward Psychiatric Treatment in Child Guidance.**
Jackson, Anna M.; And Others 1978
Subtests: Therapist's Attitude toward the Patient;
  Attitude of Other People in the Clinic; Helpful-
  ness of Therapy; Expectations of Therapy and
  Reasons for Seeking Help; Resistances; Content
  of Therapy and Techniques; Psychological
  Mindedness; Fantasy Expression; Prejudicial At-
  titudes

Descriptors: Adults; *Blacks; Children; Interviews;
  *Mental Health Clinics; *Parent Attitudes; Psy-
  chiatric Services; *Racial Attitudes; *Whites
Identifiers: TIM(E)
Availability: Tests in Microfiche; Test Collection,
  Educational Testing Service, Princeton, NJ
  08541
Target Audience: Adults
Notes: Items, 141

A parental questionnaire including items on the therapist's
attitude toward the patient, the attitudes of other people
in the clinic, the effectiveness of therapy, expectations of
therapy and reasons for seeking help, problems with having a white therapist, content of therapy and techniques,
fantasy expression, and prejudicial attitudes. The questionnaire was prepared for a study designed to test the assumption that, after terminating therapy, black parents
would have different attitudes toward psychiatric clinics
and psychotherapy than would white parents.

9368
**Edgington Attitude Scale for High School Fresh-
man Boys.** Edgington, Charles W.
Descriptors: Grade 9; *High School Freshmen;
  High Schools; *Males; *Physical Education;
  Likert Scales
Identifiers: TIM(E)
Availability: Tests in Microfiche; Test Collection,
  Educational Testing Service, Princeton, NJ
  08541
Grade Level: 9
Notes: Items, 66

Developed to determine favorable and unfavorable attitudes of high school freshman boys toward physical education. Subjects are asked to respond to attitude statements on a 6-point Likert scale.

9374
Trait and Behavior Questionnaire. Koblinsky, Sal-
ly Gentry; And Others 1978
Subtests: Children's Character Traits; Children's
  Behaviors
Descriptors: Behavior Patterns; *Elementary
  School Students; *Grade 5; *Individual Char-
  acteristics; Intermediate Grades; *Sex Role;
  *Sex Stereotypes; Social Attitudes; Student At-
  titudes
Identifiers: Sexual Attitudes
Availability: Sally Koblinsky; Family Life Dept.,
  Oregon State University, Corvallis, OR 97331
Grade Level: 5
Notes: Items, 100

Designed to assess student's attitudes concerning sex role
and sex stereotypes. Character traits and behaviors are
listed. Respondent must identify these as typical of girls,
boys, or boys and girls.

9376
**Juvenile Probationer's Behavior and Attitude Rat-
ing Scale.** Horejsi, Charles R.
Descriptors: Adults; Attitude Change; *Behavior
  Change; *Delinquent Rehabilitation; Interviews;
  *Parents; *Program Evaluation; *Rating Scales;
  *Volunteers
Identifiers: TIM(E)
Availability: Tests in Microfiche; Test Collection,
  Educational Testing Service, Princeton, NJ
  08541
Target Audience: Adults
Notes: Items, 51

Designed for use with the parents or parental surrogates of
adolescents on probation. Thirty-seven items relating to
the youngster's behavior and attitudes measure the parents' assessment of positive or negative change resulting
from a one-to-one, court-volunteer/probationer relationship. Only those changes attributed to the volunteer's influence are considered in the scoring procedure.

9383
Desire for Certainty Scale. Brim, Orville G. 1955
Subtests: Education; Recreation; Politics; Econom-
  ics; Religion; Health; Family; Transportation
  and Communication
Descriptors: *Adults; Cultural Influences;
  *Expectation; Family Attitudes; *Individual Dif-
  ferences; Political Attitudes; *Probability;
  *Security (Psychology); Social Attitudes
Availability: *American Sociological Review;*v20
  p68-78, 1955
Target Audience: Adults
Notes: Items, 32

Designed to assess individual differences in need for security that affect expectations.

9384
Parental Behavior Questionnaire. Bronfenbrenner,
Urie 1965

Subtests: Nurturance; Affective Reward; Instru-
  mental Companionship; Affiliative Companion-
  ship; Prescriptive; Social Isolation; Expressive
  Rejection; Physical Punishment; Deprivation of
  Privileges; Protectiveness; Power; Achievement
  Demands; Affective Punishment; Principled
  Discipline; Indulgence
Descriptors: Behavior Rating Scales; *Childhood
  Attitudes; Child Rearing; *Children;
  *Elementary School Students; Intermediate
  Grades; *Parent Child Relationship; *Parents
Identifiers: BPB; Bronfenbrenner Parent Behavior
  Questionnaire; *Parent Behavior
Availability: *Child Development;*v36 p163-74,
  1965
Grade Level: 4–6
Notes: Items, 45

Designed to assess children's perceptions of parental behavior toward them. Fifteen scales measure children's perceptions of their parents and thus provide a measure for
understanding the child's personality development.

9385
**Brown Scale for Measuring Attitudes toward
Computer-Assisted Instruction.** Brown, B.R. 1966
Descriptors: *Computer Assisted Instruction;
  Higher Education; Pretests Posttests; *Student
  Attitudes; *Undergraduate Students
Availability: *Journal of Educational Psychology;*v6
  n1 p46-51, Feb 1970
Grade Level: 13–16
Notes: Items, 30

Designed to assess student attitudes toward computer-
assisted instruction (CAI). Brown scale was adapted to
future tense to permit posttesting.

9387
Attitude Scale. Dutton, Wilbur H. 1968
Descriptors: Elementary Education; *Elementary
  School Mathematics; Elementary School Stu-
  dents; *Grade 6; Junior High Schools; *Junior
  High School Students; *Modern Mathematics;
  *Student Attitudes; Likert Scales
Availability: *The Elementary School Journal;*v68
  p259-64, Feb 1968
Grade Level: 6–8
Notes: Items, 27

Designed to measure students' attitudes toward modern,
or "new," mathematics.

9392
Teacher-Pupil Relationship Inventory. Lewis, Wil-
liam A.; Lovell, John T. 1965
Descriptors: *Grade 6; Intermediate Grades; Ju-
  nior High Schools; *Junior High School Stu-
  dents; Objective Tests; *Student Attitudes; Stu-
  dent Evaluation of Teacher Performance;
  *Teacher Student Relationship; Therapeutic En-
  vironment
Identifiers: TPRI
Availability: *Personnel and Guidance Journal;*v44
  n4 p396-401, Dec 1965
Grade Level: 6–9
Notes: Items, 20

Designed to assess student's perception of his/her relationship with the classroom teacher. Interpersonal relationship
between student and teacher seemed to have a greater
effect on sixth grade student's academic gains than on
junior high school students.

9393
Teacher Education Program Evaluation Scale.
Bledsoe, Joseph C.; Flowers, John D. 1977
Subtests: Pre-Professional Skills and Abilities;
  General Education; Sociological Foundations;
  Use of Teaching Materials; Personal Develop-
  ment
Descriptors: Adults; *Beginning Teachers;
  *Preservice Teacher Education; *Program Eval-
  uation; *Teacher Attitudes
Availability: Dr. John Flowers; Augusta College,
  Augusta, GA 30910
Target Audience: Adults
Notes: Items, 7

Designed to assess opinions of beginning teachers concerning their preprofessional and other college experiences.
Subjects are asked to rate their preservice education as
related to on-the-job skills.

9399
Ways of Looking at People Scale. Moursund,
Janet P. 1967
Subtests: Adults; Pity; Giving; Confidence; Liking;
  Values; Trust; Basic Nature
Descriptors: High Schools; *High School Students;
  Peer Relationship; *Social Attitudes; Social Val-
  ues; Student Attitudes; Likert Scales
Identifiers: Loyalty; WLP
Availability: Janet Moursund; Div. of Develop-
  mental Studies, College of Education, Univer-
  sity of Oregon, Eugene, OR 97403

Grade Level: 9–12
Notes: Items, 53

Designed to assess interpersonal attitudes of adolescents from grades 9-12. Assesses social maturity and perception.

9415
Compensatory Reading Project: Attitudes toward Reading, Grade 2. Trismen, Donald A.; And Others 1973
Descriptors: Compensatory Education; *Elementary School Students; *Grade 2; Primary Education; *Reading Attitudes; School Attitudes; Student Attitudes
Availability: ERIC Document Reproduction Service; 3900 Wheeler Ave., Alexandria, VA 22304 (ED130257, 424 pages).
Grade Level: 2
Notes: Items, 24

Designed to assess attitudes toward reading and books of students in second grade. Developed as part of the Compensatory Reading Project. This instrument is also included in Measuring Attitudes toward Reading ERIC/TM Report 73. (ED196938).

9428
Parental Attitudes toward Mentally Retarded Children Scale. Love, Harold D. 1967
Descriptors: Adults; *Children; *Mental Retardation; *Parent Attitudes; Parents; *Rating Scales; Likert Scales
Identifiers: P TIM(F)
Availability: Tests in Microfiche; Test Collection, Educational Testing Service, Princeton, NJ 08541
Target Audience: Adults
Notes: Items, 30

This untimed Likert scale measures parental attitudes toward mentally retarded children in work, community, and school situations.

9437
Memory Questionnaire. Perlmutter, Marion 1978
Descriptors: Adults; Age Differences; Memorization; *Memory; *Older Adults; Questionnaires; *Young Adults
Identifiers: Adult Attitudes
Availability: Developmental Psychology;v14 n4 p330-45, 1978
Target Audience: Adults
Notes: Items, 60

Designed to assess subject's thoughts about their memory such as memory problems, anticipated memory changes with age, items they found easy or difficult to remember, and what memory strategies they used.

9464
Student Deviancy Questionnaire. Heise, David R. 1968
Descriptors: *Antisocial Behavior; Higher Education; Moral Values; Questionnaires; Self Evaluation (Individuals); Social Experience; *Student Attitudes; *Undergraduate Students
Identifiers: Self Report Measures
Availability: Social Problems;v16 n1 p78-92, Sum 1968
Grade Level: 13–16
Notes: Items, 30

Designed to assess student deviant behaviors through analysis of self-report measure. Instrument assesses student's attitudes toward deviant behaviors and experience. Moral values are also measured by this instrument.

9468
JAW Board. Norton, Jeanette; And Others 1970
Descriptors: Adults; Behavior Patterns; Group Therapy; *Males; *Peer Evaluation; *Prisoners; *Problem Solving; Rehabilitation Centers; Sociometric Techniques
Availability: Bernard C. Kirby; Professor of Sociology, Dept. of Sociology, California State University at San Diego, 5402 College Ave., San Diego, CA 92115
Target Audience: Adults

Designed to enable residents of a rehabilitation center to evaluate their peers' problem-solving ability. Enabled residents to learn how their peers perceived their behavior.

9474
Change Scale. Trumbo, Don A. 1961
Descriptors: Adults; *Change; *Employee Attitudes; *Employees; Organizational Change; Work Attitudes
Availability: Journal of Applied Psychology;v45 n5 p338-44, 1961
Target Audience: Adults
Notes: Items, 9

Designed to assess employee attitudes toward work-related change.

9476
Social Episodes Test. Radke, Marian; And Others 1949
Descriptors: *Elementary School Students; Interviews; Pictorial Stimuli; Primary Education; Projective Measures; *Racial Attitudes; Racial Bias; *Social Attitudes; *Social Bias
Identifiers: *Religious Attitudes
Availability: Genetic Psychology Monographs;v40 p327-447, 1949
Grade Level: K–2

Designed to elicit social attitudes of young children. Pictures of children in simple social situations are shown to the subject. These are sufficiently ambiguous to elicit various interpretations. After initial interpretations by the child, racial and religious identification are introduced by the examiner.

9477
Liberal Conservative Scale. Coursey, Robert D. 1974
Descriptors: Adults; *Catholics; *Religious Conflict; Religious Differences; Conservatism; Liberalism
Identifiers: *Religious Attitudes
Availability: Journal of Consulting and Clinical Psychology;v42 n4 p519-28, 1974
Target Audience: Adults
Notes: Items, 55

Designed to measure liberal and conservative religious attitudes of members of the Catholic Church.

9482
Course Entry Inventory. Deaton, William L.; And Others 1977
Descriptors: Affective Measures; Course Evaluation; Graduate Students; Higher Education; *Student Attitudes; *Undergraduate Students
Availability: ERIC Document Reproduction Service; 3900 Wheeler Ave., Alexandria, VA 22304 (ED146209, 20 pages)
Grade Level: 13–20
Notes: Items, 42

Designed to assess the affective entry characteristics of college students upon beginning a course.

9485
Crossman Q Sort. Graduate Internship Program Staff, Univ. of California, Berkeley 1970
Descriptors: Adults; Preservice Teacher Education; Q Methodology; Self Evaluation (Individuals); Teacher Student Relationship; *Teacher Attitudes; *Teachers; Work Attitudes
Identifiers: Card Sort
Availability: ERIC Document Reproduction Service; 3900 Wheeler Ave., Alexandria, VA 22304 (ED083214, 161 pages)
Target Audience: Adults
Notes: Items, 98

Designed to assess attitudes toward youth and teaching. Q-sort methodology is used to enable teachers and teacher education students to assess their own attitudes and behavior.

9487
Parent Impressions of Psycho-Educational Evaluations as They Relate to Their Children. Tidwell, Romeria; Wetter, Jack 1978
Descriptors: Adults; Elementary School Students; *Parent Attitudes; *Parents; Parent School Relationship; Psychoeducational Clinics; *Psychological Evaluation; School Psychologists
Availability: Psychology in the Schools;v15 n2 p209-15, Apr 1978
Target Audience: Adults
Notes: Items, 17

Designed to assess parents' opinions concerning psychoeducational reports about their children prepared by school psychologists. The parents' satisfaction with the clarity and perceived utility of the reports was assessed.

9490
School Integration Questionnaire for Parents. Goolsby, Thomas M. 1971
Descriptors: Adults; *Desegregation Effects; Elementary School Students; *Parent Attitudes; *Parents; Primary Education; Racial Attitudes; *Racial Integration; School Desegregation
Availability: ERIC Document Reproduction Service; 3900 Wheeler Ave., Alexandria, VA 22304 (ED057096, 110 pages)
Target Audience: Adults
Notes: Items, 40

Designed to measure parents' attitudes and opinions concerning the effects of school integration on their children and the school system.

9509
Chinsky-Rappaport Adaptation of the Semantic Differential. Chinsky, Jack M.; Rappaport, Julian 1970

Subtests: Psychotherapy; Mental Patients; Nurses; Mental Illness; Psychologists; Volunteer Groups; Mental Hospital; Myself; Average Person
Descriptors: Adults; Higher Education; Mental Disorders; *Mental Health; Nurses; Patients; Psychiatric Hospitals; Psychologists; Psychotherapy; Self Concept; Semantic Differential; Undergraduate Students; Volunteers
Identifiers: TIM(E)
Availability: Tests in Microfiche; Test Collection, Educational Testing Service, Princeton, NJ 08541
Grade Level: 13–16
Notes: Time, 10; Items, 126

Semantic differential designed to measure initial attitudes and changes, of college students participating in a hospital companionship program, toward mental health concepts.

9513
Life Satisfaction Index Z. Havighurst, Robert J. 1971
Descriptors: *Attitudes; *Life Satisfaction; *Life Style; *Older Adults; Questionnaires; Self Evaluation (Individuals)
Availability: Robert J. Havighurst; Graduate School of Education, University of Chicago, 5835 Kimbark Ave., Chicago, IL 60637
Target Audience: Older Adults

Designed to measure older adults' satisfaction with their past and present lives. Three forms of the test are available.

9516
Attitude Inventory—Your Attitudes. Havighurst, Robert J. 1957
Subtests: Health (4); Family (4); Friends (4); Associations (4); Work (4); Economic Security (4); Home (4); Happiness (4)
Descriptors: Clubs; *Economic Factors; *Emotional Adjustment; *Family Life; *Friendship; *Health; *Older Adults; Security (Psychology); *Work Attitudes
Availability: Genetic Psychology Monographs;v56 p297-375, 1957
Target Audience: 65
Notes: Items, 32

Inventory to measure attitudes toward health, family, friends, associations, work, economic security, home, and happiness.

9518
Scale for Rating Manifest Complexity. Havighurst, Robert J. 1957
Subtests: Interaction with Persons (1); Range and Variety of Activities (1); Imaginative Complexity (1)
Descriptors: Affective Behavior; Human Relations; Imagination; *Interests; Middle Aged Adults; Older Adults; Rating Scales; *Retirement; Role Perception; *Social Life
Availability: Genetic Psychology Monographs;v56 p297-365, 1957
Target Audience: 40–70
Notes: Items, 3

Scale used to evaluate the complexity of interaction with persons, the numbers, and types of interactions. Also elicits information on numbers of activities and interests and the quality and variety of intellectual and emotional activity.

9519
Smoking Attitude Scale. Baer, Daniel J. 1966
Descriptors: Adults; Questionnaires; *Smoking; *Social Attitudes; Student Attitudes; Undergraduate Students
Availability: Journal of Social Psychology;v68 p65-78, Jan 1966
Target Audience: 17–23
Notes: Items, 22

Measures smokers and nonsmokers attitude. Two forms are available. A Smoking Behavior and Beliefs Questionnaire was also utilized.

9533
Scale of Non-Economic Liberalism. O'Kane, James M. 1970
Descriptors: *Civil Liberties; Grade 12; High Schools; High School Seniors; *Political Attitudes; *Liberalism; Likert Scales
Availability: James M. O'Kane; Dept. of "Sociology, Drew University, Madison, NJ 07940
Grade Level: 12
Notes: Items, 20

Measures attitudes toward civil liberties, civil rights for minorities, communism, foreign policy, Supreme Court decisions, etc.

9544
Perceptions of Other-Race Students Questionnaires. Patchen, Martin; And Others 1976

Descriptors: High Schools; High School Students; Perception; *Racial Attitudes; Racial Relations; Rating Scales
Availability: Martin Patchen; Dept. of Sociology-Anthropology, Purdue University, West Lafayette, IN 47907
Grade Level: 9–12
Notes: Items, 26

Black high school students and white high school students are asked to rate how many other-race students engage in behaviors reflective of unfriendliness, norm violations, and toughness.

9546
Black Power Sentiments Scale (Modified Form).
Tucker, Richard Dennis 1969
Descriptors: *Black Attitudes; *Black Power; College Students; Forced Choice Technique; Higher Education; Political Attitudes; *Racial Attitudes
Identifiers: Black Separatism
Availability: Richard D. Tucker; Dept. of Psychology, University of Central Florida, Orlando, FL 32816
Grade Level: 13–16
Notes: Items, 24

Revision of the Black Power Sentiment Scale (Stenfors and Woodmansee, 1968). Designed to identify black separatist extremism of the Black Panther variety.

9550
Child's Report of Parental Behavior Inventory.
Schaefer, Earl S. 1964
Descriptors: *Adolescents; Affection; Aggression; *Behavior Rating Scales; *Childhood Attitudes; Child Neglect; Discipline; Intellectual Development; Interests; Interpersonal Competence; Negative Reinforcement; *Parent Child Relationship; Positive Reinforcement; Punishment; Rejection (Psychology)
Identifiers: Child Centered; Emotional Support; Equality; Guilt; Independence; Intrusiveness; Parent Behavior; Possessiveness; Strictness; TIM(E)
Availability: Tests in Microfiche; Test Collection, Educational Testing Service, Princeton, NJ 08541
Target Audience: 12–14
Notes: Items, 260

Child rates parent's behavior in terms of its autonomy, discipline, sociability, evaluation, sharing activities, affection, independence, support, equality, intellectual stimulation, possessiveness, child-centeredness, protectiveness, intrusiveness, aggression, strictness, punishment, control by guilt, direction, nagging, irritability, rejection, neglect, ignoring. Has Mother and Father Forms.

9555
Games Choice Test. Cratty, Bryant J.; And Others 1970
Descriptors: Childhood Attitudes; *Children; *Childrens Games; *Forced Choice Technique; Minimal Brain Dysfunction
Availability: Cratty, Bryant J., and Others; *Movement Activities, Motor Ability and the Education of Children.*Springfield, IL.: Charles C. Thomas, 1970.
Target Audience: 5–12
Notes: Items, 37

Designed to measure a child's preference for one of 8 types of games: those exclusive to childhood, those in which the child imitates adults, those requiring manipulative behavior, those involving activity of larger muscles, those requiring aiming and steadiness, those paralleling adult recreational interests, musical games, and those involving aggression.

9558
Follow-up Study: Graduates of 1972, 1974, 1976.
Finn, Marie 1977
Subtests: Follow-Up Questionnaire (45); Follow-Up Study (12); Parent Survey (10); Employer Survey (7)
Descriptors: Adults; Career Choice; *Curriculum Evaluation; Educational Experience; *Followup Studies; *Graduate Surveys; *High School Graduates; Parent Attitudes; Secondary Education; Student Attitudes
Availability: ERIC Document Reproduction Service; 3900 Wheeler Ave., Alexandria, VA 22304 (ED158193, 77 pages)
Target Audience: Adults
Notes: Items, 74

Surveys high school graduates' educational and employment activities, as well as selected attitudes toward the high school experience. Separate forms for data from parents and employers.

9562
Survey of Oceanic Attitudes and Knowledge. Fortner, Rosanne White 1978

Subtests: Experiences (60); Attitudes (15); Knowledges (25)
Descriptors: *Academic Achievement; Earth Science; Grade 10; High Schools; *Knowledge Level; *Marine Biology; Multiple Choice Tests; *Oceanography; Questionnaires; Science Education; *Secondary School Science; *Student Attitudes
Availability: ERIC Document Reproduction Service; 3900 Wheeler Ave., Alexandria, VA 22304 (ED159023, microfiche only)
Grade Level: 10
Notes: Time, 45; Items, 100

Three-part instrument designed to identify the marine-related experiences students have had and the marine attitudes they express. Three forms of a test of marine knowledge are included.

9564
Experience-Interest Inventory. Davis, William J. 1978
Descriptors: Adults; *Inservice Education; *Interests; *Needs Assessment; *Principals; Professional Continuing Education; *Questionnaires; Surveys; Urban Schools
Availability: ERIC Document Reproduction Service, 3900 Wheeler Ave., Alexandria, VA 22304 (ED159143, 49 pages)
Target Audience: Adults
Notes: Items, 64

Designed to assess prospective participants' relative interests and levels of experience regarding a number of possible program topics for an inservice program for urban school principals.

9575
Work Preference Schedule. Cleland, Charles C.; Swartz, Jon D. 1968
Subtests: Work Preference (12); Pleasure Schedule (10)
Descriptors: Adults; Eating Habits; *Institutionalized Persons; *Mental Retardation; Questionnaires; Recreational Activities; *Vocational Interests; *Work Attitudes
Availability: Charles C. Cleland; University of Texas, 204 Sutton, Austin, TX 78712
Target Audience: Adults
Notes: Items, 22

Series of questionnaires designed to determine preferences in work and nonwork activities and diet in institutionalized adult retarded males. Pictures of actual work scenes in the environment were rated as liked or disliked.

9576
Daylight Saving Time Questionnaire. Cleland, Charles C.; Drew, Clifford J. 1969
Descriptors: Adults; *Employee Attitudes; *Institutionalized Persons; *Institutional Personnel; Institutional Schools; Mild Mental Retardation; Questionnaires; Severe Mental Retardation; *Time Perspective
Identifiers: *Daylight Savings Time
Availability: Charles C. Cleland; University of Texas, 204 Sutton, Austin, TX 78712
Target Audience: Adults
Notes: Items, 6

Questionnaire designed to determine whether hospital employees perceive any effects of daylight saving time on the behavior of institutionalized retarded subjects. Also assesses employee attitudes toward daylight saving time.

9601
ME. Halodyna, Tom; Thomas, Greg 1975
Subtests: ME, Grades 1-3 (30); ME, Grades 4-8 (45)
Descriptors: Art; Elementary Education; Elementary School Mathematics; Elementary School Students; Music; Physical Education; Rating Scales; Reading; *School Attitudes; Sciences; Social Studies; *Student Attitudes
Availability: Teaching Research; Monmouth, OR 97361
Grade Level: 1–8

Primary grades subtest covers reading, mathematics, physical education, art, music, and school in general. Intermediate grades subtest covers social studies and sciences in addition to the areas covered in the primary grades test. Measures attitudes toward these subjects.

9607
Pre-Transfer Interview Schedule. Steadman, Henry J.
Descriptors: Adults; *Attitudes; Criminals; Institutionalized Persons; *Interviews; Mental Disorders; *Patients; *Prisoners
Availability: Henry J. Steadman; Mental Health Research Unit, New York State Dept. of Mental Hygiene, 44 Holland Ave., Albany, NY 12208
Target Audience: Adults
Notes: Time, 25; Items, 53

Interview measure to be administered prior to patients leaving for a state mental hospital. Covers patient perceptions of institution, estimations of their own dangerousness, expectations of future situations, self-concept, interactions with patients, perceptions of stigma.

9638
Sex Attitude Survey and Profile. Trial Edition.
McHugh, Gelolo; McHugh, Thomas G. 1976
Descriptors: *Adults; Counseling; Interpersonal Relationship; Questionnaires; *Sexuality
Availability: Family Life Publications, Inc.; P.O. Box 427, Saluda, NC 28773
Target Audience: Adults
Notes: Items, 107

A communication aid and information gathering device for sex partners and prospective partners who want to have a satisfying and continuing relationship. Designed for use with a counselor.

9653
Zelig's Test on Children's Attitudes toward Annoyances. Zeligs, Rose 1962
Subtests: Personal Factors, Boys (121); Personal Factors, Girls (158); Social Factors, Boys (116); Social Factors, Girls (155); Environmental Factors, Boys (56); Environmental Factors, Girls (67)
Descriptors: Elementary School Students; *Grade 6; Intermediate Grades; *Negative Attitudes; Sex Differences; Student Problems; *Likert Scales
Identifiers: *Annoyances
Availability: Rose Zeligs; 14256 Ventura Blvd., Sherman Oaks, CA 91403
Grade Level: 6
Notes: Items, 673

Measures reactions of children to inconveniences and annoyances that they faced in daily experiences.

9691
Women's Liberation Ideology Scale. Goldschmidt, Jean; And Others 1974
Descriptors: Beliefs; College Students; Females; *Feminism; Higher Education; *Political Attitudes; *Social Attitudes; *Ideology; Likert Scales
Identifiers: *Womens Liberation
Availability: *Journal of Personality;*v42 p601-17, 1974
Grade Level: 13–16
Notes: Items, 12

Differentiates between members of a women's liberation organization and a random sample of women at the same university. Also available is a 10-item scale adapted by Jeanne Marceek.

9694
Attitudes toward Grading Questionnaire. Goldstein, Kenneth M.; Tilker, Harvey A. 1969
Subtests: Amount of Feedback (8); Motivation to Work Well (8); Anxiety and Pressure (8); Encouraging Creativity (8); True Learning (8); General Evaluation (8); Ease of Entering Graduate School (8); Fairness of the System (8)
Descriptors: Adults; *College Faculty; *Grading; Graduate Students; Higher Education; *Student Attitudes; *Teacher Attitudes; Undergraduate Students; Likert Scales
Availability: ERIC Document Reproduction Service; 3900 Wheeler Ave., Alexandria, VA 22304 (ED042408, 81 pages)
Grade Level: 13–17
Target Audience: Adults
Notes: Items, 64

Developed to measure undergraduate and graduate students' and their teachers' attitudes toward three- and five-point grading systems.

9699
Faces Inventory. Millersville State College, Pennsylvania State Dept. of Education, Harrisburg, PA 1978
Descriptors: Elementary School Students; Grade 3; Grade 5; Independent Study; Intermediate Grades; Learning Activities; Primary Education; Rating Scales; *School Attitudes; *Student Attitudes; *Student School Relationship
Availability: ERIC Document Reproduction Service; 3900 Wheeler Ave., Alexandria, VA 22304 (ED165898, 73 pages)
Grade Level: 3–5
Notes: Items, 20

Rating scale designed to measure attitudes toward school, independent study and schoolwork. Twenty statements concerning feelings are rated on a 3-point scale consisting of happy, neutral, and sad faces.

9700
Michigan Organizational Assessment Questionnaire (MOAQ). Lawler, Edward E.; And Others 1978

Subtests: General Attitudes; Job Facets; Task and Role Characteristics; Work Group Functioning; Supervisory Behavior; Pay
Descriptors: Adults; Educational Background; *Job Satisfaction; Occupational Information; *Organizational Change; *Organizational Effectiveness; Questionnaires; Salaries; Supervisory Methods; *Work Attitudes; *Work Environment
Identifiers: MOAQ
Availability: Seashore, Stanley, Ed.; *Assessing Organizational Change: A Guide to Methods, Measures and Practices.*New York: John Wiley and Sons, 1983
Target Audience: Adults
Notes: Items, 177
Designed for assessment of organizations and their changes over time; elicits objective information, beliefs, opinions and affective responses of employees covering work, work environments, and organizational activities.

9710
Political Values Measure. Bemen, F.K.; Turner, Floyd D. 1969
Descriptors: *Activism; Adults; Authoritarianism; Censorship; *Democratic Values; *Political Attitudes; Political Issues; Questionnaires; *Rating Scales; Social Action; *Values; *Dissent
Availability: ERIC Document Reproduction Service; 3900 Wheeler Ave., Alexandria, VA 22304 (ED043682, 82 pages)
Target Audience: Adults
Notes: Items, 90
Measures politically relevant values and explores the values dynamics underlying dissent.

9715
Teachers' Practices Questionnaire. Klein, Alice
Descriptors: Adults; Discipline; Questionnaires; *Role Perception; Situational Tests; Teacher Attitudes; *Teacher Behavior; *Teacher Role
Availability: ERIC Document Reproduction Service; 3900 Wheeler Ave., Alexandria, VA 22304 (ED045711, 20 pages)
Target Audience: Adults
Notes: Items, 40
A revision of the 1963 Teachers' Practices Questionnaire which measures teachers' subjective role expectations. Four role factors are represented: counselor, motivator, referees, and disciplinarian

9735
Social-Sexual Knowledge and Attitudes Questionnaire. Edmonson, Barbara; And Others 1977
Descriptors: Adults; Mild Mental Retardation; *Moderate Mental Retardation; *Opinions; Parent Attitudes; Questionnaires; Sex Education; *Sexuality; Teacher Attitudes; *Test Construction
Availability: ERIC Document Reproduction Service; 3900 Wheeler Ave., Alexandria, VA 22304 (ED160643, microfiche only).
Target Audience: Adults
Notes: Items, 22
Designed to elicit recommendations of parents, educators, and others as to which sociosexual areas should be sampled prior to the construction of a sex knowledge and attitude test for mildly and moderately mentally retarded subjects.

9736
Middle School Teacher Questionnaire. Gillan, Robert E. 1978
Subtests: Professional Description Survey (7); Middle School Employment Survey (5); Middle School Attitude Inventory (30); Middle School Concept List (20); Professional Recommendations Survey (4)
Descriptors: Adults; Elementary Secondary Education; *Job Satisfaction; *Middle Schools; *School Attitudes; *Teacher Attitudes; Teacher Certification; *Teacher Education
Availability: ERIC Document Reproduction Service; 3900 Wheeler Ave., Alexandria, VA 22304 (ED160617, 15 pages)
Target Audience: Adults
Notes: Items, 66
Used to identify differences between certified middle school teachers and those certified at another level for teaching in middle schools. Also examined included attitudes toward middle school educational programs,, educational concepts emphasis in middle schools, job satisfaction, recommendations for teacher training programs and middle school certification.

9740
Traditional Family Ideology Scale. Levinson, Daniel J.; Huffman, Phyllis E. 1949

Descriptors: Adults; *Conformity; Family (Sociological Unit); *Family Life; Family Relationship; Family Role; Family Structure; Middle Class Standards; Parent Attitudes; *Parent Child Relationship; *Parents; *Sex Role
*Availability: Journal of Personality;*v23 n3 p251-73, Mar 1955
Target Audience: Adults
Notes: Items, 40
Assesses individual's position on the democratic-autocratic continuum of family structure and functioning. Five aspects of the authoritarian personality syndrome were selected as bases for construction of the scale: conventionalism, authoritarian submission, exaggerated masculinity and femininity, extreme emphasis on discipline, and moralistic rejection of impulse life.

9741
Assumptions about Learning and Knowledge. Barth, Ronald S. 1971
Subtests: Children's Learning (24); Knowledge (5)
Descriptors: Adults; Educational Theories; Humanistic Education; *Learning Processes; Learning Theories; *Open Education; *Teacher Attitudes; Teachers; *Likert Scales
*Availability: Phi Delta Kappan;*v53 n2 p97-99, Oct 1971
Target Audience: Adults
Notes: Items, 29
Twenty-nine-item questionnaire that helps teachers examine their assumptions about learning and knowledge so that they can decide whether open learning will be compatible with their educational attitudes.

9745
Rumstein Agreement/Disagreement Test. Rumstein, Regina
Descriptors: Adults; *Educational Psychology; Elementary Education; *Elementary School Teachers; Inservice Teacher Education; *Teacher Attitudes; Teacher Characteristics; Teacher Education
Identifiers: RADT; TIM(F)
Availability: Tests in Microfiche; Test Collection, Educational Testing Service, Princeton, NJ 08541
Target Audience: Adults
Notes: Items, 34
Designed to determine the extent to which elementary school teachers agree with research findings in educational psychology. Suggested for use in evaluating inservice programs, improvement of communication with researchers, and determining relationship between teachers' agreement with findings and their practical applications in the classroom.

9747
Beliefs about Equal Rights Scale. Jacobson, Leonard I.; And Others 1976
Descriptors: *Adults; Equal Education; Equal Opportunities (Jobs); Feminism; Higher Education; Sex Discrimination; *Sex Fairness; Sex Role; Sex Stereotypes; *Social Attitudes; Undergraduate Students
Identifiers: BAERS
*Availability: Educational and Psychological Measurement;*v36 n4, p913-18, Win 1976
Grade Level: 13–16
Target Audience: Adults
Designed to measure beliefs about equal rights for men and women. Scores on the scale were related to subject, sex, age, and ethnic group as predicted.

9759
Job Satisfaction Inventory. Schmid, John, Jr. 1958
Descriptors: Adults; Employee Attitudes; Employer Employee Relationship; *Job Satisfaction; *Military Personnel; Peer Relationship; *Work Attitudes
Identifiers: *Air Force
*Availability: Educational and Psychological Measurement;*v58 n1 p189-202, 1958
Target Audience: Adults
Notes: Items, 21
Measures Air Force mechanics' expressed degree of satisfaction with their work. There are 7 classes of items related to higher organization of the Air Force; supervisor's technical competence; supervisor's leadership and social capacity; coworkers; job duties; living conditions on the base; job in general.

9801
Perceived Instrumentality of the College Test. Constantinople, Anne 1967
Descriptors: *Affective Objectives; *Cognitive Objectives; *College Role; *Educational Objectives; Higher Education; *Student Attitudes; *Undergraduate Students; Likert Scales
*Availability: Journal of Personality and Social Psychology;*v5 n2 p196-201, 1967

Grade Level: 13–16
Notes: Items, 14
Presents 14 goal statements, reflecting 9 dimensions of the college experience. Each statement is rated twice: for importance of goal and for the degree to which college helped or hindered goal attainment.

9826
McCloskey Conservative-Liberal Scale. McCloskey, H. 1958
Descriptors: Adults; *Political Attitudes
*Availability: Journal of Applied Psychology;*v54 n5 p470-72, 1970
Target Audience: Adults
Notes: Items, 13
Attempts to measure the strength of general conservative beliefs in individuals and groups.

9831
Custodial Mental Illness Ideology Scale. Gilbert, Doris C.; Levinson, Daniel J. 1956
Descriptors: Adults; *Hospital Personnel; Mental Disorders; Psychiatric Aides; *Psychiatric Hospitals; Psychiatrists
Identifiers: CMI
*Availability: Journal of Abnormal and Social Psychology;*v53 n3 p263-71, Nov 1956
Target Audience: Adults
Notes: Items, 20
Designed to assess attitudes of psychiatric hospital personnel. May be used to determine individual's ideology as custodial or humanistic. Custodial orientation provides a highly controlled setting concerned with the detention and safekeeping of its inmates. The humanistic approach is concerned with the individuality and human needs of patients and personnel. The hospital, in the humanistic view, is conceived as a therapeutic community rather than a custodial institution.

9861
Job Preferences (What Makes a Job Good or Bad?). Jurgensen, Clifford E. 1945
Descriptors: Adults; Fringe Benefits; *Job Applicants; Promotion (Occupational); Salaries; *Work Attitudes; Work Environment
*Availability: Journal of Applied Psychology;*v63 n3 p267-76, 1978
Target Audience: Adults
Designed to assess applicants' priorities in work-related factors. Respondents are asked to rank 10 factors of a job in order of importance to themselves and again rank these factors as they believe others would.

9865
Attitudes toward Public Exposure to Sexual Stimuli Scale. Crawford, JoEllen E.; Crawford, Thomas J. 1978
Descriptors: *Adults; Higher Education; *Sexuality; Social Attitudes; *Undergraduate Students; *Pornography
Identifiers: *Sexual Attitudes
*Availability: Journal of Personality Assessment;*v42 n4 p392-400, 1978
Grade Level: 13–16
Target Audience: Adults
Notes: Items, 21
Designed to measure attitudes toward public exposure to sexual stimuli. Specific variable measured is willingness to accept exposure of self and others, particularly children, to nudity and other sex-related stimuli. An abbreviated 10 item scale is also available.

9875
Manifest Alienation Measure. Gould, Laurence J. 1969
Descriptors: Affective Behavior; Apathy; Behavior; Birth Order; *Emotional Adjustment; Higher Education; Perception; Personality Problems; *Personality Traits; *Student Alienation; *Undergraduate Students
Identifiers: Cynicism; Distrust; Emotional Distance; MAM; Pessimism; TIM(F)
Availability: Tests in Microfiche; Test Collection, Educational Testing Service, Princeton, NJ 08541
Grade Level: Higher Education
Notes: Items, 20
Twenty-item measure to determine the existence in an individual of an alienation syndrome consisting of feelings of pessimism, cynicism, distrust, apathy, and emotional distance. Subjects responded from strongly agree to strongly disagree or no answer. The original study was performed on 429 male undergraduate students.

9882
Age Independence Scale. Keith, Robert Allen 1969
Descriptors: Adolescents; Cerebral Palsy; Children; Interpersonal Competence; Mental Retardation; *Parent Aspiration; *Parent Attitudes; Physical Disabilities; *Prediction; *Self Care Skills
Identifiers: *Independent Behavior; TIM(F)

Availability: Tests in Microfiche; Test Collection, Educational Testing Service, Princeton, NJ 08541
Target Audience: 2–18

Parent and professional indicate those behaviors a handicapped child now performs, the age at which it is felt the child will be able to perform other behaviors, and those behaviors the child will never be able to perform. Covers motor, cognitive, social, and self-care behaviors. Used in a study of parent's unrealistic expectations for their handicapped child. Preschool Form contains 75 items; the Elementary Form, 105 items; the Adolescent Form contains 60 items. Reliability data were available for the Preschool Form only. Some items of this form were taken from the Vineland Social Maturity Scale as well as other sources.

9883
Student Achievement Diagnostic Questionnaire. Matthews, Kenneth M.; Brown, Carvin L. 1978
Descriptors: *Academic Ability; *Elementary School Students; English; Intermediate Grades; Mathematics; *School Attitudes; Secondary Education; *Secondary School Students; *Self Concept Measures; Social Studies; Student Attitudes; *Teacher Student Relationship
Identifiers: SADQ
Availability: ERIC Document Reproduction Service; 3900 Wheeler Ave., Alexandria, VA 22304-5110 (ED178601, 13 pages)
Grade Level: 4–12
Notes: Items, 64

Designed to provide measures of students' self-concepts of ability in specific subject areas; attitudes toward teachers; perceptions of subject area teacher's expectations; and students' perceptions of the future utility of English, mathematics, science, and social studies.

9884
Health Problems Inventory. O'Daniels, Phyllis S.
Descriptors: Adults; Family Relationship; High Schools; Human Relations; Physical Health; Psychological Patterns; Security (Psychology); *Self Evaluation (Individuals); *Student Attitudes; *Student Problems; *Teacher Attitudes
Identifiers: TIM(F)
Availability: Tests in Microfiche; Test Collection, Educational Testing Service, Princeton, NJ 08541
Grade Level: High Schools
Notes: Items, 190

One-hundred ninety statements describing situations related to the social, emotional, and physical health of high school students are rated on their frequency in causing health problems on a 5-point scale from never to always. Two forms elicit student and faculty opinions.

9890
Anders Childrearing Scale. Anders, Sarah Frances 1967
Descriptors: Adults; *Attendants; *Child Rearing; *Ethnic Origins; *Institutionalized Persons; *Mental Retardation; *Residential Care; Socioeconomic Status
Identifiers: Attendant Attitudes; *Permissiveness; TIM(F)
Availability: Tests in Microfiche; Test Collection, Educational Testing Service, Princeton, NJ 08541
Target Audience: Adults
Notes: Items, 47

Consists of statements concerned with child-rearing practices and several alternative courses of action or age levels. Respondent selects choice of action or age level which corresponds to their own practices or beliefs. The scale was used in a study of the relationship between certain ethnic variables and permissive child-rearing beliefs of attendants with direct patient care in an institution for mentally retarded patients. Covers practices related to infancy, early childhood, prepuberty, and adolescence.

9892
Attitude Survey. Fiebert, Martin S. 1977
Descriptors: Beliefs; Higher Education; Individual Development; *Meditation; Pretests Posttests; Rating Scales; *Training Objectives; *Undergraduate Students
Availability: Perceptual and Motor Skills;v45 n3 p849-50, Dec 1977
Grade Level: 13–16
Notes: Items, 10

Designed to assess attitudes toward personal growth and acceptance of transpersonal beliefs. Subjects participated in a 30-minute introductory meditation session followed by a postsession questionnaire. This instrument was a rating scale to describe training experience.

9895
Adjective Rating Scale. Kelly, Edward F.; And Others 1976
Descriptors: *Course Evaluation; Higher Education; High Schools; Rating Scales; *Student Attitudes

Identifiers: ARS; TIM(F)
Availability: Tests in Microfiche; Test Collection, Educational Testing Service, Princeton, NJ 08541
Grade Level: 9–16
Notes: Items, 24

Utilizes 24 items regularly used by high school and college students in evaluating their courses. These are rated against the stimulus on a 4-point scale as being descriptive of the course.

9899
Curriculum-People Semantic Differential. Yamamoto, Kaoru 1969
Subtests: Classmates; Social Studies; Parent; Language; Teacher; Science; Myself; Arithmetic
Descriptors: Adolescents; Arithmetic; Children; Language Attitudes; Parents; *School Attitudes; Sciences; Self Concept; Semantic Differential; Social Studies; *Student Attitudes; Teachers
Identifiers: Classmates; TIM(F); Word Association Study
Availability: Tests in Microfiche; Test Collection, Educational Testing Service, Princeton, NJ 08541
Target Audience: 10–16
Notes: Items, 96

Eight concepts are rated using 12 7-point bipolar adjective scales. Four of the concepts relate to people and 4 to the school curriculum. Two forms of the scale are available.

9917
Executive Profile Survey. Lang, Virgil R. 1978
Descriptors: Adults; *Managerial Occupations; *Personality Assessment; *Personnel Selection
Availability: Institute for Personality and Ability Testing; P.O. Box 188; Champaign, IL 61820
Target Audience: Adults
Notes: Time, 60 approx.; Items, 94

Measures self-attitudes, values, and beliefs of individuals in comparison with 2,000 top level executives. Data from questions provide clear, concise, nontechnical description of the dimensions most important in business, management, and executive settings. Eleven profile dimensions assess the self-assertive, enthusiastic, creative, innovative, self-directed, receptive, adaptable, composed, perceptive, and systematic traits of the individual.

9987
Sex Knowledge Inventory, Form X. McHugh, Gelolo 1979
Descriptors: Adults; Churches; Church Programs; Clinics; Counseling Services; *Human Relations; Marriage Counseling; Outreach Programs; *Sexuality
Identifiers: Premarital Counseling; *Sexual Attitudes; SKI
Availability: Family Life Publications, Inc.; P.O. Box 427, Saluda, NC 28773
Target Audience: 18–44
Notes: Items, 80

Designed to help counselors and teachers work effectively with counselees and students toward a better understanding of the psychology of human sexual relationships. Emphasis is on interpersonal relations as a true basis for sexual relations and as an integral part of the whole marriage relationship. The inventory allows the teacher or counselor to deal with sex attitudes and feelings while working toward wholesome and enjoyable sexual self-expression.

9999
Committed-Nominal Religious Attitude Scale. Meyer, Roger A. 1976
Descriptors: Adults; *Religious Differences; Religious Discrimination; Religious Factors; *Social Attitudes; Social Bias
Availability: ERIC Document Reproduction Service; 3900 Wheeler Ave., Alexandria, VA 22304 (ED166201), 43 pages)
Target Audience: Adults
Notes: Time, 60 approx.; Items, 130

Designed to assess individual's religiosity as committed or nominal. Committed religiosity was defined as behaviors and attitudes which indicate total dedication to religious beliefs. Nominal religiosity was defined as acceptance of religious organization or philosophy so that individual receives personal or social gratification from an external source of power.

10013
Survey of Pupil Opinion. Kilbane, Marian T. 1972
Descriptors: *Compensatory Education; *Dropout Characteristics; High Schools; *High School Students; School Attitudes; *Student Attitudes; Student School Relationship
Availability: ERIC Document Reproduction Service; 3900 Wheeler Ave., Alexandria, VA 22304 (ED063329, 11 pages)
Grade Level: 9–12
Notes: Items, 30

The Survey of Pupil Opinion is an attitude-assessment instrument adapted to the reading and "palatability" levels of high school students in compensatory programs. The items are assumed to reflect "attitude toward school." Results showed that for each of 3 factors—social participation, perception of teachers, and self as student—the lowest mean score was obtained by the students who later dropped out of school. This instrument could be useful for identifying potential dropouts.

10017
Attitudes toward Underprivileged Children and Youth. Edwards, T. Bentley 1966
Descriptors: Adults; *Disadvantaged Youth; *Teacher Attitudes; *Teachers
Availability: Journal of Experimental Education;v35 n2 p80-92, 1966
Target Audience: Adults
Notes: Time, 50 approx.; Items, 72

Designed to assess teachers' attitudes toward disadvantaged youth.

10018
Disability Social Distance Scale. Tringo, John L. 1970
Descriptors: Adolescents; *Adults; *College Students; *Disabilities; Higher Education; High Schools; *High School Students; Interpersonal Relationship; Rating Scales; *Social Attitudes; Social Discrimination
Identifiers: DSDS; Social Distance
Availability: Journal of Special Education;v4 n3 p295-306, 1970
Grade Level: 9–16
Target Audience: 13–64
Notes: Items, 21

Designed to assess attitude toward specific disability groups. It was found that a hierarchy of preference exists that establishes the relative position of a specific disability in the hierarchy. Social distance refers to the degree of acceptance of disability groups.

10026
Minnesota Marking Attitude Scale. Terwilliger, James S.; And Others 1971
Subtests: Positive vs. Negative Influence of Grades; Narrow vs. Broad Basis for Grades; Objective vs. Subjective Approach to Marking; Descriptive vs. Dynamic Use of Grades; Standardized vs. Individualized Grading
Descriptors: Adults; *Grades (Scholastic); *Grading; *Teacher Attitudes; Teachers
Identifiers: MMAS; TIM(F)
Availability: Tests in Microfiche; Test Collection, Educational Testing Service, Princeton, NJ 08541
Target Audience: Adults
Notes: Time, 30 approx.; Items, 60

Instrument designed to measure teacher attitudes concerning issues and approaches in assignment of grades to students.

10030
Inventory of Student Perceptions of Instruction. Elementary, High School, and College Forms. Scott, Owen
Descriptors: *Course Evaluation; Elementary Secondary Education; Higher Education; Rating Scales; *Student Attitudes; *Student Evaluation of Teacher Performance; Likert Scales
Identifiers: ISPI; TIM(G)
Availability: Tests in Microfiche; Test Collection, Educational Testing Service, Princeton, NJ 08541
Grade Level: K–16

Students respond to statements descriptive of conditions or behaviors that characterize effective instruction including instructional objectives; classroom human relations; use of instructional resources; pupil motivation; meaningfulness of subject matter; and measurement and evaluation. There are separate forms for elementary grades (62 items); high schools (62 items); and colleges (69 items).

10045
Life Prolonging Scale. Denger, Lesley 1974
Descriptors: Adults; Patients; *Physicians
Identifiers: *Patient Care
Availability: ERIC Document Reproduction Service; 3900 Wheeler Ave., Alexandria, VA 22304-5110 (ED171763, 842 pages)
Target Audience: Adults
Notes: Items, 4

This volume consists of a series of psychosocial and physiological clinical nursing instruments. The instruments were selected from the published literature in health care, education, psychology, and the social sciences. Instruments focus upon nursing practice and stress patient variables. Designed to assess physician's attitudes toward use of life-prolonging measures for a patient.

10046
Nurse Attitudes on Sexual Counseling as a Nursing Responsibility. Green, Mary 1975
Subtests: Demographic Data; Background in Sex Education; Ability to Discuss Sexual Matters with Others; Attitudes toward Sexual Counseling as a Nursing Responsibility; Sexual Attitudes
Descriptors: Adults; Counselor Evaluation; *Nurses; *Nursing; Patients; Practical Nursing; *Sex Education; Sexuality
Identifiers: *Nurse Attitudes; Self Administered Tests
Availability: ERIC Document Reproduction Service; 3900 Wheeler Ave., Alexandria, VA 22304 (ED171763, 842 pages)
Target Audience: Adults
Notes: Time, 20 approx.; Items, 35

This volume consists of a series of psychosocial and physiological clinical nursing instruments. The instruments were selected from the published literature in health care, education, psychology, and the social sciences. Instruments focus upon nursing practice and stress patient variables. Instrument was designed to assess registered and licensed practical nurse respondents' information and attitudinal framework in the field of sex education. Useful in assessing potential candidates for effective nurse sexual counselors.

10047
Decision Scale. Guilbert, Evelyn Kelly 1970
Descriptors: Adults; *Decision Making; Hospital Personnel; *Nurses; *Nursing; Patients; *Psychiatric Hospitals
Identifiers: Independence; Psychiatric Patients; Self Administered Tests
Availability: ERIC Document Reproduction Service; 3900 Wheeler Ave., Alexandria, VA 22304 (ED171763, 842 pages)
Target Audience: Adults
Notes: Items, 34

This volume consists of a series of psychosocial and physiological clinical nursing instruments. The instruments were selected from the published literature in health care, education, psychology, and the social sciences. Instruments focus upon nursing practice and stress patient variables. Instrument assesses willingness of health care personnel in psychiatric patient settings to allocate decision making to patients. The Guttman Scale is a 6-item version of the instrument useful with persons of limited educational background.

10048
Health Care Work Powerlessness Scale (Revised).
Guilbert, Evelyn Kelly
Descriptors: Adults; Forced Choice Technique; *Health Personnel; Individual Power; Nurses; *Nursing; Patients; Psychiatric Hospitals; *Work Attitudes
Identifiers: *Nurse Attitudes; *Powerlessness
Availability: ERIC Document Reproduction Service; 3900 Wheeler Ave., Alexandria, VA 22304 (ED171763, 842 pages)
Target Audience: Adults
Notes: Items, 14

This volume consists of a series of psychosocial and physiological clinical nursing instruments. The instruments were selected from the published literature in health care, education, psychology, and the social sciences. Instruments focus upon nursing practice and stress patient variables. Instrument was designed to assess the feeling of powerlessness in health care work settings. Items are worded in general terms, not particularly related to health care settings.

10050
Parent Participation Attitude Scale. Seidl, Frederick W.; Pillitteri, Adele 1967
Descriptors: Adults; *Hospitalized Children; *Nurses; Nurses Aides; *Nursing; *Parent Participation; Patients; Pediatrics; Practical Nursing; Rating Scales
Identifiers: *Nurse Attitudes; PPAS; Self Administered Tests
Availability: ERIC Document Reproduction Service; 3900 Wheeler Ave., Alexandria, VA 22304 (ED171763, 842 pages)
Target Audience: Adults
Notes: Items, 24

This volume consists of a series of psychosocial and physiological clinical nursing instruments. The instruments were selected from the published literature in health care, education, psychology, and the social sciences. Instruments focus upon nursing practice and stress patient variables. Designed to assess nurses' attitudes toward parent participation in hospital pediatric programs.

10051
Trust Scale for Nurses. Wallston, Kenneth A.; And Others 1973
Subtests: Nurses' Trust of Patients (TS-N-P); Nurses' Trust of Other Nurses (TS-N-N)

Descriptors: Adults; Interpersonal Relationship; *Nurses; *Nursing; *Patients; Rating Scales
Identifiers: *Nurse Attitudes; Self Administered Tests; *Trust; TS(N)
Availability: ERIC Document Reproduction Service; 3900 Wheeler Ave., Alexandria, VA 22304 (ED171763, 842 pages)
Target Audience: Adults
Notes: Items, 10

This volume consists of a series of psychosocial and physiological clinical nursing instruments. The instruments were selected from the published literature in health care, education, psychology, and the social sciences. Instruments focus upon nursing practice and stress patient variables. This instrument assesses nurses' trust of patients and other nurses.

10052
Questionnaire for Understanding the Dying Person and His Family. Winget, Carolyn; And Others 1974
Descriptors: Adults; *Death; *Health Personnel; *Nurses; *Nursing; Physicians; Terminal Illness
Identifiers: Nurse Attitudes
Availability: ERIC Document Reproduction Service; 3900 Wheeler Ave., Alexandria, VA 22304 (ED171763, 842 pages)
Target Audience: Adults
Notes: Time, 40 approx.; Items, 68

This volume consists of a series of psychosocial and physiological clinical nursing instruments. The instruments were selected from the published literature in health care, education, psychology, and the social sciences. Instruments focus upon nursing practice and stress patient variables. Questionnaire was designed to obtain attitudinal and experiential data on death and dying from health care professionals.

10054
Diabetes Mellitus Patient Interview. Bowen, Rhoda G.; And Others 1961
Subtests: Knowledge of Disease; Knowledge of Insulin; Performance in Self-Administration of Insulin; Performance in Urine Testing; Knowledge of Diet and Food Exchange; Attitudes and Knowledge of Personal Hygiene; Attitudes toward the Disease
Descriptors: Adults; *Diabetes; Dietetics; Hygiene; Interviews; *Knowledge Level; Medicine; Nutrition; *Patients; Performance Tests
Identifiers: Insulin; *Patient Attitudes
Availability: ERIC Document Reproduction Service; 3900 Wheeler Ave., Alexandria, VA 22304 (ED171763, 842 pages)
Target Audience: Adults
Notes: Items, 100

This volume consists of a series of psychosocial and physiological clinical nursing instruments. The instruments were selected from the published literature in health care, education, psychology, and the social sciences. Instruments focus upon nursing practice and stress patient variables. This structured interview assesses a diabetes patient's knowledge and attitudes concerning diabetes and its treatment. The subject is also asked to demonstrate self-administration of insulin and urine testing.

10056
Labor and Delivery Tool. Aguiar, Martha B. 1974
Descriptors: Adults; *Birth; Knowledge Level; Mother Attitudes; *Mothers; *Patients; Pregnancy
Identifiers: *Labor (Birth); Postpartum Patients
Availability: ERIC Document Reproduction Service; 3900 Wheeler Ave., Alexandria, VA 22304 (ED171763, 842 pages)
Target Audience: Adults
Notes: Time, 15 approx.; Items, 41

This volume consists of a series of psychosocial and physiological clinical nursing instruments. The instruments were selected from the published literature in health care, education, psychology, and the social sciences. Instruments focus upon nursing practice and stress patient variables. Instrument was developed to assess the postpartum patient's perceptions of her labor, and delivery experience. Her general knowledge of pregnancy, labor, and delivery are also measured.

10058
Attitudes toward Sex Education in School. Bloch, Doris 1970
Descriptors: Adults; *Mother Attitudes; *Mothers; Parent Attitudes; Parents; *School Role; *Sex Education
Identifiers: Self Administered Tests; SES Attitudes
Availability: ERIC Document Reproduction Service; 3900 Wheeler Ave., Alexandria, VA 22304 (ED171763, 842 pages)
Target Audience: Adults
Notes: Time, 10 approx.; Items, 10

This volume consists of a series of psychosocial and physiological clinical nursing instruments. The instruments were selected from the published literature in health care,

education, psychology, and the social sciences. Instruments focus upon nursing practice and stress patient variables. Instrument was designed to assess parental, especially maternal, attitudes toward sex education in schools.

10059
Attitudes toward Content and Timing of Sex Education. Bloch, Doris 1970
Descriptors: Adults; *Mother Attitudes; *Mothers; Parent Attitudes; Parents; *Sex Education
Identifiers: SECT Attitudes
Availability: ERIC Document Reproduction Service; 3900 Wheeler Ave., Alexandria, VA 22304 (ED171763, 842 pages)
Target Audience: Adults
Notes: Time, 10 approx.; Items, 10

This volume consists of a series of psychosocial and physiological clinical nursing instruments. The instruments were selected from the published literature in health care, education, psychology, and the social sciences. Instruments focus upon nursing practice and stress patient variables. Instrument was designed to assess parental, especially maternal, attitudes toward the content and timing of sex education.

10063
Social Psychological Determinants of Patients Performance in Stroke Rehabilitation. Hyman, Martin D. 1972
Subtests: Feelings of Stigma; Self-Esteem; Satisfaction with Occupational Role; Satisfaction with Family Role; Feelings of Social Isolation; Dependency; Belief in Supernatural Causes of Illness; Secondary Gain in Illness
Descriptors: Adults; Individual Testing; Interviews; Loneliness; Nurses; *Nursing; *Patients; Rehabilitation; *Self Concept; Self Concept Measures; *Social Isolation; Dependency (Personality)
Identifiers: Guttman Scales; Illness; *Patient Attitudes
Availability: ERIC Document Reproduction Service; 3900 Wheeler Ave., Alexandria, VA 22304 (ED171763, 842 pages)
Target Audience: Adults
Notes: Items, 29

This volume consists of a series of psychosocial and physiological clinical nursing instruments. The instruments were selected from the published literature in health care, education, psychology, and the social sciences. Instruments focus upon nursing practice and stress patient variables. This instrument assesses patient's self-concept, attitudes toward social isolation, and attitudes toward illness. These social and psychological factors have been proven important to the success of patient rehabilitation.

10065
Semantic Differential for Health. Jenkins, C. David 1966
Descriptors: *Adults; *Beliefs; *Diseases; Interviews; Semantic Differential; *Social Attitudes; Pain
Identifiers: SDH
Availability: ERIC Document Reproduction Service; 3900 Wheeler Ave., Alexandria, VA 22304-5110 (ED171763, 842 pages)
Target Audience: Adults
Notes: Items, 15

This volume consists of a series of psychosocial and physiological nursing instruments. The instruments were selected from the published literature in health care, education, psychology, and the social sciences. Instruments focus upon nursing practice and stress patient variables. Instrument measures a subject's beliefs and feelings about diseases.

10066
Patient's Perception Scale. Palmer, Irene S. 1963
Subtests: Confidence in Family; Faith in God; Skill and Competence of Staff; Body Integrity; Acceptance of Need for Surgery; Financial Security; Understanding, Acceptance, and Support of Others; Dependency-Independency; Postoperative Living Patterns; Expectations about Surgery; Self-Awareness; Anesthesia; Painful Procedures
Descriptors: Adults; Nurses; *Nursing; *Patients; *Surgery
Identifiers: *Patient Attitudes
Availability: ERIC Document Reproduction Service; 3900 Wheeler Ave., Alexandria, VA 22304 (ED171763, 842 pages)
Target Audience: Adults
Notes: Time, 15 approx.; Items, 46

This volume consists of a series of psychosocial and physiological clinical nursing instruments. The instruments were selected from the published literature in health care, education, psychology, and the social sciences. Instruments focus upon nursing practice and stress patient variables. Instrument is designed to measure adult patient's perceptions of impending general surgery.

10067
Health-Illness (Powerlessness) Questionnaire.
Roy, Callista 1976
Descriptors: Adults; Hospitals; *Locus of Control;
Nurses; Nursing; *Opinions; *Patients; Physi-
cians; Rating Scales
Identifiers: Illness; Patient Attitudes;
*Powerlessness
Availability: ERIC Document Reproduction Ser-
vice; 3900 Wheeler Ave., Alexandria, VA 22304
(ED171763, 842 pages)
Target Audience: Adults
Notes: Items, 8

This volume consists of a series of psychosocial and physiological clinical nursing instruments. The instruments
were selected from the published literature in health care,
education, psychology, and the social sciences. Instruments
focus upon nursing practice and stress patient variables.
Instrument was designed to elicit patient's perception of
his/her control over illness, physicians, nurses, and hospitals.

10069
Health Locus of Control Scale. Wallston, Barbara
S.; And Others 1976
Descriptors: *Adults; Beliefs; *Health; *Locus of
Control; Rating Scales
Identifiers: HLC
Availability: ERIC Document Reproduction Ser-
vice; 3900 Wheeler Ave., Alexandria, VA 22304
(ED171763, 842 pages)
Target Audience: Adults
Notes: Items, 11

This volume consists of a series of psychosocial and physiological clinical nursing instruments. The instruments
were selected from the published literature in health care,
education, psychology, and the social sciences. Instruments
focus upon nursing practice and stress patient variables.
Instrument was designed to assess the type and extent of
control an individual believes he (she) has over his (her)
own state of health.

10070
Health Perception Questionnaire. Ware, John E.
1976
Descriptors: Adults; Beliefs; *Health; Rating
Scales; Self Concept Measures; *Self Evaluation
(Individuals)
Identifiers: HPQ
Availability: ERIC Document Reproduction Ser-
vice; 3900 Wheeler Ave., Alexandria, VA 22304
(ED171763, 842 pages)
Target Audience: Adults
Notes: Time, 7 approx.; Items, 32

This volume consists of a series of psychosocial and physiological clinical nursing instruments. The instruments
were selected from the published literature in health care,
education, psychology, and the social sciences. Instruments
focus upon nursing practice and stress patient variables.
Instrument elicits subject's perceptions in several areas
including current health, prior health, health outlook,
health worry/concern, resistance-susceptibility, and rejection of sick role.

10088
Washington Symptom Checklist. Wimberger,
Herbert C.; Gregory, Robert J. 1968
Descriptors: *Adolescents; Adults; Behavior Prob-
lems; Behavior Rating Scales; *Children; Emo-
tional Problems; Mental Health Clinics; *Parent
Attitudes; *Parents
Identifiers: Psychiatric Patients; WSCL
Availability: ERIC Document Reproduction Ser-
vice; 3900 Wheeler Ave., Alexandria, VA 22304
(ED171763, 842 pages)
Target Audience: 6-17
Notes: Time, 20 approx.; Items, 76

This volume consists of a series of psychosocial and physiological clinical nursing instruments. The instruments
were selected from the published literature in health care,
education, psychology, and the social sciences. Instruments
focus upon nursing practice and stress patient variables.
Instrument was developed to assess parents' perceptions of
the behaviors of their children for whom they are seeking
professional psychiatric help. Also assesses parents' motivation in seeking help. It is preferable for each parent to
complete the instrument so that the professional has 2
sources of information about the child.

10106
Prenatal Questionnaire. Lowe, Marie L. 1970
Descriptors: Adults; Behavior Patterns; Followup
Studies; *Medical Services; *Nurses; Nursing;
Nutrition; *Patients; *Pregnancy; Public Health
Identifiers: *Patient Attitudes
Availability: ERIC Document Reproduction Ser-
vice; 3900 Wheeler Ave., Alexandria, VA 22304
(ED171763, 842 pages)
Target Audience: Adults
Notes: Time, 30 approx.; Items, 83

This volume consists of a series of psychosocial and physiological clinical nursing instruments. The instruments
were selected from the published literature in health care,
education, psychology, and the social sciences. Instruments
focus upon nursing practice and stress patient variables.
Instrument was designed to measure patients' attitudes
toward, and behavioral compliance with, a regimen pre-
scribed during prenatal care. Administered at the outset of
prenatal care and near the end of pregnancy. There are
also 13 items concerning the outcome of delivery and
public health nursing followup.

10124
Religious Orientation. Allport, Gordon W. 1968
Subtests: Extrinsic; Intrinsic
Descriptors: Adults; Beliefs; *Religion; Social At-
titudes; Values
Identifiers: *Religious Attitudes
Availability: ADI Auxiliary Publications Project;
Photoduplication Service, Library of Congress,
Washington, DC 20025 (Doc. No. 9268)
Target Audience: Adults
Notes: Items, 20

Designed to assess extrinsic and intrinsic tendencies in
respondent's religious life.

10140
Socio-Sexual Knowledge and Attitudes Test.
Wish, Joel; And Others 1977
Subtests: Anatomy Terminology; Dating; Mar-
riage; Intimacy; Intercourse; Pregnancy, Child-
birth and Childbearing; Menstruation; Mastur-
bation; Homosexuality; Alcohol and Drugs;
Community Risks and Hazards; Birth Control;
Venereal Disease; Terminology Check
Descriptors: *Achievement Tests; Adjustment (to
Environment); Adults; Attitudes; Family Life
Education; Individual Testing; Institutionalized
Persons; *Mild Mental Retardation; *Moderate
Mental Retardation; Normalization
(Handicapped); *Screening Tests; Self Concept
Measures; Self Evaluation (Individuals); Sex
Differences; *Sexuality; Social Attitudes; Social
Cognition; Social Development
Identifiers: Oral Tests; Sex Knowledge and At-
titude Test; SSKAT
Availability: ERIC Document Reproduction Ser-
vice; 3900 Wheeler Ave., Alexandria, VA 22304
(ED160643, microfiche only).
Target Audience: Adults
Notes: Time, 100 approx.; Items, 250

Developed to measure a mildly or moderately retarded
person's sociosexual knowledge and attitudes as well as
how much he or she thinks that he or she knows about
each subject. Also includes evaluation on the Adaptive
Behavior Scale (Nihira et al., rev. 74). Used to determine
the sociosexual instruction needed and as an achievement
and attitude test after instruction is given. Based upon the
trend that returns mentally retarded persons to the community and the corresponding sociosexual adjustment
which this return involves. Answers require very short
statements, pointing to a picture, and/or selection among
multiple choices. Requires the use of pictures and photographs for some subtests. No more than 5 subtests
should be given in one session of approximately 30 minutes. Individually administered.

10149
Science Activities Checklist. Skinner, Ray, Jr.;
Barcikowski, Robert S. 1973
Descriptors: Biology; Earth Science; Junior High
Schools; *Junior High School Students; Physics;
Questionnaires; Rating Scales; *Science Curricu-
lum; *Student Attitudes
Availability: Journal of Research in Science Teach-
ing;v10 n2 p153-58, 1973
Grade Level: 7-8
Notes: Items, 48

The Science Activities Checklist, which was revised from
the Reed activities checklist, measures interest in biological, earth, and physical science. The questionnaire deals
with activities the students have done during the past 6
months and asks the student to indicate which of these
things the student did on his/her own because the student
wanted to and to indicate the number of times the activity
was done.

10150
**A Physical Education Attitude Scale for the Inter-
mediate Level in Elementary Schools.** Martens,
Fred L. 1979
Descriptors: *Elementary School Students; *Grade
7; Intermediate Grades; *Physical Education;
*Student Attitudes
Availability: Journal of Experimental Educa-
tion;v47 n3 p239-47, 1979
Grade Level: 4-7
Notes: Items, 29

Designed to measure student attitudes toward physical
education in grades 4-7.

10152
Sex Attitude Survey. Fretz, Bruce R. 1974
Descriptors: *Adults; *College Students; Higher
Education; Semantic Differential; Sex Educa-
tion; Sexuality
Identifiers: *Sexual Attitudes
Availability: Bruce R. Fretz; Psychology Dept.,
University of Maryland, College Park, MD
20742
Grade Level: 13-16
Target Audience: 18-64

Designed to assess respondent's attitudes toward certain
sexual behaviors. May also be used to measure changes in
attitude resulting from sex education courses.

10155
Perception of Parent Behavior Scale. Apperson,
Louise Behrens
Descriptors: Adjustment (to Environment); Adults;
Childhood Attitudes; Parent Child Relationship;
*Parent Influence; *Patients; Psychiatric Hos-
pitals; Schizophrenia
Identifiers: Psychiatric Patients
Availability: Louise B. Apperson; 1196 Dallas, Au-
rora, CO 80010
Target Audience: Adults
Notes: Items, 90

Designed to determine the relationship between perception
of parent behavior and development of mental illness or
drug and alcohol addiction in adults. Individual forms for
mothers and fathers. Each parent form has a parallel
alternate form.

10158
Attitudes toward Abortion Scale. Murray, Frank
S.; And Others 1971
Descriptors: *Abortions; Adults; *Physicians
Identifiers: TIM(G)
Availability: Tests in Microfiche; Test Collection,
Educational Testing Service, Princeton, NJ
08541
Target Audience: Adults
Notes: Items, 27

Used to measure attitudes toward abortion of physicians
residing in 2 different geographical locations with different
laws toward abortion.

10170
Child Abuse Questionnaire. Friedrich, Bill; Clark,
Linda
Descriptors: Adults; *Child Abuse; *Judges; Ques-
tionnaires
Availability: NAPS Document; Microfiche Publi-
cations, P.O. Box 3513, Grand Central Station,
New York, NY 10017 (Doc. No. 03173)
Target Audience: Adults
Notes: Items, 50

Used to survey judges concerning their opinions about
child abuse.

10172
Propositions about Reading Instruction. Duffy,
Gerald G.; Metheny, William 1978
Subtests: Basal; Linear Skills; Interest; Natural
Language; Integrated Whole
Descriptors: Adults; Rating Scales; *Reading In-
struction; Reading Processes; *Teacher Atti-
tudes; *Teachers; Likert Scales
Availability: Institute for Research on Teaching;
252 Erickson Hall, Michigan State University,
East Lansing, MI 48824
Target Audience: Adults
Notes: Items, 45

Used to assess teachers' generalized reading beliefs as
these beliefs influence both instruction practice and pupil
outcomes.

10173
First Impressions. Rosen, Sidney 1977
Descriptors: *College Students; Higher Education;
*Peer Teaching; Rating Scales; Role Theory;
*Student Attitudes; *Tutoring
Availability: Sidney Rosen; Institute for Behav-
ioral Research, University of Georgia, 624
Graduate Studies Research Center, Athens, GA
30602
Grade Level: 13-16
Notes: Items, 10

Used to test a theoretical model that attaches greater
desirability to being the tutor rather than tutee and to
being in an equitable (status congruent) rather than inequitable relationship.

10174
Second Impressions. Rosen, Sidney 1977
Descriptors: *College Students; Higher Education;
*Peer Teaching; Rating Scales; Role Theory;
*Student Attitudes; *Tutoring

Availability: Sidney Rosen; Institute for Behavioral Research, University of Georgia, 624 Graduate Studies Research Center, Athens, GA 30602
Grade Level: 13–16
Notes: Items, 12

Used to test a theoretical model that attaches greater desirability to being the tutor rather than the tutee and to being in an equitable (status congruent) rather than inequitable relationship. In addition to items paralleling those in First Impressions questionnaire (TC010173), includes items dealing with participant's own and inferred partner's estimate of felt indebtedness and desire to switch roles.

10175
Third Impressions. Rosen, Sidney 1977
Descriptors: *College Students; Higher Education; *Peer Teaching; Rating Scales; Role Theory; *Student Attitudes; *Tutoring
Availability: Sidney Rosen; Institute for Behavioral Research, University of Georgia, 624 Graduate Studies Research Center, Athens, GA 30602
Grade Level: 13–16
Notes: Items, 20

Used to test a theoretical model that attaches greater desirability to being the tutor rather than the tutee and to being in an equitable (status congruent) rather than an inequitable relationship. Contains items identical to those in Second Impressions (TC010174) and supplementary items intended to measure prior familiarity and degree of between-sessions social contact of the members within each pair.

10176
Smiley. Rosen, Sidney 1978
Descriptors: Elementary Education; *Grade 6; *Junior High School Students; *Peer Teaching; Pictorial Stimuli; Pretests Posttests; Rating Scales; Role Theory; *Student Attitudes; *Tutoring
Availability: Sidney Rosen; Institute for Behavioral Research, University of Georgia, 624 Graduate Studies Research Center, Athens, GA 30602
Grade Level: 6–8
Notes: Items, 14

Used in a study which investigated the effects of status level and status congruence on achievement and satisfaction of junior high classmates undergoing same-age peer tutoring. This attitude measure is part of a study and deals with perceptions of student's own performance and in the area of satisfaction, dealing with feelings such as enjoyment, importance, usefulness. There are 2 tests, a Pre-Smiley and a Post-Smiley, each consisting of 7 items.

10178
Criminal Attitude Scale. Taylor, A.J.W. 1968
Descriptors: Adults; Attitude Change; Crime; Criminal Law; *Criminals
Identifiers: CATS
Availability: Journal of Criminal Law, Criminology, and Political Science;v51 n1 p37-40, 1968
Target Audience: Adults
Notes: Items, 15

Measures attitudes and opinions of criminals regarding criminal justice, law enforcement, and feelings of despair. Object is to assess degree of criminality and change of attitude as a result of treatment or contamination.

10183
Transactional Analysis of Personality and Environment. Pervin, Lawrence A.; Rubin, Donald B.
Subtests: My College; My Self; Students; Faculty; Administration; Ideal College
Descriptors: *College Students; Higher Education; Peer Evaluation; *Rating Scales; *Self Concept; Semantic Differential; *Student Attitudes; *Student College Relationship; *Student Evaluation of Teacher Performance
Identifiers: TAPE; TIM(E)
Availability: Tests in Microfiche; Test Collection, Educational Testing Service, Princeton, NJ 08541
Grade Level: 13–16
Notes: Items, 336

Designed to measure student perceptions of college and his/her self. Descriptive scales are provided. Students are to decide which adjective is most appropriate and how strongly he/she would apply the adjective by circling a rating on the scale. Forms A and B are available.

10185
Dental Anxiety Scale. Corah, Norman L. 1968
Descriptors: Adults; *Anxiety; *Dentistry; Dentists; Fear; *Patients
Identifiers: *Patient Attitudes
Availability: Journal of Dental Research;v48 n4 p596, Jul-Aug 1969
Target Audience: Adults
Notes: Items, 4

Brief instrument to assess dental anxiety. Administered to patients waiting to see a dentist.

10187
Sophistication of Reading Interests Scale. Zais, Robert S. 1968
Descriptors: High Schools; *High School Students; Literature Appreciation; *Reading Interests; Secondary Education
Identifiers: SRIS; The Research Instruments Project
Availability: ERIC Document Reproduction Service; 3900 Wheeler Ave., Alexandria, VA 22304 (ED091756, 28 pages)
Grade Level: 9–12
Notes: Time, 30 approx.; Items, 29

Designed to assess high school students' maturity of reading interests in fiction.

10202
Free Speech Questionnaire. Shimkunas, Algimantas; Kime, Ronald 1973
Descriptors: *College Students; *Freedom of Speech; Higher Education; *Locus of Control; *Student Attitudes; Student Behavior
Availability: Journal of Personality Assessment;v35 n6 p561-68, 1973
Grade Level: 13–16
Notes: Items, 5

Designed to measure the degree of support of students on a freedom of speech issue by determining the level of behavior they would exhibit in support of an issue. Through the questionnaire, it was hoped to prove that student activist behavior is related to locus of control.

10203
School Performance Checklist. Macy, Daniel J.
Descriptors: Adults; *Behavior Rating Scales; Children; *Exceptional Persons; *Special Education; Student Behavior; *Student Evaluation; *Teacher Attitudes
Identifiers: TIM(E)
Availability: Tests in Microfiche; Test Collection, Educational Testing Service, Princeton, NJ 08541
Target Audience: Adults
Notes: Items, 27

Developed for use with children in special education classes. Designed to measure teacher perceptions of how special students function within the classroom and school setting.

10205
Guidance Attitude Differential. Miller, G. Dean; Boller, Jon D. 1975
Descriptors: Administrator Attitudes; *Administrators; Adults; Counselor Attitudes; *Counselor Educators; *Counselor Role; *Counselors; Semantic Differential; Teacher Attitudes; *Teachers
Identifiers: GAD
Availability: Dr. G. Dean Miller; Lincoln Square, 622 N. 3rd St., Stillwater, MN 55082
Target Audience: Adults

A semantic differential scale designed to assess attitudes toward various counselor functions.

10206
Perception of Counselor Tasks. Miller, G. Dean; Boller, Jon D. 1975
Descriptors: Adults; *Counselor Evaluation; *Counselor Role; *Counselors; Counselor Training; *Teacher Attitudes; Teachers
Identifiers: POCT
Availability: Dr. G. Dean Miller; Lincoln Square, 622 N. 3rd St., Stillwater, MN 55082
Target Audience: Adults
Notes: Items, 53

Designed to assess teachers' and institution's perceptions of counselor tasks.

10207
Student Guidance Questionnaire. Miller, G. Dean; Boller, Jon D. 1975
Descriptors: Adults; Counselor Evaluation; *Counselor Role; *Counselors; School Counselors; Secondary School Students; *Student Attitudes
Identifiers: SGQ
Availability: Dr. G. Dean Miller; Lincoln Square, 622 N. 3rd St., Stillwater, MN 55082
Grade Level: 9–12
Notes: Items, 32

Designed to assess students' opinions of various aspects of counselor's activities.

10225
Measuring Student Opinion of a College Basic Skills Program. Michaels, Linda A. 1978

Descriptors: Basic Skills; *College Freshmen; *Course Evaluation; Higher Education; *Participant Satisfaction; Skill Development; Student Attitudes
Availability: ERIC Document Reproduction Service; 3900 Wheeler Ave., Alexandria, VA 22304 (ED167628, 20 pages)
Grade Level: 13
Notes: Items, 14

Designed to measure student opinions of college basic skills course.

10226
Alpha-Omega Completed Sentence Form. Klein, Ronald; And Others 1978
Subtests: Denial; Anger; Bargaining; Depression; Acceptance
Descriptors: *Adjustment (to Environment); *College Students; *Death; Grief; Higher Education; Student Attitudes
Identifiers: AOCSF; Kubler Ross (Elisabeth)
Availability: ERIC Document Reproduction Service; 3900 Wheeler Ave., Alexandria, VA 22304 (ED167618, 27 pages)
Grade Level: 13–20
Notes: Items, 50

Developed to identify and measure individual's adaptational approaches to information concerning his or her own death or the possible death of a significant other.

10236
Client's Personal Reaction Questionnaire. Ashby, Jefferson D.; And Others 1957
Descriptors: *Adults; Affective Measures; Attitudes; *Counselor Client Relationship; *Counselor Evaluation; Rating Scales
Identifiers: Defensiveness; Positive Attitudes
Availability: Psychological Monographs;v71 n24 Whole No. 453, 1957
Target Audience: Adults
Notes: Time, 15 approx.; Items, 80

Designed to assess clients' reactions to personal counseling and their attitudes toward counselor.

10237
Human Relations Incident. Dedrick, Charles V.
Descriptors: Adults; *Attitudes; College Students; Perception; *Personality Assessment; Projective Measures
Identifiers: TIM(E)
Availability: Tests in Microfiche; Test Collection, Educational Testing Service, Princeton, NJ 08541
Target Audience: Adults

Subject describes a significant, human relations event from the past. From the thoughts and feelings related, a group of judges make inferences about the subject's perceptual or internal point of view.

10242
Questionnaire to Measure the Values of Pupils, Parents and School Personnel. Ryan, T.A. 1975
Subtests: Persistence; Competition; Success; Good Grades; Manners; Status; Risks; Work; Honesty; Religion; Authority; Family; Leadership; Materialism; Altruism; Friends; Discipline
Descriptors: Adolescents; Adults; Children; Grades (Scholastic); Intermediate Grades; *Parent Attitudes; Questionnaires; School Attitudes; *School Personnel; *School Role; Secondary Education; *Student Attitudes; *Values
Identifiers: TIM(F)
Availability: Tests in Microfiche; Test Collection, Educational Testing Service, Princeton, NJ 08541
Target Audience: 10–65
Notes: Time, 60 approx.; Items, 136

An assessment of beliefs and values that have been influenced by schools and educational goals and curricula.

10263
The Projective Assessment of Aging Method. Starr, Bernard D.; And Others 1979
Descriptors: Adult Development; *Aging (Individuals); *Gerontology; *Older Adults; Pictorial Stimuli; *Projective Measures
Identifiers: PAAM
Availability: Springer Publishing Co.; 200 Park Ave., S., New York, NY 10003
Target Audience: 65–99
Notes: Time, 45 approx.; Items, 14

A projective technique to assess feelings, attitudes, and perceptions of older adults. Respondent examines a series of pictures depicting scenes related to the aging process and themes of aging.

10293
Kelly-Tharp Marriage Role Questionnaire. Tharp, Roland 1963

Subtests: Internal Instrumentality; Division of Responsibility; Solidarity; External Relations; Sexuality
Descriptors: Adults; Marriage; *Marriage Counseling; *Role Perception; *Spouses
Identifiers: MRQ
*Availability: Marriage and Family Living;*v25 p389-404, Nov 1963
Target Audience: Adults
Notes: Items, 147

Designed to assess role expectations and role enactment of husbands and wives. Items are paired and disparity in expectation and enactment scores are determined. Separate forms for males and females.

10297
Career Behavior and Attitude Checklist Questionnaire. O'Neill, James M.; Price, Gary E. 1979
Subtests: Satisfaction with Career Planning Process; Clarity and Certainty of Ideas about Career Planning; Time Spent Thinking about Career Planning
Descriptors: *Career Counseling; *College Freshmen; Higher Education; *Interest Inventories; Questionnaires; *Student Attitudes; Student Behavior
Identifiers: TIM(G)
Availability: Tests in Microfiche; Test Collection, Educational Testing Service, Princeton, NJ 08541
Grade Level: 13
Notes: Items, 17

After administration of the Strong-Campbell Interest Inventory and the Self-Directed Search, college freshmen were tested to measure their attitudes and behaviors related to interest inventories.

10298
Career Interest Inventory Reaction Questionnaire. O'Neill, James M.; Price, Gary E. 1979
Subtests: Career Stimulation; Response to Testing; Clarity of Directions; Certainty about Career Planning
Descriptors: Career Counseling; *College Freshmen; Higher Education; *Interest Inventories; Questionnaires; *Student Attitudes; Testing; Likert Scales
Identifiers: Strong Campbell Interest Inventory; TIM(G)
Availability: Tests in Microfiche; Test Collection, Educational Testing Service, Princeton, NJ 08541
Grade Level: 13
Notes: Items, 15

Concerns subject's perceptions of interest testing immediately after a 4-hour testing workshop.

10302
Rating Scales of Children's Attitudes toward the Physically Handicapped. Rapier, Jacqueline; And Others 1969
Subtests: About Orthopedically Handicapped Children; Teacher Class Rating Scale; Orthopedically Handicapped Children-Teacher Scale
Descriptors: Adults; *Elementary Education; *Mainstreaming; Questionnaires; Rating Scales; Semantic Differential; *Student Attitudes; *Teacher Attitudes; Teachers
Identifiers: *Orthopedically Handicapped; TIM(G)
Availability: Tests in Microfiche; Test Collection, Educational Testing Service, Princeton, NJ 08541
Grade Level: 3-6
Target Audience: Adults
Notes: Items, 59

Three instruments investigate attitudes toward orthopedically handicapped children related to their integration into a regular classroom. Children select phrases they feel are descriptive of orthopedically handicapped (OH) students. Teachers rate OH children on a 7-point semantic differential and describe the behavior and difficulties in an integrated class.

10316
Inventory of Beliefs. Anthony, Sally M. 1966
Descriptors: *Beliefs; Bias; Economics; High Schools; *High School Students; Marriage; Moral Values; Patriotism; Questionnaires; Religion; Sexuality; Social Class; *Social Problems
Identifiers: Contradiction Inventory; Courtship; TIM(I)
Availability: Tests in Microfiche; Test Collection, Educational Testing Service, Princeton, NJ 08541
Grade Level: 9-12
Notes: Items, 102

Originally constructed as experimental instrument to measure contradictory beliefs in 6 controversial areas: sex, courtship, and marriage; economics; prejudice; nationalism and patriotism; social class; religion and morality. Used to measure differences between students in grade 9 and grade 12 with respect to contradictory beliefs in 6 areas and to investigate differences between male and female students. Developed by taking statements from the literature which were assumed to represent common American beliefs.

10325
Bloom Sentence Completion Survey (Student). Bloom, Wallace 1974
Subtests: Age Mates; Physical Self; Family; Psychological Self; Self-Directedness; Education; Accomplishment; Irritants
Descriptors: *Elementary School Students; Elementary Secondary Education; Family Attitudes; Individual Testing; *Mild Mental Retardation; *Projective Measures; School Attitudes; *Secondary School Students; Self Concept; *Student Attitudes
Availability: Stoelting Company; 620 Wheat Ln., Wood Dale, IL 60191
Grade Level: 1-12
Notes: Time, 25 approx.; Items, 40

Designed to reveal subject's attitudes toward important factors in everyday living. Items were constructed to reveal data of significance regarding attitudes toward age mates; physical self; family; psychological self; self-directedness; education; accomplishment and irritants. Examiner should offer to record responses so that survey will be completed more quickly; answers will be unedited and will allow subjects to enjoy opportunity to dictate to someone who will do writing for them.

10327
Job Performance Scale. E.F. Wonderlic and Associates, Northfield, IL 1977
Subtests: General Ability to Learn and Perform on Job; General Attitude toward Job
Descriptors: Ability; Adults; Behavior Rating Scales; *Employee Attitudes; *Employees; *Job Performance; Occupational Tests; Personnel Evaluation; Supervisors
Availability: E.F. Wonderlic and Associates; 820 Frontage Rd., Northfield, IL 60093
Target Audience: 18-64
Notes: Items, 55

Designed to enable ranking of employees on 3 scales: general ability to learn and perform on the job, general attitude toward job, and combined productivity-attitude ranking. Two rating forms are used. Form 2 is shorter but more detailed than Form 1.

10337
Marital Adjustment and Prediction Tests. Locke, Harvey J.; Wallace, Karl M. 1959
Subtests: Marital Adjustment; Marital Prediction
Descriptors: *Adults; *Marital Satisfaction; *Marriage; Predictive Measurement; *Spouses
Identifiers: Self Report Measures
*Availability: Marriage and Family Living;*v26 p251-55, Aug 1959
Target Audience: Adults
Notes: Items, 50

Designed to assess current marital adjustment and predict future marital adjustment. The marital adjustment section contains 15 items, and the marital prediction section consists of 35 items.

10344
Family Decision-Making Attitude Scale. Stanley, Sheila F. 1978
Descriptors: *Adolescents; Adults; *Childhood Attitudes; *Conflict Resolution; *Decision Making; Family (Sociological Unit); Family Attitudes; Family Life; *Parent Attitudes; *Parents
Identifiers: FDMAS
Availability: Sheila F. Stanley; Dir.; Contoocook Valley Mental Health Center, Box 117, Henniker, NH 03242
Target Audience: 13-64
Notes: Items, 12

Designed to measure attitudes of parents and adolescent children concerning how rules and decisions over conflicts should be made in families.

10352
Management Profiling: As Others See You. Daniels, Philip B.; And Others 1975
Subtests: Goals; Communication; Decision Making; Motivation; Influence-Interaction; Control; Leadership
Descriptors: Adults; Behavior Rating Scales; Decision Making; *Employee Attitudes; *Employees; *Employer Attitudes; *Feedback; Interpersonal Communication; Leadership Qualities; Leadership Styles; Management Development; Motivation; Peer Evaluation; Self Evaluation (Individuals); *Supervisors
Identifiers: MPQ; Supervision Attitudes; *Supervisor Evaluation; Supervisor Subordinate Relationship
Availability: Behavioral Science Resources; P.O. Box 411, Provo, UT 84603

Target Audience: Adults
Notes: Items, 43

Designed to provide feedback from subordinates to management and supervisory personnel. Employee describes manager's behavior as it is and how he/she would like it to be. Additional questionnaires permit managers to record self-perceptions and receive feedback from a superior, peer, or colleague. Four systems of management are described: passive authoritative, benevolent authoritative, consultative, participative.

10385
What Do You Believe? McLean, Milton D. 1952
Descriptors: *Adults; Beliefs; *Christianity; Higher Education; Rating Scales; *Religion; *Undergraduate Students
Identifiers: Approaches to Measurement in Religious Education; Religious World Views
Availability: ERIC Document Reproduction Service; 3900 Wheeler Ave., Alexandria, VA 22304 (ED170300, 30 pages)
Grade Level: 13-16
Target Audience: Adults
Notes: Items, 25

Designed to assess individual's theological beliefs. Scores range from "naturalistic humanism" (0-35) through "religious liberalism" (35-65) to "Christian orthodoxy" (65-100).

10410
Manager Feedback Program. Hinrichs, John R. 1978
Descriptors: Administrator Characteristics; *Administrator Evaluation; *Administrators; Adults; *Employee Attitudes; Feedback; Management Development; Rating Scales; Work Environment
Identifiers: MFP
Availability: Management Decision Systems; 108 Old Kings Hwy. N., Darien, CT 06820
Target Audience: 18-64
Notes: Items, 44

Designed to provide systematic feedback to managers concerning subordinates' evaluations of daily performance. Useful in identifying management development needs.

10428
Attitudes toward Old People Scale. Kogan, Nathan 1961
Descriptors: Higher Education; *Older Adults; Student Attitudes; *Undergraduate Students; Likert Scales
Identifiers: Old People Scale
*Availability: Journal of Abnormal and Social Psychology;*v62 n1 p44-54, 1961
Grade Level: 13-16
Notes: Items, 17

Designed to assess undergraduate students' attitudes toward old people. Two scales of 17 items each were developed. One scale contained all positive statements, and the second consisted of all negative statements.

10429
Counselor Self-Evaluation Scale. Mozee, Elliott
Descriptors: *Competence; *Counselor Role; *Interests; *Rating Scales; *Self Evaluation (Individuals); Two Year Colleges
*Availability: Personnel and Guidance Journal;*v51 n4 p285-87, Dec 1972
Grade Level: 13-14
Notes: Items, 32

Designed to enable counselors to review their professional interests and competencies, excluding counseling physically handicapped individuals or students with health problems. Self-ratings are in 2 areas: counselor's level of interest and level of competence.

10431
The Socio-Sexual Knowledge and Attitude Test. Wish, Joel; And Others 1976
Subtests: Anatomy Terminology; Menstruation; Dating; Marriage; Intimacy; Intercourse; Pregnancy; Childbirth; Child Rearing; Birth Control; Masturbation; Homosexuality; Venereal Disease; Alcohol and Drugs; Community Risks and Hazards; Terminology Check
Descriptors: Adults; Developmental Disabilities; Individual Testing; *Knowledge Level; *Language Handicaps; *Mental Retardation; *Sexuality
Identifiers: SSKAT
Availability: Stoelting Company; 620 Wheat Ln., Wood Dale, IL 60191
Target Audience: Adults
Notes: Items, 240

Developed for developmentally disabled persons, including mentally retarded individuals who are not verbally proficient or for those whose speech is unintelligible. Used to determine what this population knows or believes about areas of sociosexual functioning and what their attitudes are toward sociosexual practices. There are 14 subscores for the knowledge section. For the attitude section, there are 11 subscores: menstruation; dating; marriage; intimacy; intercourse; pregnancy; childbirth and child rearing; masturbation; homosexuality; alcohol and drugs; community risks and hazards. Individually administered.

10436
Arizona Course/Instructor Evaluation Questionnaire: Form 75. Aleamoni, Lawrence M. 1978
Subtests: General Course Attitude; Method of Instruction; Course Content; Interest and Attention; Instructor
Descriptors: *Course Evaluation; Higher Education; Student Attitudes; *Student Evaluation of Teacher Performance; Teacher Effectiveness; *Undergraduate Students
Identifiers: CIEQ
Availability: ERIC Document Reproduction Service; 3900 Wheeler Ave., Alexandria, VA 22304-5110 (ED171721, microfiche only)
Grade Level: 13–16
Notes: Items, 21
Designed to determine students' evaluation of instructor's teaching techniques and course content. Useful for instructor's self-improvement.

10440
RCA Missile Survey (Supervisory Questionnaire). Schoonmaker, Robert L. 1974
Subtests: Technical and Professional Knowledge; Organization Knowledge; Public Knowledge; Analytical and Decision-Making Skills; Interpersonal Skills
Descriptors: *Administrator Evaluation; Administrators; Adults; *Employee Attitudes; *Employees; *Management Development; Rating Scales; Supervisors
Availability: Robert L. Schoonmaker, Dir.; Training and Development, The Provident National Bank, Broad & Chestnut Sts., P.O. Box 7648, Philadelphia, PA 19101
Target Audience: Adults
Notes: Time, 20 approx.; Items, 24
Designed to provide information about manager's knowledge and skills as perceived by his subordinates. Management trainer interviews employee privately after questionnaire has been completed. Useful instrument for providing feedback to managers.

10441
Student Learning Scales. Cross, K.P. 1979
Descriptors: Course Evaluation; Higher Education; *Learning Experience; Outcomes of Education; Rating Scales; Self Evaluation (Individuals); *Student Attitudes; *Student Evaluation of Teacher Performance; *Undergraduate Students
Identifiers: SLS
Availability: ERIC Document Reproduction Service; 3900 Wheeler Ave., Alexandria, VA 22304 (ED173431, 78 pages)
Grade Level: 13–16
Notes: Items, 54
Designed for students to evaluate teacher performance, course content, and their own reactions to learning experiences.

10445
Survey of Working Relations. Wilson, Clark L. 1980
Subtests: Clarification of Goals and Objectives; Encouragement of Upward Communications and Participation; Orderly Work Planning; Expertise; Work Facilitation; Feedback; Time Emphasis; Control of Details; Goal Pressure; Delegation (Permissiveness); Fair and Enlarging Work Allocation; Approachability; Teambuilding; Interest in Subordinate Growth; Recognizing and Reinforcing Performance
Descriptors: Adults; *Employee Attitudes; Employer Employee Relationship; *Occupational Tests; Supervisors; *Supervisory Methods; Work Attitudes; Work Environment
Availability: Clark L. Wilson; Box 471, New Canaan, CT 06840
Target Audience: Adults
Notes: Items, 145
Part of a Survey of Management practices for use by managers, superiors, or peers to make observations about a particular manager. This survey is for use by subordinates. (See also TC012403 and TC012404.) All of the surveys measure 11 dimensions.

10446
Sex Attitude Scale. Rotter, George S. 1973
Subtests: Adjustment-Maladjustment; Liberal-Conservative; Sex Education; Homosexuality; Self-Image; Affective Dimension; Behavioral; Cognitive

Descriptors: Adjustment (to Environment); Adults; Behavior Patterns; Homosexuality; Knowledge Level; Self Concept; *Sex Education; *Sexuality; Teacher Attitudes; Teachers; Conservatism; Liberalism; Likert Scales
Identifiers: TIM(G)
Availability: Tests in Microfiche; Test Collection, Educational Testing Service, Princeton, NJ 08541
Target Audience: Adults
Notes: Items, 100
Designed to assess sex attitudes of teachers and potential teachers of sex education courses via a 7-point agree-disagree Likert scale.

10454
Community College Goals Inventory. American Assoc. of Community and Junior Colleges, Washington, DC; Educational Testing Service, Princeton, NJ 1979
Descriptors: Academic Freedom; Accountability; Adults; Career Guidance; *Community Colleges; Community Services; Counseling Services; Cultural Activities; Educational Attitudes; Faculty Development; Higher Education; Lifelong Learning; Organizational Climate; *Organizational Objectives; Rating Scales; Student Welfare
Identifiers: CCGI
Availability: School and Higher Education Programs; Educational Testing Service, Princeton, NJ 08541
Grade Level: 13–14
Notes: Time, 45; Items, 118
Designed to help community colleges define their goals and set priorities. Results are reported for groups, e.g., faculty students, administration. Respondents rate current degree of importance of each goal on a 5-point scale and indicate how important they feel each goal should be.

10458
Premarital Sexual Permissiveness Scales. Reiss, Ira L. 1964
Descriptors: *Adults; Dating (Social); Females; Males; Sexuality
Identifiers: Grittman Scales; Premarital Sex; *Premarital Sexual Standards; *Sexual Attitudes; Sexual Permissiveness
Availability: Journal of Marriage and the Family;v26 n2 p188-98, May 1964
Target Audience: Adults
Notes: Items, 12
Designed to assess attitudes toward premarital sexual permissiveness. Twelve-item scale may be administered in terms of male standards and female standards. Results of scale may be used to identify individual as one of several scale types.

10461
You and Death. Shneidman, Edwin S. 1970
Descriptors: *Adults; Beliefs; Biographical Inventories; *Death; Religion; Suicide; Wills
Identifiers: Death Anxiety; *Death Attitudes; Funerals; Self Administered Tests
Availability: Psychology Today;v4 n3 p67-72, Aug 1970
Target Audience: Adults
Notes: Time, 20 approx.; Items, 75
Designed to assess individuals' attitudes about death, suicide, wills, death rituals, and afterlife. The items are written at a tenth grade readability level.

10472
Interethnic Attitude Scale. Stephan, Walter G. 1973
Subtests: Attitude Scale-Mexican American; Black; White; Contact Scale; Background
Descriptors: Blacks; *Elementary School Students; *Ethnic Groups; *Ethnicity; *Ethnic Relations; Intermediate Grades; Mexican Americans; *Racial Attitudes; *Racial Integration; Semantic Differential; Social Integration; Whites
Identifiers: TIM(G)
Availability: Tests in Microfiche; Test Collection, Educational Testing Service, Princeton, NJ 08541
Grade Level: 4–5
Notes: Time, 45; Items, 30
Black, Mexican-American, and white students rate one another via 3 forms of a semantic differential describing students' temperament, social relations, work habits, and other characteristics. Also includes a scale designed to measure frequency of social contacts with other ethnic groups.

10479
Expectations about Counseling. Tinsley, Howard E.A. 1980

Subtests: Motivation; Openness; Responsibility; Realism; Acceptance; Confrontation; Directiveness; Empathy; Genuineness; Nurturance; Self-Disclosure; Attractiveness; Expertise; Tolerance; Trustworthiness; Concreteness; Immediacy; Quality of Outcome
Descriptors: Adults; *Counseling; Counseling Objectives; Counselor Attitudes; Counselor Client Relationship; Expectation; Motivation; Rating Scales
Availability: Howard E.A. Tinsley; Dept. of Psychology, Southern Illinois University, Carbondale, IL 62901
Target Audience: 18–64
Notes: Items, 152
Rating scale designed to determine future counselees' perceptions of the counseling process and of what it may consist. Covers client attitudes and behaviors, client characteristics, counselor attitudes and behaviors, counselor characteristics, characteristics of process, quality of outcome.

10532
Just World Scale. Rubin, Zick; Peplau, Letitia Anne 1975
Descriptors: *Adults; Beliefs; Higher Education; *Justice; Social Attitudes; *Undergraduate Students
Availability: Journal of Social Issues;v31 n3 p65-89, 1975
Grade Level: 13–16
Target Audience: 18–64
Notes: Items, 20
Designed to assess respondent's belief in fate and society as just. Identifies those who believe victims of unfortunate events have deserved their fate because they behaved improperly. Assesses perceptions of social justice.

10536
The Educational Forces Inventory. Rayder, Nicholas F.; Body, Bart 1975
Descriptors: Adults; Affective Measures; *Educational Environment; *Paraprofessional School Personnel; Teacher Administrator Relationship; *Teacher Attitudes; Teacher Effectiveness; *Teacher Morale; *Teachers; Teaching Conditions
Identifiers: EFI
Availability: ERIC Document Reproduction Service; 3900 Wheeler Ave., Alexandria, VA 22304 (ED179580, 28 pages)
Target Audience: Adults
Designed to assess the relative influence upon teachers of 13 forces that are important factors in the educational setting.

10537
Illinois Problems Index. Illinois State Board of Education, Springfield 1980
Subtests: Curriculum and Instruction in Basic Skills; Curriculum and Instruction in Science; Curriculum and Instruction in Home and Health Science; Curriculum and Instruction in Cultural and Social Studies; Curriculum and Instruction in the Arts; Intercurricular Concepts; Special Programs; Resource and Support Services; Program Planning and Development; Educational Administration and Policy; Research and Evaluation
Descriptors: Administrator Attitudes; Community Attitudes; *Curriculum Problems; *Educational Planning; *Elementary Secondary Education; Evaluation Methods; Needs Assessment; Parent Attitudes; Program Evaluation; *School Districts; School Surveys
Identifiers: IPI
Availability: ERIC Document Reproduction Service; 3900 Wheeler Ave., Alexandria, VA 22304-5110 (ED179606, 175 pages)
Grade Level: K–12
Notes: Items, 51
Designed for school districts to identify and evaluate educational problems relating to curriculum and services. Useful in long-range planning and program improvement.

10538
School Subjects Attitude Scales. Alberta Dept. of Education, Edmonton Minister's Advisory Committee on Student Achievement 1979
Descriptors: Course Evaluation; *Elementary School Students; Foreign Countries; *Grade 5; *Grade 8; Intermediate Grades; Junior High Schools; *Junior High School Students; *School Attitudes; Semantic Differential; *Student Attitudes
Identifiers: Canada
Availability: ERIC Document Reproduction Service; 3900 Wheeler Ave., Alexandria, VA 22304-5110 (ED179575, 74 pages)
Grade Level: 5–8
Notes: Items, 24

Designed to assess attitudes toward school subjects of students in upper elementary grades and junior high school. Instrument distinguished between students with positive and negative school attitudes.

10539
A Parent Satisfaction Survey. Scheiner, Louis 1979
Descriptors: Adults; Diagnostic Teaching; Handicap Identification; *Individualized Education Programs; *Parent Attitudes; *Parents; Preschool Children; Program Evaluation; Rating Scales
Identifiers: *Project PEACH
Availability: ERIC Document Reproduction Service; 3900 Wheeler Ave., Alexandria, VA 22304 (ED179589, 35 pages)
Target Audience: Adults
Notes: Items, 28

Designed to assess parent perception of services and degree of satisfaction with them. Questionnaire specifically sought parental attitudes about Project PEACH. The project provided diagnostic, referral, and prescriptive educational services for preschool children, ages 3-4.7 years.

10542
Teachers' Attitudes toward Research. Bengel, Rose Mary 1968
Subtests: Awareness and Understanding of Research Reports; Applying Research Results; Doing Research in the Classroom
Descriptors: Adults; *Educational Research; *Home Economics Teachers; *Teacher Attitudes
Availability: Instruments for Assessing Selected Professional Competencies for Home Economics Teachers.Ames, IA: Iowa State University Press, 1978
Target Audience: Adults
Notes: Items, 52

Developed to discriminate among teachers' attitudes toward research. Consists of 52 Likert-type statements which are descriptive of attitudes toward research.

10553
Student Expectations of Achievement through Field Experience (Pretest). Gore, Jane Stevens; Nelson, Helen Y. 1976
Descriptors: *College Students; *Expectation; *Field Experience Programs; Higher Education; *Home Economics Education; *Pretests Posttests; Rating Scales; Student Educational Objectives
Availability: Instruments for Assessing Selected Professional Competencies for Home Economics Teachers.Ames, IA: Iowa State University Press, 1978
Grade Level: 15–16
Notes: Items, 61

Used as a pretest before field work experience. Assesses extent to which students believe the coming experience will contribute to specific undergraduate educational objectives. Based on specific learning outcomes constructed from college goals related to field experiences. Items include those on general education, human ecology education, professionalism, personal qualities. A 61-item posttest, to be taken after completion of field experience, is also available.

10559
Measure of Professional Commitment. Loftis, Helen
Descriptors: Higher Education; Home Economics Education; *Home Economics Teachers; Teacher Attitudes; *Teacher Effectiveness; Teaching (Occupation)
Identifiers: MOPC; *Professional Commitment
Availability: Instruments for Assessing Selected Professional Competencies for Home Economics Teachers.Ames, IA: Iowa State University Press, 1978
Target Audience: 20–64
Notes: Items, 100

This was developed as part of a doctoral study in home economics and is intended for research use and has been used for instruction, advising, and program evaluation. It has 3 levels of response. This assessment is not recommended for use in personnel employment or advancement.

10570
Student's Estimate of Teacher Concern—Form B. Ray, Elizabeth M. 1975
Descriptors: Higher Education; Home Economics Education; Secondary Education; *Secondary School Students; *Secondary School Teachers; *Student Attitudes; *Teacher Student Relationship
Availability: Instruments for Assessing Selected Professional Competencies for Home Economics Teachers.Ames, IA: Iowa State University Press, 1978
Grade Level: 7–12
Notes: Items, 30

Designed to measure differences in teachers' ability to develop rapport with students, this device is based on Nygrens' theory of concern. The respondents are pupils of a particular teacher. Various forms of this measure have been used in studies of teacher effectiveness.

10575
Philosophy of Education. Swan, Florence 1974
Descriptors: Adults; *Beliefs; College Faculty; *Educational Philosophy; Higher Education; *Home Economics Education; *Home Economics Teachers; Rating Scales; *Values
Availability: Instruments for Assessing Selected Professional Competencies for Home Economics Teachers.Ames, IA: Iowa State University Press, 1978
Target Audience: 21–64
Notes: Items, 35

Developed concurrently with the measure, Beliefs about Curriculum, as part of doctoral research. Its purpose was to determine (1) differences in philosophic positions among college and university home economics faculty and (2) the degree of consistency of their philosophic positions with their curriculum beliefs. The responses are on a 5-point agree-disagree continuum and concern 4 major concepts around which 2 philosophic positions have been developed. The concepts are the nature of man, values for living, knowledge and learning, and the aims of education.

10576
Beliefs about Curriculum. Swan, Florence 1974
Descriptors: Adults; *Beliefs; College Faculty; *Curriculum; *Educational Philosophy; Higher Education; *Home Economics Education; *Home Economics Teachers; Questionnaires
Availability: Instruments for Assessing Selected Professional Competencies for Home Economics Teachers.Ames, IA: Iowa State University Press, 1978
Target Audience: 21–64
Notes: Items, 35

Developed concurrently with the Philosophy of Education for doctoral research. Its purpose was to determine (1) differences in philosophic positions among college and university home economics faculty and (2) the degree of consistency of their philosophic positions with their curriculum beliefs. The items are in pairs that represent different beliefs about curriculum. By checking 1 of each pair of statements that conforms best to the subject's beliefs, a pattern of responses develops that reflects the subject's position relative to one of 2 basic philosophic orientations toward education. One is toward progressive and the other is toward traditional aims for curriculum.

10588
Personal Value Systems Questionnaire. Manley, T. Roger; Manley, Eleyse T. 1980
Subtests: Ideas Associated with People; Goals of School Psychologists; Personal Information
Descriptors: *Administrators; Adults; *Educational Administration; Educational Background; *Guidance Objectives; Questionnaires; *School Psychologists; *Values
Identifiers: TIM(F)
Availability: Tests in Microfiche; Test Collection, Educational Testing Service, Princeton, NJ 08541
Target Audience: Adults
Notes: Items, 88

Questionnaire for school psychologists and educational administrators elicits information on their value concepts, goals, background, and job satisfaction. A series of concepts are rated as being of high, low, or medium importance and then described by assigning a rank to each term (pleasant, successful, or right).

10590
Masters-Wilkinson Sex Stereotypes of Toys Scale. Masters, John C.; Wilkinson, Alexander 1976
Descriptors: *Forced Choice Technique; *Parent Attitudes; Rating Scales; *Sex Stereotypes; *Toys; *Young Children
Availability: John C. Masters; Dept. of Psychology, Vanderbilt University, Nashville, TN 37240
Target Audience: 4, 7, 8, Adults
Notes: Items, 52

Fifty-two common toys were rated regarding whether they were more likely to be used by boys or girls. The toys were rated by both children and parents.

10604
Racial Attitudes and Perceptions Survey. O'Mara, Francis E.; Tierney, William 1978
Subtests: Incidence of Discriminatory Behaviors; Abridged Racial Perceptions Inventory
Descriptors: Adults; Black Attitudes; Blacks; *Military Personnel; *Racial Attitudes; Racial Bias; Racial Integration; Reverse Discrimination; Whites
Identifiers: RAPS 2

Availability: ERIC Document Reproduction Service; 3900 Wheeler Ave., Alexandria, VA 22304 (ED169098, 80 pages)
Target Audience: Adults
Notes: Items, 68

Designed for use with military personnel to assess racial climate. Racial Attitudes and Perception Survey (RAPS) consisted of 2 scales: Incidence of Discriminatory Behavior and Racial Perceptions Inventory (RPI). RAPS-2 has an abridged version of the RPI.

10634
The CATE: Children's Attitudes toward the Elderly. Jantz, Richard K.; And Others 1976
Subtests: Word Association; Picture Series; Semantic Differential; The Child's Concept of Age
Descriptors: *Affective Behavior; *Affective Measures; Age Differences; *Association Measures; *Childhood Attitudes; *Children; Cognitive Processes; *Concept Formation; Elementary Education; Interviews; *Older Adults; Preschool Education; Semantic Differential; Visual Measures
Availability: ERIC Document Reproduction Service; 3900 Wheeler Ave., Alexandria, VA 22304-5110 (ED181081, 78 pages)
Target Audience: 3–11

This instrument is designed to assess the attitudes of children, ages 3 to 11, toward older individuals through analysis of the affective, behavioral, and knowledge components of attitudes. To achieve a balanced sample of the test items for each domain, 4 measurement techniques are used: open-ended questions, semantic differential, picture series, and individual interviews, a Piaget-based technique designed to assess children's cognitive development in regard to concepts of age.

10641
My Classmates. Zeichner, Kenneth M. 1980
Descriptors: *Elementary School Students; Group Membership; Intermediate Grades; Peer Acceptance; Peer Groups; *Peer Relationship; Student Attitudes
Availability: The Journal of Experimental Education;v48 n3 p237-44, Spr 1980
Grade Level: 5–6

Designed to measure the quality of a student's perceived relationship with his peers in an elementary school classroom.

10643
Self-Perception Inventory—Student Forms. Soares, Anthony T.; Soares, Louise M. 1980
Subtests: Self-Concept; Reflected Self-Classmates; Reflected Self-Teachers; Reflected Self-Parents; Ideal Concept; Perceptions of Others; Student Self; Perceptions of Others/Student Self
Descriptors: *Disadvantaged Youth; *Elementary School Students; Elementary Secondary Education; Parent Attitudes; Peer Evaluation; Rating Scales; *Secondary School Students; *Self Concept; *Self Concept Measures; Semantic Differential
Identifiers: Classmates; Ideal Self Concept; Reflected Self Concept; Self Concept of Ability
Availability: Soares Associates; 111 Teeter Rock Rd., Trumbull, CT 06611
Grade Level: 1–12
Notes: Time, 60; Items, 288

A self-concept measure using the semantic differential format in which the student rates each concept on a 4-point scale using 2 opposite adjectives or phrases. Among the 6 components of self-perception covered are: self-concept, ideal concept, reflected self-classmates, reflected self-teachers, reflected self-parents. Included is a term called "Perceptions of Others," which is administered to those mentioned in the reflected-self terms, teachers, classmates, and parents. Administration time varies from 5 to 20 minutes per part depending on age and reading level. Norms are available for advantaged and disadvantaged students.

10644
Self-Perception Inventory, Adult Forms. Soares, Anthony T.; Soares, Louise M. 1980
Subtests: Self-Concept; Reflected Self-Friends; Reflected Self-Teachers; Reflected Self-Parents; Ideal Concept; Perceptions of Others
Descriptors: College Students; Higher Education; *High School Students; *Parent Attitudes; Peer Evaluation; Rating Scales; Research Tools; Secondary Education; *Self Concept; *Self Concept Measures; Semantic Differential; *Young Adults
Identifiers: Ideal Self Concept; Reflected Self Concept
Availability: Soares Associates; 111 Teeter Rock Rd., Trumbull, CT 06611
Target Audience: 13–30
Notes: Time, 60; Items, 180

A self-concept measure using a semantic differential format. Six components of self-perception are covered: self-concept, ideal concept, reflected self-other parents, reflected self-teachers, reflected self-friends, and perceptions of others, which is administered to significant people in the subject's life. Administration time ranges from 5-20 minutes per part, depending on reading ability. Normed on grade 12 and young working adults.

10645
Self-Perception Inventory—Teacher Forms.
Soares, Anthony T.; Soares, Louise M. 1980
Subtests: Self-Concept-Teacher; Reflected Self-Cooperating Teacher; Reflected Self-Supervisor; Ideal Self-Teacher; Teacher Perception; Reflected Teacher Perception; Student Perceptions
Descriptors: Adults; Cooperating Teachers; Rating Scales; Research Tools; *Self Concept Measures; Semantic Differential; Student Attitudes; *Student Teachers; Student Teacher Supervisors; Suburban Schools; Teacher Attitudes; *Teachers; Urban Schools
Identifiers: Ideal Self Concept; Reflected Self Concept
Availability: Soares Associates; 111 Teeter Rock Rd., Trumbull, CT 06611
Target Audience: 18–64
Notes: Time, 60; Items, 288
A self-concept measure using a semantic differential format. Self-rating forms cover self-concept as a teacher, reflected self-cooperating teacher (how the student teacher thinks he/she is seen by the cooperating teacher), reflected self-supervisor (college supervisor's view of student teacher as seen by student teacher), ideal self-teacher. Forms for rating by others cover coop teacher and supervisor rate intern, teacher rating of how intern will rate him/herself, and student perceptions of teachers. Used by teachers, student teachers, their supervisors, and students. Normed on urban and suburban student teachers.

10682
Desire for Control of Physical Environment. Jorgenson, Dale O.
Descriptors: Adults; *Individual Power; *Physical Environment; Questionnaires; Rating Scales
Identifiers: *Environmental Attitudes
Availability: Dale O. Jorgenson; Dept. of Psychology, California State University Long Beach, Long Beach, CA 90840
Target Audience: Adults
Notes: Items, 14
A scale to measure the desire to control the physical environment. Based on assumption that desire to control physical environment is a fairly stable human value orientation.

10685
Behavioral Hostility Scale. Ganzer, Victor J. 1964
Descriptors: Adults; Affective Measures; *Aggression; *Females; *Hostility; *Negative Attitudes
Identifiers: BHS
Availability: Journal of Projective Techniques and Personality Assessment;v34 n4 p302-15, 1970
Target Audience: Adults
Notes: Items, 15
Designed to assess behavioral and attitudinal aspects of hostility.

10697
Pre-School Teachers' Beliefs Inventory. Kaufman, Barry A.; And Others 1975
Descriptors: *Educational Theories; Preschool Education; *Preschool Teachers; Rating Scales; *Teacher Attitudes
Identifiers: *Piagetian Teachers Beliefs Inventory; PTBI
Availability: ERIC Document Reproduction Service; 3900 Wheeler Ave., Alexandria, VA 22304 (ED175873, 18 pages)
Target Audience: 18–64
Notes: Items, 24
Twenty-four-item inventory was constructed and standardized in order to develop an instrument which measures the degree to which a preschool teacher adheres to Piaget's epistemological belief system. The 6-point rating scale is strongly agree to strongly disagree with the statements given.

10703
Parent Education-Involvement Attitude Scale.
Pasley, Kay 1977
Descriptors: Adults; *Parent Participation; *Parent Teacher Cooperation; Preschool Education; *Preschool Teachers; Rating Scales; *Teacher Attitudes
Identifiers: PEIAS; TIM(F)
Availability: Tests in Microfiche; Test Collection, Educational Testing Service, Princeton, NJ 08541
Target Audience: Adults
Notes: Items, 53

Designed to measure the attitudes of preschool teachers relative to parent education programs in which they participate. Fifty-three items measure agreement/disagreement on a 5-point scale. Statements cover parent participation, cooperation, teacher willingness and interest, home visits, goals, techniques, worth of program.

10704
Attitude Survey of the Effects of Marijuana on Sexual Enjoyment. Dawley, Harold H.; And Others 1977
Descriptors: Adults; College Students; Drug Use; Higher Education; Participant Satisfaction; Questionnaires; *Sexuality; Surveys
Identifiers: Self Report Measures
Availability: Harold H. Dawley; Psychology Service, Veterans Administration Hospital, 1601 Perdido St., New Orleans, LA 70146
Grade Level: 13–16
Notes: Items, 57
A self-report measure of the sexual satisfaction felt by a marijuana user who uses marijuana during a sexual encounter. Also solicits background information. A lie scale is included. The 10 items directly concerned with the use of marijuana and sexual satisfaction are contained in Dawley, Harold H. and Others; "An Attitude Survey of the Effects of Marijuana on Sexual Enjoyment," in The Journal of Clinical Psychology;v35 n1 p212, Jan 1979.

10708
Empathic Fantasy Scale. Elms, Alan C. 1966
Descriptors: *Adults; *Attitude Change; *Empathy; Role Playing
Availability: Journal of Personality and Social Psychology;v4 n1 p36-43, Jul 1966
Target Audience: Adults
Notes: Items, 10
Designed to assess effectiveness of role playing in the induction of attitude change.

10742
Nutrition Attitude Scale. Byrd-Bredhenner, Carol 1980
Descriptors: *Eating Habits; Elementary School Teachers; Graduate Students; Higher Education; *Nutrition; Undergraduate Students; Likert Scales
Identifiers: *Home Economists; Nurses Attitudes; *Nutritionists; TIM(G)
Availability: Tests in Microfiche; Test Collection, Educational Testing Service, Princeton, NJ 08541
Grade Level: 13–17
Notes: Items, 25
Likert Scale designed to measure the favorableness of attitudes, toward the importance of nutrition and eating habits. Used in a study of the interrelationships of nutrition knowledge, attitudes, and behaviors.

10755
Patient Expectations and Perceptions. Chinsky, Jack M.; Rappaport, Julian 1970
Descriptors: Adults; *Patients; *Psychiatric Hospitals; Student Volunteers; Therapists
Availability: Journal of Consulting and Clinical Psychology;v35 n3 p388-94, 1970
Target Audience: Adults
Notes: Items, 25
Designed to measure psychiatric patients' perceptions of the characteristics of college student volunteers in a hospital companionship program as opposed to perceptions of their therapists.

10785
Ellis' Irrational Beliefs Questionnaire (Modification). Lee, Dong Yul; Hallberg, Ernest T. 1979
Descriptors: *Beliefs; *College Freshmen; Counseling Techniques; *Elementary School Students; *Emotional Disturbances; Higher Education; Intermediate Grades; Objective Tests; Secondary Education; *Secondary School Students
Identifiers: Irrational Belief Scale (Ellis)
Availability: Journal of Clinical Psychology;v35 n4 p754-56, Oct 1979
Grade Level: 5–13
Notes: Items, 11
Designed to assess cognitive development of younger children in an effort to determine normal developmental levels of rationality in counseling work. Decreasing endorsement of irrational beliefs is to be expected as child matures.

10788
Affective Perception Inventory, Primary Level.
Soares, Anthony T.; Soares, Louise M. 1979
Subtests: Self-Concept (as a person); Student Self; Reading Perceptions; Arithmetic Perceptions; Science Perceptions; Social Studies Perceptions; Perceptions in the Arts; Sports and Games Perceptions; School Perceptions

Descriptors: Arithmetic; *Elementary School Students; Fine Arts; Physical Education; Primary Education; Reading Attitudes; Research Tools; *School Attitudes; Sciences; *Self Concept Measures; Semantic Differential; Social Studies; *Student Attitudes
Identifiers: Self Concept of Ability
Availability: Soares Associates; 111 Teeter Rock Rd., Trumbull, CT 06611
Grade Level: 1–3
Notes: Time, 45; Items, 115
Nine scales measure feelings about the self relative to specific subject areas or classroom experiences including self as a person, student, in the school environment, or in interaction with others who are part of the educational setting. Subjects covered are reading, arithmetic, science, social studies, arts, sports, and games. Used primarily for research. Administration time depends on reading level. A semantic differential format is used. Subject scales measure attitudes toward the subject and feelings about one's ability in the subject.

10818
Older Persons Questionnaire. Gillis, Marion 1973
Descriptors: Adults; *Nurses; Nursing; *Older Adults; Patients; Rating Scales; *Social Attitudes
Identifiers: Nurse Attitudes; OPQ; Self Administered Tests
Availability: ERIC Document Reproduction Service; 3900 Wheeler Ave., Alexandria, VA 22304 (ED171763, 842 pages)
Target Audience: Adults
Notes: Time, 15 approx.; Items, 48
This volume consists of a series of psychosocial and physiological clinical nursing instruments. The instruments were selected from the published literature in health care, education, psychology, and the social sciences. Instruments focus upon nursing practice and stress patient variables. Instrument was designed to elicit information on the attitudes of nursing personnel toward the aged.

10820
Nursing Autonomy and Patients' Rights Questionnaire. Pankratz, Loren; Pankratz, Deanna 1974
Subtests: Nursing Autonomy and Advocacy; Patients' Rights; Rejection of Traditional Role Limitations
Descriptors: Adults; *Nurses; *Nursing; Patients; Rating Scales
Identifiers: Autonomy (Personal); Nurse Attitudes
Availability: ERIC Document Reproduction Service; 3900 Wheeler Ave., Alexandria, VA 22304-5110 (ED171763, 842 pages)
Target Audience: Adults
Notes: Items, 47
This volume consists of a series of psychosocial and physiological clinical nursing instruments. The instruments were selected from the published literature in health care, education, psychology, and the social sciences. Instruments focus upon nursing practice and stress patient variables. Instrument is designed to elicit information about nurses' attitudes toward their professional role and patients' rights.

10821
Patients' Bill of Rights Questionnaire. Pankrantz, Deanna
Descriptors: Adults; Nurses; *Nursing; *Patients
Identifiers: *Nurse Attitudes; Self Administered Tests
Availability: ERIC Document Reproduction Service; 3900 Wheeler Ave., Alexandria, VA 22304 (ED171763, 842 pages)
Target Audience: Adults
Notes: Items, 25
This volume consists of a series of psychosocial and physiological clinical nursing instruments. The instruments were selected from the published literature in health care, education, psychology, and the social sciences. Instruments focus upon nursing practice and stress patient variables. Designed to provide information on attitudes toward patients' rights and whether or not these rights are provided in a particular health care setting. No scoring information was provided.

10827
Importance of Nursing Actions Opinionnaire.
Walker, Laura C. 1960
Descriptors: Adults; Medical Services; *Nurses; *Nursing; *Patients
Availability: ERIC Document Reproduction Service; 3900 Wheeler Ave., Alexandria, VA 22304 (ED171763, 842 pages)
Target Audience: Adults
Notes: Time, 20 approx.; Items, 16
This volume consists of a series of psychosocial and physiological clinical nursing instruments. The instruments were selected from the published literature in health care, education, psychology, and the social sciences. Instruments focus upon nursing practice and stress patient variables.

Instrument assesses respondents' perceptions of the relative importance of specific nursing actions relative to patients. A modified q-sort technique is used.

10828
Checklist for Patients. Abdellah, Faye G.; Levine, Eugene 1957
Subtests: Events Indicating Satisfaction with Care; Rest and Relaxation; Dietary Needs; Elimination; Personal Hygiene and Supportive Care; Reaction to Therapy; Contact with Nurses
Descriptors: Adults; Attitudes; Check Lists; Hospitals; Interaction; *Medical Care Evaluation; *Nurses; *Nursing; *Patients
Identifiers: *Nursing Care
Availability: ERIC Document Reproduction Service; 3900 Wheeler Ave., Alexandria, VA 22304 (ED171763, 842 pages)
Target Audience: Adults
Notes: Items, 50

This volume consists of a series of psychosocial and physiological clinical nursing instruments. The instruments were selected from the published literature in health care, education, psychology, and the social sciences. Instruments focus upon nursing practice and stress patient variables. Instrument was developed to assess how patients feel about nursing care provided them during a hospital stay. Only events relating to nurse-patient relationship are assessed. Designed for use in conjunction with Checklist for Personnel (TC010829).

10829
Checklist for Personnel. Abdellah, Faye G.; Levine, Eugene 1957
Subtests: Administering Therapy to Patients; Carrying Out Work Assignments; Providing Needed Support Care to Patients; Contacting Patient's Family and Friends; Providing Needed Help and Equipment for Elimination; Providing for Needed Comfort and Safety Measures; Meeting the Patient's Aesthetic Needs; Providing for an Atmosphere Conducive to Rest and Relaxation; Providing Needed Nourishment for the Patient
Descriptors: Adults; Attitudes; Check Lists; *Hospital Personnel; Hospitals; Interaction; *Medical Care Evaluation; Nurses; *Nursing; *Patients
Identifiers: Nurse Attitudes; *Nursing Care
Availability: ERIC Document Reproduction Service; 3900 Wheeler Ave., Alexandria, VA 22304 (ED171763, 842 pages)
Target Audience: Adults
Notes: Items, 50

This volume consists of a series of psychosocial and physiological clinical nursing instruments. The instruments were selected from the published literature in health care, education, psychology, and the social sciences. Instruments focus upon nursing practice and stress patient variables. Instrument was developed to assess hospital personnel opinions concerning nursing care of hospital patients. Administrative, professional, and unskilled staff were asked to complete the checklist on events occurring on a specific day. Designed for use in conjunction with Checklist for Patients (TC010828).

10833
Pediatric Parents and Staff Semantic Differential Scales. Gohsman, Barbara 1975
Descriptors: Adults; Hospitalized Children; *Hospital Personnel; Nurses; *Nursing; *Parent Attitudes; *Parents; Patients; Rating Scales; Semantic Differential
Identifiers: Self Administered Tests
Availability: ERIC Document Reproduction Service; 3900 Wheeler Ave., Alexandria, VA 22304 (ED171763, 842 pages)
Target Audience: Adults
Notes: Time, 15 approx.; Items, 96

This volume consists of a series of psychosocial and physiological clinical nursing instruments. The instruments were selected from the published literature in health care, education, psychology, and the social sciences. Instruments focus upon nursing practice and stress patient variables. Instrument was designed to assess attitudes of parents of pediatric patients, as well as pediatric staff members concerning hospitalization. Attitudes in several areas are assessed including nurse, fear, time, child, pain, care, parents, doctor, nurse aide, crying, shot, and comfort.

10834
Community Mental Health Critical Issues Test. Gottesfeld, Harry 1974
Descriptors: *Adults; Community Attitudes; Community Health Services; *Mental Health Programs; Nurses; *Nursing; Patients; Social Attitudes; Likert Scales
Identifiers: CMIT; Self Administered Tests
Availability: ERIC Document Reproduction Service; 3900 Wheeler Ave., Alexandria, VA 22304 (ED171763, 842 pages)
Target Audience: Adults
Notes: Items, 72

This volume consists of a series of psychosocial and physiological clinical nursing instruments. The instruments were selected from the published literature in health care, education, psychology, and the social sciences. Instruments focus upon nursing practice and stress patient variables. This instrument assesses an individual's attitudes toward major issues in the community mental health field. Issues are community context, radicalism, traditional psychotherapy, prevention, extending the definition of mental health, and role diffusion.

10835
Postoperative Interview Guide. Hegyvary, Sue T. 1974
Subtests: Patient's Level of Understanding of Required Role; Preoperative Stress; Organizational Constraints
Descriptors: Adults; Hospitals; Interviews; *Medical Care Evaluation; Nurses; *Nursing; *Patients; Stress Variables
Identifiers: *Patient Attitudes; *Postoperative Patients
Availability: ERIC Document Reproduction Service; 3900 Wheeler Ave., Alexandria, VA 22304 (ED171763, 842 pages)
Target Audience: Adults
Notes: Items, 21

This volume consists of a series of psychosocial and physiological clinical nursing instruments. The instruments were selected from the published literature in health care, education, psychology, and the social sciences. Instruments focus upon nursing practice and stress patient variables. Designed to elicit information from postoperative patients. Should be administered by an interviewer. Developed to examine the relationship between postoperative outcomes and the type of organizational setting characteristic of a hospital.

10836
Patient Satisfaction with Health Care Survey. Linn, Lawrence 1975
Descriptors: Adults; *Clinics; *Medical Care Evaluation; Nurses; *Nursing; *Patients; Physicians; Satisfaction
Identifiers: Patient Attitudes; *Patient Care; Patient Survey
Availability: ERIC Document Reproduction Service; 3900 Wheeler Ave., Alexandria, VA 22304 (ED171763, 842 pages)
Target Audience: Adults
Notes: Time, 15 approx.; Items, 21

This volume consists of a series of psychosocial and physiological clinical nursing instruments. The instruments were selected from the published literature in health care, education, psychology, and the social sciences. Instruments focus upon nursing practice and stress patient variables. Designed for completion by patient immediately after having received medical care in an outpatient clinic or in a primary care setting. Respondent evaluates treatment received and records sources of satisfaction, or dissatisfaction, with the experience.

10837
Patient Satisfaction Scale. McGivern, Diane O. 1972
Descriptors: Adults; *Hospital Personnel; *Hospitals; Medical Care Evaluation; Nurses; *Nursing; *Patients; Satisfaction
Identifiers: *Patient Attitudes; *Patient Care
Availability: ERIC Document Reproduction Service; 3900 Wheeler Ave., Alexandria, VA 22304 (ED171763, 842 pages)
Target Audience: Adults
Notes: Time, 30 approx.; Items, 21

This volume consists of a series of psychosocial and physiological clinical nursing instruments. The instruments were selected from the published literature in health care, education, psychology, and the social sciences. Instruments focus upon nursing practice and stress patient variables. Designed to assess a patient's perceptions of hospital experiences and health care personnel. Assesses nurses' and physicians' services, hospital routines and regulations, and general hospital care.

10839
Patient's Perception of Aspects of Health Care. Pankrantz, Deanna
Descriptors: Adults; Hospital Personnel; *Hospitals; *Medical Care Evaluation; Nurses; *Nursing; *Patients; Rating Scales; Satisfaction
Identifiers: *Patient Attitudes; Patient Care
Availability: ERIC Document Reproduction Service; 3900 Wheeler Ave., Alexandria, VA 22304 (ED171763, 842 pages)
Target Audience: Adults
Notes: Items, 14

This volume consists of a series of psychosocial and psysiological clinical nursing instruments. The instruments were selected from the published literature in health care, education, psychology, and the social sciences. Instruments focus upon nursing practice and stress patient variables.

Instrument measures a patient's perceptions of the importance of aspects of health care in hospitals and his or her personal satisfaction with those aspects.

10840
Patient Interview Questionnaire. Pienschke, Darlene 1973
Descriptors: Adults; *Cancer; Hospitals; Interviews; *Medical Care Evaluation; Nurses; *Nursing; *Patients
Identifiers: Nursing Care; Patient Attitudes; Patient Care
Availability: ERIC Document Reproduction Service; 3900 Wheeler Ave., Alexandria, VA 22304 (ED171763, 842 pages)
Target Audience: Adults
Notes: Items, 28

This volume consists of a series of psychosocial and physiological clinical nursing instruments. The instruments were selected from the published literature in health care, education, psychology, and the social sciences. Instruments focus upon nursing practice and stress patient variables. Designed to obtain data for indicating the consequences of differing approaches to giving cancer patients information about their diagnosis and prognosis. Patient confidence and satisfaction with health care are assessed. First part of instrument is administered by an interviewer, and second part is self-administered by patient.

10841
Risser Patient Satisfaction Scale. Risser, Nancy 1972
Subtests: Technical-Professional; Interpersonal-Educational; Interpersonal-Trusting
Descriptors: Adults; Clinics; *Medical Care Evaluation; *Nurses; *Nursing; *Patients; Satisfaction
Identifiers: Nursing Care; *Patient Attitudes
Availability: ERIC Document Reproduction Service; 3900 Wheeler Ave., Alexandria, VA 22304 (ED171763, 842 pages)
Target Audience: Adults
Notes: Time, 15 approx.; Items, 28

This volume consists of a series of psychosocial and physiological clinical nursing instruments. The instruments were selected from the published literature in health care, education, psychology, and the social sciences. Instruments focus upon nursing practice and stress patient variables. Instrument was developed to evaluate patient care from the patient's perspective. Attitudes measured are patients' attitudes toward nurses and nursing care in a primary health care setting.

10842
Quality of Nursing Care Questionnaire-Patient. Safford, Beverly J.; And Others 1960
Subtests: Physical Care; Emotional Care; Nurse-Physician Relationship; Teaching and Preparation for Home Care; Administration; Quality of Nursing Care
Descriptors: Adults; *Hospitals; *Medical Care Evaluation; Nurses; *Nursing; *Patients; Satisfaction
Identifiers: *Nursing Care; *Patient Attitudes
Availability: ERIC Document Reproduction Service; 3900 Wheeler Ave., Alexandria, VA 22304 (ED171763, 842 pages)
Target Audience: Adults
Notes: Items, 45

This volume consists of a series of psychosocial and physiological clinical nursing instruments. The instruments were selected from the published literature in health care, education, psychology, and the social sciences. Instruments focus upon nursing practice and stress patient variables. This instrument was developed to provide information regarding relationship between hospital staffing patterns and patients' perceptions of the quality of nursing care received.

10843
Patient Perceptions of Health Services. Triplett, June L.
Subtests: Nurse Disparity; Medical Disparity; Perceived Threat-Past Experience; Social Isolation; Threat; Self-Esteem; Perceptions of Others; Demographic Data; Observation
Descriptors: Adults; *Community Health Services; Medical Care Evaluation; *Nurses; *Nursing; *Patients; Physicians; Public Health; Self Esteem
Identifiers: *Patient Attitudes
Availability: ERIC Document Reproduction Service; 3900 Wheeler Ave., Alexandria, VA 22304 (ED171763, 842 pages)
Target Audience: Adults
Notes: Time, 60 approx.; Items, 94

This volume consists of a series of psychosocial and physiological clinical nursing instruments. The instruments were selected from the published literature in health care, education, psychology, and the social sciences. Instruments focus upon nursing practice and stress patient variables.

Instrument measures patient's perceptions of health services. Designed to be read to subject during home visit by public health nurse-interviewer.

10845
Appointment-Required Clinic and No Appointment-Required Clinic Semantic Differential. Wyatt, Jane S.; Rozell, Billie 1957
Descriptors: Adults; *Clinics; Nurses; *Nursing; *Patients; Semantic Differential
Identifiers: *Appointments; *Patient Attitudes
Availability: ERIC Document Reproduction Service; 3900 Wheeler Ave., Alexandria, VA 22304 (ED171763, 842 pages)
Target Audience: Adults
Notes: Items, 27
This volume consists of a series of psychosocial and physiological clinical nursing instruments. The instruments were selected from the published literature in health care, education, psychology, and the social sciences. Instruments focus upon nursing practice and stress patient variables. Instrument designed to assess client attitudes toward clinics that do, and do not, require appointments.

10846
Neonatal Perception Inventory I and II. Broussard, Elsie R. 1964
Subtests: Average Baby; Your Baby
Descriptors: Adults; Hospitals; Infants; *Mother Attitudes; *Mothers; *Neonates; Patients
Identifiers: NPI
Availability: ERIC Document Reproduction Service; 3900 Wheeler Ave., Alexandria, VA 22304 (ED171763, 842 pages)
Target Audience: Adults
Notes: Items, 12
This volume consists of a series of psychosocial and physiological clinical nursing instruments. The instruments were selected from the published literature in health care, education, psychology, and the social sciences. Instruments focus upon nursing practice and stress patient variables. Designed to measure maternal perception of her infant. Neonatal Perception Inventory I is administered during the immediate postpartum hospital stay (1-4 days). NPI II is administered approximately 1 month postpartum (4-6 weeks). Both forms are identical in items and response format.

10855
Wife's Perception of Loss after Her Husband's Myocardial Infarction Questionnaire. Smith, Linda S. 1975
Descriptors: Adults; *Affective Measures; Attitudes; *Emotional Adjustment; Emotional Response; *Patients; *Spouses
Identifiers: *Heart Attack
Availability: ERIC Document Reproduction Service; 3900 Wheeler Ave., Alexandria, VA 22304 (ED171763, 842 pages)
Target Audience: Adults
Notes: Time, 35 approx.; Items, 33
This volume consists of a series of psychosocial and physiological clinical nursing instruments. The instruments were selected from the published literature in health care, education, psychology, and the social sciences. Instruments focus upon nursing practice and stress patient variables. This instrument assessed the wife's subjective perception of loss in the areas of financial security, emotional closeness to her husband, her husband's physical strength, open communication with her husband, and sexual relations with her husband following his myocardial infarction heart attack.

10864
Self-Perception Inventory—Student Forms, (Italian). Soares, Anthony T.; Soares, Louise M. 1980
Subtests: Self-Concept; Reflected Self-Classmates; Reflected Self-Teachers; Reflected Self-Parents; Ideal Concept; Perceptions of Others; Student Self; Perceptions of Others/Student Self
Descriptors: *Disadvantaged Youth; *Elementary School Students; Elementary Secondary Education; *Italian; Parent Attitudes; Peer Evaluation; Rating Scales; *Secondary School Students; *Self Concept; *Self Concept Measures; Semantic Differential
Identifiers: Classmates; Ideal Self Concept; Reflected Self Concept; Self Concept of Ability
Availability: Soares Associates; 111 Teeter Rock Rd., Trumbull, CT 06611
Grade Level: 1-12
Notes: Time, 60; Items, 288
A self-concept measure using a semantic differential format. Six components of self-perception are covered: self-concept, ideal concept, reflected self-classmates, reflected self-teachers, reflected self-parents, student self. Included is a term called "Perceptions of Others," which is administered to those mentioned in the reflected-self forms, teachers, classmates, and parents. Administration time varies from 5-20 minutes per part depending on age and

reading level. The student rates each concept on a 4-point scale using 2 opposite adjectives or phrases. This is a translation.

10865
Client Attitude Questionnaire, Revised. Morrison, James K. 1977
Descriptors: Adults; Institutionalized Persons; *Mental Disorders; Patients; Professional Personnel; Questionnaires; Student Attitudes
Identifiers: CAQ B; *Medical Viewpoint; *Psychosocial Viewpoint
Availability: Morrison, James K., ed.; *A Consumer Approach to Community Psychology.*Chicago: Nelson-Hall, 1979
Target Audience: Adults
Notes: Items, 20
Designed to measure the respondent's attitudes toward mental illness. Three-point response mode allows use with institutionalized mental patients as well as mental health professionals and students. Distinguishes orientation toward the psychosocial or medical views of mental illness.

10866
Semantic Differential. Morrison, James K. 1977
Descriptors: Adults; *Mental Disorders; Patients; Semantic Differential
Identifiers: *Patient Attitudes
Availability: Morrison, James K., ed.; *A Consumer Approach to Community Psychology.*Chicago: Nelson-Hall, 1979
Target Audience: Adults
Notes: Items, 30
Respondent rates the concept of "mental patient" using 30 bipolar adjectives and a 7-point scale. Used to measure attitude change related to the psychosocial approach to mental illness.

10872
Client Service Questionnaire. Becker, Roy E.; And Others 1975
Descriptors: Adults; Emotional Problems; *Mental Health Clinics; *Patients; Physical Health; Professional Personnel; *Psychotherapy; Social Problems
Identifiers: CSQ
Availability: Morrison, James K., ed.; *A Consumer Approach to Community Psychology.*Chicago: Nelson-Hall, 1979
Notes: Items, 36
Client responds true/false to items concerned with client attitudes toward staff. Concerns patients' felt needs for contact with staff, physical and emotional symptoms, social activities.

10875
Potential Interpersonal Competence Scale. Remer, Rory 1972
Subtests: Own Language; Client As an Individual; Build Client's Confidence; Establish Trust and Confidence—Post Hoc Judgment; Establish Trust and Confidence—Confidentiality; Have Rapport—Accurate Empathy; Have Rapport—Personal Communication
Descriptors: Adults; *Communication Skills; *Counselor Attitudes; *Counselor Client Relationship; *Interpersonal Competence; *Situational Tests
Identifiers: TIM(G)
Availability: Tests in Microfiche; Test Collection, Educational Testing Service, Princeton, NJ 08541
Target Audience: Adults
Notes: Items, 35
Consists of a series of simulated counseling situations and 4 possible responses to each situation. Obtainable scores include individual item scores, total instrument score; and subscale scores for each of 7 competencies measured.

10890
Kansans' Attitudes toward Education. Emporia State University, Kansas School of Education and Psychology 1980
Descriptors: Adults; Day Care; Elementary School Curriculum; *Elementary Secondary Education; Mainstreaming; Public Opinion; Questionnaires; School Taxes; Secondary School Curriculum; Surveys; Teacher Certification; Teacher Strikes
Identifiers: KATE
Availability: ERIC Document Reproduction Service; 3900 Wheeler Ave., Alexandria, VA 22304-5110 (ED191894, 79 pages)
Target Audience: Adults
Notes: Time, 15; Items, 27
Questionnaire utilized in a poll to gather information for educational decision makers. Solicits opinions on importance of various school subjects, teacher certification exams, inservice education, contract disputes, strikes, educational needs, local schools, education today, mainstreaming, child care, school taxes, and purposes of education.

10892
Krantz Health Opinion Survey. Krantz, David S. 1978
Descriptors: Adults; Information Needs; *Medical Services; *Physician Patient Relationship; *Questionnaires
Identifiers: TIM(G)
Availability: Tests in Microfiche; Test Collection, Educational Testing Service, Princeton, NJ 08541
Target Audience: Adults
Notes: Items, 16
Elicits opinions about patient preferences for an active and informed versus a relatively inactive and trusting role in the health care process.

10898
Mate Selection Questionnaire. Hendel, Darwin D. 1972
Subtests: Age; Alertness; Common Sense Knowledge; Educational Level; Family Background; Financial Status; Intelligence; Interests; Nationality; Occupational Potential; Personality; Personal Values; Physical Attractiveness; Political Beliefs; Potential as a Parent; Religious Beliefs; Sexual Appeal; Social Poise; Special Talents; Types of Friends
Descriptors: *Adults; Higher Education; Individual Characteristics; *Mate Selection; Questionnaires; Social Attitudes; *Undergraduate Students
Identifiers: MSQ
Availability: Darwin D. Hendel; 419 Walter Library, 117 Pleasant St. S.E., Minneapolis, MN 55455
Grade Level: 13-16
Target Audience: Adults
Notes: Items, 210
Designed to assess qualities respondent considers important in selecting a mate.

10925
Directiveness Scale: Mark III. Ray, John J. 1976
Descriptors: *Adults; *Authoritarianism; Behavior Patterns; Foreign Countries; Personality Measures; Personality Traits; Conservatism; Liberalism
Identifiers: Adorno (TW); *Authoritarian Behavior; Great Britain
Availability: John J. Ray; School of Sociology, University of New South Wales, Kensington, N.S.W., Australia 2033
Target Audience: Adults
Notes: Items, 14
Designed to predict authoritarian behavior and to determine the relationship between authoritarian attitudes and behavior. Authoritarian personality is not directly correlated with political attitudes—either liberal or conservative.

10955
Attitudes toward Mainstreaming Scale. Berryman, Joan D. 1981
Descriptors: Education Majors; Elementary Secondary Education; *Mainstreaming; *Teacher Attitudes; Teachers; Likert Scales
Identifiers: Education for All Handicapped Children Act 1975
Availability: Joan D. Berryman; Speech Pathology and Audiology, University of Georgia, Athens, GA 30602
Target Audience: Adults
Notes: Items, 18
Used to discover attitudes of preservice and inservice teachers toward mainstreaming elementary and secondary school students.

10962
Gifted Identification Chart. Alexander, Patricia; Muia, Joseph A. 1980
Descriptors: Abstract Reasoning; Check Lists; Communication (Thought Transfer); *Creativity; Elementary Education; *Gifted; Leadership; Reading Interests
*Availability: Reading Horizons,*v20 n4 p302-10, Sum 1980
Grade Level: 1-6
Notes: Items, 61
Observational checklist for classroom use to determine the presence of positive behaviors which have been identified as creativity or creative end products. For use with culturally dominant and subdominant students.

10966
Graduate Student Opinion Questionnaire. Feild, Hubert S. 1980

Subtests: Classification Information (15); Satisfaction with Graduate Education in Business (23); Attitudes toward Graduate School of Business (30); Evaluation of Graduate School of Business (20); Image of the Graduate School of Business (18); Evaluation of Educational Methods (12); Comments
Descriptors: *Business Administration Education; *Graduate Students; Higher Education; Questionnaires; *Student Attitudes
Identifiers: *Auburn University AL
Availability: Auburn University; Dept. of Management, Auburn, AL 36830
Grade Level: Higher Education
Notes: Items, 118
Designed to elicit feedback from graduate students about their perceptions of the program in the graduate School of Business.

10971
Group Inventory for Finding Interests. Level 1.
Rimm, Sylvia B.; Davis, Gary A. 1979
Descriptors: *Creativity; *Gifted; *Interest Inventories; Junior High Schools; *Screening Tests; Student Interests; *Talent Identification
Availability: Educational Assessment Service, Inc.; W6050 Apple Rd., Watertown, WI 53094
Grade Level: 6–9
Notes: Time, 35 approx.; Items, 60
Screening test to help select junior high school students for programs for the creatively gifted. Identifies students with attitudes and interests usually associated with creativity, such as independence, curiosity, perseverance, flexibility, breadth of interest, risk taking, and sense of humor.

10979
Group Inventory for Finding Interests. Level 2.
Rimm, Sylvia B.; Davis, Gary A. 1979
Descriptors: *Creativity; *Gifted; High Schools; *Interest Inventories; *Screening Tests; Student Interests; *Talent Identification
Availability: Educational Assessment Service, Inc.; W6050 Apple Rd., Watertown, WI 53094
Grade Level: 9–12
Notes: Time, 35 approx.; Items, 60
Screening test to help select senior high school students for creatively gifted programs. Identifies students with attitudes and interests usually associated with creativity, such as independence, curiosity, perseverance, flexibility, breadth of interest, risk taking, and sense of humor.

10980
Mathematics Self-Concept Scale. Holly, Keith A. 1971
Descriptors: Adolescents; Higher Education; *Mathematics; Mathematics Anxiety; Rating Scales; Secondary Education; *Secondary School Students; Self Evaluation (Individuals); *Undergraduate Students
Identifiers: MSCS; TIM(I)
Availability: Tests in Microfiche; Test Collection, Educational Testing Service, Princeton, NJ 08541
Grade Level: 7–14
Target Audience: 11–18
Notes: Time, 12 approx.; Items, 22
Seven-point rating scale which indicates person's feelings about mathematics. A shortened version, consisting of 10 items, can be extracted from the long form. No time limits, but average high-school student should take approximately 12 minutes to complete questionnaire.

10992
Speech in the Classroom: Assessment Instruments.
Koziol, Stephen; Cercone, Karen 1980
Subtests: Assessment of Speaking Skills (1); Inventory of Classroom Speaking Experiences Student Form A (15); Inventory of Classroom Speaking Experiences Teacher Form A (151); Inventory of Classroom Speaking Experience Student Form B (25); Inventory of Classroom Speaking Experiences Teacher Form B (25); Survey of Attitudes toward Classroom Speech Situations Form A (12); Survey of Attitudes toward Classroom Speech Situations Form B (20)
Descriptors: Classroom Communication; *Communication Skills; Elementary Secondary Education; *Measures (Individuals); *Speech Communication; *Speech Skills; *Student Attitudes
Availability: ERIC Document Reproduction Service; 3900 Wheeler Ave., Alexandria, VA 22304 (ED191112, 31 pages)
Grade Level: 1–12
Notes: Items, 113
Three speech assessment instruments that evaluate students' ability to communicate orally the context of a message; measure the amount of student participation in speaking activities and the opportunities teachers give to students for speaking experiences; and assess students'

attitudes toward participation in speech activities. Form A is intended for use in grades 1-6 and Form B is intended for grades 4-12.

11004
Student Reactions to College. Educational Testing Service, Princeton, NJ
Subtests: Quality of Instruction; Form of Instruction; Student-Centered Instruction; Academic Performance; Grading; Studying; Instructor Accessibility; Involvement with Faculty; Counseling and Advising; Planning; Programing; Registration and Scheduling; Library/Bookstore; Rules and Regulations; Administrative Procedures; Campus Climate; Organized Student Activities; Help with Living Problems; Financial and Related Problems
Descriptors: College Administration; College Environment; Counseling Effectiveness; *Institutional Evaluation; *Student Attitudes; Student Evaluation of Teacher Performance; Two Year Colleges; *Two Year College Students
Identifiers: SRC
Availability: School and Higher Education Programs; Educational Testing Service, Princeton, NJ 08541
Grade Level: 13–14
Notes: Time, 45; Items, 150
Used to help faculty and administrators at 2-year colleges understand student needs and develop programs and services to fulfill those needs. Allows students to express their opinions about many aspects of the college environment, such as instruction, counseling, administrative affairs, out-of-class activities, living arrangements, and financial matters. In addition to the basic 150 items, there is room for 20 local option questions and 9 demographic questions. Responses are reported for groups of students, and results are reported on an institutional basis.

11005
Student Reactions to College—Four-Year College Edition. Educational Testing Service, Princeton, NJ
Subtests: Quality of Instruction; Form of Instruction; Student-Centered Instruction; Academic Performance; Grading; Studying; Instructor Accessibility; Involvement with Faculty; Counseling and Advising; Planning; Programming; Registration and Scheduling; Library/Bookstore; Rules and Regulations; Administrative Procedures; Campus Climate; Organized Student Activities; Help with Living Problems; Financial and Related Problems
Descriptors: College Administration; College Environment; Educational Assessment; Higher Education; *Institutional Evaluation; Relevance (Education); *Student Attitudes; Student Evaluation of Teacher Performance; *Undergraduate Students
Identifiers: SRC
Availability: School and Higher Education Programs; Educational Testing Service, Princeton, NJ 08541
Grade Level: 13–16
Notes: Time, 45; Items, 150
Intended to provide a communications channel from students to faculty and staff and to present a systematic picture of how students perceive their college experiences. Major area of content in this survey concerns the processes of instruction as experienced by the students. Other areas covered include student goals, educational and occupational decisions, and program planning; students' perceptions of the college's administrative affairs; and out-of-class activities, problems of housing, transportation, financial support, part-time employment, and other aspects of college life. In addition to the 150 items, there is a 20-item local option section plus 9 demographic questions.

11007
Profile of Real/Ideal Scholastic Motivation. Docking, Russell A. 1979
Descriptors: *Educational Attitudes; Foreign Countries; Higher Education; High Schools; *High School Students; Rating Scales; *Student Attitudes; *Undergraduate Students; Likert Scales
Identifiers: Australia; PRISM
Availability: ERIC Document Reproduction Service; 3900 Wheeler Ave., Alexandria, VA 22304-5110 (ED194552, 42 pages)
Grade Level: 9–16
Notes: Time, 20 approx.; Items, 30
Provides an objective description of an individual's frame of reference relating to education as measured by one's responses to a series of statements about education. Suitable for group or individual administration.

11009
Future World Perspective Values Scale. Form A.
Silvernail, David L. 19(79)

Descriptors: Adolescents; Adults; Cultural Awareness; *Futures (of Society); *Global Approach; Rating Scales; *Values; Likert Scales
Availability: ERIC Document Reproduction Service; 3900 Wheeler Ave., Alexandria, VA 22304 (ED193315, 23 pages)
Target Audience: 15–64
Notes: Items, 40
Scale was designed to measure the 4 value constructs of selective economic growth; adaptive technology; international cooperation; and world economic justice. Factor analysis indicated that 28 items were valid measures of the 4 constructs.

11012
Job Involvement Questionnaire. Lodahl, Thomas M.; Kejner, Mathilde 1965
Descriptors: Adults; *Job Performance; Questionnaires; *Self Esteem; *Work Attitudes
Availability: Journal of Applied Psychology;v49 n1 p24-33, 1965
Target Audience: Adults
Notes: Items, 20
A scale to measure job involvement, which is defined as the degree to which a person's job performance affects his or her self-esteem.

11016
Institutional Functioning Inventory. Revised Edition. Peterson, Richard; And Others
Subtests: Intellectual-Aesthetic Extracurriculum; Freedom; Human Diversity; Concern for Improvement of Society; Concern for Undergraduate Learning; Democratic Governance; Meeting Local Needs; Self-Study and Planning; Concern for Advancing Knowledge; Concern for Innovation; Institutional Esprit
Descriptors: Administrator Attitudes; *Higher Education; *Self Evaluation (Groups); Student Attitudes; *Teacher Attitudes
Identifiers: IFI
Availability: School and Higher Education Programs; Educational Testing Service, Princeton, NJ 08541
Grade Level: Higher Education
Notes: Time, 30; Items, 132
Provides a means for a college or university to describe itself in terms of a number of characteristics judged important in American higher education. Normal use is with the faculty, but instrument is also appropriate for administrators or governing board members. Students may also answer Sections 1 and 2 only (72 items).

11018
Staff Attitudes and Therapeutic Styles Inventory.
Jacobs, Martin A.; Warner, Beth L. 1981
Descriptors: Adults; *Counseling Techniques; *Counselor Attitudes; *Emotional Problems; *Patients; *Psychotherapy
Availability: Journal of Clinical Psychology;v37 n1 p75-82, Jan 1981
Target Audience: Adults
Notes: Items, 10
Used to investigate whether therapeutic processes, as measured by self-reported attitudes of therapists, are differentially effective with varying levels of patient pathology. The therapeutic variables are empathetic warmth, directiveness, and uncovering.

11043
Reading Appraisal Guide. 1979
Subtests: Attitude Interview (25); Oral Reading
Descriptors: *Diagnostic Tests; Elementary Secondary Education; Miscue Analysis; *Oral Reading; *Reading Tests
Identifiers: *Australia
Availability: Northwest Regional Educational Laboratory; Office of Marketing, 101 S.W. Main St., Ste. 500, Portland, OR 97204
Grade Level: 5–12
An interview measure of attitudes toward reading in general, at home, or in school and a form for analyzing and recording errors during oral reading. Developed in Australia.

11048
Bloom Sentence Completion Survey: Adult.
Bloom, Wallace 1974
Subtests: People; Physical Self; Family; Psychological Self; Self-Directedness; Work; Accomplishment; Irritants
Descriptors: *Adults; Attitudes; *Interpersonal Relationship; Negative Attitudes; *Self Concept; *Work Attitudes
Identifiers: BSCS
Availability: Stoelting Company; 620 Wheat Ln., Wood Dale, IL 60191
Target Audience: 18–64
Notes: Time, 25 approx.; Items, 40

Designed to reveal subject's attitudes (positive, neutral, and negative) toward factors in daily living. Instrument uses sentence completion format to determine attitudes in 8 different areas.

11068
The Marlowe-Crowne Social Desirability Scale.
Crowne, Douglas P.; Marlowe, David 1964
Descriptors: Adults; Conformity; *Forced Choice Technique; *Personality Measures; Personality Traits; Prosocial Behavior; *Self Concept; *Self Evaluation (Individuals); *Social Adjustment; *Social Attitudes
Identifiers: M C Scale; MC SD Scale; Personal Reaction Inventory
Availability: Crowne, Douglas P.; and Marlowe, David; *The Approval Motive,*Westport, CT: Greenwood Press, 1964
Target Audience: Adults
Notes: Time, 15 approx.; Items, 33
Untimed, true-false instrument designed to measure individual differences in social-desirability responses. Does not measure a subject's motivated willingness or unwillingness to admit maladjusted symptoms, but does measure whether subjects do admit to such symptoms. Includes both culturally acceptable statements that are probably untrue of most people and undesirable statements.

11077
School Attitude Measure 4/6. Scott, Foresman and Co., Glenview, IL 1980
Subtests: Motivation for Schooling; Academic Self-Concept—Performance Based; Academic Self-Concept—Reference Based; Student's Sense of Control over School Performance; Student's Instructional Mastery
Descriptors: Academic Ability; *Elementary School Students; Intermediate Grades; Locus of Control; *School Attitudes; Self Concept; *Student Attitudes; Student Motivation
Identifiers: SAM
Availability: American Testronics; P.O. Box 2270, Iowa City, IA 52244
Grade Level: 4-6
Notes: Time, 30 approx.; Items, 75
Part of the Comprehensive Assessment Program. An affective self-report survey which assesses students' concepts of themselves as students. Opinions and attitudes are expressed in terms of the academic environment.

11078
School Attitude Measure 7/8. Scott, Foresman and Co., Glenview, IL 1980
Subtests: Motivation for Schooling; Academic Self-Concept—Performance Based; Academic Self-Concept—Referenced Based; Student's Sense of Control over Performance; Student's Instructional Mastery
Descriptors: Academic Ability; Junior High Schools; *Junior High School Students; Locus of Control; *School Attitudes; Self Concept; *Student Attitudes; Student Motivation
Identifiers: SAM
Availability: American Testronics; P.O. Box 2270, Iowa City, IA 52244
Grade Level: 7-8
Notes: Time, 35 approx.; Items, 85
Part of the Comprehensive Assessment Program. An affective, self-report survey which assesses students' concepts of themselves as students. Opinions and attitudes are expressed in terms of the academic environment.

11079
School Attitude Measure 9/12. Scott, Foresman and Co., Glenview, IL 1980
Subtests: Motivation for Schooling; Academic Self-Concept—Performance Based; Academic Self-Concept—Referenced Based; Student's Sense of Control over Performance; Student's Instructional Mastery
Descriptors: Academic Ability; High Schools; *High School Students; Locus of Control; *School Attitudes; Self Concept; *Student Attitudes; Student Motivation
Identifiers: SAM
Availability: American Testronics; P.O. Box 2270, Iowa City, IA 52244
Grade Level: 9-12
Notes: Time, 40 approx.; Items, 100
Part of the Comprehensive Assessment Program. An affective, self-report survey which assesses students' concepts of themselves as students. Opinions and attitudes are expressed in terms of the academic environment.

11083
Autism Attitude Scale for Teachers. Olley, J. Gregory; And Others
Descriptors: Adults; *Autism; *Teacher Attitudes; Likert Scales
Identifiers: AAST

Availability: J. Gregory Olley; Div. TEACCH, Dept. of Psychiatry, 214 Medical School Wing B, 207H, University of North Carolina, Chapel Hill, NC 27514
Target Audience: Adults
Notes: Items, 14
Used to assess teacher attitudes about admitting autistic children into their schools. Consists of 2 7-item alternate forms which may be administered separately or as 1 14-item form. Also available are an 8-item Teacher Information Questionnaire and guidelines for using alternate versus combined forms of the attitude test.

11091
Measures of Global Understanding. Educational Testing Service, Princeton, NJ 1981
Subtests: General Background; Student Opinion and Self-Perception Survey; Global Understanding Test; Foreign Language Background and Proficiency
Descriptors: *College Students; *Cultural Awareness; *Global Approach; Higher Education; Knowledge Level; Language Proficiency; Questionnaires; Second Languages; *Social Sciences; Student Attitudes; Student Interests; *World Affairs; World Problems
Identifiers: Council on Learning Education and World View Proj; Global Understanding Project
Availability: Transaction Books; Rutgers State University, Bldg. 4051, New Brunswick, NJ 08903
Grade Level: 13-16
Notes: Time, 90 approx.; Items, 133
Designed for use in a study commissioned by the Council on Learning. Test measures knowledges, attitudes, perceptions, and interests of college students related to other cultures and the political events, national policies, and other factors affecting these cultures. Also elicits students' descriptions of their own foreign language proficiency. Test items and item statistics are contained in the publication *College Students' Knowledge and Beliefs: A Survey of Global Understanding.*

11104
Attitudes toward Treatment of Disabled Students. Fonosch, Gail G. 1979
Descriptors: *Classroom Environment; *Classroom Techniques; *College Faculty; College Students; Higher Education; *Physical Disabilities; Teacher Attitudes; Likert Scales
Identifiers: ATTDS; Rehabilitation Act 1973 (Section 504); TIM(G)
Availability: Tests in Microfiche; Test Collection, Educational Testing Service, Princeton, NJ 08541
Grade Level: 13-16
Notes: Items, 32
Five-point agree/disagree Likert scale assesses teacher attitudes toward disabled students enrolled in postsecondary courses. Attitudes relate to classroom management issues pertaining to Section 504 of the Rehabilitation Act of 1973, e.g., modification of course requirements, evaluation procedure changes, provision of special course materials.

11105
Student Survey. Downey, Ronald G.; Lynch, Michael L. 1977
Subtests: General Information; Attitudes and Opinions; Purposes or Goals; Student Services; Academic Activities; Peer Interactions; Faculty Interactions; School Activities; Family Interactions; Growth and Development Activities; Community Activities; Personal Time; Work Activities
Descriptors: Background; College Curriculum; Family Relationship; Higher Education; Leisure Time; Participant Satisfaction; Peer Relationship; *School Surveys; *Student Attitudes; Student Educational Objectives; Student Personnel Services; Teacher Student Relationship; *Undergraduate Students
Identifiers: *Student Involvement; TIM(G)
Availability: Tests in Microfiche; Test Collection, Educational Testing Service, Princeton, NJ 08541
Grade Level: 13-16
Notes: Items, 119
Designed to measure student involvement in the college environment. Considers student biographical and demographic data and student satisfaction as well as attitudes and opinions. Administered by interview and via mail.

11107
Work and Family Orientation Questionnaire.
Spence, Janet T.; Helmreich, Robert L. 1978
Subtests: Work; Mastery; Competitiveness; Personal Unconcern
Descriptors: *Achievement Need; *Adults; *Family Life; *Marriage; Rating Scales; *Work Attitudes; Likert Scales
Identifiers: WOFO

Availability: Janet T. Spence; Dept. of Psychology, Mezes Hall, University of Texas, Austin, TX 78712
Target Audience: 18-65
Notes: Items, 32
Measures achievement motivation and attitudes toward family and career. Twenty-three items deal with achievement motives, and 9 items are concerned with educational aspirations, pay, prestige, advancement, attitude toward spouse employment, relative importance of marriage versus career, and number of children desired. Scales derived from factor analyses of the 23 motivational items are designated work, mastery, competitiveness, and personal unconcern. Questionnaire is also available from JSAS Catalog of Selected Documents in *Psychology,* v8 p35 1978 (MS. No. 1677).

11114
Marital Questionnaire. Haynes, S.N. 1978
Subtests: Premarital History; Descriptive Information; Marital Attitudes; Decision Making
Descriptors: Adults; Background; Decision Making; Interpersonal Relationship; *Marriage; *Marriage Counseling; *Questionnaires; Spouses
Availability: Stephen N. Haynes; Psychology Dept., Illinois Institute of Technology, 3300 S. Federal St., Chicago, IL 60616
Target Audience: Adults
Notes: Items, 66
Focuses on satisfaction in various areas: money management, communication, relationships with others, sex, decision making. Two forms are available.

11118
College Descriptive Index. Reed, Jeffrey G.; And Others 1980
Descriptors: *College Environment; *College Students; *Educational Experience; Higher Education; *Participant Satisfaction; Questionnaires; *Student Attitudes
Identifiers: CDI; TIM (H)
Availability: Tests in Microfiche; Test Collection, Educational Testing Service, Princeton, NJ 08541
Grade Level: Higher Education
Notes: Items, 8
Multidimensional measure of student satisfaction with the college experience. Uses a descriptive adjective checklist type of procedure. Adjectives are grouped in 8 areas concerning teachers, parents, self, other students, courses, finances, college administrators, and extra curricular activities.

11125
Work Relevant Attitudes Inventory. Walther, Regis H. 1975
Descriptors: Adolescents; Adults; Disadvantaged; *Individual Needs; *Labor Force Development; *Program Effectiveness; *Work Attitudes
Identifiers: TIM (H); WRAI
Availability: Tests in Microfiche; Test Collection, Educational Testing Service, Princeton, NJ 08541
Target Audience: Adolescents
Notes: Items, 26
Used to diagnose individual needs and to evaluate effectiveness of manpower programs. Can be useful in counseling process involved in manpower training programs.

11127
Body Valuation Form. Vaughan, Sandra 1977
Descriptors: Blacks; Elementary Education; Females; Grade 3; Grade 6; *Human Body; Males; Rating Scales; *Self Esteem; Values; Whites
Identifiers: *Body Esteem
Availability: Sandra Vaughan; Dept. of Psychology, Georgia State University, 33 Gilmer St. S.E., Atlanta, GA 30303
Grade Level: 3; 6
Notes: Items, 7
Public school children were asked to assign a dollar value to 7 body parts from 0 to $550 to determine whether males or females, blacks or whites have a higher body esteem.

11130
Freshman Dormitory Survey. Altman, Irwin 1975
Descriptors: *Adjustment (to Environment); Ancillary School Services; *College Freshmen; *Dormitories; Higher Education; Peer Relationship; Physical Health; Privacy; Questionnaires; Student Attitudes; Student College Relationship; Student Participation
Availability: Irwin Altman; College of Social and Behavioral Science, University of Utah, Salt Lake City, UT 84112
Grade Level: 13
Notes: Items, 65
Designed to assess students' adjustment to dormitory life, satisfaction with the university, and mechanisms used to establish privacy. Items assess participation in extracurri-

cular activities, use of student services, personal health, peer relationships, and opinions about university and dormitory life. Developed for a study on college freshmen.

11146
General Inventory for Kindergarten. Nale, Nell; And Others 1975
Subtests: Social Concepts; Motor Development; General Concepts; Memory and Problem Solving; Self-Concept and Independence; Attitude and Interest in School; Social Relationships
Descriptors: Concept Formation; *Individual Testing; *Kindergarten Children; Language Acquisition; Perceptual Motor Coordination; Primary Education; *School Readiness Tests; Social Development
Availability: McGraw Hill Book Company; School Div., 1200 N.W. 63rd St., Oklahoma City, OK 73125
Grade Level: Kindergarten
Notes: Time, 30 approx.; Items, 60
Individually administered inventory to be given at the beginning of the kindergarten year. Assesses student's current level of conceptual development, language development, social/emotional development, and perceptual/motor development.

11149
Reading Propositional Inventory. Duffy, Gerald G.; Metheny, William 1978
Descriptors: Adults; Beliefs; *Reading Attitudes; *Reading Instruction; *Teacher Attitudes; Likert Scales
Availability: ERIC Document Reproduction Service; 3900 Wheeler Ave., Alexandria, VA 22304 (ED174954, 25 pages)
Target Audience: Adults
Notes: Items, 45
Assesses teachers' beliefs about reading, which can be viewed both in terms of standard models (such as basal readers) and dimensions of observed teacher decision making. Has potential for use in teacher education at both the preservice and inservice levels.

11161
School Environment Preference Survey. Gordon, Leonard V. 1978
Subtests: Self-Subordination; Traditionalism; Rule Conformity; Uncriticalness
Descriptors: Conformity; Discipline Problems; *Educational Environment; *Elementary School Students; Elementary Secondary Education; Postsecondary Education; Rating Scales; *School Attitudes; *Secondary School Students; *Student School Relationship; Teacher Student Relationship; Work Environment
Availability: Educational and Industrial Testing Service; P.O. Box 7234, San Diego, CA 92107
Grade Level: 3-13
Notes: Time, 15; Items, 24
Designed to measure individuals' levels of commitment to the attitudes, values, and behaviors rewarded and encouraged in the school environment. High scorers seek group and institutional identification, accept authority, prefer rules, and do not question judgment. Used to gain understanding of the student in relation to disciplinary problems and in vocational education classes to determine work climate preference.

11199
Environmental Education Needs and Interests of Wisconsin Adults. Nichols, Stan; And Others 1978
Descriptors: *Adults; Continuing Education; Educational Needs; *Environment; *Environmental Education; *Individual Activities; Informal Assessment; *Information Needs; *Interest Inventories; Interviews; Older Adults; *State Surveys
Availability: University of Wisconsin—Extension; Environmental Resources Unit, 1815 University Ave., Madison, WI 53706
Target Audience: 18-90
Notes: Items, 43
A telephone survey interview used to assess the need for and interest in continuing environmental education for Wisconsin adults. Includes interest in environment and nature topics, desire to know more about topics, uses for environmental information, current environmentally related activities, likelihood of using different ways of getting information on the environment, and background information about the subject (age, education, occupation, location of home community, etc.).

11207
The Anser System. Form 4. Self-Administered Student Profile. Levine, Melvin D. 1980
Descriptors: *Data Collection; *Elementary School Students; Intermediate Grades; Interpersonal Competence; Learning Problems; *Questionnaires; Secondary Education; *Secondary School Students; Self Concept; *Self Evaluation (Individuals); Student Interests

Availability: Educators Publishing Service; 75 Moulton St., Cambridge, MA 02238
Grade Level: 4-12
Target Audience: 9-18
Integrates data in the areas of health, education, development, and behavior in order to assess children's school adjustment or learning problems. Compiled data can be used with direct assessments, including psychological evaluation, achievement tests, and health and developmental assessment. May also be used to help formulate individualized educational plans. Form 4 is a self-administered student profile covering student skills, interests, and perceptions of degree of ability in school, sports, cognitive ability, and social skills.

11229
Toy Preference Test. DeLucia, Lenore A. 1963
Descriptors: *Children; *Elementary Education; Elementary School Students; *Individual Testing; *Interest Inventories; *Pictorial Stimuli; Psychological Characteristics; *Sex Differences; *Sex Role; *Toys; Visual Measures
Identifiers: Oral Tests
Availability: Child Development;v34 n1 p107-17, Mar 1963
Grade Level: K-4
Notes: Time, 15 approx.; Items, 24
An untimed, individually administered instrument used to measure the sex-role identification of children. The child is presented with 2 pictures of toys and asked which one he or she would prefer to play with. Requires the use of a set of pictures of the toys.

11269
National Assessment of Educational Progress: Released Items. Education Commission of the States, Denver, CO 1970
Subtests: Art; Career and Occupational Development; Citizenship/Social Studies; Math; Music; Reading/Literature; Science; Writing; Energy; Health; Literacy and Reading
Descriptors: *Achievement Tests; Adolescents; Adults; Art; Career Development; Children; Citizenship; Energy; Health; *Item Banks; Knowledge Level; Literacy; Literature; Mathematics; Music; National Surveys; Reading; Sciences; Social Studies; Test Construction; Writing (Composition)
Identifiers: NAEP; National Institute of Education
Availability: National Assessment of Educational Progress; Publication Order Services, Box 2923, Princeton, NJ 08541
Target Audience: 9; 13; 17; 26-35
Items used in previous surveys of knowledges, skills, attitudes, and understandings of young Americans. Sponsored by the National Institute of Education. Constructed to aid states or other education units in building their own tests. Many are available from the Educational Resources Information Center (ERIC) (ED186231; ED145201; ED187543; ED205588; ED205589; ED161686; ED205583; ED155728).

11276
Structured Divorce Questionnaire. Reinhard, David W. 1970
Subtests: News of the Divorce; Loss of Parent; Acceptance of Parents; Changes in Family Relationships; School Performance; Peer Relationships; Behavioral Reactions; Emotional Responses; General Reactions; Post Divorce Conflict
Descriptors: *Adolescents; *Divorce; Parent Child Relationship; Peer Relationship; Rating Scales; Student School Relationship
Identifiers: TIM (H)
Availability: Tests in Microfiche; Test Collection, Educational Testing Service, Princeton, NJ 08541
Target Audience: Adolescents
Notes: Time, 20; Items, 113
Used to learn more about reactions and feelings that adolescents experience when their parents divorced. Where more than one child in a family answered the questionnaire, it was group administered. Where only one child was participating, instrument was individually administered.

11342
Personal Reaction Index. Revised Edition. Hall, Jay 1980
Descriptors: *Decision Making; *Employee Attitudes; *Organizational Climate; *Participant Satisfaction; Rating Scales
Availability: Teleometrics International; 1755 Woodstead Ct., The Woodlands, TX 77380
Target Audience: Adults
Notes: Items, 6
Designed to give managerial level employees feedback in the form of subordinate assessments regarding the decision structure that governs their work, i.e., the amount

of influence subordinates feel they have in making work-related decisions and their consequent satisfaction with and commitment to those decisions.

11348
Attitudes toward Working Mothers Scale. Tetenbaum, Toby J. 1979
Descriptors: Adults; *Employed Parents; *Mothers; Rating Scales
Identifiers: AWM Scale; TIM (H)
Availability: Tests in Microfiche; Test Collection, Educational Testing Service, Princeton, NJ 08541
Target Audience: Adults
Notes: Items, 45
Used to measure attitudes of others toward working mothers and toward women's role in society.

11370
Correctional Officers' Interest Blank. Gough, Harrison G.; Aumack, F.L. 1980
Subtests: Personal Preferences; Personal Attitudes
Descriptors: Adults; Attitudes; *Correctional Institutions; *Institutional Personnel; *Interest Inventories; Interests; *Job Applicants; *Predictive Measurement
Identifiers: COIB
Availability: Consulting Psychologists Press; 577 College Ave., Palo Alto, CA 94306
Target Audience: Adults
Notes: Time, 10 approx.; Items, 40
Contains questions about personal interests and attitudes which have been found to have modest potential for predicting performance of correctional officers. May be administered to groups or individually administered. Test is intended for use in evaluating correctional officers and job applicants. Scoring key is available only to qualified persons representing state, federal or other bona fide law enforcement or judicial agencies.

11430
Teacher Conceptions of the Educative Process. Wehling, Leslie J.; Charters, W.W., Jr. 1969
Subtests: Subject Matter; Personal Adjustment Ideology; Student Autonomy vs. Teacher Direction; Emotional Disengagement; Consideration of Student Viewpoint; Classroom Order; Student Challenge; Integrative Learning
Descriptors: Adults; Beliefs; *Classroom Environment; Course Content; Empathy; Learning Experience; Questionnaires; Social Environment; Student Interests; Student Needs; *Teacher Attitudes; *Teachers; Teaching Methods; *Teaching Styles; *Values
Identifiers: Social Distance
Availability: American Educational Research Journal;v6 n1 p7-30, Jan 1969
Target Audience: Adults
Notes: Items, 86
Questionnaire designed to determine teachers' attitudes and beliefs concerning the value of course content, student interests and needs, classroom guidance and order, teacher-student relationships and students' understanding of subject matter.

11490
Values Inventory for Children. Guilford, Joan; And Others
Subtests: Asocial; Social Conformity; Me First; Sociability; Academic; Masculinity; Adult Closeness
Descriptors: Affection; Antisocial Behavior; Assertiveness; Elementary Education; *Elementary School Students; Measures (Individuals); School Activities; Social Behavior; *Values; *Visual Measures
Identifiers: Dominant Behavior; Masculinity; Selfishness
Availability: Consulting Psychologists Press; 577 College Ave., Palo Alto, CA 94306
Grade Level: 1-7
Notes: Time, 50; Items, 47
Pictorial instrument designed to measure 7 dimensions of values of young children. Covers liking socially disapproved activities; choosing what is proper; selfishness, dominance, assertiveness; sociability; liking academic activities; liking masculine activities; close physical affection with adults. Norms are for grades 1-4.

11499
Conceptions of Personal Issues. Revised. Nucci, Larry P. 1982
Descriptors: Adolescents; Adults; Children; *Moral Issues; *Social Problems; *Values
Identifiers: Card Sort; TIM (H)
Availability: Tests in Microfiche; Test Collection, Educational Testing Service, Princeton, NJ 08541
Target Audience: 6-18
Notes: Items, 19

Card sort designed to examine the distinctions children make among moral, social, conventional, and personal issues.

11547
Modified Questionnaire on the Occupational Status of Women. Bingham, William C.; Turner, Carol J. 1980
Descriptors: Adults; *Counselor Attitudes; Counselor Educators; *Females; *Occupational Aspiration; Questionnaires
Identifiers: MQOSW; TIM (H)
Availability: Tests in Microfiche; Test Collection, Educational Testing Service, Princeton, NJ 08541
Target Audience: Adults
Notes: Items, 30

Used to measure attitudes of counselors and counselor educators toward the occupational status of women. Construct validity will be reevaluated when more data from studies become available; meanwhile, reliability and validity are adequate for research purposes. This questionnaire is a modification of the Questionnaire on the Occupational Status of Women (TC007525).

11552
Mainstreaming Opinionnaire. Schmelkin, Liora Pedhazur 1981
Descriptors: Adults; Disabilities; *Mainstreaming; Questionnaires; Special Classes; Special Education Teachers; Teachers
Identifiers: Likert Scale
Availability: Liora Pedhazur Schmelkin; Assistant Professor, Dept. of Counseling, Psychology and Research in Education, Hofstra University, Hempstead, NY 11550
Target Audience: Adults
Notes: Items, 30

A Likert-type scale consisting of 2 subscales. The Academic Costs of Mainstreaming Scale deals with possible detrimental effects of mainstreaming on the conduct of the regular classroom and the academic progress of both normal and handicapped students. The Socio-Emotional Costs of Segregation scale deals with negative aspects of segregating handicapped students in terms of their social and emotional development. Further information on this test can be found in *Exceptional Children*; v48 n1 p42-47, 1981.

11558
Mainstreaming Planning Inventory. May, Barrie Jo; Furst, Edward J. 1977
Descriptors: Adults; Higher Education; *Mainstreaming; *Student Attitudes; *Teacher Attitudes
Availability: ERIC Document Reproduction Service; 3900 Wheeler Ave., Alexandria, VA 22304 (ED160642, 37 pages)
Target Audience: Adults
Notes: Items, 40

Used to measure attitudes toward mainstreaming in education. Factors measured include acceptance of mainstreaming, resulting adjustments in the classroom, emotional demands, and sensitivities of handicapped students, teachers' confidence in coping with demands imposed by mainstreaming, positive expectations for handicapped students, treatment of students, parental attitudes, effects of mainstreaming on nonhandicapped students.

11566
A Dating Problems Checklist. Revised Edition. McHugh, Gelolo 1979
Descriptors: *Adolescents; Check Lists; Counseling; *Dating (Social); Parent Child Relationship; Physical Characteristics; Questionnaires; Self Concept; Sexuality; *Social Attitudes; *Social Problems
Identifiers: DPCL
Availability: Family Life Publications, Inc.; P.O. Box 427, Saluda, NC 28773
Target Audience: Adolescents
Notes: Time, 30 approx.; Items, 125

Teaching and counseling aid to help teachers and counselors become acquainted with current dating environment as well as with individual dating problems. The questionnaire covers the following topics: dating conditions; home, parents, and family; personality and emotional self; sex attitudes; physical self; dating and definite commitments.

11605
Children's Social Attitudes Inventory. Beardsley, Donna A. 1982
Descriptors: *Children; *Peer Acceptance; *Physical Disabilities; Pictorial Stimuli; Primary Education
Identifiers: TIM(H)
Availability: Tests in Microfiche; Test Collection, Educational Testing Service, Princeton, NJ 08541
Target Audience: 7-8
Notes: Items, 12

Designed to measure the attitudes of primary age children toward their handicapped peers. The questions represent social situations involving the interaction of a single person with 2 or 3 others, either handicapped or nonhandicapped, or with both groups.

11649
Multidimensional Fear of Death Scale. Hoelter, Jon W. 1978
Subtests: Fear of Dying; Fear of the Dead; Fear of Being Destroyed; Fear for Significant Others; Fear of the Unknown; Fear of Conscious Death; Fear for Body after Death; Fear of Premature Death
Descriptors: *Anxiety; *College Students; *Death; *Fear; Higher Education; Rating Scales; *Student Attitudes
Identifiers: *Death Anxiety; MFODS
Availability: Jon W. Hoelter; Dept. of Sociology, University of Cincinnati, Cincinnati, OH 45221
Grade Level: 13-16
Notes: Items, 42

Designed to measure different aspects of the fear of death construct (death anxiety). Provides a multidimensional conceptualization of the fear of death. Was created using a population of college students but may have applicability to other, older groups.

11652
Nutrition Attitude Instrument for Preschool. Pennsylvania State University, University Park, Nutrition Information and Resource Center 1980
Subtests: Eating New Foods; Nutrition; Vegetables
Descriptors: *Childhood Attitudes; Elementary School Curriculum; *Food; *Kindergarten Children; *Nutrition; *Pretests Posttests; Primary Education; Likert Scales
Identifiers: Oral Tests; School Nutrition Education Curriculum Study; TIM(H)
Availability: Tests in Microfiche; Test Collection, Educational Testing Service, Princeton, NJ 08541
Grade Level: K
Notes: Time, 15 approx.; Items, 18

Used to examine selected nutrition and food attitudes of kindergarten children before and after participating in a nutrition education study which examined the effect of nutrition information taught using the curriculum, Nutrition in a Changing World. Instrument includes 3 constructs: eating new foods, nutrition, and vegetables. Children respond to each statement read to them by marking 1 of 4 attitude indicators: a smiling face, a neutral face, a frowning face, or a question mark.

11657
Nutrition Attitude Instrument for the Primary Grades. Pennsylvania State University, University Park, Nutrition Information and Resource Center 1979
Subtests: Eating New Foods; Nutrition; Vegetables
Descriptors: *Childhood Attitudes; Elementary School Curriculum; *Elementary School Students; *Food; *Nutrition; *Pretests Posttests; Primary Education; Likert Scales
Identifiers: Oral Tests; School Nutrition Education Curriculum Study; TIM(H)
Availability: Tests in Microfiche; Test Collection, Educational Testing Service, Princeton, NJ 08541
Grade Level: 1-3
Notes: Time, 15 approx.; Items, 18

Used to examine selected nutrition and food attitudes before and after participating in a nutrition education study using Nutrition in a Changing World. Instrument includes 3 constructs: eating new foods, nutrition, and vegetables. The statements are read to the student who responds by marking 1 of 4 attitude indicators; a smiling face, a neutral face, a frowning face, or a question mark.

11662
Nutrition Attitude Instrument for the Intermediate Grades. Pennsylvania State University, University Park, Nutrition Information and Resource Center 1979
Subtests: Nutrition; Eating New Foods; Learning about Nutrition; Vegetables
Descriptors: *Childhood Attitudes; Elementary School Curriculum; *Elementary School Students; *Food; Intermediate Grades; *Nutrition; Nutrition Instruction; *Pretests Posttests
Identifiers: School Nutrition Education Curriculum Study; TIM(H)
Availability: Tests in Microfiche; Test Collection, Educational Testing Service, Princeton, NJ 08541
Grade Level: 4-6
Notes: Items, 25

Developed to examine selected nutrition and food attitudes of intermediate grade students before and after participating in a nutrition education study using Nutrition in a Changing World. The instrument was reviewed by nutrition education experts.

11666
Nutrition Attitude Instrument for Grades 7-12. Pennsylvania State University, University Park, Nutrition Information and Resource Center 1980
Subtests: Learning about Nutrition; Eating New Foods; Caring about Nutrition; Nutrition Affects Health
Descriptors: *Food; *Nutrition; Nutrition Instruction; *Pretests Posttests; Secondary Education; *Secondary School Students
Identifiers: School Nutrition Education Curriculum Study; TIM(H)
Availability: Tests in Microfiche; Test Collection, Educational Testing Service, Princeton, NJ 08541
Grade Level: 7-12
Notes: Items, 22

Used to examine selected nutrition-food attitudes of secondary school students before and after participating in a nutrition education study using Nutrition in a Changing World. Students rate each item on a 5-point scale.

11668
A Curriculum Survey: A Commitment Instrument for Teachers. Pennsylvania State University, University Park, Nutrition Information and Resource Center 1978
Descriptors: Adults; Elementary Education; *Elementary School Teachers; *Nutrition Instruction; *Pretests Posttests; *Teacher Attitudes; *Teacher Response
Identifiers: School Nutrition Education Curriculum Study; TIM(H)
Availability: Tests in Microfiche; Test Collection, Educational Testing Service, Princeton, NJ 08541
Grade Level: K-6
Target Audience: Adults
Notes: Items, 7

Used to assess the commitment of elementary school teachers to teaching nutrition before and after participating in a nutrition education study. Study examined the influence of 3 types of teacher preparation, using Nutrition in a Changing World. Also used to assess centrality of teachers' attitudes toward including nutrition education in the schools and to examine the effects of points of view which are incompatible with a positive attitude toward teaching nutrition.

11669
We Want Your Opinion: An Attitude Instrument for Teachers. Pennsylvania State University, University Park, Nutrition Information and Resource Center 1978
Subtests: Nutrition Is Important; Favors Nutrition Education in Schools
Descriptors: Adults; Elementary Education; *Elementary School Teachers; *Nutrition; *Nutrition Instruction; *Pretests Posttests; *Teacher Attitudes; Likert Scales
Identifiers: School Nutrition Education Curriculum Study; TIM(H)
Availability: Tests in Microfiche; Test Collection, Educational Testing Service, Princeton, NJ 08541
Grade Level: K-6
Target Audience: Adults
Notes: Items, 19

Developed to assess the attitudes of elementary school teachers toward the importance of nutrition and toward including nutrition education in the schools. Instrument used before and after teacher participation in a nutrition education study using Nutrition in a Changing World. Study also examined the influence of 3 types of teacher preparation. Each item is rated on a 5-point scale.

11670
We Want Your Opinion: An Attitude Instrument for College Students. Pennsylvania State University, University Park, Nutrition Information and Resource Center 1978
Subtests: Concern about Nutrition; Breast Feeding Is Important; Nutrition Is Important in Pregnancy; World Food Issues; Attitude about Televised Instruction
Descriptors: *College Students; *Educational Television; Higher Education; *Nutrition; *Nutrition Instruction; *Pretests Posttests; *Student Attitudes; Likert Scales
Identifiers: School Nutrition Education Curriculum Study; TIM(H)
Availability: Tests in Microfiche; Test Collection, Educational Testing Service, Princeton, NJ 08541
Grade Level: 13-16
Notes: Items, 49

Used to assess attitudes of college students enrolled in an introductory nutrition course toward nutrition and multimedia instruction. Measures their attitudes before and after receiving nutrition instruction either by traditional lecture-discussion or by multimedia method. Response to each item is made on a 5-point Likert scale.

11671
Grades 7-12 Teacher and Administrator Questionnaire. Pennsylvania State University, University Park, Nutrition Information and Resource Center 1979
Subtests: Need for Nutrition Education in Grades 7-12; Nutrition Should Be Taught As a Separate Course in Grades 7-12; Interest in Teaching Nutrition
Descriptors: *Administrator Attitudes; Adults; Curriculum Development; Inservice Teacher Education; *Nutrition Instruction; *School Administration; Secondary Education; *Secondary School Teachers; State Surveys; *Teacher Attitudes
Identifiers: Pennsylvania; School Nutrition Education Curriculum Study; TIM(H)
Availability: Tests in Microfiche; Test Collection, Educational Testing Service, Princeton, NJ 08541
Grade Level: 7–12
Target Audience: Adults
Notes: Items, 18

Developed for use in a statewide survey of junior high and senior high school administrators and teachers to assess their perspective on nutrition education for students in grades 7-12. Twelve items assess the 3 constructs of need, separate course, and interest and are rated on a 5-point Likert scale. Six items are intended to reveal opinions on the incorporation of nutrition in the overall curriculum and willingness to attend inservice session on nutrition education. Instrument was reviewed by experts in nutrition education and research methodology.

11672
Parent Attitude Questionnaire. Pennsylvania State University, University Park, Nutrition Information and Resource Center 1980
Descriptors: Adults; *Nutrition Instruction; *Parent Attitudes; Likert Scales
Identifiers: School Nutrition Education Curriculum Study; TIM(H)
Availability: Tests in Microfiche; Test Collection, Educational Testing Service, Princeton, NJ 08541
Target Audience: Adults
Notes: Items, 14

Used to assess attitudes of parents toward nutrition education and its importance. Parents were those of students who participated in a nutrition education study using Nutrition in a Changing World. Questionnaire contains statements to reflect 2 constructs: attitudes toward nutrition education and attitudes toward its importance. Most items were answered on a 5-point Likert scale.

11682
Mainstreaming Attitude Survey. Larrivee, Barbara; Cook, Linda 1979
Descriptors: Administrator Role; Adults; Class Size; *Educational Environment; Instructional Program Divisions; *Mainstreaming; Resource Teachers; School Size; *Special Classes; *Teacher Attitudes
Identifiers: Summated Rating Scale
Availability: Journal of Special Education;v13 n3 p315-24, 1979
Target Audience: Adults
Notes: Items, 30

An attitude scale, using the summated rating method that examines the effect of institutional variables on teacher attitudes. Variables include grade level taught, classroom size, school size, type of school, degree of success experienced with special needs students, level of administrative support received, availability of support services.

11716
Teacher Opinion Inventory. Revised Edition. National Study of School Evaluation, Falls Church, VA 1981
Descriptors: Curriculum Evaluation; Discipline; *Educational Assessment; *Educational Environment; Job Satisfaction; *Program Evaluation; Rating Scales; School Administration; School Community Relationship; School Counseling; School Role; *Teacher Attitudes
Identifiers: *National Study of School Evaluation
Availability: National Study of School Evaluation; 5201 Leesburg Pike, Falls Church, VA 22041
Target Audience: Adults
Notes: Items, 72

Used to assess teacher opinion toward various facets of the school; to provide teacher recommendations for improvement; and to provide data as a guide to administrative decision making. May be used by itself as an instrument or in conjunction with the Student Opinion Inventory and Parent Opinion Inventory, or as part of a complete school evaluation program. Consists of 64 multiple-choice questions covering organization and administration;

curriculum and instruction; student discipline, counseling, and advisement; school-community relations; and job satisfaction. Also has 8 open-ended questions.

11717
Student Opinion Inventory, Revised Edition. National Study of School Evaluation, Falls Church, VA 1981
Subtests: Student Teacher; Student Counselor; Student Administration; Student Curriculum and Instruction; Student Participation; Student School Image
Descriptors: Curriculum Evaluation; *Educational Assessment; Educational Counseling; School Administration; *School Attitudes; Secondary Education; *Secondary School Students; *Student Attitudes; Student Participation; Student School Relationship; Teacher Student Relationship
Identifiers: *National Study of School Evaluation
Availability: National Study of School Evaluation; 5201 Leesburg Pike, Falls Church, VA 22041
Grade Level: 7–12
Notes: Time, 45 approx.; Items, 46

Student feedback instrument which assesses student attitudes toward many facets of the school and which provides student recommendations for improvement. Can be used to collect information on individual items or items can be grouped according to various subscales and an index can be obtained for each subscale. Items in the instrument cover student attitudes toward faculty, administration, counselors, curriculum and instruction, cocurricular activities, and facilities.

11732
Parent Opinion Inventory: Revised Edition. National Study of School Evaluation, Falls Church, VA 1981
Subtests: Intrastudent Body Relationships; School Information Services; Parent Involvement; Educational Objectives; Intraschool Problems; School Program Factors; Innovative Programs; Student Activities; Support Services; Auxiliary Services; General Psychological Climate
Descriptors: Adults; Ancillary School Services; *Educational Assessment; Educational Environment; Educational Objectives; *Elementary Secondary Education; *Parent Attitudes; Parent Participation; *School Attitudes
Identifiers: *National Study of School Evaluation
Availability: National Study of School Evaluation; 5201 Leesburg Pike, Falls Church, VA 22041
Target Audience: Adults
Notes: Items, 58

Developed to assess parents' attitudes toward their children's schools and programs; to provide parents the opportunity to make specific recommendations for improvement; and to provide data to school personnel for decision making in the areas of program development, policy formulation, administrative organization, faculty development, and community relations. Instrument may be used alone, in conjunction with the Student Opinion Inventory (TC011717) and Teacher Opinion Inventory (TC011716), or as part of a complete school evaluation program.

11736
Problem-Solving Decision-Making Style Inventory. Hersey, Paul; Natemeyer, Walter E. 1982
Descriptors: Adults; *Decision Making Skills; *Peer Evaluation; *Problem Solving; *Self Evaluation (Individuals)
Availability: University Associates; 8517 Production Ave., San Diego, CA 92126
Target Audience: Adults
Notes: Items, 12

Two forms, each consisting of 12 items, which provide feedback on one's perceptions of problem-solving and decision-making styles. Perception of Self measures one's self-perceptions; Perception of Other measures perception of others with whom one interacts.

11737
Performance Levels of a School Program Survey. Williams, Frank 1979
Subtests: General Intellectual Abilities; Specific Academic Abilities; Leadership Abilities; Creative Productive Thinking Abilities; Visual and Performing Arts Abilities and Talents; Psychomotor Abilities and Talents; Affective Abilities; Vocational Career Abilities and Talents
Descriptors: Administrator Attitudes; Adults; Check Lists; *Curriculum Evaluation; *Educational Assessment; *Elementary Secondary Education; *Program Effectiveness; Rating Scales; *School Administration; *School Surveys; Teacher Attitudes; *Teachers
Identifiers: PLSPS
Availability: D.O.K. Publishers; P.O. Box 605, E. Aurora, NY 14052
Grade Level: K–12
Target Audience: Adults
Notes: Time, 60 approx.; Items, 80

Designed to evaluate 8 areas of multiple abilities relevant to developing total human potential in a school setting. Used to reflect teachers' and administrators' perceptions of how well their school program is developing these areas for all students. Can be used either individually or with groups for teachers and administrators at every grade level in a school or district.

11740
The Schutz Measures: An Integrated System for Assessing Elements of Awareness. Schutz, Will 1982
Subtests: Behavior; Feelings; Self-Concept; Relationships; Job
Descriptors: Adults; *Affective Behavior; *Affective Measures; *Emotional Response; *Employee Attitudes; *Interpersonal Relationship; Rating Scales; *Self Concept; Work Environment
Identifiers: *FIRO; *Fundamental Interpersonal Relations Orientation; Self Scoring Tests
Availability: University Associates; 8517 Production Ave., San Diego, CA 92126
Target Audience: Adults

Integrated series of instruments that measure various aspects of human functioning and human relationships. Is an extension of the FIRO system, Fundamental Interpersonal Relations Orientation. The instruments may be used separately for an investigation of one aspect of human functioning or in various combinations for a broader look at an individual. Element B, Behavior, measures respondent's behavior; element F, Feelings, measures feelings toward people in general; element S, Self-Concept, investigates how people feel about themselves; element R, Relationships, explores a person's relationship with another; element J, Job, explores the relationship between one's behavior on the job and one's self-concept. Used in various combinations, the instruments provide insight into various aspects of human behavior. For each element, 2 aspects are measured: expressed-received and perceived-wanted.

11749
Teacher Attitude toward Equal Educational Opportunity for Exceptional Children. Gickling, Edward E. 1975
Descriptors: Adults; *Mainstreaming; *Public School Teachers; *Special Education Teachers
Availability: Journal of Special Education;v9 n3 p317-28, 1975
Target Audience: Adults
Notes: Items, 46

Questionnaire designed to ask both regular teachers and special educators to indicate their personal knowledge, perceptions, and attitudes toward mainstreaming. Questionnaire was designed to investigate teacher attitudes toward how the philosophy of equal educational opportunity applies to exceptional children; teachers' willingness to commit themselves to integrating exceptional children into their classes if assistance were provided. The questions were also designed to measure the organizational mechanics whereby teachers were informed about exceptional children and were made aware of and involved with the planning for exceptional children.

11758
Learning Orientation/Grade Orientation Scale. Eison, James 1981
Descriptors: *College Students; *Grades (Scholastic); Higher Education; *Learning; *School Attitudes; *Student Attitudes
Identifiers: LOGO
Availability: Psychological Reports,v48 n3 p919-24, Jun 1981
Grade Level: 13–16
Notes: Items, 20

Designed to assess whether a student learner is oriented toward learning (LO) or toward grades (GO). Items pertain to student's reactions to various policies and experiences in class.

11800
Management Inventory on Managing Change. Kirkpatrick, Donald L. 1979
Descriptors: *Administrator Attitudes; *Administrators; Administrator Selection; Adults; Change; Change Strategies; Knowledge Level; *Management Development; *Organizational Change; *Supervisors
Identifiers: MIMC; Self Scoring Tests
Availability: Donald L. Kirkpatrick; 1080 Lower Ridgeway, Elm Grove, WI 53122
Target Audience: 18–64
Notes: Time, 20 approx.; Items, 65

Designed to measure attitudes, knowledge, and opinions regarding principles and approaches for managing change. Applicable to all levels of management with emphasis on middle and top level managers. Useful in planning and evaluating training programs.

11801
Management Inventory on Time Management. Kirkpatrick, Donald L. 1980

Descriptors: Administrative Principles;
*Administrator Attitudes; Administrators;
Adults; *Management Development;
*Supervisors; *Time Management
Identifiers: MITM
Availability: Donald L. Kirkpatrick; 1080 Lower
Ridgeway, Elm Grove, WI 53122
Target Audience: 18–64
Notes: Time, 15 approx.; Items, 60
Designed to assess opinions and attitudes toward effective time utilization and delegation techniques. May be used to plan and evaluate training courses on time management. Applicable to all levels of management with emphasis on middle and top level managers.

11803
Class Activities Questionnaire. Steele, Joe M. 1982
Subtests: Cognitive Scales; Classroom Conditions; Student Attitudes and Reactions
Descriptors: *Classroom Environment;
*Elementary School Students; *Elementary School Teachers; Elementary Secondary Education; Gifted; School Attitudes; *Secondary School Students; *Secondary School Teachers; *Student Attitudes; Teacher Student Relationship; *Teacher Attitudes
Identifiers: CAQ
Availability: Creative Learning Press; P.O. Box 320, Mansfield Center, CT 06250
Grade Level: K–12
Notes: Time, 30 approx.; Items, 30
An opinionnaire administered to both students and teachers to provide a measure of the instructional climate, both cognitive and affective, in the classroom. Provides a description of an instructional setting which can help teachers in designing an appropriate learning climate. Intended users of the results are teachers, supervisors, and researchers. May be used to characterize instructional climate on a content area, a school, or a special program, such as one for gifted students.

11804
Learning Styles Inventory: A Measure of Student Preference for Instructional Techniques. Renzulli, Joseph S.; Smith, Linda H. 1978
Subtests: Projects; Drill and Recitation; Peer Teaching; Discussion; Teaching Games; Independent Study; Programed Instruction; Lecture; Simulation
Descriptors: Discussion (Teaching Technique); Drills (Practice); Educational Games; *Elementary School Students; Elementary Secondary Education; Independent Study; Lecture Method; Peer Teaching; Programed Instruction; *Secondary School Students; Simulation; Small Group Instruction; *Student Attitudes; *Teaching Methods; *Teaching Styles
Identifiers: LSI
Availability: Creative Learning Press; P.O. Box 320, Mansfield Center, CT 06250
Grade Level: 4–12
Notes: Time, 30 approx.; Items, 65
Designed to measure student attitudes toward 9 general modes of instruction. Students indicate their reaction to each activity along a 5-point rating scale ranging from very unpleasant to very pleasant. A teacher form is also included and is designed as a tool for teachers to look at the range of instructional techniques used in their own classrooms. The profile of a teacher's instructional style can be compared to individual student preferences and serve to facilitate a closer match between how teachers instruct and the styles to which students respond most favorably.

11808
My Book of Things and Stuff: An Interest Questionnaire for Young Children. McGreevy, Ann 1982
Descriptors: *Childhood Interests; Elementary Education; *Elementary School Students; Gifted; Individualized Instruction; *Interest Inventories
Availability: Creative Learning Press; P.O. Box 320, Mansfield Center, CT 06250
Grade Level: 2–5
Target Audience: 7–11
Notes: Items, 58
Furnishes teachers, counselors, and parents with insights into children and their interest patterns. Can serve as a basis for individualized instruction. Main purposes of questionnaire are to improve or open up discussion among parents, teachers, and children and to provide a better means of planning curriculum around current and potential interests of children. Does not yield a numerical score but reveals patterns of specified interests, learning styles, abilities, preferences, and values.

11829
Famous Writers School: Your Aptitude and Interest Profile. Famous Schools, Westport, CT 1981

Descriptors: Adults; *Aptitude Tests; Correspondence Study; Interest Inventories; *Writing (Composition)
Availability: Famous Schools; P.O. Box 900, Westport, CT 06880
Target Audience: Adults
Notes: Items, 40
Designed to determine whether one has the abilities, attitudes, and interests that most writers have. For use in evaluating clients for a mail order writing course.

11832
Attitude Survey about Kids. Deich, Ruth F.; Lu, Elsie Co 1982
Descriptors: Adults; *Child Rearing; Children; *Parent Attitudes; Research Tools; *Self Concept
Identifiers: *Counseling Aids
Availability: Institute for Research in Human Growth; 1737 Finecroft Dr., Claremont, CA 91711
Target Audience: Adults
Notes: Items, 136
Gathers demographic information about parents and measures parent attitudes toward child rearing, parents' self-perceptions, and perceptions of their children. Designed for use in counseling situations or research.

11898
Teachers' Attitudes about Creativity. Treffinger, Donald; And Others 1968
Descriptors: Adults; *Creativity; *Elementary School Teachers; *Teacher Attitudes; Likert Scales
Availability: Journal of Creative Behavior;v10 n2 p242-48, 1968
Target Audience: Adults
Notes: Items, 14
A measure of the attitudes of teachers toward creativity and its expression in their pupils. Respondents indicate agreement/disagreement with statements on a 5-point Likert-type scale.

11899
Menstrual Attitude Questionnaire Forms for Adult Males and Females. Brooks-Gunn, Jeanne; Ruble, Diane 1980
Descriptors: Adults; *Menstruation
Availability: Jeanne Brooks-Gunn; Educational Testing Service, Princeton, NJ 08541
Target Audience: 18–64
Notes: Items, 33
Likert-type scales designed to investigate positive as well as negative attitudes toward aspects of menstruation. Covers menstruation as a debilitating event, a bothersome event, or a natural event; anticipation and prediction of the onset of menstruation; and denial of effects of menstruation. For information and test items, see *Psychosomatic Medicine*; v42 n5 p503-12, Sep 1980. For actual copies, see availability address.

11900
Menstrual Attitude Questionnaire Form for Adolescent Females. Brooks-Gunn, Jeanne; Ruble, Diane 1980
Descriptors: Adolescents; Elementary Education; *Grade 6; *Grade 7; Junior High Schools; *Menstruation
Availability: Jeanne Brooks-Gunn; Educational Testing Service, Princeton, NJ 08541
Grade Level: 6–7
Notes: Items, 22
Likert-type scales to investigate positive as well as negative attitudes toward aspects of menstruation. Covers menstruation as a debilitating event; a bothersome event; or a natural event; anticipation of the onset of menstruation; denial of any effect of menstruation; and embarrassment about menstruation.

11914
Children's Perceived Self-Control Scale and Teacher's Self-Control Rating Scale. Humphrey, Laura Lynn 1982
Subtests: Interpersonal Self-Control (Children); Personal Self-Control (Children); Self-Evaluation (Children); Cognitive Personal Self-Control (Teacher); Behavioral Interpersonal Self-Control (Teacher)
Descriptors: *Elementary School Students; Intermediate Grades; Rating Scales; *Self Control; Self Evaluation (Individuals); *Teacher Attitudes
Identifiers: CPSCS; TIM(I); TSCRS
Availability: Tests in Microfiche; Test Collection, Educational Testing Service, Princeton, NJ 08541
Grade Level: 4–5
Notes: Items, 26

Two scales to measure perceptions of children's self-control. The children's scale consists of 11 items with a yes-no format; the teacher's scale consists of 15 items, using a 5-point rating scale, in which teachers rate students on self-control characteristics.

11947
Pre-Marital Counseling Inventory. Stuart, Richard B.; Stuart, Freida 1975
Descriptors: Adults; *Marriage; *Marriage Counseling; *Mate Selection; Questionnaires; Rating Scales
Identifiers: *Engaged Couples; *Premarital Counseling
Availability: Compuscore Inc.; Box 7035, Ann Arbor, MI 48107
Target Audience: Adults
Structured to help couples determine the extent of their commitment to marriage by exploring their attitudes and expectations about aspects of their forthcoming marriage, personal and shared interests, work inside and outside the home, sexual interaction, desired number of children, relationships with friends and relatives, financial matters and marital roles.

11962
Attitudes toward Working with Special Education Adolescents. Plas, Jeanne M.; Cook, Valerie J. 1982
Descriptors: *Adolescents; Adults; *Professional Personnel; Rating Scales; School Psychologists; *Special Education; Special Education Teachers
Availability: Psychology in the Schools;v19 n3 p388-94, Jul 1982
Target Audience: Adults
Notes: Items, 30
Used in a study designed to identify those variables which might be associated with desire to work with special education adolescents. Study oriented toward professionals involved with special need adolescents.

11964
Personal Opinion Matrix. Hall, Jay 1977
Descriptors: *Administrator Characteristics; *Administrator Role; Adults; *Employee Attitudes; *Employees; *Leadership Styles; *Organizational Climate; Questionnaires
Identifiers: POM
Availability: Teleometrics International; 1755 Woodstead Ct., The Woodlands, TX 77380
Target Audience: Adults
Notes: Items, 36
Two-part questionnaire in that employee reads statements and selects those that best fit. Part 1 contains 18 statements describing various managerial practices. Respondent selects 8 that he or she thinks are more characteristic of the manager. In part 2, respondent chooses 8 out of 18 statements that he or she thinks most accurately reflect the organizational climate.

11970
Survey of Work Values, Revised, Form U. Bowling Green University, OH 1976
Subtests: Social Status; Activity Preference; Upward Striving; Attitude toward Earnings; Pride in Work; Job Involvement
Descriptors: Adults; Rating Scales; *Work Attitudes
Identifiers: SWV
Availability: Dr. Patricia C. Smith; Psychology Dept., Bowling Green University, Bowling Green, OH 43403
Target Audience: Adults
Notes: Items, 54
Five-point rating scale concerning the way people feel about work. Questions deal with peoples' attitudes about social status, activity preference, upward striving, attitude toward earnings, pride in work, job involvement.

11974
Medical Ethics Inventory. Stolman, Cynthia 1981
Descriptors: *Decision Making; *Ethics; Higher Education; *Medical Students; Political Attitudes; Rating Scales; Social Values; *Student Attitudes; *Values; Aesthetic Values
Identifiers: MEI; Religious Values; Theoretical Values
Availability: Cynthia Stolman; 19 Fenton Dr., Short Hills, NJ 07078
Grade Level: 13–16
Notes: Items, 72
Designed to measure the preferences of medical students for 6 value categories: aesthetic, political, economic, religious, social, and theoretical in medical decision making. Twelve patient case studies are presented. Respondent rates the importance of each of 6 factors that would influence a medical decision. Each factor represents 1 value category.

11978
Attitude toward Capital Punishment Scale. Salbod, Stephen; Mitchell, John J. 1982

Descriptors: Adults; Criminals; Prisoners; Rating Scales; *Sentencing
Identifiers: *Capital Punishment; CPS; *Death Penalty; TIM(I)
Availability: Tests in Microfiche; Test Collection, Educational Testing Service, Princeton, NJ 08541
Target Audience: 18–64
Notes: Time, 10 approx.; Items, 26

An attitude measure used to assess public's attitude toward the death penalty or capital punishment.

11980
Education for Parenthood Attitude Scale. Bridges, K. Robert 1980
Descriptors: Adolescents; *College Students; Higher Education; High Schools; *High School Students; *Parenthood Education; Rating Scales; Young Adults
Availability: K. Robert Bridges; Psychology Dept., Pennsylvania State University, New Kensington Campus, 3550 7th St. Rd., New Kensington, PA 15068
Grade Level: 9–16
Target Audience: 13–22
Notes: Items, 30

Developed to measure attitudes toward education for parenthood as a concept independent of the respondents' personal plans or expectations about parenthood.

11986
Index of Empathy for Children and Adolescents. Bryant, Brenda K. 1982
Descriptors: Adolescents; Children; *Empathy; Questionnaires; Social Attitudes
Availability: Child Development;v53 n2 p413-25, Apr 1982
Target Audience: 6–13
Notes: Items, 22

A downward extension of the Measure of Empathic Tendency (TC007186) by Mehrabian and Epstein. This paper-and-pencil test is designed to measure empathy defined as a vicarious emotional response to the perceived emotional experiences of others.

11989
Value Survey, Form G. Rokeach, Milton 1982
Descriptors: Adults; Classification; Older Adults; Surveys; *Values
Availability: Consulting Psychologists Press; 577 College Ave., Palo Alto, CA 94306
Target Audience: 20–70
Notes: Time, 15 approx.; Items, 36

Two lists of 18 alphabetically arranged terminal and instrumental values, ranked and sorted by means of sticky labels, which are arranged by the respondents in order of importance in their lives. For use in describing the values of individuals or groups in quantitative terms that can be compared and contrasted and used to measure changes over time.

11992
Oaster Stressor Scale. Oaster, Thomas R. 1982
Subtests: Perceptions of Work and Play; Actual Work and Play Behavior
Descriptors: Adults; Affective Measures; *Play; Rating Scales; *Stress Variables; Work Attitudes; Type A Behavior
Identifiers: OSS; TIM(I)
Availability: Tests in Microfiche; Test Collection, Educational Testing Service, Princeton, NJ 08541
Target Audience: Adults
Notes: Items, 48

Used in assessment of stress and Type A behavior. Two subscales are referred to as the Boredom and Overload Stressor Scales (BOSS). Identification of potential stressors are based on profiles determined by the subscale scores. Subscale A assesses perceptions of work and play; subscale B assess actual work and play behavior.

11996
College Characteristics Index, Short Form. Stern, George G.; And Others 1972
Subtests: Aspirations Level; Intellectual Climate; Student Dignity; Academic Climate; Academic Achievement; Self-Expression; Group Life; Academic Organization; Social Form; Play-Work; Vocational Climate; Intellectual Climate; Non-Intellectual Climate; Impulse Control
Descriptors: Academic Achievement; College Curriculum; College Instruction; College Students; *Educational Environment; Higher Education; Measures (Individuals); School Policy; *Social Environment; Student Interests; Work Environment
Identifiers: CCI; Murray (Henry); Need Press Paradigm
Availability: Instructional Resources Corp.; P.O. Box 545, Skaneateles, NY 13152
Grade Level: 13–17

Notes: Time, 20; Items, 92

An objective, self-administered measure of environmental climate in college. Contains items related to curriculum, teaching and classroom activities, rules, regulations, policies, student organizations, activities, interests, the campus, its services and facilities. See also TC002539 for a long form.

11999
Image of Science and Scientists Scale. Krajkovich, Joseph G. 1978
Descriptors: High Schools; *High School Students; Sciences; *Scientific Attitudes; Scientists; *Student Attitudes
Identifiers: ISSS; TIM(I)
Availability: Tests in Microfiche; Test Collection, Educational Testing Service, Princeton, NJ 08541
Grade Level: 9–12
Notes: Items, 48

Science attitude instrument. Items are based on responses of thousands of high school students to questions concerning their image of science and scientists, in a study conducted in the 1950s. Form 29 of the scale is a 29-item revision of the original ISSS and was validated in 1979.

12001
Attitude toward Mathematics Scale. Peterson, Penelope L. 1978
Descriptors: *Elementary School Students; Intermediate Grades; *Mathematics; *Student Attitudes
Identifiers: TIM(I)
Availability: Tests in Microfiche; Test Collection, Educational Testing Service, Princeton, NJ 08541
Grade Level: 4–6
Notes: Items, 15

Five-point agree-disagree scale to measure students' interest in mathematics. A higher score indicates a more positive attitude.

12022
Self-Control Rating Scale. Kendall, Philip C. 1979
Descriptors: Elementary Education; *Elementary School Students; Personality Measures; Rating Scales; *Self Control; Teacher Attitudes
Identifiers: SCRS
Availability: Journal of Consulting and Clinical Psychology;v47 n6 p1020-29, 1979
Grade Level: 3–6
Notes: Items, 33

Seven-point frequency scale which rates students' self-control and is completed by teacher. Ten items describe self-control, 13 impulsivity, and 10 both possibilities. Developed according to a cognitive-behavioral definition of self-control, which includes factors such as deliberation and problem solving, as well as having the ability to execute appropriate behaviors.

12023
Dysfunctional Attitude Scale. Weissman, Arlene N.; Beck, Aaron T. 1978
Descriptors: *Adults; Cognitive Style; *Depression (Psychology); *Emotional Adjustment; *Negative Attitudes; Rating Scales
Identifiers: DAS
Availability: ERIC Document Reproduction Service; 3900 Wheeler Ave., Alexandria, VA 22304 (ED167619, 33 pages)
Target Audience: Adults
Notes: Items, 40

Developed to measure pervasive negative attitudes of depressed individuals toward self, outside world, and future.

12025
Self-Concept Picture Inventory. Wiseman, E. Delphine; Adams, James H. 1972
Descriptors: Counseling Services; *Elementary School Students; Primary Education; School Attitudes; *Self Concept; *Self Concept Measures
Identifiers: At School; SCPI; Title I Evaluation and Reporting System
Availability: ERIC Document Reproduction Service; 3900 Wheeler Ave., Alexandria, VA 22304 (ED170299, 52 pages)
Grade Level: 1–3
Notes: Items, 48

Designed to assess impact of Title I counseling programs upon self-image and attitudes toward school and peer group. Teachers also complete SCPI for each student.

12027
Student Information Form. Cooperative Institutional Research Program, University of California, Los Angeles, CA 1982
Subtests: Demographic Characteristics; School Background; Finances; College Choice; Aspirations; Attitudes and Values

Descriptors: Academic Aspiration; College Choice; *College Freshmen; Educational Background; Family Financial Resources; Higher Education; Majors (Students); Nontraditional Students; Questionnaires; Social Values; Student Attitudes; *Student Characteristics; Transfer Students
Identifiers: Cooperative Institutional Research Program
Availability: Cooperative Institutional Research Program; Laboratory for Research on Higher Education, Graduate School of Education, University of California, Los Angeles, CA 90024
Grade Level: 13
Notes: Time, 40; Items, 52

Provides a profile on new students entering institutions of higher education including transfer and part-time students, adults, veterans, etc. Results can be used for program and policy evaluation, research, public information, and normative comparisons. Questionnaire is administered and evaluated by The Cooperative Institutional Research Program (CIRP).

12028
Survey of Organizations. Rensis Likert Associates, Ann Arbor, MI 1980
Descriptors: Adults; *Employee Attitudes; Employees; Group Behavior; Job Satisfaction; Leadership; Occupational Information; *Organizational Climate; Peer Relationship; Supervision; Surveys
Identifiers: SOO
Availability: Rensis Likert Associates, Inc.; 3001 S. State St., Ste. 401, Ann Arbor, MI 48104
Target Audience: 18–64
Notes: Items, 125

Designed to measure employee perceptions of organizational behavior including organizational climate, supervisory leadership, peer relationships, group functioning, job characteristics, and job satisfaction. Two levels are available. Level A is used with work groups and Level B, organization wide.

12029
Desegregation Questionnaire. Mullen, David J. 1971
Descriptors: *Administrator Attitudes; Administrators; Adults; *Desegregation Effects; Racial Integration; *School Desegregation; School Districts; School Personnel; Student Attitudes; Students; *Teacher Attitudes; Teachers; Satisfaction
Availability: ERIC Document Reproduction Service; 3900 Wheeler Ave., Alexandria, VA 22304 (ED057096, 110 pages)
Grade Level: 5–12
Target Audience: Adults
Notes: Items, 47

Designed to assess subject's satisfaction with school or school system after desegregation. May be used with professional as well as nonprofessional staff and students.

12030
Therapist Personal Reaction Questionnaire. Ashby, Jefferson D.; And Others 1957
Descriptors: Adults; Affective Measures; *Counselor Attitudes; *Counselor Client Relationship; *Counselors; Negative Attitudes
Identifiers: Positive Attitudes
Availability: Psychological Monographs;v71 n24 Whole No. 453, 1957
Target Audience: Adults

Designed to assess counselor's attitudes and feelings toward a specific client. Instrument is to be completed before next session with the particular client.

12031
Ames Philosophical Belief Inventory Form M-L. Ames, Kenneth A. 1979
Descriptors: Adults; *Beliefs; Existentialism; Measures (Individuals); *Philosophy; Realism; Phenomenology
Identifiers: Idealism; Pragmatism
Availability: Kenneth A. Ames; Dean, School of Education, St. Cloud State University, St. Cloud, MN 56301
Target Audience: 18–64
Notes: Items, 105

Designed to measure beliefs in 5 philosophical areas: idealism, realism, pragmatism, phenomenology, and existentialism.

12036
Arizona Course/Instructor Evaluation Questionnaire. Aleamoni, Lawrence M. 1977
Descriptors: *College Students; *Course Evaluation; Higher Education; Outcomes of Education; Questionnaires; *Student Attitudes; *Student Evaluation of Teacher Performance; Teaching Styles

Availability: Lawrence M. Aleamoni; Office of Instructional Research, 147 Harvill Bldg., University of Arizona, Tucson, AZ 85721
Grade Level: 13–16
Notes: Items, 63

Student rating covers perception of course, teacher, and teaching methods. Three hundred optional items are available covering contributions of instructors and teaching assistants in lectures and discussions, attitude toward students, student outcomes, relevance of course, use of class time, organization and preparation, clarity of presentation, instructor characteristics, interest of presentation, expectations and objectives, course attitude, examinations, visual aids, grading, assignments.

12040
Dole Vocational Sentence Completion Blank.
Dole, Arthur A. 1979
Descriptors: *Adults; Career Counseling; Higher Education; Secondary Education; *Secondary School Students; *Student Educational Objectives; *Undergraduate Students; *Vocational Interests; *Vocational Maturity; Work Attitudes
Identifiers: *Sentence Completion Tests; VSCB
Availability: Stoelting Company; 620 Wheat Ln., Wood Dale, IL 60191
Grade Level: 7–16
Target Audience: Adults
Notes: Time, 20 approx.; Items, 21

Designed for use by psychologists in assessing concerns, general emphases, and specific vocational preference areas of students. May also be used for adults in educational and vocational planning and decision making.

12047
Work Attitudes Questionnaire. Version for Research. Doty, M.S.; Betz, N.E. 1980
Subtests: Commitment; Health
Descriptors: Adults; *Employee Attitudes; *Mental Health; Rating Scales; *Work Attitudes; *Type A Behavior
Identifiers: Commitment; WAQ; *Workaholics; Work Habits
Availability: Marathon Consulting and Press; P.O. Box 09189, Columbus, OH 43209-0189
Target Audience: Adults
Notes: Items, 45

Designed to measure high degrees of work commitment and to distinguish 2 types of highly career-committed individuals; those whose commitment is high and positive and those whose commitment has adverse impact on their psychological health (workaholics or Type A personality).

12051
Anti-Negro Scale. Steckler, George A. 1957
Descriptors: Adults; *Black Attitudes; Interpersonal Competence; Moral Values; Opinions; *Racial Attitudes; Racial Integration; Racial Relations
Availability: Journal of Abnormal and Social Psychology; v54 n3 p396-99, May 1957
Target Audience: 18–64
Notes: Items, 16

Designed for use in a study investigating authoritarian ideologies in black individuals. Measures their anti-black ideologies.

12052
Anti-White Scale. Steckler, George A. 1957
Descriptors: Adults; *Black Attitudes; Interpersonal Competence; Moral Values; Opinions; *Racial Attitudes; Racial Integration; Racial Relations
Availability: Journal of Abnormal and Social Psychology; v54 n3 p396-99, May 1957
Target Audience: 18–64
Notes: Items, 18

Designed for use in a study investigating authoritarian ideologies in black individuals. Measures their anti-white ideologies.

12064
Pleasure Arousal and Dominance Inducing Qualities of Parental Attitudes. Falender, Carol A.; Mehrabian, Albert 1979
Descriptors: *Child Rearing; *Mothers; *Parent Attitudes; Questionnaires; Young Children
Identifiers: Arousal; Dominance; *Emotions; Pleasure
Availability: Albert Mehrabian; 17141 Rayen St., Northridge, CA 91325
Target Audience: 0–8
Notes: Items, 46

Questionnaire measuring child-rearing attitudes viewed as creating an emotional climate for children. Completed by mothers. Children in original sample ranged from 3 months to 8 years of age.

12073
The Leisure Interest Inventory. Hubert, Edwina E. 1969
Subtests: Games; Art; Sociability; Mobility; Immobility

Descriptors: *College Students; Forced Choice Technique; Higher Education; *Interest Inventories; *Leisure Time; *Recreational Activities
Identifiers: LII; TIM(I)
Availability: Tests in Microfiche; Test Collection, Educational Testing Service, Princeton, NJ 08541
Grade Level: 13–16
Notes: Time, 25 approx.; Items, 80

Forced choice inventory based on 5 of the 6 typologies developed by Max Kaplan in *Leisure in America: A Social Inquiry* (New York: John Wiley and Sons, 1960). Self-administered question with groups of 3 activities, in which respondents must choose activity they would like to do and activity they would least like. Separate male and female forms are available.

12089
Inventory of Job Attitudes. Third Edition. Life Insurance Marketing and Research Association, Hartford, CT 1978
Subtests: Belief in the Company; Individual Job Satisfaction; Compensation Plans; Policy Portfolio; Policy Issue, Policy Change and Commission Accounting; Home Office Training and Marketing Assistance; Home Office Practices and Procedures; Agency Physical Environment; Agency Work Environment
Descriptors: Adults; *Insurance Companies; Rating Scales; *Work Attitudes
Identifiers: *Life Insurance
Availability: Life Insurance Marketing and Research Assn.; P.O. Box 208, Hartford, CT 06141
Target Audience: Adults

The Life Insurance Marketing and Research Association offers its member companies a diagnostic job attitude survey service to help home office management appraise the effects of its policies and actions on agency personnel. Allows member companies to survey their field forces on a standard set of topics, adding or changing items to suit their needs.

12093
Children's Preference, Orientation, and Motive Scales. Solomon, Daniel; And Others 1974
Descriptors: Affective Measures; Elementary School Students; Failure; *Grade 4; *Individual Differences; Intermediate Grades; *Personality Traits; *Student Interests; Student Motivation; Teaching Methods
Availability: ERIC Document Reproduction Service; 3900 Wheeler Ave., Alexandria, VA 22304 (ED125958, 404 pages)
Grade Level: 4

Used in a research study to help identify children's individual cognitive and motivational characteristics, preferences, and orientations which help to determine their relative benefit from different kinds of educational environments. Conclusions of the study show that children benefit from a setting that requires them to experience a mode of activity they would otherwise avoid. Individual measures used are entitled Which Would You Rather Do; Why; What Kind of Class; Why Do Things Happen; Why I Do Things; What Do You Like?; How Much I Like to Do Things; and a Social Desirability Scale.

12106
Philadelphia Geriatric Center Morale Scale, Revised. Lawton, M. Powell; And Others 1975
Subtests: Agitation; Attitude toward Own Aging; Lonely Dissatisfaction
Descriptors: *Aging (Individuals); *Anxiety; *Geriatrics; *Interpersonal Relationship; *Loneliness; *Morale; *Older Adults; *Psychological Patterns; Questionnaires
Identifiers: *Oral Tests; PGC; TIM(I)
Availability: Tests in Microfiche; Test Collection, Educational Testing Service, Princeton, NJ 08541
Target Audience: 65–99
Notes: Items, 17

A multidimensional approach to assessing the psychological state of older persons. Designed to provide a measure of morale appropriate for very old or less competent individuals. Recommended that questionnaire be administered orally. Scores on this questionnaire should not be taken as an absolute judgment but should be used in a clinical setting as one factor in helping older people and their families arrive at appropriate decisions.

12107
Questionnaire for Teen-Agers and Young Adults.
Schludermann, Edward; Schludermann, Shirin 1970

Subtests: Acceptance; Childcenteredness; Possessiveness; Rejection; Control; Enforcement; Positive Involvement; Intrusiveness; Control through Guilt; Hostile Control; Inconsistent Discipline; Nonenforcement; Acceptance of Individuation; Lax Discipline; Instilling Persistent Anxiety; Hostile Detachment; Withdrawal of Relations; Extreme Autonomy
Descriptors: *Adolescents; Behavior Rating Scales; *Child Rearing; Cross Cultural Studies; *Fathers; *Mothers; *Parent Child Relationship; *Young Adults
Identifiers: Childrens Report of Parent Behavior Inventory; CRPBI; TIM (I)
Availability: Tests in Microfiche; Test Collection, Educational Testing Service, Princeton, NJ 08541
Target Audience: 13–22
Notes: Items, 108

A shortened version of Earl the Schaefers' Children's Report of Parent Behavior Inventory which is used to determine the perceptions of adolescents toward their parents' child-rearing methods. To make this shortened version suitable for cross-cultural studies, items inappropriate to ethnic, social or religious minority groups were eliminated. Factor analyses of the Schludermann's version revealed 3 major factors in children's perceptions of their parents' behavior: acceptance vs. rejection; psychological control vs. psychological autonomy; firm control vs. lax control. Separate forms are available for mothers and fathers.

12108
Mother's PARI Q4 (Parental Attitude Research Instrument). Schludermann, Edward; Schludermann, Shirin 1979
Subtests: Discouraging Verbalization; Fostering Dependence; Seclusion of The Mother; Breaking the Will; Martyrdom; Fear of Harming Baby; Marital Conflict; Strictness; Irritability; Exclusion of Outside Influences; Deification; Suppression of Aggression; Rejection of Homemaking Role; Parental Control; Approval of Actions; Avoidance of Communications; Inconsistency of Husband; Suppression of Sexuality; Ascendance of Mother; Intrusiveness; Parent Un-Involvement; Acceptance of Development; Dependence of Mother
Descriptors: Adults; *Child Rearing; *Mother Attitudes; *Mothers; Rating Scales
Identifiers: PARI; TIM(I)
Availability: Tests in Microfiche; Test Collection, Educational Testing Service, Princeton, NJ 08541
Target Audience: Adults
Notes: Items, 130

An alternate version of the Parental Attitude Research Instrument (PARI) developed originally by Schaefer and Bell as a research instrument to measure parental attitudes toward child rearing in order to see whether there was any correlation with personality development in children.

12109
Father's PARI Q4 (Parental Attitude Research Instrument). Schludermann, Edward; Schludermann, Shirin 1979
Subtests: Encouraging Verbalizing; Fosters Independence; Permits Child Self-Assertiveness; Deception; Avoid Harsh Punishment; Avoid Marital Conflict; Nonpunishment; Irresponsibility of Father; Tolerating Aggression; Avoiding Deification of Parent; Tolerance of Outside Influences; Lack of Irritability; Avoiding Strictness; Toleration Expression of Sensuality; Rejecting Ascendancy of Husband; Inconsiderateness of Wife; Encouraging Ascendancy of Wife; Encouraging Emotional Expression; Change Orientation; Forcing Independence
Descriptors: Adults; Child Rearing; *Father Attitudes; *Fathers; Rating Scales
Identifiers: PARI; TIM(I)
Availability: Tests in Microfiche; Test Collection, Educational Testing Service, Princeton, NJ 08541
Target Audience: Adults
Notes: Items, 115

An alternate version of the Parental Attitude Research Instrument (PARI) developed originally by Schaefer and Bell as a research instrument to measure parental attitudes toward child rearing in order to see if there was any correlation with personality development in children.

12119
Dental Students' Attitudes toward the Handicapped Scale. Lee, Mickey M.; Sonis, Andrew L. 1982
Descriptors: Adults; *Dental Students; *Disabilities; *Student Attitudes
Identifiers: DSATHS
Availability: ERIC Document Reproduction Service; 3900 Wheeler Ave., Alexandria, VA 22304 (ED221552, 26 pages)
Grade Level: 17–20

Target Audience: Adults
Notes: Time, 10 approx.; Items, 32

Used to assess dental students' attitudes toward working with handicapped patients. Factor analysis shows scale is composed of 2 primary factors: attitudes toward educational experiences and instructors and attitudes toward interpersonal and future interactions with handicapped patients.

12127
Revised Version of SASA. Peabody, Shelly Ann; Sedlacek, William E. 1982
Descriptors: *College Freshmen; Higher Education; Interpersonal Relationship; Negative Attitudes; Rating Scales; Student Attitudes
Identifiers: Situational Attitude Scale
Availability: Journal of College Student Personnel;v23 p140-43, 1982
Target Audience: 17-20
Notes: Items, 107

Designed to assess attitudes of young college freshmen toward mature undergraduate students. Respondents were asked to rate their reactions to 10 social or academic situations. Two forms are available. The only difference between forms is that a specific age is mentioned for the older student.

12128
Counseling Reactions Inventory. Helms, Janet E. 1976
Descriptors: Adults; *Counseling Services; *Counselor Client Relationship; Rating Scales
Identifiers: TIM(I)
Availability: Tests in Microfiche; Test Collection, Educational Testing Service, Princeton, NJ 08541
Target Audience: 18-64
Notes: Items, 9

Designed to measure subjects' reactions to a counselor in a counseling interaction. Factors concern comfort, anxiety, freedom, understanding, and liking for counselor. Scale uses 5 points from strongly agree to strongly disagree.

12142
Reasons for Living Inventory. Linehan, Marsha M.; And Others 1983
Subtests: Survival and Coping Beliefs; Responsibility to Family; Child Related Concerns; Fear of Suicide; Fear of Social Disapproval; Moral Objections
Descriptors: Adults; *Beliefs; Coping; Fear; Moral Issues; Parent Responsibility; Quality of Life; Rating Scales; Social Environment; *Suicide
Identifiers: RFL
Availability: Journal of Consulting and Clinical Psychology;v51 n2 p276-86, Apr 1983
Target Audience: Adults
Notes: Items, 48

Instrument developed to measure a range of beliefs potentially important as reasons to go on living rather than to commit suicide. Research instrument is based on cognitive-behavioral view that differentiates suicidal from nonsuicidal persons by the content of their belief systems.

12148
Attitudes toward Death Measure. Hardt, Dale V. 1975
Descriptors: Adolescents; *Death; Young Adults
Availability: Journal of School Health;v45 n2 p96-99, Feb 1975
Target Audience: 13-26
Notes: Items, 20

Developed to be a valid and reliable attitude scale to measure attitudes toward the concept of death. Measure was used in a study to assess attitudes toward death in relation to subjects' age, sex, social position, church attendance, and recency of death experience with family or friends. Limited effort was also made to interpret results of study in relation to death education as part of the school or health education curriculum.

12154
PSB-Health Occupations Aptitude Examination. Psychological Services Bureau, St. Thomas, PA 1983
Subtests: Academic Aptitude; Spelling; Reading Comprehension; Information in the Natural Sciences; Vocational Adjustment
Descriptors: *Academic Aptitude; *Allied Health Occupations; Anatomy; Aptitude Tests; Biology; Career Counseling; Chemistry; Curriculum Development; Dental Assistants; Health; Job Skills; Knowledge Level; Medical Technologists; Natural Sciences; Nonverbal Ability; Nurses Aides; Personality Traits; Pharmacology; Physics; Physiology; Postsecondary Education; Radiologic Technologists; Reading Comprehension; Safety; Secondary Education; Spelling; Student Placement; Surgical Technicians; Verbal Ability; *Vocational Adjustment; *Vocational Aptitude

Identifiers: Cytotechnologists; Electroencephalographic Technicians; Quantitative Ability; Recreational Therapists; Respiratory Therapists; *Test Batteries
Availability: Psychological Services Bureau; P.O. Box 4, St. Thomas, PA 17252
Grade Level: 10-16
Notes: Time, 120; Items, 385

A battery of tests designed to measure abilities, skills, knowledge, and attitudes important for the successful performance of students in the allied health education programs. Predictive of readiness for instruction. Also useful for placement, counseling, and curriculum planning. Measures verbal, quantitative and nonverbal ability, spelling, reading comprehension, knowledge of biology, chemistry, physics, pharmacology, anatomy, physiology, health and safety, and personal qualities indicative of adjustment.

12155
PSB Nursing School Aptitude Examination. Psychological Services Bureau, St. Thomas, PA 1980
Subtests: Academic Aptitude; Spelling; Reading Comprehension; Information in the Natural Sciences; Vocational Adjustment Index
Descriptors: *Academic Aptitude; Admission (School); Anatomy; Biology; Career Counseling; Chemistry; Health; Knowledge Level; Microbiology; Nonverbal Ability; *Nurses; Personality Traits; Pharmacology; Physics; Physiology; Postsecondary Education; Reading Comprehension; Safety; Secondary Education; Spelling; Student Placement; Verbal Ability; Vocational Adjustment; *Vocational Aptitude
Identifiers: Quantitative Ability; *Test Batteries
Availability: Psychological Services Bureau; P.O. Box 4, St. Thomas, PA 17252
Grade Level: 10-16
Notes: Time, 165; Items, 445

A battery of 5 tests for use by 2 year associate degree programs and diploma schools of nursing in admission, placement, and guidance procedures. May be used for high school counseling. Measures abilities, skills, knowledge, and attitudes of students in educational programs preparing professional nurses. Measures learning ability, spelling, reading comprehension, knowledge of biology, microbiology, chemistry, physics, pharmacology, anatomy, physiology, health and safety, and personal qualities indicative of adjustment.

12156
PSB Aptitude for Practical Nursing Examination. Psychological Services Bureau, St. Thomas, PA 1980
Subtests: General Mental Ability; Spelling; Information in the Natural Sciences; Judgement in Practical Nursing Situations; Personal Adjustment Index
Descriptors: *Academic Aptitude; Adolescents; Adults; *Aptitude Tests; Biological Sciences; Chemistry; Cognitive Ability; Decision Making Skills; Earth Science; Health; Knowledge Level; Natural Sciences; Nonverbal Ability; Personality Traits; *Practical Nursing; Safety; Spelling; Verbal Ability; Vocational Adjustment; *Vocational Aptitude
Identifiers: Quantitative Ability; *Test Batteries
Availability: Psychological Services Bureau; P.O. Box 4, St. Thomas, PA 17252
Target Audience: 16-64
Notes: Time, 180; Items, 450

A battery of 5 tests for use by schools of practical nursing in admissions, placement, and guidance procedures. Measures abilities, skills, knowledge, and attitudes important for successful performance of students in educational programs that prepare practical nurses. Measures learning ability, spelling, knowledge of life science, physics, chemistry, earth science, health and safety, and decision making related to nursing and personal qualities indicative of adjustment.

12168
Student Rights Scale. Oaster, Thomas R. 1982
Subtests: General Rights; Due Process; Academic Self-Determination; Freedom of Expression; Personal Conduct
Descriptors: Age Differences; American Indians; Comparative Analysis; *Cross Cultural Studies; Elementary School Teachers; Nonreservation American Indians; Parent Attitudes; *Parents; Reservation American Indians; Secondary Education; *Secondary School Students; *Secondary School Teachers; Student Attitudes; *Student Rights; Teacher Attitudes
Availability: Thomas R. Oaster; School of Education, Educational Research & Psychology, University of Missouri, 5100 Rockhill Rd., Kansas City, MO 64110
Grade Level: 7-12
Target Audience: 13-64
Notes: Items, 38

Designed to assess attitudes concerning student rights in junior and senior high school. Developed to gather opinions from students, teachers, and parents. Used in a study of reservation and off-reservation Native American parent, teacher, and student perceptions of student rights. Normative data are available in ERIC document ED220740.

12182
Retirement Activities Card Sort Kit. Career Research and Testing, San Jose, CA 1980
Descriptors: Aging (Individuals); Decision Making; Interests; *Older Adults; *Retirement
Identifiers: *Card Sort
Availability: Consulting Psychologists Press; 577 College Ave., Palo Alto, CA 94306
Target Audience: 65-99
Notes: Time, 120 approx.; Items, 48

Card sort that uses 48 common pastimes as an aid in planning a transition from formal employment to a fulfilling retirement lifestyle. Pastimes range from cultural events to meditation, and from entertaining to group leadership. By analyzing how they have organized and classified cards, individuals can clarify personal criteria for retirement decisions. Manual also includes 8 supplementary activities for dealing with aging and retirement.

12192
Multicultural Attitude Questionnaire. Giles, Mary B.; Sherman, Thomas M. 1981
Descriptors: College Students; *Cultural Pluralism; *Education Majors; Higher Education; *Teacher Education
Identifiers: MAQ
Availability: Mary B. Giles; College of Education, Virginia Polytechnic Institute and State University, Blacksburg, VA 24061
Grade Level: 13-16
Notes: Items, 54

Developed to measure multicultural attitudes of undergraduate education majors. Instrument contains items relating to subject's circle of family and friends, social distance, acceptance of others, and opinions on specific groups.

12194
Ames Philosophical Belief Inventory, Form L. Ames, Kenneth A. 1979
Subtests: Idealism; Realism; Pragmatism; Phenomenology; Existentialism
Descriptors: Adults; *Beliefs; Existentialism; *Philosophy; Questionnaires; Realism; Phenomenology
Identifiers: Idealism; Pragmatism
Availability: Kenneth A. Ames; Dean, School of Education, St. Cloud State University, St. Cloud, MN 56301
Target Audience: 18-64
Notes: Items, 105

Designed to measure respondent's preference for 1 of 5 philosophies. Respondent selects 1 of 2 statements describing values, existence, behavior, reality, needs, abilities, and experiences.

12208
Stuttering Problem Profile. Silverman, Franklin H. 1973
Descriptors: Adults; Behavior Modification; Counseling Objectives; Social Behavior; *Speech Therapy; *Stuttering
Availability: Journal of Speech and Hearing Disorders;v45 n1 p119-23, Feb 1980
Target Audience: 18-64
Notes: Items, 86

Designed to identify behaviors that can be modified as goals for stuttering therapy, including aspects of the moment of stuttering, word and situation avoidances, maladaptive attitudes toward stuttering, and disturbances in the personal-social sphere. No score is computed. Qualitative data are provided only. Because instrument requires subjects to indicate behaviors they would like to occur, selected behaviors would be more likely to undergo modification through counseling.

12214
Learning Environment Inventory. Anderson, Gary J.; And Others 1982
Subtests: Cohesiveness; Diversity; Formality; Speed; Material Environment; Friction; Goal Direction; Favoritism; Difficulty; Apathy; Democracy; Cliqueness; Satisfaction; Disorganization; Competitiveness
Descriptors: *Classes (Groups of Students); *Classroom Environment; High Schools; *High School Students; Rating Scales; *Student Attitudes
Identifiers: LEI
Availability: ERIC Document Reproduction Service; 3900 Wheeler Ave., Alexandria, VA 22304 (ED223649, 63 pages)
Grade Level: 10-12
Notes: Items, 105

Measures students' perceptions of 15 dimensions of the social climate in high school classrooms. Suitable for group administration. This version of LEI has statements descriptive of typical school classes that respondent rates on a 4-point agree-disagree scale. Inventory has 2 principal uses: to assess perceptions of an individual student and to measure learning environment of the class as a whole.

12215
My Class Inventory. Anderson, Gary J.; And Others 1982
Subtests: Cohesiveness; Friction; Difficulty; Satisfaction; Competitiveness
Descriptors: Children; *Classroom Environment; Elementary Education; *Elementary School Students; Questionnaires; *Social Environment; *Student Attitudes
Identifiers: Learning Environment Inventory (Anderson et al); MCI
Availability: ERIC Document Reproduction Service; 3900 Wheeler Ave., Alexandria, VA 22304-5110 (ED223649, 63 pages)
Grade Level: 2-6
Target Audience: 8-12
Notes: Items, 38
Simplified version of the Learning Environment Inventory (LEI) (TC012214). Measures 5 dimensions of social climate within the classroom. Provides teachers with feedback about their classrooms and helps in evaluating new educational programs and in investigating the effects of classroom climate on student learning. My Class Inventory originally developed for use in elementary grades but has been found useful with students in grade 7, especially those junior high school students who may have reading difficulties with the LEI.

12220
Computer Assisted Instruction Attitude Scale. Saracho, Olivia N.
Descriptors: *Computer Assisted Instruction; Elementary School Students; Intermediate Grades; Rating Scales; Secondary Education; Secondary School Students
Availability: Olivia N. Saracho; University of Maryland, College of Education, Reading Center, College Park, MD 20742
Grade Level: 5-12
Notes: Items, 7
Rating scale designed to measure attitudes toward using or learning from a computer. Two forms are available: one for groups that have used a computer, another for groups that have not.

12228
RAM Scale. Wright, Claudia R. 1983
Descriptors: *College Students; Forced Choice Technique; Higher Education; Philosophy; *Values
Availability: Claudia R. Wright; School of Communication, Research Div., P.O. Box 1211, Arcadia, CA 91006
Grade Level: 13-16
Notes: Items, 18
A forced-choice version of an instrument designed to measure students' philosophical orientations in terms of relative, absolute, or mixed biases or preferences toward issues dealing with reality (knowledge), methods, and values. For a Likert-scale version, see TC013943.

12233
STILAP: State Technical Institute's Leisure Assessment Process. Navar, Nancy H.; Peterson, Carol Ann 1979
Descriptors: Adults; Behavior Problems; Check Lists; Counseling Services; Criminals; *Disabilities; Drug Abuse; Emotional Disturbances; *Interest Inventories; Learning Disabilities; *Leisure Time; Rehabilitation Counseling
Identifiers: STILAP; TIM(I)
Availability: Tests in Microfiche; Test Collection, Educational Testing Service, Princeton, NJ 08541
Target Audience: 18-64
Notes: Items, 124
An activity checklist designed to determine those leisure activities practiced by disabled counselees in the past and present and their interests. Used with rehabilitation clients including disabled and behavioral, emotional, and learning-disordered subjects and legal offenders. Activities are oriented toward users in the state of Michigan.

12241
Pet Attitude Scale. Templer, Donald I.; And Others 1981
Descriptors: Adults; Likert Scales
Identifiers: PAS; *Pets
Availability: The Psychological Record;v31 n3 p343-48, Sum 1981
Target Audience: 18-64
Notes: Items, 18

Designed to measure the favorableness of attitudes toward pets. Yielded 3 factors: love and interaction, pets in home, joy of pet ownership. Uses 7-point Likert format.

12249
Attitudes toward Blindness. Whiteman, Martin; Lukoff, Irving F. 1964
Subtests: General Orientation toward Blindness; Dealing with Attributes of Blind People; Public Policy toward Blind People; Personal Interaction with Blind People; Information about Blindness; Acquaintance with Blind People
Descriptors: Adults; *Blindness; *College Students; Higher Education
Availability: The Journal of Social Psychology;v63 p179-91, Jun 1964
Grade Level: 13-16
Target Audience: Adults
Measure developed to help understand nature of attitudes of sighted people toward blind individuals. Used in a study with 2 groups of college students to assess attitudinal variation or similarity between them. Four aspects of attitudes toward blindness were investigated: general orientation toward blindness, perceived attributes of blind people, public policy toward blind people, readiness for interaction with blind people.

12255
Parental Modernity Inventory. Schaefer, Earl S.; Edgerton, Marianna 1981
Descriptors: Academic Achievement; Adults; *Child Rearing; *Educational Attitudes; *Parent Attitudes; Parents; Socioeconomic Status
Identifiers: Modernity
Availability: ERIC Document Reproduction Service; 3900 Wheeler Ave., Alexandria, VA 22304 (ED202605, 20 pages)
Target Audience: Adults
Notes: Items, 30
Designed to assess parental attitudes toward child rearing and education. Parental modernity in child-rearing was found to be an index of a child-rearing environment that contributes to academic competence rather than social adjustment.

12272
Test of Mathematical Abilities. Brown, Virginia L.; McEntire, Elizabeth 1984
Subtests: Attitude toward Math; Vocabulary; Computation; General Information; Story Problems
Descriptors: Academic Aptitude; *Achievement Tests; Computation; *Elementary School Students; Elementary Secondary Education; Mathematical Applications; *Mathematics Achievement; Problem Solving; *Secondary School Students; *Student Attitudes; Vocabulary
Identifiers: Story Problems (Mathematics); TOMA
Availability: PRO-ED; 8700 Shoal Creek Blvd., Austin, TX 78758
Grade Level: 3-12
Notes: Items, 107
Provides standardized information about 2 major skill areas, story problems and computation, and related information about students' attitudes toward mathematics, vocabulary of mathematical terms, and general cultural application of mathematically oriented information. There are no time requirements for the test, time required varies according to age and abilities of students. The general information subtest is individually administered; for students under the age of 11, the vocabulary subtest is not given. The test results may be used for various purposes: to identify students significantly below or above their peers in mathematics or mathematically related abilities, for diagnostic or placement purposes; to determine student's particular strengths or weaknesses; to document progress resulting from intervention strategies; to provide data and measurement to those interested in research into mathematics instruction and learning.

12282
Environmental Assessment Inventory. Conye, Robert K. 1975
Descriptors: *Campuses; *College Students; Higher Education; *Institutional Environment; Questionnaires; *Student Attitudes
Identifiers: EAI; Illinois State University
Availability: Robert K. Conyne; 340 Tangeman University Center, M.L. No. 46, University of Cincinnati, Cincinnati, OH 45221
Grade Level: 13-16
Used to provide college counseling center staff with systematic, continual data about the campus environment and its impact on students. Data can be used to evaluate existing programs, develop new ones, and help promote interaction between students and the campus environment. Questionnaire covers campus climate and staff relationships with students.

12284
Open System Assessment for Managers. Organization Renewal, Inc., Washington, DC 1980

Descriptors: Administrator Characteristics; *Administrator Evaluation; Administrator Role; Administrators; Adults; *Employee Attitudes; Personnel Evaluation; Questionnaires; Self Evaluation (Individuals)
Identifiers: *Open Systems Theory
Availability: Development Publications; 5605 Lamar Rd., Bethesda, MD 20816-1398
Target Audience: 18-64
Notes: Items, 36
Assesses the manager as an individual, as a team member, as an organization member within the healthy (open) system with unity, internal responsiveness, external responsiveness. Separate scales for managers' assessments of their own effectiveness, their supervisors' perceptions, and the cumulative results of subordinates' ratings.

12287
Sexual Jealousy Inventory. Pines, Ayala; Aronson, Elliott 1982
Descriptors: Adults; Interpersonal Relationship; *Jealousy; Social Influences; Social Psychology
Identifiers: *Sexual Attitudes
Availability: Dr. Ayala Pines; Psychology Dept., University of California, Berkeley, CA 94720
Target Audience: Adults
Notes: Items, 80
Designed to assess sexual jealousy of individuals through items including background information, questions about jealousy prevalence, attitudes and feelings that are jealousy correlates, elicitors, effects of jealousy, modes of coping with it, and reasons for it. Emphasizes situational attributes which induce feelings of jealousy.

12313
The TIP Scale. McCuiston, Velma E.; Hill, Richard L. 1979
Descriptors: Adults; Individual Characteristics; Interpersonal Competence; Job Performance; *Peer Evaluation; Rating Scales; *Self Evaluation (Individuals)
Identifiers: Task Interpersonal Personal
Availability: Development Publications; 5605 Lamar Rd., Bethesda, MD 20816-1398
Target Audience: Adults
Notes: Items, 36
A two-part inventory that explores how individuals see themselves and how they are perceived by others in terms of tasks to be performed, interpersonal and personal characteristics. Allows individuals to compare their self-evaluations with others' ratings of them. Designed for group use. Available in 2 booklets: Self Feedback Scale and Others Scale. Each booklet has 36 items divided into 3 groups: task, interpersonal, personal.

12315
Parent as a Teacher Inventory. Strom, Robert D. 1984
Subtests: Creativity Analysis; Frustration Analysis; Control Analysis; Play Analysis; Teaching-Learning Analysis
Descriptors: Adults; Arabic; Australian Aboriginal Languages; Children; Creativity; Discipline; French; German; Greek; Hopi; Italian; Navajo; *Parent Attitudes; *Parent Child Relationship; Parent Role; Play; Serbocroatian; *Spanish Speaking; Turkish; Values
Identifiers: *Child Behavior; Frustration; PAAT; Parent Restrictiveness; Parent Teaching
Availability: Scholastic Testing Service; 480 Meyer Rd., Bensenville, IL 60106
Target Audience: 18-64
Notes: Items, 50
A measure of parental attitudes toward specific parenting and child behaviors. Designed to determine parents' feeling about the importance of various behaviors, their values, and their own responses to certain child behaviors. May be used to study cross-cultural attitudes. Available in Spanish from the publisher. Has been translated into Arabic, French, German, Greek, Italian, Serbo-Croatian, Turkish, Australian Aboriginal, and American Indian (Hopi, Navajo). For information on translations, contact: Prof. R. Strom, College of Education, Arizona State University, Tempe, AZ 85287. For use with children aged 3-9.

12316
Lau-Ware Multidimensional HLC Battery. Lau, Richard R. 1981
Subtests: Self-Control over Health; Provider Control over Health; Chance Health Outcomes; General Health Threat; Health Value
Descriptors: *Adults; Experience; *Locus of Control; *Physical Health
Identifiers: Lau Ware Health Locus of Control Scale
Availability: Richard R. Lau; Carnegie-Mellon University, College of Humanities and Social Science, Dept. of Social Sciences, Schenley Park, Pittsburgh, PA 15213
Target Audience: Adults
Notes: Time, 30 approx.; Items, 30

Designed to study health locus of control beliefs and their origins. Early health habits and experiences were influential in formation of health locus of control beliefs.

12328
Mathematical Self-Concept Scale. Gourgey, Annette F. 1982
Descriptors: *Academic Ability; *College Students; Higher Education; Mathematical Concepts; *Mathematics Anxiety; Self Concept; Student Attitudes
Availability: ERIC Document Reproduction Service; 3900 Wheeler Ave., Alexandria, VA 22304 (ED223702, 18 pages)
Grade Level: 13-20
Target Audience: 18-64
Notes: Items, 27

Designed to assess attitude toward one's ability to learn mathematics. Mathematical self-concept was moderately related to mathematics anxiety but more highly correlated with arithmetic skills and number of years since last mathematics course.

12336
School Attitude Scale for Children. Randhawa, Bikkar S.; Van Hestern, Frank 1982
Descriptors: Elementary Education; Elementary School Curriculum; *Elementary School Students; Foreign Countries; *School Attitudes; Semantic Differential; *Student Attitudes
Identifiers: Canada; SASC
Availability: ERIC Document Reproduction Service; 3900 Wheeler Ave., Alexandria, VA 22304-5110 (ED223691, 23 pages)
Grade Level: 3-6
Notes: Items, 14

Designed to assess student attitudes related to the following school-related dimensions: school, teachers, arithmetic, science, social studies, language arts, music, drama, French, art, dance, religion, health, and physical education. Instrument combines the semantic differential and Likert-scale formats.

12340
Hopelessness Scale for Children. Kazdin, Alan E.; And Others 1983
Descriptors: Adolescents; Children; *Suicide
Identifiers: *Hopelessness; Psychiatric Patients
Availability: Journal of Consulting and Clinical Psychology;v51 n4 p504-10, Aug 1983
Target Audience: 8-13
Notes: Items, 17

Designed to measure hopelessness defined as negative expectancies toward oneself and the future. Subjects respond to a series of statements to determine whether each is true or not true of them. Reading level is suitable for end of first grade or above. Used with psychiatric patients.

12341
The Need for Cognition Scale. Cacioppo, John T.; Petty, Richard E. 1982
Descriptors: Adults; *Cognitive Processes; Needs; Rating Scales
Availability: Journal of Personality and Social Psychology;v42 n1 p116-31, 1982
Target Audience: 18-64
Notes: Items, 34

Designed to measure the tendency for an individual to engage in and enjoy thinking. One major factor was found. Scale consists of items that assess the tendency for individuals to gain intrinsic rewards from thinking, in a variety of situations.

12343
Death Anxiety Questionnaire. Conte, Hope R.; And Others 1982
Descriptors: Adults; *Anxiety; *Death; Fear; Older Adults; Questionnaires
Identifiers: DAQ
Availability: Journal of Personality and Social Psychology;v43 n4 p775-85, 1982
Target Audience: 30-82
Notes: Items, 15

Designed to measure attitudes toward death and dying. Covers fear of the unknown, fear of suffering, fear of loneliness, and fear of personal extinction.

12344
Adolescent Self-Concept Scale. Hofman, John E.; And Others 1982
Descriptors: Adolescents; *Arabs; Career Choice; Family Attitudes; Foreign Countries; High School Students; *Jews; Life Satisfaction; Peer Relationship; Religion; Self Concept Measures
Identifiers: ASCS; Israel
Availability: Journal of Personality and Social Psychology;v43 n4 p786-92, 1982
Target Audience: 13-17
Notes: Items, 38

Designed for use in a study comparing self-concepts of Jewish and Arab high school pupils in Israel. Items are concerned with factors common to adolescents in general

and to the above population in particular: attitudes toward family, occupational choice, life satisfaction, religion, peer relations, and the self.

12345
Attitude toward Homosexuality Scale. Leitner, L.M.; Cado, Suzana 1982
Descriptors: Adults; *Homosexuality; Rating Scales; Stress Variables; *Young Adults
Availability: Journal of Personality and Social Psychology;v43 n4 p869-72, 1982
Target Audience: 18-21
Notes: Items, 10

Designed to measure negative attitudes toward homosexuality as part of a study of homosexual stress. Statements are rated on a 13-point agree/disagree scale.

12391
Organicism-Mechanism Paradigm Inventory. Germer, Christopher; And Others 1982
Descriptors: Adults; *Beliefs; *College Students; *Forced Choice Technique; Higher Education; *Locus of Control; *Models
Identifiers: OMPI; TIM(K)
Availability: Tests in Microfiche; Test Collection, Educational Testing Service, Princeton, NJ 08541
Grade Level: 13-16
Target Audience: 18-64
Notes: Items, 26

Forced-choice inventory designed to assess individuals' tendencies to think and behave according to 1 of 2 paradigms: mechanistic or organismic. Those who subscribe to a mechanistic model believe that events are determined by the environment and are reactive and passive. Those who subscribe to an organismic model are active and autonomous and view the universe as inherently active and changing.

12392
Pregnancy Research Questionnaire and Postnatal Research Inventory. Schaefer, Earl S. 1960
Descriptors: *Adjustment (to Environment); Adults; *Females; *Mother Attitudes; *Pregnancy; Questionnaires; Rating Scales
Identifiers: *Postnatal Influence; TIM(K)
Availability: Tests in Microfiche; Test Collection, Educational Testing Service, Princeton, NJ 08541
Target Audience: 16-45

Inventories were designed to assess adjustment of women during pregnancy and the postpartum period in order to predict pregnancy outcome, maternal behavior, and the personality development of the child. There are 2 parts to the Pregnancy Research Questionnaire. Scales include dependency, fears for baby, fears for self, depression and withdrawal, irritability and tension, lack of desire for pregnancy, symptoms at menstruation, psychosomatic anxiety symptoms during pregnancy, psychosomatic anxiety symptoms before pregnancy. The Postnatal Research Inventory consists of 20 short scales of psychological response to the postpartum period: negative aspects of child rearing, intropunitiveness, length of convalescence, ignoring, depression, fear or concern for baby, irritability, need for reassurance, responsiveness to infant's needs, extrapunitiveness, confidence, happiness, need for consultation, need for assistance, need for sharing experiences, denial of problems, positive perception of others, protectiveness, acceptance, and fears for self.

12400
Minnesota School Attitude Survey: Lower Form. Ahlgren, Andrew 1983
Subtests: Basic Subjects; Other Subjects; Fine Arts; Learning Activities; Extra-Class Activities; Student Role; Autonomy; Self-Expression; School Personnel; Other Students; Local Items; Academic Support; Personal Support; Acceptance; Fairness; Academic Pressure; Competition; External Motivation; Personal Worth as a Student; Need for Structure; Cooperation; Internal Motivation
Descriptors: Achievement Need; Curriculum Evaluation; Educational Experience; Elementary Education; *Elementary School Students; Primary Education; *School Attitudes; Self Concept; *Student Attitudes
Identifiers: MSAS; Oral Testing
Availability: Science Research Associates; 155 N. Wacker Dr., Chicago, IL 60606
Grade Level: 1-6
Notes: Time, 40 approx.; Items, 89

Designed to assess attitudes of students in elementary grades, especially grades 1-3, toward several facets of their educational experience. Survey results are scored by SRA and may be returned to school district on a minicomputer diskette for Apple II. Survey results were designed to provide help for school personnel in making curriculum and instruction decisions. This form may be used with students in grades 4-6. Part 2 of this form is not suitable for students in grade 1. Answer sheet allows 5 blank spaces for items of local concern.

12401
Minnesota School Attitude Survey: Upper Form. Ahlgren, Andrew 1983
Subtests: Basic Subjects; Other Subjects; Fine Arts; Learning Activities; Extra-Class Activities; Student Role; Autonomy; Self-Expression; School Personnel; Other Students; Local Items; Academic Support; Personal Support; Acceptance; Fairness; Academic Pressure; Competition; External Motivation; Personal Worth as a Student; Need for Structure; Cooperation; Internal Motivation
Descriptors: Achievement Need; Curriculum Evaluation; Educational Experience; *Elementary School Students; Intermediate Grades; *School Attitudes; Secondary Education; *Secondary School Students; *Student Attitudes
Identifiers: MSAS
Availability: Science Research Associates; 155 N. Wacker Dr., Chicago, IL 60606
Grade Level: 4-12
Notes: Time, 40 approx.; Items, 94

Designed to assess attitudes of students in grades 4-12 toward several facets of their educational experience. Survey results were designed to provide assistance for school personnel in making curriculum and instruction decisions. Results are scored by SRA and may be returned to school district on a minicomputer diskette for Apple II. The answer sheet for this form contains 5 blank spaces which may be used for items for local concern.

12403
Survey of Management Practices, Form JE. Wilson, Clark L. 1982
Descriptors: *Administration; Administrative Principles; Administrators; Adults; Behavior Rating Scales; *Occupational Tests; *Supervisory Methods; *Surveys
Availability: Clark L. Wilson; Box 471, New Canaan, CT 06840
Target Audience: Adults
Notes: Items, 100

Designed to measure manager,ial and supervisory practices and attitudes. Form is completed by the manager, the manager's own supervisor, one who is supervised by the manager, and another manager who is a peer. Questions are concerned with communication and relationships. Each behavior is rated on a 7-point scale of frequency.

12404
Survey of Management Practices, Form JQ. Wilson, Clark L. 1981
Descriptors: *Administration; Administrative Principles; Administrators; Adults; Behavior Rating Scales; *Occupational Tests; *Supervisory Methods; *Surveys
Identifiers: Self Scoring Tests
Availability: Clark L. Wilson; Box 471, New Canaan, CT 06840
Target Audience: Adults
Notes: Items, 100

Designed to measure managerial and supervisory practices and attitudes. Form is completed by the manager, the manager's own supervisor, one who is supervised by the manager, and another manager who is a peer. Questions are concerned with communication and relationships. Each behavior is rated on a 7-point scale of frequency. Has attached answer sheet with a self-scoring, pressure-sensitive answer sheet.

12413
Classroom Behavior Description Checklist. Aaronson, May; And Others 1979
Descriptors: Academic Ability; Adjustment (to Environment); Affective Behavior; Behavior Problems; *Behavior Rating Scales; *Preschool Children; Social Behavior; *Student Behavior; Teacher Attitudes; Young Children
Identifiers: CBD; Task Orientation
Availability: ERIC Document Reproduction Service; 3900 Wheeler Ave., Alexandria, VA 22304 (ED183599, 46 pages)
Target Audience: 2-6
Notes: Items, 10

Checklist for obtaining teacher ratings of preschool children's behavior considered likely to influence school performance. Useful to identify children needing intervention. Covers child's ability, classroom adjustment, and social, emotional and task-oriented behaviors. Suggested for use as a companion measure to the Preschool Preposition Test (TC005994), a screening measure for developmental delay.

12424
Smoker's Self-Testing Kit, Revised. Public Health Service (DHEW), Washington, DC, Center for Disease Control 1973

Subtests: Do You Want to Change Your Smoking Habits; What Do You Think the Effects of Smoking Are; Why Do You Smoke; Does the World around You Make It Easier or Harder to Change Your Smoking Habits
Descriptors: Adolescents; Adults; Knowledge Level; Older Adults; Rating Scales; Self Evaluation (Individuals); *Smoking
Identifiers: Self Administered Tests
Availability: Superintendent of Documents; U.S. Government Printing Office, Washington, DC 20402
Target Audience: 12–99
Notes: Items, 55

Four-part test that helps people find out what they know about smoking and how they feel about it. Provides an explanation of what the scores mean.

12428
Addiction Research Center Inventory (ARCI). Haertzen, C.A. 1974
Subtests: General Information; Interests & Drives; Sensation & Perception; Bodily Symptoms & Processes; Feelings & Attitudes
Descriptors: Adults; Affective Measures; Drug Abuse; Drug Addiction; *Illegal Drug Use; *Pharmacology; Social Attitudes
Identifiers: ARCI; Drug Addicts; Self Report Measures
Availability: Dr. Charles A. Haertzen; NIDA Addiction Research Center, c/o Baltimore City Hospital, Bldg D-5W, 4940 Eastern Ave., Baltimore, MD 21224
Target Audience: Adults
Notes: Items, 600

Designed to assess physical, emotive, cognitive, and subjective effects of various drugs. Applicable to any literate English-speaking population, not just opiate addicts.

12436
General Anxiety Scale for Children. Sarason, Seymour; And Others 1960
Descriptors: *Anxiety; Elementary Education; *Elementary School Students; Junior High Schools; *Junior High School Students; Student Attitudes
Identifiers: GASC
Availability: Sarason, Seymour B., et al.; *Anxiety in Elementary School Children: A Research Report.*New York: Wiley, 1960
Grade Level: 1–9
Notes: Items, 45

Designed to assess child's anxiety in various situations. Should be administered in one sitting with the Test Anxiety Scale for Children (TC008529). Instrument includes an 11-item lie scale.

12447
Cross Genders Majors Questionnaire. Rea, Julie S.; Strange, C. Carney 1981
Subtests: Current Satisfaction; Interaction with Professors; Future Expectations
Descriptors: Higher Education; Interpersonal Relationship; *Majors (Students); *Participant Satisfaction; Self Concept; *Sex Role; *Undergraduate Students; Likert Scales
Availability: Journal of College Student Personnel;v24 n4 p356-63, Jul 83
Grade Level: 13–16
Notes: Items, 14

Designed as part of a study to examine the relationship between gender, sex-role self-concept, and experiences students report following enrollment in same and cross-gender academic majors. The study indicated students in cross-gender majors, particularly females, seem to have difficulty gaining access to the usual socialization mechanisms afforded other students through interaction with peers and faculty.

12450
Persistence/Dropout Rating Scale. Pascarella, Ernest T.; Terenzini, Patrick T. 1980
Subtests: Peer Group Interactions; Interactions with Faculty; Faculty Concern for Student Development and Teaching; Academic and Intellectual Development; Institutional and Goal Commitments
Descriptors: *Academic Persistence; *College Freshmen; *Dropout Research; *Dropouts; Higher Education; Interpersonal Relationship; Predictive Measurement; Student Attitudes; Student Educational Objectives
Availability: Journal of Higher Education;v51 n1 p60-75, Jan-Feb 1980
Grade Level: 13
Notes: Items, 30

Designed to assess academic and social integration of college freshmen. Attempts to identify those students with a high probability of becoming dropouts.

12451
Traditional-Liberated Social Stereotype and Self-Concept Scales. Cartwright, Rosalind D.; And Others 1983
Descriptors: Adults; Employed Women; *Females; Personality Traits; *Self Concept Measures; *Social Attitudes; Spouses; *Stereotypes
Identifiers: Liberated Women; TLSC; TLSS; Traditional Women
Availability: Journal of Personality and Social Psychology;v44 n3 p581-88, 1983
Target Audience: 18–64
Notes: Items, 86

Two scales derived from the Adjective Checklist (TC002498), designed to measure traits associated with the traditional-liberated dimension for women. Traditional is defined as one whose major interest is a part of a marital dyad, and liberated as one who is also interested in work outside the home. The TLSS has 45 items. The TLSC has 41 items.

12452
Fear of Personal Death Scale. Florian, Victor; Kravetz, Shlomo 1983
Descriptors: Adults; *Death; Fear
Availability: Journal of Personality and Social Psychology;v44 n3 p600-07, 1983
Target Audience: 18–30
Notes: Items, 31

Measures which of 31 supposed consequences of death cause a person to fear death. Respondent rates each consequence in response to the statement "Death frightens me because..." on a 7-point scale ranging from "totally correct for me" to "totally incorrect."

12503
Parent Attitudinal Questionnaire. Matthews, Doris B.; Casteel, Jim Frank 1983
Descriptors: Adults; Elementary Secondary Education; *Parent Attitudes; Rating Scales; *School Districts; *School Effectiveness; Teacher Attitudes; Likert Scales
Identifiers: School District Questionnaire
Availability: ERIC Document Reproduction Service; 3900 Wheeler Ave., Alexandria, VA 22304 (ED230587, 27 pages)
Target Audience: Adults
Notes: Items, 51

Content-based questionnaire developed for Orangeburg, South Carolina, School District. Intended to provide school district with feedback from parents and teachers about the quality of the school programs. Particularly useful for districts interested in self-improvement programs and for continued monitoring of such programs. Can be used as a pretest posttest following implementation of planned changes.

12533
IEP Educational Diagnostic Inventories: Behavior Reinforcement Inventory. Sedlak, Joseph E. 1979
Descriptors: Educational Diagnosis; Elementary Education; *Elementary School Students; Emotional Disturbances; *Exceptional Persons; Gifted; *Individualized Education Programs; Individual Testing; Learning Disabilities; Mild Mental Retardation; Questionnaires; *Student Attitudes
Identifiers: IEP Educational Diagnostic Inventories
Availability: National Press Publishing Company; P.O. Box 237, Belle Vernon, PA 15012
Grade Level: K–6
Notes: Time, 5 approx.; Items, 6

One instrument in a test battery developed to enable classroom teachers to screen and diagnose those students with potential learning problems. The instrument may be used to develop an Individual Education Program for gifted, educable mentally retarded, emotionally disturbed, or learning-disabled students. Designed to assess student preferences. Useful in planning reinforcement of behaviors associated with learning. Results may aid teacher in selecting materials and rewards that stimulate effective learning.

12567
Attitudes toward Seeking Professional Psychological Help. Fischer, Edward H.; Turner, John 1970
Subtests: Recognition of Need for Psychotherapeutic Help; Stigma Tolerance; Interpersonal Openness; Confidence in Mental Health Practitioner
Descriptors: Adults; Emotional Problems; *Psychotherapy
Availability: Journal of Consulting and Clinical Psychology;v35 n1 p79-90, 1970
Target Audience: Adults
Notes: Items, 29

A measure of attitudes toward seeking professional help for psychological disturbances was developed and standardized. Four factors were identified when the instrument was administered to college and nursing students: recognition of the need for professional psychological help;

tolerance of the stigma associated with psychiatric help; interpersonal openness regarding subject's problems; and confidence in the mental health professional.

12568
Effective Schools Questionnaires. Austin Independent School District, Texas Office of Research and Evaluation 1981
Descriptors: *Administrator Attitudes; *Educational Improvement; *Elementary School Students; *Parent Attitudes; Questionnaires; *School Attitudes; *School Effectiveness; *Secondary School Students; *Teacher Attitudes
Identifiers: Austin Independent School District TX
Availability: ERIC Document Reproduction Service; 3900 Wheeler Ave., Alexandria, VA 22304-5110 (ED228258, 18 pages)
Target Audience: 6–64

Five questionnaires are based on Ronald Edmonds' work on "Effective Schools." They were designed to assess the perceptions of each group on the 5 areas identified by Edmonds as distinguishing effective and ineffective schools for students from low-income families. The groups are prinicpals, parents, teachers, elementary, and secondary students. The characteristics represent areas to which the schools may look for improvement. They are The Principal Is a Strong Instructional Leader; Pupil Progress Is Monitored Frequently; There Is an Emphasis on Basic Skills; School Staff Have Positive Expectations for All Students; and The Schools' Climate Is Safe, Orderly, and Business-like. The questionnaires were designed for optional use by the principals themselves.

12574
Interpersonal Orientation Scale. Swap, Walter C.; Rubin, Jeffrey 1983
Descriptors: Adults; Interests; *Interpersonal Relationship; Rating Scales; Responses; Self Evaluation (Individuals); Likert Scales
Identifiers: Self Report Measures
Availability: Journal of Personality and Social Psychology;v44 n1, p208-19, Jul 1983
Target Audience: Adults
Notes: Items, 29

A self-report measure of high and low interest in and reactions to people. Subjects with low interest are more concerned with economic features of relationships. Items are Likert-type and deal with responses to the behaviors of others directly affecting the respondent.

12576
Paranormal Belief Scales. Tobacyk, Jerome; Milford, Gary 1983
Descriptors: Adults; Beliefs; Questionnaires; Religion; *Self Evaluation (Individuals)
Identifiers: *Paranormal Beliefs; Parapsychology
Availability: Journal of Personality and Social Psychology;v44 n5 p1029-37, May 1983
Target Audience: Adults
Notes: Items, 25

Self-report questionnaire designed to assess belief in the paranormal. Seven different factors emerged: Traditional Religious Belief, Psi Belief, Witchcraft, Superstition, Spiritualism, Extraordinary Life Forms, and Precognition.

12579
Planning for Educational Computing Questionnaire. Poirot, Jim 1982
Descriptors: *Administrator Attitudes; *Administrators; Adults; Computer Literacy; Inservice Teacher Education; *Microcomputers; *Teacher Attitudes; *Teachers
Availability: Electronic Learning;v2 n1 p34-38, Sep 1982
Target Audience: Adults
Notes: Items, 39

Designed to assess faculty's attitudes toward computers in education and types of educational computing applications respondents feel are important. Background data on respondent is used to assess his/her current level of computer expertise.

12582
Self-Reinforcement Attitudes Questionnaire. Heiby, Elaine M. 1983
Descriptors: Adults; *Reinforcement; *Self Concept; Self Concept Measures; Self Evaluation (Individuals); Self Reward
Identifiers: Self Report Measures
Availability: Journal of Personality and Social Psychology;v44 n6 p1304-07, Jun 1983
Target Audience: Adults
Notes: Items, 30

A measure of the frequency with which individuals reinforce their own self-esteem. Low frequency of self-reinforcement is hypothesized to make an individual more prone to depression when outside reinforcements are withdrawn. This self-report, true-false measure was administered to undergraduate psychology students.

12585
Attitudes toward Pharmacy as a Profession. Nuessle, Noel O.; Levine, Daniel U. 1982
Subtests: Pharmacy as a Profession; Patient Medication Records; Pharmacist Advisement Concerning OTC Drugs; Prescription Medication Advisement; Patient-Pharmacist Relationships; Physician-Pharmacist Relationship; Management of a Pharmacy; Pharmacist's Responsibility for Drug Use; Adequacy of Preparation; School of Pharmacy Curriculum
Descriptors: *College Students; Higher Education; *Pharmaceutical Education; *Pharmacists; *Pharmacy; Rating Scales
Availability: American Journal of Pharmaceutical Education;v46 n1 p60-67, Spr 1982
Grade Level: 13–16
Notes: Items, 66

Developed to measure students' attitudes toward pharmacy as a profession, professional principles, and preparation for a pharmacy career.

12590
Zones of Indifference Questionnaire. Wilkes, Sam T.; Blackbourn, Joe M. 1981
Descriptors: Elementary School Teachers; *Power Structure; Questionnaires; Secondary School Teachers; *Teacher Administrator Relationship; Teacher Attitudes
Availability: ERIC Document Reproduction Service; 3900 Wheeler Ave., Alexandria, VA 22304 (ED212063, 31 pages)
Target Audience: 18–64
Notes: Items, 78

This instrument measures the zones of indifference of teachers to typical directives issued by administrators. The zones describe the extent to which people will respond to orders or directives issued by authority figures. Two sets of items were identified: one set explains variables describing teacher determined practices and the other covers administrator determined policy.

12596
Measures in Assessment of Innovation Fidelity. Syracuse University, New York Center for Instructional Development 1981
Subtests: Psychology Student Questionnaire; English Poetry Course Questionnaire
Descriptors: Educational Innovation; *Grade 12; *Instructional Improvement; Questionnaires; Rating Scales; Secondary Education; *Student Attitudes
Identifiers: Project Advance
Availability: ERIC Document Reproduction Service; 3900 Wheeler Ave., Alexandria, VA 22304-5110 (ED202866, 47 pages)
Grade Level: 12
Notes: Items, 109

These questionnaires were developed by Syracuse University Project Advance. They are used in high school introductory courses in psychology and English but at the college freshman level. College credit is given for them. The questionnaire in the English course has 5 categories: materials, structure, behavior, knowledge, and values. The characteristics of the psychology questions are based on activities found in most personalized system of instruction course designs. There are 71 items on the psychology instrument and 38 on the English poetry. These questionnaires were developed to assess educational innovation. Both instruments were used in a report, "A Methodology for Assessing the Implementation of Educational Innovations: Analysis and Revision. Final Report."

12612
PRIDE: Preschool and Kindergarten Interest Descriptor. Rimm, Sylvia B. 1983
Descriptors: *Creativity; *Gifted; *Kindergarten Children; *Preschool Children; Preschool Education; Rating Scales; *Screening Tests; Talent Identification
Identifiers: PRIDE
Availability: Educational Assessment Service, Inc.; W6050 Apple Rd., Watertown, WI 53094
Target Audience: 3–6
Notes: Time, 35 approx.; Items, 50

Developed to provide an easily administered, reliable, and valid instrument to screen preschool and kindergarten children for programs for the creatively gifted. Purpose of PRIDE is to identify children with attitudes and interests usually associated with preschool and kindergarten creativity, such as a variety of interests, curiosity, independence, perseverance, imagination, playfulness, humor, and originality. It is recommended that parents complete the inventory at a parent meeting or during a preschool or kindergarten screening for their child. There is no time limit to complete the inventory, but it usually takes between 20 and 35 minutes.

12616
The Computer Appreciator-Critic Attitude Scales. Mathews, Walter M.; Wolf, Abraham W. 1983
Descriptors: Adults; *Computers; Rating Scales; Undergraduate Students; Likert Scales
Identifiers: TIM(J)
Availability: Tests in Microfiche; Test Collection, Educational Testing Service, Princeton, NJ 08541
Target Audience: Adults
Notes: Items, 40

A measure of one's attitude toward computers. Group or individually administered. Responses are ratings of statements reflecting appreciation or criticism of computers on a 5-point Likert-type scale.

12626
Alumni Association Survey, University of Pittsburgh. Pittsburgh University, PA
Descriptors: *Alumni; College Graduates; Graduate Surveys; Higher Education; *Opinions; Questionnaires; *School Attitudes
Availability: ERIC Document Reproduction Service; 3900 Wheeler Ave., Alexandria, VA 22304 (ED187251, microfiche only)
Target Audience: 18–64
Notes: Items, 76

Comprehensive survey of alumni opinion regarding the role and activities of the alumni association and the university. It includes questions on specifics of alumni association programing and publications and on personal data to permit correlations by academic and social background. This questionnaire is in "Attitude and Opinion Research: Why You Need It/How You Do It" (ED187251). An alternate source for the entire document is Council for Advancement and Support of Education, Suites 530/600, 1 Dupont Circle, Washington, DC 20036.

12627
UBC Alumni Association Survey. British Columbia University, Vancouver 1971
Descriptors: *Alumni; College Graduates; Foreign Countries; Graduate Surveys; Higher Education; *Opinions; Questionnaires; *School Attitudes; Teacher Attitudes
Identifiers: British Columbia (Vancouver)
Availability: ERIC Document Reproduction Service; 3900 Wheeler Ave., Alexandria, VA 22304 (ED187251, microfiche only)
Target Audience: 18–64
Notes: Items, 65

The University of British Columbia questionnaire surveys the alumni attitudes toward the university, the alumni association, and higher education in general. It also includes percentage responses. This questionnaire is in "Attitude and Opinion Research: Why You Need It/How You Do It" (ED187251). An alternate source for the entire document is Council for Advancement and Support of Education, Suites 530/600, 1 Dupont Circle, Washington, DC 20036.

12628
Hofstra University Questionnaire. Hofstra University, Hempstead, NY 1975
Descriptors: *College Freshmen; Higher Education; *Opinions; Questionnaires; *Recruitment; *School Attitudes; *Student Attitudes; Student Characteristics; *Transfer Students
Availability: ERIC Document Reproduction Service; 3900 Wheeler Ave., Alexandria, VA 22304-5110 (ED187251, microfiche only)
Grade Level: 13–16
Notes: Items, 25

This questionnaire was given to all entering Freshmen and transfer students in 1975 to measure the effectiveness of various communications tools used in student recruitment. This questionnaire is in "Attitude and Opinion Research: Why You Need It/How You Do It" (ED187251). An alternate source for the entire document is Council for Advancement and Support of Education, Suites 530/600, 1 Dupont Circle, Washington, DC 20036.

12629
Hood College Alumnae Association Evaluation. Hood College, Frederick, MD 1975
Descriptors: *Alumni; College Graduates; Fund Raising; Graduate Surveys; Higher Education; *Opinions; Questionnaires; *School Attitudes
Availability: ERIC Document Reproduction Service; 3900 Wheeler Ave., Alexandria, VA 22304-5110 (ED187251, microfiche only)
Target Audience: 18–64
Notes: Items, 25

This questionnaire was used to obtain alumnae evaluations of the college, its communications, alumni programing, and fund raising. It includes employment and other information useful to the development office. This questionnaire is in "Attitude and Opinion Research: Why You Need It/How You Do It" (ED187251). An alternate source for the entire document is Council for Advancement and Support of Education, Suites 530/600, 1 Dupont Circle, Washington, DC 20036.

12630
St. John's University Alumni Survey. St. John's University, Jamaica, NY 1975
Descriptors: *Alumni; College Graduates; Fund Raising; Graduate Surveys; Higher Education; *Opinions; Questionnaires; *School Attitudes; Student Attitudes
Availability: ERIC Document Reproduction Service; 3900 Wheeler Ave., Alexandria, VA 22304-5110 (ED187251, microfiche only)
Target Audience: 18–64
Notes: Items, 21

This survey was used to obtain biographical data for alumni and fund-raising records as well as attitudes toward the university. This questionnaire is in "Attitude and Opinion Research: Why You Need It/How You Do It" (ED187251). An alternate source for the entire document is Council for Advancement and Support of Education, Suites 530/600, 1 Dupont Circle, Washington, DC 20036.

12631
West Virginia University Faculty-Staff Survey. West Virginia University, Morgantown 1972
Descriptors: Administrative Policy; College Faculty; Higher Education; *Opinions; Questionnaires; *School Attitudes; Teacher Attitudes
Availability: ERIC Document Reproduction Service; 3900 Wheeler Ave., Alexandria, VA 22304 (ED187251, microfiche only)
Target Audience: 18–64
Notes: Items, 16

This faculty-staff opinion survey covers university policies, programs, and administrative procedures. This questionnaire is in "Attitude and Opinion Research: Why You Need It/How You Do It" (ED187251). An alternate source for the entire document is Council for Advancement and Support of Education, Suites 530/600, 1 Dupont Circle, Washington, DC 20036.

12632
West Virginia University Student Survey. West Virginia University, Morgantown 1972
Descriptors: *College Students; Higher Education; *Opinions; Questionnaires; *School Attitudes; *Student Attitudes; Student Characteristics; Student College Relationship
Availability: ERIC Document Reproduction Service; 3900 Wheeler Ave., Alexandria, VA 22304 (ED187251, microfiche only)
Grade Level: 13–16
Notes: Items, 17

This survey was used to obtain student opinions about a variety of university policies and programs. It includes reasons for choosing the institution and opinion on student participation in decision making in specific areas. This questionnaire is in "Attitude and Opinion Research: Why You Need It/How You Do It" (ED187251). An alternate source for the entire document is Council for Advancement and Support of Education, Suites 530/600, 1 Dupont Circle, Washington, DC 20036.

12633
Opinion Poll—State University of New York at Buffalo. State University of New York, Buffalo
Descriptors: *Community Attitudes; *Community Characteristics; Community Involvement; Higher Education; *Opinions; Questionnaires; *School Attitudes
Availability: ERIC Document Reproduction Service; 3900 Wheeler Ave., Alexandria, VA 22304 (ED187251, microfiche only)
Target Audience: 18–64
Notes: Items, 33

This poll was used for an institutional image study among county voters. It includes involvement with the university, knowledge about faculty data such as enrollment and financing, opinion of the university's value to the community and feelings about the university. This questionnaire is in "Attitude and Opinion Research: Why You Need It/How You Do It" (ED187251). An alternate source for the entire document is Council for Advancement and Support of Education, Suites 530/600, 1 Dupont Circle, Washington, DC 20036.

12634
University of Richmond Survey. Richmond University, Richmond, VA
Descriptors: Adults; *Community Attitudes; *Fund Raising; *Opinions; Questionnaires
Availability: ERIC Document Reproduction Service; 3900 Wheeler Ave., Alexandria, VA 22304 (ED187251, microfiche only)
Target Audience: 18–64
Notes: Items, 16

This institutional image survey in the local business community was used preceding a capital campaign. It includes comparisons with selected institutions, assessments of different aspects of the university, and donation history, including reasons for not donating. This questionnaire is in "Attitude and Opinion Research: Why You Need It/How You Do It" (ED187251). An alternate source for the entire document is Council for Advancement and Support of Education, Suites 530/600, 1 Dupont Circle, Washington, DC 20036.

12635
Maryland Readership Survey. Maryland University, College Park
Descriptors: *Alumni; College Graduates; Graduate Surveys; Higher Education; *Opinions; Publications; Questionnaires; Reading Interests; *School Attitudes
Availability: ERIC Document Reproduction Service; 3900 Wheeler Ave., Alexandria, VA 22304 (ED187251, microfiche only)
Target Audience: Adults
Notes: Items, 10

This is an alumni readership survey on the quarterly magazine and includes specific preferences, evaluation of content, design, and coverage and past gift support to the institution. This questionnaire is in "Attitude and Opinion Research: Why You Need It/How You Do It" (ED187251). An alternate source for the entire document is Council for Advancement and Support of Education, Suites 530/600, 1 Dupont Circle, Washington, DC 20036.

12639
Ethnic Attitude Test. Martinez, Roger D. 1979
Descriptors: Adults; American Indians; Blacks; *Cultural Background; *Elementary Secondary Education; Ethnicity; Ethnic Relations; Ethnic Studies; *Learning Experience; Mexican Americans; Minority Groups; *Multicultural Education; Questionnaires; *Teacher Attitudes; Teacher Education; Teacher Improvement
Identifiers: Colorado; Ethnic Heritage Studies Program
Availability: ERIC Document Reproduction Service; 3900 Wheeler Ave., Alexandria, VA 22304 (ED180739, 12 pages)
Target Audience: 18–64
Notes: Items, 40

This instrument is designed to be a learning experience in which Colorado elementary and secondary teachers can share ideas, change attitudes if need be, clarify information, and/or reinforce what they knew to be true all along about the multicultural heritage of the state. Participants are asked to indicate the extent of their agreement with 40 statements concerning ethnic or cultural studies and then compare their choices to the point of view expressed by the Colorado State Department of Education, a position that supports the view that children should, as an integral part of their education, learn about their own and their neighbor's ethnic heritage and learn to respect cultural differences. The statements probe teacher attitudes concerning special programs for American Indians, blacks, and Mexican Americans; ethnic stereotypes and cliches; self-determination rights of minorities to control their own programs; and the role of teachers, ethnic leaders, and parents in program planning.

12641
Wisconsin Reading Program Assessment Scale and Attitudes Scale. Wisconsin State Dept. of Public Instruction, Madison 1979
Descriptors: Adults; Needs Assessment; *Program Development; Rating Scales; Reading Attitudes; *Reading Improvement; *Reading Programs
Identifiers: Right to Read; Wisconsin
Availability: ERIC Document Reproduction Service; 3900 Wheeler Ave., Alexandria, VA 22304 (ED178891, 43 pages)
Target Audience: 18–64

These scales were developed as part of the fifth resource guide to assist Wisconsin Public Schools in offering quality reading instruction. The scales are used in Planning a Local Right to Read Program. There are 10 scales: Reading Program Assessment Scale; Planning and Management; Goals and Objectives; Instruction; Staff; Staff Development; Materials and Facilities; Leadership Development; Community Involvement; Program Evaluation; and Scale to Measure Attitudes toward Reading which has 20 items and uses a 5-point rating scale. The scales are part of the *Wisconsin Handbook for Reading Improvement: Section E, Assessment.*

12643
Administrator Professional Leadership Scale. Thompson, Bruce 1974
Descriptors: *Administrator Evaluation; Adults; *Leadership Qualities; *Principals; Program Implementation; Rating Scales; *Teacher Administrator Relationship; Teacher Attitudes
Identifiers: APLS
Availability: ERIC Document Reproduction Service; 3900 Wheeler Ave., Alexandria, VA 22304 (ED175911, 15 pages)
Target Audience: Adults
Notes: Items, 18

The Administrator Professional Leadership Scale (APLS) was developed to measure the perceived professional leadership quality of a school principal, and to provide principals with anonymous feedback on teachers' perceptions of their leadership. Further refinement was carried out to increase its reliability; to discover categories of administrator behavior considered by teachers when evaluating leadership; and to improve the evaluation of principals according to these dimensions of leadership. The revised instrument may be appropriate for use by school principals who wish to obtain information about how the faculty perceive them or for program evaluation efforts when leadership provided by the principals may produce variations in program implementation. These influences need to be quantified.

12656
Attitudes toward Reading Scale: Primary Scale. Deck, Dennis; Barnette, J. Jackson 1976
Descriptors: *Elementary School Students; Family Influence; Primary Education; *Reading Attitudes; Reading Habits; Student Attitudes
Identifiers: Measuring Attitudes toward Reading; Oral Testing; Pennsylvania
Availability: ERIC Document Reproduction Service; 3900 Wheeler Ave., Alexandria, VA 22304 (ED128407, 21 pages)
Grade Level: 1–3
Notes: Items, 29

Designed to assess reading attitudes of students in primary grades. Developed for Pennsylvania Right to Read Project. This instrument is also included in Measuring Attitudes toward Reading ERIC/TM Report 73 (ED196938).

12657
Attitudes toward Reading Scale: Intermediate Scale. Deck, Dennis; Barnette, J. Jackson 1976
Descriptors: *Elementary School Students; Family Influence; Intermediate Grades; *Reading Attitudes; Reading Habits; Student Attitudes
Identifiers: Measuring Attitudes toward Reading; Pennsylvania
Availability: ERIC Document Reproduction Service; 3900 Wheeler Ave., Alexandria, VA 22304 (ED128407, 21 pages)
Grade Level: 4–6
Notes: Items, 30

Designed to assess attitudes toward reading and books of students in grades 4 to 6. Developed for the Pennsylvania Right to Read Project. This instrument is also included in Measuring Attitudes Toward Reading ERIC/TM Report 73 (ED196938).

12658
Seventy Item Attitude Instrument. Kennedy, Larry D.; Halinski, Ronald S. 1975
Descriptors: *Reading Attitudes; Secondary Education; *Secondary School Students; Student Attitudes
Identifiers: Measuring Attitudes toward Reading
Availability: *Journal of Reading;*v18 n7 p518-22, Apr 1975
Grade Level: 7–12
Notes: Items, 70

Designed to measure secondary school students' attitudes toward reading. Instrument is also included in Measuring Attitudes toward Reading ERIC/TM Report 73, available from ERIC Document Reproduction Service, 3900 Wheeler Avenue, Alexandria, VA 22304 (ED196938, 145 pages).

12659
Mikulecky Behavioral Reading Attitude Measure. Mikulecky, Larry 1979
Descriptors: *Adults; *Reading Attitudes; *Reading Habits; Self Evaluation (Individuals)
Identifiers: Measuring Attitudes toward Reading
Availability: ERIC Document Reproduction Service; 3900 Wheeler Ave., Alexandria, VA 22304 (ED196938, 145 pages)
Target Audience: Adults

Designed for self-assessment of attitudes toward books and reading. Further information about this instrument is available in *Adult Reading Habits, Attitudes and Motivations: A Cross-Sectional Study* by Larry Mikulecky and others. Monographs in Teaching and Learning, No. 2, available from School of Education, Indiana University, June 1979. This instrument is included in Measuring Attitudes toward Reading ERIC/TM Report 73 (ED196938).

12660
Primary Reading Attitude Index. Powell, Annelle 1971
Descriptors: Attitude Change; *Elementary School Students; Family Influence; Primary Education; *Reading Attitudes; Recreational Reading; Student Attitudes
Identifiers: Measuring Attitudes toward Reading
Availability: ERIC Document Reproduction Service; 3900 Wheeler Ave., Alexandria, VA 22304 (ED091738, 29 pages)
Grade Level: 1–3
Notes: Items, 32

Designed to measure students' attitudes toward reading for pleasure. May also be used to assess changing reading attitudes over a period of time. This instrument is included in Measuring Attitudes toward Reading ERIC/TM Report 73 (ED196938).

12661
Children's Attitude toward Reading Test. Redelheim, Paul S. 1975
Descriptors: *Elementary School Students; *Kindergarten Children; Nonverbal Tests; Pictorial Stimuli; Primary Education; *Reading Attitudes; Recreational Reading; *Student Attitudes
Identifiers: CHART; Measuring Attitudes toward Reading; Self Report Measures
Availability: ERIC Document Reproduction Service; 3900 Wheeler Ave., Alexandria, VA 22304 (ED195580, 71 pages)
Grade Level: K–2
Notes: Items, 37

Designed to assess young children's attitudes toward reading. Instrument consists of pictures that represent instructional, school, or home recreational reading. Student is instructed to mark 1 of 3 boxes beneath the picture to indicate whether the scene depicts something she/he would like to do, not like to do, or is unsure about. This instrument is included in Measuring Attitudes toward Reading ERIC/TM Report 73 (ED196938).

12662
The Reading Attitudes Inventory. Sartain, Harry W. 1970
Subtests: Recreational Reading; Work-Type Reading; Learning to Read; Social Values
Descriptors: Elementary Education; *Elementary School Students; *Reading Attitudes; Reading Interests; Recreational Reading
Identifiers: Measuring Attitudes toward Reading
Availability: ERIC Document Reproduction Service; 3900 Wheeler Ave., Alexandria, VA 22304 (ED045219, 9 pages)
Target Audience: 6–11
Notes: Time, 30 approx.; Items, 37

Designed to assess children's attitudes toward instructional and recreational reading. This instrument is included in Measuring Attitudes toward Reading ERIC/TM Report 73 (ED196938).

12663
Reading Attitude Scales. Teale, William H.; Lewis, Ramon
Subtests: Individual Development Scale; Utilitarian Scale; Enjoyment Scale
Descriptors: *Elementary School Students; Elementary Secondary Education; *Reading Attitudes; Recreational Reading; *Secondary School Students; Student Attitudes
Identifiers: Measuring Attitudes toward Reading; Oral Testing
Availability: ERIC Document Reproduction Service; 3900 Wheeler Ave., Alexandria, VA 22304 (ED196938, 145 pages)
Grade Level: 3–12
Notes: Items, 33

Designed to assess student's attitudes toward instructional and recreational reading. Items are read aloud to students. Responses to items produce scales of individual development, utility, and enjoyment. This instrument is included in Measuring Attitudes toward Reading ERIC/TM Report 73.

12664
Rhody Secondary Reading Attitude Assessment. Tullock-Rhody, Regina; Alexander, J. Estill 1980
Descriptors: *Reading Attitudes; Secondary Education; *Secondary School Students; *Student Attitudes
Identifiers: Measuring Attitudes toward Reading
Availability: *Journal of Reading;*v23 p609-14, Apr 1980
Grade Level: 7–12
Notes: Items, 25

Designed to assess reading attitudes of secondary school students. This instrument is included in Measuring Attitudes toward Reading ERIC/TM Report 73, available from ERIC Document Reproduction Service, P.O. Box 190, Arlington, VA 22210 (ED196938, 145 pages).

12665
Reading Attitudes Questionnaire. Fiddler, Jerry B. 1974
Descriptors: Elementary School Students; *Grade 6; Intermediate Grades; *Reading Attitudes; *School Attitudes; Student Attitudes
Identifiers: Measuring Attitudes toward Reading
Availability: ERIC Document Reproduction Service; 3900 Wheeler Ave., Alexandria, VA 22304 (ED196938, 145 pages)
Grade Level: 6
Notes: Items, 100

Designed to assess attitudes of sixth grade students concerning reading and other subjects. More descriptive information is available in Jerry Ben Fiddler's *The Standardization of a Questionnaire to Ascertain the Attitude toward Reading of Sixth-Grade Pupils,* Ed.D. dissertation, State University of New York at Buffalo, 1974 (University

Microfilms International Order No. DCJ74-14298, 203 pages). This instrument is included in Measuring Attitudes toward Reading ERIC/TM Report 73 (ED196938).

12680
An Opinionnaire on Race, Sex and Multicultural Education, for School Personnel. Community Change, Inc., Reading, MA 1978
Descriptors: Adults; Ethnic Stereotypes; *Multicultural Education; *Opinions; Questionnaires; *Racial Attitudes; *School Personnel; Sex Discrimination; *Sex Stereotypes
Availability: ERIC Document Reproduction Service; 3900 Wheeler Ave., Alexandria, VA 22304-5110 (ED163149, 7 pages)
Target Audience: Adults
Notes: Items, 52

In this questionnaire, 52 statements related to attitudes concerning race, sex, and multicultural education are presented. Respondents (school personnel) register their agreement or disagreement with the statements. The questions are designed to stimulate discussions between groups and to help to establish program goals in school systems. The questionnaire does not ask respondents to state facts. The intent is to secure a composite picture of how people employed in a given school or school system feel and think about the statements presented.

12686
The SOCO Scale: A Measure of the Customer Orientation of Salespeople. Saxe, Robert; Weitz, Barton A. 1982
Descriptors: Adults; Rating Scales; *Salesmanship; *Sales Workers
Identifiers: *Customer Satisfaction; SOCO
Availability: Marketing Science Institute; Publications Dept., 1000 Massachusetts Ave., Cambridge, MA 02138
Target Audience: Adults
Notes: Items, 24

Developed to measure the degree to which salespersons engage in customer-oriented selling. Customer-oriented selling is defined as the degree to which salespeople practice the technique whereby they try to help their customers make purchase decisions which will satisfy customer needs. Highly customer-oriented behavior aims at increasing long-term customer satisfaction. Nomological validity indicates that the use of customer-oriented selling is related to the ability of salespeople to help their customers and the quality of the customer-salesperson relationship.

12687
The TLC Teaching Style Inventory. Silver, Harvey F.; Hanson, J. Robert 1980
Subtests: Sensing Feeling; Sensing Thinking; Intuitive Feeling; Intuitive Thinking
Descriptors: Adults; Classroom Environment; Educational Objectives; Lesson Plans; Rating Scales; *Self Evaluation (Individuals); Student Behavior; Student Evaluation; Teacher Student Relationship; Teacher Attitudes; Teacher Role; *Teachers; *Teaching Styles
Identifiers: Jung (Carl G); Self Administered Tests; TLC Learning Preference Inventory Kit; TSI
Availability: Educational Performance Associates; 600 Broad Ave., Ridgefield, NJ 07657
Target Audience: Adults
Notes: Items, 40

A self-description test based on Carl Jung's Theory of Psychological Types (1921). Designed to help teachers identify their own teaching profile based on their preferences for particular behaviors. The teaching aspects covered include classroom atmosphere, teaching techniques, planning, what teachers value in students, teacher-student interaction, classroom management, student behaviors, teaching behaviors, evaluation, educational goals. The 4 behaviors are sensing, thinking, feeling, intuitive.

12691
Compensatory Reading Project: Attitudes toward Reading, Grades 4 and 6. Trismen, Donald A.; And Others 1973
Descriptors: Compensatory Education; *Elementary School Students; *Grade 4; *Grade 6; Intermediate Grades; *Reading Attitudes; School Attitudes; Student Attitudes
Availability: ERIC Document Reproduction Service; 3900 Wheeler Ave., Alexandria, VA 22304 (ED130257, 424 pages)
Grade Level: 4; 6
Notes: Items, 45

An attitude measure developed as part of the Compensatory Reading Project. Measures attitudes toward reading and books.

12703
The Institutional Renewal Scale. Crowley, Robert J. 1976
Descriptors: Adults; Educational Attitudes; *Educational Innovation; Individual Characteristics; Rating Scales; Secondary Education; *Secondary School Teachers; *Teacher Attitudes
Identifiers: IRS
Availability: ERIC Document Reproduction Service; 3900 Wheeler Ave., Alexandria, VA 22304-5110 (ED156678, 33 pages)
Grade Level: 9-12
Target Audience: 18-64
Notes: Items, 12

The Institutional Renewal Scale (IRS) is designed to measure attitudes toward the general and intuitive concept of educational innovation in schools. It is a 12-item attitude scale which was intended for schools, but its use may be extended to those concerned with educational innovations. Developed for secondary school teachers, but it is applicable to teachers at all levels. The IRS is a relatively brief scale that approximates the best qualities of a cumulative scale.

12718
Survey Questionnaire for Teacher Education Developmental Service. State University of New York, Albany. Teacher Education Developmental Service 1976
Descriptors: *Administrator Attitudes; Beginning Teachers; Research Projects; *State Surveys; *Teacher Attitudes; *Teacher Certification
Identifiers: New York
Availability: ERIC Document Reproduction Service; 3900 Wheeler Ave., Alexandria, VA 22304 (ED143665, microfiche only)
Target Audience: 18-64
Notes: Items, 18

This is a survey questionnaire sent to educators in New York state to assess their attitudes toward some projected possibilities for a different mode of certification for beginning educators. It was done as part of the project for the Teacher Education Developmental Service. An alternate source is the Office of Education, Washington, DC Teacher Corps. Not available in hardcopy because of the marginal legibility of original document.

12728
The ACT Evaluation/Survey Service for Educational Institutions and Agencies: Student Opinion Survey. American College Testing Program, Iowa City, IA 1981
Descriptors: College Environment; College Programs; *College Students; Higher Education; *Institutional Research; *Organizational Objectives; Questionnaires; *Student Attitudes
Identifiers: ACT Evaluation Survey Service; ESS
Availability: ACT; Evaluation/Survey Service, P.O. Box 168, Iowa City, IA 52243
Grade Level: 13-16
Notes: Time, 20 approx.; Items, 81

Primary purpose of the ACT Evaluation/Survey Service (ESS) is to assist postsecondary educational institutions and agencies in the collection, interpretation, and use of student survey data for such purposes as institutional planning, research, evaluation, and self-study. There are 9 survey instruments currently available, and each is designed to address a single educational topic and audience. Items are broad enough in scope to be applicable to most postsecondary institutions but specific enough to provide data that may be readily translatable into institutional action. The Student Opinion Survey is used to explore perceptions of enrolled students regarding the college's programs, services, and environment. Untimed instrument that takes about 20 minutes to complete and covers background information, college services, college environment. There is room for an institution to add up to 30 additional questions and for respondent to write in suggestions or comments.

12729
The ACT Evaluation/Survey Service for Educational Institutions and Agencies: Student Opinion Survey (2-Year College Form). American College Testing Program, Iowa City, IA 1981
Descriptors: College Environment; College Programs; *Institutional Research; *Organizational Objectives; Postsecondary Education; Questionnaires; *Student Attitudes; *Two Year Colleges; *Two Year College Students
Identifiers: ACT Evaluation Survey Service; ESS
Availability: ACT; Evaluation/Survey Service, P.O. Box 168, Iowa City, IA 52243
Grade Level: 13-14
Notes: Time, 20 approx.; Items, 96

Primary purpose of the ACT Evaluation/Survey Service (ESS) is to assist postsecondary educational institutions and agencies in the collection, interpretation, and use of student survey data for such purposes as institutional planning, research, evaluation, and self-study. There are 9 survey instruments currently available, and each is designed to address a single educational topic and audience. Items are broad enough in scope to be applicable to most postsecondary institutions but specific enough to provide data that may be readily translatable into institutional action. The Student Opinion Survey for 2-year colleges is used to explore perceptions of enrolled students regarding the institution's programs, environment, and services. Untimed instrument that takes about 20 minutes to complete and covers background information, college impressions, college services, and college environment. There is room for an institution to add up to 30 additional items and for respondents to write in suggestions and comments.

12733
Dimensions of Self-Concept, Form E. Michael, William B.; Smith, Robert A. 1977
Subtests: Aspiration; Anxiety; Academic Interest and Satisfaction; Leadership and Initiative; Identification vs. Alienation
Descriptors: Academic Aspiration; Anxiety; *Educational Environment; *Elementary School Students; Identification (Psychology); Intermediate Grades; Leadership Qualities; Learning Motivation; Rating Scales; *Self Concept; *Self Concept Measures; Student Motivation
Identifiers: DOSC
Availability: Educational and Industrial Testing Service; P.O. Box 7234, San Diego, CA 92107
Grade Level: 4-6
Notes: Time, 40 approx.; Items, 70

Developed to measure noncognitive factors associated with self-esteem or self-concept in a school setting. The items were constructed to represent an activity or attitude in the school learning situation or environment. Is a self-report instrument that reflects perceptions students have of their place within the educational setting. There are 2 purposes to using the instrument: to identify students who may have difficulty in their schoolwork because of low self-esteem or to diagnose those dimensions and associated activities that might contribute to low self-esteem and to impaired learning capabilities for purposes of guidance or counseling. The inventory is not timed but should take between 20 and 40 minutes.

12734
Dimensions of Self-Concept, Form S. Michael, William B.; Smith, Robert A. 1977
Subtests: Aspiration; Anxiety; Academic Interest and Satisfaction; Leadership and Initiative; Identification vs. Alienation
Descriptors: Academic Aspiration; Anxiety; *Educational Environment; Identification (Psychology); Leadership Qualities; Learning Motivation; Rating Scales; Secondary Education; *Secondary School Students; *Self Concept; *Self Concept Measures; Student Motivation
Identifiers: DOSC
Availability: Educational and Industrial Testing Service; P.O. Box 7234, San Diego, CA 92107
Grade Level: 7-12
Notes: Time, 35 approx.; Items, 70

Developed to measure noncognitive factors associated with self-esteem or self-concept in a school setting. The items were constructed to represent an activity or attitude in the school learning situation or environment. Is a self-report instrument that reflects perceptions students have of their place within the educational setting. There are 2 purposes to using the instrument: to identify students who may have difficulty in their schoolwork because of low self-esteem or to diagnose those dimensions and associated activities that might contribute to low self-esteem and to impaired learning capabilities for purposes of guidance or counseling. The inventory is not timed but should take between 15 and 35 minutes.

12814
Student Questionnaire, Form C. American Institutes for Research in the Behavioral Sciences, Palo Alto, CA 1977
Descriptors: Elementary Education; *Elementary School Students; Grade 3; Grade 4; Grade 5; *Longitudinal Studies; Questionnaires; *Student Attitudes; Student Behavior; *Student Characteristics
Identifiers: Longitudinal Study of Educational Practices; Project Longstep
Availability: ERIC Document Reproduction Service; 3900 Wheeler Ave., Alexandria, VA 22304 (ED133369, 59 pages)
Grade Level: 3-5
Notes: Items, 28

This questionnaire is 1 of several developed for use in Project Longstep. . It is used for grades 3, 4, and 5 to assess student characteristics and is completed by the student. The general emphasis of Project Longstep (Longitudinal Study of Educational Practices) was on the identification of changes in student achievement that occur as a result of intensive educational innovation. The instruments used in this project provided information on student cognitive performance, student characteristics, student attitudes, teacher characteristics, and educational treatments. Student cognitive achievement was measured by standard, commercially developed instruments. Student characteristics and attitudes and teacher characteristics were assessed by questionnaires developed specifically for the study.

12815
Student Questionnaire, Form D. American Institutes for Research in the Behavioral Sciences, Palo Alto, CA 1977
Descriptors: Elementary School Students; Elementary Secondary Education; *Grade 6; Grade 7; Grade 8; *Junior High School Students; *Longitudinal Studies; Questionnaires; Student Attitudes; *Student Characteristics
Identifiers: Longitudinal Study of Educational Practices; Project Longstep
Availability: ERIC Document Reproduction Service; 3900 Wheeler Ave., Alexandria, VA 22304 (ED133369, 59 pages)
Grade Level: 6–8
Notes: Items, 35

This questionnaire is one of several developed for use in Project Longstep. It is used to assess student characteristics and attitudes in grades 6-8. The general emphasis of Project Longstep (Longitudinal Study of Educational Practices) was on the identification of changes in student achievement that occur as a result of intensive educational innovation. The instruments used in this project provided information on student cognitive performance, student characteristics, student attitudes, teacher characteristics, and educational treatments. Student cognitive achievement was measured by standard, commercially developed instruments. Student characteristics and attitudes and teacher characteristics were assessed by questionnaires developed specifically for the study.

12816
Student Questionnaire, Form E. American Institutes for Research in the Behavioral Sciences, Palo Alto, CA 1977
Descriptors: High Schools; *High School Students; *Longitudinal Studies; Questionnaires; *Student Attitudes; *Student Characteristics
Identifiers: Longitudinal Study of Educational Practices; Project Longstep
Availability: ERIC Document Reproduction Service; 3900 Wheeler Ave., Alexandria, VA 22304 (ED133369, 59 pages)
Grade Level: 9–12
Notes: Items, 39

This questionnaire is one of several developed for use in Project Longstep. It is used to assess student characteristics and attitudes in grades 9-12. The general emphasis of Project Longstep (Longitudinal Study of Educational Practices) was on the identification of changes in student achievement that occur as a result of intensive educational innovation. The instruments used in this project provided information on student cognitive performance, student characteristics, student attitudes, teacher characteristics, and educational treatments. Student cognitive achievement was measured by standard, commercially developed instruments. Student characteristics and attitudes and teacher characteristics were assessed by questionnaires developed specifically for the study.

12817
Student Questionnaire, Form E. American Institutes for Research in the Behavioral Sciences, Palo Alto, CA 1977
Descriptors: Adults; Elementary School Teachers; Elementary Secondary Education; *Longitudinal Studies; Questionnaires; Secondary School Teachers; *Student Attitudes; *Student Characteristics; *Teacher Attitudes; *Teacher Characteristics
Identifiers: Longitudinal Study of Educational Practices; Project Longstep
Availability: ERIC Document Reproduction Service; 3900 Wheeler Ave., Alexandria, VA 22304-5110 (ED133369, 59 pages)
Grade Level: 1–12
Notes: Items, 40

This questionnaire is one of several developed for use in Project Longstep. It is used to assess student characteristics and attitudes. The general emphasis of Project Longstep (Longitudinal Study of Educational Practices) was on the identification of changes in student achievement that occur as a result of intensive educational innovation. The instruments used in this project provided information on student cognitive performance, student characteristics, student attitudes, teacher characteristics, and educational treatments. Student cognitive achievement was measured by standard, commercially developed instruments. Student characteristics and attitudes and teacher characteristics were assessed by questionnaires developed specifically for the study.

12841
Student Questionnaire (Harvard Project Physics). Welch, Wayne W.; Ahlgren, Andrew 1968
Subtests: Attitude toward Physics; Career Interest; Student Characteristics
Descriptors: High Schools; High School Students; *Physics; Questionnaires; Science Course Improvement Projects; Secondary School Science; *Student Characteristics; *Vocational Interests
Identifiers: Harvard Project Physics
Availability: ERIC Document Reproduction Service; 3900 Wheeler Ave., Alexandria, VA 22304 (ED127121, microfiche only)
Grade Level: 9–12
Notes: Time, 45; Items, 60

This questionnaire was designed to gather general background information from students who had used the Harvard Project Physics curriculum. The instrument includes 3 20-item subscales: (1) attitude toward physics, (2) career interest, and (3) student characteristics. Items are multiple choice with 5 options. This is not available from EDRS in hardcopy because of the colored pages throughout the original document. An alternate source is Harvard University, Cambridge, MA.

12843
Energy Environment Opinionnaire. Wert, Jonathan M. 1975
Descriptors: Adults; *Energy; *Environment; Environmental Education; High Schools; High School Students; Natural Resources; Opinions; *Student Attitudes; *Teacher Attitudes; Teachers
Availability: ERIC Document Reproduction Service; 3900 Wheeler Ave., Alexandria, VA 22304-5110 (ED125865, 10 pages)
Grade Level: 9–12
Target Audience: 18–64
Notes: Items, 85

This questionnaire is designed to assess the opinions of students, teachers, and citizens about energy and the environment. It is composed of 85 energy and environment-oriented statements about which the examinee gives an opinion. Choices provided on the answer sheet given are strongly agree, mildly agree, not sure or don't know, mildly disagree, and strongly disagree. There is a respondent's information sheet included.

12844
Mexican American Youth and Vocational Education in Texas Questionnaire. Houston University Texas Center for Human Resources 1976
Descriptors: *Academic Aspiration; Career Choice; High Schools; *High School Students; *Mexican Americans; *Occupational Aspiration; *Student Attitudes; Student Educational Objectives; *Vocational Education; Youth
Identifiers: Texas
Availability: ERIC Document Reproduction Service; 3900 Wheeler Ave., Alexandria, VA 22304 (ED124368, 39 pages)
Grade Level: 9–12
Notes: Items, 287

This questionnaire was used to survey the attitudes, program at school, and plans for the future of Mexican-American high school students in Texas. Almost all of the questions consist of circling a number or checking one or more answers. A few require written answers. Topics covered by the questions are the student's family background; school activities; attitudes about school, work, and life in general; what their parents do, feel, and think about their school, kinds of problems encountered while job hunting; careers, jobs, and the labor market; how to go about getting a job; and employers' attitudes about high school students, students' attitudes about employers, education or training necessary for certain jobs, and future educational and employment plans. There is one section for vocational students only.

12845
The Instructional Improvement Questionnaire. Pohlmann, John T.; Elmore, Patricia B. 1976
Descriptors: College Faculty; College Students; *Course Evaluation; *Feedback; *Higher Education; Participant Satisfaction; Questionnaires; Rating Scales; *Student Evaluation of Teacher Performance; Teacher Effectiveness
Identifiers: IIQ
Availability: ERIC Document Reproduction Service; 3900 Wheeler Ave., Alexandria, VA 22304-5110 (ED121828, 131 pages)
Grade Level: 13–16
Notes: Items, 100

The Instructional Improvement Questionnaire (IIQ) is a student rating form designed to provide evaluative feedback to instructors about their teaching. The IIQ was developed at Southern Illinois University at Carbondale in 1969 and revised in 1972. Results from the IIQ may be used for teacher promotion and annual salary reviews, student course selection, and evaluating course effectiveness. Results are released only on authorization of the instructor. There are 4 sections: a student biographical section, an instructor evaluation section, a course evaluation section, and an optional section where instructors can have students respond to as many as 60 items prepared by individual departments or faculty. Students respond directly on opscan answer sheets which are computer processed.

12868
Mathematics Achievement Questionnaire: Parent Forms and Student Forms. Parsons, Jacquelynne Eccles 1980
Descriptors: Adults; *Elementary School Students; Intermediate Grades; *Mathematics Achievement; *Parent Attitudes; Rating Scales; Secondary Education; *Secondary School Students; *Self Concept; *Student Attitudes
Identifiers: TIM(K)
Availability: Tests in Microfiche; Test Collection, Educational Testing Service, Princeton, NJ 08541
Grade Level: 5–11
Target Audience: Adults

Series of questionnaires to assess the impact of parents on children's achievement self-concept in mathematics. Also forms for children in grade 5 through 11 to assess their attitudes and beliefs regarding their mathematics achievement.

12870
Questionnaire on Eradicating Sexism in Vocational Education. Weitz, Anna D. 1971
Subtests: Career Options; Family Role; Aptitudes and Traits; Leadership and Authority; Education
Descriptors: Adults; *College Faculty; Higher Education; Sex Bias; *Sex Discrimination; *Sex Stereotypes; *Student Attitudes; *Teacher Attitudes; *Undergraduate Students; Vocational Education
Identifiers: Self Administered Tests
Availability: ERIC Document Reproduction Service; 3900 Wheeler Ave., Alexandria, VA 22304-5110 (ED147564, 101 pages)
Grade Level: 13–16
Target Audience: 18–64
Notes: Time, 5 approx.; Items, 18

Designed to identify nature and extent of sex role stereotyping by college faculty and students.

12871
Affective Perception Inventory, Intermediate Level. Soares, Anthony T.; Soares, Louise M. 1979
Subtests: Self-Concept (as a person); Student Self; Perceptions in Language Arts; Mathematics Perceptions; Science Perceptions; Social Studies Perceptions; Perceptions in the Arts; Perceptions in Physical Education; School Perceptions
Descriptors: *Elementary School Students; Fine Arts; Intermediate Grades; Junior High Schools; *Junior High School Students; Language Arts; Mathematics; Physical Education; Research Tools; *School Attitudes; Sciences; *Self Concept Measures; Semantic Differential; Social Studies; *Student Attitudes
Identifiers: Self Concept of Ability
Availability: Soares Associates; 111 Teeter Rock Rd., Trumbull, CT 06611
Grade Level: 4–8
Notes: Time, 45; Items, 115

Nine scales measure feelings about the self relative to specific subject areas or classroom experiences including self as a person, as a student, in the school environment, or in interaction with others who are part of the educational setting. Subjects covered are language arts, mathematics, science, social studies, arts, physical education. Used primarily for research. Administration time depends on reading level. A semantic differential format is used. Subject scales measure attitudes toward the subject and feelings about one's ability in the subject.

12872
Affective Perception Inventory, Advanced Level. Soares, Anthony T.; Soares, Louise M. 1979
Subtests: Self-Concept (as a person); Student Self; English Perceptions; Mathematics Perceptions; Science Perceptions; Perceptions in Social Studies; Perceptions in the Arts; Perceptions in Physical Education; School Perceptions
Descriptors: English Curriculum; Fine Arts; High Schools; *High School Students; Mathematics; Physical Education; Research Tools; *School Attitudes; Sciences; *Self Concept Measures; Semantic Differential; Social Studies; *Student Attitudes; Self Concept
Availability: Soares Associates; 111 Teeter Rock Rd., Trumbull, CT 06611
Grade Level: 9–12
Notes: Time, 45; Items, 115

Nine scales measure feelings about the self relative to specific subject areas or classroom experiences including self as a person, as a student, in the school environment, or in interaction with others who are part of the educational setting. Subjects covered are English, mathematics, science, social studies, arts, physical education. Used primarily for research. A semantic differential format is used. Subject scales measure attitudes toward the subject and feelings about one's ability in the subject.

12873
Affective Perception Inventory, Advanced Level, Italian. Soares, Anthony T.; Soares, Louise M. 1980

Subtests: Self-Concept (as a person); Student Self; English Perceptions; Mathematics Perceptions; Science Perceptions; Perceptions in Social Studies; Perceptions in the Arts; Perceptions in Physical Education; School Perceptions
Descriptors: English Curriculum; Fine Arts; High Schools; *High School Students; *Italian; Mathematics; Physical Education; Research Tools; *School Attitudes; Sciences; *Self Concept Measures; Semantic Differential; Social Studies; *Student Attitudes
Identifiers: Self Concept of Ability
Availability: Soares Associates; 111 Teeter Rock Rd., Trumbull, CT 06611
Grade Level: 9–12
Notes: Time, 45; Items, 115
Nine scales measure feelings about the self relative to specific subject areas or classroom experiences including self as a person, as a student, in the school environment, or in interaction with others who are part of the educational setting. Subjects covered are English, mathematics, science, social studies, arts, physical education. Used primarily for research. A semantic differential format is used. This version is a translation.

12874
Affective Perception Inventory, Intermediate Level, Italian. Soares, Anthony T.; Soares, Louise M. 1980
Subtests: Self-Concept (as a person); Student Self; Perceptions in Language Arts; Mathematics Perceptions; Science Perceptions; Social Studies Perceptions; Perceptions in the Arts; Perceptions in Physical Education; School Perceptions
Descriptors: *Elementary School Students; Fine Arts; Intermediate Grades; *Italian; Junior High Schools; *Junior High School Students; Language Arts; Mathematics; Physical Education; Research Tools; *School Attitudes; Sciences; *Self Concept Measures; Semantic Differential; Social Studies; *Student Attitudes
Identifiers: Self Concept of Ability
Availability: Soares Associates; 111 Teeter Rock Rd., Trumbull, CT 06611
Grade Level: 4–8
Notes: Time, 45; Items, 115
Nine scales measure feelings about the self relative to specific subject areas or classroom experiences including self as a person, as a student, in the school environment, or in interaction with others who are part of the educational setting. Subjects covered are language arts, mathematics, science, social studies, arts, physical education. Used primarily for research. Administration time depends on reading level. A semantic differential format is used. This version is a translation.

12875
Affective Perception Inventory, Primary Level, Italian. Soares, Anthony T.; Soares, Louise M. 1980
Subtests: Self-Concept (as a person); Student Self; Reading Perceptions; Arithmetic Perceptions; Science Perceptions; Social Studies Perceptions; Perceptions in the Arts; Sports and Games Perceptions; School Perceptions
Descriptors: Arithmetic; *Elementary School Students; Fine Arts; *Italian; Physical Education; Primary Education; Reading Attitudes; Research Tools; *School Attitudes; Sciences; *Self Concept Measures; Semantic Differential; Social Studies; *Student Attitudes
Identifiers: Self Concept of Ability
Availability: Soares Associates; 111 Teeter Rock Rd., Trumbull, CT 06611
Grade Level: 1–3
Notes: Time, 45; Items, 115
Nine scales measure feelings about the self relative to specific subject areas or classroom experiences including self as a person, as a student, in the school environment, or in interaction with others who are part of the educational setting. Subjects covered are reading, arithmetic, science, social studies, arts, sports and games. Used primarily for research. Administration time depends on reading level. A semantic differential format is used. This is a translation.

12876
Self-Perception Inventory, Adult Form (Italian). Soares, Anthony T.; Soares, Louise M. 1980
Subtests: Self-Concept; Reflected Self-Friends; Reflected Self-Teachers; Reflected Self-Parents; Ideal Concept; Perceptions of Others
Descriptors: College Students; Higher Education; *High School Students; *Italian; *Parent Attitudes; Peer Evaluation; Rating Scales; Research Tools; Secondary Education; *Self Concept; *Self Concept Measures; Semantic Differential; *Young Adults
Identifiers: Ideal Self Concept; Reflected Self Concept
Availability: Soares Associates; 111 Teeter Rock Rd., Trumbull, CT 06611

Target Audience: 18–64
Notes: Time, 60; Items, 218
A self-concept measure using a semantic differential format. Six components of self-perception are covered self-concept, ideal concept, reflected self-other parents, reflected self-teachers, reflected self-friends, and perceptions of others, which is administered to significant people in the subject's life. Administration time ranges from 5-20 minutes per part, depending on reading ability. This version is a translation. No norms are included. The English version (TC010644) was normed on grade 12 and college students and young working adults.

12877
Self-Perception Inventory—Teacher Forms (Italian). Soares, Anthony T.; Soares, Louise M. 1980
Subtests: Self-Concept-Teacher; Reflected Self-Cooperating Teacher; Reflected Self-Supervisor; Ideal Self-Teacher; Teacher Perception; Reflected Teacher Perception; Student Perceptions
Descriptors: Adults; Cooperating Teachers; *Italian; Rating Scales; Research Tools; *Self Concept; *Self Concept Measures; Semantic Differential; Student Attitudes; *Student Teachers; Student Teacher Supervisors; Suburban Schools; Teacher Attitudes; *Teachers; Urban Schools
Identifiers: Ideal Self Concept; Reflected Self Concept
Availability: Soares Associates; 111 Teeter Rock Rd., Trumbull, CT 06611
Target Audience: 18–64
Notes: Time, 60; Items, 288
A self-concept measure used by teachers, student teachers, their supervisors, and students. Self-rating forms cover self-concept as a teacher, reflected self-cooperating teaching (how the student teacher thinks he/she is seen by the cooperating teacher), reflected self-supervisor (college supervisor's view of student teacher as seen by student teacher), ideal-self-teacher. Forms for rating by others are coop teacher and supervisor rate intern, teacher rating of how intern will rate him/herself and student perceptions of teachers. This version is a translation. The English version (TC010645) is normed on urban and suburban student teachers. No norms are included in this version.

12880
Self-Perception Inventory—Student Forms, (Spanish). Soares, Anthony T.; Soares, Louise M. 1980
Subtests: Self-Concept; Reflected Self-Classmates; Reflected Self-Teachers; Reflected Self-Parents; Ideal Concept; Perceptions of Others; Student Self; Perceptions of Others/Student Self
Descriptors: *Disadvantaged Youth; *Elementary School Students; Elementary Secondary Education; Parent Attitudes; Peer Evaluation; Rating Scales; *Secondary School Students; *Self Concept; *Self Concept Measures; Semantic Differential; *Spanish
Identifiers: Classmates; Ideal Self Concept; Reflected Self Concept; Self Concept of Ability
Availability: Soares Associates; 111 Teeter Rock Rd., Trumbull, CT 06611
Grade Level: 1–12
Notes: Time, 60; Items, 288
A self-concept measure using a semantic differential format in which the student rates each concept on a 4-point scale using 2 opposite adjectives or phrases. Six components of self-perception are covered: self-concept, ideal concept, reflected self-classmates, reflected self-teachers, reflected self-parents, student self. Included is a term called "Perceptions of Others", which is administered to those mentioned in the reflected-self forms, teachers, classmates, and parents. Administration time varies from 5-20 minutes per part depending on age and reading level. Norms on the English version (TC010643) are for advantaged and disadvantaged students.

12881
Self-Perception Inventory, Adult Forms (Spanish). Soares, Anthony T.; Soares, Louise M. 1980
Subtests: Self-Concept; Reflected Self-Friends; Reflected Self-Teachers; Reflected Self-Parents; Ideal Concept; Perceptions of Others
Descriptors: Adults; College Students; Higher Education; *High School Students; *Parent Attitudes; Peer Evaluation; Rating Scales; Research Tools; Secondary Education; *Self Concept; *Self Concept Measures; Semantic Differential; *Spanish; *Young Adults
Identifiers: Ideal Self Concept; Reflected Self Concept
Availability: Soares Associates; 111 Teeter Rock Rd., Trumbull, CT 06611
Target Audience: 18–64
Notes: Time, 60; Items, 288
A self-concept measure using a semantic differential format. Six components of self-perception are covered: self-concept, ideal concept, reflected self-other parents, reflected self-teachers, reflected self-friends, and perceptions of others, which is administered to significant people in the subject's life. Administration time ranges from 5-20 minutes per part, depending on reading ability. This version is

a translation. No norms are included. The English version (PTC010644) was normed on grade 12 and college students and young working adults.

12882
Self-Perception Inventory—Teacher Forms (Spanish). Soares, Anthony T.; Soares, Louise M. 1980
Subtests: Self-Concept-Teacher; Reflected Self-Cooperating Teacher; Reflected Self-Supervisor; Ideal Self-Teacher; Teacher Perception; Reflected Teacher Perception; Student Perceptions
Descriptors: Adults; Cooperating Teachers; Rating Scales; Research Tools; Self Concept; *Self Concept Measures; Semantic Differential; *Spanish; Student Attitudes; *Student Teachers; Student Teacher Supervisors; Suburban Schools; Teacher Attitudes; *Teachers; Urban Schools
Identifiers: Ideal Self Concept; Reflected Self Concept
Availability: Soares Associates; 111 Teeter Rock Rd., Trumbull, CT 06611
Target Audience: 18–64
Notes: Time, 60; Items, 288
A self-concept measure using a semantic differential format. Self-rating forms cover self-concept as a teacher, reflected self-cooperating teacher (how the student teacher thinks he/she is seen by the cooperating teacher), reflected self-supervisor (college supervisor's view of student teacher as seen by student teacher), ideal self-teacher. Forms for rating by others cover coop teacher and supervisor rate intern, teacher rating of how intern will rate him/herself, and student perceptions of teachers. Used by teachers, student teachers, their supervisors and students. This version is a translation. No norms are included.

12883
Self-Perception Inventory—Student Forms, (French). Soares, Anthony T.; Soares, Louise M. 1980
Subtests: Self-Concept; Reflected Self-Classmates; Reflected Self-Teachers; Reflected Self-Parents; Ideal Concept; Perceptions of Others; Student Self; Perceptions of Others/Student Self
Descriptors: *Disadvantaged Youth; *Elementary School Students; Elementary Secondary Education; *French; Parent Attitudes; Peer Evaluation; Rating Scales; *Secondary School Students; *Self Concept; *Self Concept Measures; Semantic Differential
Identifiers: Classmates; Ideal Self Concept; Reflected Self Concept; Self Concept of Ability
Availability: Soares Associates; 111 Teeter Rock Rd., Trumbull, CT 06611
Grade Level: 1–12
Notes: Time, 60; Items, 288
A self-concept measure using a semantic differential format. Six components of self-perception are covered: self-concept, ideal concept, reflected self-classmates, reflected self-teachers, reflected self-parents, student self. Included is a term called "Perceptions of Others," which is administered to those mentioned in the reflected-self forms, teachers, classmates, and parents. Administration time varies from 5-20 minutes per part depending on age and reading level. The student rates each concept on a 4-point scale using 2 opposite adjectives or phrases. No norms are provided.

12884
Self-Perception Inventory, Adult Form (French). Soares, Anthony T.; Soares, Louise M. 1980
Subtests: Self-Concept; Reflected Self-Friends; Reflected Self-Teachers; Reflected Self-Parents; Ideal Concept; Perceptions of Others
Descriptors: Adults; College Students; *French; Higher Education; *High School Students; *Parent Attitudes; Peer Evaluation; Rating Scales; Research Tools; Secondary Education; *Self Concept; *Self Concept Measures; Semantic Differential; *Young Adults
Identifiers: Ideal Self Concept; Reflected Self Concept
Availability: Soares Associates; 111 Teeter Rock Rd., Trumbull, CT 06611
Target Audience: 18–64
Notes: Time, 60; Items, 288
A self-concept measure using a semantic differential format. Six components of self-perception are covered: self-concept, ideal concept, reflected self-other parents, reflected self-teachers, reflected self-friends, and perceptions of others, which is administered to significant people in the subject's life. Administration time ranges from 5-20 minutes per part, depending on reading ability. This version is a translation. No norms are included. The English version (TC010644) was normed on grade 12 and college students and young working adults.

12885
Self-Perception Inventory—Teacher Forms (French). Soares, Anthony T.; Soares, Louise M. 1980

Subtests: Self-Concept-Teacher; Reflected Self-Co-operating Teacher; Reflected Self-Supervisor; Ideal Self-Teacher; Teacher Perception; Reflected Teacher Perception; Student Perceptions
Descriptors: Adults; Cooperating Teachers; *French; Rating Scales; Research Tools; *Self Concept; *Self Concept Measures; Semantic Differential; Student Attitudes; *Student Teachers; Student Teacher Supervisors; Suburban Schools; Teacher Attitudes; *Teachers; Urban Schools
Identifiers: Ideal Self Concept; Reflected Self Concept
Availability: Soares Associates; 111 Teeter Rock Rd., Trumbull, CT 06611
Target Audience: 18–64
Notes: Time, 60; Items, 288

A self-concept measure used by teachers, student teachers, their supervisors and students. Self-rating forms cover self-concept as a teacher, reflected self cooperating teacher (how the student teacher thinks he/she is seen by the cooperating teacher), reflected self-supervisor (college supervisor's view of student teacher as seen by student teacher), ideal-self-teacher. Forms for rating by others are coop teacher and supervisor rate intern, teacher rating of how intern will rate him/herself and student perceptions of teachers. This version is a translation. The English version (TC010645) is normed on urban and suburban student teacher. No norms are included in this version.

12886
Attitudes toward Men in Society Scale. Falkenberg, Steven D.; And Others 1983
Descriptors: Adults; College Students; *Males; Rating Scales; *Sex Role
Identifiers: AMS
Availability: ERIC Document Reproduction Service; 3900 Wheeler Ave., Alexandria, VA 22304 (ED223287, 16 pages)
Target Audience: 18–64
Notes: Items, 14

Developed to measure attitudes of males and females toward male roles in society. Analysis of the responses of male and female college students to the rating scale showed that females had a slightly more liberated view than males of male roles in society and that older women were more liberal than younger women. Among males, there was no differences based on age.

12894
Feminine Role Behavior Scale. Kammeyer, Kenneth 1961
Descriptors: Adults; Birth Order; *College Students; Family Role; Females; Personality Traits; *Sex Role; *Traditionalism
Identifiers: Guttman Scales; Kammeyer Feminine Role Behavior Scale
Availability: American Sociological Review;v31 n4 p508-15, Aug 1966
Target Audience: Adults
Notes: Time, 4 approx.; Items, 5

Designed to assess female sex role perception. The relationship between birth order and orientation toward feminine role seemed to indicate first-born females were more traditional and in greater agreement with parents' views.

12896
Parent Self-Appraisal Inventory. Project KIDS, Dallas, TX
Descriptors: Adults; Needs Assessment; *Parent Attitudes; Parent Child Relationship; Questionnaires; Rating Scales; *Self Evaluation (Individuals)
Identifiers: PSAI
Availability: Project KIDS; Dr. Ruth Turner, Special Education Dept., Dallas Independent School District, Dallas, TX 75269
Target Audience: 18–64
Notes: Items, 14

The Parent Self-Appraisal Inventory (PSAI) lists 14 areas in which parents rate themselves using a 3-level scale; strong, average, or weak. Included are statements concerning care of the child's physical and emotional needs, behavior management, instruction, family life, and personal skills. The PSAI is both a measure of progress and a needs assessment tool. It includes an extensive list of suggestions for strengthening skills in each area.

12898
Marriage Type and Domestic Responsibility Scales. Pendleton, Brian F.; And Others 1977
Descriptors: *Dual Career Family; *Employed Women; Family Financial Resources; *Females; Heads of Households; Marital Satisfaction; Rating Scales; Self Evaluation (Individuals); Social Attitudes; Social Influences; Vocational Maturity; *Work Attitudes
Availability: Brian F. Pendleton; Sociology Dept., University of Akron, Akron, OH 44325
Target Audience: 18–64
Notes: Items, 60

This instrument is used to assess the consequences of dual-career marriages. This questionnaire is for the woman in the dual-career family. The first part asks for vital statistics, and the second section asks the subject to answer the statements in terms of whether she agrees or disagrees with them. The scale is from strongly agree to strongly disagree, and a not applicable choice is given. The scale has a 6-point range.

12900
Affective Perception Inventory, Advanced Level, Spanish. Soares, Anthony T.; Soares, Louise M. 1979
Subtests: Self-Concept (as a person); Student Self; English Perceptions; Mathematics Perceptions; Science Perceptions; Perceptions in Social Studies; Perceptions in the Arts; Perceptions in Physical Education; School Perceptions
Descriptors: English Curriculum; Fine Arts; High Schools; *High School Students; Mathematics; Physical Education; Research Tools; *School Attitudes; Sciences; *Self Concept Measures; Semantic Differential; Social Studies; *Spanish; *Student Attitudes
Identifiers: Self Concept of Ability
Availability: Soares Associates; 111 Teeter Rock Rd., Trumbull, CT 06611
Grade Level: 9–12
Notes: Time, 45; Items, 115

Nine scales measure feelings about the self relative to specific subject areas or classroom experiences including self as a person, as a student, in the school environment, or in interaction with others who are part of the educational setting. Subjects covered are English, mathematics, science, social sciences, arts, physical education. Used primarily for research. A semantic differential format is used. Subject scales measure attitudes toward the subject and feelings about one's ability in the subject.

12901
Affective Perception Inventory, Intermediate Level, Spanish. Soares, Anthony T.; Soares, Louise M. 1979
Subtests: Self-Concept (as a person); Student Self; Perceptions in Language Arts; Mathematics Perceptions; Science Perceptions; Social Studies Perceptions; Perceptions in the Arts; Perceptions in Physical Education; School Perceptions
Descriptors: *Elementary School Students; Fine Arts; Intermediate Grades; Junior High Schools; *Junior High School Students; Language Arts; Mathematics; Physical Education; Research Tools; *School Attitudes; Sciences; *Self Concept Measures; Semantic Differential; Social Studies; *Spanish; *Student Attitudes
Identifiers: Self Concept of Ability
Availability: Soares Associates; 111 Teeter Rock Rd., Trumbull, CT 06611
Grade Level: 4–8
Notes: Time, 45; Items, 115

Nine scales measure feelings about the self relative to specific subject areas or classroom experiences including self as a person, as a student, in the school environment, or in interaction with others who are part of the educational setting. Subjects covered are language arts, mathematics, science, social studies, arts, physical education. Used primarily for research. Administration time depends on reading level. A semantic differential format is used. Subject scales measure attitudes toward the subject and feelings about one's ability in the subject.

12902
Affective Perception Inventory, Primary Level, Spanish. Soares, Anthony T.; Soares, Louise M. 1979
Subtests: Self-Concept (as a person); Student Self; Reading Perceptions; Arithmetic Perceptions; Science Perceptions; Social Studies Perceptions; Perceptions in the Arts; Sports and Games Perceptions; School Perceptions
Descriptors: Arithmetic; *Elementary School Students; Fine Arts; Physical Education; Primary Education; Reading Attitudes; Research Tools; *School Attitudes; Sciences; *Self Concept Measures; Semantic Differential; Social Studies; *Spanish; *Student Attitudes
Identifiers: Self Concept of Ability
Availability: Soares Associates; 111 Teeter Rock Rd., Trumbull, CT 06611
Grade Level: 1–3
Notes: Time, 45; Items, 115

Nine scales measure feelings about the self relative to specific subject areas or classroom experiences including self as a person, as a student, in the school environment, or in interaction with others who are part of the educational setting. Subjects covered are reading, arithmetic, science, social studies, arts, sports and games. Used primarily for research. Administration time depends on reading level. A semantic differential format is used.

12903
Affective Perception Inventory, Advanced Level, French. Soares, Anthony T.; Soares, Louise M. 1980
Subtests: Self-Concept (as a person); Student Self; English Perceptions; Mathematics Perceptions; Science Perceptions; Perceptions in Social Studies; Perceptions in the Arts; Perceptions in Physical Education; School Perceptions
Descriptors: English Curriculum; Fine Arts; *French; High Schools; *High School Students; Mathematics; Physical Education; Research Tools; *School Attitudes; Sciences; *Self Concept Measures; Semantic Differential; Social Studies; *Student Attitudes
Identifiers: Self Concept of Ability
Availability: Soares Associates; 111 Teeter Rock Rd., Trumbull, CT 06611
Grade Level: 9–12
Notes: Time, 45; Items, 115

Nine scales measure feelings about the self relative to specific subject areas or classroom experiences including self as a person, as a student, in the school environment, or in interaction with others who are part of the educational setting. Subjects covered are English, mathematics, science, social studies, arts, physical education. Used primarily for research. A semantic differential format is used. This version is a translation.

12904
Affective Perception Inventory, Intermediate Level, French. Soares, Anthony T.; Soares, Louise M. 1980
Subtests: Self-Concept (as a person); Student Self; Perceptions in Language Arts; Mathematics Perceptions; Science Perceptions; Social Studies Perceptions; Perceptions in the Arts; Perceptions in Physical Education; School Perceptions
Descriptors: *Elementary School Students; Fine Arts; *French; Intermediate Grades; Junior High Schools; *Junior High School Students; Language Arts; Mathematics; Physical Education; Research Tools; *School Attitudes; Sciences; *Self Concept Measures; Semantic Differential; Social Studies; *Student Attitudes
Identifiers: Self Concept of Ability
Availability: Soares Associates; 111 Teeter Rock Rd., Trumbull, CT 06611
Grade Level: 4–8
Notes: Time, 45; Items, 115

Nine scales measure feelings about the self relative to specific subject areas or classroom experiences including self as a person, as a student, in the school environment, or in interaction with others who are part of the educational setting. Subjects covered are language arts, mathematics, science, social studies, arts, physical education. Used primarily for research. Administration time depends on reading level. A semantic differential format is used. This version is a translation.

12905
Affective Perception Inventory, Primary Level, French. Soares, Anthony T.; Soares, Louise M. 1980
Subtests: Self-Concept (as a person); Student Self; Reading Perceptions; Arithmetic Perceptions; Science Perceptions; Social Studies Perceptions; Perceptions in the Arts; Sports and Games Perceptions; School Perceptions
Descriptors: Arithmetic; *Elementary School Students; Fine Arts; *French; Physical Education; Primary Education; Reading Attitudes; Research Tools; *School Attitudes; Sciences; *Self Concept Measures; Semantic Differential; Social Studies; *Student Attitudes
Identifiers: Self Concept of Ability
Availability: Soares Associates; 111 Teeter Rock Rd., Trumbull, CT 06611
Grade Level: 1–3
Notes: Time, 45; Items, 115

Nine scales measure feelings about the self relative to specific subject areas or classroom experiences including self as a person, as a student, in the school environment, or in interaction with others who are part of the educational setting. Subjects covered are reading, arithmetic, science, social studies, arts, sports and games. Used primarily for research. Administration time depends on reading level. A semantic differential format is used. This is a translation.

12907
Student Survey and Attitude Inventory: Form A. South Carolina State Dept. of Education, Columbia Office of Research 1975
Descriptors: *Grade 7; *Grade 9; *Grade 11; High School Students; Junior High School Students; Questionnaires; Rating Scales; *Self Concept Measures; *State Programs; Student Attitudes; Surveys; Testing Programs
Identifiers: South Carolina; SSAI

Availability: ERIC Document Reproduction Service; 3900 Wheeler Ave., Alexandria, VA 22304 (ED111876, 43 pages)
Grade Level: 7; 9; 11
Notes: Items, 114

The Student Survey and Attitude Inventory (SSAI) is an instrument that measures how students feel about themselves, other people, and the world; it is seen as having potential for examining the attitudes of students and obtaining an indication of change in their self-concept. There are 2 parts to Form A. The first contains a 25-question study survey which elicits information about the students, their background, and attitudes. In the second section, the respondent is asked to indicate the degree of agreement on a 4-point scale. The inventory includes statements relating to nine different aspects of personality. These provide subscores in the areas of self-reliance, work orientation, identity, communication skills, enlightened trust, knowledge of major roles, social commitment, openness to sociopolitical change, and tolerance of individual and cultural differences. Self-concept is measured by the items in the self-reliance, work orientation, and identity subscales, which, when looked at together, form the individual adequacy scale. This test was administered to most seventh graders and a sample of ninth and eleventh graders in South Carolina.

12909
Revision of the Child Raising Opinion Questionnaire. Conrad, Rowan W. 1975
Descriptors: Adults; *Child Rearing; *Parent Attitudes; Questionnaires; Rating Scales; *Rural Population; Student Attitudes
Identifiers: CROQ; Mountain Plains Program
Availability: ERIC Document Reproduction Service; 3900 Wheeler Ave., Alexandria, VA 22304 (ED110832, 16 pages)
Target Audience: 18–64
Notes: Items, 91

The Child Raising Opinion Questionnaire (CROQ) assesses attitudes toward child rearing, in the Mountain-Plains student population. This revision has added 2 new scales to the questionnaire. One measures resistance to learning about children in particular and resistance to outside influences in the area of child rearing generally. The other measures confidence/adequacy in dealing with children. New items were included in the section dealing with general child-rearing practice.

12910
Project PRIMES (Progress Research in Meeting Elementary Standards) Language Arts Evaluation. Brierley, Miriam; Conard, Susan M. 1974
Descriptors: *Curriculum Evaluation; Elementary Education; *Elementary Schools; *Language Arts; Parent Attitudes; Principals; Questionnaires; *Reading Instruction; *State Standards; *Student Evaluation; *Teacher Attitudes
Identifiers: Elementary Secondary Education Act Title III; Ohio; Project PRIMES
Availability: ERIC Document Reproduction Service; 3900 Wheeler Ave., Alexandria, VA 22304 (ED110474, 21 pages)
Grade Level: K–8
Notes: Items, 85

The Project PRIMES (Progress Research in Meeting Elementary Standards) system examines elementary schools in light of minimum standards set by the Ohio State Department of Education. This evaluation instrument includes sections on the use of test results, pupil evaluation, teacher profile, administrator strengths and weaknesses, instructional equipment and materials, areas of instructional emphasis, program components, factors enhancing the optional reading program, and a parent opinionnaire. The questions pertain to the elementary language arts programs.

12912
Project PRIMES (Progress Research in Meeting Elementary Standards) Creative Arts and Physical Education Evaluation. Martin, Cecil; Cook, Gary 1974
Descriptors: *Art Activities; Curriculum Evaluation; *Dance; *Dramatics; Elementary Education; *Elementary Schools; *Music; *Physical Education; Principals; Questionnaires; *State Standards; *Teacher Attitudes
Identifiers: Elementary School Education Act Title III; Ohio; Project Primes
Availability: ERIC Document Reproduction Service; 3900 Wheeler Ave., Alexandria, VA 22304 (ED110472, 16 pages)
Grade Level: K–8
Notes: Items, 35

The Project PRIMES (Progress Research in Meeting Elementary Standards) system examines elementary schools in light of minimum standards set by the Ohio State Department of Education. This evaluation instrument is divided into 4 sections: (1) teacher strengths and weaknesses, (2) principal's strengths and weaknesses, (3) instructional components, and (4) evaluation. Questions concern the curriculum areas of art, music, drama, physical education, dance, and the applied arts.

12913
Project PRIMES (Progress Research in Meeting Elementary Standards) School/Community Relations Evaluation Instrument, Staff Opinionnaire. Fourman, Louis; Cook, Gary 1974
Descriptors: Curriculum Evaluation; *Elementary Education; *Elementary Schools; *Employee Attitudes; Opinions; Questionnaires; *School Community Relationship; *School Personnel; *State Standards
Identifiers: Elementary Secondary Education Act Title III; Ohio; Project PRIMES
Availability: ERIC Document Reproduction Service; 3900 Wheeler Ave., Alexandria, VA 22304 (ED110471, 17 pages)
Target Audience: Adults
Notes: Items, 15

This Staff Opinionnaire is 1 of 3 used to provide an indepth look at the strengths and weaknesses of the school/community relations programs. The 3 instruments are part of Project PRIMES (Progress Research in Meeting Elementary Standards) system which examines elementary schools in light of minimum standards set by the Ohio State Department of Education. The other 2 forms are a Parent Survey and a Community Survey. The questions are about school policy, organizations, sources of information/communication, and assistance programs.

12914
Project PRIMES (Progress Research in Meeting Elementary Standards) School/Community Relations Evaluation Instrument, Parent Survey. Fourman, Louis; Cook, Gary 1974
Descriptors: Elementary Education; *Elementary Schools; Opinions; *Parent Attitudes; *School Community Relationship; *State Standards; Surveys
Identifiers: Elementary Secondary Education Act Title III; Ohio; Project PRIMES
Availability: ERIC Document Reproduction Service; 3900 Wheeler Ave., Alexandria, VA 22304 (ED110471, 17 pages)
Target Audience: Adults
Notes: Items, 12

This Parent Survey is 1 of 3 used to provide an indepth look at the strengths and weaknesses of the school/community relations programs. The 3 instruments are part of Project PRIMES (Progress Research in Meeting Elementary Standards) system which examines elementary schools in light of minimum standards set by the Ohio State Department of Education. The other 2 forms are a Staff Opinionnaire and a Community Survey. In the belief that good communication with parent community is in the best interest of both the child and the development of the school program to meet the child's individual needs, the parents were asked to respond. The questions deal with sources of information, the P.T.A., and topics of interest in the schools.

12915
Project PRIMES (Progress Research in Meeting Elementary Standards) School/Community Relations Evaluation Instrument, Community Survey. Fourman, Louis; Cook, Gary 1974
Descriptors: *Community Surveys; Elementary Education; *Elementary Schools; Questionnaires; *School Community Relationship; *State Standards
Identifiers: Elementary Secondary Education Act Title III; Ohio; Project PRIMES
Availability: ERIC Document Reproduction Service; 3900 Wheeler Ave., Alexandria, VA 22304 (ED110471, 17 pages)
Target Audience: Adults
Notes: Items, 6

This instrument may be used by community members other than parents of children attending the local school. These members will be defined by the building principals, and this survey may or may not be used, depending on needs, with the other 2 instruments. The other instruments are a Parent Survey and a Staff Opinionnaire. All 3 instruments are used to provide an indepth look at the strengths and weaknesses of the school/community relations programs. The 3 instruments are part of Project PRIMES system which examines elementary schools in light of minimum standards set by the Ohio State Department of Education.

12916
Project PRIMES (Progress Research in Meeting Elementary Standards) ESEA Title III Instrument to Evaluate Standards for Ohio Elementary Schools, Organization and Administration Questionnaire. Martin, Cecil 1974
Subtests: Policies and Procedures; School Records and Reports; Instruction; Statements of Philosophy and Objectives; Statutory Requirements
Descriptors: Curriculum Evaluation; Elementary Education; *Elementary Schools; Questionnaires; School Administration; School Law; *School Organization; *State Standards
Identifiers: Elementary Secondary Education Act Title III Ohio; Project PRIMES
Availability: ERIC Document Reproduction Service; 3900 Wheeler Ave., Alexandria, VA 22304 (ED110470, 21 pages)
Target Audience: Adults
Notes: Items, 37

The Project PRIMES (Progress Research in Meeting Elementary Standards) system examines elementary schools in light of minimum standards set by the Ohio State Department of Education. Respondents indicate the degree to which a stated condition exists in the schools and to what degree they think that condition should exist. There is also a Teacher Questionnaire and a Parent Reaction Form to evaluate the standards.

12917
Project PRIMES (Progress Research in Meeting Elementary Standards) ESEA Title III Instrument to Evaluate Standards for Ohio Elementary Schools, Teacher Questionnaire. Martin, Cecil 1974
Descriptors: Curriculum Evaluation; Elementary Education; *Elementary Schools; Questionnaires; *School Organization; *State Standards; *Teacher Attitudes
Identifiers: Elementary Secondary Education Act Title III Ohio; Project PRIMES
Availability: ERIC Document Reproduction Service; 3900 Wheeler Ave., Alexandria, VA 22304 (ED110470, 21 pages)
Target Audience: Adults
Notes: Items, 10

The Project PRIMES (Progress Research in Meeting Elementary Standards) system examines elementary schools in light of minimum standards set by the Ohio State Department of Education. Respondents indicate the degree to which a stated condition exists in the schools and to what degree they think that condition should exist. There is also an Organization and Administration Questionnaire and a Parent Reaction Form to evaluate the standards.

12918
Project PRIMES (Progress Research in Meeting Elementary Standards) ESEA Title III Instrument to Evaluate Standards for Ohio Elementary Schools, Parent Reaction Form. Martin, Cecil 1974
Descriptors: Educational Philosophy; Educational Quality; Elementary Education; *Elementary Schools; *Parent Attitudes; Questionnaires; School Organization; *State Standards
Identifiers: Elementary Secondary Education Act Title III Ohio; Project PRIMES
Availability: ERIC Document Reproduction Service; 3900 Wheeler Ave., Alexandria, VA 22304 (ED110470, 21 pages)
Target Audience: Adults
Notes: Items, 5

The Project PRIMES (Progress Research in Meeting Elementary Standards) system examines elementary schools in light of minimum standards set by the Ohio State Department of Education. Respondents indicate the degree to which a stated condition exists in the schools and to what degree they think that condition should exist. There is also an Organization and Administration Questionnaire and a Teacher Questionnaire to evaluate the standards. This instrument asks for information about the appearance of the school, the philosophy, and the instructional quality which their child(ren) receives.

12929
Attitude Inventory on Sewing. Wenzel, Patricia; Kramer, Phyllis 1974
Descriptors: High School Students; *Home Economics Education; Junior High School Students; Secondary Education; *Secondary School Students; *Sewing Instruction
Identifiers: Indiana Home Economics Association
Availability: ERIC Document Reproduction Service; 3900 Wheeler Ave., Alexandria, VA 22304 (ED109334, 151 pages)
Grade Level: 7–12

The Attitude Inventory on Sewing identifies students' interest, experiences, and needed guidance in sewing by the teacher. The student completes the statements that are given. This is one instrument in Evaluation in Home Economics published by the IN Home Economics Association. Included in the publication are a variety of instruments appropriate for evaluating to some degree the progress toward attainment of objectives in the several areas of home economics for junior and senior high school students, adults, and out-of-school youth. Along with the evaluation form are suggestions for their use in the following areas of home economics: child development, clothing and textiles, consumer education, foods and nutrition, family relationships, housing and home decorating, health of the family and home care of the sick, interpersonal relations, and occupational home economics. Another source is University Book Store, 360 State Street, West Lafayette, IN 47906.

12942
Foods' Interest Questionnaire. Decker, Marilyn 1974
Descriptors: *Eating Habits; High School Students; *Home Economics Education; Junior High School Students; Knowledge Level; *Nutrition; Questionnaires; Secondary Education; *Secondary School Students; Student Attitudes
Identifiers: Indiana Home Economics Association
Availability: ERIC Document Reproduction Service; 3900 Wheeler Ave., Alexandria, VA 22304 (ED109334, 151 pages)
Grade Level: 7–12
Notes: Items, 22

This questionnaire is used to identify the interests and knowledge of food of students. There are 2 areas covered: "Introducing You" and "Your Food IQ." This is one instrument in Evaluation in Home Economics published by the IN Home Economics Association. Included in the publication are a variety of instruments appropriate for evaluating to some degree the progress toward attainment of objectives in the several areas of home economics for junior and senior high school students, adults, and out-of-school youth. Along with the evaluation form are suggestions for their use in the following areas of home economics: child development, clothing and textiles, consumer education, foods and nutrition, family relationships, housing and home decorating, health of the family and home care of the sick, interpersonal relations, and occupational home economics. Another source is University Book Store, 360 State Street, West Lafayette, IN 47906.

12955
Inventory of Teacher Concerns. Wick, John W.; Smith, Jeffrey K. 1981
Subtests: Classroom Inventory; Individual Inventory
Descriptors: Behavior Standards; Check Lists; Elementary School Students; Individual Needs; Primary Education; Student Behavior; Student Characteristics; *Student Evaluation; *Teacher Attitudes
Identifiers: Comprehensive Assessment Program
Availability: American Testronics; P.O. Box 2270, Iowa City, IA 52244
Grade Level: 1–3
Notes: Items, 35

The Classroom Inventory and the Individual Inventory are 2 components of the Inventory of Teacher Concerns. Each is structured with the acknowledgment that a wide range of variation exists with a group of children and within an individual child. The Individual Inventory is designed to help the teacher delineate specific areas of concern about a child and will show a range of concerns or characteristics from which the teacher can make specific decision.

12956
Multidimensional Measurement of Death Attitudes. Nelson, Lynn D. 1978
Subtests: Death Avoidance; Disengagement from Death; Death Fear
Descriptors: *Death; Higher Education; Student Attitudes; *Undergraduate Students
Identifiers: 3 DAF
Availability: The Psychological Record; v28 p525-33, 1978
Grade Level: 13–16
Notes: Items, 15

Designed to assess 3 factors of attitudes toward death, death avoidance, disengagement from death, and death fear.

12965
Employee Attitude Inventory. London House, Park Ridge, IL 1982
Subtests: Theft Admissions Scale; Theft Attitude Scale; Theft Knowledge and Suspicion Scale; Drug Scale; Job Burnout Scale; Job Dissatisfaction Scale; Validity Scale
Descriptors: Adults; *Antisocial Behavior; Burnout; Drug Use; *Employee Attitudes; *Employees; Job Satisfaction; Predictive Measurement; *Stealing
Identifiers: Drug Attitudes; EAI; *Honesty
Availability: London House Management Consultants; 1550 Northwest Hwy., Park Ridge, IL 60068
Target Audience: Adults
Notes: Time, 30 approx.; Items, 179

Designed to predict theft and other forms of counterproductivity of current employees. Assesses attitudes of employees concerning theft, drug use, job burnout, and job dissatisfaction. Validity scale assesses employees' tendencies to "fake good" on the instrument by answering items in a socially acceptable direction.

12969
Writing Attitude Survey. Coleman, Dona R. 1980
Descriptors: *Gifted; Primary Education; Student Evaluation; Surveys; *Writing (Composition)
Identifiers: Faces Scale

Availability: Dona R. Coleman; Friends University, 2100 University, Wichita, KS 67213
Grade Level: 1–3
Notes: Items, 12

Measures student attitudes toward writing, prewriting, teacher evaluation of writing, and students' evaluation of their own writing. A face scale is used with 5 points ranging from happy face to sad face. The test was designed to measure change after student participation in a writing project for gifted students. A discussion of the project evaluation can be found in *Gifted Child Quarterly*; v27 n3 p114-21, Sum 1983.

12971
Group Leader Self-Disclosure Scale. Dies, Robert R. 1977
Subtests: Personal History; Personal Characteristics; Here and Now Reactions
Descriptors: Adults; Groups; *Leaders; *Personality Traits; Personal Narratives; Rating Scales; Responses; Sensitivity Training; *Therapy
Identifiers: Facilitators; Openness; *Self Disclosure
Availability: University Associates, Inc.; 8517 Production Ave., P.O. Box 26240, San Diego, CA 92126
Target Audience: Adults
Notes: Items, 45

Designed to enable group members to indicate how helpful or harmful it would be for a group leader in a therapy or encounter group to disclose information about him- or herself-on scales of Personal History, Personal Characteristics, and Here-and-Now Reactions. Self-disclosure by the leader is evaluated by group members. This instrument is available in the *1977 Annual Handbook for Group Facilitators.*

12972
TORI Group Self-Diagnosis Scale. Gibb, Jack R. 1977
Descriptors: *Adults; Attitudes; Behavior Patterns; Groups; *Organizational Effectiveness; *Self Evaluation (Groups)
Identifiers: Facilitators; Interdependence; Openness; *Trust
Availability: University Associates, Inc.; 8517 Production Ave., P.O. Box 26240, San Diego, CA 92126
Target Audience: Adults
Notes: Items, 96

Designed to assess individual's trust level of a group. Measures the 4 aspects of trust: Trust, Openness, Realization, and Interdependence (TORI). When group trust level is high, behavior of group members is more personal, open, interdependent, and self-determining. This instrument is available in the *1977 Annual Handbook for Group Facilitators.*

12973
Organizational Norms Opinionnaire. Alexander, Mark 1978
Subtests: Organizational/Personal Pride; Performance/Excellence; Teamwork/Communication; Leadership/Supervision; Profitability/Cost Effectiveness; Colleague/Associate Relations; Customer/Client Relations; Innovativeness/Creativity; Training/Development; Candor/Openness
Descriptors: Adults; *Employee Attitudes; *Employees; Management Development; *Norms; *Organizations (Groups); Rating Scales; Self Evaluation (Groups); Sensitivity Training
Identifiers: Facilitators
Availability: University Associates, Inc.; 8517 Production Ave., P.O. Box 26240, San Diego, CA 92126
Target Audience: Adults
Notes: Items, 42

Designed to identify positive and negative organizational norms of behavior that influence the effectiveness and job satisfaction of employees. This instrument is available in the *1978 Annual Handbook for Group Facilitators.*

12974
Critical Consulting Incidents Inventory. Jones, John E.; Banet, Anthony G. 1978
Descriptors: Administrator Attitudes; Administrators; Adults; *Consultants; Human Relations; Management Development; Self Evaluation (Individuals); Situational Tests
Identifiers: CCII
Availability: University Associates, Inc.; 8517 Production Ave., P.O. Box 26240, San Diego, CA 92126
Target Audience: Adults
Notes: Items, 20

Designed to assist human relations consultants to assess their style of response to critical incidents. Major options available to consultants in response to critical situations

are support, direction, and problem solving. This instrument is available in the *1978 Annual Handbook for Group Facilitators.*

12975
Mach V Attitude Inventory. Christie, Richard 1978
Subtests: Nature of Interpersonal Tactics; Views of Human Nature; Abstract or Generalized Morality
Descriptors: Adults; Forced Choice Technique; Individual Development; *Interpersonal Competence; *Interpersonal Relationship; *Management Development; Personality Measures; *Personality Traits
Identifiers: *Machiavellianism
Availability: University Associates, Inc.; 8517 Production Ave., P.O. Box 26240, San Diego, CA 92126
Target Audience: Adults
Notes: Items, 20

Designed for use in personal growth groups to help raise individual's awareness of their own and others' interpersonal styles and beliefs. Leadership and management development programs would find data useful to the understanding of characteristics and behavior of supervisors and subordinates. Inventory was adapted from Christie, Richard; Geis, Florence L., *Studies in Machiavellianism*, New York; Academic Press, 1970. This instrument is available in the *1978 Annual Handbook for Group Facilitators.*

12982
Increasing Employee Self-Control. Harvey, Barron H. 1977
Descriptors: *Administrator Attitudes; *Administrators; Adults; *Employee Responsibility; Employees; Management by Objectives; *Power Structure
Identifiers: IESC
Availability: University Associates, Inc.; 8517 Production Ave., P.O. Box 26240, San Diego, CA 92126
Target Audience: Adults
Notes: Time, 20 approx.; Items, 16

Designed to assess manager's receptiveness toward increasing employees' self-control in organizations. This instrument is available in the *1980 Annual Handbook for Group Facilitators.*

12983
Organizational Diagnosis Questionnaire. Preziosi, Robert C. 1980
Subtests: Purposes; Structure; Relationships; Rewards; Leadership; Helpful Mechanisms
Descriptors: Adults; *Employee Attitudes; *Employees; *Organizational Climate; *Organizational Development; Organizations (Groups); Rating Scales; *Self Evaluation (Groups)
Identifiers: ODQ
Availability: University Associates, Inc.; 8517 Production Ave., P.O. Box 26240, San Diego, CA 92126
Target Audience: Adults
Notes: Items, 35

Designed to enable employees to assess the functioning of their organization. Measures attitudes on Weisbord's Six Box Organizational Model. This instrument is available in the *1980 Annual Handbook for Group Facilitators.*

12987
Organizational-Process Survey. Burns, Frank; Gragg, Robert L. 1981
Descriptors: Administrator Attitudes; *Administrators; Adults; *Management Development; Management Teams; *Organizational Effectiveness; Rating Scales
Availability: University Associates, Inc.; 8517 Production Ave., P.O. Box 26240, San Diego, CA 92126
Target Audience: Adults
Notes: Items, 10

Designed for use in organization survey, team building with executives, and management development. This instrument is available in the *1981 Annual Handbook for Group Facilitators.*

12988
Learning-Group Process Scale. Burns, Frank; Gragg, Robert L. 1981
Descriptors: Adults; Group Dynamics; *Self Evaluation (Groups)
Availability: University Associates, Inc.; 8517 Production Ave., P.O. Box 26240, San Diego, CA 92126
Target Audience: Adults
Notes: Items, 10

Designed for use in group self-assessment, clarification of expectations, and comparative study of groups. This instrument is available in the *1981 Annual Handbook for Group Facilitators.*

12994
Managerial Attitude Questionnaire. Roskin, Rick 1982
Descriptors: *Administrator Attitudes; Administrators; Adults; *Ambiguity; *Leadership Styles; Management Development; Situational Tests
Identifiers: Self Administered Tests; Self Scoring Tests
Availability: University Associates, Inc.; 8517 Production Ave., P.O. Box 26240, San Diego, CA 92126
Target Audience: Adults
Notes: Time, 40 approx.; Items, 10

Designed to assess a manger's ability to cope with ambiguous work situations. Respondent is asked to distribute 100 points over 6 responses for each of 10 situations. This instrument is available in the *1982 Annual Handbook for Group Facilitators.*

12995
Learning-Style Inventory (Trainee). Jacobs, Ronne Toker; Fuhrmann, Barbara Schneider 1984
Subtests: Dependence; Collaboration; Independence
Descriptors: Adults; Check Lists; Cognitive Style; Management Development; *Participant Satisfaction; *Trainees; Trainers
Availability: University Associates, Inc.; 8517 Production Ave., P.O. Box 26240, San Diego, CA 92126
Target Audience: Adults
Notes: Items, 36

Designed to elicit trainee's opinions about a positive training experience. Three scales are scored. These include dependence in a learning situation, collaboration, and independence. This instrument is available in the *1984 Annual Handbook for Group Facilitators.*

12999
Quality of Work Life-Conditions/Feelings. Sashkin, Marshall; Lengermann, Joseph J. 1984
Subtests: Autonomy; Personal Growth Opportunity; Work Speed and Routine; Work Complexity; Task Related Interaction; Feelings
Descriptors: Adults; *Employees; Job Analysis; *Job Satisfaction; *Work Attitudes; *Work Environment
Identifiers: QWL (C F)
Availability: University Associates, Inc.; 8517 Production Ave., P.O. Box 26240, San Diego, CA 92126
Target Audience: Adults
Notes: Time, 15 approx.; Items, 35

Two-part instrument designed to measure objective conditions of one's work setting and one's personal reactions to those conditions. The QWL-C consists of 25 items, and the QWL-F consists of 10 items. This instrument is available in the *1984 Annual Handbook for Group Facilitators.*

13000
Relationship Belief Inventory. Eidelson, Roy J.; Epstein, Norman 1981
Subtests: Disagreement Is Destructive; Mindreading Is Expected; Partners Cannot Change; Sexual Perfectionism; Sexes Are Different
Descriptors: Adults; *Beliefs; Counseling Techniques; *Interpersonal Relationship; Marital Instability; Marriage; Marriage Counseling; *Spouses
Identifiers: RBI; Self Report Measures
Availability: Norman B. Epstein, Ph.D.; Dept. of Family and Community Development, University of Maryland, College Park, MD 20742
Target Audience: Adults
Notes: Items, 40

Designed to assess some beliefs about intimate relationships that may contribute to marital problems. May be used to diagnose cognitive components of relationship dysfunction, assess cognitive changes in evaluating treatment outcome, initiate discussion of relationship beliefs in marital therapy sessions, and anticipate individual's resistance to treatment.

13012
National Assessment of Educational Progress, Released Exercises: Mathematics. Education Commission of the States, Denver, CO 1983
Subtests: Mathematics in School; Mathematics and Oneself; Mathematics and Society; Mathematics As a Discipline; Experiences in Mathematics; Mathematical Process; Content
Descriptors: Achievement Tests; Adolescents; Adults; Algebra; Children; Computers; Geometry; *Item Banks; *Mathematics; Mathematics Anxiety; Measurement; Metric System; Motivation; *National Surveys; Numbers; Probability; Self Concept; Statistics; Trigonometry
Identifiers: Customized Tests; NAEP; National Institute of Education
Availability: National Assessment of Educational Progress; Box 2923, Princeton, NJ 08541
Target Audience: 9; 13; 17; 26–35
Notes: Items, 227

Contains items used in the National Assessment of Educational Progress (NAEP), which conducts yearly surveys of the knowledge, skills and attitudes of individuals aged 9, 13, 17, and 26-35. All items are in the public domain and may be used to build customized tests. Areas covered are attitudes toward math; perceptions of self in relation to math, including math anxiety and motivation; attitudes toward the usefulness and importance of math; views of mathematics as a discipline and process; experience with metric system, calculators, computers. Content areas are numbers, numeration, algebra, trigonometry, geometry measurement, probability, and statistics, use of calculator, computer literacy. Not all exercises are used with all age groups.

13014
Attitudes toward Women Survey. Englehard, Patricia Aver 1968
Descriptors: Adults; Career Counseling; *Counselor Attitudes; *Counselors; Employed Women; *Females; Feminism; Sex Fairness; *Sex Role
Identifiers: Self Administered Tests
Availability: *Impact;*p31-34, Win 1972
Grade Level: 13–16
Target Audience: 18–65
Notes: Time, 30 approx.; Items, 68

Designed for use with high school and college counselors, as well as college students. Assesses sex role perception and attitudes toward female participation in traditionally masculine areas and sex fairness.

13029
Philosophy of Glasser Questionnaire. Masters, James R.; Laverty, Grace E. 1974
Descriptors: Adults; Elementary Education; *Elementary School Teachers; Humanistic Education; Opinions; Questionnaires; Rating Scales; *Teacher Attitudes
Identifiers: Glasser (William); New Castle School District PA; Schools without Failure; SWF
Availability: ERIC Document Reproduction Service; 3900 Wheeler Ave., Alexandria, VA 22304 (ED107681, 161 pages)
Target Audience: 18–64
Notes: Items, 15

This questionnaire has 15 items that measures attitudes toward the philosophy of William Glasser. After reading each statement, one is to circle the group of words that best shows how he/she feels about it. The responses range from completely agree to completely disagree. This instrument is part of the instrumentation to assess the effectiveness of the Schools without Failure (SWF) program in 10 elementary schools in the New Castle, PA, school district.

13030
Satisfaction with Teaching Questionnaire. Merwin, J.C.; Divesta, F.J. 1974
Descriptors: Adults; Elementary Education; *Elementary School Teachers; *Job Satisfaction; Rating Scales; *Teacher Attitudes
Identifiers: Glasser (William); New Castle School District PA; Schools without Failure; SWF
Availability: ERIC Document Reproduction Service; 3900 Wheeler Ave., Alexandria, VA 22304 (ED107681, 161 pages)
Target Audience: 18–64
Notes: Items, 11

The Satisfaction with Teaching Questionnaire was used to discriminate between students choosing to be teachers and those choosing other careers. The scale was developed for preservice teachers. For the New Castle Study, slight revisions were made in 3 items for use with teachers. This instrument is part of the instrumentation to assess the effectiveness of the Schools without Failure (SWF) program in 10 elementary schools in the New Castle, PA, school district.

13031
Opinionnaire on Attitudes toward Education. Lindgren, H.D.; Patton, G.M. 1974
Descriptors: Discipline; Elementary Education; *Elementary School Teachers; Humanistic Education; Opinions; Rating Scales; Student Behavior; *Teacher Attitudes
Identifiers: Glasser (William); New Castle School District PA; Schools without Failure; SWF
Availability: ERIC Document Reproduction Service; 3900 Wheeler Ave., Alexandria, VA 22304 (ED107681, 161 pages)
Target Audience: 18–64
Notes: Items, 50

This opinionnaire was used as a measure of teacher attitudes toward child-centered education, discipline, and the desirability of understanding pupils' behaviors. Statements were given, and the teacher was to indicate on a 1-5 scale his/her agreement. The scale ranged from strongly agree to strongly disagree. This instrument is part of the instrumentation to assess the effectiveness of the Schools without Failure (SWF) program in 10 elementary schools in the New Castle, PA, school district.

13032
Acceptance of Ideas of Others (Number Form). Masters, James R.; Laverty, Grace E. 1974
Descriptors: Elementary Education; *Elementary School Students; *Peer Relationship; Rating Scales; *Student Attitudes
Identifiers: Glasser (William); New Castle School District PA; Schools without Failure; SWF
Availability: ERIC Document Reproduction Service; 3900 Wheeler Ave., Alexandria, VA 22304-5110 (ED107681, 161 pages)
Grade Level: 4–6

This instrument was developed to determine pupils' attitudes toward classmates. Given a list of all class members, pupils are asked to circle a number from 1 to 5 to rate classmates on who usually has the best ideas. The better a person's ideas are, the higher the number circled. This instrument is part of the instrumentation to assess the effectiveness of the Schools without Failure (SWF) program in 10 elementary schools in the New Castle, PA, school district.

13033
Acceptance of Ideas of Others (Star Form). Masters, James R.; Laverty, Grace E. 1974
Descriptors: Elementary Education; *Elementary School Students; *Peer Relationship; Rating Scales; *Student Attitudes
Identifiers: Glasser (William); New Castle School District PA; Schools without Failure; SWF
Availability: ERIC Document Reproduction Service; 3900 Wheeler Ave., Alexandria, VA 22304-5110 (ED107681, 161 pages)
Grade Level: 1–6

This instrument was developed to determine pupils' attitudes toward classmates. Given a list of all class members, pupils are asked to color in number of stars. If the class member has good ideas, the pupil should decide to color in 3, 4, or 5 stars. The scale is from 1 star to 5. This instrument is part of the instrumentation to assess the effectiveness of the Schools without Failure (SWF) program in 10 elementary schools in the New Castle, PA, school district.

13034
School Attitude Scale (Grades 4-6). Masters, James R.; Laverty, Grace E. 1974
Descriptors: *Elementary School Students; *Intermediate Grades; Rating Scales; *School Attitudes; *Student Attitudes
Identifiers: Glasser (William); New Castle School District PA; Schools without Failure; SWF
Availability: ERIC Document Reproduction Service; 3900 Wheeler Ave., Alexandria, VA 22304-5110 (ED107681, 161 pages)
Grade Level: 4–6
Notes: Items, 30

This 30-item School Attitude Scale was developed to measure children's attitudes toward school in grades 4-6. A verbal response form was used. The 5 choices were from "Don't like it at all" to "Like it a lot." This instrument is part of the instrumentation to assess the effectiveness of the Schools without Failure (SWF) program in 10 elementary schools in the New Castle, PA, school district.

13035
Acceptance of Others (Numbers Form). Masters, James R.; Laverty, Grace E. 1974
Descriptors: *Elementary School Students; Intermediate Grades; *Peer Relationship; Rating Scales; *Student Attitudes
Identifiers: Glasser (William); New Castle School District PA; Schools without Failure; SWF
Availability: ERIC Document Reproduction Service; 3900 Wheeler Ave., Alexandria, VA 22304-5110 (ED107681, 161 pages)
Grade Level: 4–6

The Acceptance of Others (Number Form) was prepared to determine pupils' attitudes toward classmates. Pupils are asked to circle a number from 1 to 5 to rate classmates on how much fun it would be to do something with each person. This instrument is part of the instrumentation to assess the effectiveness of the Schools without Failure (SWF) program in 10 elementary schools in the New Castle, PA, school district.

13036
Pennsylvania Educational Quality Assessment Attitude toward School Instrument. Pennsylvania State Dept. of Education, Harrisburg 1974
Descriptors: *Elementary School Students; *Intermediate Grades; Rating Scales; *School Attitudes; *Student Attitudes
Identifiers: Glasser (William); New Castle School District PA; Schools without Failure; SWF
Availability: ERIC Document Reproduction Service; 3900 Wheeler Ave., Alexandria, VA 22304-5110 (ED107681, 161 pages)

Grade Level: 4–6
Notes: Items, 17
This assessment scale has 5 different ratings and is used to find what students in grades 4-6 think is important in their schoolwork and to assess what students like in their classrooms. This instrument is part of the instrumentation to assess the effectiveness of the Schools without Failure (SWF) program in 10 elementary schools in the New Castle, PA, school district.

13037
School Attitude Scale (Grades 1-3). Masters, James R.; Laverty, Grace E. 1974
Descriptors: *Elementary School Students; *Primary Education; Rating Scales; *School Attitudes; *Student Attitudes
Identifiers: Glaser (William); New Castle School District PA; Schools without Failure; SWF
Availability: ERIC Document Reproduction Service; 3900 Wheeler Ave., Alexandria, VA 22304-5110 (ED107681, 161 pages)
Grade Level: 1–3
Notes: Items, 30
This 30-item school attitude scale was developed to measure children's attitudes toward school in grades 1-3. It is part of the instrumentation to assess the effectiveness of the Schools without Failure (SWF) program in 10 elementary schools in the New Castle, PA, school district. A faces response form was used with the faces ranging from very sad to very happy.

13038
School Attitude Scale for Beginning 1st Graders. Masters, James R.; Laverty, Grace E. 1974
Descriptors: *Elementary School Students; *Grade 1; Primary Education; Rating Scales; *School Attitudes; *Student Attitudes
Identifiers: Glasser (William); New Castle School District PA; Schools without Failure; SWF
Availability: ERIC Document Reproduction Service; 3900 Wheeler Ave., Alexandria, VA 22304-5110 (ED107681, 161 pages)
Grade Level: 1
Notes: Items, 18
This instrument is part of the instrumentation to assess the effectiveness of the Schools without Failure (SWF) program in 10 elementary schools in the New Castle, PA, school district. This 18-item school attitude scale was developed to measure beginning first graders attitudes toward school. The rating scale is a 5-point one using faces ranging from very sad to very happy.

13039
Questionnaire on Teacher Practices (Abridged). Furst, Edward J. 1974
Descriptors: Adults; Classrooms; College Students; Elementary Secondary Education; *Higher Education; Human Relations; Questionnaires; Rating Scales; *Situational Tests; Student Attitudes; Student Behavior; Student Evaluation; *Teacher Attitudes; *Teacher Behavior; Teacher Role; Teacher Student Relationship; Teaching Methods; Values
Availability: ERIC Document Reproduction Service; 3900 Wheeler Ave., Alexandria, VA 22304-5110 (ED106318, 50 pages)
Grade Level: 13–16
Target Audience: 18–64
Notes: Items, 10
The abridged questionnaire is used to gather the data for "Measuring Human Relations Attitudes and Values with Situational Inventories." Its contents are 10 problematic situations that might be faced in an elementary or high school classroom. Following each situation there is a list of possible alternatives that a teacher might take. The abridged questionnaire includes only the alternatives from the original that became part of the final analysis of data. The questionnaire should be viewed as a tentative form built originally for research on attitudes and values. Although it can be used informally for self-evaluation and instruction with prospective teachers, this form should not be used for decisions about the selection or retention of students or teachers. The questionnaire should only be used for research or for the informal purposes stated above.

13044
IEA Six-Subject Survey Instruments: Student Questionnaire, Populations II, IV. International Association for the Evaluation of Educational Achievement, Stockholm (Sweden) 1975
Descriptors: *Academic Achievement; *Background; College Bound Students; *Comparative Education; *Cross Cultural Studies; Foreign Countries; Questionnaires; Secondary Education; *Secondary School Students; Student Attitudes
Identifiers: International Evaluation Education Achievement; Sweden
Availability: ERIC Document Reproduction Service; 3900 Wheeler Ave., Alexandria, VA 22304 (ED102190, 60 pages)

Target Audience: 14–15; 17–18
Notes: Items, 48
In 1965, the International Association for the Evaluation of Educational Achievement (IEA) inaugurated a cross-national survey of achievement in 6 subjects: science, reading comprehension, literature, English as a foreign language, French as a foreign language, and civic education. The overall aim of the project was to use international tests in order to relate student achievement and attitudes to instructional, social, and economic factors and, from the results, to establish generalizations of value to policymakers worldwide. This questionnaire is for Population II students, consisting of students aged 14 and 15 years, and Population IV students, consisting of students enrolled in the final year of preuniversity training.

13045
IEA Six-Subject Survey Instruments: General Attitudes and Descriptive Scales. International Association for the Evaluation of Educational Achievement, Stockholm (Sweden) 1975
Descriptors: *Academic Achievement; *Background; College Bound Students; *Comparative Education; *Cross Cultural Studies; Elementary School Students; Foreign Countries; Questionnaires; Secondary School Students; Student Attitudes
Identifiers: International Evaluation Education Achievement; Sweden
Availability: ERIC Document Reproduction Service; 3900 Wheeler Ave., Alexandria, VA 22304 (ED102190, 60 pages)
Target Audience: 10–11; 14–15; 17–18
In 1965, the International Association for the Evaluation of Educational Achievement (IEA) inaugurated a cross-national survey of achievement in 6 subjects: science, reading comprehension, literature, English as a foreign language, French as a foreign language, and civic education. The overall aim of the project was to use international tests in order to relate student achievement and attitudes to instructional, social, and economic factors and, from the results, to establish generalizations of value to policymakers worldwide. This attitude and descriptive scale is for Population I, II, and IV surveying what students think about themselves and the schools they attend. Population I consists of students aged 10 to 11 years; Population II, 14 to 15 years; and Population IV, students in the final year of preuniversity training.

13048
IEA Six-Subject Survey Instruments: Civic Education, Affective Scales. International Association for the Evaluation of Educational Achievement, Stockholm (Sweden) 1975
Descriptors: *Academic Achievement; *Affective Measures; Background; *Civics; College Bound Students; *Comparative Education; *Cross Cultural Studies; Elementary School Students; Elementary Secondary Education; Foreign Countries; Governmental Structure; High School Students; Political Science; Questionnaires; Rating Scales; Secondary School Students; Student Attitudes; Surveys
Identifiers: International Evaluation Education Achievement; Sweden
Availability: ERIC Document Reproduction Service; 3900 Wheeler Ave., Alexandria, VA 22304 (ED102188, 66 pages)
Target Audience: 10–11; 14–15; 17–18
Notes: Items, 64
In 1965, the International Association for the Evaluation of Educational Achievement (IEA) inaugurated a cross-national survey of achievement in 6 subjects: science, reading comprehension, literature, English as a foreign language, French as a foreign language, and civic education. The overall aim of the project was to use international tests in order to relate student achievement and attitudes to instructional, social, and economic factors and, from the results, to establish generalizations of value to policymakers worldwide. The areas covered in this Affective Scales instrument are "How would you describe your local council?" "How would you describe your national government?" Other areas cover how laws are made, how the nation should be governed, general agreement with the government, and what a good citizen is. The student is given a statement and then must check on a 1-5 rating scale the extent to which he/she agrees. This questionnaire is 1 of 3 instruments for the civic education students at populations I, II, IV. Population I consists of students aged 10 to 11 years; population II, 14 to 15 years, and population IV, students enrolled in the final year of preuniversity training.

13049
IEA Six-Subject Survey Instruments: Civic Education Background Questionnaire. International Association for the Evaluation of Educational Achievement, Stockholm (Sweden) 1975

Descriptors: Background; *Civics; College Bound Students; *Comparative Education; *Cross Cultural Studies; Elementary School Students; Elementary Secondary Education; Foreign Countries; High School Students; Opinions; Questionnaires; Rating Scales; Secondary School Students; *Student Attitudes
Identifiers: International Evaluation Education Achievement; Sweden
Availability: ERIC Document Reproduction Service; 3900 Wheeler Ave., Alexandria, VA 22304 (ED102188, 66 pages)
Target Audience: 10–11; 14–15; 17–18
Notes: Items, 79
In 1965, the International Association for the Evaluation of Educational Achievement (IEA) inaugurated a cross-national survey of achievement in 6 subjects: science, reading comprehension, literature, English as a foreign language, French as a foreign language, and civic education. The overall aim of the project was to use international tests in order to relate student achievement and attitudes to instructional, social, and economic factors and, from the results, to establish generalizations of value to policymakers worldwide. This background questionnaire is 1 of 3 instruments for the civic education students at populations I, II, IV. Population I consists of students aged 10 to 11 years; population II, 14 to 15 years, and population IV, students enrolled in the final year of preuniversity training. The questionnaire has statements covering film and TV watching, political ideas and opinions, attitudes about parents/friends/school, and classes related to civics/history/current events.

13075
PEECH Parent Questionnaire. Peech Project, Champaign, IL
Descriptors: Adults; *Disabilities; Elementary Education; *Handicap Identification; *Parent Attitudes; Parent Participation; *Parents; Parent School Relationship; *Preschool Children; *Program Evaluation
Identifiers: PEECH Outreach Project
Availability: PEECH Project; Colonel Wolfe School, 403 E. Healey St., Champaign, IL 61820
Target Audience: Adults
Notes: Items, 15
Designed for completion by parents of children in the PEECH project. Assesses parents' satisfaction with program for their child; their perceptions of the child's progress and the usefulness of parent involvement activities; and the level of parent involvement. Program PEECH (Program for Early Identification of Children with Handicaps) is a home-based program for handicapped preschool children.

13076
Measure of Achievement Motivation. Castenell, Louis A. 1980
Subtests: Peer; Home; School
Descriptors: *Achievement Need; *Adolescents; High Schools; *High School Students; Student Attitudes; *Student Motivation
Availability: Louis Castenell; Xavier University, 7325 Palmetto St., New Orleans, LA 70125
Grade Level: 9–12
Target Audience: 13–17
Notes: Items, 9
Designed to assess general achievement motivation of adolescents.

13080
The Morale Index for Supervisors/Managers. Bedell, Ralph; Lippitt, Gordon L. 1981
Descriptors: *Administrator Attitudes; *Administrators; Adults; Job Satisfaction; *Morale; *Self Evaluation (Individuals); *Supervisors; *Supervisory Training; Work Attitudes
Identifiers: Self Report Measures
Availability: Development Publications; 5605 Lamar Rd., Bethesda, MD 20816-1398
Target Audience: Adults
Notes: Items, 25
Designed to enable supervisors and managers to record feelings toward important aspects of their organizational life or supervisory work. Useful for self-evaluation in training programs.

13081
Productivity Index for Supervisors/Managers. Ericson, Richard F.; Lippitt, Gordon L. 1981
Descriptors: *Administrator Attitudes; Administrators; Adults; Efficiency; *Organizational Effectiveness; *Productivity; Self Evaluation (Individuals); Supervisors; *Supervisory Training
Identifiers: Self Report Measures
Availability: Development Publications; 5605 Lamar Rd., Bethesda, MD 20816-1398
Target Audience: Adults
Notes: Items, 25

Designed to enable supervisory personnel to record their feelings or attitudes toward elements affecting the efficiency of their own and their organization's operations. A stimulus for self-examination and group discussion.

13101
IEA Six-Subject Survey Instruments: General Attitude and Descriptive Scale, Populations I. International Association for the Evaluation of Educational Achievement, Stockholm (Sweden) 1975
Descriptors: *Academic Achievement;
  *Background; *Comparative Education; *Cross Cultural Studies; *Elementary School Students; Foreign Countries; Questionnaires; *Student Attitudes
Identifiers: International Evaluation Educational Achievement; Sweden
Availability: ERIC Document Reproduction Service; 3900 Wheeler Ave., Alexandria, VA 22304 (ED102178, 56 pages)
Target Audience: 10–11
Notes: Items, 36

In 1965 the International Association for the Evaluation of Educational Achievement (IEA) inaugurated a cross-national survey of achievement in 6 subjects: science, reading comprehension, literature, English as a foreign language, French as a foreign language and civic education. The overall aim of the project was to use international tests in order to relate student achievement and attitudes to instructional, social, and economic factors and, from the results, to establish generalizations of value to policymakers worldwide. This questionnaire is for Population I students, aged 10 to 11. It surveys what students think about themselves and their schools. Information concerning this questionnaire can be found in ED084503.

13102
IEA Six-Subject Survey Instruments: General Attitude and Descriptive Scale, Populations II, IV. International Association for the Evaluation of Educational Achievement, Stockholm (Sweden) 1975
Descriptors: *Academic Achievement;
  *Background; College Bound Students; *Comparative Education; *Cross Cultural Studies; Foreign Countries; Questionnaires; Secondary Education; *Secondary School Students; *Student Attitudes
Identifiers: International Evaluation Educational Achievement; Sweden
Availability: ERIC Document Reproduction Service; 3900 Wheeler Ave., Alexandria, VA 22304 (ED102178, 56 pages)
Target Audience: 14–15; 17–18
Notes: Items, 36

In 1965, the International Association for the Evaluation of Educational Achievement (IEA) inaugurated a cross-national survey of achievement in 6 subjects: science, reading comprehension, literature, English as a foreign language, French as a foreign language and civic education. The overall aim of the project was to use international tests in order to relate student achievement and attitudes to instructional, social, and economic factors and, from the results, to establish generalizations of value to policymakers worldwide. This questionnaire is for Populations II and IV surveying what students think about themselves and the schools they attend. Population II consists of students aged 14-15 years, and Population IV, students enrolled in the final year of preuniversity training. Information concerning this questionnaire can be found in ED084503.

13106
IEA Six-Subject Survey Instruments: Literature Student Questionnaires, Populations II, IV. International Association for the Evaluation of Educational Achievement, Stockholm (Sweden) 1975
Subtests: Literature; Section R
Descriptors: *Academic Achievement; College Bound Students; *Comparative Education; *Cross Cultural Studies; Foreign Countries; Grade 12; *Literature; Questionnaires; Secondary Education; *Secondary School Students; *Student Attitudes
Identifiers: International Evaluation Educational Achievement; Sweden
Availability: ERIC Document Reproduction Service; 3900 Wheeler Ave., Alexandria, VA 22304 (ED102176, 23 pages)
Target Audience: 14–15; 17–18
Notes: Items, 55

In 1965, the International Association for the Evaluation of Educational Achievement (IEA) inaugurated a cross-national survey of achievement in 6 subjects: science, reading comprehension, literature, English as a foreign language, French as a foreign language and civic education. The overall aim of the project was to use international tests in order to relate student achievement and attitudes to instructional, social, and economic factors and, from the results, to establish generalizations of value to policymakers worldwide. These instruments are a student literature questionnaire and a literature attitude scale for student populations II and IV. These 2 measures sur-

vey information about the study and his/her study of literature including background, study time and habits, and what part books, films, etc., play in the lives of these students. Population II consists of students aged 14 to 15 years; Population IV, those students enrolled in the final year of preuniversity training. The answer keys can be found in ED085709.

13117
IEA Six-Subject Survey Instruments: Teacher Questionnaire, Science. International Association for the Evaluation of Educational Achievement, Stockholm (Sweden) 1975
Descriptors: *Academic Achievement; Adults; Background; *Comparative Education; *Cross Cultural Studies; Foreign Countries; Questionnaires; *Science Teachers; *Teacher Attitudes
Identifiers: International Evaluation Educational Achievement; Sweden
Availability: ERIC Document Reproduction Service; 3900 Wheeler Ave., Alexandria, VA 22304 (ED102171, 17 pages)
Target Audience: 18–64
Notes: Items, 24

In 1965, the International Association for the Evaluation of Educational Achievement (IEA) inaugurated a cross-national survey of achievement in 6 subjects: science, reading comprehension, literature, English as a foreign language, French as a foreign language and civic education. The overall aim of the project was to use international tests in order to relate student achievement and attitudes to instructional, social, and economic factors and, from the results, to establish generalizations of value to policymakers worldwide. This questionnaire is for science teachers, measuring teacher background, attitudes, and how they regard the job of science teaching. Answer keys can be found in ED081639.

13120
IEA Six-Subject Survey Instruments: The Place of Science in the School and in the World Outside, Population I. International Association for the Evaluation of Educational Achievement, Stockholm (Sweden) 1975
Descriptors: *Academic Achievement; Background; *Comparative Education; *Cross Cultural Studies; Elementary Education; *Elementary School Students; Foreign Countries; Questionnaires; *Student Attitudes; Student Interests
Identifiers: International Evaluation Educational Achievement; Sweden
Availability: ERIC Document Reproduction Service; 3900 Wheeler Ave., Alexandria, VA 22304 (ED102170, 36 pages)
Target Audience: 10–11
Notes: Items, 22

In 1965, the International Association for the Evaluation of Educational Achievement (IEA) inaugurated a cross-national survey of achievement in 6 subjects: science, reading comprehension, literature, English as a foreign language, French as a foreign language and civic education. The overall aim of the project was to use international tests in order to relate student achievement and attitudes to instructional, social, and economic factors and, from the result, to establish generalizations of value to policymakers worldwide. This questionnaire is a science attitude and descriptive scale that measures the part science plays in the students' lives. Population I consists of students aged 10 to 11 years old. Answer keys can be found in ED018639.

13121
IEA Six-Subject Survey Instruments: The Place of Science in the School and in the World Outside. International Association for the Evaluation of Educational Achievement, Stockholm (Sweden) 1975
Descriptors: *Academic Achievement; Background; College Bound Students; *Comparative Education; *Cross Cultural Studies; Foreign Countries; Questionnaires; Secondary Education; *Secondary School Students; *Student Attitudes; Student Interests
Identifiers: International Evaluation Educational Achievement; Sweden
Availability: ERIC Document Reproduction Service; 3900 Wheeler Ave., Alexandria, VA 22304 (ED102170, 36 pages)
Target Audience: 14–15; 17–18
Notes: Items, 48

In 1965, the International Association for the Evaluation of Educational Achievement (IEA) inaugurated a cross-national survey of achievement in 6 subjects: science, reading comprehension, literature, English as a foreign language, French as a foreign language and civic education. The overall aim of the project was to use international tests in order to relate student achievement and attitudes to instructional, social, and economic factors and, from the results, to establish generalizations of value to policymakers worldwide. This questionnaire is used to find out what students think about science. It is for Population II, students aged 14 to 15 years, and Population IV, students enrolled in the final year of preuniversity train-

ing. Answer keys can be found in ED081639. The second part of this questionnaire asks about science in the school and is a descriptive scale that measures the part science plays in the students' lives.

13125
IEP Attitude Questionnaire. Morgan, Daniel P.; Rhode, Ginger 1983
Descriptors: Adults; *Individualized Education Programs; *Special Education Teachers
Identifiers: IEP
Availability: Exceptional Children;v50 n1 p64-67, Sep 1983
Target Audience: Adults
Notes: Items, 27

Measures attitudes of special education teachers toward individual education programs and the IEP requirement. Items are in a 7-point Likert-type format. Items concern help received from school sources in planning IEPs, results of IEPs, time constraints, parent involvement.

13134
Parent's Questionnaire. Educational Testing Service, Princeton, NJ 1973
Descriptors: Adults; Grade 12; High Schools; Income; *Longitudinal Studies; *National Surveys; Occupations; Parent Attitudes; Parent Background; *Parents; Questionnaires
Identifiers: National Longitudinal Study High School Class 1972
Availability: ERIC Document Reproduction Service; 3900 Wheeler Ave., Alexandria, VA 22304-5110 (ED097370, 7 pages)
Target Audience: 18–64
Notes: Items, 12

This questionnaire, designed to elicit information for the National Longitudinal Study of the High School Class of 1972, is completed by the parents or guardians of students participating in the study. Questions concern parent attitudes toward higher education, financial support, ethnic and demographic information, income level, occupation, and educational background.

13135
Student Questionnaire. Educational Testing Service, Princeton, NJ 1972
Descriptors: Career Planning; College Planning; *Grade 12; High Schools; *High School Seniors; *Longitudinal Studies; *National Surveys; Questionnaires; Student Attitudes; Student Experience
Identifiers: National Longitudinal Study High School Class 1972
Availability: ERIC Document Reproduction Service; 3900 Wheeler Ave., Alexandria, VA 22304-5110 (ED097369, 40 pages)
Grade Level: 12
Notes: Items, 104

Designed to elicit information for the National Longitudinal Study of the High School Class of 1972, this objective questionnaire is divided into sections of questions, some to be answered by all twelfth grade students and some to be answered only by those whose future plans correspond to the question category. All students answer questions in the sections high school experiences, attitudes and opinions, and plans for the future. In the remaining sections, students answer only the section or sections that correspond with their plans for the year after they leave high school: the apprenticeship or on-the-job training program, to enter military service, to be full-time housekeepers, to take vocational or technical courses at a trade or business school, to go to a 4-year college or university, and for those who plan to work part-time.

13147
Sexual Compatibility Test. Foster, Arthur L. 1974
Descriptors: Adults; Marital Satisfaction; Questionnaires; *Sexuality
Identifiers: SCT; Sex Therapy
Availability: Arthur L. Foster, Dir.; The Phoenix Institute of California, 248 Blossom Hill Rd., Los Gatos, CA 95030
Target Audience: 18–64
Notes: Items, 101

The Sexual Compatibility Test (SCT) appears to be a useful tool in the initial evaluation of couples who present themselves for sexual counseling or sexual therapy. Its structure is such that it can collect a large amount of information in a short amount of time. All the items of the SCT were composed to describe behaviors that are important in achieving a satisfying sexual relationship between heterosexual individuals. The following content areas were assessed: caressing, nudity, variety, intercourse activities, embracing, loving verbalizations, manual-genital caressing, manual-genital caressing to orgasm, oral-genital caressing, oral genital caressing to orgasm, breasts, kissing, physical discomfort or pain, impotence, ejaculatory incompetence, premature ejaculation, orgasmic insufficiency, sexual satisfaction, deception, and problem-solving verbalizations.

13178
Situational Attitude Scale—Handicapped. Sedlacek, William E.; Stovall, Carol 1970
Descriptors: *Blindness; *College Students; Higher Education; *Physical Disabilities; Rating Scales; Social Bias
Identifiers: SASH
Availability: William Sedlacek; Counseling Center, University of Maryland, College Park, MD 20742
Grade Level: 13-16
Notes: Items, 10

This questionnaire was designed to measure how people think and feel about a number of social and personal incidents and situations. Each item or situation is followed by 10 descriptive word scales, and the subject is to select the rating which best describes his/her feelings toward the item. There are 3 forms. All 3 forms are identical in situations, except that form A does not specify a disability, form B specifies blindness, and Form C specifies a wheelchair.

13186
Classroom Preference Scale, Non-Picture Interview. Cohen, Sandra R. 1968
Descriptors: Child Development; *Childhood Attitudes; Interviews; *Primary Education; Projective Measures; *School Attitudes
Availability: Archives, Educational Testing Service; Princeton, NJ 08541 (PR 68-10, microfiche only)
Grade Level: 1-2
Notes: Items, 8

This instrument was developed to measure children's attitudes toward school and learning in the primary grades and should be considered an experimental instrument. The category system is the current working version. The student was asked a "do you" and "what do" questions. The responses were then classified. If the first response was inappropriate or ambiguous, the first codable response was scored. The categories for responses differ for the different items. This is an experimental instrument.

13189
Barclay Classroom Assessment System. Barclay, James R. 1983
Subtests: Self-Competency; Group Nomination; Vocational; Teacher Rating; Reinforcer; Attitude; Factor
Descriptors: *Affective Measures; Check Lists; Elementary Education; *Elementary School Students; *High Risk Students; *Peer Evaluation; Questionnaires; *Screening Tests; *Self Concept; *Self Evaluation (Individuals); Sociometric Techniques; Student Characteristics; *Student Evaluation; *Vocational Interests
Identifiers: BCAS
Availability: Western Psychological Services; 12031 Wilshire Blvd., Los Angeles, CA 90025
Grade Level: 3-6
Notes: Time, 40 approx.; Items, 192

Developed to assist educators in early identification of potential problems that may interfere with learning progress of children. Provides information from 3 viewpoints: child, child's classmates, and teachers. Measures are obtained from self, peer, and teacher ratings on a broad range of skills, feelings, and attitudes that child displays in classroom setting. Provides means of assessing individual social and affective interactions of children in the classroom. Highest purpose is early identification of at-risk children for learning-related problem. BCAS is scored by computer only, using the Western Psychological Services Test Report Service. In addition to the items completed by the students, there is a 63-item checklist of be completed by the teacher for each student. Sections that the student completes cover vocational interests, assessment of skills and ability to complete various activities, attitudes toward school, preferred activities, description of peers' characteristics. Formerly known as the Barclay Classroom Climate Inventory.

13206
Needs of University Commuter Students Questionnaire. Bare, Alan C. 1983
Descriptors: *Ancillary School Services; Black Students; *College Environment; *College Students; Commuter Colleges; *Commuting Students; Females; Higher Education; Institutional Characteristics; Males; Nontraditional Students; Student Attitudes; Student Characteristics; Student College Relationship; *Student Needs; Student Transportation
Availability: ERIC Document Reproduction Service; 3900 Wheeler Ave., Alexandria, VA 22304 (ED234683, 36 pages)
Grade Level: 13-16
Notes: Items, 124

This instrument was developed to profile students' perceptions of 30 aspects of the college environment. By comparing the student characteristics to environmental characteristics, it is hoped to improve the fit between college and student. Some of the aspects surveyed are academic advising, courses and class size, business office/registrar, facilities, student services, staff, and activities.

13214
Alumni Survey '80, NIU. Northeastern Illinois University, Chicago 1983
Descriptors: Adults; *Alumni; *Biographical Inventories; College Graduates; *Graduate Surveys; Higher Education; Questionnaires
Identifiers: NIU
Availability: ERIC Document Reproduction Service; 3900 Wheeler Ave., Alexandria, VA 22304 (ED234659, microfiche only)
Target Audience: 18-64
Notes: Items, 22

This questionnaire was used in the first universitywide effort to find out how the alumni experience at Northeastern affected their lives. The responses were to be used to better serve future students as well as alumni. The responses would also allow Northeastern to strengthen its case as it approached legislatures, federal agencies, and private foundations for support of university programs. An alternate source for this document is Council for Advancement and Support of Education, 1 Dupont Circle, Suite 400, Washington, DC 20036.

13216
Institutional Programming Inventory—Alumni. Alfred University, New York 1983
Descriptors: Adults; *Alumni; *Biographical Inventories; College Graduates; *Graduate Surveys; Higher Education; Opinions; Questionnaires
Availability: ERIC Document Reproduction Service; 3900 Wheeler Ave., Alexandria, VA 22304-5110 (ED234659, microfiche only)
Target Audience: 18-64
Notes: Items, 26

This instrument was sent to a random sample of 10 percent of the Alfred alumni. The information was to ascertain Alfred's relationship with the alumni and to set its course for the future. The data would have an impact on student recruitment, fund raising, alumni programing, and institutional communications. An alternate source for this document is Council for Advancement and Support of Education, 1 Dupont Circle, Suite 400, Washington, DC 20036.

13217
Bradley University Alumni Records Survey, 1983. Bradley University, Peoria, IL 1983
Descriptors: Adults; *Alumni; *Biographical Inventories; College Graduates; *Graduate Surveys; Higher Education; Questionnaires
Availability: ERIC Document Reproduction Service; 3900 Wheeler Ave., Alexandria, VA 22304-5110 (ED234659, microfiche only)
Target Audience: 18-64
Notes: Items, 25

This survey instrument was used to update alumni records and help the university form long-range development plans influenced by the views on the directions Bradley should consider in the future. An alternate source for this document is Council for Advancement and Support of Education, 1 Dupont Circle, Suite 400, Washington, DC 20036.

13218
CSPP 1981 Alumni Survey. California School of Professional Psychology, Los Angeles 1983
Descriptors: Adults; *Alumni; *Biographical Inventories; College Graduates; *Graduate Surveys; Higher Education; Questionnaires
Identifiers: California School of Professional Psychology; CSPP
Availability: ERIC Document Reproduction Service; 3900 Wheeler Ave., Alexandria, VA 22304 (ED234659, microfiche only)
Target Audience: 18-64
Notes: Items, 33

This survey asked for background information about the alumni, present and future plans, and their attitudes about CSSP. An alternate source for this document is Council for Advancement and Support of Education, 1 Dupont Circle, Suite 400, Washington, DC 20036.

13219
1980 Canisius College Alumni/Alumnae Survey. Canisius College, Buffalo, NY 1983
Descriptors: Adults; *Alumni; *Biographical Inventories; College Graduates; *Graduate Surveys; Higher Education; Questionnaires
Availability: ERIC Document Reproduction Service; 3900 Wheeler Ave., Alexandria, VA 22304-5110 (ED234659, microfiche only)
Target Audience: 18-64
Notes: Time, 20 approx.; Items, 32

The information on this questionnaire was used for 2 purposes: to update alumni records and compile an accurate statistical picture of the alumni and to help the college in evaluating its current programs to provide better services to students and alumni. An alternate source for this document is Council for Advancement and Support of Education, 1 Dupont Circle, Suite 400, Washington, DC 20036.

13220
Iowa State University Alumni Questionnaire. Iowa State University of Science and Technology, Ames 1983
Descriptors: Adults; *Alumni; *Biographical Inventories; College Graduates; *Graduate Surveys; Higher Education; Questionnaires
Availability: ERIC Document Reproduction Service; 3900 Wheeler Ave., Alexandria, VA 22304 (ED234659, microfiche only)
Target Audience: 18-64
Notes: Items, 43

The Iowa State Alumni office used this instrument to survey the alumni. The information was to be used in evaluating services and establishing goals. An alternate source for this document is Council for Advancement and Support of Education, 1 Dupont Circle, Suite 400, Washington, DC 20036.

13221
The New School for Social Research Alumni Survey. New School for Social Research, New York, NY 1983
Descriptors: Adults; *Alumni; *Biographical Inventories; College Graduates; *Graduate Surveys; Higher Education; Questionnaires
Availability: ERIC Document Reproduction Service; 3900 Wheeler Ave., Alexandria, VA 22304-5110 (ED234659, microfiche only)
Target Audience: 18-64
Notes: Items, 31

When the New School established an Office of Alumni Affairs, it sent this questionnaire to the alumni. The information would be used for alumni records, to bring alumni concerns and suggestions to the attention of the administration and Board of Trustees, and to create programs and services responsive to alumni interests and needs. An alternate source for this document is Council for Advancement and Support of Education, 1 Dupont Circle, Suite 400, Washington, DC 20036.

13222
1980 Alumni Survey, Portland State University. Portland State University, Oregon 1983
Descriptors: Adults; *Alumni; *Biographical Inventories; College Graduates; *Graduate Surveys; Higher Education; Questionnaires
Availability: ERIC Document Reproduction Service; 3900 Wheeler Ave., Alexandria, VA 22304-5110 (ED234659, microfiche only)
Target Audience: 18-64
Notes: Items, 24

This survey and questionnaire was developed by Portland State graduates working with an alumni steering committee to explore avenues for strengthening the relationship between the alumni community and the university while creating opportunities for alumni to interact with one another through educational, recreational, and social activities. An alternate source for this document is Council for Advancement and Support of Education, 1 Dupont Circle, Suite 400, Washington, DC 20036.

13223
Alumni Survey, University of Central Florida. University of Central Florida, Alumni Relations Office, Orlando 1983
Descriptors: Adults; *Alumni; *Biographical Inventories; College Graduates; *Graduate Surveys; Higher Education; Questionnaires
Availability: ERIC Document Reproduction Service; 3900 Wheeler Ave., Alexandria, VA 22304 (ED234659, microfiche only)
Target Audience: 18-64
Notes: Items, 58

This questionnaire was sent to a random sample of the alumni to survey alumni opinions and suggestions concerning the University of Central Florida and the Alumni Association. The responses would be helpful to improve the quality of the educational programs for future students along with improving alumni services. An alternate source for this document is Council for Advancement and Support of Education, 1 Dupont Circle, Suite 400, Washington, DC 20036.

13224
Nebraska Alumni Census and Questionnaire. Nebraska University Lincoln 1983
Descriptors: Adults; *Alumni; *Biographical Inventories; College Graduates; *Graduate Surveys; Higher Education; Questionnaires; Rating Scales
Availability: ERIC Document Reproduction Service; 3900 Wheeler Ave., Alexandria, VA 22304-5110 (Ed234659, microfiche only)
Target Audience: 18-64
Notes: Items, 41

In addition to asking for background information of the alumni, this survey sought information about the alumni's relationship with the university. The alumni were to rate statements on a scale of strongly agree to strongly disagree. An alternate source for this document is Council for Advancement and Support of Education, 1 Dupont Circle, Suite 400, Washington, DC 20036.

13225
University of New Hampshire Alumni Survey. New Hampshire University Durham 1983
Descriptors: Adults; *Alumni; *Biographical Inventories; College Graduates; *Graduate Surveys; Higher Education; Questionnaires
Availability: ERIC Document Reproduction Service; 3900 Wheeler Ave., Alexandria, VA 22304 (ED234659, microfiche only)
Target Audience: 18–64
Notes: Items, 29

This questionnaire was used to survey the alumni of the University of New Hampshire about their attitudes toward the alumni office and its programs/publications. An alternate source for this document is Council for Advancement and Support of Education, 1 Dupont Circle, Suite 400, Washington, DC 20036.

13226
University of Oklahoma Association, Inc., Members Opinion Survey. Oklahoma University, Norman 1983
Descriptors: Adults; *Alumni; *Biographical Inventories; College Graduates; *Graduate Surveys; Higher Education; Opinions; Questionnaires
Availability: ERIC Document Reproduction Service; 3900 Wheeler Ave., Alexandria, VA 22304 (ED234659, microfiche only)
Target Audience: 18–64
Notes: Items, 50

This questionnaire asked the alumni what they really thought about the Sooners, the football newsletter, local community activities, on-campus activities, travel and Sooner keepsakes, communications, and the reaction to an if section; e.g., "what your reaction would be if the items listed were made available to you." An alternate source for this document is Council for Advancement and Support of Education, 1 Dupont Circle, Suite 400, Washington, DC 20036.

13227
Wake Forest University Alumni Survey. Wake Forest University, Winston Salem, NC 1983
Descriptors: Adults; *Alumni; *Biographical Inventories; College Graduates; *Graduate Surveys; Higher Education; Questionnaires
Availability: ERIC Document Reproduction Service; 3900 Wheeler Ave., Alexandria, VA 22304-5110 (ED234659, microfiche only)
Target Audience: 18–64
Notes: Items, 27

The Wake Forest Alumni used this questionnaire for a telephone survey of their alumni. The interviewing was done by an independent contractor and the Alumni Office was most interested in the areas of the university that most interested the alumni and their attitudes about Wake Forest. An alternate source for this document is Council for Advancement and Support of Education, 1 Dupont Circle, Suite 400, Washington, DC 20036.

13228
Mount Saint Mary's Alumni Questionnaire. Thompson and Pendel Associates 1983
Descriptors: Adults; *Alumni; *Biographical Inventories; College Graduates; *Graduate Surveys; Higher Education; Questionnaires
Availability: ERIC Document Reproduction Service; 3900 Wheeler Ave., Alexandria, VA 22304 (ED234659, microfiche only)
Target Audience: 18–64
Notes: Items, 88

This questionnaire, used by Mount Saint Mary's in Emmitsburg, MD, was developed by Thompson and Pendel Associates in consulting with several clients. It is to provide biographical and attitudinal information. This instrument involves a number of open-ended questions not so much to find out what the alumni think, as to find out how certain individuals react. The developers of this questionnaire say that it should be used only if there is adequate preparation. An alternate source for this document is Council for Advancement and Support of Education, 1 Dupont Circle, Suite 400, Washington, DC 20036.

13229
Teenage Cigarette Smoking Self-Test. Public Health Service (DHHS), Rockville, Md. 1982
Subtests: Teenagers' Knowledge of Smoking; Social Awareness and Self-Understanding
Descriptors: *Adolescents; Decision Making; Health Education; Personal Autonomy; Secondary Education; *Self Evaluation (Individuals); *Smoking
Availability: ERIC Document Reproduction Service; 3900 Wheeler Ave., Alexandria, VA 22304 (ED234301, 14 pages)
Target Audience: 13–17
Notes: Items, 40

This self-test was designed to help teenagers understand their feelings about cigarette smoking. This test can be self-administered and self-scored. The items are statements that some teenagers have made about cigarette smoking and cigarette smokers. The student is to show whether he/she agrees, disagrees, or does neither about each statement.

13244
Judgment Extremity Confidence Procedure. Kogan, Nathan; Wallach, Michael A. 1964
Descriptors: Adults; Attitudes; Cognitive Style; Evaluative Thinking; Risk
Identifiers: *Confidence
Availability: Kogan, Nathan, and Wallach, Michael A.; *Risk Taking: A Study in Cognition and Personality.*New York: Holt, Rinehart and Winston, 1964
Target Audience: Adults
Notes: Items, 50

Designed to assess examinee's confidence in his/her judgment.

13269
The Pictorial Scale of Perceived Competence and Social Acceptance for Young Children (Grades 1-2). Harter, Susan; Pike, Robin 1981
Subtests: Cognitive Competence; Physical Competence; Peer Acceptance; Maternal Acceptance
Descriptors: *Cognitive Ability; Elementary School Students; Individual Testing; Interpersonal Competence; *Parent Child Relationship; *Peer Acceptance; Pictorial Stimuli; *Primary Education; *Psychomotor Skills; Rating Scales; Self Concept; Self Concept Measures; Self Esteem; *Self Evaluation (Individuals); Teacher Attitudes
Identifiers: Self Report Measures
Availability: Susan Harter; Dept. of Psychology, University of Denver, University Park, Denver, CO 80208
Grade Level: 1–2
Target Audience: 6–7
Notes: Items, 24

Designed to assess young child's perceptions of his/her general competence and social acceptance. A domain-specific assessment of the young child's self-judgment. This instrument is a downward extension of the Self-Perception Profile for Children (TC013325). Separate scales are used for boys and girls. A teacher's rating scale permits the rating of a child's actual competence and social acceptance for comparison with the child's self-evaluation.

13270
The Pictorial Scale of Perceived Competence and Social Acceptance for Young Children (Preschool-Kindergarten). Harter, Susan; Pike, Robin 1980
Subtests: Cognitive Competence; Physical Competence; Peer Acceptance; Maternal Acceptance
Descriptors: *Cognitive Ability; Individual Testing; Interpersonal Competence; Kindergarten; *Kindergarten Children; *Parent Child Relationship; *Peer Acceptance; Pictorial Stimuli; *Preschool Children; Preschool Education; *Psychomotor Skills; Rating Scales; Self Concept; Self Concept Measures; Self Esteem; *Self Evaluation (Individuals); Teacher Attitudes
Identifiers: Self Report Measures
Availability: Susan Harter; Dept. of Psychology, University of Denver, University Park, Denver, CO 80208
Grade Level: K
Target Audience: 4–5
Notes: Items, 24

A domain-specific assessment of the young child's self-judgment. This instrument is a downward extension of the Self-Perception Profile for Children (TC013325). Separate scales are used for boys and girls. A teacher's rating scale permits the rating of a child's actual competence and social acceptance for comparison with the child's self-evaluation.

13325
Self-Perception Profile for Children. Harter, Susan 1983
Subtests: Scholastic Competence; Social Acceptance; Athletic Competence; Physical Appearance; Behavior/Conduct; Self-Worth
Descriptors: Academic Ability; Elementary Education; *Elementary School Students; Junior High Schools; *Junior High School Students; Peer Acceptance; Physical Characteristics; Physical Fitness; Rating Scales; *Self Concept; Self Concept Measures; Student Behavior; Teacher Attitudes
Identifiers: Self Report Measures; What I Am Like
Availability: Susan Harter; Dept. of Psychology, University of Denver, University Park, Denver, CO 80208
Grade Level: 3–9
Notes: Items, 36

An instrument designed to assess children's perceptions of themselves in the domains of scholastic and athletic competence, social acceptance, physical appearance, behavior/conduct, and self-worth. Scholastic and athletic competence subscales assess competency in each area. The other subscales refer to various forms of adequacy which do not necessarily imply competence. Items were designed to encourage students to think about the global perception of their worth as individual persons. A teacher rating scale consisting of 15 items parallels the student form for each domain. The teacher rates the child's actual behavior and makes an independent judgment of the child's adequacy. This scale consists of subscales including scholastic and athletic competence, social acceptance, physical appearance, and behavior/conduct. Domain scores are calculated and compared to the child's self-evaluation scores. Test items are in the manual and may be reproduced as needed. This instrument is a revision of the Perceived Competence Scale for Children.

13326
Subjective Stress Scale. Kerle, Robert H. 1958
Descriptors: Adults; Affective Behavior; Behavior Patterns; Check Lists; *Emotional Response; *Stress Variables
Identifiers: SSS; Thurstone Scales
Availability: National Technical Information Service; 5285 Port Royal Rd., Springfield, VA 22161 (Order No. 489-875).
Target Audience: 18–64
Notes: Items, 100

The Subjective Stress Scale (SSS) was constructed to obtain measures of subjective reactions under field experimental conditions. The 100 words describe an individual's emotional or affective state. The scale was used in field studies, i.e., at the Atomic Energy Commission's summer test exercises, at the Navy Fire Fighting School at Treasure Island, CA, and at the rope suspension bridge built in Pilarcitos Canyon, Fort Ord, CA. The test is easily administered, and the subjects check how they felt at particular times in the studies. The construction of the scale was based on the Thurstone scaling technique.

13328
Personal Values Inventory, Revised 1983. Porter, Elias H.; Maloney, Sara E. 1983
Descriptors: Adults; *Affective Behavior; *Behavior Patterns; Conflict; *Perspective Taking; Self Concept; Self Evaluation (Individuals); *Values
Availability: Personal Strengths Publishing; P.O. Drawer 397, Pacific Palisades, CA 90272
Target Audience: 18–64
Notes: Items, 20

This inventory was developed to help individuals understand what it is they want from others and what it is they don't want from others. It is to help them see their own personal strengths, the ways they act that make them feel good about themselves. It will also help them see some ways in which they may make trouble for themselves. There are 2 forms to the Personal Values Inventory; the second is the mirror edition in which individuals answer the same items but think of another person they are describing when he/she is faced with conflict and opposition. When the Personal Values Inventory is answered, the subject answers the question thinking about situations at work, at school, at home, or with friends but is always thinking of situations where he/she is feeling good about himself/herself.

13329
Inventaire du Deploiement des Forces de la Personnalite. Porter, Elias H. 1977
Descriptors: Adults; *Affective Behavior; *Behavior Patterns; Conflict; *French; *Perspective Taking; Self Concept; Self Evaluation (Individuals); *Values
Identifiers: Personal Values Inventory
Availability: Personal Strengths Publishing; P.O. Drawer 397, Pacific Palisades, CA 90272
Target Audience: 18–64
Notes: Items, 20

This is a French version of an inventory developed to help individuals understand what it is they want from others and what it is they don't want. It is to help them see their own personal strengths, the ways they act that make them feel good about themselves. It will also help them see some ways in which they may make trouble for themselves. When this inventory is answered, the subject answers the question thinking about situations at work, at school, at home, or with friends, but always thinking of situations where things are going well for the individual and he/she is feeling good about him/herself.

13330
The Children's Version of the Family Environment Scale. Pino, Christopher J.; And Others 1984
Subtests: Cohesion; Expressiveness; Conflict; Independence; Achievement Orientation; Intellectual-Cultural Orientation; Active-Recreational Orientation; Moral-Religious Emphasis; Organization; Control

Descriptors: *Affective Measures; *Childhood Attitudes; *Children; *Counseling Techniques; *Family Environment; *Family Relationship; Self Concept; Visual Measures
Identifiers: CVFES
Availability: Slosson Educational Publications; P.O. Box 280, East Aurora, NY 14052
Target Audience: 5–12
Notes: Items, 30

This Scale is an objective measure covering 10 areas of family functioning: cohesion, expressiveness, conflict, independence, achievement orientation, intellectual-cultural orientation, active-recreational orientation, moral-religious emphasis, organization, and control. This is a 30-question, pictorial nonprojective measure. This is a useful measure for counselors, psychologists, and clinicians.

13332
Other Nations Other Peoples. Pike, Lewis; And Others 1976
Subtests: Background and Interest Questionnaire; Knowledge Test; Attitudes toward and Perceptions of Other Nations and Peoples
Descriptors: Achievement Tests; Cultural Awareness; Elementary Secondary Education; Foreign Culture; *Global Approach; High Schools; Intermediate Grades; Junior High Schools; Student Attitudes; Student Interests; World Geography; World Problems
Availability: ERIC Document Reproduction Service; 3900 Wheeler Ave., Alexandria, VA 22304 (ED189190, 177 pgs)
Grade Level: 4; 8; 12
Notes: Time, 60 approx.

Designed to measure students' interests, knowledge, attitudes, and perceptions regarding other nations including United States, Mexico, France, Egypt, People's Republic of China, and the U.S.S.R. Many items are no longer useful because the responses contain outdated information.

13370
Seriousness of Illness Rating Scale. Wyler, Allen R.; And Others 1967
Descriptors: *Adults; *Diseases; *Physicians
Availability: Journal of Psychosomatic Research;v11 p363-74, 1968
Target Audience: Adults
Notes: Time, 30 approx.; Items, 126

Designed to establish a magnitude estimation of the "seriousness of illness." Respondent rates severity of diseases. Studies were conducted to compare physicians' responses to lay people with no medical training.

13378
Meier Burnout Assessment. Meier, Scott; Davis, Susan 1983
Descriptors: *Burnout; *Expectation; Higher Education; Negative Attitudes; Questionnaires; *Student Attitudes; *Undergraduate Students
Identifiers: MBA
Availability: ERIC Document Reproduction Service; 3900 Wheeler Ave., Alexandria, VA 22304 (ED235437, 12 pages)
Grade Level: 13–16
Notes: Items, 25

Based on author's cognitive behavioral model of burnout in that burnout is defined as a state in which individuals expect little reward and considerable punishment from work because of a lack of valued reinforcement, controllable outcomes, or personal competence. The questionnaire is a 25-item true-false test that assesses respondents' conditions and expectations related to burnout.

13405
Personal Adjustment Index: A Vocational Adjustment Index, Test 8-A. Hadley, S. Trevor; Stouffer, George A.W., Jr. 1984
Subtests: Community Spirit; Attitude toward Cooperation with Employers; Attitude toward Health; Attitude toward Authority; Lack of Nervous Tendencies; Leadership; Job Stability
Descriptors: *Adjustment (to Environment); Adults; *Employee Attitudes; Employees; *Job Applicants; *Personality Measures; *Screening Tests; Self Evaluation (Individuals); Work Attitudes
Identifiers: ETSA Tests
Availability: Employers' Tests and Services Associates; 341 Garfield St., Chambersburg, PA 17201
Target Audience: Adults
Notes: Time, 45 approx.; Items, 105

Part of the ETSA series of occupational aptitude tests. Essentially a vocational adjustment inventory that measures certain aspects of the examinee's characteristic mode of adjustment to the environment. A self-report measure that yields a sampling of examinee's attitudes and feelings in relation to certain factors significant in the world of work. Findings may also be useful in counseling present employees. ETSA tests are a series of aptitude tests and a

personality inventory, designed to be administered, scored, and interpreted in one's own business, industry, organization, or institution. Tests emphasize power rather than speed. Each test has a time limit long enough to permit examinees to attempt all items. For a complete profile of an applicant, it is recommended that the General Mental Ability Test 1-A (TC013400) and the Personal Adjustment Index Test 8-A (TC013405) be administered with the additional ETSA test designed for the particular job under consideration.

13406
Lifestyles for Women Attitude Scale. Burns, Marie Susan A. 1974
Descriptors: Career Choice; *College Students; *Females; Higher Education; *Life Style; Males; *Sex Role; *Student Attitudes; Traditionalism
Availability: Psychological Reports;v35 p227-30, 1974
Grade Level: 13–16
Notes: Items, 28

Designed to assess attitudes of men and women concerning lifestyles for women. Samples attitudes with respect to a career or traditional (motherhood) orientation.

13407
The Alcoholism Questionnaire. Ferneau, E.; Mueller, S. 1971
Descriptors: Alcohol Education; *Alcoholism; *College Students; Higher Education; Rating Scales; *Student Attitudes
Identifiers: Alcoholism Questionnaire; Marcus (A)
Availability: ERIC Document Reproduction Service; 3900 Wheeler Ave., Alexandria, VA 22304-5110 (ED071091, 18 pages)
Grade Level: 13–16
Notes: Time, 20 approx.; Items, 40

This questionnaire was used in a study of college students' attitudes toward alcohol abuse and the alcohol abuser. The subject responds to the 40 statements by checking a position on the 1-7 rating scale. It takes about 20 minutes to complete this instrument. It is identical to the drug-abuse questionnaire except for word changes appropriate to the subject matter.

13408
The Drug-Abuse Questionnaire. Ferneau, E.; Mueller, S. 1971
Descriptors: *College Students; *Drug Abuse; Drug Addiction; Drug Education; Higher Education; Rating Scales; *Student Attitudes
Identifiers: Alcoholism Questionnaire; Marcus (A)
Availability: ERIC Document Reproduction Service; 3900 Wheeler Ave., Alexandria, VA 22304 (ED071091, 18 pages)
Grade Level: 13–16
Notes: Time, 20 approx.; Items, 40

This questionnaire was used to survey college student attitudes on drug-abuse. It is identical to the alcoholism questionnaire except for word changes appropriate to the subject matter. The subject responds to the 40 statements by checking a position on the 1-7 rating scale. It takes about 20 minutes to complete this instrument.

13416
Study of High School Educational Climates: Teachers' Questionnaire. McDill, Edward L.; Rigsby, Leo C. 1973
Descriptors: Adults; *Educational Environment; Educational Philosophy; *High Schools; Occupational Aspiration; Questionnaires; *Secondary School Teachers; Social Background; Student Behavior; Teacher Student Relationship; *Teacher Attitudes; Teaching Styles; Values
Availability: McDill, Edward L., and Rigsby, Leo C.; Structure and Process in Secondary Schools: The Academic Impact of Educational Climates.Baltimore, MD: Johns Hopkins University Press, c1973
Target Audience: Adults
Notes: Items, 234

Elicits information on social background, intellectual values, and norms and how these values affect the teacher's relationship with students. Also covers teacher's career aspirations for students and dominant values, norms, and behavior patterns of student body and colleagues. A group of true-false items measure environmental "press" of teachers toward scientism, intellectualism, etc.

13417
Study of High School Educational Climates: Boys' Attitude Questionnaire. McDill, Edward L.; Rigsby, Leo C. 1973
Descriptors: Academic Achievement; Academic Aspiration; *Educational Environment; Educational Philosophy; *High School Students; *Males; Occupational Aspiration; Peer Relationship; Questionnaires; Social Background; Social Behavior; Social Influences; *Student Attitudes; Teaching Styles; Values

Availability: McDill, Edward L., and Rigsby, Leo C.; Structure and Process in Secondary Schools: The Academic Impact of Educational Climates.Baltimore, MD: Johns Hopkins University Press, c1973
Grade Level: 9–12
Notes: Items, 440

Requests information about social background, intellectual attitudes and values, educational and occupational aspirations, academic and interpersonal behavior in the school setting and outside of school. Students also provide sociometric information on peer group structure and perceptions of environmental "press" of teachers toward scientism, intellectualism, etc.

13418
Study of High School Educational Climates: Girls' Attitude Questionnaire. McDill, Edward L.; Rigsby, Leo C. 1973
Descriptors: Academic Achievement; Academic Aspiration; *Educational Environment; Educational Philosophy; *Females; *High School Students; Occupational Aspiration; Peer Relationship; Questionnaires; Social Background; Social Behavior; Social Influences; *Student Attitudes; Teaching Styles; Values
Availability: McDill, Edward L., and Rigsby, Leo C.; Structure and Process in Secondary Schools: The Academic Impact of Educational Climates.Baltimore, MD: Johns Hopkins University Press, c1973
Grade Level: 9–12
Notes: Items, 440

Requests information about social background, intellectual attitudes and values, educational and occupational aspirations, academic and interpersonal behavior in the school setting and outside of school. Students also provide sociometric information on peer group structure and perceptions of environmental "press" of teachers toward scientism, intellectualism, etc.

13469
Homosexual Threat Inventory. Mosher, Donald L.; O'Grady, Kevin E. 1979
Descriptors: Adults; Anxiety; *Homosexuality; *Males
Identifiers: *Sexual Attitudes
Availability: Journal of Consulting and Clinical Psychology;v47 n5 p863-64, 1979
Target Audience: Adults
Notes: Items, 21

Designed to assess degree to which a male subject is threatened by contact with homosexual males. Measures sexual attitudes.

13484
The Chin Inventory on Content Area Reading Instruction. Chin, Beverly Ann 1975
Descriptors: Adults; *Content Area Reading; Elementary Secondary Education; Inservice Teacher Education; Preservice Teacher Education; Rating Scales; *Reading Instruction; *Reading Teachers; *Teacher Attitudes; *Teacher Effectiveness; Likert Scales
Identifiers: *The Research Instruments Project
Availability: ERIC Document Reproduction Service; 3900 Wheeler Ave., Alexandria, VA 22304 (ED236657, 13 pages)
Target Audience: 18–64
Notes: Items, 27

This instrument is to assess attitudes and perceptions of competency in teaching reading in the content areas of pre- and inservice teachers of elementary and secondary content area subjects. Teachers respond to 27 specific skill statements on a 5-point Likert-type scale. Each statement represents and illustrates the integration of reading instruction with content instruction. There are 2 independent sections: Part A assesses teachers' attitudes toward content area reading instruction, and Part B assesses teachers' perceptions of competency in content area reading instruction.

13485
Gary-Brown Writing Opinionnaire for College Instructors. Gary, Melvin; Brown, Sandra 1981
Descriptors: *College Faculty; Higher Education; Inservice Teacher Education; Rating Scales; *Teacher Attitudes; *Writing Instruction
Identifiers: *The Research Instruments Project
Availability: ERIC Document Reproduction Service; 3900 Wheeler Ave., Alexandria, VA 22304-5110 (ED236660, 11 pages)
Target Audience: 18–64
Notes: Items, 47

This instrument was designed to assess teachers' attitudes toward teaching writing, evaluating writing, and teaching course content through writing. The first part of this 2-part measure is a 35-item Likert-type scale representing the opinionnaire's 3 purposes. The second part asks for professional opinions in 12 categories, including extent of marginal comment on student papers, nature of writing assignments, peer evaluation, percentage of college students with severe writing problems, most common student writing errors, rewriting, and recommendations for improvement of instruction.

13486
The DeFord Theoretical Orientation to Reading Profile (TORP). DeFord, Diane E. 1979
Descriptors: Adults; Educational Philosophy; Inservice Teacher Education; Measures (Individuals); Preservice Teacher Education; Rating Scales; *Reading Instruction; *Reading Teachers; *Teacher Attitudes; Teaching Methods; *Teaching Styles; Likert Scales
Identifiers: *The Research Instruments Project
Availability: ERIC Document Reproduction Service; 3900 Wheeler Ave., Alexandria, VA 22304 (ED236661, 12 pages)
Target Audience: 18-64
Notes: Time, 30 approx.; Items, 28
Designed to differentiate preservice and inservice teachers according to their theoretical orientation to reading, the TORP consists of 28 items reflecting practices and beliefs about reading instruction. The items, which require a Likert-type response, fall into 3 categories: phonics (smaller than word emphasis), skills (whole words with multiple skills for dealing with this unit), and whole language (larger than word segments). The resulting score is a general indicator of the respondent's orientation.

13491
Story Preference Inventory. Swayne, Philip E. 1975
Subtests: Fantasy versus Realism; Past versus Contemporary; Geographically Remote versus Near-at-Hand
Descriptors: *Childhood Interests; Childrens Literature; Elementary Education; *Elementary School Students; Forced Choice Technique; *Interest Inventories; Literature Appreciation; Measures (Individuals); *Reading Attitudes; *Reading Interests; Reading Material Selection
Identifiers: *Story Setting; The Research Instruments Project
Availability: ERIC Document Reproduction Service; 3900 Wheeler Ave., Alexandria, VA 22304 (ED236639, 64 pages)
Grade Level: K-6
Notes: Items, 36
This inventory was designed to assess children's preferences for story settings and requires children to indicate their preference for a story setting in each of 36 pairs of contrasting pictures, 12 pairs in each of the following categories: (1) fantasy versus realism, (2) past versus contemporary, and (3) geographically remote versus the near-at-hand. The inventory yields 3 scores, 1 in each of the 3 categories.

13505
Spanish-English Bilingual Program Needs Assessment: Parent Survey. Tucson Unified School District, Tucson, AZ 1978
Descriptors: Adults; *Bilingual Education; Elementary Education; English (Second Language); Junior High Schools; *Needs Assessment; *Parent Attitudes; Parents; Spanish Speaking; Student Placement; Surveys
Availability: ERIC Document Reproduction Service; 3900 Wheeler Ave., Alexandria, VA 22304-5110 (ED173429, 29 pages)
Grade Level: K-8
Target Audience: Adults
Notes: Items, 8
Elicits parents' perceptions of the child's competence in English and Spanish and their preference of program placement for the child, either bilingual or all English.

13506
Student Questionnaire: Opinions about Sahuaro High School. Tucson Unified School District, Tucson, AZ 1978
Descriptors: Academic Standards; Athletics; Counseling Services; Courses; Curriculum; Extracurricular Activities; Grading; High Schools; *High School Students; Library Services; *Program Attitudes; Questionnaires; School Policy; *Student Attitudes; Student Needs; Study Habits
Availability: ERIC Document Reproduction Service; 3900 Wheeler Ave., Alexandria, VA 22304-5110 (ED173429, 29 pages)
Grade Level: 9-12
Notes: Items, 35
Elicits information on student attitudes toward high school programs and how well these programs meet student needs. Covers activities, sports, library, subjects, courses, school policy, counseling, academic standards, and grading. Also elicits information on students' study habits and post-high school plans.

13507
School Parent Survey: Team Teaching. Tucson Unified School District, Tucson, AZ 1978

Descriptors: Adults; *Parent Attitudes; Parents; Surveys; *Team Teaching
Availability: ERIC Document Reproduction Service; 3900 Wheeler Ave., Alexandria, VA 22304 (ED173429, 29 pages)
Target Audience: Adults
Notes: Items, 7
Measures parent attitudes toward team teaching. No psychometric data or technical information are included.

13508
Staff Questionnaire: Your Opinions about Sahuaro High School. Tucson Unified School District, Tucson, AZ 1978
Descriptors: Administration; Adults; Counseling Services; High Schools; *Noninstructional Responsibility; Questionnaires; School Attitudes; School Policy; Student Behavior; *Teacher Attitudes
Availability: ERIC Document Reproduction Service; 3900 Wheeler Ave., Alexandria, VA 22304 (ED173429, 29 pages)
Target Audience: Adults
Notes: Items, 38
Elicits teachers' opinions concerning routine administrative duties, counseling, resources, school policies concerning students, nonteaching assignments, student behavior and attitudes, and attitudes of teachers in general toward the school.

13509
Student Counseling Survey. Tucson Unified School District, Tucson, AZ 1978
Descriptors: Career Planning; *Counseling Services; Extracurricular Activities; Family Environment; High Schools; *High School Students; School Counselors; *Student Attitudes; Student Characteristics; Surveys
Availability: ERIC Document Reproduction Service; 3900 Wheeler Ave., Alexandria, VA 22304 (ED173429, 29 pages.)
Grade Level: 9-12
Notes: Items, 40
Information-gathering tool for and use by guidance office to compile data on student characteristics, activities, home environment, future plans, and use of opinions about counseling and counselors.

13510
Girls High School Sports Survey. Tucson Unified School District, Tucson, AZ 1978
Descriptors: *Athletics; *Females; High Schools; *High School Students; Interest Inventories; *Student Attitudes; Student Problems; Surveys
Availability: ERIC Document Reproduction Service; 3900 Wheeler Ave., Alexandria, VA 22304 (ED173429, 29 pages.)
Grade Level: 9-12
Notes: Items, 9
Elicits information on female students' interest in the athletic program and what problems they may have encountered with it.

13511
Quarter Credit System: Staff Questionnaire. Tucson Unified School District, Tucson, AZ 1978
Descriptors: High Schools; *Quarter System; Questionnaires; *Teachers
Availability: ERIC Document Reproduction Service; 3900 Wheeler Ave., Alexandria, VA 22304 (ED173429, 29 pages.)
Target Audience: Adults
Notes: Items, 10
Measure attitudes concerning the effects of quarter courses on students, such as student failures, and evaluation of student progress over a short time period.

13512
Quarter Credit System: Student Questionnaire. Tucson Unified School District, Tucson, AZ 1978
Descriptors: High Schools; *High School Students; *Quarter System; Questionnaires
Availability: ERIC Document Reproduction Service; 3900 Wheeler Ave., Alexandria, VA 22304 (ED173429, 29 pages.)
Grade Level: 9-12
Notes: Items, 7
Elicits information on the number and quality of courses taken, reasons for dropping a course, and other problems with the quarter system.

13518
Coping with Death Scale. Jones, Paul L.; Young, Patricia 1983
Descriptors: College Students; *Coping; *Death; Higher Education; Rating Scales; Likert Scales
Availability: ERIC Document Reproduction Service; 3500 Wheeler Ave., Alexandria, VA 22304 (ED237542, microfiche only)
Grade Level: 13-16
Notes: Items, 25

There are 4 dimensions to the Coping with Death Scale: Relating to Others about Death, Preparedness for One's Own Death, Coping with Personal Losses, and Knowledge of Funeral Arrangements. The 25 items are scored on a 5-point Likert scale.

13519
Questionnaire for Identifying Writer's Block. Rose, Mike 1981
Subtests: Blocking; Lateness; Premature Editing; Strategies for Complexity; Attitudes
Descriptors: Adults; College Students; Postsecondary Education; Questionnaires; Secondary Education; Secondary School Students; *Student Attitudes; *Writing (Composition); *Writing Apprehension; *Writing Processes
Identifiers: QIWB; *The Research Instruments Project
Availability: ERIC Document Reproduction Service; 3900 Wheeler Ave., Alexandria, VA 22304-5110 (ED236652, 8 pages)
Grade Level: 9-16
Notes: Items, 24
This is an attitude questionnaire which is designed to identify students with writer's block. The 24 items are separated into 5 subscales: blocking, lateness, premature editing, strategies for complexity, and attitudes. If a teacher wishes to identify blockers, only the items within the behavioral subscales, blocking and lateness, need be administered. If further cognitive diagnosis is desired, then the items in the cognitive/behavioral and cognitive/attitudinal subscales can be administered. This instrument was designed for the senior high student through postsecondary and adults.

13529
Salamon-Conte Life Satisfaction in the Elderly Scale. Salamon, Michael J.; Conte, Vincent A. 1984
Subtests: Daily Activities; Meaning; Goals; Mood; Self-Concept; Health; Finances; Social Contacts
Descriptors: Adults; *Life Satisfaction; *Older Adults; Rating Scales; *Self Evaluation (Individuals)
Identifiers: LSES; Self Report Measures
Availability: Psychological Assessment Resources; P.O. Box 998, Odessa, FL 33556
Target Audience: 55-90
Notes: Time, 25 approx.; Items, 40
Designed to measure reliably life satisfaction among aged persons in a variety of settings. Assesses older adult reactions to their ecological, emotional, and social environments. Key areas found to be significant to this age group and which are evaluated by the LSES include taking pleasure in daily activities, regarding life as meaningful, goodness of fit between desired and achieved goals, positive mood, positive self-concept, and perceived health, financial security, and satisfaction with number and quality of social contacts.

13538
Work Itself/Work Environment Preference Questionnaire. Cascio, Wayne F. 1973
Descriptors: Adults; *Employees; Occupational Information; Rating Scales; Work Attitudes; Work Environment
Identifiers: WIWE
Availability: University of Rochester; Graduate School of Management, Rochester, NY 14627
Target Audience: Adults
Notes: Items, 19
Designed to identify elements that reflect the intrinsic and extrinsic motivational properties of jobs. Ten elements are related to the work environment, and 9 are related to the job itself. For each element, respondents select 1 or more of 5 statements that are indicative of the conditions for a particular element.

13539
Sex Role Differentiation in Physical Education Attitude Measure. Chrietzberg, Agnes L. 1981
Descriptors: Adults; *Equal Education; *Physical Education; *Physical Education Teachers; Preservice Teacher Education; Rating Scales; Secondary School Teachers; *Sex Bias; *Teacher Attitudes; Likert Scales
Identifiers: SRDPE; TIM(J)
Availability: Tests in Microfiche; Test Collection, Educational Testing Service, Princeton, NJ 08541
Target Audience: Adults
Notes: Items, 42
Inventory was constructed to evaluate attitudes of preservice and inservice teachers toward differential treatment of boys and girls in secondary physical education programs. SRD/PE was developed as part of a validation plan to determine the effectiveness of instructional modules designed to help teachers reduce sex bias in physical education.

13545
Staff Burnout Scale for Health Professionals.
Jones, John W. 1980
Subtests: Burnout; Lie Scale
Descriptors: Adults; *Burnout; *Health Personnel;
Hospital Personnel; Job Satisfaction; Nurses;
Self Concept
Identifiers: SBSHP; Self Report Measures
Availability: London House Management Consultants; 1550 N. Northwest Hwy., Park Ridge, IL
60068
Target Audience: Adults
Notes: Time, 15 approx.; Items, 30
This inventory of attitudes is designed to assess staff
burnout among health professionals. It measures degree of
work stress experienced by hospital-related personnel.

13546
Staff Burnout Scale for Police and Security Personnel. Jones, John W. 1980
Subtests: Burnout; Lie Scale
Descriptors: Adults; *Burnout; Job Satisfaction;
*Police; *Security Personnel; Self Concept
Identifiers: SBSPS; Self Report Measures
Availability: London House Management Consultants; 1550 N. Northwest Hwy., Park Ridge, IL
60068
Target Audience: Adults
Notes: Time, 15 approx.; Items, 30
An inventory of attitudes designed to assess staff burnout
among police and security officers. Measures acute stress
reactions of examinees and how they currently feel.

13551
Engagement Schedule E. Marriage Council of
Philadelphia, PA 1950
Descriptors: Adults; Counseling Techniques;
*Marriage Counseling; Sexuality
Identifiers: *Premarital Counseling; Self Report
Measures
Availability: Marriage Council of Philadelphia,
Inc.; 4025 Chestnut St., Ste. 210, Philadelphia,
PA 19104
Target Audience: Adults
Notes: Items, 41
Designed to aid counselor in premarital counseling of
engaged couples. Clients are asked to provide facts about
the engagement; feelings about future in-laws, own parents, confiding, affection, need for information about sex,
number of children planned, and sharing of interests and
activities. May also be used with married couples recalling
their engagement period.

13552
Marriage Adjustment Schedule 1A. Marriage
Council of Philadelphia, PA 1950
Descriptors: Adults; Counseling Techniques; Marriage; *Marriage Counseling; *Sexuality;
*Spouses
Identifiers: Self Report Measures
Availability: Marriage Council of Philadelphia,
Inc.; 4025 Chestnut St., Ste. 210, Philadelphia,
PA 19104
Target Audience: Adults
Notes: Items, 34
Designed for completion by married couples to provide
marriage counselor with information about shared activities, problem areas in the relationship, and sharing of
responsibilities.

13562
Sex Role Learning Index. Edelbrock, Craig; Sugawara, Alan I. 1978
Descriptors: *Individual Testing; Pictorial Stimuli;
*Sex Role; Sex Stereotypes; *Young Children
Identifiers: SERLI; TIM(J)
Availability: Tests in Microfiche; Test Collection,
Educational Testing Service, Princeton, NJ
08541
Target Audience: 3–8
Notes: Time, 15 approx.; Items, 30
A picture choice instrument for measuring sex role acquisition in young children, ages 3 through 8. It is individually administered. Designed to measure 3 concepts: sex
role discrimination, sex role preference, and sex role confirmation. There are separate forms for boys and girls.

13571
Marriage Adjustment Schedule 1B. Marriage
Council of Philadelphia, PA 1950
Descriptors: Adults; Counseling Techniques; Counselors; Interviews; *Marriage Counseling;
*Sexuality; Spouses
Identifiers: Sexual Adjustment; *Sexual Attitudes
Availability: Marriage Council of Philadelphia,
Inc.; 4025 Chestnut St., Ste. 210, Philadelphia,
PA 19104
Target Audience: Adults
Notes: Items, 36

This questionnaire is always used by the counselor during
the counseling hour. Designed to provide information
about married couple's feelings, attitudes, and behaviors
concerning marital sexual relationship.

13583
Women in Science Scale. Erb, Thomas Owen;
Smith, Walter S. 1983
Descriptors: *Adolescents; *Females; High Schools;
Intermediate Grades; Junior High Schools;
*Preadolescents; Rating Scales; *Science Careers; *Sex Role
Identifiers: WISS
Availability: Walter S. Smith; Dept. of Curriculum
and Instruction, University of Kansas, Lawrence, KS 66045
Target Audience: 10–16
Notes: Items, 27
Developed to measure attitudes of early adolescents toward women in science careers. The items are also available in an article appearing in *Journal of Research in
Science Teaching*; v21 n4 p391-97, 1984. The WISS has
several uses: to evaluate a science career education program for early adolescents; to evaluate programs intended
to affect attitudes toward women in science in students in
middle and junior high schools, to compare attitudes of
various groups of early adolescents, and to study developmental changes in attitude over a wider age range.

13627
Attitudes toward Increased Participation by Women Questionnaire. Storrs, Sally 1972
Descriptors: *Elementary School Students; Elementary Secondary Education; *Equal Opportunities (Jobs); *Females; *Secondary School Students; *Student Attitudes
Availability: The Journal of Educational Research; v67 n4 p147-48, Dec 1973
Grade Level: 4–10
Notes: Items, 20
Developed to examine the views of elementary and secondary school students concerning women's increased participation in fields typically thought of as dominated by
males. When used in a study, results showed differences in
response were almost always a function of the sex of the
respondent, except for slight increments in egalitarian responses as students got older.

13641
**Aiken's Enjoyment of Mathematics and Value of
Mathematics Scales.** Aiken, L.R. 1974
Subtests: Enjoyment of Mathematics; Value of
Mathematics
Descriptors: *College Students; Foreign Countries;
Higher Education; *Mathematics; *Rating
Scales; *Self Evaluation (Individuals); Values;
Likert Scales
Identifiers: Australia (Tasmania)
Availability: Educational and Psychological Measurement; v43 n4 p1247-53, Win 1983
Grade Level: 13–16
Notes: Items, 21
This instrument was used in connection with a wider
study on instructional methods at the University of Tasmania. The 2 scales are scored on a 5-point Likert-style
format ranging from zero to 4 on each response along a
continuum from "strongly disagree" to "strongly agree."
There are 11 items on the Enjoyment of Mathematics
Scale and 10 items on the Value of Mathematics. The
instrument is used to measure different aspects of attitude
toward mathematics. Although used for college students, it
could be used for secondary school students.

13651
Standardized Test of Computer Literacy. Montag,
Mary; And Others 1984
Descriptors: *Achievement Tests; Adults;
*Anxiety; College Students; *Computer Literacy;
*Computers; Higher Education; High School
Students; Programing; Screening Tests; Secondary Education
Identifiers: Computer Applications; Computer Systems; STCL
Availability: Michael Simonson; Professor, College
of Education, Instructional Resources Center,
Quadrangle Bldg., Iowa State University, Ames,
IA 50011
Grade Level: 9–16
Target Audience: Adults
Notes: Items, 96
Composed of 2 separate parts. Part 1 is an achievement
test of student competence in computer systems, computer
applications, and computer programing principles. Part 2
is a standardized measure of computer anxiety, the fear of
using computers, or the apprehension felt while using
them. Part 1 has 70 items, and each of the subtests within
it can be administered separately. Parts 1 and 2 can be
purchased as separate tests. May be used with anyone who
has taken a computer literacy course. Part 2 may be used
to identify those who might have trouble succeeding in a
computer literacy course.

13663
**ACT Evaluation Survey/Service: The High School
Student Opinion Survey.** American College Testing Program, Iowa City, IA 1983
Subtests: Background Information; High School
Environment; Occupational Preparation; Educational Preparation; High School Characteristics
Descriptors: Background; Career Counseling; Educational Environment; Educational Planning; Institutional Characteristics; *Institutional Research; Opinions; *Organizational Objectives;
Program Evaluation; Secondary Education;
*Secondary School Students; Student Attitudes;
Surveys
Identifiers: ACT; HSSOS
Availability: American College Testing Program;
Evaluation Survey Service, P.O. Box 168, Iowa
City, IA 52243
Grade Level: 7–12
Notes: Time, 25; Items, 70
Part of a system of survey instruments and scoring/reporting services designed to assist educational institutions in
collecting and using information on students. The HSSOS
is designed to explore the perceptions of students regarding programs, characteristics, and environment of the
school. For use in institutional planning and decision
making, to identify strengths and weaknesses in programs,
to determine student interests, concerns, and opinions.
Additional questions can be added by the user.

13681
Studies in Personal Adjustment. Indiana University, Institute for Sex Research, Bloomington 1967
Descriptors: Adults; Biographical Inventories;
*Emotional Adjustment; *Homosexuality;
*Individual Characteristics; *Individual Development; *Individual Differences; *Males;
*Personality Assessment; Questionnaires;
*Sexuality
Identifiers: Kinsey (Alfred)
Availability: Kinsey Institute for Research in Sex,
Gender, and Reproduction; Morrison Hall 416,
Bloomington, IN 47405
Target Audience: 18–64
Notes: Items, 165
This questionnaire is used to obtain biographical information from homosexuals. It also asks questions about sexual
background, preferences, and practices. The instrument is
for subjects 20 to 50 years of age and was used for those
living in the Chicago Ethnographic area.

13682
College Youth Study: An Interview Schedule. Simon, William; Gagnon, John 1967
Descriptors: *College Students; Family Characteristics; Higher Education; Interpersonal Relationship; Interviews; Opinions; Questionnaires; *Self
Evaluation (Individuals); *Sexuality
Identifiers: Kinsey (Alfred)
Availability: The Kinsey Institute for Research in
Sex, Gender, and Reproduction; Morrison Hall
313, Indiana University, Bloomington, IN
47405
Grade Level: 13–17
Notes: Items, 292
This instrument is used to interview college students who
have completed the first semester of their freshman year
and are attending school on a regular basis or had regular
status and expect to return to regular status but are on
special status now. The questions cover background,
friends, social activities, relationships, feelings about sex,
and sex habits. Items also cover family background, physical development, religion, and high school. This document may be found in the report, "Youth Cultures and
Aspects of the Socialization Process."

13683
Adolescent Sex Education: A Questionnaire. Mooney, Elizabeth; Elias, James
Subtests: Background Information; Attitudes; Level of Sex Knowledge; Source of Sex Knowledge;
Handout
Descriptors: College Students; Elementary School
Students; Elementary Secondary Education;
Higher Education; High School Students; Questionnaires; Rating Scales; *Self Evaluation
(Individuals); Sex Education; *Sexuality
Identifiers: Kinsey (Alfred)
Availability: Kinsey Institute for Research in Sex,
Gender, and Reproduction; Morrison Hall 416,
Bloomington, IN 47405
Grade Level: 6–14
Notes: Items, 163
This questionnaire was developed for use in the sixth
grade to sophomores in college. It was used in a study to
determine the attitudes of different age students about sex.
There are questions about dating behavior, biographical
and background, the knowledge of words used in discussing sexual life, and the source of sex knowledge. The

handout section has questions about the subject's reaction to sexual magazines, pictures, and movies. There is also a section for subjects who have had a sex education course.

13686
Attitudes to Foods Scale. Rozin, Paul; And Others 1984
Descriptors: Adults; *Food; *Hygiene
Identifiers: Food Additives
Availability: *Developmental Psychology;*v20 n2 p309-14, Mar 1984
Target Audience: Adults
Notes: Items, 24

Explores attitudes toward food, especially sensitivity to cleanliness and contamination of foods. Elicits information on food preferences (soup) and how much one would like to eat it after being stirred with a flyswatter, out of a dog dish, with a bug in it.

13688
Goldberg Anorectic Attitude Scale. Goldberg, Solomon C. 1980
Descriptors: Adolescents; Adults; *Anorexia Nervosa; Body Weight; Eating Habits; *Emotional Disturbances; *Females; *Preadolescents; *Rating Scales; *Self Evaluation (Individuals)
Identifiers: GAAS
Availability: *Journal of Psychiatric Research;*v15 p239-51, 1980
Target Audience: 10–30
Notes: Items, 63

This scale is part of a study designed to evaluate the effectiveness of drug treatment and of behavior modification on anorexia nervosa patients. The items were constructed from a number of attitude dimensions hypothesized on the basis of clinical experience. The scale was given to female anorexia nervosa patients in 3 hospitals: University of Iowa, University of Minnesota, and the Illinois State Psychiatric Institute. The factors covered are staff, fear of fat, parents, denial, hunger, hypothermia, bloated, self-care, effort for achievement, food sickens me, my problems—mental or physical—helpful authority, physical problems, hobby cooking, and heterosexual disinterest. The responses were on a 4-point scale in which the patient indicated the extent to which the statement reflected her feelings. The patients had to be between 10 and 40 years of age and had to have had the onset of their illness between 10 and 30 years.

13698
Behavioral Pediatrics Questionnaire. Spiegel, Nancy; Reis, Harry T. 1983
Descriptors: Adults; *Graduate Medical Students; *Medical Students; *Pediatrics; Rating Scales; *Student Attitudes
Identifiers: BPQ; TIM(K)
Availability: Tests in Microfiche; Test Collection, Educational Testing Service, Princeton, NJ 08541
Target Audience: Adults

Designed for use with medical students and pediatric residents to evaluate attitudes toward a broad range of topics pertaining to behavioral pediatrics. The questionnaire is divided into 2 parts. Part I, Attitudes toward Pediatric Medicine, consists of the following scales: Attitudes toward the Profession, Attitudes toward Patients, Attitudes toward Mental Health Counseling, and Attitudes toward Behavioral Pediatrics. Part II deals with interpersonal attitudes and consists of the following scales: Attitudes toward Mental Illness, Attitudes toward Physical Disabilities, Attitudes toward Parenting, Empathy Scale, and Attitudes toward Human Sexuality. May be used to select these residents and students who might benefit from a behavioral program.

13701
Maturation of the Concept of Death, Revised. Thornburg, Kathy R.; Townley, Kimberly F. 1980
Descriptors: Children; *Death; Elementary Education; *Elementary School Students
Availability: Kimberly F. Townley; 110 CDL, University of Nebraska, Lincoln, NE 68503
Grade Level: 1–6
Target Audience: 6–12

Questionnaire to assess the level of understanding of the concept of death of elementary school children. Questions deal with children's perception of causes, images, and finality of death. There is also a brief questionnaire for parents to complete.

13733
Parent's Consumer Satisfaction Questionnaire. Forehand, Rex L.; McMahon, Robert J. 1981
Descriptors: Adults; *Behavior Problems; Children; Clinics; *Parent Attitudes; Parent Child Relationship; Parent Materials; *Parents; *Parent Workshops; *Program Evaluation; Rating Scales; Socialization
Identifiers: *Parenting Techniques
Availability: Forehand, Rex L., and McMahon, Robert J.; *Helping the Noncompliant Child: A Clinician's Guide to Parent Training.*New York: The Guilford Press, 1981
Target Audience: Adults
Notes: Items, 47

A rating scale designed to measure parents' satisfaction with a clinical treatment program in parenting techniques. It covers satisfaction with the overall program, teaching format, specific parenting techniques, and therapists. Children of these parents were exhibiting noncompliant and other oppositional behavior problems.

13736
Attitudinal Test. Karmos, Ann H.; Karmos, Joseph S. 1984
Descriptors: *Achievement Tests; *Grade 6; Intermediate Grades; Junior High Schools; *Junior High School Students; *Standardized Tests; *Student Attitudes
Availability: *Measurement and Evaluation in Counseling and Development;*v17 n2 p56-66, Jul 84
Grade Level: 6–9
Notes: Items, 12

Developed to assess the attitudes of students in grades 6 through 9 toward standardized achievement tests.

13745
The Personal Value Statement: An Experiential Learning Instrument. Oliver, John E.
Descriptors: Adults; *Organizational Development; Rating Scales; Training Objectives; *Values
Identifiers: PVS
Availability: University Associates; 8517 Production Ave., San Diego, CA 92121
Target Audience: Adults
Notes: Items, 20

Development of instrument is based on Edward Spranger's 1929 book *Types of Men* that describes 6 basic value systems which motivate people's thoughts and behaviors: political, aesthetic, social, theoretical, economic, and religious. Instrument is intended as a learning device in organizational behavior. It is not meant to be used as a counseling, selection, or placement instrument. This instrument is available in the *1985 Annual Handbook for Group Facilitators: Developing Human Resources*, published by University Associates.

13746
Attitudes toward Women as Managers. Yost, Edward B.; Herbert, Theodore T. 1977
Descriptors: *Administrators; Adults; *Females; *Managerial Occupations; *Sex Role
Identifiers: ATWAM
Availability: University Associates; 8517 Production Ave., San Diego, CA 92121
Target Audience: Adults
Notes: Time, 15 approx.; Items, 12

Developed to measure subjects' attitudes toward women in managerial positions. A paper-and-pencil instrument that can be administered in a group or as a take-home questionnaire. Can be used as a practical tool or as a research instrument in management training situations, as a pre- and posttest to help increase one's self-awareness, or as the basis for discussions of biased or discriminatory behavior. This instrument is available in the *1985 Annual Handbook for Group Facilitators: Developing Human Resources*, published by University Associates.

13753
Sex Role Attitudes Scale. Osmond, Marie Withers; Martin, Patricia Yancey 1972
Descriptors: Adults; Background; Questionnaires; Rating Scales; *Self Evaluation (Individuals); *Sex Role; *Sex Stereotypes; Likert Scales
Identifiers: SRA
Availability: Marie Withers Osmond; Dept. of Sociology, Florida State University, Tallahassee, FL 32306
Target Audience: 18–64
Notes: Items, 80

The Sex-Role Attitudes Scale (SRA) is a 32-item Likert Scale that is aimed at gaining a better understanding of the opinions and feelings of persons toward the changing roles of men and women. The items are statements and the one taking the SRA responds to the item using a 5-point scale, from strongly disagree to strongly agree. There are 4 general components: (1) familial roles of males and females, (2) extra-familial roles of each sex, (3) stereotypes of male/female characteristics and behaviors, and (4) social change as related to sex roles. In addition to the 32 items, there are 48 questions asking for background information.

13754
The Idea Inventory: A Test of Irrational Beliefs. Kassinove, Howard 1977
Descriptors: Adults; Dogmatism; Elementary School Students; Elementary Secondary Education; *Emotional Response; *Opinions; Questionnaires; Rating Scales; Secondary School Students; *Self Evaluation (Individuals); Likert Scales
Identifiers: Irrational Belief Scale (Ellis)
Availability: Howard Kassinove; 10 Ingold Dr., Dix Hills, NY 11746
Grade Level: 4–12
Notes: Items, 33

This instrument uses a 3-point Likert Scale, and the test taker reacts to each statement by marking agree, uncertain, or disagree. The test was developed to measure how elementary students to adults reacted to irrational ideas. The inventory was part of a study which found that, based on rational-emotive theory, school mental health programs can be effective. Another source for the inventory is the *Journal of Community Psychology*; v5 p266-74, 1977.

13757
Quality of Life Dimensions. Flanagan, John C.
Descriptors: Adults; Interpersonal Relationship; *Life Satisfaction; Living Standards; Older Adults; Physical Fitness; *Quality of Life; Questionnaires; Rating Scales; Self Evaluation (Individuals); Socioeconomic Status; *Values
Availability: *Education;*v100 n3 p194-202, Spr 1980
Target Audience: 30; 50; 70
Notes: Items, 15

This instrument was used to define the main determinants of quality of life. It is an empirical approach, and 3 groups of Americans were surveyed: 30 year olds, 50 year olds, and 70 year olds. Both males and females were in the 3 age groups. The items covered physical and material well-being; relations with other people; social, community, and civic activities; personal development and fulfillment; and recreation. The adults were asked to respond to 2 questions: At this time in your life, how important is (the list of items)? and How well are your needs and wants being met in this regard? (for those aged 30, the question read How satisfied are you with your status in this respect?)

13795
Life Satisfaction Index. Neugarten, Bernice; And Others 1961
Descriptors: Check Lists; *Life Satisfaction; Middle Aged Adults; *Older Adults; Questionnaires; *Self Evaluation (Individuals); *Well Being
Identifiers: LSI
Availability: *Journal of Gerontology;*v16 n2 p134-43, Apr 1961
Target Audience: 50–90
Notes: Items, 18

The Life Satisfaction Index is an attitude inventory that is used to measure psychological well-being of older people. The subjects respond to statements about life in general, about which people feel differently, by checking agree, disagree, or not sure. The LSI was used for men and women aged 50 to 90.

13826
Kulm Mathematics Self-Concept Test. Kulm, Gerald 1973
Subtests: Satisfaction; Change
Descriptors: College Students; *Education Majors; *Elementary Education; Higher Education; *Mathematics; Pretests Posttests; *Self Concept; *Student Attitudes
Identifiers: TIM(K)
Availability: Tests in Microfiche; Test Collection, Educational Testing Service, Princeton, NJ 08541
Grade Level: 13–16
Notes: Items, 27

Developed to assess specific aspects of self-concepts of students enrolled in a mathematics course for prospective elementary school teachers. Designed for pre- and posttesting to assess the effects of a mastery learning approach used in the class.

13828
Social and Athletic Readjustment Rating Scale. Bramwell, Steven T.; And Others
Descriptors: *Athletes; *College Students; *Football; Higher Education; *Injuries; Rating Scales; Self Evaluation (Individuals)
Identifiers: SARRS
Availability: *Journal of Human Stress;*v1 n2 p6-20, Jun 1975
Grade Level: 13–17
Notes: Items, 57

This Social and Athletic Readjustment Rating Scale (SARRS) was used in a study at the University of Washington of the perception of life change events in athletic injuries. Those using the rating scale were college football players. The 57 experiences encountered by athletes were ranked by the football players. The players rank ordered the life events, including injuries, as how important the event was to each of them.

13841
Children's Perception of Sex Stereotyping in Elementary School. Sheridan, E. Marcia 1978
Descriptors: Bias; Elementary Education; *Elementary School Students; Questionnaires; *Sex Role; *Sex Stereotypes; *Student Attitudes

Availability: ERIC Document Reproduction Service; 3900 Wheeler Ave., Alexandria, VA 22304-5110 (ED159262, 26 pages)
Grade Level: 2–6
Notes: Items, 18

This instrument was developed to use with children to determine how children perceive sex roles related to school and classroom situations. The questions were read to the students who responded by marking a box on an answer sheet that visually represented only girls, only boys, mostly girls, mostly boys, or both boys and girls. The items were about activities involving strength or mechanical ability, activities related to domestic or academic ability, perceptions regarding negative treatment from teachers, perceptions regarding positive treatment from teachers, behavior, and intelligence.

13884
The Effective School Battery. Gottfredson, Gary D. 1984
Descriptors: *Educational Environment; *Secondary Education; Secondary School Students; Secondary School Teachers; *Student Attitudes; *Teacher Attitudes
Identifiers: ESB
Availability: Psychological Assessment Resources; P.O. Box 998, Odessa, FL 33556
Grade Level: 7–12
Notes: Time, 50 approx.

Instrument to assess climates of secondary schools. Can be used to identify a school's strengths and weaknesses, to develop improvement plans, and to evaluate improvement projects. To assess school climate, students and teachers answer questions about their school. Answers are analyzed by a computer. The student inventory has 4 parts: what about you, how do you spend your time, your school, and what do you think. The teacher inventory has 12 parts: background information, involvement of parents, classroom management and teaching practices, resources, job satisfaction, training and other activities, interaction with students, school rules and discipline, how different groups get along, personal safety, your opinions, and school climate.

13890
General Attitudes toward Mathematics. Merkel-Keller, Claudia 1974
Descriptors: *Grade 9; Junior High Schools; Junior High School Students; *Mathematics; Rating Scales; Sex Differences; *Student Attitudes
Identifiers: TIM(K)
Availability: Tests in Microfiche; Test Collection, Educational Testing Service, Princeton, NJ 08541
Grade Level: 9
Notes: Items, 25

Developed as part of a study to determine outcomes in mathematics in the affective and cognitive areas of students in grade 9. To determine outcomes in the affective domain, an attitude measure was constructed.

13891
Geriatric Depression Scale. Brink, T.L.; And Others 1982
Descriptors: Aging (Individuals); *Depression (Psychology); *Older Adults; Psychological Evaluation
Identifiers: GDS
Availability: Clinical Gerontologist;v1 n1 p37-43, Fall 1982
Target Audience: 65–90
Notes: Items, 30

A self-rating scale used to identify depression in elderly people. Items represent core of geriatric depression and include items on lowered affect, inactivity, irritability, withdrawal, distressing thoughts, and negative outlook on past, present, and future. A copy of the scale can also be found in *Journal of Psychiatric Research*; v17 n1 p37-49, 1983.

13892
Emig-King Attitude Scale for Students. Emig, Janet; King, Barbara 1979
Descriptors: Rating Scales; Secondary Education; Secondary School Students; *Student Attitudes; *Writing (Composition); *Writing Processes
Identifiers: New Jersey; The Research Instruments Project
Availability: ERIC Document Reproduction Service; 3900 Wheeler Ave., Alexandria, VA 22304 (ED236630, 12 pages)
Grade Level: 7–12
Notes: Time, 30 approx.; Items, 40

This scale contains 40 items and is designed to assess students' attitudes toward writing. The items represent 3 categories: preference for writing, perception of writing, and process of writing. Students circle 1 of 5 points on the scale, ranging from almost always to almost never. This instrument is a revision of the Emig Writing Attitude Scale (Student Version) constructed in 1977 for the New Jersey Writing Project.

13893
Emig-King Attitude Scale for Teachers. Emig, Janet; King, Barbara 1979
Descriptors: Adults; *Attitude Change; Inservice Teacher Education; Preservice Teacher Education; Rating Scales; *Teacher Attitudes; Writing (Composition); *Writing Instruction; Writing Processes
Identifiers: New Jersey; The Research Instruments Project
Availability: ERIC Document Reproduction Service; 3900 Wheeler Ave., Alexandria, VA 22304 (ED236629, 12 pages)
Target Audience: 18–64
Notes: Time, 30 approx.; Items, 50

This instrument is designed to measure attitudes toward writing and changes in attitudes toward writing held by preservice and inservice teachers. There are 50 statements representing 3 categories: preference for writing, perception of writing, and process of writing. Respondents circle 1 of 5 points on a scale ranging from almost always to almost never. This attitude scale is a revision of the Emig Writing Attitude Scale (Teacher Version) constructed for the New Jersey Writing Project in 1977.

13936
Teacher Role Survey. Maes, Wayne R.; Anderson, Darrell E. 1983
Descriptors: Adults; *Locus of Control; *Teacher Role; *Teachers
Identifiers: TRS
Availability: Wayne R. Maes; Counselor Education, University of New Mexico, 4021 Mesa Vista, Albuquerque, NM 87131
Target Audience: Adults
Notes: Items, 32

Designed to measure teacher expectancies for internal or external control of important aspects of the teacher role. Four categories of job satisfiers are represented in the measure: responsibility, recognition, attitudes of parents and society, and relations with teachers.

13943
RAM Scale, Revised. Wright, Claudia R. 1983
Descriptors: *College Students; Higher Education; Philosophy; *Values; Likert Scales
Availability: Claudia R. Wright; School of Communication, Research Div., P.O. Box 1211, Arcadia, CA 91006
Grade Level: 13–16
Notes: Items, 18

A Likert version of an instrument designed to measure students' philosophical orientations in terms of relative, absolute, or mixed biases or preferences toward issues dealing with reality (knowledge), methods, and values. For a forced-choice version, see TC012228.

13944
Preschool Play Materials Preference Inventory. Wolfgang, Charles H.; Phelps, Pamela 1983
Descriptors: Interest Inventories; *Play; Preschool Education; Toys; *Young Children
Availability: Early Child Development and Care;v12 p127-41, 1983
Target Audience: 3–5
Notes: Items, 20

The test administrator asks each child which of 2 paired toys he or she would prefer. Toys are categorized as sensory-motor play, symbolic play, fluid construction, structured construction, and letter and numbers.

13957
Attitude toward Energy Conservation Scale. Koballa, Thomas R. 1984
Descriptors: Adults; Elementary School Teachers; *Energy Conservation; Preservice Teacher Education; Rating Scales; *Teacher Attitudes
Availability: Journal of Research in Science Teaching;v20 n7 p709-23, Oct 1984
Target Audience: Adults

Developed to measure attitudes of teachers toward energy conservation. Developed using data from samples of preservice elementary teachers but is suggested for use with both preservice and inservice elementary teachers.

13962
Illinois Quality Schools Index. Illinois State Board of Education, Springfield, Program Planning and Development Section 1984
Descriptors: Educational Quality; *Elementary Secondary Education; *School Effectiveness; *School Surveys; State Programs
Identifiers: IQSI
Availability: ERIC Document Reproduction Service; 3900 Wheeler Ave., Alexandria, VA 22304 (ED251493, 72 pages)
Grade Level: 1–12

Designed for use by local school districts as the beginning of a process for developing and maintaining quality schooling. Uses a 5-step, 3-meeting schedule of activities in which a coordinator and a committee of school district

personnel, students, parents, and community members complete survey instruments, review the data, place items in a priority list, and summarize the findings. There are 8 instruments, each representing a characteristic of effective schools: leadership, mission, expectations, time on task, monitoring, basic skills, climate, parent-community participation. Respondents rate each characteristic on 2 scales: perception on whether the school or district is demonstrating the characteristic and the perception of the importance of the characteristic to quality education.

13966
Irenometer. Bardis, Panos D. 1984
Descriptors: Adolescents; Adults; *Peace; Rating Scales
Identifiers: *Irenology
Availability: Panos D. Bardis; Sociology Dept., University of Toledo, Toledo, OH 43606
Target Audience: 12–65
Notes: Items, 10

An attitude measure by which subjects assess their own values and attitudes concerning peace. Self-administered, 5-point rating scale.

13968
Vasectomy Scale: Attitudes. Bardis, Panos D. 1974
Descriptors: Adults
Identifiers: *Vasectomy
Availability: Society and Culture;v5 n2 p177-91, Jul 1974
Target Audience: Adults
Notes: Items, 25

Five-point agree/disagree Likert scale discussing issues related to vasectomy.

13969
A Violence Scale. Bardis, Panos D. 1973
Descriptors: Adults; *Violence
Availability: Journal of Political and Military Sociology;v1 n1 p121-46, Spr 1973
Target Audience: Adults
Notes: Items, 25

Five-point agree/disagree scale concerned with violence defined as words and actions aimed at property damage and personal injury. Items are concerned with punishing a child, war and rioting, criminal punishment.

13973
A Religion Scale. Bardis, Panos D. 1961
Descriptors: Adults; *Religion
Availability: Panos D. Bardis; Sociology Dept., University of Toledo, Toledo, OH 43606
Target Audience: Adults
Notes: Items, 25

A measure of agreement/disagreement with statements concerning religious issues such as church attendance, tithing, and prayer.

13974
A Pill Scale. Bardis, Panos D. 1969
Descriptors: Adults; *Contraception
Availability: Panos D. Bardis; Sociology Dept., University of Toledo, Toledo, OH 43606
Target Audience: Adults
Notes: Items, 25

A measure of agreement/disagreement with issues concerning birth control pills including restrictions, sin, decline of the family.

13976
Abortion Scale. Bardis, Panos D. 1972
Descriptors: *Abortions; Adults
Availability: Panos D. Bardis; Sociology Dept., University of Toledo, Toledo, OH 43606
Target Audience: Adults
Notes: Items, 25

A measure of agreement/disagreement with issues concerning abortion.

13977
Borromean Family Index: For Married Persons. Bardis, Panos D. 1975
Descriptors: Adults; *Family Life; *Spouses
Availability: Panos D. Bardis; Sociology Dept., University of Toledo, Toledo, OH 43606
Target Audience: Adults
Notes: Items, 18

A measure of attitudes toward one's own family spouse, and children, specifically the positive and negative aspects of family life, e.g., companionship, financial problems.

13978
Borromean Family Index: For Single Persons. Bardis, Panos D. 1975
Descriptors: Adults; *Family Life
Availability: Panos D. Bardis; Sociology Dept., University of Toledo, Toledo, OH 43606
Target Audience: Adults
Notes: Items, 15

A measure of the intensity of the attachment to one's family based on benefits or problems associated with family life.

13980
A Dating Scale. Bardis, Panos D. 1962
Descriptors: Adolescents; Beliefs; *Dating (Social)
Availability: Panos D. Bardis; Sociology Dept., University of Toledo, Toledo, OH 43606
Target Audience: 13–17
Notes: Items, 25

A measure of beliefs about dating. Covers adult supervision, going steady, sex.

13981
Erotometer. Bardis, Panos D. 1971
Descriptors: Adults; *Dating (Social); Interpersonal Relationship
Availability: Panos D. Bardis; Sociology Dept., University of Toledo, Toledo, OH 43606
Target Audience: Adults
Notes: Items, 50

A measure of feelings toward another in a heterosexual relationship.

13984
A Familism Scale. Bardis, Panos D. 1959
Descriptors: Adults; *Extended Family; Family Influence; *Family Involvement; Family Relationship; *Nuclear Family
Availability: Panos D. Bardis; Sociology Dept., University of Toledo, Toledo, OH 43606
Target Audience: Adults
Notes: Items, 16

A measure of agreement/disagreement with statements concerning nuclear and extended family integration. Items are concerned with obedience, children's contribution of earnings, and similarity of beliefs. Separate forms dealing with only the nuclear family or only the extended family are available.

13992
Energy Opinionnaire. Kuhn, David 1980
Subtests: Energy Conservation and Development; Public Responsibility and Government Controls
Descriptors: Citizenship Responsibility; *Energy Conservation; Federal Regulation; Government Role; High Schools; *High School Students
Availability: *The Journal of Environmental Education;*v15 n2 p42-44, 1983-84
Grade Level: 9–12
Notes: Items, 25

Developed to assess opinions of high school students on energy conservation and citizen responsibility and governmental role in conserving energy resources.

13998
Torabi-Veenker Alcohol Attitude Scale. Torabi, Mohammad R.; Veenker, C. Harold 1983
Subtests: Feeling; Belief; Intention to Act
Descriptors: Adults; *Alcoholic Beverages; *College Students; *Drinking; Higher Education; Likert Scales
Availability: Dr. Mohammad R. Torabi; 116 HPER, Indiana University, Bloomington, IN 47405
Grade Level: 13–16
Target Audience: 18–64
Notes: Items, 54

A Likert-type summated rating scale was developed to measure college students' attitudes toward alcohol use and abuse. Includes 3 subscales to measure feeling, belief, and intention to act.

14006
Supervisory Practices Inventory, Form A. Canfield, Judith S.; Canfield, Albert A. 1981
Descriptors: Administrator Attitudes; Adults; Business Administration; Occupational Tests; *Supervision; *Supervisory Methods
Availability: Humanics Media; 5457 Pine Cone Rd., La Crescenta, CA 92124
Target Audience: Adults
Notes: Items, 20

Designed to measure the emphasis that an administrator places on people, the task, or achieving results when performing the job of a supervisor and whether a laissez-faire, democratic, or autocratic style is predominant. A "dissonance score" also shows whether the administrators see themselves as functioning in a way they prefer or far from their own ideal of an administrator.

14031
School Climate Assessment of Learning Environments, Scale I. Sandrini, James V. 1982
Descriptors: Adults; Educational Environment; Elementary Secondary Education; *Individualized Instruction; Rating Scales; Student Teachers; *Teacher Attitudes; Teachers
Availability: ERIC Document Reproduction Service; 3900 Wheeler Ave., Alexandria, VA 22304 (ED214254, 32 pages)

Target Audience: Adults
Notes: Items, 30

Designed to assess a school's readiness for individualizing instruction. Consists of items representing beliefs about individualization of instruction, responded to by teachers on a 5-point agree/disagree scale.

14034
Language Attitude Inventory. Byrd, Marquita; Williams, Hampton S. 1981
Descriptors: Adults; *Black Dialects; Classroom Communication; Elementary Secondary Education; *Teacher Attitudes
Availability: ERIC Document Reproduction Service; 3900 Wheeler Ave., Alexandria, VA 22304 (ED213062, 15 pages)
Target Audience: Adults
Notes: Items, 15

A measure of teachers' attitudes toward the use of black dialect. Covers teachers' perceptions of the dialect itself and their perceptions of the usage of black dialect and its effects on students in the classroom.

14035
Youth Employment Questionnaire. Gilbert, Patricia J. 1980
Descriptors: *College Students; Higher Education; Job Skills; *Occupations; Rating Scales; Sex Role; *Sex Stereotypes; *Student Attitudes; Technical Institutes; Vocational Aptitude
Availability: ERIC Document Reproduction Service; 3900 Wheeler Ave., Alexandria, VA 22304 (ED193474, 70 pages)
Grade Level: 13–16

Designed to measure stereotypes people have concerning various jobs and worker traits. A series of work-related abilities are evaluated on a 5-point scale as being male or female, followed by a list of jobs to be rated similarly.

14036
Hawk Adolescent Literature Attitude Scale. Hawk, Jane Ward 1983
Descriptors: *Adolescent Literature; Adolescents; Adults; *Censorship; Parent Attitudes; Secondary Education; Secondary School Students; Student Attitudes; Teacher Attitudes
Availability: University Microfilms International; Dissertation Copies, P.O. Box 1764, Ann Arbor, MI 48106 (Order No. DA8402900)
Grade Level: 7–12
Notes: Items, 59

This scale was designed to measure the attitudes of educators, students, and parents toward potentially censorable topics found in literature read by adolescents. Six factors covered are interpersonal/intrapersonal conflicts, adherence to conventional stereotypes, sexual relationships, drug abuse, aggressive behavior and language, and commonly perceived traditional values. Items are rated on a 5-point scale, first as they pertain to required reading and again for self-selected reading.

14037
Student Behaviors Questionnaire. Brozo, William G.; Schmelzer, Ronald V. 1985
Descriptors: *College Students; Higher Education; Rating Scales; *Student Behavior; *Teacher Attitudes; *Teacher Student Relationship
Identifiers: SBQ
Availability: *Journal of College Student Personnel;*v26 n3 p229-34, May 1985
Grade Level: 13–16
Notes: Items, 57

Fifty-seven-item questionnaire requiring faculty members to rate student behaviors on a scale ranging from very undesirable to very desirable. Research using this scale could be useful in providing a basis for information given to students in academic assistance programs, providing a basis for mutual examination of educational goals and values of students and faculty, and encouraging more widespread use of this questionnaire.

14038
Course Orientations of Staff and Students: A Procedure for Curriculum Evaluation Questionnaire. Lynch, P.P.; And Others 1980
Descriptors: *Chemistry; *College Students; *Course Evaluation; Higher Education; Questionnaires; Sciences; Scientific Attitudes; Student Attitudes
Availability: *Higher Education;*v9 n4 p409-18, Jul 1980
Grade Level: 13–16
Notes: Items, 32

Designed to evaluate first-year science courses at a university level. Measures expectations of students, influences upon students, and aims of staff.

14047
Eating Attitudes Test. Garner, David M.; Garfinkel, Paul E. 1982

Descriptors: Adolescents; *Anorexia Nervosa; *Eating Habits; *Females; Rating Scales; Young Adults
Identifiers: EAT
Availability: Dr. David M. Garner; Toronto General Hospital, 101 College St., Toronto, Ontario M5G 9Z9 Canada
Target Audience: 13–25
Notes: Items, 26

Data suggest EAT is an objective and valid index of symptoms frequently seen in cases of anorexia nervosa. Has been used to detect abnormal eating habits in female adolescents and young adults. An earlier 40-item version can be found in *Psychological Medicine;* v9 p278, 1979.

14055
Scale for the Measurement of Attitudes toward the Social, Educational, and Economic Roles of Women. Arnold, Vanessa D. 1976
Descriptors: Adults; *Females; Rating Scales; *Sex Role
Availability: *Journal of Business Education;*p216-17, Feb 1976
Target Audience: Adults
Notes: Items, 35

Questionnaire designed to elicit attitudes toward women's role in society.

14072
Miner Sentence Completion Scale, Form H, Multiple Choice Version. Miner, John B. 1977
Descriptors: Adults; College Faculty; Counseling; *Employee Attitudes; Employees; *Motivation; Multiple Choice Tests; Occupational Tests; Professional Occupations; Work Attitudes
Availability: Organizational Measurement Systems Press; P.O. Box 81, Atlanta, GA 30301
Target Audience: Adults
Notes: Items, 40

A measure of an individual's bureaucratic motivation. For use in employee counseling and organizational development. Normative data derive from a sample of professors in business schools involved in teaching, writing, and consulting. A projective sentence completion version is also available (TC014073).

14073
Miner Sentence Completion Scale, Form P. Miner, John B. 1981
Subtests: Acquiring Knowledge; Independent Action; Accepting Status; Providing Help; Professional Commitment
Descriptors: Adults; College Faculty; Counseling; *Employee Attitudes; Employees; *Motivation; Occupational Tests; Professional Occupations; *Projective Measures; Work Attitudes
Availability: Organizational Measurement Systems Press; P.O. Box 81, Atlanta, GA 30301
Target Audience: Adults
Notes: Items, 40

A measure of an individual's professional motivation. Used for employee counseling and organizational development. Normative data derive from a sample of professors in business schools involved in teaching, writing, and consulting.

14108
Therapy Attitude Inventory. Eyberg, Sheila M. 1974
Descriptors: Adults; *Mothers; *Parent Child Relationship; Parenting Skills; Parent Workshops; *Program Evaluation; Therapy; Training
Availability: Sheila M. Eyberg; Oregon Health Sciences University, School of Medicine, Dept. of Medical Psychology, OP336, 3181 S.W. Sam Jackson Park Rd., Portland, OR 97201
Target Audience: Adults
Notes: Items, 12

A questionnaire eliciting the opinions of mothers involved in a program of training to help them improve their facilitative behaviors with their child. Covers mothers' feelings about the program, how much they have learned, and whether their relationship with the child has improved.

14129
Academic Motivation Scale. Baker, Robert W.; Siryk, Bohdan 1979
Descriptors: *College Freshmen; Higher Education; *Learning Motivation; Rating Scales
Availability: *Journal of College Student Personnel;*v25 n5 p459-64, Sep 1984
Grade Level: 13
Notes: Items, 20

Designed to measure academic motivation of college students. Uses items to reflect a variety of relevant behavioral outcomes taken from high school performance and from several points in the students' college careers. Used in several studies of college freshmen to assess scales reliability and validity. Scales of 46 items, 35 items, and 20 items are included in the article.

14139
The Affective Perception Inventory: College Level. Soares, Anthony T.; Soares, Louise M. 1985
Subtests: Self-Concept; Student-Self; English Perceptions; Mathematics Perceptions; Science Perceptions; Social Science Perceptions; Perceptions in the Fine Arts; Perceptions in the Humanities; College Perceptions
Descriptors: Affective Measures; *College Students; Higher Education; Intellectual Disciplines; Rating Scales; *Research Tools; *School Attitudes; *Self Concept Measures; Semantic Differential; *Student Attitudes
Availability: Soares Associates; 111 Teeter Rock Rd., Trumbull, CT 06611
Grade Level: 13-16
Notes: Time, 45 approx.; Items, 255

Primary purpose of the instrument is as a research tool. Instrument may also be used to describe present affective dimension of students and their interpersonal perceptions related to educational experiences, to determine perceptions of self as a person, self as a student, self in various academic disciplines and self in the school environment; to compare self-ratings with others' ratings; and to obtain an indirect measure of needs assessment programs. Scales measure attitudes toward the subject and individuals' feelings about their ability in the subject.

14148
Inventory of Career Attitudes. Pinkney, James W.; Ramirez, Marty 1985
Descriptors: *Career Planning; *Cultural Traits; High Schools; *High School Students; *Mexican Americans; Rating Scales; *Student Attitudes
Identifiers: *Chicanos; ICA
Availability: *Journal of College Student Personnel;*v26 n4 p300-05, Jul 1985
Grade Level: 11-12
Notes: Items, 28

Developed to study the career planning assumptions and beliefs of Chicano high school students and the cultural influences that affect their career planning process. Findings from using the inventory in a research study indicated Chicano students were less realistic in their career-planning attitudes than white students.

14149
Attitudes toward College Inventory. Johanson, Roger P.; Vopava, Judy R. 1985
Descriptors: *College Attendance; *Disadvantaged Youth; *Economically Disadvantaged; High Schools; *High School Students; Rating Scales; *Student Attitudes
Identifiers: ATCI
Availability: *Journal of College Student Personnel;*v26 n4 p339-42, Jul 1985
Grade Level: 9-12
Notes: Items, 30

Developed to assess high school students' attitudes toward college. Used in a study that investigated college attendance of economically disadvantaged students.

14232
Statistics Attitude Survey. Roberts, Dennis M. 1980
Descriptors: College Students; Higher Education; *Mathematics; Predictive Measurement; *Statistics
Availability: Dennis M. Roberts; Pennsylvania State University, College of Education, Carpenter Bldg., University Park, PA 16802
Grade Level: 13-16
Notes: Items, 33

This scale is designed to sample attitudes of students taking a beginning statistics course, for the purpose of predicting performance in statistics, especially at the introductory level. It uses a 5-point agree/disagree Likert-type format.

14237
Classroom Teachers' Self-Reported Attitudes toward Mainstreaming Emotionally Disturbed Children. Vacc, Nicholas A.; Kirst, Nancy 1977
Descriptors: Adults; Depression (Psychology); Elementary Education; Elementary School Teachers; *Emotional Disturbances; Hyperactivity; *Mainstreaming; Rating Scales; *Teacher Attitudes; Withdrawal (Psychology)
Availability: *Elementary School Journal;*v77 n4 p309-17, Mar 1977
Target Audience: Adults
Notes: Items, 20

A measure of elementary school teachers' attitudes toward the mainstreaming of emotionally disturbed children, those who exhibit deviant behavior such as hyperactivity, impulsive or depressive behavior, or withdrawal. Ratings were made on a 5-point Likert scale. Items covered special class versus mainstreaming; effects of mainstreaming on the nonhandicapped children, and effects of mainstreaming on the regular classroom teacher.

14281
Sex Equity Opinion Survey. Frary, Robert B.; And Others 1985
Descriptors: Adults; Females; Feminism; Opinions; *Sex Bias; Sex Discrimination; Surveys; Women Faculty
Identifiers: *Sex Equity
Availability: *Educational Researcher;*v14 n2 p12-17, Feb 1985
Target Audience: Adults
Notes: Items, 15

This 4-point agree/disagree scale covers professional versus homemaking issues; equity issues in education; verbal forms of sex bias; and women in professions. Data were gathered from a sample of college-affiliated nonstudent, AERA members.

14284
Attitudes toward Statistics. Wise, Steven L. 1985
Subtests: Attitude toward Course; Attitude toward the Field
Descriptors: *College Students; Higher Education; Pretests Posttests; *Statistics; *Student Attitudes
Identifiers: ATS
Availability: Steven Wise; Ed 4, 26 Teachers College, University of Nebraska, Lincoln, NE 68588
Grade Level: 13-16
Notes: Items, 29

Constructed to provide a measure of attitudes held by college students toward an introductory course in statistics. Items were designed to be attitudinal questions, to be as answerable on the first day of class as at the end of the course, and to measure the 2 domains of attitudes toward the course and toward the use of statistics in their field of study. Inventory may prove useful in evaluating courses or the effects of changes in course structure. May also serve as a measure in identifying influences on student achievement and on the development of positive student attitudes toward statistics and research.

14286
Heathington Primary Attitude Scale. Heathington, Betty S. 1975
Descriptors: Early Childhood Education; Elementary School Students; Independent Reading; *Primary Education; Rating Scales; *Reading; Recreational Reading
Availability: Alexander, J. Estill, and Filler, Ronald Claude; *Attitude and Reading: Reading Aides Series.*Newark, DE: International Reading Assn., 1976
Grade Level: 1-3
Notes: Items, 20

Uses a rating scale composed of faces ranging from happy to unhappy to measure attitudes toward free reading in the classroom, organized reading in the classroom, reading at the library or at home, other recreational reading, and general reading.

14287
Heathington Intermediate Attitude Scale. Heathington, Betty S. 1975
Descriptors: Elementary Education; Elementary School Students; Independent Reading; *Intermediate Grades; *Reading; Recreational Reading
Availability: Alexander, J. Estill, and Filler, Ronald Claude; *Attitude and Reading: Reading Aides Series.*Newark, DE: International Reading Assn., 1976
Grade Level: 4-6
Notes: Items, 20

Uses a rating scale composed of faces ranging from happy to unhappy to measure attitudes toward reading free time in the classroom, organized reading in the classroom, reading at the library, reading at home, other recreational reading, and general reading. Uses a 5-point (face) agree/disagree format.

14302
Alcohol Expectancy Questionnaire-III (Adult). Brown, Sandra 1981
Subtests: Global, Positive Changes; Enhanced Sexual Performance and Experience; Physical and Social Pleasure; Increased Social Assertiveness; Relaxation and Tension Reduction; Arousal and Power
Descriptors: Adults; *Alcoholic Beverages; *Drinking
Availability: Sandra A. Brown; Psychological Services, Veterans Administration Medical Center, 3350 La Jolla Village Dr., San Diego, CA 92161
Target Audience: Adults
Notes: Items, 120

Series of statements concerning effects of alcohol to which subjects respond based on their personal thoughts, feelings, and beliefs about alcohol at the time they complete the questionnaire. A 90-item version questionnaire was used in a research study with college students to examine their alcohol expectancies as a function of their drinking patterns and to compare expectancies to demographic/background variables for their ability to predict problematic and nonproblematic drinking patterns.

14308
Affective Work Competencies Inventory. Brauchle, Paul; Petty, Gregory C. 1983
Subtests: Ambition; Self-Control; Organization; Enthusiasm; Conscientiousness (Lack of)
Descriptors: *Administrators; Adults; Aspiration; Behavior Patterns; *Employees; Job Skills; Organization; Personality; Self Control; *Teachers; Vocational Education; *Work Attitudes
Identifiers: AWCI; Work Attitudes Inventory
Availability: Gregory C. Petty; University of Tennessee, Knoxville, TN 37996-3400
Target Audience: Adults
Notes: Items, 45

The scale is des,igned to measure work behaviors, attitudes, and characteristics of industrial workers, supervisors, and vocational educators. It is a self-report, Likert-type questionnaire. These work behaviors are said to be important for work success. Information on the scale can be found in *Educational and Psychological Measurement;* v43 n2 p603-09, Sum 1983.

14328
T.A. Survey: Trustworthiness Attitude Survey. Cormack, Robert W.; Strand, Alan L.
Descriptors: Adults; *Credibility; *Job Applicants; *Personality Traits; *Personnel Selection; Psychological Evaluation
Identifiers: *Honesty; PASS; Personnel Assessment Selection System
Availability: Psychological Surveys Corp.; 900 Jorie Blvd., Ste. 130, Oak Brook, IL 60521
Target Audience: Adults
Notes: Time, 15 approx.; Items, 118

Designed to measure attitudes and personality characteristics related to trustworthiness. Developed as a company inhouse placement tool and is administered and scored within companies licensed by the test publisher. May be used in combination with A.I. Survey and E.S. Survey in the Personnel Assessment Selection System (PASS) or may be used with A.I. Survey in the Personnel Assessment Selection System II (PASS II). There is also a Personnel Assessment Selection System III with youth norms that consists of a no-template, instant, graded 100-question digest of the T.A. Survey, A.I. Survey, and additional D.A. (Drug Attitude) questions designed as a projective attitude trust-risk screening instrument for part-time/hourly candidates.

14330
A.I. Survey: Alienation Index Survey. Cormack, Robert W.; Strand, Alan L. 1982
Descriptors: Adults; *Alienation; *Job Applicants; *Personality Traits; *Personnel Selection; Psychological Evaluation
Identifiers: PASS; Personnel Assessment Selection System
Availability: Psychological Surveys Corp.; 900 Jorie Blvd., Ste. 130, Oak Brook, IL 60521
Target Audience: Adults
Notes: Items, 52

Designed to identify alienated attitudes of job applicants toward employers, supervisors, coworkers, work conditions, and benefits and salary. A preemployment survey designed to be administered, scored, and interpreted by personnel or human resources staff licensed by the test publisher. May be used in combination with T.A. Survey, and E.S. Survey in the Personnel Assessment Selection System (PASS). Or may be used with T.A. Survey in the Personnel Assessment Selection System II (PASS II). There is also a Personnel Assessment Selection System III with youth norms that consists of a no-template, instant, graded 100-question digest of the T.A. Survey, A.I. Survey, and additional D.A. (Drug Attitude) questions designed as a projective attitude trust risk screening instrument for part-time/hourly candidates.

14341
Kilmann-Saxton Culture-Gap Survey. Kilmann, Ralph H.; Saxton, Mary J. 1983
Descriptors: Adults; *Cultural Influences; Group Behavior; *Group Dynamics; Social Values; *Work Attitudes
Availability: XICOM Incorporated; Sterling Forest, Tuxedo, NY 10987
Target Audience: Adults
Notes: Items, 28

A measure of the social and motivational factors present in the environment of a work group. Items cover intergroup communication, socializing within the group, peer pressure to conform, receptivity to change, dividing work tasks fairly, competition. Used to identify forces outside of policies and rules that affect work group morale and performance.

14361
Small Business Assessment. Rensis Likert Associates, Ann Arbor, MI 1984

Descriptors: Adults; Employee Attitudes; Group Dynamics; Job Satisfaction; *Organizational Climate; *Small Businesses; Supervisory Methods
Availability: Rensis Likert Associates, Inc.; 3001 S. State St., Ste. 401, Ann Arbor, MI 48104
Target Audience: Adults
Notes: Items, 60

An inventory derived from Likert's Survey of Organizations (TC012028), designed to measure organizational climate, including group functioning; supervisory leadership; and job satisfaction. Items are general and could be applied to many types of businesses.

14377
Personal Problem-Solving Inventory. Heppner, P. Paul
Subtests: Problem-Solving Confidence; Approach-Avoidance Style; Personal Control
Descriptors: Adults; *Problem Solving; Rating Scales; *Self Evaluation (Individuals)
Identifiers: PSI
Availability: Keller, Peter A., and Ritt, Lawrence G., eds.; *Innovations in Clinical Practice: A Source Book.*Volume 1. Sarasota, FL: Professional Resource Exchange, 1982
Target Audience: Adults
Notes: Items, 35

Basic purpose is to assess people's perceptions of their problem-solving behaviors and attitudes. Is a self-rating questionnaire, and results should not be considered synonymous with actual problem-solving skills. Assesses how individuals perceive themselves generally reacting to personal problems in their daily life. Has been used primarily as a research tool and with groups of people. The publisher of *Innovations in Clinical Practice: A Source Book*, is Professional Resource Exchange, P.O. Box 15560, Sarasota, FL 33579. This instrument was included in this volume by permission of the original publisher and can be found also in *Journal of Counseling Psychology*; v29 n1 p66-75, 1982.

14379
Parent and Teacher Rating Forms for the Assessment of Hyperkinesis in Children. Conners, C. Keith
Descriptors: Adolescents; Children; *Hyperactivity; *Minimal Brain Dysfunction; Parent Attitudes; Rating Scales; Teacher Attitudes
Availability: Keller, Peter A., and Ritt, Lawrence G., eds.; *Innovations in Clinical Practice: A Source Book.*Volume 1. Sarasota, FL: Professional Resource Exchange, 1982
Target Audience: 3–17

Useful in assessment of children diagnosed as hyperkinetic resulting from minimal brain dysfunction. May also be useful to clinician in identifying other symptoms which appear as factors on the scale. The parent's questionnaire consists of 48 items and assesses 5 primary factors: conduct problems, learning problems, psychosomatic, impulsive hyperactive, and anxiety. The teacher's questionnaire has 28 items and assesses 3 primary factors: conduct problems, hyperactivity, and inattentive-passive. The publisher of *Innovations in Clinical Practice: A Source Book*, is Professional Resource Exchange, P.O. Box 15560, Sarasota, FL 33579.

14383
Current Symptom Checklist for Children. Walker, C. Eugene
Descriptors: *Affective Behavior; *Behavior Problems; *Children; Parent Attitudes; *Psychological Evaluation; Psychotherapy; Questionnaires
Availability: Keller, Peter A., and Ritt, Lawrence G., eds.; *Innovations in Clinical Practice: A Source Book.*Volume 2, Sarasota, FL: Professional Resource Exchange, 1983
Target Audience: 6–12
Notes: Time, 10 approx.; Items, 71

Developed for use in an outpatient clinic for children to serve as an interview guide during the initial diagnostic assessment of child therapy cases. Questionnaire is completed by child's parents. Questionnaire is to serve only as a guide to interviewing child and makes no claims for reliability, validity, or other psychometric properties. The publisher of *Innovations in Clinical Practice: A Source Book*, is Professional Resource Exchange, P.O. Box 15560, Sarasota, FL 33579.

14416
Children of Alcoholics Screening Test. Jones, John W. 1983
Descriptors: Adolescents; Adults; *Affective Measures; *Alcoholism; Children; Parent Child Relationship; Screening Tests
Identifiers: CAST
Availability: Camelot Unlimited; 17 N. State St., Ste. 1222, Dept. 18, Chicago, IL 60602
Target Audience: 6–35
Notes: Time, 10 approx.; Items, 30

Measures children's attitudes, feelings, perceptions, and experiences related to their parent's drinking behavior. Assesses children's psychological distress, perceptions of drinking-related marital discord between the parents, attempts to control a parent's drinking, efforts to escape from the alcoholism, exposure to drinking-related family violence, tendencies to perceive parents as alcoholic, and desire for professional counseling. Inventory can be used to identify children of alcoholics, to assist in the diagnosis of a parent's alcoholism, as a clinical counseling tool, and as a valid and reliable research instrument.

14430
The Children's Fear Expression and Research Survey. Davies, Michael H. 1982
Descriptors: *Affective Measures; *Childhood Attitudes; Elementary Education; *Elementary School Students; *Fear; Self Evaluation (Individuals)
Identifiers: FEARS; Self Report Measures
Availability: ERIC Document Reproduction Service; 3900 Wheeler Ave., Alexandria, VA 22304 (ED260092, 18 pages.)
Grade Level: 2–6
Notes: Items, 24

Self-report measure designed to meet current psychometric standards and to be used in both clinical and research settings. The measure contains 4 components: death and destruction, social acceptance, social conflict, and imagination. Age difference analysis indicated that death and destruction fears decreased with age, but social acceptance fears increased.

14432
Hogan Personnel Selection Series: Sales Potential Inventory. Hogan, Robert; Hogan, Joyce 1985
Subtests: Validity Scale; Reliability; Stress Tolerance; Service Orientation; Sales Potential
Descriptors: Adults; *Career Counseling; Interpersonal Competence; Job Applicants; Motivation; Objective Tests; *Personnel Selection; *Salesmanship; *Sales Occupations; *Screening Tests; Values
Availability: National Computer Systems; Professional Assessment Services, P.O. Box 1416, Minneapolis, MN 55440
Target Audience: Adults
Notes: Items, 218

Used to assist psychologists and personnel professionals in personnel screening and vocational counseling settings. Assesses interpersonal attitudes, values, and motivations to help predict and identify types of people who will perform well in various roles in an organization. Vocational counselors can use the inventory to evaluate the effectiveness of training in specialized areas and to help an individual's vocational development in specific occupational areas. The Sales Potential subtest aids in identifying individuals who are persistent, persuasive, socially skilled, and self-starting.

14433
Hogan Personnel Selection Series: Managerial Potential Inventory. Hogan, Robert; Hogan, Joyce 1985
Subtests: Validity Scale; Reliability; Stress Tolerance; Service Orientation; Managerial Potential
Descriptors: Adults; *Career Counseling; Decision Making Skills; Interpersonal Competence; Job Applicants; Leadership Qualities; *Managerial Occupations; Motivation; Objective Tests; *Personnel Selection; *Screening Tests; Values
Identifiers: HPSS
Availability: National Computer Systems; Professional Assessment Services, P.O. Box 1416, Minneapolis, MN 55440
Target Audience: Adults
Notes: Items, 223

Used to assist psychologists and personnel professionals in personnel screening and vocational counseling settings. Assesses interpersonal attitudes, values, and motivations to help predict and identify types of people who will perform well in various roles in an organization. Vocational counselors can use the inventory to evaluate the effectiveness of training in specialized areas and to help an individual's vocational development in specific occupational areas. Managerial potential subtest identifies individuals with leadership ability, planning, and decision-making skills.

14434
Hogan Personnel Selection Series: Clerical Potential Inventory. Hogan, Robert; Hogan, Joyce 1985
Subtests: Validity Scale; Reliability; Stress Tolerance; Service Orientation; Clerical Potential
Descriptors: Adults; *Career Counseling; *Clerical Occupations; Interpersonal Competence; Job Applicants; Motivation; Objective Tests; *Personnel Selection; *Screening Tests; Values
Identifiers: HPSS
Availability: National Computer Systems; Professional Assessment Services, P.O. Box 1416, Minneapolis, MN 55440
Target Audience: Adults
Notes: Items, 215

Used to assist psychologists and personnel professionals in personnel screening and vocational counseling settings. Assesses interpersonal attitudes, values, and motivations to help predict and identify types of people who will perform well in various roles in an organization. Vocational counselors can use the inventory to evaluate the effectiveness of training in specialized areas and to help an individual's vocational development in specific occupational areas. The Clerical Potential subtest identifies individuals willing to follow directions, pay attention to details, and communicate accurately and well. This scale is associated with overall rated performance in clerical jobs and reflects individuals who show compliance, maturity, and industriousness.

14435
Hogan Personnel Selection Series: Prospective Employee Potential Inventory. Hogan, Robert; Hogan, Joyce 1985
Subtests: Validity Scale; Reliability; Stress Tolerance; Service Orientation
Descriptors: Adults; *Career Counseling; Interpersonal Competence; Job Applicants; Motivation; Objective Tests; *Personnel Selection; *Screening Tests; Values
Identifiers: HPSS
Availability: National Computer Systems; Professional Assessment Services, P.O. Box 1416, Minneapolis, MN 55440
Target Audience: Adults
Notes: Items, 198

Used to assist psychologists and personnel professionals in personnel screening and vocational counseling settings. Assesses interpersonal attitudes, values, and motivations to help predict and identify types of people who will perform well in various roles in an organization. Vocational counselors can use the inventory to evaluate the effectiveness of training in specialized areas and to help an individual's vocational development in specific occupational areas.

14441
View Sharing Inventory. Guerney, Bernard, Jr. 1982
Descriptors: Adults; Interpersonal Relationship; *Marriage Counseling; Questionnaires; *Spouses
Identifiers: *Premarital Counseling; VSI
Availability: Keller, Peter A., and Ritt, Lawrence G., eds.; *Innovations in Clinical Practice: A Source Book.*Volume 4, Sarasota, FL: Professional Resource Exchange, 1985
Target Audience: Adults

Developed for use by mental health professionals, clergy, and others to aid couples in preparation for marriage or in problem prevention. May also be useful for couples engaged in marital counseling. Used to provide clients with a rationale for discussing areas of agreement or disagreement to identify areas where changes are desired or to provide counselor with a means of selecting areas for discussion. The inventory consists of 2 parts. Part 1 assesses the client's views in 10 areas: leisure-vacations, job-community, financial, friends-relatives, sex, children, housekeeping-grooming, religion, communication, and roles or division of labor. Part 2 covers 2 areas: the way in which a couple interacts with each other and attitudes and behaviors not directed toward the partner but which could have a significant impact on the relationship now or in the future. The publisher of *Innovations in Clinical Practice: A Source Book* is Professional Resource Exchange, P.O. Box 15560, Sarasota, FL 33579.

14445
Supervisory and Leadership Beliefs Questionnaire. Rao, T. Venkateswara
Subtests: Benevolent; Critical; Self-Dispensing
Descriptors: *Administrator Attitudes; Adults; *Leadership Styles; Professional Development; Rating Scales; *Self Evaluation (Individuals); *Supervisory Methods
Availability: Pfeiffer, J. William, and Goodstein, Leonard D., eds.; *The 1986 Annual: Developing Human Resources.*San Diego, CA: University Associates, 1986
Target Audience: Adults
Notes: Items, 9

A rating scale used to determine a supervisor's style of supervising and interacting with subordinates. Scores are indicative of the strength of the beliefs or orientations underlying each 1 of 3 styles: benevolent, critical, or self-dispensing. This inventory is intended for professional development work and is not intended for indepth personal growth, psychodiagnostic use, or therapeutic work. The instrument is available from University Associates, 8517 Production Avenue, San Diego, CA 92121.

14446
Motivational Analysis of Organizations-Behavior. Pareek, Udai
Subtests: Achievement; Affiliation; Influence; Control; Extension; Dependence

Descriptors: *Administrator Characteristics; Adults; *Employee Attitudes; *Interprofessional Relationship; Professional Development; Rating Scales; *Work Environment
Identifiers: MAOB
Availability: Pfeiffer, J. William, and Goodstein, Leonard D., eds.; *The 1986 Annual: Developing Human Resources.*San Diego, CA: University Associates, 1986
Target Audience: Adults
Notes: Items, 60

Enables respondents to identify which of 6 primary factors motivates their behavior in their organizational settings. Instrument can be used in managerial and supervisory training, as part of a human resource development or team-building program, and for personal growth and development. It is not intended for indepth personal awareness, psychodiagnostic use, or therapeutic work. Can also be used in organization development and consulting work to obtain group profiles, to search for organizational factors to explain the profiles, to develop organizational strategies to improve the profiles, and to develop individual strategies to increase employees' effectiveness. The instrument is available from University Associates, 8517 Production Avenue, San Diego, CA 92121.

14454
Parent Education Design Scale. Bridges, K. Robert 1985
Descriptors: Adults; *Parent Education; Rating Scales
Availability: *Educational and Psychological Measurement;*v45 n4 p729-35, Win 1985
Target Audience: Adults
Notes: Items, 42

Scale developed to identify the outstanding issues involved in parent education program design and to measure the attitudes of participants toward these issues. Seven factors were identified and concerned curriculum content, attendance, enrollment of course clientele, program development and administration, and program outcomes.

14455
Computer Attitude Scale. Bannon, Susan H.; And Others 1985
Descriptors: Adolescents; Adults; *Computers; Rating Scales
Availability: *Educational and Psychological Measurement;*v45 n3 p679-81, Fall 1985
Target Audience: 16-65
Notes: Items, 14

Developed to determine attitudes toward computers among students, teachers, educational administrators, and other educators. Two factors were identified: cognitive and affective.

14458
Attitudes toward Bilingual Education. Krus, David J.; Brazelton, J.M. 1983
Descriptors: Adults; *Bilingual Education
Identifiers: ABE
Availability: *Educational and Psychological Measurement;*v45 n3 p693-98, Fall 1985
Target Audience: Adults
Notes: Items, 23

Used in a study to present additional evidence for the scale's construct validity and to assess its potential to provide valid discrimination between a defined group of bilingual education proponents and a group randomly selected from the general population.

14461
Adult Career Concerns Inventory. Super, Donald E.; And Others 1985
Descriptors: Adults; *Attitude Change; *Career Development; *Interest Inventories; Midlife Transitions; Self Evaluation (Individuals); *Vocational Interests
Identifiers: ACCI
Availability: Consulting Psychologists Press; 577 College Ave., Palo Alto, CA 94306
Target Audience: Adults
Notes: Items, 61

Consists of 61 statements of career concerns based on Donald Super's theory of life stages. The stages are exploration, establishment, maintenance, disengagement, and a special scale on career change status. Inventory can be self-scored to yield a profile based on the clusters of career development tasks of most importance to the individual. Inventory may be valuable for counselors in measuring subject's career stage and growth. Researchers may use it to examine the impact of an individual's life stage on such factors as productivity, creativity, and turnover.

14473
ASSETS: A Survey of Students' Educational Talents and Skills-Later Elementary. Grand Rapids Public Schools, MI 1978
Descriptors: *Elementary School Students; *Enrichment Activities; Gifted; Intermediate Grades; Needs Assessment; Parent Attitudes; Rating Scales; Student Attitudes; *Student Interests; *Talent Identification; Teacher Attitudes
Availability: Learning Publications; P.O. Box 1326, Holmes Beach, FL 33509
Grade Level: 4-6

Helps in identification of children's gifts and talents and in planning enrichment activities and experiences for these students. Provides a means of surveying individual student interests and creative abilities as well as academic strengths and talents. Can serve a variety of purposes such as selecting students for special programs, individualizing curricula in the classroom, enhancing curriculum planning, discovering knowledge and skills students bring to the classroom, and helping parents and teachers to discuss student's needs. There are separate forms for parents, students, and teachers to fill out. Information from all 3 sources is combined in a single profile and can be viewed together to obtain a thorough and balanced assessment of each student's educational talents and skills, including academic aptitude, motivational characteristics, creative thinking ability, and visual and performing arts aptitude/talent.

14474
ASSETS: A Survey of Students' Educational Talents and Skills-Early Elementary. Grand Rapids Public Schools, MI 1979
Descriptors: Elementary School Students; *Enrichment Activities; Gifted; Needs Assessment; Parent Attitudes; *Primary Education; Rating Scales; Student Attitudes; *Student Interests; *Talent Identification; Teacher Attitudes
Availability: Learning Publications; P.O. Box 1326, Holmes Beach, FL 33509
Grade Level: K-3

Helps in identification of children's gifts and talents and in planning enrichment activities and experiences for these students. Provides a means of surveying individual student interests and creative abilities as well as academic strengths and talents. Can serve a variety of purposes such as selecting students for special programs, individualizing curricula in the classroom, enhancing curriculum planning, discovering knowledge and skills students bring to the classroom, and helping parents and teachers to discuss student's needs. There are separate forms for parents, students, and teachers to fill out. Information from all 3 sources is combined in a single profile and can be viewed together to obtain a thorough and balanced assessment of each student's educational talents and skills, including academic aptitude, motivational characteristics, creative thinking ability, and visual and performing arts aptitude/talent.

14494
Children's Intervention Rating Profile. Witt, J.C.; Elliott, S.N. 1985
Descriptors: Adolescents; *Antisocial Behavior; Behavior Modification; Children; *Intervention; Rating Scales; Student Attitudes; *Student Behavior; *Student Evaluation of Teacher Performance; Teachers
Identifiers: CIRP
Availability: *Journal of School Psychology;*v24 n1 p23-35, Spr 1986
Target Audience: 6-18
Notes: Items, 7

A scale to measure children's reactions to 12 interventions by a teacher for classroom misbehavior involving a male student who either destroyed property or frequently talked out of turn. Written at a fifth grade reading level.

14495
Scales for Investigation of the Dual-Career Family, Revised. Glass, Carol R.; And Others 1982
Descriptors: Adults; *Dual Career Family; Family Involvement; Family Life; *Females; Life Satisfaction; Marriage; Occupational Aspiration; Parent Role; Responsibility; Self Concept; Spouses
Availability: *Measurement and Evaluation in Counseling and Development;*v18 n3 p120-27, Oct 1985
Target Audience: Adults
Notes: Items, 44

A revision of the original Pendleton et al. scale developed in 1980. See *Journal of Marriage and the Family*; v42 p269-76, 1980. Thirteen new items were added. Covers career aspiration, traditional versus equalitarian marriage type, domestic responsibility, importance of career, satisfaction with dual career roles, and self-image in dual-career roles. Items are responded to only by the female spouse in the dual-career family.

14510
Achievement Identification Measure. Rimm, Sylvia B. 1985
Subtests: Competition; Responsibility; Control; Achievement; Communication; Respect
Descriptors: *Elementary School Students; Elementary Secondary Education; Gifted; Identification; *Parent Attitudes; Rating Scales; *Secondary School Students; *Underachievement
Identifiers: AIM
Availability: Educational Assessment Service, Inc.; W6050 Apple Rd., Watertown, WI 53094
Grade Level: K-12
Notes: Time, 20 approx.; Items, 77

Developed to identify students who have characteristics of underachievers. Purpose of inventory is to determine the degree to which children exhibit the characteristics of underachievers, so that preventive or remedial efforts can be administered. Parents complete the inventory by marking the responses that best describe their child's present behavior and environment. There is no time limit for completing the questionnaire. It usually takes about 20 minutes for each child.

14514
Protestant Ethic Scale. Mirels, Herbert; Garrett, James B. 1971
Descriptors: Rating Scales; *Work Attitudes; *Work Ethic
Availability: *Journal of Consulting and Clinical Psychology;*v36 n1 p40-44, 1971
Target Audience: Adults
Notes: Items, 19

Series of statements to be rated from strongly agree to strongly disagree which views the Protestant work ethic as a dispositional variable. Used in a research project in which attempt was made to characterize psychological meaning of work ethic in terms of its relationship with other personality variables and with vocational interests. The scale is also available from Herbert Mirels, Department of Psychology, Ohio State University, 1885 Neil Ave., Columbus, OH 43210.

14525
Student Athlete Recruitment Decision Making Survey. Mathes, Sharon; Gurney, Gerald 1984
Descriptors: *Athletics; *College Choice; *Higher Education; Questionnaires
Availability: *Journal of College Student Personnel;*v26 n4 p327-33, Jul 1985
Grade Level: 13-16
Notes: Items, 114

A survey designed to identify the factors that influenced the selection of a college by female and male athletes receiving full and partial scholarships for participating in revenue- and nonrevenue-producing sports. The sample consisted of 182 students who all attended the same large midwestern university. Results showed that, contrary to popular belief, the athletes were more influenced by the academic characteristics of their prospective college than by its athletic aspects. One of the purposes of this questionnaire was to use the results as an aid in the athletic recruitment process.

14526
Attitudes toward Self. Carver, Charles S. 1983
Subtests: Overgeneralization; High Standards; Self-Criticism
Descriptors: Adults; *Depression (Psychology); Rating Scales; *Self Evaluation (Individuals)
Identifiers: ATS; Self Punitiveness
Availability: *Journal of Abnormal Psychology;*v92 n3 p330-37, 1983
Target Audience: Adults
Notes: Items, 18

Developed to use in a research study in which 3 variables were examined to determine whether they are possible contributors to the depressive tendency to be self-punitive. The 3 factors are holding high standards, making harsh self-judgments, and overgeneralizing self-judgments.

14535
Dimensions of Self-Concept, Form H-College. Michael, William B.; And Others 1985
Subtests: Level of Aspiration; Anxiety; Academic Interest and Satisfaction; Leadership and Initiative; Identification versus Alienation
Descriptors: Academic Aspiration; Anxiety; *College Students; *Educational Environment; Higher Education; Identification (Psychology); Learning Motivation; Rating Scales; *Self Concept; *Self Concept Measures; Student Motivation
Identifiers: DOSC
Availability: Educational and Industrial Testing Service; P.O. Box 7234, San Diego, CA 92107
Grade Level: 13-16
Notes: Items, 80

Developed to measure noncognitive factors associated with self-esteem or self-concept in a school setting. Each item was prepared to represent an activity or attitude in the school environment. This is a self-report instrument that reflects perceptions students have of their place within the educational setting. Instrument serves 2 purposes: to identify students who may have difficulty in their schoolwork because of low self-esteem and to diagnose, for purposes of guidance or counseling, those dimensions and associated activities that might contribute to low self-esteem and to impaired learning capabilities.

14540
The Manifest Needs Questionnaire. Bramson Parlette Associates, Berkeley, CA 1980
Descriptors: Achievement Need; Adults; Affiliation Need; *Employment; *Motivation; Personal Autonomy; Rating Scales; *Work Attitudes
Identifiers: Dominant Behavior; MNQ
Availability: Bramson-Parlette Associates; P.O. Box 10213, North Berkeley Station, Berkeley, CA 94709
Target Audience: Adults
Notes: Items, 20

A measure of the relative power of 4 work-related motivating factors: need for achievement, need for affiliation, need for autonomy, and need for dominance.

14550
The Facts on Aging Quiz, Alternate Form. Palmore, Erdman B.
Descriptors: Adults; *Aging (Individuals); Aging Education; *Knowledge Level; Older Adults; Social Bias
Identifiers: FAQ
Availability: The Gerontologist;v21 n4 p431-37, 1981
Target Audience: Adults
Notes: Items, 25

Designed for use in assessing knowledge level about the aging process for use in stimulating discussion, for identifying misconceptions, and for measuring the effects of education in gerontology. Also measures bias toward the aged. Also available in Erdman B. Palmore's *The Facts on Aging Quiz: A Handbook of Uses and Results.* New York: Springer Publishing Company, 1988.

14551
Feedback Questionnaire. Miller, Mark J.; Springer, Thomas P. 1986
Descriptors: *Career Guidance; Cognitive Processes; College Students; *Computer Assisted Testing; Costs; Higher Education; Cognitive Dissonance
Identifiers: DISCOVER
Availability: Journal of College Student Personnel;v27 n2 p142-46, Mar 1986
Grade Level: 13-16
Notes: Items, 14

Designed to measure student satisfaction with a computerized vocational guidance system called DISCOVER. Measure is based on the theory of cognitive dissonance that concerns how behaviors such as paying for a service affect attitudes. In this case, the hypothesis was that, the more money clients spend for the use of the DISCOVER system, the more worthwhile they will perceive the experience to be. The scale items cover usefulness of the system, amount of learning, interest.

14555
Employer Attitudes toward Hiring Cooperative Education Students. Kane, Stephen Mark 1981
Descriptors: College Students; *Cooperative Education; *Employer Attitudes; Higher Education; Personnel Selection
Identifiers: TIM(N)
Availability: Tests in Microfiche; Test Collection, Educational Testing Service, Princeton, NJ 08541
Grade Level: 13-16
Notes: Items, 33

Five-point Likert-type measure of the attitudes of employers involved in cooperative education programs to cooperative education itself. Factors identified were development (items related to employer responsibility, career development, etc.); cost effectiveness; recruitment; communication; and benefits. Additional items elicit background information on the employer's company and history of involvement with cooperative education.

14556
Reading Preference Survey. Bundy, Barbara Ann 1983
Descriptors: Elementary School Students; *Intermediate Grades; Rating Scales; *Reading Attitudes; Reading Interests
Availability: University Microfilms International; 300 N. Zeeb Rd., Ann Arbor, MI 48106 (Order No. DA8312392)
Grade Level: 4-6
Notes: Items, 44

Developed for research for a doctoral degree. Purpose was to develop a valid and reliable survey instrument to assess the group reading preferences of students in grades 4, 5, and 6 and to use the instrument to examine the relationship between grade, sex, and reading preference. General categories of reading preferences included history, biography, science, how-to-do-it or craft books, fairy tales, sports, mystery, jokes, riddles, puzzles, adventure, animals, and poetry.

14563
Speech Dialect Attitudinal Scale. Mulac, Anthony 1974
Descriptors: Adults; *Dialects; Semantic Differential; *Speech Communication; Speech Evaluation; Status
Identifiers: SDAS
Availability: Anthony Mulac; Communication Studies Program, University of California, Santa Barbara, CA 93106
Target Audience: Adults
Notes: Items, 12

A semantic differential consisting of 12 pairs of bipolar adjectives evaluated on a 7-point scale. It is designed to quantify listener attitudes that result from variations in the dialect of a speaker. Factor analysis identified 3 independent dimensions: sociointellectual status, aesthetic quality, and dynamism.

14564
Teacher Contingency Scale. Kennelly, Kevin 1975
Descriptors: Discipline; Elementary Education; Elementary School Students; Grade 6; Helplessness; *Negative Reinforcement; *Positive Reinforcement; *Student Attitudes; Student Behavior; *Teacher Behavior
Availability: Kevin J. Kennelly; Dept. of Psychology, North Texas State University, Denton, TX 76203
Grade Level: 6
Notes: Items, 40

This scale was devised to measure students' perceptions of relationships between students' good and poor behaviors and teachers' rewards or punishments that follow whether rewards/punishments are contingent/noncontingent upon student behaviors. Ten items show teachers as contingently rewarding, 10 as contingently punitive, 10 as noncontingently rewarding, 10 as noncontingently punitive. Students indicate whether behaviors are very false to very true on a 5-point scale. May be related to concept of learned helplessness. Information on validity and reliability of the scale can be found in *Psychology in the Schools;* v22 n4 p465-69, Oct 1985.

14568
Beliefs about Computers Scale. Ellsworth, Randy; Bowman, Barbara E. 1982
Descriptors: Beliefs; College Students; *Computers; *Higher Education
Availability: The Computing Teacher; v10 n4 p32-34, 1982
Grade Level: 13-16
Notes: Items, 17

A series of questions about computers for use as a scale to measure junior and senior college students' beliefs. Norm sample consisted of computer science and biology majors. Responses are on a 5-point scale from strongly agree to strongly disagree.

14578
Teacher's Evaluation of Student's Creativity. Runco, Mark A. 1984
Descriptors: Adults; *Creativity; Observation; *Rating Scales; Teacher Attitudes; Teachers; Likert Scales
Availability: Perceptual and Motor Skills;v59 p711-17, 1984
Target Audience: Adults
Notes: Items, 25

This measure of a teacher's subjective judgment of a child's creativity was used in a study of the validity of tests of divergent thinking. The instrument consists of a list of synonyms for creativity. The teacher indicates, on a scale of 1 through 7, whether a typical child exhibits characteristics typical of each descriptive word from rarely to extremely. The scale can be reconstructed from the information contained in the journal source.

14580
Students' Attitude toward the Mentally Handicapped. Campbell, N. Jo; And Others 1982
Descriptors: Disabilities; Elementary Education; *Elementary School Students; *Mental Retardation; Middle Schools; Social Attitudes; *Student Attitudes
Identifiers: Harth (R); Multidimensional Attitude Scale Mental Retardation; TIM(M)
Availability: Tests in Microfiche; Test Collection, Educational Testing Service, Princeton, NJ 08541
Grade Level: 4-8
Notes: Items, 40

Designed for use with upper elementary and middle school students to measure attitudes toward mainstreamed mentally handicapped students. The upper elementary form assesses 4 components of these attitudes: overfavorableness; integration-segregation opinion; social distance, and private rights concerned with mentally handicapped persons. The middle school form measures all of the above except overfavorableness and includes another component measuring subtle derogatory evaluations of retarded people.

14584
Study Attitudes and Methods Survey, Short Form. Michael, William B.; And Others 1985
Descriptors: *College Students; Counseling Techniques; Higher Education; Rating Scales; Secondary Education; *Secondary School Students; *Student Attitudes; Student Motivation; *Study Habits
Availability: Educational and Industrial Testing Service, P.O. Box 7234, San Diego, CA 92107
Grade Level: 7-16
Notes: Items, 90

Developed to assess motivational, noncognitive dimensions that are related to school achievement and that contribute to a student's performance beyond those factors measured by traditional ability tests. May be used to identify those students who might benefit from individual counseling by diagnosing those habits and attitudes that inhibit a student from achieving full academic potential. Results can provide aid in working on students' study habit improvement.

14614
Organizational Change Readiness Scale. Conner, Daryl R. 1983
Descriptors: Adults; *Change Agents; Diagnostic Tests; *Employee Attitudes; Occupational Tests; *Organizational Change; Readiness
Identifiers: OCRS
Availability: University Associates; 8517 Production Ave., San Diego, CA 92121
Target Audience: Adults
Notes: Items, 23

Designed as an aid in dealing with the human aspects of an organization's adaptation to change. Can be used as a diagnostic tool to determine the overall acceptance level of an organizational change and to identify the resistance factors present that should be addressed when developing an implementation strategy.

14625
Liberal Arts Career Interest Inventory. Flores-Esteves, Manuel 1984
Descriptors: *College Students; Higher Education; *Interest Inventories; *Liberal Arts; Majors (Students); *Vocational Interests
Identifiers: LCA II
Availability: Manuel Flores-Esteves; 11926 Laurelwood Dr., Ste. 6, Studio City, CA 91604
Grade Level: 13-16
Notes: Items, 186

Designed to assist liberal arts majors in choosing fields of interest that are applicable to their degree or major. Accompanies the book *In Search of Liberal Arts Careers*, by Viking-Penguin Publishing Co., 1985. A profile is plotted and compared to 14 related fields of interest.

14627
Claydon College Drinking Questionnaire. Claydon, Peter D. 1982
Descriptors: *Alcohol Education; Alcoholic Beverages; Alcoholism; Background; Citizenship Responsibility; *College Students; *Drinking; Fraternities; Higher Education; Knowledge Level; Responsibility; Sororities
Availability: Journal of Alcohol and Drug Education;v31 n1 p51-64, Fall 1985
Grade Level: 13-16
Notes: Items, 80

Five-part survey used to evaluate the effectiveness of alcohol education programs. It covers demographic information, knowledge of alcohol and alcoholism, responsible and irresponsible attitudes, and attitudes about sorority/fraternity membership and alcohol. This group was used because it has been identified as being at risk for developing alcohol-related problems.

14634
Study Behavior Inventory, Form D. Mueller, Richard J. 1984
Descriptors: Adults; Adult Students; Higher Education; *Metacognition; Rating Scales; Self Evaluation (Individuals); Student Behavior; *Study Habits
Identifiers: Study Habits Inventory (Wrenn)
Availability: ERIC Document Reproduction Service; 3900 Wheeler Ave., Alexandria, VA 22304 (ED254535, 28 pages)
Target Audience: Adults
Notes: Items, 46

An inventory developed to measure the study habits and behaviors of adult students in a variety of college settings. It covers general study habits and behaviors, reading and note taking techniques, coping with examinations. Data were collected on over 1,000 students. Statements about general study attitudes and behavior are rated on a 4-point frequency scale. It is the third revision on an instrument first developed by C. Gilbert Wrenn.

14641
High School Survey on Drugs. Pascale, Pietro 1985

Descriptors: *Drug Abuse; Drug Education; *Drug Use; High Schools; *High School Students; Secondary Education; *Student Attitudes
Availability: ERIC Document Reproduction Service; 3900 Wheeler Ave., Alexandria, VA 22304 (ED255558, 8 pages)
Grade Level: 9–12
Notes: Time, 15; Items, 72

Developed to assess the drug attitudes of and usage, by high school students, as a determination of drug education program needs. Thirteen drugs are covered by questions assessing prevalence, frequency of usage, and perception of harmfulness. Questions also solicit information on family drug use.

14644
Opinion Survey toward Statistics and Research Methodology. Wolfe, Mary L. 1985
Descriptors: Academic Failure; *College Students; Higher Education; Mathematics Anxiety; Nursing Education; *Research Design; *School Attitudes; *Statistics; Student Attitudes; Student Interests
Identifiers: *Nursing Students
Availability: ERIC Document Reproduction Service; 3900 Wheeler Ave., Alexandria, VA 22304 (ED254556, 13 pages)
Grade Level: 13–16
Notes: Items, 16

An instrument designed to measure general attitudes toward research design and statistics for use with students in an undergraduate nursing research course. Factors were fear of failure, challenge and relevance, lack of interest, intrinsic value.

14645
Comfortability Scale in Special Education. Norlander, Key A.; Reich, Melvyn 1984
Descriptors: Adults; Emotional Disturbances; Knowledge Level; Mental Retardation; *Self Esteem; Self Evaluation (Individuals); Special Education; *Special Education Teachers; Teachers
Availability: ERIC Document Reproduction Service; 3900 Wheeler Ave., Alexandria, VA 22304 (ED252599, 26 pages)
Target Audience: Adults
Notes: Items, 44

A self-evaluation instrument measuring special-education teachers' perceptions of comfort or self-confidence in their skills, ability, and knowledge of tasks related to teaching special education students and with pertinent issues. Each item is rated on a 7-point Likert scale from not comfortable to very comfortable. Subscales are written information, team approach, mental retardation, emotional disturbance, and several as yet unnamed scales.

14653
Evaluation Guidelines for Multicultural-Multiracial Education: Teacher Questionnaire. National Study of School Evaluation, Falls Church, VA 1973
Descriptors: Administrator Attitudes; Community Role; High Schools; Instructional Materials; *Multicultural Education; *Program Evaluation; Questionnaires; Racial Attitudes; Racial Composition; School Community Relationship; *Secondary Education; *Secondary School Teachers; *Teacher Attitudes; Teaching Methods
Availability: National Study of School Evaluation; 5201 Leesburg Pike, Falls Church, VA 22041
Target Audience: Adults

Designed to accompany a series of guidelines for conducting a self-evaluation of the multicultural-multiracial education program in a secondary school. Individual agree-disagree questionnaires cover attitudes toward multicultural-multiracial education, teacher and administrator attitudes toward multicultural-multiracial education as perceived by the teacher, use of related curriculum materials, and racial tension.

14654
Evaluation Guidelines for Multicultural-Multiracial Education: Student. National Study of School Evaluation, Falls Church, VA 1973
Descriptors: High Schools; High School Students; *Multicultural Education; *Program Evaluation; Questionnaires; Racial Attitudes; Racial Composition; *Secondary Education; *Secondary School Students; *Student Attitudes; Teacher Attitudes
Availability: National Study of School Evaluation; 5201 Leesburg Pike, Falls Church, VA 22041
Grade Level: 7–12

Designed to accompany a series of guidelines for conducting a self-evaluation of the multicultural-multiracial education program in a secondary school. This agree/disagree format questionnaire covers racial differences within the school; curriculum materials, favoritism; staff and student attitudes toward multiracial education as perceived by the students.

14669
Student Perceptions of Teaching Effectiveness. Burdsal, Charles A.; Bardo, John W. 1986
Descriptors: *College Students; Course Content; Course Organization; Curriculum; Grading; Higher Education; Instructional Materials; Multivariate Analysis; *Student Attitudes; *Student Evaluation of Teacher Performance; Teacher Attitudes
Identifiers: SPTE
Availability: Educational and Psychological Measurement;v46 n1 p63-79, Spr 1986
Grade Level: 13–16
Notes: Items, 56

A Likert-type agree/disagree scale responded to by students. It is designed to measure student perceptions of teacher attitudes toward students; work load; value of the course to students; course organization/structure; grading quality; level of learning materials. It differs from other instruments in that it uses a multivariate approach.

14717
Thinking about My School—A Practical Tool for Assessing Student Attitudes and Feelings about Their School. Whitmore, Joanne Rand 1985
Subtests: Power; Social; Work; Teachers; Liking for School
Descriptors: *Educational Environment; *Elementary School Students; *Intermediate Grades; Learning Motivation; Power Structure; *School Attitudes; Social Environment; *Student Attitudes; Teacher Effectiveness
Identifiers: TAMS
Availability: United Educational Services; P.O. Box 605, East Aurora, NY 14052
Grade Level: 4–6
Notes: Time, 30 approx.; Items, 47

Questionnaire designed to measure student perceptions of the school environment and feelings about their school. Developed to be a practical tool to assess student attitudes and perceptions that may be useful in program planning, designing interventions with problem students, or engaging students in discussions of feelings and desires relative to their school experience.

14721
Perceptions of Parental Role Scales. Gilbert, Lucia A.; Hansen, Gary R. 1982
Subtests: Cognitive Development; Handling of Emotions; Social Skills; Norms and Social Values; Physical Health; Personal Hygiene; Survival Skills; Health Care; Material-Food, Clothing, Shelter; Meeting the Emotional Needs of the Child; Child Care; Interface between Child and Social Institutions; Interface between Child and the Family
Descriptors: Adults; Cognitive Development; Daily Living Skills; Emotional Development; Family Life; Interpersonal Competence; *Parent Child Relationship; *Parent Role; Physical Health; Rating Scales; Social Values
Identifiers: PPRS
Availability: Marathon Consulting and Press; P.O. Box 09189, Columbus, OH 43209-0189
Target Audience: Adults
Notes: Time, 15 approx.; Items, 78

Designed to measure perceived parental responsibilities. The 78 items assess 13 parental areas in 3 major areas: teaching the child, meeting the child's basic needs, and serving as a connection between the child and the family and the child and other social institutions. The instrument is self-administered. Respondents indicate how important they believe each item is as a parental responsibility on a 5-point rating scale.

14724
Computer Anxiety Questionnaire. Toris, Carol 1984
Descriptors: Anxiety; *College Students; *Computer Literacy; Computers; Higher Education; Knowledge Level; Projective Measures
Identifiers: *Computer Anxiety
Availability: ERIC Document Reproduction Service; 3900 Wheeler Ave., Alexandria, VA 22304 (ED254540, 19 pages.)
Grade Level: 13–16
Notes: Time, 10

This questionnaire measure of computer anxiety is in 4 parts: the projective Toris Draw-a-Computer Test, a computer knowledge test, a measure of behaviors toward computers, and another of attitudes toward computers. It has been used with students at the College of Charleston in South Carolina. The knowledge level test is based on information presented in a college level introductory computing course.

14758
Love and Liking Scales. Rubin, Zick 1969
Descriptors: Adults; College Students; *Dating (Social); Interpersonal Competence; Significant Others; *Love

Identifiers: *Liking
Availability: Journal of Personality and Social Psychology;v16 n2 p265-73, 1970
Target Audience: Adults
Notes: Items, 27

The love scale measures romantic love as an interpersonal attitude with 3 components affiliative and dependent need, a predisposition to help, an orientation of exclusiveness and absorption. Respondent indicates level of agreement/disagreement on a 9-point scale. Each scale is scored separately. The liking scale measures favorable evaluation, respect, and perception that the other is similar to oneself. The scale items were administered together for study purposes.

14759
Scale to Measure Attitudes toward Physicians and Primary Medical Care. Hulka, Barbara S.; And Others 1970
Descriptors: Adults; Medical Services; *Physicians
Availability: Medical Care; v3 n5 p429-36, Sep-Oct 1970
Target Audience: Adults
Notes: Items, 41

This scale is designed to measure attitudes toward medical care and satisfaction with it. Items cover professional competence, personal qualities and cost/convenience. Data were collected on mothers attending a pediatric clinic at Duke University. The scale uses an agree/disagree format.

14768
Women as School District Administrators Survey. Educational Research Service, Arlington, VA 1981
Subtests: General Acceptance of Women as School District Administrators; Stereotypic Feminine Barriers to Full-Time Employment; Possession by Women of Traits of Effective School District Administrators
Descriptors: Administrators; Adults; Females; *Sex Stereotypes; Surveys; *Women Faculty
Identifiers: WASDA
Availability: WEEA Publishing Center; Education Development Center, 55 Chapel St., Newton, MA 02160
Target Audience: Adults
Notes: Items, 21

Survey used to measure the strength of sex-role stereotypes that might act against women in the position of school district administrator. Based on the theory that sex-role stereotypes may lead to the exclusion of women in management positions. About half of the items reflect women favorably, the other half unfavorably. The favorable items are reverse scored so as to use a consistent numerical base. Also measures 3 factors: General Acceptance of Women as School District Administrators, Stereotypic Feminine Barriers to Full-Time Employment, and Possession by Women of the Traits of Effective School District Administrators. The survey is a modification of the items used in the Women as Managers Scale: A Measure of Attitudes toward Women in Management Positions (WAMS).

14770
Career Education Affective Assessment Questionnaire, Grades 1-3. Minnesota Research Coordinating Unit for Vocational Education, Minneapolis, MN 1975
Descriptors: *Career Education; Elementary School Students; *Primary Education; Questionnaires; *Student Attitudes
Identifiers: TIM(M)
Availability: Tests in Microfiche; Test Collection, Educational Testing Service, Princeton, NJ 08541
Grade Level: 1–3
Notes: Items, 57

Group-administered questionnaire designed to measure students' attitudes toward the world of work. Most of the items have 3 possible responses. The response choice of the first half consists of 3 faces ranging in expression from happy to neutral to sad. The teacher or test administrator reads each item to the students.

14771
Career Education Affective Assessment Questionnaire, Grades 4-6. Minnesota Research Coordinating Unit for Vocational Education, Minneapolis, MN 1974
Descriptors: *Career Education; *Elementary School Students; Intermediate Grades; *Student Attitudes
Identifiers: TIM(M)
Availability: Tests in Microfiche; Test Collection, Educational Testing Service, Princeton, NJ 08541
Grade Level: 4–6
Notes: Time, 45 approx.; Items, 105

Designed to measure the feelings and attitudes of students toward a wide range of concepts related to the world of work. Students respond to each item on a 3-point scale.

14778
Nuclear Weapons Policies Questionnaire. Nelson, Linden L.; Slem, Charles M. 1984
Descriptors: *College Students; *Disarmament; Higher Education; *Nuclear Warfare; Questionnaires; *Student Attitudes
Availability: ERIC Document Reproduction Service; 3900 Wheeler Ave., Alexandria, VA 22304 (ED257699, 19 pages)
Grade Level: 13–16
Notes: Items, 18
This questionnaire was designed to investigate relationships between attitude toward arms control and beliefs about nuclear weapon effects, probability of war, Soviet goals, and the importance of nuclear arms superiority.

14796
Employee Effectiveness Profile. Pfeiffer, William J. 1986
Descriptors: Administration; Adults; Employee Attitudes; Job Performance; *Occupational Tests; *Personnel Evaluation; Personnel Management; Profiles; Rating Scales; Supervisors; Supervisory Methods; Work Attitudes
Availability: University Associates; 8517 Production Ave., San Diego, CA 92121
Target Audience: Adults
Notes: Items, 19
This profile is designed to assist managers in identifying the overall effectiveness of individual employees. It is completed by the supervisor. Uses a variation of the Productivity-Potential Model to describe employees as stars, workhorses, marginal, deadwood, trainees, or problem children. Uses a 4-point Likert-type agree/disagree scale. Strategies are suggested to deal with each type of employee.

14805
Salience Inventory. Super, Donald E.; Nevill, Dorothy D. 1985
Descriptors: Adolescents; Adults; *Career Counseling; Children; *Life Style; *Values; Work Attitudes
Identifiers: Life Roles
Availability: Consulting Psychologists Press; 577 College Ave., Palo Alto, CA 94306
Target Audience: 12–65
Notes: Time, 45; Items, 170
This inventory is scored for participation in, commitment to, and value expectations of 5 major life roles: student, worker, homemaker (spouse and parent); leisureite, and community service. It was designed to assess the relative importance of 5 major life roles in individuals and cultures. May be used for individual counseling as well as survey work.

14809
The OD Kit. Training House, Inc., Princeton, NJ 1984
Descriptors: Administrators; Adults; Business Communication; Career Planning; *Industrial Training; Job Performance; Leadership; *Management Development; Motivation; Needs Assessment; *Occupational Tests; Organizational Climate; Organizational Communication; *Organizational Development; Personnel Management; Planning; Productivity; Self Evaluation (Groups); Time Management; Vocational Evaluation; Work Attitudes
Availability: Training House, Inc.; P.O. Box 3090, Princeton, NJ 08543
Target Audience: Adults
This kit includes assessments, surveys, and self-inventory exercises for use in training sessions; to identify strengths and weaknesses of a work group during the needs analysis that precedes a management development program; for personnel management and career planning. Instruments cover organizational climate, time management, motivation, leadership, management style, work attitudes, productivity, communication, performance review, job orientation, career planning goals.

14824
Forms for Behavior Analysis with Children. Cautela, Joseph R.; And Others 1983
Descriptors: *Adolescents; Anxiety; Assertiveness; *Behavior Problems; *Children; *Clinical Diagnosis; Fear; Medical Case Histories; Parent Attitudes; Physical Health; Rating Scales; Records (Forms); Reinforcement; Student Behavior
Availability: Research Press; 2612 N. Mattis Ave., Champaign, IL 61820
Target Audience: 6–17
These forms are part of a compilation for use in assessing children's problems and in generating treatment prescriptions for use in clinical work with children and adolescents. Included are instruments that measure behavior, reinforcement, assertiveness, tension and anxiety, fear, medical history, physical complaints, parent reactions, and school behavior. Several instruments are used during intervention to assess behaviors, motivation, and progress.

Some are completed by children, others by parent, school, or personnel or therapy givers. They may be copied as needed for clinical use.

14827
Teacher Attitude Inventory. Whitmore, Joanne Rand 1985
Descriptors: Adults; Classroom Techniques; *Educational Philosophy; Research Tools; *Teacher Attitudes; Teacher Behavior; *Teachers; Teaching Methods; Teaching Styles
Identifiers: TAI
Availability: United Educational Services; P.O. Box 605, East Aurora, NY 14052
Target Audience: Adults
Notes: Time, 10; Items, 24
Designed for use as an indicator of teacher attitudes concerning philosophical issues and educational practices. Can be used to determine a teacher's instructional style, indicate need for faculty development or provide a research tool for investigating practices within the school system. Teachers indicate their position on a continuum of 2 dichotomous styles, traditional teacher-centered or experimental-flexible behaviors concerning rigidity, control, professionalism, and individualism.

14844
Personal Resource Assessment Battery. Aposhyan, Joseph 1985
Descriptors: Adults; Antisocial Behavior; *Career Planning; Cognitive Ability; *Intelligence Tests; Personality Traits; Reading Comprehension; Self Evaluation (Individuals); Values; Visual Perception
Availability: Palmer Testing Service; 93 Main St., Andover, MA 01810
Target Audience: 18–65
Notes: Time, 20
This untimed scale is designed to measure mental ability, perceptual ability, reading comprehension, occupational interest, personality traits and deviances, moral attitudes or values. It is said to correlate with the Wonderlic Personnel Test and the Wechsler Adult Intelligence Scale for I.Q. A technical manual is not offered. The test is mailed to individuals free of charge. The test is then returned to the publisher for scoring. Separate fees are charged for scoring for I.Q. and for the other factors. Said to be useful for career planning.

14847
Bulimia Attitude Survey. Kapoor, Sandy 1986
Descriptors: Adults; *Bulimia; Rating Scales; *Significant Others
Identifiers: TIM(M)
Availability: Tests in Microfiche; Test Collection, Educational Testing Service, Princeton, NJ 08541
Target Audience: Adults
Notes: Time, 30 approx.; Items, 30
Developed to measure attitudes toward supporting the recovery of a bulimic and managing dilemmas and situations produced by involvement with a bulimic. Scoring is designed so that a high score indicates a favorable attitude toward helping a bulimic.

14868
Irrational Beliefs Test, Revised. Jones, R. Gainer 1977
Descriptors: Adults; *Affective Measures; *Beliefs; Rating Scales; Social Values
Identifiers: IBT; Irrational Beliefs (Ellis)
Availability: Test Systems International; P.O. Box 18347, Wichita, KS 67218
Target Audience: Adults
Notes: Time, 15 approx.; Items, 100
Designed to measure the extent to that an individual has incorporated certain socially communicated values or beliefs that are essentially irrational and inconsistent. Based on Ellis' irrational belief system. Uses 5-point agree/disagree scale. Contains reliability and validity statistics.

14904
Parent Behavior Form, Elementary. Worrell, Leonard; Worrell, Judith 1986
Subtests: Acceptance; Active Involvement; Equalitarianism; Cognitive Independence; Curiosity; Cognitive Competence; Lax Control; Conformity; Achievement; Strict Control; Punitive Control; Hostile Control; Rejection
Descriptors: Behavior Patterns; *Childhood Attitudes; Child Rearing; Children; Elementary Education; *Elementary School Students; *Parent Child Relationship; Parenting Skills; Personality; Rating Scales; *Rejection (Psychology)
Identifiers: Acceptance; PBF; TIM(N)
Availability: Tests in Microfiche; Test Collection, Educational Testing Service, Princeton, NJ 08541
Grade Level: 3–8
Notes: Items, 117

This version of the Parent Behavior Form uses all 13 subscales with simplified wording. Each scale consists of 9 items of parenting behavior. The scales correlate positively and negatively with acceptance and are arranged roughly on an acceptance-rejection dimension. Form C-B (TC014905) is similar, using only 10 scales. Measures child's perception of parent behavior. Measures the presence of various positive and negative parenting behaviors.

14905
Parent Behavior Form, Form C-B. Worrell, Leonard; Worrell, Judith 1986
Subtests: Acceptance; Active Involvement; Cognitive Independence; Curiosity; Cognitive Competence; Lax Control; Conformity; Achievement; Strict Control; Punitive Control
Descriptors: Behavior Patterns; *Childhood Attitudes; Child Rearing; Children; Elementary Education; *Elementary School Students; *Parent Child Relationship; Parenting Skills; Personality; Rating Scales; *Rejection (Psychology)
Identifiers: Acceptance; PBF; TIM(N)
Availability: Tests in Microfiche; Test Collection, Educational Testing Service, Princeton, NJ 08541
Grade Level: 3–8
Notes: Items, 90
This version of The Parent Behavior Form is for elementary school students. It has 10 scales. Each scale consists of 9 items of parenting behavior. Measures child's perceptions of parent behavior. The scales correlate positively and negatively with acceptance and are arranged roughly on an acceptance-rejection dimension. This version has simplified wording. It differs from the elementary version (TC014904) in that it omits 3 scales, one that is equivalent to Active Involvement (Equalitarianism) and Hostile Control and Rejection said to have low frequency in a normal child population. Measures the presence of various positive and negative parenting behaviors.

14910
Cognitive Self-Management Test. Rude, Stephanie 1980
Descriptors: *Ability; Adults; Change; Cognitive Processes; *Competence; *Depression (Psychology); *Females; Negative Reinforcement; Positive Reinforcement; Self Esteem; Self Evaluation (Individuals)
Identifiers: TIM(N)
Availability: Tests in Microfiche; Test Collection, Educational Testing Service, Princeton, NJ 08541
Target Audience: Adults
Notes: Items, 26
This scale was designed to determine feelings of how capable a person is when he or she is ready to undertake a new task or move into a new situation and also whether the thinking and self-examination going on at this time is positive or negative. The scale was designed primarily for use with depressed women. Subscales are positive focus; systematic problem solving and task efficacy; self-blame; and reasonable goal setting.

14920
Values Inventory: A Process for Clarifying Institutional Culture. Whitcomb, David B.; Deshler, David
Descriptors: Adults; *College Environment; College Faculty; College Role; Decision Making; *Faculty College Relationship; Higher Education; *Institutional Characteristics; *Organizational Climate; Questionnaires; School Personnel; State Universities; *Values
Identifiers: *California State University Long Beach
Availability: ERIC Document Reproduction Service; 3900 Wheeler Ave., Alexandria, VA 22304 (ED252639, 11 pages)
Target Audience: Adults
Notes: Time, 60 approx.; Items, 25
An open-ended questionnaire used to interview 83 faculty and staff at California State University, Long Beach about perceptions of institutional culture, values, and issues. The Values Inventory was part of a project that sought to (1) identify institutional values shaping decision making and (2) promote awareness of value issues in higher education. After analyzing the results of the questionnaire, it was concluded that it would be useful for administrators in higher education as a barometer of organizational culture, as a catalyst for value-laden dialogue, and as a bridge to new possibilities of perceptions for the institution.

14926
Faculty and Student Attitudes toward the Mixed-Age College Class. Mishler, Carol; Davenport, Margaret 1984
Descriptors: *Adult Students; *Age Differences; Classroom Environment; *College Faculty; *College Students; Higher Education; *Student Attitudes; Student Characteristics; *Teacher Attitudes

Availability: ERIC Document Reproduction Service; 3900 Wheeler Ave., Alexandria, VA 22304 (ED250988, 47 pages)
Grade Level: 13–16
Target Audience: Adults

A survey of the attitudes of students and teachers at 7 University of Wisconsin campuses toward mixed-age college courses. Approximately 200 faculty members and 1,000 students (60 percent under 25) participated in the study. Results indicate that both students and faculty prefer the age-mix in classes. Faculty cited an improved intellectual environment and more mature class discussion as some of the reasons for their preference. Students felt, among other reasons, that their classes were more interesting. This survey is comprised of 2 parts: a Faculty Opinion Survey and a Student Opinion Survey.

14928
Vocational Opinion Index Transition System. Associates for Research in Behavior, Philadelphia, PA 1976
Descriptors: Adults; *Disadvantaged; *Employee Attitudes; Employment Patterns; Motivation; Occupational Tests; *Spanish Speaking; *Vocational Education
Identifiers: VOI; VOITS
Availability: ARBOR, Inc.; The Science Center, 3401 Market St., Philadelphia, PA 19104
Target Audience: Adults
Notes: Items, 23

This diagnostic and prescriptive system was designed to help vocational training staff to determine individuals' attitudes, perceptions, and motivations that impact on their ability to get and hold a job. Learning activities designed to improve job holding skills and attitudes are included. Training for personnel planning to use the system, is suggested. Norms were based on a disadvantaged population. A Spanish version is available.

14938
Inventory of Affective Aspects of School. Haladyna, Thomas; Shaughnessy, Joan 1982
Subtests: Attitudes toward School; Attitudes toward Language Arts; Attitudes toward Mathematics; Attitudes toward Science; Attitudes toward Social Studies
Descriptors: Educational Environment; *Elementary School Students; Elementary Secondary Education; Language Arts; Mathematics; School Administration; *School Attitudes; Sciences; *Secondary School Students; Social Studies; *Student Attitudes; *Teacher Attitudes; Teaching (Occupation)
Identifiers: IAAS; TIM(M)
Availability: Tests in Microfiche; Test Collection, Educational Testing Service, Princeton, NJ 08541
Grade Level: 4–12
Notes: Time, 30 approx.

Three versions of this instrument measure attitudes of students in grades 4, 7, and 9 and teachers. They are said to be useful across grades 4-12. The grade 4-6 version measures 34 variables, and for grades 7-12, 45 variables. Scales are said to be useful in measuring changes in the classroom over time but not for measuring individual student change. A small computer and program can be used for scoring. Some of the variables include satisfaction with the class, fatalism, teacher enthusiasm and support, cohesiveness, friction. These tools were designed for use in research on correlates of attitudes toward subjects.

15001
The Values Scale. Super, Donald E.; Nevill, Dorothy D. 1985
Subtests: Ability Utilization; Achievement; Advancement; Aesthetics; Altruism; Authority; Autonomy; Creativity; Economic Rewards; Life Style; Personal Development; Physical Activity; Prestige; Risk; Social Interaction; Social Relations; Variety; Working Conditions; Cultural Identity; Physical Prowess; Economic Security
Descriptors: Adolescents; Adults; Job Satisfaction; Life Satisfaction; Rating Scales; *Values
Identifiers: VS
Availability: Consulting Psychologists Press; 577 College Ave., Palo Alto, CA 94306
Target Audience: 13–65
Notes: Time, 45 approx.; Items, 106

Measures a number of intrinsic and extrinsic values not assessed by existing measures. Objectives are to understand the values that individuals seek in various life roles and to assess the relative importance of the work role as a means of value realization in the context of other life roles. Yields 21 separate scales of values or satisfactions that people seek in life. Can be administered to middle school students through adults who read at an eighth grade level. Values Scale can be used in individual counseling, group assessment, career-development workshops, needs surveys, and research with other variables such as interests, career maturity, sex and socioeconomic status.

15012
Individual-Team-Organization Survey. Anderson, Will 1987
Descriptors: Adults; Behavior Patterns; Business Communication; Conflict Resolution; Employee Assistance Programs; *Employee Attitudes; Industrial Structure; Interpersonal Communication; Leadership; *Occupational Tests; *Organizational Climate; Planning; Problem Solving; Productivity; Staff Meetings; Stress Variables; Teamwork; Time Management; Work Attitudes; *Work Environment
Identifiers: ITO; Risk Taking
Availability: University Associates; 8517 Production Ave., San Diego, CA 92121
Target Audience: Adults
Notes: Items, 56

Designed to create an awareness of differences in perceptions of employees concerning how various parts of the organization work together through hidden agreements. Items relate to the individual, the team, and the organization. Each respondent indicates the frequency of behaviors related to role clarity, job satisfaction, rewards, communication, collaboration, time management, risk taking, employee assistance, influence, purpose, leadership, meeting effectiveness, conflict management, problem solving, productivity, planning, structure, procedures, climate, stress. This scale is available in *The 1987 Annual: Developing Human Resources.*

15038
Modified World Affairs Questionnaire. Mayton, Daniel M., II 1984
Descriptors: Adults; *Disarmament; *Nuclear Warfare; Public Opinion; *Rating Scales
Identifiers: MWAQ
Availability: ERIC Document Reproduction Service; 3900 Wheeler Ave., Alexandria, VA 22304 (ED273679, 27 pages)
Target Audience: Adults
Notes: Items, 23

A Likert-type scale to assess respondents' views on various aspects of nuclear war (probability, outcome, level of concern), arms control (perceived impact, issues preference), and national defense. This instrument is a composite of items from 3 other scales, developed, respectively, by Novak and Lerner (1966), Mayton and Delomater (1983), and Jeffries (1974).

15039
Attitudes toward Nuclear Disarmament. Larsen, Knud 1985
Descriptors: Adults; *Disarmament; Public Opinion; Rating Scales
Identifiers: AND
Availability: Journal of Social Psychology;v125 n1 p17-21, 1985
Target Audience: Adults
Notes: Items, 21

A reliable and valid Likert-type scale intended to measure attitudes toward nuclear disarmament. Developed as part of a study by social psychologists to determine public opinion on this topic.

15057
Colorado Educational Interest Inventory. Whetstone, Robert D.; Taylor, Ronald G. 1975
Subtests: Educational Area; Educational Cluster; Personal Characteristics; School and College; Academic Major; Academic Achievement Interest; Educational Level and Check
Descriptors: *College Students; Educational Counseling; Higher Education; *High School Students; *Interest Inventories; *Majors (Students); *Student Educational Objectives
Identifiers: CEII
Availability: Consulting Psychologists Press; 577 College Ave., Palo Alto, CA 94306
Grade Level: 10–15
Notes: Items, 399

An interest inventory composed of 399 items related to postsecondary education. Supplies educational interest information specifically for the academic decision-making concerns. Designed to identify for students those academic majors in which there is a pattern of interest similar to that of successful students who have earned degrees in that major. Most useful for high school students in grades 11 and 12, freshmen and sophomores in college, and older students coming back to college. Items are arranged in 6 sections each of which focuses on a specific aspect of the educational experience of most students: course titles, educational experiences, instructor characteristics, personal preferences, educational preferences, educational self-concept. Because there are about 150 scales, it is necessary to use computer scoring. The scales are divided into 6 areas: educational area, educational cluster, school and college, academic major, academic achievement interest, educational level and check.

15080
Family Assessment Device, Version 3. Epstein, Nathan B.; And Others 1983

Descriptors: Adolescents; Adults; Affective Behavior; Behavior Patterns; *Family Attitudes; *Family Counseling; *Family Life; Interpersonal Communication; Problem Solving; Questionnaires; Rating Scales; Role Perception
Identifiers: FAD
Availability: Brown University/Butler Hospital Family Research Program; Butler Hospital, 345 Blackstone Rd., Providence, RI 02906
Target Audience: 12–65
Notes: Time, 20 approx.; Items, 60

Sixty-item questionnaire used to assess family functioning. Meant to be used as a screening device, it allows therapists or researchers to identify problem areas in a simple and efficient manner. Measures family members' respective perceptions of their family. These perceptions are divided into 7 dimensions: problem solving, communication, role, affective responsiveness, affective involvement, behavior control, and general functioning. Can be used with a variety of family situations, including families of patients with affective or physical disorders, psychotic patients, children with behavior disorders, and families without any specific problem. Based on the McMaster Model of Family Functioning.

15083
Management Inventory on Modern Management. Kirkpatrick, Donald L. 1984
Descriptors: *Administrators; Adults; *Aptitude Tests; *Job Skills; *Management Development; Managerial Occupations; Personnel Selection
Availability: Donald Kirkpatrick; 1920 Hawthorne Dr., Elm Grove, WI 53122
Target Audience: Adults
Notes: Time, 20 approx.; Items, 80

Covers 8 different topics of importance to managers: Leadership Styles; Selecting and Training; Communicating; Motivating; Managing Change; Delegating; Decision Making; and Managing Time. There are 10 items for each topic. They cover philosophy, principles, and approaches related to the effective performance of managers. Can be used to determine the need for training, as a tool for conference discussions, to evaluate the effectiveness of a training course, to provide information for on-the-job coaching, and to assist in the selection of managers.

15104
Mindmaker 6. Brain Technologies Corp., Ft. Collins, CO 1987
Subtests: Self; Substance; Social; Work; Intimates; Cosmic
Descriptors: Adults; Behavior Patterns; *Beliefs; *Brain Hemisphere Functions; Change Agents; Interpersonal Competence; Personality; Self Concept; Social Behavior; *Values; Work Attitudes
Availability: Brain Technologies Corp.; 414 Buckeye St., Ft. Collins, CO 80524
Target Audience: Adults
Notes: Items, 25

Uses hemispheric dominance theories to identify group members' values and beliefs in 6 areas. Said to be useful for management, employees, markets, regulators, and critics to determine coinciding viewpoints and as an information gathering tool for change agents. Assists in matching employees with available positions.

15117
Managerial Values Profile, Japanese Version. Sashkin, Marshall 1986
Descriptors: Administrator Attitudes; *Administrators; Adults; Beliefs; Business; *Ethics; *Japanese; Occupational Tests; Values
Availability: Organization Design and Development; 2002 Renaissance Blvd., Ste. 100, King of Prussia, PA 19406-2746
Target Audience: Adults
Notes: Time, 10; Items, 24

Japanese-language version of a survey designed for use in determining a respondent's beliefs and values relating to business ethics. Three ethical positions are presented: utilitarian, the greatest good for the greatest number; moral rights, personal rights are inviolable; and justice, benefits and burdens must be allocated fairly. For use in stimulating discussions during training sessions.

15118
Managerial Values Profile. Sashkin, Marshall 1986
Descriptors: Administrator Attitudes; *Administrators; Adults; Beliefs; Business; *Ethics; Occupational Tests; Values
Availability: Organization Design and Development; 2002 Renaissance Blvd., Ste. 100, King of Prussia, PA 19406-2746
Target Audience: Adults
Notes: Time, 10; Items, 24

Designed for use in determining a respondent's beliefs and values relating to business ethics. Three ethical positions are presented: utilitarian, the greatest good for the greatest number; moral rights, personal rights are inviolable; and justice, benefits and burdens must be allocated fairly. For use in stimulating discussion during training sessions. A Japanese version is available (TC015117).

15182
Nuclear Attitudes Questionnaires and Nuclear I.Q. Test. Kierulff, Stephen 1985
Descriptors: Adults; Disarmament; *Knowledge Level; National Defense; *Nuclear Warfare
Identifiers: TIM(M)
Availability: Tests in Microfiche; Test Collection, Educational Testing Service, Princeton, NJ 08541
Target Audience: Adults

Combines attitude measures with a measure of knowledge about nuclear warfare, nuclear weapons, and a nuclear freeze and/or disarmament. Instruments were used in a study of the relationship between knowledge and beliefs or attitudes. Based on the hypotheses of the study and the scores on the questionnaires of the population sampled, it was concluded that those with more accurate knowledge of nuclear issues showed a statistically significant tendency toward supporting a halt in nuclear escalation.

15183
Children's Health Locus of Control. Parcel, Guy S. 1977
Descriptors: *Children; Elementary School Students; *Health; Health Education; *Locus of Control
Identifiers: CHLC
Availability: *Health Education Monographs;*v6 n1 p149-59, Spr 1978
Target Audience: 7-12
Notes: Items, 20

A questionnaire measuring children's health locus of control. When used as one component of a health-related behavior model, can help predict health behavior. Results useful in understanding the relationship between health education and subsequent attitude and behavioral changes. Findings indicate that this instrument has acceptable levels of reliability, internal consistency, and construct validity.

15184
Mathematics Attitude Scale. Aiken, L.R. 1979
Descriptors: *Elementary School Mathematics; *Elementary School Students; Intermediate Grades; Mathematics; Mathematics Anxiety; Middle Schools
Identifiers: Iran
Availability: *School Science and Mathematics;*v79 p229-34, 1979
Grade Level: 4-6
Notes: Items, 24

Twenty-four-item scale that measures attitudes toward mathematics in Iranian middle schools. The total score is based on 4 subscores in the following areas: enjoyment, motivation, importance, and fear.

15185
Questionnaire on Nuclear War. Zweigenhaft, Richard L.
Descriptors: Adolescents; Adults; *Anxiety; Black Attitudes; Civil Defense; College Students; High School Students; *Knowledge Level; *Nuclear Warfare; Older Adults; Questionnaires; Racial Differences; Sex Differences; Social Studies
Availability: Richard L. Zweigenhaft; Psychology Dept., Guilford College, Greensboro, NC 27410
Target Audience: 13-80
Notes: Items, 40

Questionnaire used to measure people's attitudes toward and knowledge about nuclear weapons and nuclear war, its history and its effects. Used to study the differences in knowledge and attitude between whites and blacks and between males and females. Also used with high school and college students from the United States and foreign countries to compare responses of the groups. Could be used by civil defense planners and antinuclear activists to determine the extent to which people are informed about nuclear war so they may be instructed accordingly.

15191
Marriage and Family Attitude Survey. Martin, Donald V.; Martin, Maggie
Descriptors: *College Students; *Diagnostic Tests; *Family Life; Higher Education; *Marriage; *Marriage Counseling; Secondary Education; *Secondary School Students
Availability: Psychologists and Educators; P.O. Box 513, St. Louis, MO 63017
Target Audience: 13-65
Notes: Time, 10 approx.; Items, 58

A diagnostic and educational instrument for understanding relationship attitudes in adolescents and adults. Attitude items cover 10 basic components necessary to understand marriage and family life: cohabitation and premarital sexual relations; marriage and divorce; childhood and child rearing; division of household labor and professional employment; marital and extramarital sexual relations; privacy rights and social needs; religious needs; communication expectations; parental relationships; and professional counseling services. Developed for use with many different types of populations and/or settings. Can be used in counseling with individuals or couples. Also useful as discussion tool in junior high, senior high or college.

15199
Conceptual Systems Test. Harvey, O.J.; Hoffmeister, James K. 1971
Subtests: Divine Fate Control; Need for Structure-Order; General Pessimism; Need to Help People; Need for People; Interpersonal Aggression
Descriptors: Abstract Reasoning; Adults; Aggression; Altruism; *Beliefs; *Concept Formation; *Interpersonal Relationship; Rating Scales; *Self Evaluation (Individuals)
Identifiers: Concrete Operations; CST; Pessimism
Availability: Test Analysis and Development Corp.; 855 Inca Pwy., Boulder, CO 80303
Target Audience: Adults
Notes: Items, 48

Instrument used to measure subjects' levels of conceptual functioning. On a 5-point scale, subjects rate the extent to which they agree or disagree with statements concerning their beliefs, interactions with others, and need for order in their life. The Divine Fate Control section of the instrument may be used to determine whether the person is functioning on an abstract or concrete level.

15212
Family Relations Indicator, Revised and Enlarged Edition. Howells, John G.; Lickorish, John R. 1967
Descriptors: Adults; Childhood Attitudes; Children; *Family Attitudes; *Family Characteristics; *Family Relationship; Parent Attitudes; Parents; *Projective Measures
Identifiers: FRI
Availability: International Universities Press; 300 Raritan Center, CN94, Edison, NJ 08818
Target Audience: 7-12; Adults
Notes: Items, 40

A projective measure consisting of unstructured drawings of family members used to assess the relationships between members of a family and to determine their feelings and attitudes. Some of the 40 plates are for use with families having children of one sex. If both sexes occur, then the whole set can be used with the parents. This administration takes one hour. Cards depict a white middle-class family. Clothing is outdated and appears to be continental. Interviews should be taped. Responses are analyzed and scored.

15230
Bricklin Perceptual Scales: Child Perception of Parents Series. Bricklin, Barry 1984
Subtests: Mother; Father
Descriptors: *Adolescents; *Child Custody; *Children; Family Attitudes; Family Problems; *Parent Child Relationship; *Parents
Identifiers: BPS
Availability: Village Publishing; Village Barn Center, Furlong, PA 18925
Target Audience: 6-17
Notes: Items, 64

This instrument yields information on a child's perception of his or her parents in 4 major areas: competence, supportiveness, follow-up consistency, and possession of admirable personality traits. Each of its 64 items makes use of a continuum stimulus—a straight line scale with values of "very well" and "not so well" at its extremes—on which the child assesses the parents in a specific area. Verbal responses to each item are also elicited. Developed to help assist those involved in solving child custody decisions by taking into account the "best interests of the child" principle. This scale can also be useful to psychotherapists and psychodiagnosticians working with children and their families in varied situations.

15252
Comprehensive Assessment of School Environments. Kelley, Edgar A.; And Others 1987
Subtests: School Climate Survey; Student Satisfaction Survey; Teacher Satisfaction Survey; Parent Satisfaction Survey
Descriptors: *Educational Environment; Elementary Secondary Education; Parents; Rating Scales; School Surveys; Students; Teachers; Likert Scales
Identifiers: CASE
Availability: National Assn. of Secondary School Principals; 1904 Association Dr., Reston, VA 22091-1598
Grade Level: 6-12
Target Audience: 10-65

Instrument consists of 4 surveys. The first is the School Climate Survey. It may be used with students in grades 6 through 12, parents, teachers, and citizen groups. It is recommended that all major stakeholder groups are assessed. Individuals are asked to respond as to how they think most people feel about the school environment than how the individual being questioned feels. Responses are made according to a 6-point Likert Scale. The last 3 surveys are the Student Satisfaction Survey, Teacher Satisfaction Survey, and Parent Satisfaction Survey. Each survey is administered to the proper group. Individuals are asked to make personal, affective responses about the situations or conditions indicated. Instrument may be used singly or in any combination, but use within context of model is encouraged. Used to foster school improvement. Should be related to a school instruction management. May also be used to prepare school reports.

15259
Body Elimination Attitude Scale. Corgiat, Mark D.; And Others 1986
Descriptors: Adults; *Human Body
Identifiers: BEAS; *Body Elimination
Availability: Donald I. Templer; California School of Professional Psychology, 1350 M St., Fresno, CA 93721
Target Audience: Adults
Notes: Items, 26

A self-rating scale developed and administered as part of a study to assess body elimination and to determine the structure and correlates of measured attitude in contemporary American society. Found to have good internal consistency and temporal stability. Seven factors identified: fecal smell, personal hygiene, sight, dirty hair, animal feces, mucous-like discharge, and sound. Greater disgust was found to be associated positively with psychopathology and to be related to various demographic variables. Future research appears to have promise in theoretical areas such as Freudian and other personality theories, in addition to having practical applications such as the selection of persons for certain occupations (physicians or veterinarians, for example).

15275
Organizational Beliefs Questionnaire: Pillars of Excellence. Sashkin, Marshall 1984
Descriptors: Administration; Adults; Business Communication; *High Achievement; *Institutional Environment; Occupational Tests; *Organizational Climate; Questionnaires; Values; Work Attitudes
Identifiers: OBQ
Availability: Organization Design and Development; 2002 Renaissance Blvd., Ste. 100, King of Prussia, PA 19406-2746
Target Audience: Adults
Notes: Time, 20; Items, 50

Designed to measure the overall "excellence" culture of any organization as described in the book *In Search of Excellence.* This tool covers 10 important beliefs that contribute to excellence: work should be fun; one is being the best; risk-taking; attention to detail; people are worthwhile and valuable; quality; communication; growth, profit and other indicators of success; hands-on management; the importance of a shared philosophy. Discussion time is suggested at 1 to 2 hours.

15287
Hypochondriasis Scale: Institutional Geriatric. Brink, T.L. 1978
Descriptors: Diseases; French; *Individual Testing; *Institutionalized Persons; *Older Adults; Spanish
Identifiers: HSIG; *Hypochondria
Availability: T.L. Brink; 1044 Sylvan, San Carlos, CA 94070
Target Audience: 65-99
Notes: Time, 3 approx.; Items, 6

Measures hypochondrial attitudes rather than behaviors of the institutionalized elderly. May be administered in oral or written format, but former is preferred. Spanish and French translations are available. Can be administered to noninstitutionalized elders, adolescents, and young adults, but no validity studies are available.

15295
Mathematics Attitude Inventory. Sandman, Richard 1972
Subtests: Perception of the Mathematics Teacher; Anxiety toward Mathematics; Value of Mathematics in Society; Self-Concept in Mathematics; Enjoyment of Mathematics; Motivation in Mathematics
Descriptors: *High School Students; *Junior High School Students; *Mathematics; Mathematics Anxiety; Rating Scales; Secondary Education; *Secondary School Students; *Student Attitudes
Identifiers: MAI
Availability: Minnesota Research and Evaluation Center; 210 Burton Hall, University of Minnesota, Minneapolis, MN 55455
Grade Level: 7-12
Notes: Items, 48

Measures attitudes toward mathematics of secondary school students in grades 7 through 12. Determines group attitudes toward mathematics and the changes in these attitudes.

15301
Job Descriptive Index, Revised. Smith, Patricia C. 1985
Subtests: Work on Present Job; Present Pay; Opportunities for Promotion; Supervision; Coworkers; Job in General
Descriptors: Adults; Employment; *Job Satisfaction; Promotion (Occupational); Questionnaires; Supervision; Wages
Identifiers: Coworkers; JDI
Availability: Dr. Patricia C. Smith; Psychology Dept., Bowling Green State University, Bowling Green, Ohio 43403
Target Audience: Adults

Brief measures of satisfaction with work, pay, promotions, supervision, and coworkers. Areas are measured separately. Sensitive to differences in the situation and the nature of the work force. Vocabulary level is low and is easily administered.

15305
Invitational Teaching Survey. Amos, Lundee W.; And Others 1984
Subtests: Commitment; Consideration; Coordination; Proficiency; Expectation
Descriptors: *College Students; Dental Hygienists; *Graduate Students; Higher Education; Interpersonal Competence; Nurses; Rating Scales; *Student Attitudes; *Student Evaluation of Teacher Performance; Teacher Behavior; *Teacher Effectiveness; Teacher Student Relationship; Teaching Styles
Identifiers: *Invitational Education; ITS; TIM(N)
Availability: Tests in Microfiche; Test Collection, Educational Testing Service, Princeton, NJ 08541
Grade Level: 13–17
Notes: Items, 43

Designed to identify student perceptions of their instructors "invitational teaching" behavior. Invitational teaching is defined as those "signal systems" that cordially encourage individuals to grow. Teacher behaviors are rated on a 5-point frequency scale from very seldom to very often. Norms are included for dental hygienists and master's-level nurses. Validity and reliability are discussed. Items cover teaching style, interpersonal competence, and student/teacher relationships.

15306
Student Attitudinal Outcome Measures. Amos, Lundee W. 1984
Subtests: Course; Subject Matter; Instructor; Self as Learner
Descriptors: *College Students; Course Content; Courses; Dental Hygienists; *Graduate Students; Higher Education; Nurses; Rating Scales; *Student Attitudes; Teachers
Identifiers: *Invitational Education; Learner Self Concept; SAOM; TIM(N)
Availability: Tests in Microfiche; Test Collection, Educational Testing Service, Princeton, NJ 08541
Grade Level: 13–17
Notes: Items, 20

Measures student attitudes related to being a student in the classroom within the context of invitational teaching which is defined as those signal systems that cordially encourage individuals to grow. Norms are included for dental hygienists and master-level nurses. The SOAM uses a 4-point agree/disagree scale. Reliability is discussed.

15310
Instrument Timbre Preference Test. Gordon, Edwin E. 1984
Descriptors: Bands (Music); *Elementary School Students; Elementary Secondary Education; *Interest Inventories; Magnetic Tape Cassettes; *Musical Instruments; Music Education; Orchestras; *Secondary School Students
Identifiers: ITPT; *Timbre
Availability: G.I.A. Publications; 7404 S. Mason Ave., Chicago, IL 60638
Grade Level: 5–12
Notes: Time, 30 approx.; Items, 42

Helps students in grades 5-12 choose an appropriate woodwind or brass instrument to learn to play in beginning instrumental music and band. Results indicate students' likes and dislikes associated with various woodwind and brass instruments. If a student likes the sound of a particular instrument, he or she will be more successful on that instrument. Seven timbres are organized into 42 recorded test items on a cassettes tape. Students indicate preference on an answer sheet.

15318
Station Employee Applicant Inventory. London House, Park Ridge, IL 1988
Subtests: Honesty; Interpersonal Cooperation; Drug Avoidance; Arithmetic Skills; Job-Specific Skills and Abilities
Descriptors: Adults; Arithmetic; Computer Software; Cooperation; Drug Use; Interpersonal Competence; Job Skills; *Occupational Tests; Personality; *Personnel Selection; Predictive Measurement; *Sales Workers; Scoring
Identifiers: *Cashiers; *Gas Station Employees; Honesty; SEAI
Availability: London House; 1550 Northwest Hwy., Park Ridge, IL 60068
Target Audience: Adults
Notes: Time, 45; Items, 144

Designed to predict on-the-job attitudes and behaviors of prospective gas station or convenience store cashiers. Said to select those who will be less often late or absent; safeguard money; be accurate and honest with cash or changes; use safe work habits; perform well when rushed and distracted; give the company a positive image. A lie scale is included to detect faked responses. Administered on-site by company personnel with no special training. Scoring is by mail, via phone, or via IBM compatible PC. Said to be highly valid, that is, correlates with future performance evaluation.

15319
Attitude Survey Program for Business and Industry. London House, Park Ridge, IL 1988
Subtests: Organization Survey; Managerial Survey; Professional Survey; Sales Survey
Descriptors: Adults; Business Communication; Job Performance; *Job Satisfaction; Leadership; *Occupational Tests; *Organizations (Groups); *Professional Personnel; Salaries; *Sales Occupations; *Supervisors; Supervisory Methods
Identifiers: Coworkers
Availability: London House; 1550 Northwest Hwy., Park Ridge, IL 60068
Target Audience: Adults

Designed to measure attitudes of employee groups: hourly employees; managers above first line; staff; and field sales personnel. Said to be useful in measuring causes for low morale and productivity; employee acceptance of change; determining training needs for managers. Consists of Organization Survey, Managerial Survey, Professional Survey, Sales Survey. Modifications and customized versions can be made to specifications. Profiles compare results to a national norm. Scoring is done by the publisher. Covers organization identification, job satisfaction, material rewards, leadership, supervision, work efficiency, communication, and sales-related factors for that survey.

15320
Attitude Survey Program for Health Care. London House, Park Ridge, IL 1988
Descriptors: Adults; *Allied Health Occupations; Business Communication; Job Performance; *Job Satisfaction; Leadership; *Nurses; *Occupational Tests; Organizations (Groups); Paraprofessional Personnel; *Physicians; Salaries; Supervisory Methods
Availability: London House; 1550 Northwest Hwy., Park Ridge, IL 60068
Target Audience: Adults

Designed to measure attitudes of staff members in hospitals, health maintenance organizations (HMOs), clinics, and nursing care facilities. Surveys focus on organizational efficiency, harmony, and factors that influence patient care. Said to uncover attitudes that could result in absenteeism, excessive lateness, and high turnover. The following surveys are available: Nursing Staff; Physicians; Paraprofessionals; Nonmedical Professionals; Health Care Employees. Some areas covered are organization identification; job satisfaction; salaries and benefits; supervisory practices; work efficiency; communication; and other matters directly related to concerns of medical staff.

15322
Personnel Selection Inventory. London House, Park Ridge, IL
Descriptors: Adults; Background; Drug Use; Emotional Problems; *Employee Attitudes; Interpersonal Competence; *Job Applicants; *Job Performance; Personnel Evaluation; *Personnel Selection; *Predictive Measurement; Productivity; Questionnaires; Self Evaluation (Individuals); Validity; *Work Attitudes
Identifiers: Honesty; PSI
Availability: London House; 1550 Northwest Hwy., Park Ridge, IL 60068

Designed to screen out job applicants who fall into the high-risk employee categories of dishonesty, neglect of duties, and disruptive behavior. Items cover the areas of honesty, drug avoidance, nonviolence, employee customer relations, emotional stability, safety, work values, supervision attitudes, and applicant employability. Includes 2 scales which measure the validity of job applicants' answers. There are 8 versions of the inventory. Employers may choose the version which best suits their needs. Another 2 versions are available for selection of bank employees.

15327
Audit of Principal Effectiveness. Valentine, Jerry W.; Bowman, Michael L. 1986
Descriptors: *Administrator Evaluation; Elementary Secondary Education; Feedback; Instructional Leadership; *Organizational Climate; *Principals; *Teacher Attitudes
Availability: ERIC Document Reproduction Service; 3900 Wheeler Ave., Alexandria, VA 22304 (ED281319, 21 pages)
Target Audience: Adults
Notes: Items, 80

Designed to determine teachers' perceptions of principal effectiveness, to allow principals to obtain feedback from teachers regarding strengths and weaknesses, and to provide a useful tool for teachers studying principals. Focuses on 3 broad domains of administration: organizational development, organizational environment, and educational reform. In addition, each of these domains is broken down into its respective discrete factors. Statistical reliability for factors is indicated.

15352
Invitational Teaching Survey. Amos, Lundee W. 1984
Subtests: Disclosing; Supporting; Investing; Attending; Affirming; Cheering; Clarifying; Informing; Managing; Relying; Expectation
Descriptors: Behavior Rating Scales; College Students; *Higher Education; *Student Attitudes; *Student Evaluation of Teacher Performance; Surveys; *Teacher Behavior; *Teacher Effectiveness; Teachers; Teacher Student Relationship; Teaching Methods
Identifiers: *Invitational Teaching
Availability: ERIC Document Reproduction Service; 3900 Wheeler Ave., Alexandria, VA 22304-5110 (ED281891, 23 pages)
Grade Level: 13–16
Notes: Items, 63

A self-administered student-rating questionnaire designed to give teachers feedback about classroom interactions. "Invitational" teaching is a concept that emphasizes factors that invite or encourage students to learn. The instrument assesses which of these factors is present or absent in the teacher from the students' points of view. There are 2 major dimensions—personally inviting, and professionally inviting, and 5 clusters of teaching skills—commitment skills, consideration skills, coordination skills, proficiency skills, and expectations for students. Normed on dental hygiene and nursing students.

15364
Assertion-Rights Questionnaire. Woodcock, Mike; Francis, Dave 1981
Descriptors: Adults; *Assertiveness; Behavior Patterns; Group Counseling; *Human Resources; *Industrial Training; *Labor Force Development; Occupational Tests; Personnel Evaluation; Rating Scales
Identifiers: ARQ
Availability: University Associates; 8517 Production Ave., San Diego, CA 92121
Target Audience: Adults
Notes: Items, 12

Designed to assist participants in evaluating their own attitudes about personal assertion. Part of a kit of instruments that may be reproduced as needed without permission (up to 100 copies) by human resources development personnel for educational and training activities. This 5-point agree/disagree scale elicits the participants' perceptions of their rights and how this is translated into behavior.

15385
Life-Style Preference Evaluation. Adams, John D. 1980
Descriptors: Adults; *Human Resources; *Industrial Training; *Life Style; Locus of Control; *Management Development; Needs; Occupational Tests; Stress Management; *Values
Identifiers: LSPE
Availability: University Associates; 8517 Production Ave., San Diego, CA 92121
Target Audience: Adults
Notes: Items, 24

Designed to measure an individual's lifestyle preference and whether it conforms to 1 of 3 different approaches: personalistic, sociocentric, or formalistic. Personalistic is defined by items related to self as having responsibility and being a motivating force. The sociocentric approach references others as important. The formalistic approach refers to society as a whole and established procedures and policies. Part of a large kit of instruments that may be reproduced as needed (up to 100 copies) without permission. For use by human resources development professionals in educational and training activities.

15387
Male-Female Role Questionnaire. Carney, Clark G.; McMahon, Sarah Lynne 1977

Descriptors: Adults; *Human Resources; *Industrial Training; *Management Development; Occupational Tests; *Sensitivity Training; *Sex Bias; Sex Differences; *Sex Discrimination; *Sex Role
Identifiers: MFRQ
Availability: University Associates; 8517 Production Ave., San Diego, CA 92121
Target Audience: Adults
Notes: Items, 50

A measure of the perception of the roles, characteristics, and issues involving the sexes in our society. Four separate scales require the respondent to describe the opposite sex and oneself; rate various traits as common to one sex and either cultural or biological; agree/disagree with statements about differences and similarities in the treatment of the sexes in society; and approve/disapprove of equality issues. Part of a large kit of instruments that may be reproduced as needed (up to 100 copies) without permission. For use by human resources development professionals in educational and training activities.

15389
Manager's Dilemma Work Sheet. Glaser, Rollin; Glaser, Christine 1983
Descriptors: Administration; *Administrators; Adults; Employees; Employer Attitudes; *Human Resources; *Industrial Training; Job Performance; *Management Development; Managerial Occupations; Occupational Tests; *Supervisors; Theories
Identifiers: McGregor (Douglas); MDWS; Theory X; Theory Y
Availability: University Associates; 8517 Production Ave., San Diego, CA 92121
Target Audience: Adults
Notes: Items, 11

Designed to measure a manager's agreement with McGregor's Theory X and Theory Y that deal with a supervisor's perceptions of employees as capable, achieving, responsible (Theory Y) or avoiding, incapable and indifferent (Theory X). Part of a large kit of instruments that may be reproduced as needed (up to 100 copies) without permission. For use by human resources development professionals in educational and training activities.

15394
Organizational Performance-Appraisal Questionnaire Evaluation. Sashkin, Marshall 1981
Descriptors: Adults; *Employee Attitudes; Employer Attitudes; *Human Resources; *Industrial Training; *Occupational Tests; Organizational Development; *Personnel Evaluation; Supervisors
Identifiers: OPAQUE; *Performance Appraisal
Availability: University Associates; 8517 Production Ave., San Diego, CA 92121
Target Audience: Adults
Notes: Items, 6

A measure of the respondent's perception of performance appraisal in an organization. Some items refer to the experience of appraising others and some of the experiences of being appraised. Uses an agree/disagree response format. Part of a large kit of instruments that may be reproduced as needed (up to 100 copies) without permission. For use by human resources development professionals in educational and training activities.

15395
Performance Appraisal System Evaluation. Sashkin, Marshall 1981
Descriptors: Adults; *Employer Attitudes; *Human Resources; *Industrial Training; *Occupational Tests; Organizational Development; *Personnel Evaluation
Identifiers: PASE; *Performance Appraisal
Availability: University Associates; 8517 Production Ave., San Diego, CA 92121
Target Audience: Adults
Notes: Items, 15

Designed to elicit respondent's perceptions about the general practices in an organization that are related to the performance appraisal system. Uses a 5-point agree/disagree response format. Part of a large kit of instruments that may be reproduced as needed (up to 100 copies) without permission. For use by human resources development professionals in educational and training activities.

15399
Self-Assessment Inventory: Behavior in Groups. Thayer, Louis 1976
Descriptors: Adults; Behavior Patterns; *Group Dynamics; Groups; *Human Resources; *Industrial Training; *Occupational Tests; Self Evaluation (Individuals)
Identifiers: SAI
Availability: University Associates; 8517 Production Ave., San Diego, CA 92121
Target Audience: Adults
Notes: Time, 30; Items, 25

Designed to assist a member of a training group to assess his or her attitudes and behavior during the sessions. Attitudes are concerned with the learning process, expression of feelings, and behaviors occurring within the group. Part of a large kit of instruments that may be reproduced as needed (up to 100 copies) without permission. For use by human resources development professionals in educational and training activities.

15403
Training Philosophies Profile. Beamish, G.E.H. 1983
Descriptors: Adults; Behavior Patterns; *Human Resources; *Industrial Training; *Occupational Tests; *Philosophy; Self Concept; Self Evaluation (Individuals); *Trainers
Identifiers: TPP
Availability: University Associates; 8517 Production Ave., San Diego, CA 92121
Target Audience: Adults
Notes: Time, 60; Items, 36

Designed to determine the philosophies of participants in management training about the training itself and to help participants clarify their perceptions about the relationship between training and management. Used a pair comparison format. Respondent allocates 3 points between statements in each pair. Scored to reveal the trainers' behaviors, self-images, and underlying attitudes. Part of a large kit of instruments that may be reproduced as needed (up to 100 copies) without permission. For use by human resources development professionals in educational and training activities.

15406
Work-Needs Assessment Inventory: Achievement, Affiliation and Power. Doyle, Patrick 1985
Descriptors: Achievement Need; Adults; Affiliation Need; Employee Attitudes; *Human Resources; *Industrial Training; Management Development; *Needs; *Needs Assessment; *Occupational Tests; Work Attitudes
Identifiers: Power Need; WNAI
Availability: University Associates; 8517 Production Ave., San Diego, CA 92121
Target Audience: Adults
Notes: Items, 18

Designed to identify the needs in the workplace that motivate people, and the respondents' own needs. Statements are rank ordered. The ordering reveals whether the respondents desire achievement, affiliation, or power as first, second, or third priorities. Part of a large kit of instruments that may be reproduced as needed (up to 100 copies) without permission. For use by human resources development professionals in educational and training activities.

15409
Student Attitudes toward Economics. Duchastel, Philippe 1985
Subtests: Satisfaction with Current Grasp of Economics; Capability for Understanding Economics; Attraction to Economics; Economics as a Field; General Need for Economics; Economics Courses
Descriptors: Adults; *Adult Students; *Economics; Higher Education; *Professional Continuing Education; Questionnaires; *Student Attitudes; *Undergraduate Students
Availability: ERIC Document Reproduction Service; 3900 Wheeler Ave., Alexandria, VA 22304 (ED266187, 19 pages)
Grade Level: 13–16
Target Audience: Adults
Notes: Items, 49

Designed for use in a study and administered to adult students in continuing education programs in financial services and to two groups of undergraduate students. Technical information is in terms of item scores, subscale scores, full-form scores, interscale correlations, and item scale correlations. The questionnaire is said to be reliable, as are subscales. Strong differences between subscales are not present.

15412
Orientation to Learning. Shapiro, Stewart B. 1985
Subtests: Process-Orientation; Self-Determination; Connectedness: Relevancy; Integration; Context; Affective Bias; Innovation; Democrative Participation; Personal Growth Orientation; People Orientation; Individualism; Reality Claims; Evaluation; Variety-Creativity
Descriptors: College Students; *Educational Objectives; Higher Education; *Learning; Learning Experience; Learning Processes; Student Role; *Teacher Behavior; Teacher Role; *Teacher Student Relationship; *Teaching Styles; Values
Identifiers: OTL; TIM(N)
Availability: Tests in Microfiche; Test Collection, Educational Testing Service, Princeton, NJ 08541
Grade Level: 13–16
Notes: Items, 135

A series of 3 forms of a measure of orientation to learning based on a humanistic value orientation to the principles of instruction. Fifteen major humanistic instructional values were identified and serve as subscales. Each subscale contains 19 items except in shorter form B1-B2. Instruction based on the humanistic paradigm is described as person-centered and growth-oriented. Each scale uses a 5-point Likert-type strongly agree to strongly disagree format. Several types of reliability and validity are presented. Percentile norms are available for several student groups. Items pertain to teaching style and behaviors, the teacher-student relationship, and educational goals.

15421
Comparative Guidance and Placement Program. Educational Testing Service, Princeton, NJ
Descriptors: Achievement Tests; Biographical Inventories; Cognitive Tests; *College Students; *Educational Counseling; Higher Education; *Postsecondary Education; Student Interests; *Student Placement; *Two Year College Students; *Undergraduate Students
Identifiers: CGP; MAPS; Multiple Assessment Programs and Services
Availability: Educational Testing Service; Comparative Guidance and Placement Program/ MAPS, Princeton, NJ 08541
Grade Level: 13–16

Comprehensive information gathering and interpretation system to meet counseling and placement needs of community colleges, vocational-technical institutes, and 4-year institutions. Program consists of several components. The Biographical Inventory provides information on students' background, attitudes, plans, needs, and aspirations in personal and academic areas. The Comparative Interest Index asks students to indicate their degree of interest in numerous academic and related fields. It may be self-administered by the student. The English and Mathematics Achievement/Placement Tests are useful for determining students who are adequately prepared for regular placement and those who may need developmental work. There are achievement/placement tests in reading and written English expression and 3 levels of mathematics tests, depending the the student's background in high school algebra. The achievement/placement tests are also available in self-scoring format. In addition, there are 3 special abilities tests which are less dependent than others on knowledge obtained in a formal setting: Year 2000 Test, Mosaic Comparisons Test, and Letter Groups Test. To meet the varying needs of users, CGP offers 3 options: full CGP program, modified CGP program, or English and Mathematics Achievement/Placement Test in self-scoring form.

15424
Follow-up Survey of College Freshmen. Higher Education Research Institute, University of California, Los Angeles, CA 1987
Subtests: Demographic Information; College Satisfaction; Goals (Personal); Activities; Career Choice; Major Field; Change of Institution by Student; Student Perception of Institutional Values; Postcollegiate Plans
Descriptors: Career Choice; College Freshmen; *College Students; *Followup Studies; Higher Education; Majors (Students); Objectives; Organizational Objectives; *Participant Satisfaction; Planning; School Choice; *Surveys; Values
Availability: Higher Education Research Institute; Graduate School of Education, University of California, Los Angeles, 320 Moore Hall, Los Angeles, CA 90024
Grade Level: 13–16

Designed for use in conducting longitudinal studies of entering students. The survey focuses on student experiences during college and includes items that measure satisfaction with aspects of the college experience. The questionnaire also repeats items from the freshman survey (TC012027) so that change can be measured. Said to be particularly useful for retention studies, accreditation reports, and self-study. Users must be participants in the Cooperative Institutional Research Program annual freshman survey. Norms are available for 2 and 4 years after college entry.

15431
Survey of Field Attitudes. Life Insurance Marketing and Research Association, Hartford, CT 1987
Descriptors: *Administrative Policy; Adults; *Insurance Companies; *Sales Workers; Surveys; Work Attitudes
Availability: Life Insurance Marketing and Research Association; P.O. Box 208, Hartford, CT 06141
Target Audience: Adults

A diagnostic job attitude survey service to help home-office management appraise the effects of its policies and actions on its sales personnel. Companies can survey their sales forces with the prepared items and add others to suit their needs. The survey is specifically tailored to the insurance industry.

15503
Preschool Reading Attitudes Scale. Saracho, Olivia N. 1986
Subtests: School Reading Activities; Library Reading Activities; Nonschool Reading Activities; General Reading Activities
Descriptors: Beginning Reading; *Reading Attitudes; Recreational Reading; *Young Children
Identifiers: PRAS
Availability: Olivia N. Saracho; University of Maryland, Dept. of Curriculum and Instruction, Reading Center, College Park, MD 20742
Target Audience: 3-5
Notes: Items, 12
Designed to assess attitudes toward reading. Scale was found to be reliable and valid with children aged 3 to 5 years. Is a group-administrered instrument consisting of 12 statements that are read to the children. The statements indicate specific areas of a child's reading environment: school reading activities, nonschool reading activities, library reading activities, and general reading activities.

15505
Money Attitude Scale. Yamauchi, Kent T.; Templer, Donald I. 1982
Subtests: Retention Time; Distrust; Quality; Anxiety; Power-Prestige
Descriptors: Adults; *Money Management
Identifiers: MAS
Availability: Journal of Personality Assessment;v46 n5 p522-28, 1982
Target Audience: Adults
Notes: Items, 29
This standardized measure uses a 7-point Likert-Type scale with always and never as end points. Normed on a general adult population. Said to provide a reliable assessment of the 5 factors measured. For use in investigating the compatibility of couples or evaluating the efficacy of clinical procedures designed to identify and change irrational or problem behaviors related to money.

15521
Hall-Tonna Inventory of Values. Hall, Brian P.; Tonna, Benjamin 1986
Descriptors: Adults; *Forced Choice Technique; Institutional Characteristics; Self Concept; *Self Concept Measures; *Values; *Values Clarification; Life Style
Identifiers: Discern
Availability: Behaviordyne; 994 San Antonio Rd., P.O. Box 10994, Palo Alto, CA 94303-0997
Target Audience: Adults
Notes: Items, 77
A self-administered, computerized assessment instrument that measures the value priorities of individuals, documents, and institutions and places, each in the context of spiritual and human development. The Hall-Tonna Report consists of 2 components: a computerized printout based on responses to the inventory and a workbook that enables the subject, through a series of reflective questions, to integrate the information from the printout. Together they guide the subject in the exploration of choices and goals and in the development of insight into personal values. Several specialized supplemental reports can be ordered. The workbook is available in 2 forms: "Discern," for religious use, and "Lifestyle," the secular form.

15525
Clinical Teaching Survey for Nursing. Ripley, Delia McKeithan 1985
Subtests: Commitment; Consideration; Coordination; Proficiency; Expectation; Course; Subject Matter; Instructor; Self as Learner
Descriptors: Higher Education; *Nurses; Rating Scales; *Student Attitudes; *Student Evaluation of Teacher Performance; Surveys; Teacher Effectiveness
Identifiers: TIM(N)
Availability: Tests in Microfiche; Test Collection, Educational Testing Service, Princeton, NJ 08541
Grade Level: 13-16
Notes: Items, 44
This student rating was designed to provide clinical nursing instructors with feedback about student perceptions of their teaching in the clinical setting. Uses items adapted from the Invitational Teaching Survey (TC015305) and the Student Attitudinal Outcome Measures (TC015306). Teaching behaviors are rated on a 5-point frequency scale.

15543
Thanatometer. Bandis, Panos D. 1986
Descriptors: Adults; Behavior Patterns; *Death; *Social Problems
Availability: Panos D. Bardis; Sociology Dept., University of Toledo, Toledo, OH 43606
Target Audience: Adults
Notes: Items, 20

Five-point Likert-type agree/disagree scale concerning a list of issues related to death. Issues cover terminal illness, funerals, grieving and mourning, and social conventions or mores concerning practices surrounding these death-related behaviors, such as the need for long elaborate funerals.

15544
Black Ethnocentrism Scale. Chang, Edward C.; Ritter, Edward H. 1976
Descriptors: Adults; *Black Attitudes; Black Power; College Students; *Ethnocentrism; Racial Attitudes; *Racial Relations; Whites
Identifiers: BES
Availability: Journal of Social Psychology;v100 p89-98, 1976
Target Audience: Adults
Notes: Items, 40
This Likert-type scale was developed with 2 subscales: pro-black sentiment and anti-white sentiment. Data gathered are based on the responses of black college students, and norms are reported. It was developed for a study that assumed that blacks are becoming more ethnocentric and that black ethnocentrism involves both pro-black and anti-white components.

15568
Educational Process Questionnaire. Institute for Behavioral Research in Creativity, Salt Lake City, UT 1987
Subtests: Reinforcement of Self-Concept; Academic Learning Time; Feedback; Expectations; Development of Multiple Talents
Descriptors: *Classroom Environment; *Elementary School Students; Elementary Secondary Education; Rating Scales; *Secondary School Students; *Student Evaluation of Teacher Performance; *Teaching Styles
Identifiers: EPQ
Availability: Institute for Behavioral Research in Creativity; 1570 South 1100 East, Salt Lake City, UT 84105
Grade Level: 3-12
Notes: Time, 35 approx.; Items, 54
Intended primarily to aid teachers in their own self-development by providing objective information about the processes used in teacher's own classroom. The questionnaire gathers student descriptions of classroom activities. By seeing classroom activities as perceived by the students, the teacher can focus on teaching skills that influence student behaviors. Helps provide direction to a teacher's self-improvement effort by identifying 5 educational processes as target areas for continuing effort. The Reinforcement of Self-Concept Scale concerns feedback students receive from the teacher. Academic Learning Time Scale assesses how much class time teachers actually spend teaching. Feedback assesses how quickly they receive feedback from teachers. Expectations scale assesses whether students are expected to do their best. Development of Multiple Talents Scale assesses emphasis on classroom activities to foster creativity, decision making, planning. This questionnaire should not be used as an evaluation of overall teaching performance. Questions are written at late third grade level.

15615
Life Role Salience Scales. Amatea, Ellen S.; And Others 1986
Subtests: Occupation Role Reward Value; Occupational Role Commitment; Parental Role Reward Value; Parental Role Commitment; Marital Role Reward Value; Marital Role Commitment; Homecare Role Reward Value; Homecare Role Commitment
Descriptors: Adults; College Students; Expectation; Family Role; Higher Education; Marriage; Occupational Aspiration; Parent Role; Rating Scales; *Role Perception; Likert Scales
Identifiers: LRSS
Availability: Journal of Marriage and the Family;v48 n4 p831-38, Nov 1986
Target Audience: Adults
Notes: Items, 40
Rating scale by which men and women assess their personal expectations concerning occupational, marital, parental, and home-care roles. Scale assesses personal importance or value of the roles and intended level of commitment of time and energy to the enactment of the role. May be used with men and women who are either engaged in particular roles or those anticipating entry into the roles. May be used to measure attitude changes as a result of role changes. Has been tested for validity and reliability.

15641
Personality Assessment Questionnaire, Mother. Rohner, Ronald P. 1979
Subtests: Hostility/Aggression; Dependency; Self-Esteem; Self-Adequacy; Emotional Responsiveness; Emotional Stability; World View
Descriptors: Adults; Behavior; Child Caregivers; *Children; *Mothers; *Personality Traits; Questionnaires; Self Concept
Identifiers: PAQ

Availability: University of Connecticut; Center for the Study of Parental Acceptance and Rejection, Storrs, CT 06268
Target Audience: Adults
Notes: Items, 42
A self-report instrument designed to assess an individual's perception of his or her child with respect to 7 behavioral dispositions: hostility/aggression, dependency, self-esteem, self-adequacy, emotional responsiveness, emotional stability and world view. The mother's version asks mothers or other caretakers, such as teachers, to reflect on the child's behavioral dispositions. Developed to complement Parental Acceptance-Rejection Questionnaire but may be used in other contexts.

15642
Personality Assessment Questionnaire, Child. Rohner, Ronald P. 1977
Subtests: Hostility/Aggression; Dependency; Self-Esteem; Self-Adequacy; Emotional Responsiveness; Emotional Stability; World View
Descriptors: Behavior; *Children; *Personality Traits; Questionnaires; *Self Concept; Self Evaluation (Individuals)
Identifiers: PAQ
Availability: University of Connecticut; Center for the Study of Parental Acceptance and Rejection, Storrs, CT 06268
Target Audience: 7-18
Notes: Items, 42
A self-report instrument designed to assess an individual's perception of himself or herself with respect to 7 behavioral dispositions: hostility/aggression, dependency, self-esteem, self-adequacy, emotional responsiveness, emotional stability, and world view. Children's version asks children to reflect on their behavioral dispositions. Developed to complement Parental Acceptance-Rejection Questionnaire but may be used in other contexts.

15643
Personality Assessment Questionnaire, Adult. Rohner, Ronald P. 1977
Subtests: Hostility/Aggression; Dependency; Self-Esteem; Self-Adequacy; Emotional Responsiveness; Emotional Stability; World View
Descriptors: Adults; Behavior; *Personality Assessment; *Personality Traits; Questionnaires; *Self Concept; Self Evaluation (Individuals)
Identifiers: PAQ
Availability: University of Connecticut; Center for the Study of Parental Acceptance and Rejection, Storrs, CT 06268
Target Audience: Adults
Notes: Items, 63
A self-report instrument designed to assess an individual's perception of himself or herself with respect to 7 behavioral dispositions: hostility/aggression, dependency, self-esteem, self-adequacy, emotional responsiveness, emotional stability, and world view. Adult version asks adults to reflect on their own behavioral dispositions. Developed to complement Parental Acceptance-Rejection Questionnaire but may be used in other contexts.

15695
Reid Survey. Reid Psychological Systems, Chicago, IL 1985
Descriptors: Adults; *Employee Attitudes; Questionnaires; *Values
Identifiers: *Honesty
Availability: Psychological Surveys Corp.; 900 Jorie Blvd., Ste. 130, Oak Brook, IL 60521
Target Audience: Adults
Notes: Time, 40 approx.; Items, 90
Is designed to be used only with employees who have worked in their positions for at least 2 years. Questionnaire yields the following assessments of current employees: their attitudes toward honesty; information on any wrongdoing by the employee; employees' knowledge and views of coworkers' honesty and performance; employees' propensity to use drugs and alcohol; employees' contentment or unhappiness in the job; the employees' degree of cooperativeness related to the job and the company.

15698
Student Developmental Task and Lifestyle Inventory. Winston, Roger B.; And Others 1987
Subtests: Establishing and Clarifying Purpose Task; Developing Mature Interpersonal Relationships Task; Developing Academic Autonomy Task; Salubrious Life-Style Scale; Intimacy Scale; Response Bias Scale
Descriptors: *College Students; *Developmental Tasks; Higher Education; Questionnaires; Self Evaluation (Individuals); *Student Attitudes; *Student Behavior; *Student Development
Identifiers: SDTLI
Availability: Student Development Associates; 110 Crestwood Dr., Athens, GA 30605
Grade Level: 13-16
Notes: Time, 35 approx.; Items, 140

Questionnaire represents behaviors, attitudes, and activities common to college students. Developed to help students look at themselves objectively and to use the information to help them gain the most they can from their college experience. Items represent a sample of behaviors and reports of feelings and attitudes that students can be expected to demonstrate when they have satisfactorily achieved certain developmental tasks common to young adults who are in college. Item content of the questionnaire is written at the grade 11.1 reading level. Instrument was originally developed as a counseling tool but has been expanded to serve also as a research and program evaluation tool.

15706
Exchange-Orientation Scale for Friends. Murstein, Bernard I.; Azar, James A. 1986
Descriptors: Adolescents; Adults; Anxiety; *Friendship; Rating Scales; Self Evaluation (Individuals); Likert Scales
Identifiers: *Exchange Orientation; *Roommates
*Availability: Small Group Behavior;*v17 n1 p3-17, Feb 1986
Grade Level: 13-16
Notes: Items, 21

Measures the exchange-orientation of roommates. The hypothesis is that the less each individual worries about what he or she should be getting in return for good turns done for his or her roommate, the better the roommates will get along. The scale measures the individuals' attitudes toward interpersonal exchange. Each member of the roommate pair completes the scale along with rating the roommate on a dimension of compatibility, which ranges from 1 to 7. The scale was found to be valid in making predictions regarding the roommates' compatibility according to the attitude on exchange for each member of the pair. The scale also showed that exchange-orientation and anxiety were correlated for women subjects but not for men.

15708
Self-Reported Self-Appraisal. Westbrook, Bert W.; And Others 1987
Descriptors: Adolescents; Career Choice; *Career Planning; High Schools; *High School Students; *Self Evaluation (Individuals); Values; Vocational Aptitude; *Vocational Interests; Work Environment; Likert Scales
*Availability: Measurement and Evaluation in Counseling and Development;*v20 n2 p51-61, Jul 1987
Grade Level: 10-12
Target Audience: Adolescents
Notes: Items, 5

A self-report scale of one's ability to appraise himself or herself. Using Likert-type scales, individuals assess their own interests, values and aptitudes in the context of career choice. Data on reliability and validity are included.

15709
Women in the Military Questionnaire. Rustad, Michael L. 1982
Descriptors: Adults; *Females; *Military Personnel; Organizational Climate; Problems; Questionnaires; Rating Scales; Role Perception; Self Esteem; Self Evaluation (Individuals); Social Attitudes; Likert Scales
*Availability: Rustad, Michael L., Women in Khaki: The American Enlisted Woman.*New York: Praeger Publishers, 1982
Target Audience: Adults
Notes: Time, 45 approx.; Items, 136

Questionnaire designed to assess individual's feelings about women in the military. May be issued to both military and nonmilitary personnel and to both men and women. Subjects who are military personnel are asked to respond to extra items pertaining to their military experience which others are not. All subjects respond to items concerning background information, feelings about self, societal attitudes, and women's roles.

15735
PeopleFacts: The Opinion Processor. Shamrock Press, San Diego, CA 1985
Descriptors: Adults; *Computer Software; *Microcomputers; *Surveys; *Test Construction
Identifiers: *Opinionnaires
*Availability: Shamrock Press; Div. of Karl Albrecht and Associates, 1277 Garnet Ave., P.O. Box 90699, San Diego, CA 92109
Target Audience: Adults

Personal computer software package for use on an IBM-PC that allows people to construct their own surveys, print and record them, enter survey data, and print the results.

15737
Security Aptitude Fitness Evaluation. Taccarino, John R.
Subtests: Numerical Ability; Language Skills; Attitudes (Honesty)

Descriptors: Adults; *Job Skills; Language Skills; Mathematics; Microcomputers; *Personality Traits; *Personnel Selection; *Screening Tests
Identifiers: *Honesty; SAFE
*Availability: SAFE, Inc.; 141 Briarwood N., Oak Brook, IL 60521
Target Audience: Adults
Notes: Time, 30 Approx.; Items, 130

Identifies theft-prone job applicants and measures an individual's capability and suitability to do the job. Assesses individuals' attitudes about work and theft and tests their basic math and language skills. Provides an evaluation of an applicant's total potential job suitability and performance. Scored and interpreted automatically through the SAFE hand-held computer or using special software on an IBM PC.

15738
Security Aptitude Fitness Evaluation—Resistance. Taccarino, John R.
Subtests: Numerical Ability; Language Skills; Attitudes (Honesty)
Descriptors: Adults; *Job Skills; Language Skills; Mathematics; Microcomputers; *Personality Traits; *Personnel Selection; *Screening Tests
Identifiers: *Honesty; SAFE(R)
*Availability: SAFE, Inc.; 141 Briarwood N., Oak Brook, IL 60521
Target Audience: Adults
Notes: Time, 30 Approx.; Items, 164

Assesses individuals' attitudes about work and theft, their psychological and personality characteristics, and life experiences relating to substance-abuse potential and tests their basic math and language skills. Provides information for the employer to hire suitable, honest, and drug-free employees. May be scored using a SAFE hand-held computer or using special software on an IBM PC.

15746
Marital Satisfaction Scale. Roach, Arthur J.; And Others 1981
Descriptors: Adults; Intervention; *Marital Satisfaction; Rating Scales; Self Evaluation (Individuals); Likert Scales
Identifiers: MSS
*Availability: Journal of Marriage and the Family;*v43 p537-46, Aug 1981
Target Audience: Adults
Notes: Items, 48

Instrument designed to assess one's level of satisfaction toward his or her own marriage. Satisfaction is measured in terms of greater or lesser favorability at a given point in time. Aims to measure attitudes toward the marriage rather than success or happiness in the marriage. Answers are made according to a 5-point Likert-type scale. May be used before and after various types of helping interventions to assess change in marital satisfaction resulting from the intervention. Shown to have high internal consistency and to be reliable and valid.

15752
Friendship Intensity Questionnaire. Marsden, Edith N. 1966
Subtests: Friendship Value Inventory; General Value Inventory; Friendship Questionnaire
Descriptors: *College Students; Dormitories; *Females; Forced Choice Technique; *Friendship; Group Experience; Higher Education; Questionnaires; Rating Scales; *Values; Young Adults
*Availability: Connecticut College Psychology Journal;*v3 p3-13, Spr 1966
Grade Level: 13-16
Target Audience: 18-22
Notes: Items, 41

Uses 3 scales, Friendship Value Inventory, General Value Inventory, and Friendship Questionnaire to determine whether people become friends on the basis of similar values. Written for college women living in dormitories. Both the Friendship Value Inventory and the General Value Inventory ask subjects to rank 15 items according to what is most valued in a friend, and one's own interests and values. The Friendship Scale is completed by the subject, who rates every other person in the dormitory. From it, each pair is labeled as having high, low, or medium friendship. Correlation tests are then performed on each pair of scales to determine whether similar roles play a significant role in friendship.

15780
Attitudes toward Computer Usage Scale. Popovich, Paula M.; And Others 1987
Descriptors: Adults; *Computers; Rating Scales; Likert Scales
Identifiers: ATCUS
*Availability: Educational and Psychological Measurement;*v47 n1 p261-69, Spr 1987
Target Audience: Adults
Notes: Items, 20

Scale designed to assess how people react to using computers and other devices which are computer-related. On a 7-point Likert-type scale, people indicate their attitudes toward computer usage. Scale is divided into 4 factors: negative reactions to computers, positive reactions to computers, computers and children/education, and reaction to (familiar) computer-related mechanisms. Demographic information on the subjects may be gathered to assess factors that may be related to attitudes toward computers. Found to be reliable.

15781
Communication Profile for the Hearing Impaired. Demorest, Marilyn E.; Erdman, Sue Ann 1987
Subtests: Communication Performance; Communication Environment; Communication Strategies; Personal Adjustment
Descriptors: Adjustment (to Environment); Adults; Affective Behavior; *Communication Problems; Communication Skills; *Deafness; Environmental Influences; *Hearing Impairments; Hearing Therapy; Needs Assessment; Partial Hearing; Psychological Needs; Self Evaluation (Individuals); Likert Scales
Identifiers: CPHI
*Availability: Journal of Speech and Hearing Disorders;*v52 n2 p129-43, May 1987
Target Audience: Adults
Notes: Items, 145

Designed to assess the environmental, behavioral, emotional, and attitudinal factors that affect communication problems of hearing-impaired adults. Scale is divided into 3 parts. In one part, respondents answer items according to how accurately the item reflects their feelings about their situation. In another part, respondents indicate how frequently they have experienced the event described. In the third section, items are responded to in both manners. Covers 4 areas: Communication Performance, Communication Environment, Communication Strategies, and Personal Adjustment. May be used to facilitate intervention.

15795
Army Battalion Unit Morale Measure. Kimmel, Melvin J.; And Others 1984
Descriptors: Adults; Job Satisfaction; *Military Organizations; *Military Service; *Morale; Occupational Tests; *Organizational Climate
*Availability: National Technical Information Service; 5285 Port Royal Rd., Springfield, VA 22161 (AD-A168311)
Target Audience: 18-55
Notes: Items, 73

Designed for use as a measure of organizational morale for military personnel within battalions. Was administered to a sample of service personnel, noncommissioned officers, and other officers. A general satisfaction score is calculated. To develop a morale score, all individual scores are averaged. Items cover organizational climate in 4 domains: unit, supervisor, coworker, and job domain.

15798
Stereotypes about Male Sexuality Scale. Snell, William E. Jr.; And Others 1986
Descriptors: Adults; Beliefs; *Males; Measures (Individuals); *Sexuality; Spouses; *Stereotypes; Therapists
Identifiers: SAMSS
*Availability: Select Press; P.O. Box 9838, San Rafael, CA 94912
Target Audience: Adults
Notes: Items, 60

This inventory was designed to measure the 10 stereotypes about male sexuality. Subscales are inexpressiveness, sex equals performance, males orchestrate sex, always ready for sex, touching leads to sex, sex equals intercourse, sex requires erection, sex requires orgasm, sex is spontaneous, men are sexually aware. Focuses on misconceptions of therapists and others about male sexuality and what others should believe about it. Available as *Social and Behavioral Sciences Documents*, 1986, v16 n1, 9(Ms. No. 2746) 57 pages.

15806
Trust Assessment Survey. Goodloe, Alfred; And Others 1984
Descriptors: *Administrator Attitudes; Administrators; Adults; Interpersonal Relationship; Questionnaires; *Trust (Psychology)
*Availability: Goodloe, Alfred, and Others; Managing Yourself: How to Control Emotion, Stress, and Time.*New York: Franklin Watts, 1984
Target Audience: Adults
Notes: Items, 25

Designed to measure the level of trust managers have in their subordinates and colleagues. Managers complete the survey by responding to questions about each of their coworkers in turn. Gives an overall picture of how managers think about their subordinates and colleagues. May be used to help managers enhance their trust in others.

15811
Beliefs about Women Scale. Belk, Sharyn S.; Snell, William E., Jr. 1986

Descriptors: Adults; Affective Behavior; Behavior Patterns; Beliefs; *Females; Interpersonal Competence; Males; Personality Traits; *Sex Stereotypes; Sexuality; Undergraduate Students
Identifiers: BAWS
Availability: Select Press; P.O. Box 9838, San Rafael, CA 94912
Target Audience: Adults
Notes: Items, 75

A self-report measure of 15 stereotypes about women designed for use in the investigation of women's and men's personal functioning and their interpersonal relationships. The 15 subscales cover dominance, passivity, vulnerability, emotional insight, interpersonal ability, career interest, intelligence, decisiveness, sexuality, menstruation, emphasis on appearance, sexual teasing, morality, acting silly, and using manipulation. Two types of stereotypes are measured: those dealing with women's characteristics and those dealing with women vis-a-vis men. Normed on undergraduate psychology students.

15816
Attitudes toward the Male's Role Scale. Doyle, James A.; Moore, Robert J. 1978
Subtests: Male-Female Sex Roles; Appropriate Male Behavior; Chivalry; Male Role in the Family and Occupations; Attitudes toward Homosexuality
Descriptors: Adults; Behavior Patterns; College Students; Family Environment; Females; Higher Education; Homosexuality; *Males; *Sex Role; Sexuality; Work Environment
Identifiers: AMR
Availability: Select Press; P.O. Box 9838, San Rafael, CA 94912
Target Audience: Adults
Notes: Items, 45

This 4-point agree/disagree scale was designed to investigate male dominance, general and vocational pursuits, interests and skills, sexuality, emotionality, courtesies toward women, and interpersonal relations. Norms are available for sectarian college males and females; public university males and females; junior-senior high school females and males; adult females/males. Responses reflect a progression from extremely conservative traditional attitudes to nontraditional, liberal attitudes.

15834
EASY: Employee Attitude Study. Wolfe Personnel Services, Oradell, NJ 1988
Subtests: Interpersonal Harmony; People Orientation; Excitement; Involvement; Action Bias; Work Pressure; Control; Communications; Autonomy; Innovation; Hygiene Factors; Physical Environment
Descriptors: Adults; *Computer Assisted Testing; Computers; Computer Software; *Employee Attitudes; *Work Attitudes; *Work Environment
Identifiers: EASY
Availability: Wolfe Personnel Services; Box 319, Oradell, NJ 07649
Target Audience: Adults
Notes: Time, 60; Items, 84

Assesses employee attitudes toward actual work environment using true/false format. The employee then responds to the same statements with respect to an ideal work environment. A group's manager completes the same scale. The instrument is offered as a PC-based system for corporatewide use only. It is IBM compatible. Can be generalized to work groups at various levels to allow comparison. A report is produced for each group to integrate all input.

15839
Parent Outcome Interview. Magura, Stephen; Moses, Beth Silverman 1986
Descriptors: Adults; *Child Welfare; *Interviews; *Parent Attitudes; *Program Effectiveness
Availability: Child Welfare League of America; 440 1st St. N.W., Ste. 310, Washington, DC 20001-2085
Target Audience: Adults

Evaluation instrument designed to obtain client's assessment of agency services and case outcomes in child welfare cases. Interview covers 11 areas: referral situation, out-of-home placement, housing and economic conditions, physical child care, discipline and emotional care of children, children's academic adjustment, children's conduct, children's symptomatic behavior, victimization of children, parental coping, and relationship with social worker. Checklist is intended to indicate relative changes in types and numbers of problems between referral and the interview, and the ratings are intended to indicate changes in the degree of the problems in each content area. The various parts of the interview constitute the method of measuring case change for each problem content area.

15945
Wellness Index, Second Edition. Travers, John W. 1988
Subtests: Wellness, Self-Responsibility and Love; Wellness and Breathing; Wellness and Sensing; Wellness and Eating; Wellness and Moving; Wellness and Feeling; Wellness and Thinking; Wellness and Playing/Working; Wellness and Communicating; Wellness and Sex; Wellness and Finding Meaning; Wellness and Transcending
Descriptors: Adults; Rating Scales; Self Evaluation (Individuals); *Well Being
Identifiers: *Wellness
Availability: Wellness Associates; Box 5433, Mill Valley, CA 94942
Target Audience: Adults
Notes: Items, 378

Measures individuals' perceptions of their degree of wellness rather than their degree of illness. Recommended by publisher for classes and clinics where wellness is a major topic of interest.

15946
Wellness Inventory, Third Edition. Travers, John W. 1988
Subtests: Wellness, Self-Responsibility and Love; Wellness and Breathing; Wellness and Sensing; Wellness and Eating; Wellness and Moving; Wellness and Feeling; Wellness and Thinking; Wellness and Playing/Working; Wellness and Communicating; Wellness and Sex; Wellness Finding Meaning; Wellness and Transcending
Descriptors: Adults; Computer Assisted Testing; Rating Scales; Self Evaluation (Individuals); *Well Being
Identifiers: Hypercard; *Wellness
Availability: Wellness Associates; Box 5433, Mill Valley, CA 94942
Target Audience: Adults
Notes: Items, 120

Measures individuals' perceptions of their degree of wellness rather than the degree of illness. This is an abridged version of the Wellness Index (TC015945). Has a graphic self-scoring wheel to give respondent a picture of his or her self-perceptions of wellness. Provides an introduction to the concept and practice of wellness. Can also be self-administered interactively on a microcomputer, including IBM and compatibles, Macintosh Plus, SE, and II. HyperCard software comes with new computers.

16027
Bath County Computer Attitudes Survey. Bear, George; And Others 1987
Descriptors: *Computers; *Elementary School Students; Elementary Secondary Education; Questionnaires; *Secondary School Students; *Student Attitudes; Likert Scales
Identifiers: BCCAS
Availability: *Journal of Educational Computing Research;*v3 n2 p207-18, 1987
Grade Level: 4-12
Notes: Items, 26

Designed to measure the attitudes of students in grades 4 through 12 toward computers. May be used in conjunction with 2 other instruments to determine the factors in the students' background which affect their attitudes toward computers. The first is a questionnaire concerning students' computer experience and usage, educational and career plans, and favorite school subjects. The second is the Elementary Form of the Estes Attitude Scales (TC011265), which is used to assess students' attitudes toward school subjects.

16030
Computer Attitudes Questionnaire. Zoltan, Elizabeth; Chapanis, Alphonse 1982
Subtests: Background Information; General Attitudes; General Statements
Descriptors: Adults; Attitudes; *Computers; *Professional Personnel; Questionnaires; Semantic Differential; Likert Scales
Availability: *Behaviour and Information Technology;*v1 n1 p55-68, 1982
Target Audience: Adults
Notes: Items, 64

Designed to measure professional persons' attitudes toward computers. Consists of a Background Information section, which may be tailored to each person's profession, a General Attitudes section, and a General Statements section. The General Attitudes section consists of 41 pairs of adjectives in a semantic differential format. Participants choose how closely each adjective corresponds to their attitudes about computers. The General Statements section consists of 23 statements to which participants respond as to how strongly they agree or disagree with each statement. Factor analysis provided. May be used to examine differences among professions and between experienced and inexperienced users.

16043
Personal Expectations Inventory. Forisha-Kovach, Barbara; And Others 1980
Descriptors: Adults; Behavior Patterns; *Employee Attitudes; Group Behavior; Interpersonal Relationship; *Occupational Tests; Personality Measures; Productivity; Social Integration; *Work Attitudes
Identifiers: PXI
Availability: Organization Design and Development; 2002 Renaissance Blvd., Ste. 100, King of Prussia, PA 19406-2746
Target Audience: Adults
Notes: Items, 72

Designed to measure individual employees' expectations and perceptions that are the framework of their behaviors. Identifies employees who are producers (getting things done), processors (being with others), integrators (making all the parts fit). Said to assist in determining who is "in synchrony" with the employee group, which may lead to increased productivity, depending on the norms of the group.

16046
Career Profile Inventory. Nowack, Kenneth W. 1986
Descriptors: Adults; *Career Development; *Employees; Individual Needs; Interests; *Occupational Tests; Organizational Climate; Power Structure; Values; Work Attitudes
Availability: Organization Design and Development; 2002 Renaissance Blvd., Ste. 100, King of Prussia, PA 19406-2746
Notes: Time, 30; Items, 10

This inventory is designed to assist the respondent in gaining insight into present career stage, career path preference, organizational political style orientation. Covers career concerns, activities, values, needs and behaviors, interests, political style. Designed for use in group or individual career development sessions.

16048
Managerial Interest Audit. Nowack, Kenneth W. 1986
Descriptors: *Administrators; Adults; Affiliation Need; Computer Assisted Testing; *Interests; Interpersonal Competence; *Job Satisfaction; Leadership; Management Development; *Managerial Occupations; *Occupational Tests; *Personnel Selection; Values; *Work Attitudes
Identifiers: MIA
Availability: Organization Design and Development; 2002 Renaissance Blvd., Ste. 100, King of Prussia, PA 19406-2746
Notes: Items, 150

Designed to measure an employee's interest in 15 job-relevant areas: autonomy, variety, innovation, achievement, self-assessment, persuasion, affiliation, people perception, group communication, leading, negotiation, problem analysis, planning, and organizing, coaching, and delegation. May be used for employee selection, placement, training and development, presupervisory development, and succession planning. This instrument is said to be predictive of job satisfaction. May be administered and scored via a software package.

16049
Employee Interest Audit. Nowack, Kenneth W. 1986
Descriptors: Adults; Affiliation Need; *Computer Assisted Testing; *Employees; *Interests; Interpersonal Competence; *Job Satisfaction; *Occupational Tests; Personnel Selection; Problem Solving; Values; *Work Attitudes
Identifiers: EIA
Availability: Organization Design and Development; 2002 Renaissance Blvd., Ste. 100, King of Prussia, PA 19406-2746
Notes: Items, 130

Measures an employee's interests in 13 job-relevant areas: variety, autonomy, achievement, persuasion, affiliation, people perception, group communication, leading, negotiating, problem solving, planning and organizing, coaching, administering. This instrument is said to be predictive of job satisfaction. May be administered and scored via a software package.

16062
Teacher Problem-Solving Interview. Burns, Robert B.; Lash, Andrea A. 1988
Descriptors: Classroom Techniques; Elementary Education; *Elementary School Teachers; Grade 7; *Interviews; *Mathematics Instruction; *Mathematics Teachers; *Problem Solving; *Teacher Attitudes; Teaching Methods
Availability: *Elementary School Journal;*v88 n4 p369-86, Mar 1988
Target Audience: Adults
Notes: Time, 60 approx.; Items, 22

Semistructured teacher interview investigating teachers' views on teaching mathematics and problem-solving, as well as everyday classroom operation. May be used to measure teachers' knowledge of how to manage and organize classroom instruction and how to teach problem-solving techniques in mathematics. Interviews may be audio taped and transcribed so that responses may be analyzed at a later time. May be used in conjunction with Teacher Planning Interview (TC016063) which investigates the ways in which teachers plan lessons for the problem-solving area of mathematics.

16111

Brief Measure of Activism Regarding the Nuclear Arms Race. Warner, Paul D.; Roy, Paul J. 1984
Subtests: Pro-Nuclear Acts; Anti-Nuclear Acts; Bipolar Activism; 14-Item Intensity
Descriptors: *Activism; Adults; Attitudes; *Disarmament; *Nuclear Warfare; Questionnaires; Self Evaluation (Individuals); Likert Scales
*Availability: Journal of Personality Assessment;*v49 n2 p181-86, 1985
Target Audience: Adults
Notes: Items, 14

Questionnaire designed to measure individuals' behavioral responses to the nuclear arms race. A bipolar questionnaire in which 7 statements concern actions taken for nuclear weapons, and 7 statements concern actions taken against nuclear weapons. Participants indicate on a Likert-type scale the frequency with which they have performed the actions in the last 4 years. May be analyzed according to 4 scales: Bipolar Activism, Anti-Nuclear Act; Pro-Nuclear Acts; and Fourteen Item Intensity. Validity of the entire scale was examined by studying responses of 5 groups whose ideologies range from pronuclear weapons to antinuclear weapons: defense industry workers, Republicans; psychology students; religious teachers; and peace activists. Results indicate expected results were recorded for each group. A 50 item form of this questionnaire is available.

16163

Methodology Interest Questionnaire. Schiefele, Urlich; Krapp, Andreas 1988
Descriptors: *College Students; *Education Majors; Higher Education; *Interest Inventories; *Research Methodology; *Student Interests
Identifiers: MIQ
Availability: ERIC Document Reproduction Service; 3900 Wheeler Ave., Alexandria, VA 22304 (ED292886, 25 pages)
Grade Level: 13-16
Notes: Items, 6

Developed for use in a research study to examine the relationship between the extent of interest in research methodology of education students and knowledge in this area. Objective of the study was to gain a better understanding of the role of specific and qualitative cognitive measures in the examination of the interest-achievement relationship.

16164

Omega Scale. Staik, Irene M. 1984
Descriptors: Adults; Beliefs; *College Students; *Death; Higher Education; Rating Scales; Religion; *Student Attitudes
Identifiers: Funerals
Availability: ERIC Document Reproduction Service; 3900 Wheeler Ave., Alexandria, VA 22304 (ED292820, 13 pages)
Grade Level: Higher Education
Target Audience: 18-65
Notes: Items, 25

The Omega Scale is a 25-item Likert-type scale developed to assess the attitudes of college students toward their own deaths, burial practices, traditional vs. nontraditional funeral options, and preferences regarding the disposition of their bodies after death. The factors analyzed include non-traditional secular funeral, personal funeral arrangement, traditional funeral, and preferred disposition of the body. Factor analysis of the Omega Scale is included.

16169

Supervisory Style Evaluation Instrument. Didactic Systems, Cranford, NJ 1979
Descriptors: Adults; *Employee Attitudes; Feedback; *Supervisory Methods
Availability: Didactic Systems; Box 457, Cranford, NJ 07016
Target Audience: Adults
Notes: Items, 18

The primary purpose of this questionnaire is to provide a vehicle for introspection. It attempts to connect task and people orientation through a Task Scale and People Scale included on the Supervisory Style Scale. This evaluation instrument gives a general view of how a supervisor is likely to be perceived by subordinates and peers.

16172

Coping Inventory: Self-Rated Form. Zeitlin, Shirley 1985
Subtests: Coping with Self; Coping with Environment
Descriptors: *Adjustment (to Environment); Adolescents; Adults; *Coping; Rating Scales; *Self Evaluation (Individuals); Well Being
Availability: Scholastic Testing Service; 480 Meyer Rd., Bensenville, IL 60106

Target Audience: 13-65
Notes: Items, 48

The Coping Inventory is a self-rating instrument used to assess the behavior patterns and skills that a person uses to meet individual needs and to adapt to the demands of the environment. The 48 items in the inventory are equally divided into 2 categories, Coping with Self and Coping with Environment. The items in each of these categories are further divided into 3 dimensions, productive, active, and flexible. These describe the learned behaviors an individual uses to meet personal needs and to adapt to the demands of the environment.

16230

New Environmental Paradigm Scale. Dunlap, Riley E.; Van Liere, Kent 1978
Descriptors: Adults; Conservation (Environment); Ecology; *Global Approach; *Models; *Physical Environment; Rating Scales
Identifiers: NEP Scale
*Availability: Journal of Environmental Education;*v17 n1 p9-12, Fall 1985
Target Audience: Adults
Notes: Items, 12

Scale used to measure the paradigm shifts in the public's orientation toward the physical environment. The paradigm, the New Environmental Paradigm, views humans as a part of nature, recognizing the limits of an ecosystem and its balance. Factor analysis information included. May be administered to different populations, specifically people living in different parts of the country, or in rural or urban settings, to assess differences in attitude toward the physical environment among those populations.

16235

Student Opinionnaire of Teachers. Wright, Theodore H. 1971
Descriptors: *Listening Skills; Rating Scales; Secondary Education; *Secondary School Students; *Secondary School Teachers; Speech Skills; Student Attitudes; *Student Behavior
*Availability: Phi Delta Kappan;*v52 p625-28, July 1971
Grade Level: 7-12
Notes: Items, 10

Questionnaire to be administered by teachers to the students in their classes to assess students' listening ability. Students respond to questions concerning their reactions to the teacher's speaking. Teachers may use the results to improve their own speaking and listening skills as well as the listening skills of their students.

16239

Family Belief Interview Schedule. Alessandri, Steven M.; Wozniak, Robert H. 1987
Descriptors: Adolescents; Adults; Behavior Patterns; *Beliefs; *Childhood Attitudes; Children; *Family Attitudes; Interviews; *Parent Attitudes; Parents
*Availability: Child Development;*v58 n2 p316-23, Apr 1987
Target Audience: 10-65
Notes: Items, 15

This instrument consists of 15 short vignettes designed to assess parental beliefs about the child and the child's beliefs about parental beliefs. Vignettes describe situations a child may encounter at home. Parents are asked to describe what they think the child might do in that situation, and children are asked for either parent's point of view or what the child might "really" do in that situation. Data are available derived from a sample of 10-11 year olds and 15-16 year olds, males and females.

16318

Employability Attitudes Assessment. PREP, Inc., Trenton, NJ 1986
Descriptors: Adults; *Audiovisual Aids; Behavior Problems; Employment Potential; Industrial Training; Job Applicants; Job Search Methods; Multiple Choice Tests; *Occupational Tests; Pictorial Stimuli; *Work Attitudes
Availability: PREP, Inc.; 1007 Whitehead Rd. Extension, Trenton, NJ 08638
Target Audience: Adults
Notes: Items, 360

This audiovisual program and paper-and-pencil test is designed to assess individuals' employability-related attitudes. Uses a self-paced system. Uses an instrument with 36 behavior categories, 13 job seeking and 23 job keeping, based on a survey of hiring, firing, and promotion-inspiring behaviors seen in industry. The assessment is presented on audiovisual cartridges for individual or small group administration. For each attitude assessed, there are 10 behavioral incidents portrayed followed by a multiple-choice test item. Respondent chooses from among 7 behavioral solutions to the incident. Prescriptive and training materials included.

16362

Employee Opinion Survey. Talico, Inc., Jacksonville Beach, FL 1987

Descriptors: Adults; *Employee Attitudes; *Feedback; Job Satisfaction; *Organizational Climate; *Organizational Development; *Quality of Working Life; *Work Environment
Availability: Talico, Inc.; 2320 S. 3rd St., Ste. 5, Jacksonville Beach, FL 32250
Target Audience: Adults
Notes: Time, 35 approx.; Items, 46

This instrument measures and evaluates employees' attitudes, perceptions, and beliefs about their jobs, their organization, and other work-related issues. Items dealing with 12 key organization impact areas are included. They are management effectiveness, supervisory practices, communication effectiveness, nondiscrimination, pay, benefits, interpersonal relations, policies, work rules, job interest, work performance, and general level of job satisfaction. The test includes 3 items calling for written comments or suggestions. The test may be used for employee opinion surveys, employee attitude studies, and organization climate surveys.

16367

Human Resource Survey. Talico, Inc., Jacksonville Beach, FL 1988
Subtests: Communication; Cost and Performance Consciousness; (EEO) Non-Discrimination; Growth and Advancement; Interpersonal Relationships; Management Effectiveness; Organization Policy; Pay and Benefits; Safety and Work Conditions; Supervisory Effectiveness
Descriptors: Adults; *Employee Attitudes; *Employer Employee Relationship; Equal Opportunities (Jobs); Fringe Benefits; *Organizational Climate; *Quality of Working Life; Rating Scales; *Work Environment
Identifiers: HRS; *Human Resource Management
Availability: Talico, Inc.; 2320 S. 3rd St., Ste. 5, Jacksonville Beach, FL 32250
Target Audience: Adults
Notes: Time, 45 approx.; Items, 50

This instrument measures employees' opinions and attitudes about those aspects of the job and work environment that impact on morale, performance, and productivity. Employee perceptions are gathered in 10 categories which include communications, cost and performance, consciousness, nondiscrimination (EEO), growth and advancement, relationships, management and supervisory effectiveness, policies and work rules, pay and benefits, and safety and work conditions. The instrument includes a write-in comment section as well. The instrument may be used in morale and motivation studies, climate studies, organizational analysis, and human resource management audits.

16369

Participative Climate Diagnosis. Talico, Inc., Jacksonville Beach, FL 1988
Subtests: Creative Climate; Communication; Productivity Consciousness; Participative Climate; Interpersonal Climate; Goals and Standards; Motivation; Change; Problem Solving; Union Relations (Optional)
Descriptors: Adults; *Change Strategies; *Employee Attitudes; Informal Organization; *Organizational Climate; *Organizational Development; *Organizational Effectiveness; *Organizational Objectives; *Participative Decision Making; Quality Circles; Self Evaluation (Groups)
Availability: Talico, Inc.; 2320 S. 3rd St., Ste. 5, Jacksonville Beach, FL 32250
Target Audience: Adults
Notes: Time, 20 approx.; Items, 50

This diagnostic instrument helps to assess the readiness of organizational climates for participative or employee involvement programs. Employees' perceptions about working conditions and the organizational environment which impact on their performance and productivity are categorized into 10 participative and performance categories. These categories include creative climate, communications, productivity consciousness, participative climate, interpersonal climate, goals, stands, motivation change, problem solving, union relations. The test may be self- or facilitator administered. This instrument may be used for quality circle programs, productivity teams, attitude and climate studies, participative management training.

16370

Survey of Organizational Effectiveness. Talico, Inc., Jacksonville Beach, FL 1988
Subtests: Collaboration; Commitment; Creativity
Descriptors: Adults; *Creativity; *Employee Attitudes; *Organizational Development; *Organizational Effectiveness; *Organizational Objectives; *Participative Decision Making; Rating Scales; Self Evaluation (Groups); *Teamwork
Identifiers: *Organizational Competence Theory; SOE
Availability: Talico, Inc.; 2320 S. 3rd St., Ste. 5, Jacksonville Beach, FL 32250
Target Audience: Adults

Notes: Time, 20 approx.; Items, 24

This diagnostic tool, based on the organizational competency theory, helps management evaluate the effectiveness and performance competence at all levels of the organization by measuring current levels of collaboration, commitment, and creativity. Specifically, it measures the commitment of the workers to the organization's goals and objectives as well as the workers' sense of their individual contributions. It also measures how the employees work together as a team and use their full creative capability to problem solve and make decisions. The survey is administered by a facilitator. The survey may be used for climate studies, organization change and renewal, performance and productivity improvement, and organizational competence studies.

16388
Career Values Scale. Talico, Inc., Jacksonville Beach, FL 1987
Descriptors: Adults; *Management Development; *Managerial Occupations; *Occupational Aspiration; Values; *Vocational Interests
Identifiers: CVS
Availability: Talico, Inc.; 2320 S. 3rd St., Ste. 5, Jacksonville Beach, FL 32250
Target Audience: Adults

Developed to help managerial staff gain a clearer understanding about the values they assign to various career-related factors and to aid in career planning and counseling activites. Helps to measure career interests, goals, needs, and aspirations in 4 major dimensions: work environment, position preference, growth-ambition, and career introspection. Self- or facilitator administered. Normative and reliability data are under development. Can be used for career planning, self-professional-career development, coaching and counseling, and selection and advancement.

16389
Clerical Productivity Analysis. Talico, Inc., Jacksonville Beach, FL 1987
Descriptors: Adults; *Clerical Workers; Productivity; Rating Scales; *Work Environment
Identifiers: CPA
Availability: Talico, Inc.; 2320 S. 3rd St., Ste. 5, Jacksonville Beach, FL 32250
Target Audience: Adults
Notes: Time, 25 approx.; Items, 40

Developed to help office managers and supervisors evaluate those factors that influence clerical work force productivity most significantly. Included are factors relating to physical environment and human resources, such as training, staffing, and morale/motivation. May be self- or administrator administered. Useful for office supervision training and development, aiding clerical worker productivity and improvement, and coaching and counseling. Clerical staff rates each item on 2 factors: importance to the job and personal opinions.

16395
Safety Practices Audit. Talico, Inc., Jacksonville Beach, FL 1987
Descriptors: Adults; *Employees; Knowledge Level; Questionnaires; Rating Scales; *Safety; *Work Environment
Identifiers: SPA
Availability: Talico, Inc.; 2320 S. 3rd St., Ste. 5, Jacksonville Beach, FL 32250
Target Audience: Adults
Notes: Time, 45 approx.; Items, 40

Used to measure awareness and attitudes regarding personal and organizational safety and to improve and develop employee safety consciousness. Measures employees' knowledge and awareness of such issues as safety and emergency care procedures, safety practices, facilities, safety training, accident rates, causes, and related issues. Also aids in the identification of safety problems and elicits suggestions for improvement. Experimental instrument for which reliability and normative data are being collected. Can be used for safety program evaluation, organization analysis, or safety training and needs analysis.

16420
Beck Hopelessness Scale. Beck, Aaron T.; Steer, Robert A. 1988
Descriptors: Adolescents; Adults; Clinical Diagnosis; *Depression (Psychology); Multiple Choice Tests; Personality Problems; *Suicide
Identifiers: BHS; Future; *Hopelessness; *Pessimism
Availability: Psychological Corp.; 555 Academic Ct., San Antonio, TX 78204-0952
Target Audience: 13–65
Notes: Items, 20

This scale is designed to measure the extent of the respondent's negative attitudes, or pessimism, about the future. May be used as an indicator of suicidal risk in depressed persons who have made suicide attempts. The test is multiple choice. It is not designed for use as a measure of the hopelessness construct but has been used as such. Sufficient data about the use of the test with those younger than 17 has not been collected. May be administered and scored by paraprofessionals. May be used and interpreted only by clinically trained professionals, who can employ psychotherapeutic interventions. Norms are available for suicidal patients and depressed patients and drug abusers.

16426
Attitudinal Listening Profile System. Performax Systems International, Minneapolis, MN 1988
Descriptors: Adults; *Listening Habits
Availability: Carlson Learning Company; 12805 State Hwy. 55, Minneapolis, MN 55451
Target Audience: Adults

This instrument aids in identifying individuals' predominant listening attitudes; comparing their listening attitudes in task and human relations settings; describing different listening attitudes; and increasing flexibility in listening habits. Listening attitudes are said to be directly related to individual needs. People develop inflexible listening habits if they perceive their needs as static. Listening attitudes are defined as leisure (pleasurable), inclusive (comprehensive), stylistic (mannerisms-medium), technical (systematic), empathetic (emotions), and nonconforming (analytical).

16463
Goldfarb Fear of Fat Scale. Goldfarb, Lori A. 1985
Descriptors: *Adolescents; *Anorexia Nervosa; *Bulimia; *Fear; *Females; *Obesity; Rating Scales; *Screening Tests; Likert Scales
Identifiers: GFFS
Availability: *Journal of Personality Assessment;*v49 n3 p329-32, 1985
Target Audience: 12–18
Notes: Items, 10

Ten-item scale designed to assess females' fears of becoming overweight. Scale may be administered to people who suffer from bulimia or anorexia nervosa, repeat dieters and nondieters to examine the differences in fear of weight gain among the groups. Respondents indicate on a 4-point Likert-type scale how closely each statement represents their beliefs and feelings. May be used for early identification of bulimic individuals. Information on correlations among groups is included as well as information on analysis of variance.

16513
Attitudes toward Alcohol and Alcoholism. Weir, W.R. 1969
Descriptors: Adolescents; *Alcohol Education; *Alcoholism; *Attitude Change; Pretests Posttests; Questionnaires; Secondary Education
Availability: *Journal of Alcohol Education;*v15 p1-8, 1969

An attitude measure for use as part of an educational program on alcohol and alcoholism. Purpose of the instrument is to determine individuals' attitudes toward alcohol before participating in the program and any changes in attitude that may occur as a result of the program. Consists of 3 groups of 7 statements each. Individuals indicate the statements they agree and disagree with and indicate the statement within each group that they agree with most and the one they disagree with most. Individuals' age, sex, intelligence, involvement in a family alcohol problem and ego-involvement in the issue may be focused on to determine differences that might occur among these groups. Variations in presentation of the program may also be made to examine how each type of presentation affects attitudes. Instrument has been used primarily with high school students.

16527
FAMACT. Funch, Donna P.; And Others 1986
Descriptors: Adults; *Eating Habits; *Family Attitudes; Questionnaires; Responses; *Social Support Groups
Availability: *Social Science and Medicine;*v23 n3 p337-44; 1986
Target Audience: Adults
Notes: Items, 6

Instrument to be completed by individuals who are dieting to assess the attitudes and behaviors of members of the individuals' families to their dieting. Respondents indicate whether the actions noted in 6 statements are applicable to their families. May be used in conjunction with the Social Support Scale (TC016515) to measure support given to dieting individuals by their families.

16551
Survey of AIDS Information. Goodwin, Megan P.; Roscoe, Bruce 1988
Descriptors: Adults; *College Students; Fear; Higher Education; *Homosexuality; *Knowledge Level; Objective Tests; *Acquired Immune Deficiency Syndrome
Availability: *Journal of American College Health;*v36 p214-21, Jan 1988
Grade Level: 13–16
Target Audience: Adults
Notes: Items, 49

True-false instrument to measure college students' knowledge and attitudes concerning Acquired Immunodeficiency Syndrome (AIDS). Consists of 3 sections: knowledge of AIDS (32 items); fear of contracting AIDS (9 items); and attitudes toward homosexuality (8 items). Used to study whether relationships exist between or among the 3 issues focused upon. Results may be used to assist educators in setting up programs concerning AIDS and programs educating about homosexuality.

800126
Test of Perception of Scientists and Self. Mackay, L.D.; White, R.T. 1976
Subtests: Self; Scientists
Descriptors: Behavior Patterns; Foreign Countries; High Schools; *High School Students; Personality Traits; Sciences; *Scientists; Self Concept; Self Concept Measures; *Student Attitudes
Identifiers: Australia; TOPOSS
Availability: Tests in Microfiche; Test Collection, Educational Testing Service, Princeton, NJ 08541
Grade Level: 9–12
Notes: Time, 20 approx.; Items, 40

Designed to measure effects of instruction on students' perception of scientists; students' self-perception; and similarity between scientists' perception of scientists and students' perception of scientists. Useful in measuring attributes of groups of students.

800191
Test of Science-Related Attitudes. Fraser, Barry J. 1981
Subtests: Social Implications of Science; Normality of Scientists; Attitude to Scientific Inquiry; Adoption of Scientific Attitudes; Enjoyment of Science Lessons; Leisure Interest in Science; Career Interest in Science
Descriptors: Adoption (Ideas); Foreign Countries; Leisure Time; Rating Scales; Science Curriculum; *Sciences; Scientific Methodology; Scientists; *Secondary School Students; Social Values; Vocational Interests
Identifiers: Australia; TOSRA
Availability: Australian Council for Educational Research; P.O. Box 210, Hawthorn, Victoria Australia 3122
Grade Level: 7–10
Notes: Items, 70

Designed to measure 7 distinct science-related attitudes of secondary school students. Suitable for group administration. Can be administered within the duration of a normal class lesson.

800194
Transmission Interpretation Scale, Short Form. Gardner, P.L.; Taylor, S.M. 1979
Descriptors: Foreign Countries; High Schools; *High School Students; Questionnaires; Rating Scales; *Secondary School Teachers; *Speech Communication; *Student Attitudes; *Teaching Styles
Identifiers: Australia
Availability: *British Journal of Educational Psychology;*v50 p186-87, 1980
Grade Level: High Schools
Notes: Items, 20

Attempts to measure style of teachers' verbal behavior, conceptualized as transmission-interpretation, as perceived by students.

800234
Library of Test Items: Home Science, Volume 1. New South Wales Dept. of Education, Sydney (Australia) 1980
Descriptors: Achievement Rating; Consumer Education; Criterion Referenced Tests; Foods Instruction; Foreign Countries; *Geography; *Home Economics; *Item Banks; Mastery Tests; Multiple Choice Tests; Nutrition Instruction; Secondary Education; *Secondary School Students; Student Evaluation; Test Construction; Values
Identifiers: Assessment Instruments; Australia (New South Wales)
Availability: ERIC Document Reproduction Service; 3900 Wheeler Ave., Alexandria, VA 22304 (ED219285, 111 pages)
Grade Level: 7–10

One of a series of test-item collections developed by the Assessment and Evaluation Unit of the Directorate of Studies. Designed for use by secondary school teachers for the construction of tests or as the basis for classroom discussions. Items in this volume measure attitudes and values, knowledge of consumer economics, nutrition and foods.

800258
Attitude Scales towards Institutional Authorities, Mother, Father, Parents in General. Rigby, Ken; Rump, E.E. 1980

Descriptors: *Adolescents; Fathers; Foreign Countries; Institutional Role; Justice; Military Organizations; Mothers; Parent Role; Police Community Relationship; Rating Scales; Teacher Student Relationship
Identifiers: Australia
Availability: Ken Rigby; School of Social Studies, S. Australian Institute of Technology, N. Terrace, Adelaide, S. Australia 5000
Target Audience: 13–17
Notes: Items, 84

Developed to assess attitudes of adolescents toward parents and institutional authorities, including police, teachers, the army, and the law. When used in a research study, it was found that adolescents' feelings toward their own parents had a bearing upon their attitudes toward authorities only during early adolescence.

800274
Goal and Mode Value Systems Inventories. Braithwaite, Valerie 1979
Subtests: Goal Values; Social Values; Mode Values
Descriptors: Adults; Foreign Countries; *Moral Values; Rating Scales; *Social Values; Values
Identifiers: Australia
Availability: *Journal of Personality and Social Psychology;*v49 n1 p250-63, 1985
Target Audience: Adults
Notes: Items, 125

Multi-item instrument measuring personal and social values using a rating scale. Divided into 3 parts: principles that you live by, behavior used as a guiding principle in your life, and principles that guide your judgments and actions.

800275
School-Level Environment Questionnaire, Modified Version. Williamson, John C.; And Others 1986
Descriptors: *Educational Environment; Foreign Countries; *High Schools; Organizational Climate; Rating Scales; *Secondary School Teachers; *Teacher Attitudes; *Teaching Conditions
Identifiers: Australia; SLEQ
Availability: ERIC Document Reproduction Service; 3900 Wheeler Ave., Alexandria, VA 22304 (ED274693, 31 pages)
Target Audience: Adults
Notes: Items, 56

A simple, fast, and valid measure of the educational climate at the high school level. Yields 8 scales which indicate teacher perceptions of their institutions in the following areas: Affiliation (support from colleagues), Professional interest (coworkers' interest in each others' professional activities), Achievement Orientation (expectation of student achievement), Formalization, Centralization, Innovativeness, Resource Adequacy, and Work Pressure

800276
College and University Classroom Environment Inventory. Treagust, David F.; Fraser, Barry J. 1986
Subtests: Personalization; Involvement; Student Cohesiveness; Task Orientation; Innovation; Individualization; Satisfaction
Descriptors: *Classroom Environment; *College Students; Foreign Countries; Higher Education; Rating Scales; *Seminars; *Student Attitudes; *Teacher Attitudes
Identifiers: Australia; CUCEI
Availability: ERIC Document Reproduction Service; 3900 Wheeler Ave., Alexandria, VA 22304 (ED274692, 25 pages)
Grade Level: 13–16
Notes: Items, 49

Used to assess college students' and faculty's perceptions of 7 psychosocial dimensions of actual or preferred classroom environment. To be used with small classes or seminars. Has been used in 2 research studies: an investigation of the relationship between student outcomes and the nature of the classroom environment and a study of the difference between students and instructors in their perceptions of actual and preferred classroom environments.

800277
Learning Process Questionnaire. Biggs, John 1987
Subtests: Surface Motive; Surface Strategy; Deep Motive; Deep Strategy; Achieving Motive; Achieving Strategy
Descriptors: *Cognitive Style; Individual Testing; *Learning Motivation; Learning Processes; *Learning Strategies; Secondary Education; *Secondary School Students; *Student Attitudes
Identifiers: LPQ
Availability: Australian Council for Educational Research; P.O. Box 210, Hawthorn, Victoria, Australia 3122
Grade Level: 9–12
Notes: Time, 20 approx.; Items, 36

Questionnaire designed to assess a student's general attitude toward learning. For students in grades 9 through 12. Provides scores on 3 basic motives for learning and 3 learning strategies and on the approaches to learning that are formed by these motives and strategies. Individual student profiles are generated. Profiles provide information for teachers and counselors in planning intervention programs and teaching strategies.

800282
School-Level Environment Questionnaire. Rentoul, A. John; Fraser, Barry J. 1983
Subtests: Affiliation; Student Supportiveness; Professional Interest; Achievement Orientation; Formalization; Centralization; Innovativeness; Resource Adequacy
Descriptors: *Educational Environment; Elementary Secondary Education; Foreign Countries; Psychological Characteristics; Rating Scales; Social Environment; Social Influences; *Teacher Attitudes
Identifiers: Australia; SLEQ
Availability: *Journal of Educational Administration;*v21 n1 p21-39, Win 1983
Target Audience: Adults
Notes: Items, 56

Measures teacher's perceptions of 8 psychosocial dimensions of the environment of primary or secondary schools: affiliation, student supportiveness, professional interest, achievement orientation, formalization, centralization, innovativeness, and resource adequacy. Useful in providing information on the effects of school-level environment and on teacher's pedagogical attitudes.

810098
Family Relations Test: Children's Version. Bene, Eva; Anthony, James 1978
Descriptors: *Adolescents; Affective Measures; *Childhood Attitudes; *Children; *Family Relationship; Foreign Countries; Individual Testing; Interpersonal Relationship; Psychological Testing
Identifiers: England; FRT; Great Britain
Availability: NFER-Nelson Publishing Company Ltd.; Darville House, 2 Oxford Rd. E., Windsor, Berkshire SL4 1DF, England
Target Audience: 3–15
Notes: Time, 25 approx.

Designed as an objective device for the exploration of the child's emotional relations with family members. Form for younger children, ages 3-7 years, consists of 47 items. Form for older children, ages 8-15, consists of 99 items.

810375
Family Relations Test: Married Couples Version. Bene, Eva 1976
Descriptors: Adults; Affective Measures; Child Rearing; Foreign Countries; Individual Testing; Interpersonal Relationship; *Marriage; *Parent Attitudes; *Parent Child Relationship; Parents; Psychological Testing; *Spouses
Identifiers: England; FRT; Great Britain
Availability: NFER-Nelson Publishing Company Ltd.; Darville House, 2 Oxford Rd. E., Windsor, Berkshire SL4 1DF, England
Target Audience: 18–64
Notes: Time, 25 approx.; Items, 78

Designed as an objective measure for the exploration of feelings between spouses and between parents and children.

810406
Personal Questionnaire Rapid Scaling Technique. Mulhall, David J. 1977
Descriptors: Adults; *Attitudes; Behavior Rating Scales; *Beliefs; Counseling Techniques; Foreign Countries; Questionnaires
Identifiers: England; Great Britain; *Personal Experiences; PQ10; PQ14; PQRST
Availability: NFER-Nelson Publishing Company Ltd.; Darville House, 2 Oxford Rd. E., Windsor, Berkshire SL4 1D7, England
Target Audience: Adults
Notes: Time, 15 approx.

Designed to monitor fluctuations in the intensity of personal experiences such as feelings, beliefs, symptoms. Has use in therapy, counseling, educational contexts, and various types of research. Comprised of 2 scales that differ in their range. PQ14; is a 14-point scale and uses a set of 8 adjectives, and PQ10 is a 10-point scale and uses 6 adjectives. With PQ14, variations in symptoms can be monitored more closely. PQ10 can be used more rapidly and makes less demands upon the patient. Can be given on several occasions so that a graph can be drawn showing changes which occur over time.

810477
The Claybury Selection Battery. Caine, T.M.; And Others 1982
Descriptors: Adults; *Counselor Attitudes; Expectation; Foreign Countries; *Interests; Patients; *Psychotherapy; Questionnaires; Rating Scales
Identifiers: ATQ; DIQ; England; Great Britain; Psychiatric Patients; TEQ; *Treatment Expectancies
Availability: NFER-Nelson Publishing Company Ltd.; Darville House, 2 Oxford Rd. E., Windsor, Berkshire SL4 1DF, England
Target Audience: Adults

Battery consists of 3 measures that assess elements of personal style that research has demonstrated to have clinical implications, particularly in the area of treatment selection. Based on evidence that patient expectancies and staff attitudes are a major influence on the outcome of treatment for psychological therapies, the Direction of Interest Questionnaire (DIQ) is a 14-item forced-choice questionnaire that distinguishes between an interest in ideas, theories, emotions, and an interest in facts, practical problems, common sense, power, and action. The Treatment Expectancies Questionnaire (TEQ) is a 15-item factor-analytically derived questionnaire that measures patients' expectancies regarding psychological and psychiatric treatment. The Attitudes to Treatment Questionnaire (ATQ) is a 19-item factor-analytically derived scale incorporated in a 24-item questionnaire that measures staff attitudes toward approaches to psychological and psychiatric treatment. Intended for psychologists, psychiatrists, occupational therapists, nurses, educational counselors, personnel, and training officers.

810499
Occupational Values. Educational and Industrial Test Services, Hempstead, England 1971
Descriptors: Adolescents; Adults; Career Guidance; Educational Counseling; Foreign Countries; Rating Scales; *Work Attitudes
Identifiers: England; Great Britain
Availability: Educational and Industrial Test Services, Ltd.; 83 High St., Hemel, Hempstead, Hertfordshire HP1 3AH, England
Target Audience: 13–64
Notes: Time, 5 approx.; Items, 8

Rating scale that indicates subject's attitudes to various aspects of job security or achievement and risk. Areas covered include travel, meeting people, salary, job security, pay versus interesting work, decision making, size of organization, responsibility. This rating scale is also included in the Personal Questionnaire (TC810498). Useful in vocational and educational guidance.

810500
Choosing A Career. Educational and Industrial Test Services, Hempstead, England 1968
Subtests: Rewards; Interests; Security; Pride and Recognition; Autonomy
Descriptors: Adolescents; Adults; Career Guidance; Educational Counseling; Foreign Countries; Needs Assessment; Preadolescents; Rating Scales; *Work Attitudes
Identifiers: England; Great Britain
Availability: Educational and Industrial Test Services, Ltd.; 83 High St., Hemel, Hempstead, Hertfordshire HP1 3AH, England
Target Audience: 11–64
Notes: Time, 10 approx.; Items, 50

Designed to supplement the Rothwell-Miller Interest Blank (TC800056) by providing a measure of attitudes toward work by investigating 5 factors: rewards; interests; security; pride and recognition; autonomy. Subject ranks statements in order of importance and from this the relative importance of each of the 5 categories can be determined. Useful for vocational and educational guidance.

810509
Family Relations Test: Adult Version. Bene, Eva 1965
Descriptors: Adults; Affective Measures; *Emotional Response; *Family Relationship; Parent Child Relationship; *Psychological Testing
Availability: NFER-Nelson Publishing Company Ltd.; Darville House, 2 Oxford Rd. E., Windsor, Berkshire SL4 1D7, England
Target Audience: Adults
Notes: Items, 96

To focus adults' attention on feelings they had as children toward their parents and other family members and on the attitudes the adults felt that family members had toward them as children. Two purposes of test are to facilitate recollection of childhood family feelings and to obtain these recollections in a systematic and quantifiable way. Test materials consist of 20 cardboard figures representing family members of various ages, sizes, and shapes to give a concrete representation of the testee's childhood family. There are 96 items, each printed on individual cards which the subject is asked to read and place into a box-like base attached to the family member who best fits the item description. Test may be used as a diagnostic, clinical instrument or as a research tool.

810569
Life Style Questionnaire. Barrett, James S.

Subtests: Expressive/Imaginative; Logical/Analytical; Managerial/Enterprising; Precise/Administrative; Active/Concrete; Supportive/Social; Risk Taking/Uncertainty; Perseverance/Determination; Self-Evaluation; Sensitivity/Other Awareness; Affiliation; Degree to which Vocation Is Associated with Self-Fulfillment; Degree of Certainty
Descriptors: Adolescents; Adults; Behavior; Career Counseling; Foreign Countries; *Life Style; Questionnaires; *Vocational Interests; *Work Attitudes
Identifiers: England; LSQ
Availability: The Test Agency; Cournswood House, North Dean, High Wycombe HP14 4NW, England
Target Audience: 14–65
Notes: Items, 132

Provides, information regarding the interests, attitudes, and likely behaviors of people at work. Intended for use in vocational guidance, counseling, recruitment, selection, and related areas. The LSQ presents 13 scales which are divided into 2 groups. Six of the scales are concerned with established areas of vocational choice. These 6 are expressive/imaginative, logical/analytical, managerial/enterprising, precise/administrative, active/concrete, and supportive/social. The other 7 scales provide insight regarding how the subject may be expected to cope with activities and situations with careers. These are risk taking/uncertainty, perseverance/determination, self-evaluation, sensitivity/other awareness, affiliation, degree to which vocation is associated with self-fulfillment, and degree of certainty. Intended for persons from age 14 upward. Graphs are provided as the best way of giving such information, one relating to interests and one to attitudes.

810573
Questionnaire to Investigate Attitudes to Infant Feeding and Post Natal Infant Feeding Questionnaire. Manstead, A.S.R. 1980
Descriptors: *Adolescents; *Adults; Foreign Countries; *Mother Attitudes; Questionnaires; Rating Scales; Self Evaluation (Individuals); *Breastfeeding
Identifiers: *Bottle Feeding; England
Availability: A.S.R. Manstead; Dept. of Psychology, University of Manchester, Manchester, M13 9PL, England
Target Audience: 13–64

This questionnaire was used in Manchester, England, to see whether mothers' attitudes to infant-feeding methods before the birth of a child to determine the feeding method; i.e., breast or bottle method. The attitudes were measured on mothers aged 16 to 40 years and with women having their first or subsequent child. These attitudes, beliefs, were measured during the last 3 months of pregnancy and again 6 weeks after the birth of the child. The rating scale was a 7-point one ranging from very unlikely to very likely. Two slightly different questionnaires were used; one administered prenatal and the other 6 weeks postnatal.

810574
Family Relations Test: Children's Version, Revised 1978 Edition. Bene, Eva; Anthony, James 1978
Descriptors: *Adolescents; *Children; *Emotional Disturbances; *Family Counseling; Family Influence; *Family Relationship; Foreign Countries; *Parent Child Relationship; *Parent Role
Identifiers: England; Great Britain
Availability: NFER-Nelson Publishing Company Ltd.; Darville House, 2 Oxford Rd. E., Windsor, Berkshire SL4 1DF, England
Target Audience: 3–15
Notes: Time, 25 approx.

The test material of the Family Relations Test was designed to give a concrete representation of the child's family. It consists of 20 figures representing people of various ages shapes, and sizes, sufficiently stereotyped to stand for members of any child's family, yet ambiguous enough to become, under suggestion, a specific family. They range from grandparents to a baby in a carriage, and from these, the child is able to create his or her own significant circle. There is also a figure "Nobody" that serves to accommodate those items that are not felt to apply to any in the family. Each figure is attached to a box-like base which has a slit in the top. The items are printed on small individual cards. The child is told that the cards contain messages and that his or her task is to put each card "into the person" for whom the message fits best. This is an objective technique for exploring emotional attitudes in children. There are 2 scoring sheets, one for younger children, ages 3-7, and another for older children, ages 7-15. There are 3 tests in the series: The Children's Version, The Adult Version, and The Married Couples' Version of the Family Relations Test. There are 99 items on the older children's test and 47 on the younger children's.

810600
Belief in Human Benevolence Scale. Thornton, D.; Kline, P. 1982
Descriptors: Adolescents; Adults; *Beliefs; Delinquency; Foreign Countries; Human Relations; Prisoners; Research Tools
Identifiers: Benevolence; Great Britain
Availability: *British Journal of Social Psychology*;v21 p57-62, 1982
Target Audience: 18–65
Notes: Items, 20

This scale was designed for use in research with juvenile delinquents and assesses the degree to which someone expects people to be generally malevolent or benevolent. It was used with undergraduate students and prisoners.

830213
Organization Health Survey. Kehoe, P.T.; Reddin, W.J. 1970
Subtests: Productivity; Leadership; Organization Structure; Communication; Conflict Management; Participation; Human Resource Management; Creativity
Descriptors: *Administrator Attitudes; *Administrators; Adults; Foreign Countries; *Management Systems; *Organizational Climate; *Organizational Communication
Identifiers: Canada; OHS
Availability: Organizational Tests, Ltd.; P.O. Box 324, Fredericton, NB E3B 4Y9, Canada
Target Audience: Adults
Notes: Time, 30 approx.; Items, 80

Untimed instrument used to discover the attitudes of managers to the organization in 8 areas: productivity, leadership, organization structure, communication, conflict management, participation, human resource management, and creativity. The manager answers true or false to each given statement. If used as part of a management training and development program, the authors recommended setting aside between 1.5 and 4.5 hours for taking the test, scoring, and discussion of the test itself and of the individual response to the organization. The authors recommend its use as an organizational survey in order to provide management with information on current opinion and as an in-company training device using the consensus method; it is particularly useful for sequential administrations over the life of an organizational change.

830218
Supervisory Human Relations. Stewart, E. Keith; Reddin, W.J. 1970
Descriptors: Adults; Employer Attitudes; *Employer Employee Relationship; Foreign Countries; Humanization; *Human Relations; *Interprofessional Relationship; Management Development; Occupational Tests; *Supervisors; Work Attitudes
Identifiers: Canada; SHR; *Supervisor Attitudes
Availability: Organizational Tests, Ltd.; P.O. Box 324, Fredericton, NB E3B 4Y9, Canada
Target Audience: Adults
Notes: Time, 30 approx.; Items, 80

An untimed, true-false instrument used to evaluate a supervisor's attitudes toward others. Includes relations with superiors, coworkers, subordinates. Used for both blue- and white-collar supervisors. When used as part of a supervisory training and development program, the authors recommend setting aside from 1.5 to 4.5 hours for the testing, the scoring, and for the discussion of the test itself and of related matters such as motivation, attitudes toward work, etc.

830220
Supervisory Union Relations. Reddin, W.J.; Stewart, E. Keith 1970
Descriptors: Adults; *Employer Employee Relationship; Foreign Countries; *Labor Relations; *Supervisors; *Unions; Work Attitudes; *Work Environment
Identifiers: Canada; *Supervisor Attitudes; SUR
Availability: Organizational Tests, Ltd.; P.O. Box 324, Fredericton, NB E3B 4Y9, Canada
Target Audience: Adults
Notes: Time, 30 approx.; Items, 80

An untimed, true-false instrument to determine a supervisor's attitudes toward unions. Includes motives of union leadership, why workers join unions, how best to work with unions, management rights, role of shop steward, foreman union relationship, labor benefits, and company benefits. Suitable for either blue- or white-collar supervisors. When used as part of supervisory training and development programs, the authors recommend setting aside from 1.5 to 4.5 hours for taking the test, scoring it, and discussing the test items, test score and other matters regarding labor relations, unions, etc.

830224
Supervisory Job Safety. Stewart, E. Keith 1970
Descriptors: Adults; Blue Collar Occupations; Foreign Countries; Knowledge Level; *Occupational Safety and Health; Safety Education; *Supervisors
Identifiers: Canada; SJS
Availability: Organizational Tests Ltd.; P.O. Box 324, Fredericton, NB E3B 4Y9, Canada
Target Audience: Adults
Notes: Items, 80

Designed to assess knowledge and attitudes toward safety practices. Useful for blue-collar supervision. Topics assessed include safety instruction, safety devices, safety responsibilities, safety causes, corrective practices, work methods, types of accidents, hazard analysis, accident investigation, and role of supervisors.

830228
Culture Shock Inventory. Reddin, W.J.; Rowell, K.R. 1970
Subtests: Western Ethnocentrism; Cross-Cultural Experience; Cognitive Flex; Behavioral Flex; Cultural Knowledge Specific; Cultural Knowledge General; Customs Acceptance; Interpersonal Sensitivity
Descriptors: Adolescents; Adults; Cultural Differences; Culture; *Culture Conflict; Foreign Countries; *Social Attitudes
Identifiers: Canada; CSI; Culture Shock Test
Availability: Organizational Tests Ltd.; P.O. Box 324, Fredericton, NB E3B 4Y9, Canada
Target Audience: 13–64
Notes: Items, 80

Designed to assess cross-cultural attitudes. May be used with those who expect to work outside their own culture or work with people from other cultures.

830229
Managerial Values Inventory. Reddin, W.J.; Rowell, K.R. 1970
Descriptors: Achievement Need; *Administrator Attitudes; *Administrators; *Adults; Foreign Countries; Higher Education; *Undergraduate Students; *Values
Identifiers: Canada; MVI; Values Inventory
Availability: Organizational Tests; P.O. Box 324, Fredericton, NB E3B 4Y9, Canada
Grade Level: 13–16
Target Audience: Adults
Notes: Items, 28

Designed to reveal the respondent's value system. Values assessed include theoretical, power, effectiveness, achievement, human, industry, and profit. May be used in colleges as well as industry.

830245
French Language Questionnaire. Randhawa, Bikkar S.; Korpan, Susan M. 1972
Descriptors: Elementary Education; *Elementary School Students; Foreign Countries; *French; *Junior High School Students; *Language Attitudes; Rating Scales; *Second Language Learning
Identifiers: ALFS; Canada; TIM(A)
Availability: Tests in Microfiche; Test Collection, Educational Testing Service, Princeton, NJ 08541
Grade Level: 1–8
Notes: Items, 26

Designed to measure attitudes toward learning French as a second language, this questionnaire encompasses 4 attitude factors: utilitarianism, aestheticism, tolerance, and projection.

830265
Teacher Questionnaire. Ontario Institute for Studies in Education, Toronto 1973
Subtests: Attitude toward Education; Attitude toward Teaching; Attitude toward Pupils; Attitude toward Innovations
Descriptors: Educational Attitudes; Elementary Education; *Elementary School Teachers; Foreign Countries; Innovation; *Teacher Attitudes; Work Attitudes
Identifiers: Canada; Educational Evaluation Instruments
Availability: Educational Evaluation Center, Ontario Institute for Studies in Education, Dept. of Measurement and Evaluation; 252 Bloor St. W., Toronto, ON M5S 1V6, Canada
Target Audience: Adults
Notes: Items, 108

One of a series of instruments developed for use in a descriptive study of elementary schools. Designed to measure teacher attitudes toward education, teaching, pupils, and innovations.

830284
Reaction Inventory-Guilt. Evans, David R. 1970
Subtests: Intentional Behavior Disrupting Interpersonal Relations; Self-Destructive Behavior; Behavior Contrary to Moral or Ethical Principles; Unintentional Behavior Disrupting Interpersonal Relationships
Descriptors: Adults; *Emotional Response; Foreign Countries; *Interpersonal Relationship; *Moral Development; Rating Scales; *Responses; Self Evaluation (Individuals); *Social Attitudes; Likert Scales

Identifiers: Canada; *Guilt; TIM(C)
Availability: Tests in Microfiche; Test Collection,
Educational Testing Service, Princeton, NJ
08541
Target Audience: Adults
Notes: Items, 50

Development of an instrument to index guilt-producing situations. The respondent is presented with 50 situations to which his or her is to respond with his or her level of guilt feelings, from not-at-all to very much.

830286
Scales of Alienated Attitude. Nettler, Gwynn
Subtests: Vs. Mass Culture; Vs. Familism; A-Religiosity; A-Politicalism
Descriptors: Adults; *Alienation; Foreign Countries; Groups; Opinions; Social Values
Identifiers: Canada; Prediction Of Human Conduct; Study of Opinions; TIM(C)
Availability: Tests in Microfiche; Test Collection,
Educational Testing Service, Princeton, NJ
08541
Target Audience: Adults
Notes: Items, 72

Designed to assess estrangement from some of the principal values of American culture. The author advises (1) rescale for each individual group and time; (2) may be useful for group-ordering purposes; (3) should NOT be used for assessment of individuals; and (4) always administered in the context of some other purpose such as the enclosed questionnaire entitled The Prediction of Human Conduct. This questionnaire has 3 sections. In the first section, one is to respond as he or she thinks most others would respond. The second section, entitled A Study of Opinions, asks the respondent for his or her own opinions. The third section gathers information about the respondent's age, sex, marital status, occupation, etc.

830288
Clarke Parent/Child Relations Questionnaire.
Paitich, Daniel 1976
Subtests: Mother's Aggression to Subject; Father's Aggression to Subject; Subject's Aggression to Mother; Subject's Aggression to Father; Mother's Aggression to Father; Father's Aggression to Mother; Mother's Competence; Father's Competence; Mother's Affection; Father's Affection; Mother's Strictness; Father's Strictness; Mother Identification; Father Identification; Mother's Indulgence; Father's Indulgence; Denial (Mother); Denial (Father)
Descriptors: Adults; Affection; Aggression; *Childhood Attitudes; Foreign Countries; *Interpersonal Relationship; *Parent Child Relationship; Parent Role
Identifiers: Canada; PCR; TIM(D)
Availability: Tests in Microfiche; Test Collection,
Educational Testing Service, Princeton, NJ
08541
Target Audience: Adults
Notes: Items, 131

Designed to sample the content areas of parent-child relations that have been found significant in clinical research. Includes 18 scales dealing with aggression, competence, affection, strictness, identification, indulgence, denial.

830398
A Curriculum Orientation Profile. Babin, Patrick
1979
Descriptors: Administrator Attitudes; Adults; *Check Lists; *Curriculum; *Educational Philosophy; Foreign Countries; *Self Evaluation (Individuals); Teacher Attitudes
Identifiers: Canada; Self Administered Tests; Self Scoring Tests
Availability: Education Canada;v19 n3 p38-43,
Fall 1979
Target Audience: Adults
Notes: Items, 57

Used to help educators identify particular curricular orientations. The subject agrees or disagrees with the statements concerning the content, goals, and organization of the curriculum. The inventory can be self-scored to reveal the individual's specific orientation to curriculum as one of the following: development of cognitive processes, curriculum as technology, self-actualization or curriculum as consummatory experience, social reconstruction-relevance, or academic rationalism.

830436
Intermediate Attitude Scale. Shapson, Stan; And
Others 1980
Descriptors: *Elementary School Students; Foreign Countries; *French; *Grade 7; Intermediate Grades; Junior High Schools; Rating Scales; *Student Attitudes
Identifiers: Canada
Availability: Simon Fraser University; Faculty of
Education, B.C. French Study, Burnaby, BC
V5A 1S6, Canada
Grade Level: 4-7
Notes: Time, 20 approx.; Items, 21

Designed for use with students in grades 4 through 7 to measure their attitudes toward the French language and culture. One item measures attitudes toward school in general.

875044
**Measurement of Masculinity-Femininity: Attitude
Interest Schedule.** Gottfries, Ingrid; Marke, Sven
1967
Descriptors: Adults; Affective Behavior; Foreign Countries; Interests; *Sex Role; Vocational Interests
Identifiers: Adjective Scales; *Femininity; *Masculinity; Sweden
Availability: Psychological Research Bulletin;v7 n4
p1-51, 1967
Target Audience: Adults
Notes: Items, 151

A measure of masculinity/femininity using subscales measuring preferences for occupations, hobbies, books, plays, and drawings. Emotionality-sensitivity is measured using items concerned with fear, disgust, pity, ethics, toughness, and emotions. Two other scales measure the subject's identification with animals and elicit a self-description via an adjective checklist. The *Psychological Research Bulletin* is published by Lund University in Sweden.

922000
**Cognitive Orientation Questionnaire of Defensive
Behavior.** Kreitler, Hans; Kreitler, Shulamith
1976
Subtests: Norms; General Beliefs; Beliefs about Self; Beliefs about Goals
Descriptors: Adults; *Attitudes; *Cognitive Style; Foreign Countries; Hebrew; *Predictive Measurement; Self Concept
Identifiers: Israel; TIM(D)
Availability: Tests in Microfiche; Test Collection,
Educational Testing Service, Princeton, NJ
08541
Target Audience: Adults
Notes: Items, 60

Designed to measure 4 types of beliefs (beliefs about norms and goals, general beliefs, and beliefs about self) that may orient an adult toward behavior corresponding to the defense mechanisms of rationalization, denial, and projection. The questionnaire is translated from Hebrew.

922001
Cognitive Orientation Questionnaire of Curiosity.
Kreitler, Shulamith; Kreitler, Hans 1974
Subtests: Beliefs about Self; General Beliefs; Beliefs about Goals; Beliefs about Norms
Descriptors: Attitudes; Behavior; *Cognitive Style; *Curiosity; Foreign Countries; Individual Testing; Primary Education; *Self Concept; *Young Children
Identifiers: Israel; TIM(D)
Availability: Tests in Microfiche; Test Collection,
Educational Testing Service, Princeton, NJ
08541
Target Audience: 4-8
Notes: Items, 73

Ten-part questionnaire designed to assess beliefs that may orient a child toward behavior identified as curiosity. The 73 items refer to 4 belief types: norms, general beliefs, beliefs about self, and goals. Responses are scored in terms of 3 categories: procuriosity orientation, anticuriosity orientation, and indeterminate position. Basic form is altered to suit boys or girls. Individually administered.

922002
Cognitive Orientation Questionnaire of Achievement. Kreitler, Hans; Kreitler, Shulamith
Subtests: Norms; Beliefs about Self; General Beliefs; Beliefs about Goals
Descriptors: *Achievement Need; *Adolescents; Cognitive Processes; *Cognitive Style; Foreign Countries; Hebrew; *Motivation; Secondary Education; Self Concept; Student Attitudes
Identifiers: Israel; TIM(D)
Availability: Tests in Microfiche; Test Collection,
Educational Testing Service, Princeton, NJ
08541
Target Audience: 15-18
Notes: Items, 45

Designed to assess 4 types of beliefs that may orient an adolescent toward achieving behavior. The belief types include norms, general beliefs, beliefs about self, and goals. The questionnaire is translated from Hebrew.

922004
**Cognitive Orientation Questionnaire for Quitting
Smoking.** Kreitler, Hans; Kreitler, Shulamith
1976
Subtests: Goals; Beliefs about Self; Beliefs about Norms; General Beliefs
Descriptors: Adults; Attitudes; Cognitive Style; Foreign Countries; Hebrew; Questionnaires; *Smoking
Identifiers: Israel; Oral Testing; TIM(D)

Availability: Tests in Microfiche; Test Collection,
Educational Testing Service, Princeton, NJ
08541
Target Audience: Adults
Notes: Items, 12

Questionnaire deals with quitting smoking. It is based on the cognitive orientation theory, and the items encompass 4 components of cognitive orientation: goals, beliefs about self, beliefs about norms, and general beliefs.

SUBJECT INDEX

AUTHOR INDEX

BOWMAN, BARBARA E. Beliefs about Computers Scale 14568

BOWMAN, MICHAEL L. Audit of Principal Effectiveness 15327

BRADLEY UNIVERSITY, PEORIA, IL Bradley University Alumni Records Survey, 1983 13217

BRAIN TECHNOLOGIES CORP., FT. COLLINS, CO Mindmaker 6 15104

BRAITHWAITE, VALERIE Goal and Mode Value Systems Inventories 800274

BRAMSON PARLETTE ASSOCIATES, BERKELEY, CA The Manifest Needs Questionnaire 14540

BRAMWELL, STEVEN T. Social and Athletic Readjustment Rating Scale 13828

BRAUCHLE, PAUL Affective Work Competencies Inventory 14308

BRAZELTON, J.M. Attitudes toward Bilingual Education 14458

BREED, GEORGE Scales to Measure Attitudes toward Marijuana and Marijuana Users 7944

BRICKLIN, BARRY Bricklin Perceptual Scales: Child Perception of Parents Series 15230

BRIDGES, K. ROBERT Education for Parenthood Attitude Scale 11980
——. Parent Education Design Scale 14454

BRIERLEY, MIRIAM Project PRIMES (Progress Research in Meeting Elementary Standards) Language Arts Evaluation 12910

BRIM, ORVILLE G. Desire for Certainty Scale 9383

BRINK, T.L. Geriatric Depression Scale 13891
——. Hypochondriasis Scale: Institutional Geriatric 15287

BRITISH COLUMBIA UNIVERSITY, VANCOUVER UBC Alumni Association Survey 12627

BRODSKY, ANNETTE Attitudes toward Feminist Issue Scale 9162

BRONFENBRENNER, URIE Parental Behavior Questionnaire 9384

BROOKS-GUNN, JEANNE Menstrual Attitude Questionnaire Form for Adolescent Females 11900
——. Menstrual Attitude Questionnaire Forms for Adult Males and Females 11899

BROUSSARD, ELSIE R. Neonatal Perception Inventory I and II 10846

BROWN, BOB BURTON Personal Beliefs Inventory: Forms A and B 7168

BROWN, B.R. Brown Scale for Measuring Attitudes toward Computer-Assisted Instruction 9385

BROWN, CARVIN L. Student Achievement Diagnostic Questionnaire 9883

BROWN, JOHN D. Semantic Differential Instrument for Measuring Attitude toward Mathematics 9074

BROWN, SANDRA Alcohol Expectancy Questionnaire-III (Adult) 14302
——. Gary-Brown Writing Opinionnaire for College Instructors 13485

BROWN, VIRGINIA L. Test of Mathematical Abilities 12272

BROZO, WILLIAM G. Student Behaviors Questionnaire 14037

BRUNKAN, R. The Family Relations Inventory 5568

BRYANT, BRENDA K. Index of Empathy for Children and Adolescents 11986

BUES, H.W. Scale for Measuring Attitudes toward Any Practice 2777

BUNDA, MARY ANNE Evaluation Characteristics Survey 8949

BUNDY, BARBARA ANN Reading Preference Survey 14556

BURBACH, HAROLD J. University Alienation Scale 5224

BURDSAL, CHARLES A. Student Perceptions of Teaching Effectiveness 14669

BURNS, FRANK Learning-Group Process Scale 12988
——. Organizational-Process Survey 12987

BURNS, MARIE SUSAN A. Lifestyles for Women Attitude Scale 13406

BURNS, ROBERT B. Teacher Problem-Solving Interview 16062

BYRD, MARQUITA Language Attitude Inventory 14034

BYRD-BREDHENNER, CAROL Nutrition Attitude Scale 10742

CACIOPPO, JOHN T. The Need for Cognition Scale 12341

CADO, SUZANA Attitude toward Homosexuality Scale 12345

CAHALAN, DON American Drinking Practices Questionnaire 9290

CAINE, T.M. The Claybury Selection Battery 810477

CALIFORNIA SCHOOL OF PROFESSIONAL PSYCHOLOGY, LOS ANGELES CSPP 1981 Alumni Survey 13218

CAMPBELL, E.Q. North Carolina Study of Seniors Questionnaire 9178
——. North Carolina Study of Youth Questionnaire 9177

CAMPBELL, N. JO Students' Attitude toward the Mentally Handicapped 14580

CANDEE, DAN Political and Cultural Elicitation Routine 5829

CANFIELD, ALBERT A. Supervisory Practices Inventory, Form A 14006

CANFIELD, JUDITH S. Supervisory Practices Inventory, Form A 14006

CANISIUS COLLEGE, BUFFALO, NY 1980 Canisius College Alumni/Alumnae Survey 13219

CARDON, B.W. Attitudes Inventory for Youth 4811

CAREER RESEARCH AND TESTING, SAN JOSE, CA Retirement Activities Card Sort Kit 12182

CARNEGIE-MELLON UNIVERSITY., PITTSBURGH, PA, PROJECT AFRICA World Regions Perception Survey 6471

CARNEY, CLARK G. Male-Female Role Questionnaire 15387

CARTWRIGHT, ROSALIND D. Traditional-Liberated Social Stereotype and Self-Concept Scales 12451

CARVER, CHARLES S. Attitudes toward Self 14526

CASCIO, WAYNE F. Work Itself/Work Environment Preference Questionnaire 13538

CASTEEL, JIM FRANK Parent Attitudinal Questionnaire 12503

CASTENELL, LOUIS A. Measure of Achievement Motivation 13076

CATLIN, NANCY Croake-Hinkle Children's Fears Assessment Instrument 8840

CAUTELA, JOSEPH R. Forms for Behavior Analysis with Children 14824

CENTER FOR EDUCATIONAL RESEARCH, SEATTLE, WA Student Evaluation of Teaching 7318

CERCONE, KAREN Speech in the Classroom: Assessment Instruments 10992

CHABASSOL, DAVID J. Chabassol Adolescent Structure Inventory 7892

CHAMBERS, DAVID W. Dental Auxiliary Image Test 6777

CHANG, EDWARD C. Black Ethnocentrism Scale 15544

CHAPANIS, ALPHONSE Computer Attitudes Questionnaire 16030

CHARTERS, W.W., JR. Teacher Conceptions of the Educative Process 11430

CHASEN, BARBARA Chasen Diagnostic Sex-Role Bias Scale 8000

CHEEK, JIMMY G. Secondary School Counselor Opinionnaire Form 9166
——. Secondary School Principal Opinionnaire 9165
——. Vocational Counselor Opinionnaire Form 9164
——. Vocational Director Opinionnaire Form 9163

CHEONG, GEORGE S.C. Pupil Situational Inventory: A Measure of Experimental Attitude 6358

CHICAGO AREA BILINGUAL CENTERS, ILLINOIS Bilingual Center Parent Questionnaire 7839

CHIN, BEVERLY ANN The Chin Inventory on Content Area Reading Instruction 13484

CHINSKY, JACK M. Chinsky-Rappaport Adaptation of the Semantic Differential 9509
——. Patient Expectations and Perceptions 10755

CHRIETZBERG, AGNES L. Sex Role Differentiation in Physical Education Attitude Measure 13539

CHRISTIANSEN, JAMES E. Secondary School Counselor Opinionnaire Form 9166
——. Secondary School Principal Opinionnaire 9165
——. Vocational Counselor Opinionnaire Form 9164
——. Vocational Director Opinionnaire Form 9163

CHRISTIE, RICHARD Mach V Attitude Inventory 12975

CHURCHMAN, DAVID UCLA Drug Abuse Questionnaire 8944

CICIRELLI, VICTOR G. Purdue Interview Schedule for Parents of Primary Grade Children 8100
——. Purdue Social Attitude Scales for Preschool Children 8096
——. Purdue Social Attitude Scales for Primary Grade Children 8097

CINCINNATI PUBLIC SCHOOLS, OHIO DEPT. OF PROGRAM RESEARCH AND DESIGN Attitudes toward Self and School 6746

CLARK, LINDA Child Abuse Questionnaire 10170

CLAYDON, PETER D. Claydon College Drinking Questionnaire 14627

CLELAND, CHARLES C. Daylight Saving Time Questionnaire 9576
——. Work Preference Schedule 9575

CLIFFORD, EDWARD When I Was Born 9200

COAN, RICHARD W. General Beliefs 7662
——. Personal Opinion Survey 7663

COFFER, J. HENRY A Religious Attitudes Inventory 2464

COHEN, DONALD Family Background 7869

COHEN, SANDRA R. Classroom Preference Scale, Non-Picture Interview 13186

COHLER, BERTRAN J. Maternal Attitude Scale 7319

COLAIUTA, VICTORIA Scales to Measure Attitudes toward Marijuana and Marijuana Users 7944

COLEMAN, DONA R. Writing Attitude Survey 12969

COLLETT, LORA-JEAN The Collett-Lester Fear of Death Scale 1720

COLWELL, DAVID Student Attitude Measure 7814

COMMUNITY CHANGE, INC., READING, MA An Opinionnaire on Race, Sex and Multicultural Education, for School Personnel 12680

CONARD, SUSAN M. Project PRIMES (Progress Research in Meeting Elementary Standards) Language Arts Evaluation 12910

CONNER, DARYL R. Organizational Change Readiness Scale 14614

CONNERS, C. KEITH Parent and Teacher Rating Forms for the Assessment of Hyperkinesis in Children. 14379

CONNOR, R.G. Attitudes of Parents Questionnaire 9175
——. Questionnaire on Alcoholism 9174

CONRAD, ROWAN W. Revision of the Child Raising Opinion Questionnaire 12909

CONSTANTINOPLE, ANNE Perceived Instrumentality of the College Test 9801

CONTE, HOPE R. Death Anxiety Questionnaire 12343

CONTE, VINCENT A. Salamon-Conte Life Satisfaction in the Elderly Scale 13529

CONYE, ROBERT K. Environmental Assessment Inventory 12282

COOK, GARY Project PRIMES (Progress Research in Meeting Elementary Standards) Creative Arts and Physical Education Evaluation 12912
——. Project PRIMES (Progress Research in Meeting Elementary Standards) School/Community Relations Evaluation Instrument, Community Survey 12915
——. Project PRIMES (Progress Research in Meeting Elementary Standards) School/Community Relations Evaluation Instrument, Parent Survey 12914
——. Project PRIMES (Progress Research in Meeting Elementary Standards) School/Community Relations Evaluation Instrument, Staff Opinionnaire 12913

COOK, LINDA Mainstreaming Attitude Survey 11682

COOK, STUART Judging Arguments: Form C-2 7401
——. Multifactor Racial Attitude Inventory: Short Form 7404

COOK, STUART W. Multifactor Racial Attitude Inventory: Form C-8 7400

COOK, VALERIE J. Attitudes toward Working with Special Education Adolescents 11962

COOPER, EUGENE B. Parent Attitudes toward Stuttering Checklist 8365
——. Stuttering Attitudes Checklist 8363

COOPER, JOSEPH B. Parent Evaluation Scales 8403

COOPERATIVE INSTITUTIONAL RESEARCH PROGRAM, UNIVERSITY OF CALIFORNIA, LOS ANGELES, CA Student Information Form 12027

COOPERSMITH, STANLEY Self-Esteem Inventory: Adult Form 8274
——. Self-Esteem Inventory: School Form 6457

CORAH, NORMAN L. Dental Anxiety Scale 10185

CORBETT, LOIS STILWELL A Semantic Differential for Measurement of Global and Specific Self-Concepts 5774

CORGIAT, MARK D. Body Elimination Attitude Scale 15259

CORMACK, ROBERT W. A.I. Survey: Alienation Index Survey 14330
——. T.A. Survey: Trustworthiness Attitude Survey 14328

COSTIN, FRANK The Knowledge about Psychology Test 7281

COTTLE, WILLIAM C. School Interest Inventory 706

COURSEY, ROBERT D. Liberal Conservative Scale 9477

COWEN, EMORY L. Teacher's Evaluation Form 7485

CRAIN, WILLIAM C. Political World Interview (Short Version) 9018

CRANDALL, JAMES E. Social Interest Scale 8333

CRANDALL, VIRGINIA C. Children's Social Desirability Questionnaire 6099
——. Intellectual Achievement Responsibility Questionnaire 6098

CRANE, WILLIAM E. A Religious Attitudes Inventory 2464

CRATTY, BRYANT J. Games Choice Test 9555

CRAWFORD, JOELLEN E. Attitudes toward Public Exposure to Sexual Stimuli Scale 9865

CRAWFORD, THOMAS J. Attitudes toward Public Exposure to Sexual Stimuli Scale 9865

CRITES, JOHN O. The Family Relations Inventory 5568

CROAKE, JAMES W. Attitudes toward Child Rearing Scale 8841
——. Croake-Hinkle Children's Fears Assessment Instrument 8840

CROSS, HERBERT J. Parental Attitude Research Instrument: Short Form 7701

CROSS, K.P. Student Learning Scales 10441

CROWLEY, ROBERT J. The Institutional Renewal Scale 12703

CROWNE, DOUGLAS P. The Marlowe-Crowne Social Desirability Scale 11068

CRUMBAUGH, JAMES C. Purpose in Life Test 4936
——. Seeking of Noetic Goals Test 5869

DALY, JOHN A. Writing Apprehension Measure 6172

DANIELS, PHILIP B. Management Profiling: As Others See You 10352

DAVENPORT, MARGARET Faculty and Student Attitudes toward the Mixed-Age College Class 14926

DAVIES, MICHAEL H. The Children's Fear Expression and Research Survey 14430

DAVIS, GARY A. Group Inventory for Finding Interests. Level 1. 10971
——. Group Inventory for Finding Interests. Level 2 10979

DAVIS, SUSAN Meier Burnout Assessment 13378

DAVIS, WILLIAM J. Experience-Interest Inventory 9564

DAWLEY, HAROLD H. Attitude Survey of the Effects of Marijuana on Sexual Enjoyment 10704

DEAN, DWIGHT G. Alienation Scale 7343

DEATON, WILLIAM L. Course Entry Inventory 9482

DECK, DENNIS Attitudes toward Reading Scale: Intermediate Scale 12657
——. Attitudes toward Reading Scale: Primary Scale 12656

TITLE INDEX